EYEWITNESS *TRAVEL GUIDES*

LONDON

DK EYEWITNESS *TRAVEL GUIDES*

LONDON

Main Contributor: MICHAEL LEAPMAN

DORLING KINDERSLEY
LONDON • NEW YORK • MUNICH
DELHI • MELBOURNE
www.dk.com

A DORLING KINDERSLEY BOOK

www.dk.com

PROJECT EDITOR Jane Shaw
ART EDITOR Sally Ann Hibbard
EDITOR Tom Fraser
DESIGNERS Pippa Hurst, Robyn Tomlinson
DESIGN ASSISTANT Clare Sullivan

CONTRIBUTORS
Christopher Pick, Lindsay Hunt

PHOTOGRAPHERS
Max Alexander, Philip Enticknap,
John Heseltine, Stephen Oliver

ILLUSTRATORS
Brian Delf, Trevor Hill, Robbie Polley

This book was produced with the assistance of
Websters International Publishers.

Reproduced by Colourscan (Singapore)
Printed and bound by South China Printing Co. Ltd. (China)

First published in Great Britain in 1993
by Dorling Kindersley Limited
80 Strand, London WC2R 0RL
**Reprinted with revisions 1994, 1995, 1996, 1997,
1999, 2000 (twice), 2001, 2002**

Copyright 1993, 2002 © Dorling Kindersley Limited, London
A Penguin Company

A CIP CATALOGUE RECORD IS AVAILABLE FROM THE BRITISH LIBRARY.

ISBN 0 7513 4705 1

**The information in every DK Eyewitness Travel Guide is
checked regularly.**
Every effort has been made to ensure that this book is as up-to-
date as possible at the time of going to press. Some details,
however, such as telephone numbers, prices, gallery hanging
arrangements and travel information, are liable to change. The
publishers cannot accept responsibility for any consequences
arising from the use of this book, nor for any material on third-
party websites, and cannot guarantee that any website address in
this book will be a suitable source of travel information. We value
the views and suggestions of our readers highly. Please write to:
Senior Publishing Manager, DK Eyewitness Travel Guides,
Dorling Kindersley, 80 Strand, London WC2R 0RL.

CONTENTS

Portrait of Sir Walter Raleigh (1585)

INTRODUCING
LONDON

Bedford Square doorway (1775)

The Broadwalk at Hampton Court (c.1720)

Beefeater at the Tower of London

Bandstand in St James's Park

Houses of Parliament

SURVIVAL GUIDE

St Paul's Church: Covent Garden

TRAVELLERS' NEEDS

HOW TO USE THIS GUIDE

THIS EYEWITNESS TRAVEL GUIDE helps you get the most from your stay in London with the minimum of practical difficulty. The opening section, *Introducing London,* locates the city geographically, sets modern London in its historical context and describes the regular highlights of the London year. *London at a Glance* is an overview of the city's specialities. *London Area by Area* takes you round the city's areas of interest. It describes all the main sights with maps, photographs and detailed illustrations. In addition, five planned walking routes take you to parts of London you might otherwise miss.

Well-researched tips on where to stay, eat, shop, and on entertainments are in *Travellers' Needs. Children's London* lists highlights for young visitors, and *Survival Guide* tells you how to do anything from posting a letter to using the Underground.

LONDON AREA BY AREA

The city has been divided into 17 sightseeing areas, each with its own section in the guide. Each section opens with a portrait of the area, summing up its character and history and listing all the sights to be covered. Sights are numbered and clearly located on an *Area Map*. After this comes a large-scale *Street-by-Street Map* focusing on the most interesting part of the area. Finding your way about the area section is made simple by the numbering system. This refers to the order in which sights are described on the pages that complete the section.

Sights at a Glance lists the sights in the area by category: Historic Streets and Buildings, Churches, Museums and Galleries, Monuments, Parks and Gardens.

The area covered in greater detail on the *Street-by-Street Map* is shaded red.

Numbered circles pinpoint all the listed sights on the area map. St Margaret's Church, for example, is ❻

1 The Area Map

For easy reference, the sights in each area are numbered and located on an Area Map. *To help the visitor, the map also shows* Underground *and mainline stations and car parks.*

Photographs of facades and distinctive details of buildings help you to locate the sights.

Colour-coding on each page makes the area easy to find in the book.

Travel tips help you reach the area quickly by public transport.

2 The Street-by-Street Map

This gives a bird's-eye view of the heart of each sightseeing area. The most important buildings are picked out in stronger colour, to help you spot them as you walk around.

A locator map shows you where you are in relation to surrounding areas. The area of the *Street-by-Street Map* is shown in red.

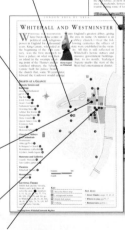

A suggested route for a walk takes in the most attractive and interesting streets in the area.

St Margaret's Church is shown on this map as well.

Red stars indicate the sights that no visitor should miss.

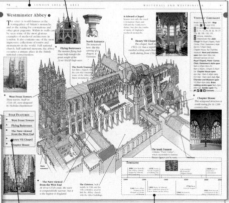

LONDON AT A GLANCE

Each map in this section concentrates on a specific theme: *Celebrated Londoners, Museums and Galleries, Churches, Parks and Gardens, Ceremonies*. The top sights are shown on the map; others are described on the following two pages and cross-referenced to their full entries in the *Area by Area* section.

Each sightseeing area is colour-coded.

The theme is explored in greater detail on the pages following the map.

3 Detailed information on each sight

All important sights in each area are described in depth in this section. They are listed in order, following the numbering on the Area Map. *Practical information is also provided.*

PRACTICAL INFORMATION

Each entry provides all the information needed to plan a visit to the sight. The key to the symbols is inside the back cover.

Telephone number

Address

Map reference to Streetfinder at back of book

St Margaret's Church ❻ — Sight Number

Parliament Sq SW1. **Map** 13 B5.
📞 020-7222 5152. ⊖ *Westminster.*
Open *9:30am–3:45pm Mon–Sat, 1–5:30pm Sun.* 🕭 *11am Sun.*
🚫 🔥 🎵 *Concerts.*

Opening hours

Services and facilities available

Nearest Underground station

4 London's major sights

These are given two or more full pages in the sightseeing area in which they are found. Historic buildings are dissected to reveal their interiors; museums and galleries have colour-coded floor plans to help you find important exhibits.

The Visitors' Checklist provides the practical information you will need to plan your visit.

The facade of each major sight is shown to help you spot it quickly.

Red stars indicate the most interesting architectural details of the building, and the most important works of art or exhibits on view inside.

A timeline charts the key events in the history of the sight.

INTRODUCING
LONDON

Putting London on the Map

L ONDON, THE CAPITAL of the United
Kingdom, is a city of seven million
people covering 620 sq miles (1,606 sq
km) of southeast England. It is built on
the River Thames and is at the centre of
the UK road and rail networks. From
London visitors can easily reach the
country's other main tourist attractions.

View east over the Thames from Southwark

WESTERN EUROPE

NORWAY

SWEDEN

REPUBLIC
OF
IRELAND   UNITED
KINGDOM

DENMARK

London   NETHERLANDS

BELGIUM   GERMANY

LUXEMBOURG

FRANCE

SWITZERLAND   AUSTRIA

ITALY

SPAIN

PORTUGAL

The Midlands

*The Midlands
The North*

Stratford-
upon-Avon

M40   A43

A40

Thames   Oxford   M40   *Chiltern Hills*

Western Europe

*London is in northwest
Europe, on the same
latitude as Warsaw. It
is Europe's biggest city
and the business centre
of the continent. London
has five airports and is
about an hour's flying
time from Scandinavia,
Germany, Holland and
France. It is also linked
to northern Europe
through nearby ports.*

The West   M4

Bath   M4   Reading

Windsor

M3

Stonehenge   A30   A34

A36   Salisbury

A30   Winchester   A3

The West   S o u
D o w

A35   Southampton   M27   A3(M)   A27

Poole   Portsmouth

Isle of Wight

Le Havre

Caen

Channel Islands   *Cherbourg*   *St Malo*   *Cherbourg*   E N G L I S H

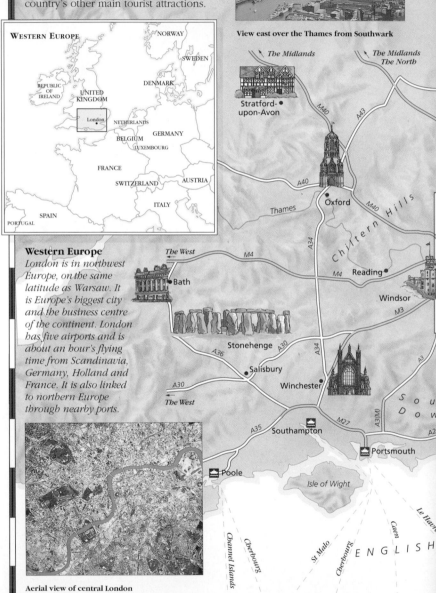

Aerial view of central London

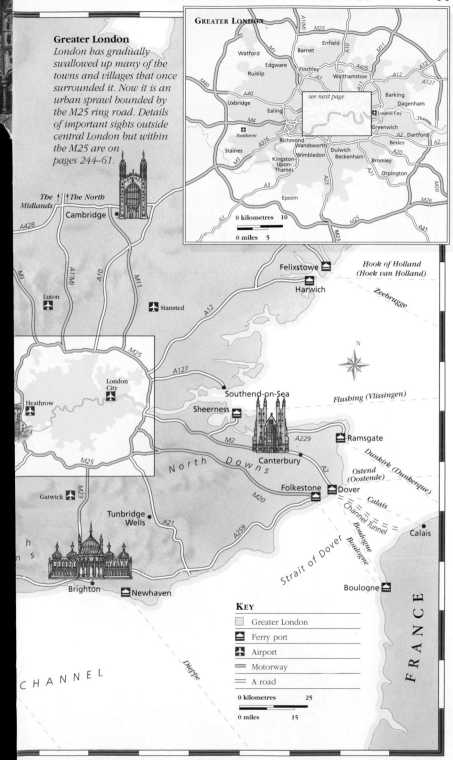

Greater London

London has gradually swallowed up many of the towns and villages that once surrounded it. Now it is an urban sprawl bounded by the M25 ring road. Details of important sights outside central London but within the M25 are on pages 244–61.

GREATER LONDON

Watford
Enfield
Barnet
Edgware
Finchley
Walthamstow
Ruislip
Uxbridge
Ealing
Heathrow
Richmond
Wandsworth
Staines
Wimbledon
Dulwich
Beckenham
Kingston-Upon-Thames
Epsom

Barking
Dagenham
London City
Greenwich
Dartford
Bexley
Bromley
Orpington

see next page

0 kilometres 10

0 miles 5

The North
The Midlands

Cambridge

Luton
Stansted

Felixstowe
Harwich

Hook of Holland
(Hoek van Holland)

Zeebrugge

N

London City

Heathrow

Southend-on-Sea
Sheerness

Flushing (Vlissingen)

Gatwick

Canterbury

Ramsgate

Dunkirk (Dunkerque)

Ostend
(Oostende)

Folkestone
Dover

Calais

Channel Tunnel

Calais

Tunbridge Wells

North Downs

Brighton
Newhaven

Strait of Dover

Boulogne

Boulogne

FRANCE

CHANNEL

Dieppe

KEY

	Greater London
⚓	Ferry port
✈	Airport
═	Motorway
═	A road

0 kilometres 25

0 miles 15

Central London

M OST OF THE SIGHTS described in this book lie within 14 areas of central London plus two outlying districts of Hampstead and Greenwich. Each of these has its own chapter. If you are short of time you may decide to restrict yourself to the five areas that are packed with most of London's famous sights: Whitehall and Westminster, The City, Bloomsbury and Fitzrovia, Soho and Trafalgar Square, and South Kensington and Knightsbridge.

PAGES 220–27
*Street Finder maps
3–4, 11–12*

PAGES 236–43
*Street Finder maps
23–24*

Hampstead

PAGES 228–35
*Street Finder maps
1–2*

*Regent's Park
and
Marylebone*

*Greenwich and
Blackheath*

*South Kensington
and
Knightsbridge*

*Kensington
and
Holland Park*

*Piccadilly
and
St James's*

PAGES 214–19
*Street Finder maps
9–10, 17*

Chelsea

PAGES 198–213
*Street Finder maps
10–11, 18–19*

PAGES 192–7
*Street Finder maps
18–19*

| 0 kilometres | 1 |
| 0 miles | 0.5 |

PAGES 98–109
*Street Finder maps
12–13*

PAGES 120–31
*Street Finder maps
4–5, 13*

PAGES 110–19
*Street Finder maps
13–14*

PAGES 132–41
*Street Finder maps
5–6, 13–14*

N

Bloomsbury
and
Fitzrovia

Smithfield
and
Spitalfields

PAGES 160–71
*Street Finder maps
6–7, 14, 16*

Soho and
Trafalgar
Square

Holborn
and the
Inns of Court

Covent
Garden
and the
Strand

The City

RIVER THAMES

Southwark
and Bankside

South Bank

PAGES 142–59
*Street Finder maps
14–16*

Whitehall
and
Westminster

PAGES 68–85
*Street Finder maps
13, 20–1*

PAGES 86–97
*Street Finder maps
12–13, 20*

PAGES 184–91
*Street Finder maps
13–14, 21–2*

PAGES 172–83
*Street Finder maps
6, 16*

THE HISTORY OF LONDON

IN 55 BC, JULIUS CAESAR'S Roman army invaded England, landed in Kent and marched northwest until it reached the broad River Thames at what is now Southwark. There were a few tribesmen living on the opposite bank but no major settlement. However, by the time of the second Roman invasion 88 years later, a small port and mercantile community had been established here. The Romans bridged the river and built their administrative headquarters on the north bank, calling it Londinium – a version of its old Celtic name.

The griffon: the City of London's symbol

settlements around it. These included the royal city of Westminster which had long been London's religious and political centre. The explosive growth of commerce and industry during the 18th and 19th centuries made London the biggest and wealthiest city in the world, creating a prosperous middle class who built the fine houses that still grace parts of the capital. The prospect of riches also lured millions of the dispossessed from the countryside and from abroad. They crowded into insanitary dwellings, many just east of the City, where docks provided employment.

LONDON AS CAPITAL

London was soon the largest city in England and, by the time of the Norman Conquest in 1066, it was the obvious choice for national capital.

Settlement slowly spread beyond the original walled city, which was virtually wiped out by the Great Fire of 1666. The post-Fire rebuilding formed the basis of the area we know today as the City but, by the 18th century, London enveloped the

By the end of the 19th century, 4.5 million people lived in inner London and another 4 million in its immediate vicinity. Bombing in World War II devastated many central areas and led to substantial rebuilding in the second half of the 20th century, when the docks and other Victorian industries disappeared.

The following pages illustrate London's history by giving snapshots of significant periods in its evolution.

A map of 1580 showing the City of London and, towards the lower left corner, the City of Westminster

A 15th-century manuscript showing the Tower of London with London Bridge in the background

Roman London

W HEN THE ROMANS invaded Britain in the 1st century AD, they already controlled vast areas of the Mediterranean, but fierce opposition from local tribes (such as Queen Boadicea's Iceni) made Britain difficult to control. The Romans persevered, however, and had consolidated their power by the end of the century. Londinium, with its port, developed into a capital city; by the 3rd century, there were some 50,000 people living there. But, as the Roman Empire crumbled in the 5th century, the garrison pulled out, leaving the city to the Saxons.

1st-century Roman coin

EXTENT OF THE CITY
☐ 125 AD   ☐ Today

Public Baths
Bathing was an important part of Roman life. This pocket-sized personal hygiene kit (including a nail pick) and bronze pouring dish date from the 1st century.

Site of present-day Museum of London

Roman fort

Site of present-day St. Paul's

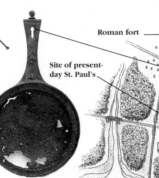

Basilica

Forum

LONDINIUM
Roman London was an important center on the site of the present-day City (see pp142–59). On the Thames, it was in a good position to trade with the rest of the Empire.

Forum and Basilica
About 600 ft (200 m) from London Bridge was the forum (the chief market and meeting place) and the basilica (the town hall and court of justice).

Temple of Mithras
Mithras protected the good from evil. This 2nd-century head was in his temple.

TIMELINE

55 BC Julius Caesar invades Britain

AD 61 Boadicea attacks

200 City wall built

410 Roman troops begin to leave

| 100 | 200 | 300 | 400 | 50 |

AD 43 Claudius establishes Roman London and builds the first bridge

☐ Roman London

London Wall
The tombstone of a Roman legionnaire was built into the city wall. The writing tablets in his left hand suggest he did clerical work.

Amphitheatre
Entertainment was brutal. A popular spectacle was gladiators, dressed like this figurine, fighting to the death.

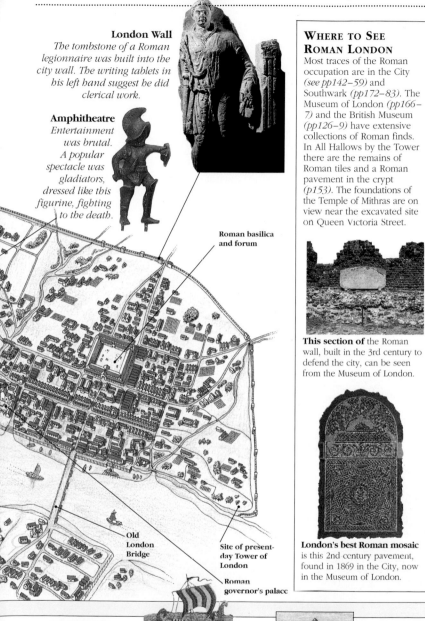

Roman basilica and forum

Old London Bridge

Site of present-day Tower of London

Roman governor's palace

WHERE TO SEE ROMAN LONDON

Most traces of the Roman occupation are in the City (*see pp142–59*) and Southwark (*pp172–83*). The Museum of London (*pp166–7*) and the British Museum (*pp126–9*) have extensive collections of Roman finds. In All Hallows by the Tower there are the remains of Roman tiles and a Roman pavement in the crypt (*p153*). The foundations of the Temple of Mithras are on view near the excavated site on Queen Victoria Street.

This section of the Roman wall, built in the 3rd century to defend the city, can be seen from the Museum of London.

London's best Roman mosaic is this 2nd-century pavement, found in 1869 in the City, now in the Museum of London.

604 King Ethelbert builds first St Paul's

834 First Viking raids

1014 Norse invader Olaf pulls down London Bridge to take the city

600   700   800   1000

884 Alfred the Great, King of Wessex, takes power

Medieval London

THE HISTORIC DIVISION between London's centres of commerce (the City) and government (Westminster) started in the mid-11th century when Edward the Confessor established his court and sited his abbey *(see pp76–9)* at Westminster. Meanwhile, in the City, tradesmen set up their own institutions and guilds, and London appointed its first mayor. Disease was rife and the population never rose much above its Roman peak of 50,000. The Black Death (1348) reduced the population by half.

EXTENT OF THE CITY

☐ *1200*   ☐ *Today*

St Thomas à Becket
As Archbishop of Canterbury he was murdered in 1170, at the request of Henry II with whom he was quarrelling. Thomas was made a saint and pilgrims visited his Canterbury shrine.

LONDON BRIDGE
The first stone bridge was built in 1209 and lasted 600 years. It was the only bridge across the Thames in London until Westminster Bridge (1750).

The Chapel of St Thomas, erected the year the bridge was completed, was one of its first buildings.

Iron railings

Houses and shops projected over both sides of the bridge. Shopkeepers made their own merchandise on the premises and lived above their shops. Apprentices did the selling.

THE CORPORATION OF
THE HOUSE OF
RICHARD
WHITTINGTON
MAYOR OF LONDON
STOOD ON THIS SITE
1423
THE CITY OF LONDON

Dick Whittington
The 15th-century trader was thrice mayor of London (see p39).

The piers were made from wooden stakes rammed into the river bed and filled with rubble.

Stag Hunting
Such sports were the chief recreation of wealthy landowners.

The arches ranged from 4.5 m (15 ft) to 10 m (35 ft) in width.

TIMELINE

1042 Edward the Confessor becomes king	**1086** Domesday Book, England's first survey, published		**1191** Henry Fitzalwin becomes London's first mayor	**1215** King John's Magna Carta gives City more powers	
1050	1100	1150	1200		1250
	1066 William I crowned in Abbey	**1176** Work starts on the first stone London Bridge		**1240** First parliament sits at Westminster	
	1065 Westminster Abbey completed				

☐ **Medieval London**

Chivalry
Medieval knights were idealized for their courage and honour. Edward Burne-Jones (1833–98) painted George, patron saint of England, rescuing a maiden from this dragon.

Geoffrey Chaucer
The poet and customs controller (see p39), *is best remembered for his* Canterbury Tales *which creates a rich picture of 14th-century England.*

WHERE TO SEE MEDIEVAL LONDON

There were only a few survivors of the Great Fire of 1666 *(see pp22–3)* – the Tower *(pp154–7)*, Westminster Hall *(p72)* and Westminster Abbey *(pp76–9)*, and a few churches *(p46)*. The Museum of London *(pp166–7)* has artefacts while Tate Britain *(pp82–5)* and the National Gallery *(pp104–7)* have paintings. Manuscripts, including the Domesday Book, are found at the British Library *(p125)*.

The Tower of London was started in 1078 and became one of the few centres of royal power in the largely self-governing City.

A 14th-century rose window is all that remains of Winchester Palace near the Clink *(see p177)*.

Plan of the Bridge
The bridge had 19 arches to span the river making it, for many years, the longest stone bridge in England.

Many 13th-century pilgrims went to Canterbury.

1350	1400	1450

1348 Black Death kills thousands

1381 Peasants' Revolt defeated

1394 Westminster Hall remodelled by Henry Yevele

1397 Richard Whittington becomes mayor

1476 William Caxton sets up first printing press at Westminster

The Great Seal of Richard I shows us what medieval kings looked like.

Elizabethan London

IN THE 16TH CENTURY the monarchy was stronger than ever before. The Tudors established peace throughout England, allowing art and commerce to flourish. This renaissance reached its zenith under Elizabeth I as explorers opened up the New World, and English theatre, the nation's most lasting contribution to world culture, was born.

EXTENT OF THE CITY
▨ *1561*   ☐ *Today*

SHAKESPEARE'S GLOBE
Elizabethan theatres were built of wood and only half covered, so plays had to be cancelled in bad weather.

A balcony on the stage was part of the scenery.

The apron stage had a trap door for special effects.

Curtain

Death at the Stake
The Tudors dealt harshly with social and religious dissent. Here Bishops Latimer and Ridley die for so-called heresy in 1555, when Elizabeth's sister, Mary I, was queen. Traitors could expect to be hung, drawn and quartered.

In the pit, below the level of the stage, commoners stood to watch the play.

Hunting and Hawking
Popular 16th-century pastimes are shown on this cushion cover.

TIMELINE

Rat catchers, and other pest controllers, could not prevent epidemics of plague.

1535 Sir Thomas More executed for treason

1536 Henry VIII's second wife, Anne Boleyn, executed

1530

1534 Henry VIII breaks with the Roman Catholic church

1553 Edward dies, succeeded by his sister Mary I

1547 Henry dies, succeeded by his son Edward VI

1550

☐ **Elizabethan London**

The galleries were for rich theatre-goers who could watch from the comfort of seats.

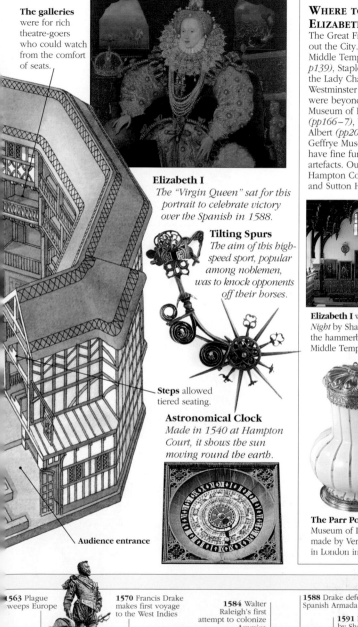

Elizabeth I
The "Virgin Queen" sat for this portrait to celebrate victory over the Spanish in 1588.

Tilting Spurs
The aim of this high-speed sport, popular among noblemen, was to knock opponents off their horses.

Steps allowed tiered seating.

Astronomical Clock
Made in 1540 at Hampton Court, it shows the sun moving round the earth.

Audience entrance

WHERE TO SEE ELIZABETHAN LONDON

The Great Fire of 1666 wiped out the City. Fortunately, Middle Temple Hall (*see p139*), Staple Inn (*p141*) and the Lady Chapel inside Westminster Abbey (*pp76–9*) were beyond its reach. The Museum of London (*pp166–7*), Victoria and Albert (*pp202–205*), and Geffrye Museums (*p248*) have fine furniture and artefacts. Out of town are Hampton Court (*pp254–7*) and Sutton House (*p248*).

Elizabeth I watched *Twelfth Night* by Shakespeare under the hammerbeam roof of Middle Temple Hall in 1603.

The Parr Pot, now in the Museum of London, was made by Venetian craftsmen in London in 1547.

1563 Plague sweeps Europe

1570 Francis Drake makes first voyage to the West Indies

1584 Walter Raleigh's first attempt to colonize America

1588 Drake defeats Spanish Armada

1591 First play by Shakespeare produced

| 1560 | 1570 | 1580 | 1590 |

1558 Mary I's death makes Elizabeth queen

Gloves made from imported silk and velvet

1603 Elizabeth dies, James I accedes

Restoration London

CIVIL WAR HAD BROKEN out in 1642 when the mercantile class demanded that some of the monarch's power be passed to Parliament. The subsequent Commonwealth was dominated by Puritans under Oliver Cromwell. The Puritans outlawed simple pleasures, such as dancing and theatre, so it was small wonder that the restoration of the monarchy under Charles II in 1660 was greeted with rejoicing and the release of pent-up creative energies. The period was, however, also marked with two major tragedies: the Plague (1665) and the Great Fire (1666).

EXTENT OF THE CITY

■ 1680   □ Today

St Paul's was destroyed in the fire that raged as far east as Fetter Lane *(map 14 E1).*

London Bridge itself survived, but many of the buildings on it were burned down.

Oliver Cromwell
He led the Parliamentarian army and was Lord Protector of the Realm from 1653 until his death in 1658. At the Restoration, his body was dug up and hung from the gallows at Tyburn, near Hyde Park (see p207).

Charles I's Death
The king was beheaded for tyranny on a freezing day (30 January 1649) outside Banqueting House (see p80).

Charles I
His belief in the Divine Right of Kings angered Parliament and was one of the causes of civil war.

TIMELINE

1623 Shakespeare's first folio published

1625 James I dies, succeeded by his son Charles I

1642 Civil war starts when Parliament defies king

1620	1640	1650

1605 Guy Fawkes leads failed attempt to blow up the King and Parliament

Feathered helmet worn by Royalist cavaliers

1649 Charles I executed, Commonwealth established

□   **Restoration London**

Newton's Telescope
Physicist and astronomer Sir Isaac Newton (1642–1727) discovered the law of gravity.

Samuel Pepys
His exuberant diaries tell us much about courtly life of the time.

The Tower of London was just out of the fire's reach.

WHERE TO SEE RESTORATION LONDON

Wren's churches and his St Paul's Cathedral *(see p47 and pp148–51)* are, with Inigo Jones's Banqueting House *(p80)*, London's most famous 17th-century buildings. On a more modest scale are Lincoln's Inn *(p136)* and Cloth Fair *(p165)*. There is a fine period interior at the Museum of London *(pp166–7)*. The British Museum *(pp126–9)* and the Victoria and Albert *(pp202–205)* have pottery, silver and textile collections.

Ham House *(p252)* was built in 1610 but much enlarged later in the century. It has the finest interior of its time in England.

Peter Paul Rubens painted the ceiling in 1636 for Inigo Jones's Banqueting House *(p80)*. This is one of its panels.

THE GREAT FIRE OF 1666
An unidentified Dutch artist painted this view of the fire that burned for 5 days, destroying 13,000 houses.

The Plague
During 1665, carts collected the dead and took them to communal graves outside the city.

1664–5 Plague kills 100,000

1666 Great Fire

1685 Charles II dies, Catholic James II becomes king

1692 First insurance market opens at Lloyd's

1660   1670   1690

1660 Monarchy restored under Charles II

A barber's bowl made by London potters in 1681

1688 James ousted in favour of Protestant William of Orange

1694 First Bank of England set up by William Paterson

Georgian London

George I (reigned 1714–27)

THE FOUNDATION of the Bank of England in 1694 spurred the growth of London and, by the time George I came to the throne in 1714, it had become an important financial and commercial centre. Aristocrats with West End estates began laying out elegant squares and terraces to house newly-rich merchants. Architects such as the Adam brothers, John Soane and John Nash developed stylish medium-scale housing. They drew inspiration from the great European capitals, as did English painters, sculptors, composers and craftsmen.

EXTENT OF THE CITY

☐ 1810   ☐ Today

Manchester Square was laid out in 1776–8.

Portman Square was on the town's outskirts when it was started in 1764.

Great Cumberland Place
Built in 1790, it was named after a royal duke and military commander.

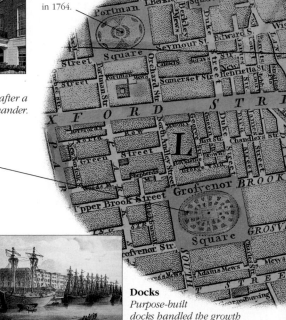

Grosvenor Square
Few of the original houses remain on one of the oldest and largest Mayfair squares (1720).

Docks
Purpose-built docks handled the growth in world trade.

TIMELINE

1714 George I becomes king

1727 George II becomes king

1759 Kew Gardens established

1768 Royal Academy of Art established

| 1720 | 1740 | 1760 | 177 |

1717 Hanover Square built, start of West End development

1729 John Wesley (1703–91) founds the Methodist Church

1760 George III becomes king

☐ Georgian London

John Nash
Stylish Nash shaped 18th-century London with variations on Classical themes, such as this archway in Cumberland Terrace, near Regent's Park.

WHERE TO SEE GEORGIAN LONDON

The portico of the Theatre Royal, Haymarket *(see pp328–9)* gives a taste of the style of fashionable London in the 1820s. In Pall Mall *(p92)* Charles Barry's Reform and Travellers' Clubs are equally evocative. Most West End squares have some Georgian buildings, while Fournier Street *(p170)* has good small-scale domestic architecture. The Victoria and Albert Museum (V&A *pp202–205*) has silver, as do the London Silver Vaults *(p141)* where it is for sale. Hogarth's pictures, at Tate Britain *(pp82–5)* and Sir John Soane's Museum *(pp136–7)*, show the social conditions.

This English long case clock
(1725), made of oak and pine with Chinese designs, is in the V&A.

GEORGIAN LONDON
The layout of much of London's West End has remained very similar to how it was in 1828, when this map was published.

Captain Cook
This Yorkshire-born explorer discovered Australia during a voyage round the world in 1768–71.

Berkeley Square
Built in the 1730s and 1740s in the grounds of the former Berkeley House, several characteristic original houses remain on its west side.

Ironwork
Crafts flourished. This ornate railing is on Manchester Square.

Signatories of the American Declaration of Independence

1811 George III goes mad, his son George is made Regent

1820 George III dies, Prince Regent becomes George IV

1830 George IV dies, brother William IV is king

| 1800 | 1810 | 1820 | 1830 |

1776 Britain loses American colonies with Declaration of Independence

1802 Stock Exchange formally established

1829 London's first horse bus

Victorian London

MUCH OF LONDON TODAY is Victorian. Until the early 19th century, the capital had been confined to the original Roman city, plus Westminster and Mayfair to the west, ringed by fields and villages such as Brompton, Islington and Battersea. From the 1820s these green spaces filled rapidly with terraces of houses for the growing numbers attracted to London by industrialization. Rapid expansion brought challenges to the city. The first cholera epidemic broke out in 1832, and in 1858 came the Great Stink, when the smell from the Thames became so bad that Parliament had to go into recess. But Joseph Bazalgette's sewerage system (1875), involving banking both sides of the Thames, eased the problem.

Queen Victoria in her coronation year (1838)

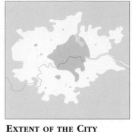

EXTENT OF THE CITY

▨ *1900*   ☐ *Today*

The building was 560 m (1,850 ft) long and 33 m (110 ft) high.

Nearly 14,000 exhibitors came from all over the world, bringing more than 100,000 exhibits.

Pantomime
The traditional family Christmas entertainment – still popular today (see p328) *– started in the 19th century.*

Soldiers marched and jumped on the floor to test its strength before the exhibition opened.

Massive elm trees growing in Hyde Park were left standing and the exhibition was erected around them.

The Crystal Fountain was 8 m (27 ft) high.

Carpets and stained glass were hung from the galleries.

TIMELINE

1837 Victoria becomes queen

1851 Great Exhibition

Season ticket for Great Exhibition

A Wedgwood plate in typical florid Victorian style

1861 Prince Albert dies

1860

1836 First London rail terminus opens at London Bridge

1840 Rowland Hill introduces the Penny Post

1863 Metropolitan Railway, world's first Underground system, is opened

1870 First Peabody Buildings, to house the poor, built in Blackfriars Road

☐ **Victoria's reign**

Railways
By 1900 fast trains, such as this Scotch Express, *were crossing the country.*

WHERE TO SEE VICTORIAN LONDON
Grandiose buildings best reflect the spirit of the age, notably the rail termini, the Kensington Museums (see pp198–213) and the Royal Albert Hall (p207). Leighton House (p218) has a well-preserved interior. Pottery and fabrics are in the Victoria and Albert Museum, and the London Transport Museum (p114) has buses, trams and trains.

Telegraph
Newly-invented communications technology, like this telegraph from 1840, made business expansion easier.

Crystal Palace
Between May and October 1851, six million people visited Joseph Paxton's superb feat of engineering. In 1852 it was dismantled and reassembled in south London where it remained until destroyed by fire in 1936.

The Victorian Gothic style suited buildings like the Public Record Office in Chancery Lane.

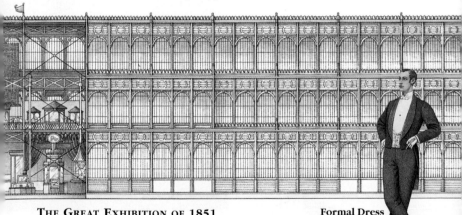

THE GREAT EXHIBITION OF 1851
The exhibition, held in the Crystal Palace in Hyde Park, celebrated industry, technology and the expanding British Empire.

Formal Dress
Under Victoria, elaborate men's attire was replaced by more restrained evening wear.

A special box for carrying top hats

1889 London County Council (LCC) established

1891 First LCC public housing built, in Shoreditch

1899 First motor buses introduced

1901 Queen Victoria dies, Edward VII accedes

1880

1890

1900

1890 First electric Underground line, from Bank to Stockwell, opens

Commemorative fan for the Boer War, which ended in 1903

London Between the World Wars

Art Deco china by Clarice Cliff

T HE SOCIETY THAT emerged from World War I grasped eagerly at the innovations of early 20th-century London – the motor car, the telephone, commuter transport. The cinema brought transatlantic culture, especially jazz and swing music. Victorian social restraints were discarded as people flocked to dance in restaurants, clubs and dance halls. Many left the crowded inner city for new suburban estates. Then came the 1930s global Depression, whose effects had barely worn off when World War II began.

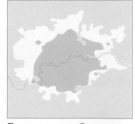

EXTENT OF THE CITY

☐ *1938*   ☐ *Today*

METRO-LAND
PRICE TWO-PENCE

Commuting
London's new outer suburbs were made popular by the under- ground railway. In the north was "Metroland", named after the Metro- politan line which penetrated Hertfordshire.

High Fashion
The sleek flowing new styles contrasted with the fussy elaboration of the Victorians and Edwardians. This tea gown is from the 1920s.

Formal evening wear, including hats for both sexes, was still compulsory when going to smart West End night spots.

A LONDON STREET SCENE
Maurice Greiflenhagen's painting (1926) captures the bustle of London after dark.

TIMELINE

Medals, like this from 1914, were struck during the campaign for women's votes.

1921 North Circular Road links northern suburbs

1922 First BBC national radio broadcast

1910

1920

1910 George V succeeds Edward VII

Cavalry was still used in the Middle Eastern battles of World War I (1914–18).

☐ **Interwar period**

Early Cinema

London-born Charlie Chaplin (1889–1977), seen here in City Lights, *was a popular star of both silent and talking pictures.*

Seven new theatres were built in central London from 1924 to 1931.

George VI
Oswald Birley painted this portrait of the king who became a model for wartime resistance and unity.

Early motor buses had open tops, like the old horse-drawn buses.

Communications
The radio provided home entertainment and information. This is a 1933 model.

Throughout the period newspaper circulations increased massively. In 1930 *The Daily Herald* sold 2 million copies a day.

WORLD WAR II AND THE BLITZ
World War II saw large-scale civilian bombing for the first time, bringing the horror of war to Londoners' doorsteps. Thousands were killed in their homes. Many people took refuge in Underground stations and children were evacuated to the safety of the country.

WOMEN OF BRITAIN
COME INTO THE FACTORIES

As in World War I, women were recruited for factory work formerly done by men who were away fighting.

Bombing raids in 1940 and 1941 (the Blitz) caused devastation all over the city.

1929 US stock market crash brings world Depression

1939 World War II begins

25   1930

1927 First talking pictures

1936 Edward VIII abdicates to marry US divorcée Wallis Simpson. George VI accedes

1940 Winston Churchill becomes Prime Minister

Postwar London

MUCH OF LONDON was flattened by World War II bombs. Afterwards, the chance for imaginative rebuilding was missed – some badly designed postwar developments are already being razed. But, by the 1960s, London was such a dynamic world leader in fashion and popular music that *Time* magazine dubbed it "swinging London". Skyscrapers sprang up, but some stayed empty as 1980s boom gave way to 1990s recession.

EXTENT OF THE CITY

☐ 1959	☐ Today

The Beatles
The Liverpool pop group, pictured in 1965, had rocketed to stardom two years earlier with songs of appealing freshness and directness. The group symbolized carefree 1960s London.

Festival of Britain
After wartime, the city's morale was lifted by the Festival, marking the 1851 Great Exhibition's centenary (see pp26–7).

Margaret Thatcher
Britain's first woman Prime Minister (1979–90) promoted the market-led policies that fuelled the 1980s boom.

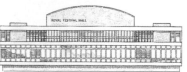

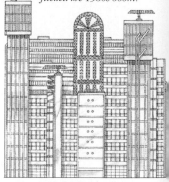

The Royal Festival Hall (1951) was the Festival's centrepiece and is still a landmark *(see p189).*

Telecom Tower (1964), at 189 m (620 ft) high, dominates the Fitzrovia skyline.

The Lloyd's Building (1986) is Richard Rogers's Post-Modernist emblem *(see p159).*

TIMELINE

1948 Olympic Games held in London

1952 George VI dies; his daughter Elizabeth II accedes

Minis became a symbol of the 1960s; small and manoeuvrable, they typified the go-as-you-please mood of the decade.

1945	1950	1955	1960	1965	1970	1975

1951 Festival of Britain

1945 End of World War II

1954 Food rationing, introduced during World War II, abolished

1963 National Theatre founded at the Old Vic

1971 New London Bridge built

1977 Queen's silver jubilee; work starts on Jubilee line underground

Postwar London

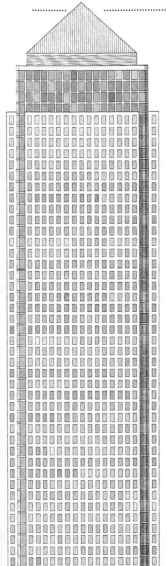

Canada Tower (1991) is London's tallest building. It was designed by César Pelli *(see p249)*.

Docklands Light Railway
In the 1980s, new, driver-less trains started to transport people to the developing Docklands.

POST-MODERN ARCHITECTURE
The new wave of architects since the 1980s are reacting against the bleak and stark shapes of the Modernists. Some, like Richard Rogers, are masters of high-tech, emphasizing structural features in their designs. Others, Terry Farrell for example, adopt a more playful approach using pastiches of Classical features such as columns.

Charing Cross (1991) has Terry Farrell's glasshouse on top of the Victorian station *(see p119)*.

YOUTH CULTURE
With their new mobility and spending power, young people began to influence the development of British popular culture in the years after World War II. Music, fashion and design were increasingly geared to their rapidly changing tastes.

Punks were a phenomenon of the 1970s and 1980s. Their clothes, music, hair and habits were designed to shock.

The Prince of Wales
As heir to the throne, he is outspokenly critical of much of London's recent architecture. He prefers Classical styles.

1984 Thames Barrier completed	**1986** Greater London Council abolished	*Vivienne Westwood's clothes won prizes in the 1980s and 1990s.*		*The observation wheel, British Airways London Eye, was raised during the spring of 2000.*		
1980	1985	1990	1995	2000	2005	2010
1982 Last of the London docks closes	**1985** Ethiopian famine leads to Live Aid relief campaign	**1992** Canary Wharf development opens	**2000** Ken Livingstone wins the battle to be London's first directly elected mayor			
			1997 Princess Diana's funeral procession brings London to a halt			

Kings and Queens in London

LONDON HAS BEEN the royal capital of England since 1066, when William the Conqueror began a tradition of holding coronations in Westminster Abbey. Since then, successive kings and queens have left their mark on London and many of the places described in this book have royal associations: Henry VIII hunted at Richmond, Charles I was executed on Whitehall and the young Queen Victoria rode on Queensway. Royalty is also celebrated in many of London's traditional ceremonies – for more details on these turn to pages 52–5.

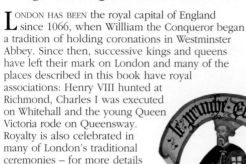

1413–22 Henry V

1509–47 Henry VIII

1399–1413 Henry IV

1485–1509 Henry VII

1066–87 William the Conqueror

1087–1100 William II

1100–35 Henry I

1135–54 Stephen

1327–77 Edward III

1483–5 Richard III

1050	1100	1150	1200	1250	1300	1350	1400	1450	1500
NORMAN		PLANTAGENET					LANCASTER	YORK	TUDOR
1050	1100	1150	1200	1250	1300	1350	1400	1450	1500

1154–89 Henry II

1189–99 Richard I

1199–1216 John

1216–72 Henry III

1307–27 Edward II

1272–1307 Edward I

1461–70 and 1471–83 Edward IV

1422–61 and 1470–1 Henry VI

1377–99 Richard II

Matthew Paris's 13th-century chronicle showing Kings Richard I, Henry II, John and Henry III

1483 Edward V

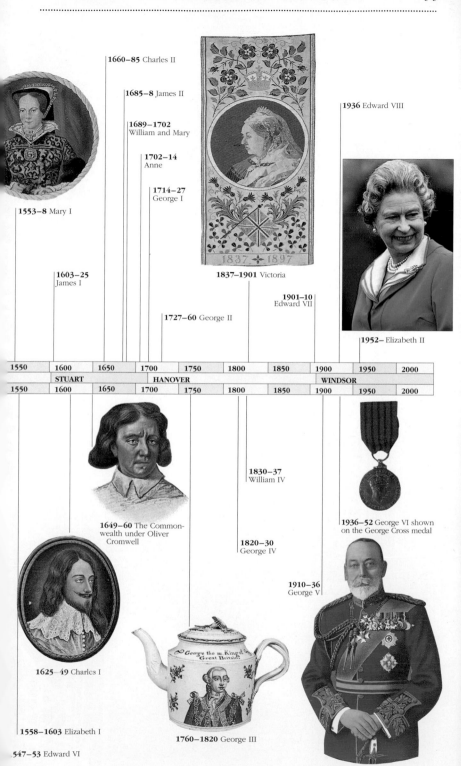

1660–85 Charles II

1685–8 James II

1689–1702
William and Mary

1702–14
Anne

1714–27
George I

1936 Edward VIII

1553–8 Mary I

1603–25
James I

1837–1901 Victoria

1901–10
Edward VII

1727–60 George II

1952– Elizabeth II

1550	1600	1650	1700	1750	1800	1850	1900	1950	2000
	STUART		HANOVER				WINDSOR		
1550	1600	1650	1700	1750	1800	1850	1900	1950	2000

1830–37
William IV

1649–60 The Common-
wealth under Oliver
Cromwell

1936–52 George VI shown
on the George Cross medal

1820–30
George IV

1910–36
George V

1625–49 Charles I

1558–1603 Elizabeth I

1760–1820 George III

547–53 Edward VI

LONDON AT A GLANCE

THERE ARE NEARLY 300 places of interest described in the Area by Area section of this book. These range from the magnificent National Gallery *(see pp104–7)* to gruesome Old St Thomas's Operating Theatre *(p176)*, and from ancient Charterhouse *(p164)* to modern Canary Wharf *(p249)*. To help you make the most of your stay, the following 20 pages are a time-saving guide to the best London has to offer. Museums and galleries, churches, and parks and gardens each have a section, and there are guides to famous Londoners and ceremonies in London. Each sight mentioned is cross-referenced to its own full entry. Below are the ten top tourist attractions to start you off.

LONDON'S TOP TEN TOURIST ATTRACTIONS

St Paul's
See pp148–51.

Hampton Court
See pp254–7.

Changing the Guard
Buckingham Palace, see pp94–5.

British Museum
See pp126–9.

National Gallery
See pp104–7.

Westminster Abbey
See pp76–9.

Madame Tussaud's
See p224.

Houses of Parliament
See pp72–3.

Tower of London
See pp154–7.

Victoria and Albert Museum
See pp202–205.

The British Airways London Eye and Big Ben

Celebrated Visitors and Residents

MANY FAMOUS LONDONERS are famous for *being* Londoners – Samuel Pepys, Christopher Wren, Dr Samuel Johnson, Charles Dickens and countless others *(see pp38–9)*. However, as a centre of international culture, commerce and politics, the English capital has also always attracted celebrated people from overseas. Some famous visitors were escaping war or persecution at home, others came to work or study, or as tourists. In some cases, their association with London is little-known and surprising.

Mary Seacole *(1805–81)*
The Jamaican-born writer and nurse in the Crimean War lodged first in Tavistock Street, then Cambridge Street, Paddington.

Regent's Park and Marylebone

Richard Wagner
(1813– 83)
In 1877 the German opera composer lived at No. 12 Orme Square, Bayswater, from where he would walk across the park to conduct at the Royal Albert Hall (see p207).

South Kensington and Knightsbridge

Kensington and Holland Park

Henry James *(1843–1916)*
The American novelist lived at No. 3 Bolton Street, Mayfair then at No. 34 de Vere Gardens, Kensington (1886–92). He died at Carlyle Mansions, Cheyne Walk.

Dwight Eisenhower
(1890–1969)
During World War II he planned the North African invasion in a house on Grosvenor Square, Mayfair.

Chelsea

Mark Twain
(1835–1910)
Huckleberry Finn's American creator lived from 1896 until 1897 at No. 23 Tedworth Square.

Jenny Lind
(1827–87)
The "Swedish Nightingale" lived for a time at No. 189 Old Brompton Road, Kensington.

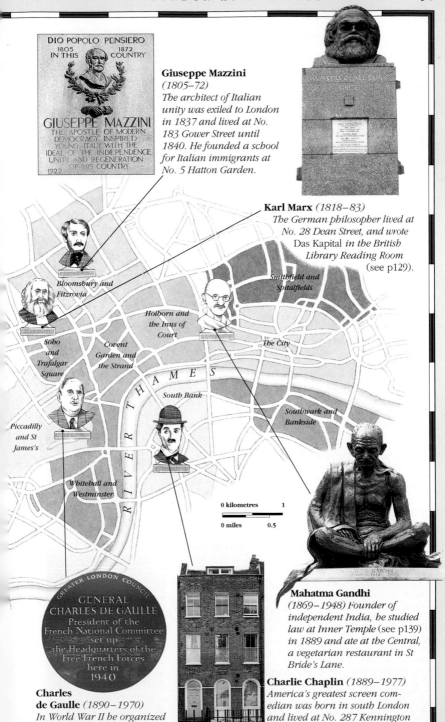

Giuseppe Mazzini
(1805–72)
The architect of Italian unity was exiled to London in 1837 and lived at No. 183 Gower Street until 1840. He founded a school for Italian immigrants at No. 5 Hatton Garden.

Karl Marx *(1818–83)*
The German philosopher lived at No. 28 Dean Street, and wrote Das Kapital *in the British Library Reading Room* (see p129).

Bloomsbury and Fitzrovia

Holborn and the Inns of Court

Smithfield and Spitalfields

The City

Soho and Trafalgar Square

Covent Garden and the Strand

South Bank

Southwark and Bankside

Piccadilly and St James's

Whitehall and Westminster

R I V E R   T H A M E S

0 kilometres   1

0 miles   0.5

Mahatma Gandhi
(1869–1948) Founder of independent India, he studied law at Inner Temple (see p139) in 1889 and ate at the Central, a vegetarian restaurant in St Bride's Lane.

Charlie Chaplin *(1889–1977)*
America's greatest screen comedian was born in south London and lived at No. 287 Kennington Road. He began his career in London's music halls.

Charles de Gaulle *(1890–1970)*
In World War II he organized the French resistance from Carlton House Terrace.

Remarkable Londoners

Caricature of the
Duke of Wellington

LONDON HAS ALWAYS been a gathering place for the most prominent and influential people of their times. Some of these figures have come to London from other parts of Britain or from countries further afield; others have been Londoners, born and bred. All of them have left their mark on London, by designing great and lasting buildings, establishing institutions and traditions, and by writing about or painting the city they knew. Most of them have also had an influence on their times that spread out from London to the rest of the world.

Venus Venticordia by Dante Gabriel Rossetti

ARCHITECTS AND ENGINEERS

John Nash's Theatre Royal Haymarket (1821)

A NUMBER OF people who built London still have works standing. Inigo Jones (1573–1652), London-born, was the father of English Renaissance architecture. He was also a landscape painter and a stage designer. Jones lived and worked at Great Scotland Yard, Whitehall, then the residence of the royal architect – the post in which he was later succeeded by Sir Christopher Wren (1632–1723).

Wren's successors as the prime architects of London were his protégé Nicholas Hawksmoor (1661–1736) and James Gibbs (1682–1754). Succeeding generations each produced architects who were to stamp their genius on the city: in the 18th century the brothers Robert (1728–92) and James Adam (1730–94), then John Nash (1752–1835), Sir Charles Barry (1795–1860), Decimus Burton (1800–81), and the Victorians Alfred Waterhouse (1830–1905),

Norman Shaw (1831–1912) and Sir George Gilbert Scott (1811–78). The engineer Sir Joseph Bazalgette (1819–91) built London's sewer system and the Thames Embankment.

ARTISTS

P AINTERS IN LONDON, as elsewhere, often lived in enclaves, for mutual support and because they shared common priorities. During the 18th century, artists clustered around the court at St James's

to be near their patrons. Thus both William Hogarth (1697–1764) and Sir Joshua Reynolds (1723–92) lived and worked in Leicester Square, while Thomas Gainsborough (1727–88) lived in Pall Mall. (Hogarth's Chiswick house was his place in the country.)

Later, Cheyne Walk in Chelsea, with its river views, became popular with artists, including the masters J M W Turner (1775–1851), James McNeill Whistler (1834–1903), Dante Gabriel Rossetti (1828–82), Philip Wilson Steer (1860–1942) and the sculptor

HISTORIC LONDON HOMES

Four writers' homes that have been recreated and are open to visitors are those of the romantic poet **John Keats** (1795–1821), where he fell in love with Fanny Brawne; the historian **Thomas Carlyle** (1795–1881); the lexicographer **Dr Samuel Johnson** (1709–84); and the prolific and popular novelist **Charles Dickens** (1812–70). The house that the architect **Sir John Soane** (1753–1837) designed for himself remains largely as it was when he died, as does the house where the psychiatrist **Sigmund Freud** (1856–1939) settled after fleeing from the Nazis before the outbreak of World War II.

The Hyde Park Corner house of the **Duke of Wellington** (1769–1852), hero of the Battle of Waterloo, has been lovingly refurbished. Finally, the rooms of Sir Arthur Conan Doyle's fictional detective **Sherlock Holmes** have been created in Baker Street.

Dickens House

Carlyle's House

PLAQUES

All over London the former homes of well-known figures are marked by plaques. Look out for these, especially in Chelsea, Kensington and Mayfair, and see how many names you recognize.

No. 3 Sussex Square, Kensington

No. 27b Canonbury Square, Islington

No. 56 Oakley Street, Chelsea

Sir Jacob Epstein (1880–1959). Augustus John (1879–1961) and John Singer Sargent (1856–1925) had studios in Tite Street. John Constable (1776–1837) is best known as a Suffolk painter but lived for a while at Hampstead, from where he painted many fine views of the heath.

WRITERS

GEOFFREY CHAUCER (c.1345–1400), author of *The Canterbury Tales*, was born in Upper Thames Street, the son of an innkeeper. Both the playwrights William Shakespeare (1564–1616) and Christopher Marlowe (1564–93) were associated with the theatres in Southwark, and may have lived nearby.

The poets John Donne (1572–1631) and John Milton (1608–74) were both born in Bread Street in the City. Donne, after a profligate youth, became Dean of St Paul's. The diarist Samuel Pepys (1633–1703) was born off Fleet Street.

The young novelist Jane Austen (1775–1817) lived briefly off Sloane Street, near the Cadogan Hotel, where the flamboyant Oscar Wilde (1854–1900) was arrested in 1895 for homosexuality. Playwright George Bernard Shaw (1856–1950) lived at No. 29 Fitzroy Square in Bloomsbury. Later the same house was home to Virginia Woolf (1882–1941) and

George Bernard Shaw

became a meeting place for the Bloomsbury Group of writers and artists, which included Vanessa Bell, John Maynard Keynes, E M Forster, Roger Fry and Duncan Grant.

LEADERS

IN LEGEND, a penniless boy named Dick Whittington came to London with his cat seeking streets paved with gold, and later became Lord Mayor. In fact, Richard Whittington (1360?–1423), Lord Mayor three times between 1397 and 1420 and one of London's most celebrated early politicians, was the son of a noble. Sir Thomas More (1478–1535), a Chelsea resident, was Henry VIII's chancellor until they quarrelled over the king's break with the Catholic church and Henry ordered More's execution. More was canonized in 1935. Sir Thomas Gresham (1519?–79) founded the Royal Exchange. Sir Robert Peel (1788–1850) started the London police force, who were known as "bobbies" after him.

ACTORS

NELL GWYNNE (1650–87) won more fame as King Charles II's mistress than as an actress. However, she did appear on stage at Drury Lane Theatre; she also sold oranges there. The Shakespearean actor Edmund Kean (1789–1833) and the great

tragic actress Sarah Siddons (1755–1831) were more distinguished players at Drury Lane. So were Henry Irving (1838–1905) and Ellen Terry (1847–1928), whose stage partnership lasted 24 years. Charlie Chaplin (1889–1977), born in Kennington, had a poverty-stricken childhood in the slums of London.

In the 20th century, a school of fine actors blossomed at the Old Vic, including Sir John Gielgud (1904–2001), Sir Ralph Richardson (1902–83), Dame Peggy Ashcroft (1907–91) and Laurence (later Lord) Olivier (1907–89), who was appointed the first director of the National Theatre.

Laurence Olivier

WHERE TO FIND HISTORIC LONDON HOMES

London's Best: Museums and Galleries

LONDON'S MUSEUMS ARE FILLED with an astonishing diversity of treasures from all over the world. This map highlights 15 of the city's most important galleries and museums whose exhibits cater to most interests. Some of these collections started from the legacies of 18th- and 19th-century explorers, traders and collectors. Others specialize in one aspect of art, history, science or technology. A more detailed overview of London's museums and galleries is on pages 42–3.

British Museum
This Anglo-Saxon helmet is part of a massive collection of antiquities.

Wallace Collection
Frans Hals's Laughing Cavalier *is a star attraction in this museum of art, furniture, armour and* objets d'art.

Royal Academy of Arts
Major international art exhibitions are held here, and the renowned Summer Exhibition, when works are on sale, takes place every year.

Regent's Park and Marylebone

Kensington and Holland Park

South Kensington and Knightsbridge

Piccadilly and St James

Science Museum
Newcomen's steam engine of 1712 is just one of many exhibits that cater for both novice and expert.

Chelsea

Natural History Museum
All of life is here, with vivid displays on everything from dinosaurs (like this Triceratops skull) to butterflies.

Victoria and Albert
It is the world's largest museum of decorative arts. This Indian vase is 18th-century.

0 kilometres   1

0 miles   0.5

National Portrait Gallery
Important British figures are documented in paintings and photographs. This is Vivien Leigh, by Angus McBean (1954).

National Gallery
The world-famous paintings in its collection are mainly European and date from the 15th to the 19th centuries.

Museum of London
London's history since prehistoric times is told with exhibits like this 1920s lift door.

Tower of London
The Crown Jewels and the Royal Armouries are here. This armour was worn by a 14th-century Italian knight.

Design Museum
New inventions and prototypes sit next to familiar, everyday objects from past and present.

Bloomsbury and Fitzrovia

Smithfield and Spitalfields

Holborn and the Inns of Court

The City

Soho and Trafalgar Square

Covent Garden and the Strand

RIVER THAMES

Southwark and Bankside

South Bank

Whitehall and Westminster

Tate Modern
Works of the 20th century, such as Dali's Lobster Telephone, *are celebrated here.*

Tate Britain
Formerly the Tate Gallery, this museum showcases an outstanding collection of British art covering the 16th century to the present.

Imperial War Museum
It uses displays, film and special effects to recreate 20th-century battles. This is one of the earliest tanks.

Courtauld Gallery
Well-known works, such as Manet's Bar at the Folies-Bergère, *line its galleries.*

Exploring Museums and Galleries

Austin Mini, exhibited at the Design Museum

LONDON BOASTS astonishingly rich and diverse museums, the product, in part, of centuries at the hub of world-wide trade and a far-flung Empire. The world-renowned collections cannot be missed, but do not neglect the city's range of smaller museums. From buses to fans, these cover every imaginable speciality and are often more peaceful than their grander counterparts.

Geffrye Museum: Art Nouveau Room

ANTIQUITIES AND ARCHAEOLOGY

SOME OF THE most celebrated artefacts of ancient Asia, Egypt, Greece and Rome are housed in the **British Museum**. Other antiquities, including books, manuscripts, paintings, busts and gems, are displayed in **Sir John Soane's Museum**, which is one of the most idiosyncratic to be found in London.

The **Museum of London** contains much of archaeological interest from all periods of the city's history.

FURNITURE AND INTERIORS

THE MUSEUM OF LONDON recreates typical domestic and commercial interiors from the Roman period right up to the present day. The **Victoria and Albert Museum** (or V&A) contains complete rooms rescued from now vanished buildings, plus a magnificent collection of furniture ranging from the 16th century to work by contemporary designers.

Design Museum display of chairs

Eclectic collection at Sir John Soane's Museum

On a more modest scale, the **Geffrye Museum** consists of fully-furnished period rooms dating from 1600 to the 1990s. Writers' houses, such as the **Freud Museum**, give insights into the furniture of specific periods, while the **Linley Sambourne House** offers visitors a perfectly preserved example of a late Victorian interior.

COSTUME AND JEWELLERY

THE V&A'S VAST collections include English and European clothes of the last 400 years, and some stunning jewellery from China, India and Japan. The priceless Crown Jewels, at the **Tower of London**, should also not be missed. **Kensington Palace** Court Dress Collection opens a window on Court uniforms and protocol from about 1750. The **Theatre Museum** has displays of costumes, props and other memorabilia, while the **British Museum** displays ancient Aztec, Mayan and African costume.

CRAFTS AND DESIGN

ONCE AGAIN, the **Victoria and Albert Museum** (V&A) is the essential first port of call; its collections in these fields remain unrivalled. The **William Morris Gallery** shows every aspect of the 19th-century designer's work within the Arts and Crafts movement. For more modern craft and design, the **Design Museum** focuses on mass-produced goods, while the **Crafts Council Gallery** displays (and sometimes sells) contemporary British craftwork.

MILITARY ARTEFACTS

THE NATIONAL ARMY MUSEUM uses vivid models and displays to narrate the history of the British Army from the reign of Henry VII to the present. The crack regiments of Foot Guards, who are the elite of the British Army, are the main focus of the **Guards' Museum**. The Royal Armouries in the **Tower of London**, Britain's oldest public museum, hold part of the national collection of arms and armour; the **Wallace Collection** also has a display. In the **Imperial War Museum** re-creations of World War I trenches and the 1940 Blitz show war as it really was. The **Florence Nightingale Museum** illustrates the hardships of 19th-century warfare.

TOYS AND CHILDHOOD

TEDDY BEARS, toy soldiers and dolls' houses are some of the toys that can be seen in **Pollock's Toy Museum**. The collection includes Eric, "the oldest known teddy-bear". The **Bethnal Green Museum of Childhood** and the **Museum of London** are a little more formal, but still fun, and illustrate aspects of the social history of childhood with the former offering some interesting children's activities.

SCIENCE AND NATURAL HISTORY

COMPUTERS, ELECTRICITY, space exploration, industrial processes and transport can all be studied at the **Science Museum**. Forms of transport enthusiasts are also catered for at the **London Transport Museum**. In addition, there are other specialized museums such as the **Faraday Museum** concerning the development of electricity, and the **Kew Bridge Steam Museum**. The **National Maritime Museum** and the **Royal Observatory** in Greenwich chart both maritime history and the creation of GMT, by which the world still sets its clocks.

Samson and Delilah (1620) by Van Dyck at the Dulwich Picture Gallery

The **Natural History Museum** mixes displays of animal and bird life with ecological exhibits. The **Museum of Garden History** is devoted to the favourite British pastime.

Imperial War Museum

VISUAL ARTS

THE PARTICULAR STRENGTHS of the **National Gallery** are early Renaissance Italian and 17th-century Spanish painting and a wonderful collection of Dutch masters. **Tate Britain** specializes in British paintings spanning all periods, while **Tate Modern** has displays of international modern art from 1900 to the present day. The **V&A** is strong on European art from 1500–1900 and British art of 1700–1900. The **Royal Academy** and the **Hayward Gallery** specialize

Stone Dancer (1913) by Gaudier-Brzeska at Tate Britain

in major temporary exhibitions. The **Courtauld Institute** at Somerset House contains Impressionist and Post-Impressionist works, while the **Wallace Collection** has 17th-century Dutch and 18th-century French paintings. The **Dulwich Picture Gallery** includes works by Rembrandt, Rubens, Poussin and Gainsborough, while **Kenwood House** is home to paintings by Reynolds, Gainsborough and Rubens in fine Adam interiors. Details of temporary exhibitions are in listings magazines *(see p326)*.

WHERE TO FIND THE COLLECTIONS

London's Best: Churches

IT IS WORTH stopping to look at London's churches and going in, if they are open. They have a special atmosphere unmatched elsewhere in the city, and they can often yield an intimate glimpse of the past. Many churches have replaced earlier buildings in a steady succession, dating back to pre-Christian times. Some began life in outlying villages beyond London's fortified centre, and were absorbed into suburbs when the city expanded in the 18th century. The memorials in the capital's churches and church-yards are a fascinating record of local life, liberally peppered with famous names. A more detailed overview of London churches is on pages 46–7.

All Souls
This plaque comes from a tomb in John Nash's Regency church of 1824.

St Paul's Covent Garden
Inigo Jones's Classical church was known as "the handsomest barn in England".

Bloomsbury and Fitzrovia

Regent's Park and Marylebone

Soho and Trafalgar Square

Piccadilly and St James's

St Martin-in-the-Fields
James Gibbs's church of 1722–6 was originally thought "too gay" for Protestant worship.

South Kensington and Knightsbridge

| 0 kilometres | | 1 |
| 0 miles | 0.5 | |

Whitehall and Westminster

Westminster Cathedral
The Italian-Byzantine Catholic cathedral's red-and-white brick exterior conceals a rich interior of multicoloured marbles.

Brompton Oratory
This sumptuous Baroque church was decorated with works by Italian artists.

Westminster Abbey
The famous abbey has the most glorious medieval architecture in London, and highly impressive tombs and monuments.

St Mary-le-Strand
Now on a traffic island, this ship-like church was built by James Gibbs in 1714–17 to a lively Baroque design. Featuring high windows and rich interior detailing, it was made solid enough to keep out the noise from the street.

St Mary Woolnoth
The jewel-like interior of Nicholas Hawksmoor's small Baroque church (1716–27) appears larger than the outside.

Smithfield and Spitalfields

Holborn and the Inns of Court

Covent Garden and the Strand

The City

R I V E R   T H A M E S

South Bank

Southwark and Bankside

St Stephen Walbrook
Wren was at his best with this domed interior of 1672–7. Its carvings include Henry Moore's austere modern altar.

St Paul's
At 110 m (360 ft) high, the dome of Wren's cathedral is the world's second largest after St Peter's in Rome.

Temple Church
Built in the 12th and 13th centuries for the Knights Templar, this is one of the few circular churches to survive in England.

Southwark Cathedral
This largely 13th-century priory church was not designated a cathedral until 1905. It has a fine medieval choir.

Exploring Churches

St Paul's, Covent Garden

THE CHURCH SPIRES that puncture London's skyline span nearly a thousand years of the city's history. They form an index to many of the events that have shaped the city – the Norman Conquest (1066); the Great Fire of London (1666); the great restoration, led by Wren, that followed it; the Regency period; the confidence of the Victorian era; and the devastation of World War II. Each has had its effect on the churches, many designed by the most influential architects of their times.

MEDIEVAL CHURCHES

THE MOST FAMOUS old church to survive the Great Fire of 1666 is the superb 13th-century **Westminster Abbey**, the church of the Coronation, with its tombs of British monarchs and heroes. Less well known are the well-hidden Norman church of **St Bartholomew-the-Great**, London's oldest church, (1123), the circular **Temple Church** founded in 1160 by the Knights Templars and **Southwark Cathedral**, set amid Victorian railway lines and warehouses. **Chelsea Old Church** is a charming village church near the river.

CHURCHES BY JONES

INIGO JONES (1573–1652) was Shakespeare's contemporary, and his works were almost as revolutionary as the great dramatist's. Jones's Classical churches of the 1620s and 1630s shocked a public used to conservative Gothic finery. By far the best-known is **St Paul's Church** of the 1630s, the centrepiece of Jones's Italian-style piazza in Covent Garden. **Queen's Chapel, St James** was built in 1623 for Queen Henrietta Maria, the Catholic wife of Charles I. It was the first Classical church in England and has a magnificent interior but is, unfortunately, usually closed to the public.

CHURCHES BY HAWKSMOOR

NICHOLAS HAWKSMOOR (1661–1736) was Wren's most talented pupil, and his churches are among the finest

SPIRES

Look out for London's richly-decorated church steeples. Here are four of the city's most distinctive to get you started.

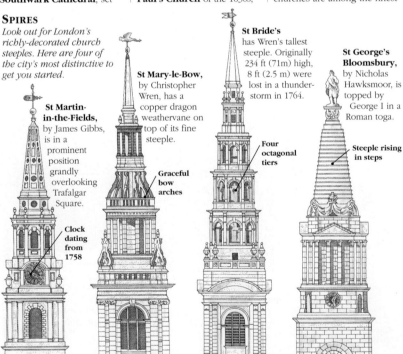

St Martin-in-the-Fields, by James Gibbs, is in a prominent position grandly overlooking Trafalgar Square.

Clock dating from 1758

St Mary-le-Bow, by Christopher Wren, has a copper dragon weathervane on top of its fine steeple.

Graceful bow arches

St Bride's has Wren's tallest steeple. Originally 234 ft (71m) high, 8 ft (2.5 m) were lost in a thunderstorm in 1764.

Four octagonal tiers

St George's Bloomsbury, by Nicholas Hawksmoor, is topped by George I in a Roman toga.

Steeple rising in steps

Baroque buildings to be found in Britain.

St George's, Bloomsbury (1716–31) has an unusual centralized plan and a pyramid steeple topped by a statue of King George I. **St Mary Woolnoth** is a tiny jewel of 1716–27, and further east **Christ Church, Spitalfields** is a Baroque tour-de-force of 1714–29, now being restored.

Among Hawksmoor's East End churches are the stunning **St Anne's, Limehouse** and **St Alfege**, of 1714–17, which is across the river in Greenwich. The tower on this temple-like church was added later by John James in 1730.

St Anne's, Limehouse

CHURCHES BY GIBBS

JAMES GIBBS (1682–1754) was more conservative than his Baroque contemporaries such as Hawksmoor, and he also kept his distance from the Neo-Classical trend so popular after 1720. His idiosyncratic London churches were enormously influential. **St Mary-le-Strand** (1714–17) is an island church which appears to be sailing down the Strand. The radical design of **St Martin-in-the-Fields** (1722–6) predates its setting, Trafalgar Square, by a hundred years.

REGENCY CHURCHES

THE END OF the Napoleonic Wars in 1815 brought a flurry of church building. The need for churches in London's new suburbs fused with a Greek Revival. The

CHRISTOPHER WREN

Sir Christopher Wren (1632–1723) was leader among the many architects who helped restore London after the Great Fire of London. He devised a new city plan, replacing the narrow streets with wide avenues radiating from piazzas. His plan was rejected, but he was commissioned to build 52 new churches; 31 have survived various threats of demolition and the bombs of World War II, although six are shells. Wren's great masterpiece is the massive **St Paul's**, while nearby is splendid **St Stephen Walbrook**, his domed church of 1672–77. Other landmarks are **St Bride's**, off Fleet Street, said to have inspired the traditional shape of wedding cakes, **St Mary-le-Bow** in Cheapside and **St Magnus Martyr** in Lower Thames Street. Wren's own favourite was **St James's, Piccadilly** (1683–4). Smaller gems are **St Clement Danes**, Strand (1680–82) and **St James, Garlickhythe** (1674–87).

results may lack the exuberance of Hawksmoor, but they have an austere elegance of their own. **All Souls, Langham Place** (1822–4), at the north end of Regent Street, was built by the Prince Regent's favourite, John Nash, who was ridiculed at the time for its unusual combination of design styles. Also worth visiting is **St Pancras**, a Greek Revival church of 1819–22, which is typical of the period.

VICTORIAN CHURCHES

LONDON HAS SOME of the finest 19th-century churches in Europe. Grand and colourful, their riotous decoration is in marked contrast to the chaste Neo-Classicism of the preceding Regency era. Perhaps the best of the capital's late Victorian churches is **Westminster Cathedral**, a

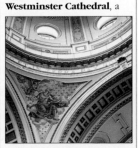

Brompton Oratory

stunningly rich, Italianate Catholic cathedral built in 1895–1903, with architecture by J F Bentley and *Stations of the Cross* reliefs by Eric Gill. **Brompton Oratory** is a grand Baroque revival, based on a church in Rome and filled with magnificent furnishings from all over Catholic Europe.

London's Best: Parks and Gardens

Since MEDIEVAL TIMES London has had large expanses of green. Some of these, such as Hampstead Heath, were originally common land, where small-holders could graze their animals. Others, such as Richmond Park and Holland Park, were royal hunting grounds or the gardens of large houses; several still have formal features dating from those times. Today you can cross much of central London by walking from St James's Park in the east to Kensington Gardens in the west. Purpose-built parks, like Battersea, and botanical gardens, like Kew, appeared later.

Hampstead Heath
This breezy, open space is located in the midst of north London. Nearby Parliament Hill offers views of St Paul's, the City and the West End.

Hampstead

Kensington Gardens
This plaque is from the Italian Garden, one of the features of this elegant park.

Kensington and Holland Park

South Kensington Knightsbri

Holland Park
The former grounds of one of London's grandest homes are now its most romantic park.

Kew Gardens
The world's premier botanic garden is a must for anyone with an interest in plants, exotic or mundane.

0 kilometres 1

0 miles 0.5

Richmond Park
The biggest royal park in London remains largely unspoiled, with deer and magnificent river views.

Regent's Park
In this civilized park, surrounded by fine Regency buildings, you can stroll around the rose garden, visit the open-air theatre, or simply sit and admire the view.

Greenwich Park
Its focal point is the National Maritime Museum, well worth a visit for its architecture as well as its exhibits. There are also fine views.

Hyde Park
The Serpentine is one of the highlights of a park which also boasts restaurants, an art gallery and Speakers' Corner.

Regent's Park and Marylebone

Bloomsbury and Fitzrovia

Holborn and the Inns of Court

Smithfield and Spitalfields

Soho and Trafalgar Square

The City

Piccadilly

THAMES

South Bank

Southwark and Bankside

Whitehall and Westminster

RIVER THAMES

N

Greenwich and Blackheath

Green Park
Its leafy paths are favoured by early-morning joggers from the Mayfair hotels.

St James's Park
People come here to feed the ducks, or watch the pelicans. A band plays throughout the summer.

Battersea Park
Visitors can hire a rowing boat for the best view of the Victorian landscaping around the lake.

Exploring Parks and Gardens

L ONDON HAS ONE of the the world's greenest city centres, full of tree-filled squares and grassy parks. From the intimacy of the Chelsea Physic Garden to the wild, open spaces of Hampstead Heath, every London park has its own charm and character. For those looking for a specific outdoor attraction – such as sports, wildlife or flowers – here are some of the most interesting London parks.

Camilla japonica

FLOWER GARDENS

T HE BRITISH are famed for their gardens and love of flowers and this is reflected in several of London's parks. Really keen gardeners will find all they ever wanted to know at **Kew Gardens** and the **Chelsea Physic Garden**, which is especially strong on herbs. Closer to the centre of town, **St James's Park** boasts some spectacular flower beds, filled with bulbs and bedding plants, which are changed every season. **Hyde Park** sports a magnificent show of daffodils and crocuses in the spring and London's best rose garden is Queen Mary's in

Regent's Park. **Kensington Gardens'** flower walk has an exemplary English mixed border, and there is also a delightful small 17th-century garden at the **Museum of Garden History**.

Battersea Park also has a charming flower garden, and indoor gardeners should head to the **Barbican Centre**'s well-stocked conservatory.

FORMAL GARDENS

T HE MOST SPECTACULAR formal garden is at **Hampton Court**, which has a network of gardens from different periods, starting with Tudor. The gardens at **Chiswick**

Embankment Gardens

House remain dotted with their 18th-century statuary and pavilions. Other restored gardens include 17th-century **Ham House**, and **Osterley Park**, whose 18th-century layout was retraced through the art of dowsing. **Fenton House** has a really fine walled garden; **Kenwood** is less formal, with its woodland area. **The Hill** is great in summer. The sunken garden at **Kensington Palace** has a formal layout and **Holland Park** has flowers around its statues.

RESTFUL CORNERS

L ONDON'S SQUARES are cool, shady retreats but, sadly, many are reserved for key-holders, usually residents of the surrounding houses. Of those open to all, **Russell Square** is the largest and most secluded. **Berkeley Square** is open but barren. **Green Park**, with its shady trees and deck chairs, offers a cool picnic spot right in central London. The Inns of Court provide some really pleasant havens: **Gray's Inn** gardens, **Middle Temple**

Sunken garden at Kensington Palace

GREEN LONDON

In Greater London there are 1,700 parks covering a total of 67 sq miles (174 sq km). This land is home to some 2,000 types of plant and 100 bird species who breed in the trees. Trees help the city to breathe, manu-facturing oxygen from the polluted air. Here are some of the species you are most likely to see in London.

The London plane, now the most common tree in London, grows along many streets.

The English oak grows all over Europe. The Royal Navy used to build ships from it.

gardens and **Lincoln's Inn Fields**. **Soho Square,** which is surrounded by streets, is more urban and animated.

MUSIC IN SUMMER

STRETCHING OUT on the grass or in a deck chair to listen to a band is a British tradition. Military and other bands give regular concerts throughout the summer at **St James's** and **Regent's Parks** and also at **Parliament Hill Fields**. The concert schedule will usually be found posted up close to the bandstand in the park.

Open-air festivals of classical music are held in the summer in several parks *(see p333)*.

WILDLIFE

THERE IS A LARGE and well-fed collection of ducks and other water birds, even including a few pelicans, in **St James's Park**. Duck lovers will also appreciate **Regent's, Hyde** and **Battersea Parks,** as well as **Hampstead Heath**. Deer roam in **Richmond** and **Greenwich Parks.** For a wide variety of captive animals, **London Zoo** is in **Regent's Park** and there are aviaries or aquariums at several parks and gardens, including **Kew Gardens** and **Syon House**.

Geese in St James's Park

HISTORIC CEMETERIES

In the late 1830s a ring of private cemeteries was established around London to ease the pressure on the monstrously overcrowded and unhealthy burial grounds of the inner city. Today some of these (notably **Highgate Cemetery** and Kensal Green – Harrow Road W10) are worth visiting for their air of repose and their Victorian monuments. **Bunhill Fields** is earlier; it was first used during the plague of 1665.

Kensal Green cemetery

Boating pond at Regent's Park

SPORTS

CYCLING IS NOT universally encouraged in London's parks, and footpaths tend to be too bumpy to allow much rollerskating. However, most parks have tennis courts, which normally have to be reserved in advance with the attendant. Rowing boats may be hired at **Hyde, Regent's** and **Battersea Parks,** among others. Athletics tracks are at both Battersea Park and also **Parliament Hill**. The public may swim at the ponds on **Hampstead Heath** and in the Serpentine in Hyde Park. Hampstead Heath is also ideal kite-flying territory.

The common beech has a close relation, the copper beech, with reddish purple leaves.

The horse chestnut's hard round fruits are used by children for a game called conkers.

London's Best: Ceremonies

MUCH OF LONDON'S rich inheritance of tradition and ceremony centres on royalty. Faithfully enacted today, some of these ceremonies date back to the Middle Ages, when the ruling monarch had absolute power and had to be protected from opponents. This map shows the venues for some of the most important ceremonies in London. For more details on these and other ceremonies please turn to pages 54–5; information on all sorts of events taking place in London throughout the year can be found on pages 56–9.

St James's Palace and Buckingham Palace
Members of the Queen's Life Guard stand at the gates of these two palaces.

Bloomsbury and Fitzrovia

Soho and Trafalgar Square

South Kensington and Knightsbridge

Piccadilly and St James's

Whitehall and Westminster

Hyde Park
Royal Salutes are fired by six guns of the King's Troop Royal Horse Artillery on royal anniversaries and ceremonial occasions.

Chelsea

Chelsea Hospital
In 1651 Charles II hid from parliamentary forces in an oak tree. On Oak Apple Day, Chelsea Pensioners decorate his statue with oak leaves and branches.

Horse Guards
At Trooping the Colour, the most elaborate of London's royal ceremonies, the Queen salutes as a battalion of Foot Guards parades its colours before her.

The City and Embankment

At the Lord Mayor's Show, pikemen and musketeers escort the newly elected Lord Mayor through the City in a gold state coach.

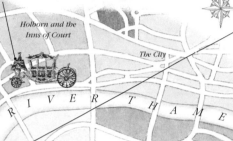

Holborn and the
Inns of Court

Covent
arden and
be Strand

The City

The Cenotaph

On Remembrance Sunday the Queen pays homage to the nation's war dead.

R I V E R T H A M E S

South Bank

Southwark and
Bankside

0 kilometres   1

0 miles   0.5

Tower of London

In the nightly Ceremony of the Keys, a Yeoman Warder locks the gates. A military escort ensures the keys are not stolen.

Houses of Parliament

Each autumn the Queen goes to Parliament in the Irish State Coach to open the new parliamentary session.

Attending London's Ceremonies

ROYALTY AND COMMERCE provide the two principal sources of London's rich calendar of ceremonial events. Quaint and old-fashioned these events may be, but what may seem arcane ritual has real historical meaning – many of the capital's ceremonies originated in the Middle Ages.

ROYAL CEREMONIES

ALTHOUGH THE Queen's role is now largely symbolic, the Guard at Buckingham Palace still actively patrols the palace grounds. The impressive ceremony of **Changing the Guard** – dazzling uniforms, shouted commands, military music – consists of the Old Guard, which forms up in the palace forecourt, going off duty and handing over to the New Guard. The Guard consists of three officers and 40 men when the Queen is in residence, but only three officers and 31 men when she is away. The ceremony takes place in front of the palace. In another changeover ceremony, the Queen's Life Guards travel daily from Hyde Park Barracks to Horse Guards' Parade.

One of the Queen's Life Guards

The **Ceremony of the Keys** at the Tower of London is one of the capital's most timeless ceremonies. After each of the Tower gates has been locked, the last post is sounded by a trumpeter before the keys are secured in the Queen's House.

The Tower of London and Hyde Park are also the scene of **Royal Salutes** which take place on birthdays and other occasions throughout the year. At such times 41 rounds are fired in Hyde Park at noon, and 62 rounds at the Tower at 1pm. The spectacle in Hyde Park is a stirring one as 71 horses and six 13-pounder cannons swirl into place and the roar of the guns begins.

The combination of pageantry, colour and music makes the annual **Trooping the Colour** the high point of London's ceremonial year. The Queen takes the Royal Salute, and after her troops have marched past, she leads them to Buckingham Palace where a second march past takes place. The best place to watch this spectacle is from the Horse Guards Parade side of St James's Park.

Bands of the Household Cavalry and the Foot Guards stage the ceremony of **Beating the Retreat** at

A Queen's Guard in winter

Horse Guards Parade. This takes place three or four evenings a week in the fortnight leading up to Trooping the Colour.

The spectacular **State Opening of Parliament**, when the Queen opens the annual parliamentary session in the House of Lords – usually in November – is not open to the general public, although it is now televised. The huge royal procession, which moves from Buckingham Palace to Westminster, is, however, a magnificent sight, with the Queen travelling in the highly ornate Irish State Coach drawn by four horses.

MILITARY CEREMONIES

THE CENOTAPH in Whitehall is the setting for a ceremony held on **Remembrance Sunday**, to give thanks to those who died fighting in the two World Wars.

National **Navy Day** is commemorated by a parade down the Mall, followed by a service held at Nelson's Column in Trafalgar Square.

Royal salute, Tower of London

Trooping the Colour

Silent Change ceremony at Guildhall for the new Lord Mayor

CEREMONIES IN THE CITY

NOVEMBER IS THE focus of the City of London's ceremonial year. At the **Silent Change** in Guildhall, the outgoing Lord Mayor hands over symbols of office to the new Mayor in a virtually wordless ceremony. The following day sees the rumbustious **Lord Mayor's Show**. Accompanying the Lord Mayor in his gold state coach a procession of bands, decorated floats and military detachments makes its way through the City from Guildhall past the Mansion House to the Law Courts, and back again along the Embankment.

Lord Mayor's chain of office

Many of the ceremonies that take place in the City are linked to the activities of the Livery Companies *(see p152)*. These include the Worshipful Companies of **Vintners' and Distillers'** annual celebration of the wine harvest and the Stationers' **Cakes and Ale Sermon**, held in St Paul's. Cakes and ale are provided according to the will of a 17th-century stationer.

NAME-DAY CEREMONIES

EVERY 21 MAY **King Henry VI**, who was murdered in the Tower of London in 1471, is still remembered by the members of his two famous foundations, Eton College and King's College, Cambridge,

who meet for a ceremony at the Wakefield Tower where he was killed. **Oak Apple Day** commemorates King Charles II's lucky escape from the Parliamentary forces of Oliver Cromwell in 1651. The King managed to conceal himself in a hollow oak tree, and today Chelsea Pensioners honour his memory by decorating his statue at Chelsea Royal Hospital with oak leaves and branches. On 18 December, the diarist **Dr Johnson** is commemorated in an annual service held at Westminster Abbey.

INFORMAL CEREMONIES

EACH JULY, six guildsmen from the Company of Watermen compete for the prize in **Doggett's Coat and Badge Race**. In autumn, the **Pearly Kings and Queens**, representatives of east London's traders, meet at St Martin-in-the-Fields. In March children are given oranges and lemons at the **Oranges and Lemons service** at St Clement Danes Church. In February, clowns take part in a service for **Joseph Grimaldi** (1779–1837) at the Holy Trinity Church in Dalston E8.

Pearly Queen

LONDON THROUGH THE YEAR

SPRINGTIME IN London carries an almost tangible air of a city waking up to longer days and outdoor pursuits. The cheerful yellow of daffodils studs the parks, and less-hardy Londoners turn out for their first jog of the year to find themselves puffing in the wake of serious runners in training for the Marathon. As spring turns into summer, the royal parks reach their full glory, and in Kensington Gardens

nannies gather to chat under venerable chestnut trees. As autumn takes hold, these same trees are ablaze with red and gold and Londoners' thoughts turn to afternoons in museums and art galleries, followed by tea in a café. The year draws to a close with Guy Fawkes parties and shopping in the West End. Contact the London Tourist Board (see *p347*) or check the listings magazines (*p326*) for details of seasonal events.

SPRING

THE WEATHER during the spring months may be raw, and an umbrella is a necessary precaution. Druids celebrate the Spring Equinox in a subdued ceremony on Tower Hill. Painters compete to have their works accepted by the Royal Academy. Footballers close their season with the FA Cup Final at Wembley, while cricketers don their sweaters to begin theirs. Oxford and Cambridge Universities row their annual boat race along the Thames, and Marathon runners pound the streets.

Runners in the London Marathon passing Tower Bridge

MARCH

Chelsea Antiques Fair (*second week*), Chelsea Old Town Hall, King's Rd SW3.
Ideal Home Exhibition (*second week*), Earl's Court, Warwick Rd SW5. It is a long-established show with the latest in domestic gadgetry and state-of-the-art technology.
Oranges and Lemons Service, St Clement Danes (*p55*). Service for school-children; each child is given an orange and a lemon.
Oxford v Cambridge boat race (*Sat before Easter, or Easter*), Putney to Mortlake (*p339*).
Spring Equinox celebration (*21 Mar*), Tower Hill EC3. Historic pagan ceremony with modern-day druids.

EASTER

Good Fri and following Mon are public holidays. **Easter parades**, Covent Garden (*p112*), Battersea Park (*p251*).

Kite flying, Blackheath (*p243*) and Hampstead Heath (*p234*).
Easter procession and hymns (*Easter Mon*), Westminster Abbey (*pp76–9*). One of London's most evocative religious celebrations.
International Model Railway Exhibition (*Easter weekend*), Royal Horticultural Hall, Vincent Sq SW1. Of real interest to everyone, not just railway enthusiasts.

A London park in the spring

APRIL

Queen's Birthday gun salutes (*21 Apr*), Hyde Park, Tower of London (*p54*).
London Marathon (*Sun in Apr or May*), Greenwich to Westminster (*p339*).

MAY

First and last Mon are public holidays.
FA Cup Final, football season's climax (*p338*).
Henry VI Memorial (*p55*).
Beating the Bounds (*Ascension Day*), throughout the City. Young boys selected from the City parish beat certain buildings, marking the parish boundaries.
Oak Apple Day, at the Royal Hospital, Chelsea (*p55*).
Funfairs (*late May public hol weekend*), various commons.
Chelsea Flower Show (*late May*), Royal Hospital, Chelsea.
Beating the Retreat (*p54*).
Royal Academy Summer Exhibition (*May–Jul*), Piccadilly (*p90*).

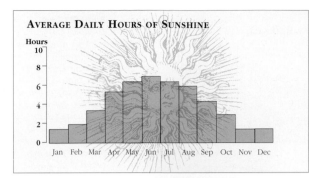

AVERAGE DAILY HOURS OF SUNSHINE

Hours

Jan Feb Mar Apr May Jun Jul Aug Sep Oct Nov Dec

Sunshine Chart
London's longest and hottest days fall between May and August. In the height of summer, daylight hours can extend from well before 5am to after 9pm. Daytime is much shorter in the winter, but London can be stunning in the winter sunshine.

SUMMER

Lorem ipsum — LONDON'S SUMMER season is packed full of indoor and outdoor events. The weather is very unreliable, even at the height of summer, but unless you are notably unlucky there should be enough fine days to sample what is on offer.

The selection includes many traditional events, such as the Wimbledon tennis championships and the cricket test matches at Lord's and the Oval. Well out of view from the general public and prying photographers, the Queen holds garden parties for favoured subjects in the splendid grounds of Buckingham Palace. The summer public holiday is also marked with funfairs in some of London's parks.

JUNE

Morris dancing *(Wed eves, all summer)*, Westminster Abbey *(pp76–9)*. Traditional English folk-dancing.
Coronation Day gun salutes *(2 Jun)*, Hyde Park and Tower of London *(p54)*.
Ceramics fair, Dorchester Hotel, Park Lane W1.
Fine Art and Antiques fair, Olympia, Olympia Way W14.
Trooping the Colour, Horse Guards Parade *(p54)*.
Charles Dickens memorial service *(9 Jun)*, Westminster Abbey *(pp76–9)*. Celebration of London's famous author.
Duke of Edinburgh's Birthday gun salutes *(10 Jun)*, Hyde Park and Tower of London *(p54)*.
Wimbledon Lawn Tennis Championships *(two weeks in late Jun; p338)*.

Revellers at Notting Hill Carnival

Cricket test match, Lord's *(p338)*.
Open-air theatre season *(throughout the summer)*, Regent's Park and Holland Park. Shakespeare, Shaw and others offer the perfect opportunity for a picnic *(p328)*.
Open-air concerts, Kenwood, Hampstead Heath, Crystal Palace, Marble Hill, St James's Park *(p333)*.
Street theatre festival *(Jun–Jul)*, Covent Garden *(pp112–3)*. Street performers of every kind gather to flaunt their various talents.
Summer festivals *(late Jun)*, Greenwich, Spitalfields and Primrose Hill. Contact the London Tourist Board *(p347)* or see the listings magazines *(p326)* for times and venues of all these events.

JULY

Summer festivals, City of London and Richmond.
Sales. Price reductions across London's shops *(p313)*.

Doggett's Coat and Badge Race *(p55)*.
Hampton Court Flower Show, Hampton Court Palace *(pp254–7)*.
Capital Radio Jazz Festival, Royal Festival Hall *(p188)*.
Henry Wood Promenade Concerts *(late Jul–Sep)*, Royal Albert Hall *(p207)*.

AUGUST

Last Monday in August is a public holiday.
Queen Mother's Birthday gun salutes *(4 Aug)*, Hyde Park and Tower of London *(p54)*.
Notting Hill Carnival *(late Aug holiday weekend)*. An internationally famous and well attended celebration organized mainly by the area's various ethnic communities *(p219)*.
Funfairs *(Aug holiday)*. These tend to run throughout London's parks during the summer months.

Regimental band, St James's Park

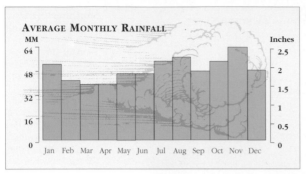

AVERAGE MONTHLY RAINFALL

MM		Inches
64		2.5
48		2
32		1.5
16		1
		0.5
0		0

Jan Feb Mar Apr May Jun Jul Aug Sep Oct Nov Dec

Rainfall Chart
London's average monthly rainfall remains much the same throughout the year. July and August, the capital's warmest months, are also two of its wettest. Rain is less likely in spring, but visitors should be prepared for a shower at any time of year.

AUTUMN

THERE IS A SENSE of purpose about London in autumn. The build-up to the busiest shopping season, the start of the academic year, and the new parliamentary session, opened by the Queen, inject some life into the colder months. The cricket season comes to an end in mid-September, while food-lovers may be interested in the spectacular displays of fresh fish that are laid out in the vestry of St Mary-at-the-Hill, celebrating the harvest of this island nation.

Memories of a more turbulent opening of Parliament are revived on 5 November, when there are bonfires and fireworks to commemorate the failure of a conspiracy led by Guy Fawkes to blow up the Palace of Westminster in 1605. A few days later the dead of two World Wars are commemorated at a ceremony held in Whitehall.

Pearly Kings gathering for the harvest festival at St Martin-in-the-Fields

SEPTEMBER

National Rose Society Annual Show, Royal Horticultural Hall, Vincent Sq SW1.
Great River Race, Thames.
Chelsea Antiques Fair *(third week)*, Chelsea Old Town Hall, King's Road SW3.
Horse of the Year Show *(25–9 Sep)*, Wembley *(p339)*. London's equestrian showpiece.
Last Night of the Proms *(mid-Sep)*, Royal Albert Hall *(p207)*.

OCTOBER

Pearly Harvest Festival *(first Sun)*, St Martin-in-the-Fields.
Punch and Judy Festival Covent Garden WC2. Celebration of puppet duo.
Harvest of the Sea *(second Sun)*, St Mary-at-Hill Church *(p152)*.
Vintners' and Distillers' Wine Harvest *(p55)*.
Navy Day *(p54)*.

State Opening of Parliament *(p54)*.

NOVEMBER

Guy Fawkes Night *(5 Nov)*. Listings magazines give details of firework displays *(p326)*.
Remembrance Day Service *(p54)*.
Silent Change *(p55)*.
Lord Mayor's Show *(p55)*.
London to Brighton veteran car rally *(first Sun)*.
Christmas lights *(late Nov–6 Jan)*. The West End *(p315)* lights up for the festive season.

London-to-Brighton veteran car run

Autumn colours in a London park

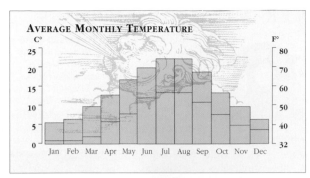

AVERAGE MONTHLY TEMPERATURE

Temperature Chart
The chart shows the average minimum and maximum temperatures for each month. Top temperatures averaging 22° C (75° F) belie London's reputation for year-round chilliness, although November through to February can be icy.

WINTER

SOME OF THE most striking images of London are drawn from winter: paintings of frost fairs in the 17th and 18th centuries, when the River Thames froze over completely; and Claude Monet's views of the river and its bridges.

For centuries thick "pea-souper" fogs were an inevitable part of winter, until the Clean Air Act of 1956 barred coal-burning in open grates.

Christmas trees and lights twinkle everywhere – from the West End shopping streets to construction sites. The scent of roasting chestnuts pervades as street pedlars sell them from glowing mobile braziers.

Seasonal menus feature roast turkey, mince pies and rich, dark Christmas pudding. Traditional fare in theatres includes colourful family pantomimes (where the customary cross-dressing between the sexes baffles many visitors – *p328*) and popular ballets such as *Swan Lake* or *The Nutcracker*.

Skaters use the open-air rink at the Broadgate Centre in the City, and sometimes it is safe to venture on to the frozen lakes in the parks.

Winter in Kensington Gardens

DECEMBER

Oxford v Cambridge rugby union match Twickenham *(p339)*.
Dr Johnson memorial service *(18 Dec)*, Westminster Abbey *(p55)*.
Festival of Showjumping *(late Dec)*, Olympia.

CHRISTMAS, NEW YEAR

25–26 Dec and **1 Jan** are public hols. There is no train service on Christmas Day.

Carol services *(leading up to Christmas)*, Trafalgar Square *(p102)*, St Paul's *(pp148–51)*, Westminster Abbey *(pp76–9)* and other churches.
Turkey auction *(24 Dec)*, Smithfield Market *(p164)*.
Christmas Day swim Serpentine, Hyde Park *(p211)*.
New Year's Eve celebrations *(31 Dec)*, Trafalgar Square, St Paul's.

JANUARY

Sales *(p313)*.
International Boat Show, Earl's Court, Warwick Rd SW5.
International Mime Festival *(mid Jan–early Feb)*, various venues.
Charles I Commemoration *(last Sun)*, procession from St James's Palace *(p91)* to Banqueting House *(p80)*.
Chinese New Year *(late Jan–early Feb)*, Chinatown *(p108)* and Soho *(p109)*.

FEBRUARY

Clowns' Service *(first Sun)*, Dalston *(p55)*.
Queen's Accession gun salutes *(6 Feb)*, 41-gun salute Hyde Park; 62-gun salute Tower of London *(p54)*.
Pancake races *(Shrove Tue)*, Lincoln's Inn Fields *(p137)* and Covent Garden *(p112)*.

PUBLIC HOLIDAYS
New Year's Day (1 Jan); **Good Friday; Easter Monday; May Day** (first Monday in May); **Whit Monday** (last Monday in May); **August Bank Holiday** (last Monday in August); **Christmas** (25–26 December).

Christmas illuminations in Trafalgar Square

A RIVER VIEW OF LONDON

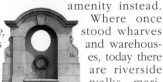

IN OLD Celtic the word for river was *teme*, and the Romans adopted this as the name for the great waterway upon which they founded the city

Decoration on Southwark Bridge

of *Londinium (see pp16–17)* nearly 2,000 years ago. The Roman settlers built their new city along the most easterly point at which the river could be bridged using the technology of the time. Since then, the Thames has continued to play a critical role in London's history. It was the route taken by the Viking invaders of the 8th and 9th centuries, the birthplace of the Royal Navy in Tudor times, and the artery for much of the country's commerce until well into the 1950s.

Now changing trade patterns have moved the big ships elsewhere, and the river has become the capital's foremost leisure amenity instead. Where once stood wharves and warehouses, today there are riverside walks, marinas, bars and restaurants.

One of the most interesting ways of seeing the capital is by boat, and several companies offer sightseeing cruises from central London. These vary in length from 30 minutes to four hours. The most popular section of the river to travel runs downstream from the Houses of Parliament to Tower Bridge. A river view gives you a very different perspective of London's major sites, including Traitors' Gate, the infamous river entrance to the Tower of London, which was used for prisoners brought from trial in Westminster Hall *(see pp72–3)*. You can also take longer journeys past the varied architectural styles found between Hampton Court and the Thames Barrier.

The Thames in London
Passenger boat services cover about 30 miles (50 km) of the Thames, from Hampton Court in the west to the Thames Barrier in the former Docklands of the east.

Houseboats at Chelsea

Kew Rail Bridge
Kew Bridge
Kew
Chiswick Bridge
Twickenham Rail Bridge
Twickenham Bridge
Richmond Bridge
Richmond
Teddington Foot Bridge
Kingston Bridge
Hampton Court

TOUR OPERATORS

Most of these services run from 1 April until the end of September, when they revert to winter schedules, but phone first to check times, which are subject to change. During the winter there are no upriver services.

A circular cruise on *Mercedes*

Westminster Pier
Map 13 C5.
🚇 *Westminster.*

Downriver to Tower Pier
📞 *020-7930 9933.*

Departures
9.40am daily in peak season (end May–beg Sep). 10am, 10.20am, 10.40am and every 20 minutes until 6pm. Then twice per hour until 9.20pm peak season only.
Duration 30 minutes.

Downriver to Greenwich
📞 *020-7930 9033 or 4097.*
Departures 9.40am daily in peak season (end May–beg Sep). 10.20am, 10.30am, 11am, 11.30am, 11.40am, noon. Then three times per hour until 4.30pm, 5pm peak season.
Duration 1 hour.

Downriver to the Thames Barrier
📞 *020-7930 4097.*
Departures 11am, 12pm, 1pm (2pm peak season).
Duration about 1½ hours.

Upriver to Kew
📞 *020-7930 4721 or 2062.*
Departures 10.15am, 10.30am, 11.15am, noon and 2pm.
Duration 1½ hours.

Upriver to Richmond
📞 *020-7930 4721 or 2062.*
Departures 10.30am, 11.15am and noon.
Duration about 2 hours.

Upriver to Hampton Court
📞 *020-7930 4721.*

Private party on a chartered boat

The River Thames is at its most romantic at dusk. The view east from Waterloo Bridge shows St Paul's and the City on the north bank and the Oxo Tower on the south.

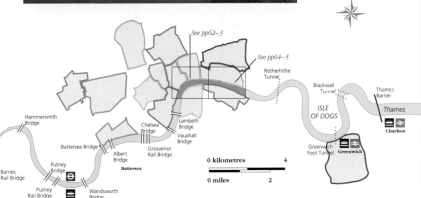

See pp62–3

See pp64–5

Rotherhithe Tunnel

Blackwall Tunnel

Thames Barrier

ISLE OF DOGS

Thames

Charlton

Hammersmith Bridge

Chelsea Bridge

Lambeth Bridge

Vauxhall Bridge

Battersea Bridge

Albert Bridge

Grosvenor Rail Bridge

Battersea

Greenwich Foot Tunnel **Greenwich**

Putney Bridge

Barnes Rail Bridge

Putney Rail Bridge

Wandsworth Bridge

Putney

0 kilometres 4

0 miles 2

KEY

Underground station

Railway station

River boat stop

The river at Twickenham

The view from Richmond Hill

Open-decked boat

Departures *11am and noon end-Mar–mid-Apr. 10.30am, 11.15am and noon mid-Apr–Sep.* **Duration** *about 3¹/₂ hours.*

Circular service to St. Katharine's
020-7936 2033.
Departures *11am, 11.40am, 12.20pm, 1pm, 1.40pm and every 40 minutes until 5pm Apr–May. 11am, 11.30am and every*

30 minutes until 6.30pm Jun–Aug. **Duration** *1 hour.*

Embankment Pier
Map 13 C3. Charing Cross, Embankment.
Downriver to Tower Pier
020-7987 1185.
Departures *every 45 minutes 10am–4pm Mon–Fri Apr–Jun, Sep–Oct. Every 30 minutes 10am–4pm daily Jul–Aug and Sat–Sun Apr–Jun, Sep–Oct.* **Duration** *30 minutes.*

Downriver to Greenwich
020-7987 1185.

Departures *As Embankment to Tower Pier above.* **Duration** *1 hour.*

Tower Pier
Map 16 D3. Tower Hill.

Upriver to Westminster
020-7930 9033.
Departures *10.35am, 10.55am, 11.15am, 11.35am and every 20 minutes until 6.35pm. Then 6.55pm, 7.15pm, 7.35pm, 7.55pm, 8.20pm, 8.50pm in peak season (end May–beg Sep).* **Duration** *30 minutes.*

Downriver to Greenwich
020-7930 9033 or 020-7987 1185.
Departures *10.10am, 10.30am, 10.50am, 11am, 11.30am, noon, then three per hour until 5.30pm Jul–Aug. 10.30am, 10.50am, 11.15am, 11.30am then three per hour until 4.50pm Apr–Jun, Sep–Oct.* **Duration** *30 minutes.*

Sightseeing boat

Westminster Bridge to Blackfriars Bridge

UNTIL WORLD WAR II, this stretch of the Thames marked the division between rich and poor London. On the north bank were the offices, shops, luxury hotels and apartments of Whitehall and the Strand, the Inns of Court and the newspaper district. To the south were smoky factories and slum dwellings. After the war, the Festival of Britain in 1951 started the revival of the South Bank (see pp184–91) which now has some of the capital's most interesting modern buildings.

Savoy Hotel
This hotel is on the site of a medieval palace (p116).

Shell Mex House
Offices for the oil company were built in 1931 on the site of the vast Cecil Hotel.

Somerset House is an office complex built in 1786 *(p117).*

Cleopatra's Needle was made in ancient Egypt and given to London in 1819 *(p118).*

Embankment Gardens is the site of many open-air concerts held in the bandstand during the summer months *(p118).*

Charing Cross

Embankment

Festival Pier

Embankment Pier

Waterloo Bridge

Hungerford Railway Bridge

The South Bank Centre was the site of the 1951 Festival of Britain and is London's most important arts complex. It is dominated by the Festival Hall, the National Theatre and the Hayward Gallery *(pp184–91).*

Charing Cross
The rail terminus is encased in a Post-Modernist office complex with many shops (p119).

British Airways London Eye offers breathtaking views over London *(p189).*

The Banqueting House is one of Inigo Jones's finest works, built as part of Whitehall Palace *(p80).*

The Ministry of Defence is a bulky white fortress completed in the 1950s.

Westminster Pier

Westminster

Westminster Bridge

London Aquarium
The former seat of London's government is now home to a state-of-the-art aquarium (p188).

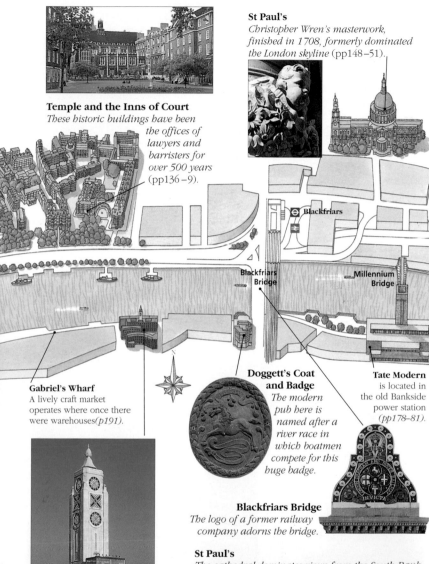

Temple and the Inns of Court
These historic buildings have been the offices of lawyers and barristers for over 500 years (pp136–9).

St Paul's
Christopher Wren's masterwork, finished in 1708, formerly dominated the London skyline (pp148–51).

Blackfriars

Blackfriars Bridge

Millennium Bridge

Gabriel's Wharf
A lively craft market operates where once there were warehouses *(p191)*.

Doggett's Coat and Badge
The modern pub here is named after a river race in which boatmen compete for this huge badge.

Tate Modern
is located in the old Bankside power station *(pp178–81)*.

Blackfriars Bridge
The logo of a former railway company adorns the bridge.

St Paul's
The cathedral dominates views from the South Bank.

OXO Tower
The windows were designed to spell the brand name of a popular meat extract.

KEY

Underground station
Railway station
River boat boarding point

Southwark Bridge to St Katharine's Dock

FOR CENTURIES THE STRETCH just east of London Bridge was the busiest part of the Thames, with ships of all sizes jostling for position to unload at the wharves on both banks. Then, in the 19th century, the construction of the docks to the east eased congestion. Today most landmarks on this section hark back to that commercial past.

Old Billingsgate
Note the flying fish weather vanes on what was London's main fish market (p152).

Fishmongers' Hall
The hall (1834) of this ancient City guild dominates the view north from London Bridge (p152).

Monument
The Great Fire of 1666 started near this spot (p152).

A Custom House has been here since 1272. This version dates from 1825.

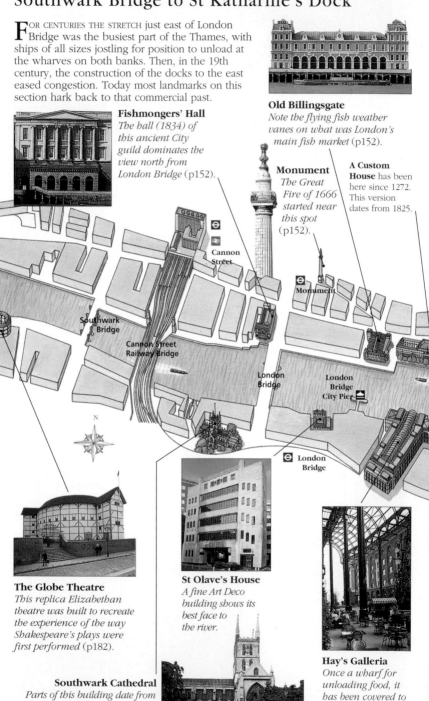

Cannon Street

Monument

Southwark Bridge

Cannon Street Railway Bridge

London Bridge

London Bridge City Pier

N

London Bridge

The Globe Theatre
This replica Elizabethan theatre was built to recreate the experience of the way Shakespeare's plays were first performed (p182).

St Olave's House
A fine Art Deco building shows its best face to the river.

Hay's Galleria
Once a wharf for unloading food, it has been covered to house shops and restaurants.

Southwark Cathedral
Parts of this building date from the 12th century. It contains memorials to Shakespeare (p176).

Southwark Wharves
Now there are walkways with river views where ships used to dock.

Tower Bridge
It still opens to let tall ships pass, but not as often as it did when cargo vessels came through (p153).

Tower of London
Look out for Traitors' Gate, where prisoners would be taken into the Tower by boat (pp154–7).

St Katharine's Dock
The former dock is now a lively attraction for visitors. Its yacht marina is a highlight (p158).

Tower Pier

Tower Bridge

Victorian warehouses
on Butlers Wharf have been converted into apartments.

HMS Belfast
This World War II cruiser has been a museum since 1971 (p183).

Design Museum
Opened in 1989, this ship-like building is a shining example of Docklands' renaissance (p183).

LONDON AREA BY AREA

WHITEHALL AND WESTMINSTER

WHITEHALL AND WESTMINSTER have been at the centre of political and religious power in England for a thousand years. King Canute, who ruled at the beginning of the 11th century, was the first monarch to have a palace on what was then an island in the swampy meeting point of the Thames and its vanished tributary, the Tyburn. Canute built his palace beside the church that, some 50 years later, Edward the Confessor would enlarge

Horse Guard on Whitehall

into England's greatest abbey, giving the area its name. (A minster is an abbey church.) Over the following centuries the offices of state were established in the vicinity. All this is still reflected in Whitehall's heroic statues and massive government buildings. But, to its north, Trafalgar Square marks the start of the West End entertainment district.

SIGHTS AT A GLANCE

Historic Streets and Buildings
Houses of Parliament pp72–3 ❶
Big Ben ❷
Jewel Tower ❸
Dean's Yard ❺
Parliament Square ❼
Downing Street ❾
Cabinet War Rooms ❿
Banqueting House ⓫
Horse Guards Parade ⓬
Queen Anne's Gate ⓮
St James's Park Station ⓰
Blewcoat School ⓱

Churches, Abbeys and Cathedrals
Westminster Abbey pp76–9 ❹
St Margaret's Church ❻
Westminster Cathedral ⓲
St John's, Smith Square ⓳

Museums and Galleries
Guards' Museum ⓯
Tate Britain pp82–5 ⓴

Theatres
Whitehall Theatre ⓭

Monuments
Cenotaph ❽

GETTING THERE
Rail services and the Victoria, Jubilee, District and Circle lines all serve the area. Bus numbers 3, 11, 12, 24, 29, 53, 77, 77A, 88, 109, 159, 170 and 184 go to Whitehall; 2, 2B, 16, 25, 36A, 38, 39, 52, 52A, 73, 76, 135, 507 and 510 serve Victoria.

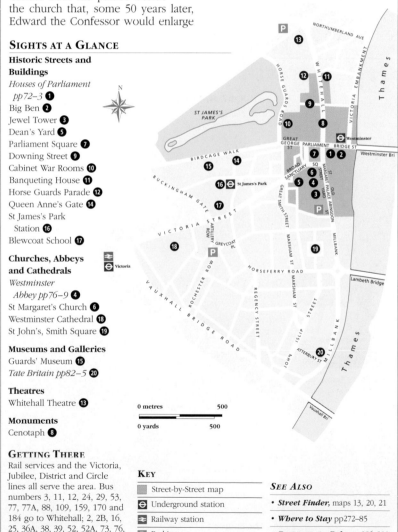

KEY

▢	Street-by-Street map
Ⓔ	Underground station
⇌	Railway station
Ⓟ	Parking

SEE ALSO
- *Street Finder,* maps 13, 20, 21
- *Where to Stay* pp272–85
- *Restaurants, Pubs* pp286–311

Looking down Whitehall towards Big Ben

Street-by-Street: Whitehall and Westminster

COMPARED WITH MANY capital cities, London has little monumental architecture designed to overawe with pomp. Here, at the historic seat both of the government and of the established church, it most closely approaches the broad, stately avenues of Paris, Rome and Madrid. On weekdays the streets are crowded with members of the civil service, as most of their work is based in this area. At weekends, however, it is deserted, apart from tourists visiting some of London's most famous sights.

Earl Haig, the British World War I chief, was sculpted by Alfred Hardiman in 1936.

Downing Street
British Prime Ministers have lived here since 1732 **9**

Central Hall is a florid example of the Beaux Arts style, built in 1911 as a Methodist meeting hall. In 1946 the first General Assembly of the United Nations was held here.

★ **Cabinet War Rooms**
Now open to the public, these were Winston Churchill's World War II headquarters **10**

★ **Westminster Abbey**
The Abbey is London's oldest and most important church **4**

The Sanctuary
was a medieval safe place for those escaping the law.

Richard I's Statue, by Carlo Marochetti (1860), depicts the 12th-century *Coeur de Lion* (Lionheart).

Dean's Yard
Westminster School was founded here in 1540 **5**

Jewel Tower
Kings once stored their most valuable possessions here **3**

The Burghers of Calais
is a cast of Auguste Rodin's original in Paris.

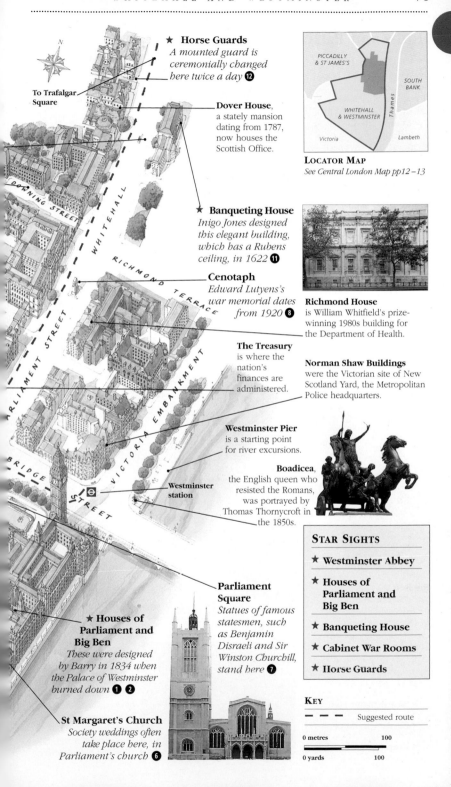

★ **Horse Guards**
A mounted guard is ceremonially changed here twice a day ⓬

To Trafalgar Square

Dover House, a stately mansion dating from 1787, now houses the Scottish Office.

LOCATOR MAP
See Central London Map pp12–13

★ **Banqueting House**
Inigo Jones designed this elegant building, which has a Rubens ceiling, in 1622 ⓫

Cenotaph
Edward Lutyens's war memorial dates from 1920 ❽

Richmond House
is William Whitfield's prize-winning 1980s building for the Department of Health.

The Treasury
is where the nation's finances are administered.

Norman Shaw Buildings
were the Victorian site of New Scotland Yard, the Metropolitan Police headquarters.

Westminster Pier
is a starting point for river excursions.

Boadicea,
the English queen who resisted the Romans, was portrayed by Thomas Thornycroft in the 1850s.

Westminster station

Parliament Square
Statues of famous statesmen, such as Benjamin Disraeli and Sir Winston Churchill, stand here ❼

★ **Houses of Parliament and Big Ben**
These were designed by Barry in 1834 when the Palace of Westminster burned down ❶ ❷

St Margaret's Church
Society weddings often take place here, in Parliament's church ❻

STAR SIGHTS

★ Westminster Abbey

★ Houses of Parliament and Big Ben

★ Banqueting House

★ Cabinet War Rooms

★ Horse Guards

KEY

– – – Suggested route

0 metres　　　　100

0 yards　　　　100

Houses of Parliament ❶

Sɪɴᴄᴇ 1512 the Palace of Westminster has been the seat of the two Houses of Parliament, called the Lords and the Commons. The Commons is made up of elected Members of Parliament (MPs) of different political parties; the party with the most MPs forms the Government, and its leader becomes Prime Minister. MPs from other parties make up the Opposition. Commons' debates can become heated and are impartially chaired by an MP designated as Speaker. The Commons formulates legislation which is first debated in both Houses before becoming law.

The mock-Gothic building was designed by Victorian architect Sir Charles Barry. Victoria Tower, on the left, contains 1.5 million Acts of Parliament passed since 1497.

★ **Commons' Chamber**
The room is upholstered in green. The Government sits on the left, the Opposition on the right, and the Speaker presides from a chair between them.

Big Ben
The vast bell was hung in 1858 and chimes on the hour; four smaller ones ring on the quarter hours (see p74).

Members' entrance

★ **Westminster Hall**
The only surviving part of the original Palace of Westminster, it dates from 1097; its hammerbeam roof is from the 14th century.

Sᴛᴀʀ Fᴇᴀᴛᴜʀᴇs
★ Westminster Hall
★ Lords' Chamber
★ Commons' Chamber

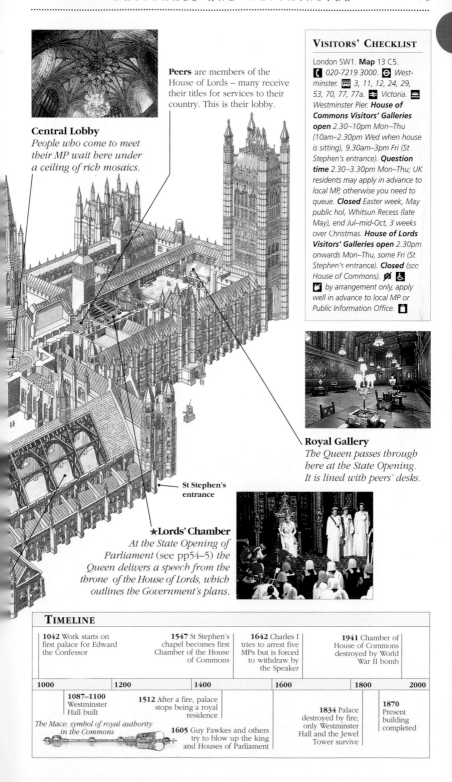

Central Lobby
People who come to meet their MP wait here under a ceiling of rich mosaics.

Peers are members of the House of Lords – many receive their titles for services to their country. This is their lobby.

St Stephen's entrance

★ Lords' Chamber
At the State Opening of Parliament (see pp54–5) the Queen delivers a speech from the throne of the House of Lords, which outlines the Government's plans.

Royal Gallery
The Queen passes through here at the State Opening. It is lined with peers' desks.

VISITORS' CHECKLIST

London SW1. **Map** 13 C5.
☎ 020-7219 3000. ⊖ *Westminster.* 🚌 *3, 11, 12, 24, 29, 53, 70, 77, 77a.* 🚆 *Victoria.* 🚤 *Westminster Pier.* **House of Commons Visitors' Galleries open** *2.30–10pm Mon–Thu (10am–2.30pm Wed when house is sitting), 9.30am–3pm Fri (St Stephen's entrance).* **Question time** *2.30–3.30pm Mon–Thu; UK residents may apply in advance to local MP, otherwise you need to queue.* **Closed** *Easter week, May public hol, Whitsun Recess (late May), end Jul–mid-Oct, 3 weeks over Christmas.* **House of Lords Visitors' Galleries open** *2.30pm onwards Mon–Thu, some Fri (St Stephen's entrance).* **Closed** *(see House of Commons).* Ø ♿ 📷 *by arrangement only, apply well in advance to local MP or Public Information Office.* 🚻

TIMELINE

1042 Work starts on first palace for Edward the Confessor

1547 St Stephen's chapel becomes first Chamber of the House of Commons

1642 Charles I tries to arrest five MPs but is forced to withdraw by the Speaker

1941 Chamber of House of Commons destroyed by World War II bomb

1000	1200	1400	1600	1800	2000

1087–1100 Westminster Hall built

The Mace: symbol of royal authority in the Commons

1512 After a fire, palace stops being a royal residence

1605 Guy Fawkes and others try to blow up the king and Houses of Parliament

1834 Palace destroyed by fire; only Westminster Hall and the Jewel Tower survive

1870 Present building completed

Houses of Parliament ❶

See pp72–3.

Big Ben ❷

Bridge St SW1. **Map** 13 C5.
🚇 Westminster.
***Not open** to the public.*

To be pedantic, Big Ben is not the name of the world-famous four-faced clock in the 106-m (320-ft) tower that rises above the Houses of Parliament, but of the resonant 14-tonne bell on which the hours are struck. It was named after Sir Benjamin Hall, Chief Commissioner of Works when the bell was hung in 1858. Cast at White-chapel, it was the second giant bell made for the clock, the first having become cracked during a test ringing. (The present bell also has a slight crack.) The clock is the largest in Britain, its four dials 7.5 m (23 ft) in diameter and the minute hand 4.25 m (14 ft) long, made in hollow copper for lightness. It has kept exact time for the nation more or less continuously since it was first set in motion in May 1859. The deep chimes have become a symbol of Britain all over the world and are broadcast daily on BBC radio.

Jewel Tower ❸

Abingdon St SW1. **Map** 13 B5.
📞 020-7222 2219. 🚇 Westminster.
Open Apr–Sep: 10am–6pm daily; Oct: 10am–5pm; Nov–Mar: 10am–4pm daily. **Closed** 24–26 Dec, 1 Jan and state occasions. **Adm charge.** 📷 🚻

This and Westminster Hall *(see p72)* are the only vestiges of the old Palace of Westminster. The tower was built in 1366 as a stronghold for Edward III's treasure and is today a small museum containing relics relating to the palace, pottery dug from the moat, and fascinating drawings of some of the best losing designs for rebuilding the Houses of Parliament after the fire of 1834.

The tower served as the weights and measures office from 1869 until 1938 and another display relates to that era. Alongside are the remains of the moat and a medieval quay.

Westminster Abbey ❹

See pp76–9.

Dean's Yard ❺

Broad Sanctuary SW1. **Map** 13 B5.
🚇 Westminster. **Buildings not open** to the public.

Entrance to the Abbey and cloisters from Dean's Yard

An arch near the west door of the Abbey leads into this secluded grassy square, surrounded by a jumble of buildings from many different periods. A medieval house on the east side has a distinctive dormer window and backs on to Little Dean's Yard, where the monks' living quarters used to be. Dean's Yard is private property. It belongs to the Dean and Chapter of Westminster and is close to Westminster School, whose famous former pupils include poet John Dryden and play-wright Ben Jonson. Scholars are, by tradition, the first to acknowledge a new monarch.

St Margaret's Church ❻

Parliament Sq SW1. **Map** 13 B5.
📞 020-7222 5152. 🚇 Westminster.
Open 9:30am–3:45pm Mon–Fri, 9:30am–1:45pm Sat, 2–5pm Sun.
🕙 11am Sun. 🚫 ♿

Statue of Charles I overlooking St Margaret's doorway

Overshadowed by the Abbey, this early-15th-century church has long been a favoured venue for political and society weddings, such as Winston and Clementine Churchill's. Although much restored, the church retains some Tudor features, notably a stained-glass window that celebrates the engagement of Catherine of Aragon to Arthur, Henry VIII's eldest brother.

Parliament Square ❼

SW1. **Map** 13 B5. 🚇 Westminster.

Laid out in the 1840s to provide a more open aspect for the new Houses of Parliament, the square became Britain's first official roundabout in 1926. Today it is hemmed in by heavy traffic. Statues of statesmen and soldiers are dominated by Winston Churchill in his greatcoat, glowering at the House of Commons. On the north side Abraham Lincoln sits in front of the mock-Gothic Middlesex Guildhall, completed in 1913.

Cenotaph ❽

Whitehall SW1. **Map** 13 B4.
🚇 Westminster.

This suitably bleak and pale monument, completed in 1920 by Sir Edwin Lutyens to commemorate the dead of World War I, stands in the middle of Whitehall. On Remembrance Day every year – the Sunday nearest 11 November – the monarch and other dignitaries place wreaths of red poppies on the Cenotaph. This solemn ceremony, commemorating the 1918 armistice, honours the victims of World Wars I and II (see pp54–5).

The Cenotaph

Cabinet War Rooms ❿

Clive Steps, King Charles St SW1. **Map** 13 B5. ☎ 020-7930 6961. ⊖ Westminster. **Open** Apr–Sep: 9.30am–6pm; Oct–Mar: 10am–6pm daily (last adm: 5.15pm). **Closed** 24–26 Dec. **Adm charge.** ⊡ ⬥ ⬛

Telephones in the Map Room of the Cabinet War Rooms

THIS INTRIGUING slice of 20th-century history is a warren of cellar rooms below the Government Office Building north of Parliament Square. It is where the War Cabinet – first under Neville Chamberlain, then Winston Churchill – met during World War II when German bombs were falling on London. The War Rooms include living quarters for key ministers and military leaders and a sound-proofed Cabinet

Room, where many strategic decisions were taken. All rooms are protected by a layer of concrete about a metre (3 ft) thick. They are laid out as they were when the war ended, complete with period furniture, including Churchill's desk, some old-fashioned communications equipment and maps with markers for plotting complex military strategy.

Downing Street ❾

SW1. **Map** 13 B4. ⊖ Westminster. **Not open** to the public.

SIR GEORGE DOWNING (1623–84) spent part of his youth in the American colonies. He was the second graduate from the nascent Harvard College before returning to fight for the Parliamentarians in the English Civil War. In 1680 he

bought some land near Whitehall Palace and built a street of houses. Four of these survive, though they are much altered. George II gave No. 10 to Sir Robert Walpole in 1732. Since then it has been the official residence of the Prime Minister and contains offices as well as a private apartment. In 1989, for security reasons, iron gates were erected at the Whitehall end.

The famous front door of No. 10

No. 12, the Whips' Office, is where Party campaigns are organized.

Government policy is decided in the Cabinet Room at No. 10.

No. 11 is the Chancellor of the Exchequer's official residence.

No. 10 is the official home of the Prime Minister.

The Prime Minister entertains official guests in the State Dining Room.

Westminster Abbey ④

THE ABBEY is world-famous as the resting-place of Britain's monarchs, and as the setting for coronations and other great pageants. Within its walls can be seen some of the most glorious examples of medieval architecture in London. It also contains one of the most impressive collections of tombs and monuments in the world. Half national church, half national museum, the abbey occupies a unique place in the British national consciousness.

★Flying Buttresses
The massive flying buttresses help transfer the great weight of the 31-m (102-ft) high nave.

North Entrance
The stonework here, like this carving of a dragon, is Victorian.

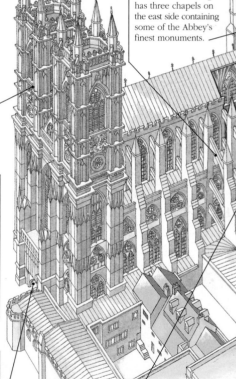

The North Transept has three chapels on the east side containing some of the Abbey's finest monuments.

★West Front Towers
These towers, built in 1734–45, were designed by Nicholas Hawksmoor.

STAR FEATURES

★ **West Front Towers**

★ **Flying Buttresses**

★ **The Nave viewed from the West End**

★ **The Lady Chapel**

★ **Chapter House**

Main entrance

★ The Nave viewed from the West End
At 10 m (35 ft) wide, the nave is comparatively narrow, but it is the highest in England.

The Cloisters, built mainly in the 13th and 14th centuries, used to link the Abbey church with the other buildings.

St Edward's Chapel
houses not only the royal
Coronation Chair and
Edward the Confessor's
shrine, but also the tombs
of many of England's
medieval monarchs.

★ **The Lady Chapel**
*The chapel, built in
1503–12, has a superb
vaulted ceiling and choir
stalls dating from 1512.*

★ **Chapter House**
*This octagonal structure is
worth seeing for its 13th-
century tiles.*

The South Transept
contains "Poets' Corner",
where memorials to famous
literary figures can be seen.

Museum

TIMELINE

*13th-century
tile from the
Chapter House*

1050 New Benedic-tine abbey church begun by Edward the Confessor	**1376** Henry Yevele begins rebuilding the nave				**1838** Queen Victoria's coronation
1000	1200	1400	1600	1800	2000
	1245 New abbey begun to the designs of Henry of Rheims	**1269** Body of Edward the Confessor moved to new shrine in the abbey	**1734** West towers begun **1540** Monastery dissolved	**1953** Most recent coronation in the abbey: Elizabeth II's	

A Guided Tour of Westminster Abbey

THE ABBEY'S INTERIOR presents an exceptionally diverse array of architectural and sculptural styles. These range from the austere French Gothic of the nave to the stunning complexity of Henry VII's Tudor chapel and the riotous invention of the later 18th-century monuments. Many English monarchs were buried here; some of their tombs are deliberately plain, while others are lavishly decorated. At the same time, there are monuments to a number of Britain's greatest public figures – ranging from politicians to poets – crowded into the aisles and transepts.

② **Lady Nightingale's Memorial**
The North Transept chapels contain some of the abbey's finest monuments – this one, by Roubiliac, is for Lady Nightingale (1761).

HISTORICAL PLAN OF THE ABBEY

The first abbey church was established as early as the 10th century, when St Dunstan brought a group of Benedictine monks to the area. The present structure dates largely from the 13th century; the new, French-influenced design was begun in 1245 at the behest of Henry III. Because of its unique role as the royal coronation church, the abbey survived Henry VIII's mid-16th-century onslaught on Britain's monastic buildings.

KEY

- ▨ Built before 1400
- ▨ Added in 15th century
- ▨ Built in 1503–19
- ▨ Completed in 1745
- ☐ Restored after 1850

Main entrance

① **The Nave**
The nave is 10.5 m (35 ft) wide and 31 m (102 ft) high. It took 150 years to build.

The Choir houses a gilded 1840s screen, which contains remnants of the 13th-century original.

The Jericho Parlour, added in the early 16th century, contains some fine panelling.

The Jerusalem Chamber has a 17th-century fireplace, fine tapestries and an interesting painted ceiling.

⑧ **Tomb of the Unknown Warrior**
This plain but moving memorial serves to commemorate the many thousands killed in World War I who had no formal resting place. One un-named soldier is actually buried here.

The Deanery is where the monastery's abbot used to live.

CORONATION

The abbey has been the fittingly sumptuous setting for all royal coronations since 1066. The last occupant of the Coronation Chair was the present monarch, Elizabeth II. She was crowned in 1953 in the first televised coronation.

The Chapel of St John the Baptist is full of tombs dating from the 14th to the 19th centuries.

The St Faith Chapel contains works of art that date back to the 13th century.

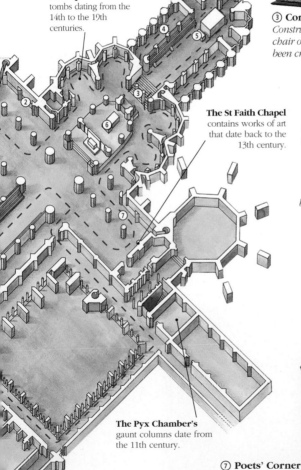

The Pyx Chamber's gaunt columns date from the 11th century.

Dean's Yard entrance

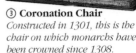

③ **Coronation Chair**
Constructed in 1301, this is the chair on which monarchs have been crowned since 1308.

④ **Tomb of Elizabeth I**
Inside Henry VII's Chapel you will find Elizabeth I's (reigned 1558–1603) huge tomb. It also houses the body of her sister, "Bloody" Mary I.

⑤ **Henry VII Chapel**
The undersides of the choir stalls, dating from 1512, are beautifully carved with exotic and fantastic creatures.

⑥ **St Edward's Chapel**
The shrine of the Saxon king Edward the Confessor and the tombs of many medieval monarchs are here.

⑦ **Poets' Corner**
Take time to explore the memorials to countless literary giants, such as Shakespeare and Dickens, which are gathered here.

Banqueting House ⓫

Whitehall SW1. **Map** 13 B4. ⓒ *020-7839 8919.* ⓒ *Charing Cross, Embankment, Westminster.* **Open** *10am–5pm Mon–Sat (last adm: 4.30).* **Closed** *public hols, 24 Dec–2 Jan, at short notice for functions.* **Adm charge.** 🕭 📷 *Video presentations.*

T HIS DELIGHTFUL BUILDING is of great architectural importance. It was the first in central London to embody the Classical Palladian style that designer Inigo Jones brought back from his travels in Italy. Completed in 1622, its disciplined stone facade marked a startling change from the Elizabethans' fussy turrets and unrestrained external decoration. It was the sole survivor of the fire that destroyed most of the old Whitehall Palace in 1698.

The ceiling paintings by Rubens, a complex allegory on the exaltation of James I, were commissioned by his son, Charles I, in 1630. This blatant glorification of royalty was despised by Oliver Cromwell and the Parliamentarians, who executed King Charles I on a scaffold outside Banqueting House in 1649. Ironically, Charles II celebrated his restoration to the throne here 20 years later. The building is occasionally used for official functions.

Mounted sentries stationed outside Horse Guards Parade

Horse Guards Parade ⓬

Whitehall SW1. **Map** 13 B4. 🕭 *0906 866 3344.* ⓒ *Westminster, Charing Cross.* **Open** *8am–6pm daily.* **Changing the Guard** *11am Mon–Sat, 10am Sun.* **Dismounting Ceremony** *4pm daily. Times for both are subject to change (phone for details).* **Trooping the Colour** *see* **Ceremonial London** *pp52–5.*

O NCE HENRY VIII's tiltyard (tournament ground), nowadays the Changing of the Guard takes place here every morning. The elegant buildings, completed in 1755, were designed by William Kent. On the left is the Old Treasury, also by Kent, and Dover House, completed in 1758 and now used as the Scottish

Office. Nearby is a trace of the "real tennis" court where Henry VIII is said to have played the ancient precursor of modern lawn tennis. On the opposite side, the view is dominated by the ivy-covered Citadel. This is a bomb-proof structure that was erected in 1940 beside the Admiralty. During World War II it was used as a communications headquarters by the Navy.

Whitehall Theatre ⓭

Whitehall SW1. **Map** 13 B3. 🕭 *020-7369 1735.* ⓒ *Charing Cross.* **Open** *for performances only.* *See* **Entertainment** *pp328–9.*

Detail of a Whitehall Theatre box

B UILT IN 1930, the plain white front seems to emulate the Cenotaph *(see p74)* at the other end of the street, but, inside, the theatre boasts some excellent Art Deco detailing. From the 1950s to the 1970s it was noted for staging a wide range of farces.

Queen Anne's Gate ⓮

SW1. **Map** 13 A5. ⓒ *St James's Park.*

T HE SPACIOUS terraced houses at the west end of this well-preserved enclave date from 1704 and are notable for the ornate canopies over their front doors. At the other end are houses built some 70 years later, sporting blue plaques that record former residents, such as Lord Palmerston, the Victorian Prime Minister. Until recently, the British Secret Service, MI5, was allegedly based in this unlikely spot. A small statue of Queen Anne stands in front of the wall separating Nos. 13 and 15. To the west, situated at the corner of Petty France, Sir Basil Spence's Home Office building (1976)

Panels from the Rubens ceiling, Banqueting House

is an architectural incongruity. Cockpit Steps, leading down to Birdcage Walk, mark the site of a 17th-century venue for the popular, yet blood-thirsty, sport of cockfighting.

Guards Museum ⑮

Birdcage Walk SW1. **Map** 13 A5. 020-7930 4466 x 3271. St James's Park. **Open** 10am–4pm daily. **Closed** 25 Dec, 1 Jan, ceremonies. **Adm charge**.

ENTERED FROM Birdcage Walk, the museum is under the parade ground of Wellington Barracks, head-quarters of the five Guards regiments. A must for military buffs, the museum uses tableaux and dioramas to illustrate various battles in which the Guards have taken part, from the English Civil War (1642– 8) to the present. Weapons and row after row of colourful uniforms are on display, as well as a fascin-ating collection of models.

St James's Park Station ⑯

55 Broadway SW1. **Map** 13 A5. St James's Park.

Epstein sculpture outside St James's Park Station

THE STATION is built into Broadway House, Charles Holden's 1929 headquarters for London Transport. It is notable for its sculptures by Jacob Epstein and reliefs by Henry Moore and Eric Gill.

Blewcoat School ⑰

23 Caxton St SW1. **Map** 13 A5. 020-7222 2877. St James's Park. **Open** 10am –5.30pm Mon– Wed, Fri, 10am –7pm Thu. **Closed** public hols.

Statue of a Blewcoat pupil above the Caxton Street entrance

A RED-BRICK GEM hemmed in by the office towers of Victoria Street, it was built in 1709 as a charity school to teach pupils how to "read, write, cast accounts and the catechism". It remained as a school until 1939, then became an army store during World War II and was bought by the National Trust in 1954. The beautifully proportioned interior now serves as a National Trust gift shop.

Westminster Cathedral ⑱

Ashley Place SW1. **Map** 20 F1. 020-7798 9055. Victoria. **Open** 7am–7pm Sun–Fri, 8am–7pm Sat **Adm charge** for bell tower lift (Apr– Nov: 9am–5pm daily, Dec–Mar: 9am– 5pm Thu–Sun). 5.30pm Mon–Fri, 10.30am Sat, Sun, sung Mass (phone 020-7798 9097 to check for other services). **Concerts.**

ONE OF LONDON'S rare Byzantine buildings, it was designed by John Francis Bentley for the Catholic diocese and completed in 1903 on the site of a former prison. Its 87-m (285-ft) high, red-brick tower, with horizontal stripes of white stone, stands out on the skyline in sharp contrast to the Abbey nearby. A restful piazza on the north side

provides a good view of the cathedral from Victoria Street. The rich interior decoration, with marble of varying colours and intricate mosaics, makes the domes above the nave seem incongruous. They were left bare because the project ran out of money.

Eric Gill's dramatic reliefs of the 14 Stations of the Cross, created during World War I, adorn the pier of the nave. The organ is one of the finest in Europe, and a series of concerts is held here every second Tuesday from June until September.

St John's, Smith Square ⑲

Smith Sq SW1. **Map** 21 B1. 020-7222 1061. Westminster. **Open** 10am–5pm Mon–Fri and for evening concerts. **Concerts**. See **Entertainment** pp332–3.

Premiere Ensemble at St John's, Smith Square

DESCRIBED BY artist and art historian Sir Hugh Casson as one of the masterpieces of English Baroque architecture, Thomas Archer's plump church, with its turrets at each corner, looks as if it is trying to burst from the confines of the square, and rather over-powers the pleasing 18th-century houses on its north side. It has an accident-prone history: completed in 1728, it was burned down in 1742, struck by lightning in 1773 and destroyed again by a World War II bomb in 1941. There is a reasonably priced restaurant in the basement – a rarity in this area – that is open daily for lunch and on the evenings of concerts.

Tate Britain ⑳

See pp82–5.

Tate Britain ⑳

FORMERLY THE Tate Gallery, Tate Britain displays the world's largest collection of British art from the 16th to the 21st century. The international modern art once housed here is now held at Tate Modern *(see pp178–181)*. In the adjoining Clore Gallery is the magnificent Turner Bequest, left to the nation by the great landscape artist J M W Turner in 1851. The Clore Gallery has its own entrance giving direct access to the Turner Collection and allowing a full appreciation of the architect Sir James Stirling's witty post-modernist design for the building.

Loan exhibitions covering all manner of British art are installed here and on the lower floor.

Main floor

The Saltonstall Family *(1637)*
David des Granges's life-size family portrait includes the dead first Lady Saltonstall as the second shows off her new baby.

Lower floor

Atterbury St entrance

Flatford Mill (Scene on a Navigable River) *(1816–17)*
John Constable was among the first to paint finished landscapes direct from nature. This work typifies his masterly observation of light and shadow.

GALLERY GUIDE

The permanent collection displays occupy threequarters of the main floor. Starting in the northwest corner, the displays follow a broad chronological sweep from the early 16th century to the present. Each room explores an historical theme or is devoted to a major artist. Major loan exhibitions are installed in the remaining quarter of the main floor and in the lower-floor galleries.

KEY TO FLOORPLAN

- [ ] 1500-1800
- [ ] 1800-1900
- [ ] 1900-1960
- [ ] 1960 to present
- [ ] Duveen Sculpture Gallery
- [ ] Clore Gallery
- [ ] Loan Exhibitions
- [ ] Non-exhibition space

★ **Nocturne in Blue and Gold: Old Battersea Bridge** *(c. 1872–5)*
J A M Whistler's atmospheric night scenes of the Thames in London marked the arrival of modern art in Britain.

THE ART OF GOOD FOOD

On the lower floor Tate Britain boasts a café and an espresso bar, as well as a restaurant. Celebrated murals by Rex Whistler adorn the walls of the restaurant, telling the tale of the mythical inhabitants of Epicuriana and their expedition in search of rare foods. The extensive wine list has won awards and is known for its fair pricing. Open for lunch only.

VISITORS' CHECKLIST

Millbank SW1. **Map** 21 B2.
☎ 020-7887 8000.
📠 020-7887 8008. ⊖ Pimlico.
🚌 C10, 36, 77a, 88, 159, 185, 507. 🚆 Victoria, Vauxhall.
Open 10am–5.50pm daily.
Closed 24–26 Dec. **Adm charge** for special exhibitions only. 📷
♿ Atterbury St. 🗄 🎧 🍴 🛍
📽 **Lectures, film presentations, exhibitions, children's activities.**
ⓦ www.tate.org.uk

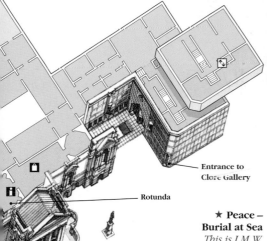

Entrance to Clore Gallery

Rotunda

Millbank entrance

Stairs to lower floor

Lady of Shalott *(1888)*
J W Waterhouse's work reflects the Pre-Raphaelite fascination with Arthurian myth.

★ **Peace – Burial at Sea**
This is J M W Turner's tribute to his friend and rival David Wilkie. It was painted in 1842, the year after Wilkie died at sea.

★ **Three Studies for Figures at the Base of a Crucifixion**
(1944, detail)
Francis Bacon's famous triptych encapsulates an anguished vision of human existence. When first displayed, its savagery deeply shocked audiences.

STAR PAINTINGS

★ **Peace – Burial at Sea by Turner**

★ **Nocturne in Blue & Gold by Whistler**

★ **Three Studies for Figures at the Base of a Crucifixion by Bacon**

Exploring Tate Britain

Tate Britain draws its pieces from the massive Tate Collection. The variety of works on show, coupled with a rigorous programme of loan exhibitions, results in a selection of pieces to suit all tastes – from Elizabethan portraiture to cutting edge installation. Although Tate Britain was recently expanded, the number of British works in the collection still outstrips the space available in the gallery, necessitating some rotation of displays.

The Cholmondeley Sisters (c. 1600–10), **British School**

1500–1800

This group of galleries traces the emergence of a distinctively British school of art. "English Renaissance" looks at the decorative and stylized art of the age of Queen Elizabeth I, typified by the rigid poses and exquisite detail of *The Cholmondeley Sisters*. William Hogarth, often called the father of British painting, is celebrated in "Hogarth and Modern Life", while the grand portrait tradition exemplified in the work of Joshua Reynolds and Thomas Gainsborough is traced in the "Courtly Portraiture" gallery. The rise of what is often seen as the most typical form of British

art, landscape, is set out in "Landscape and Empire". At the end of this period one of the great eccentric geniuses of British art appeared, William Blake. Inspired by Michelangelo, Blake made paintings and poetry that expressed his highly personal vision of man and god.

Satan Smiting Job with Sore Boils (c.1826) **by William Blake**

1800–1900

From the end of the eighteenth century, paintings of scenes from British history, theatre and literature became increasingly popular. The sweeping display of "Making British History" ranges from the Shakespeare-inspired fantasies of Henry Fuseli to paintings of historical events by John Singleton Copley and J M W Turner. The sharply focused literary and contemporary life subjects of the Pre-Raphaelites are also found in this large gallery.

No fewer than three rooms are given to John Constable, Turner's rival as the greatest British landscapist. One of these presents contextual and biographical material while the other two, "Constable and Outdoor Painting 1800–1817" and "Constable's Later Years 1818–1837", follow the development of his painting through his career.

Large-scale paintings by John Martin and Francis Danby are displayed in "John Martin and Visions of the Apocalypse". The popularity of these artists' paintings of Biblical fantasies was fuelled by the religious revivalism of the period. "Art and Victorian Society" looks at the image of women in Victorian art. Finally the impact of French Impressionism, brought to Britain by the great painter J A M Whistler and his followers, is examined in "British Art and France".

TURNER AT THE CLORE GALLERY

The Turner Bequest comprises some 300 oil paintings and about 20,000 watercolours and drawings left to the nation by the great landscape painter J M W Turner on his death in 1851. Turner's will had specified that a gallery be built to house his pictures and this was finally done in 1987 with the opening of the Clore Gallery. All the oils in the Bequest are on view in the main galleries, while the wonderful watercolours are the subject of changing displays.

The Scarlet Sunset: A Town on a River (c. 1830–40)

Mr. and Mrs. Clark and Percy (1970–1) by David Hockney

1900–1960

IN THIS SECTION, the displays are arranged by theme, each exploring the response of British artists to the changing world around them. "War and Memory" looks at the extraordinary and lasting impact of the First World War. Images of the war by the futurist C R W Nevinson and

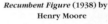

Recumbent Figure (1938) by Henry Moore

the sculptor Charles Sargent Jagger are displayed here, along with post-war works such as the haunted landscapes of Paul Nash.

"Modern Art and Tradition" sets the pioneering modernist work of sculptors Henry Moore and Barbara Hepworth in the 1930s against more traditional artists such as Cecil Collins. The more extreme developments of modernism in the 1930s in Britain are shown in "An International Abstract Art".

From the Second World War onwards the story of British art is traced in a series of rotating displays that feature Francis Bacon and Graham Sutherland, the angst-ridden post-war sculpture characterized as "the geometry of fear", the realist painting of the Kitchen Sink school, and the work of the Independent Group, led by Richard Hamilton and Eduardo Paolozzi, which foreshadowed Pop art.

1960 TO PRESENT

FROM THE 1960s, Tate's funding for the purchase of works began to increase substantially, while artistic activity continued to pick up speed, encouraged by public funding. As a result, the Tate Collection is particularly rich for this time period, necessitating the frequent rotation of displays.

British art in the 1960s was characterized by the lively development of Pop art, seen in the early work of David Hockney, the paintings and constructions of Peter Blake which celebrate fairground

Cold Dark Matter: An Exploded View (1991) by Cornelia Parker

culture and pop music, and the more intellectual Pop art of Richard Hamilton. At the same time there was a huge flowering of large-scale, brightly coloured abstract art in both painting and sculpture. A revolt against this movement took place at the end of the 1960s with the emergence of conceptual artists such as Gilbert and George, known as the Living Sculptures, and Richard Long, who created a whole new approach to landscape art by importing landscape materials into the gallery. Conceptual art was in turn rejected at the start of the 1980s by the School of London painters, including Howard Hodgkin, Lucian Freud and Kitaj, while Francis Bacon came into fresh focus as the godfather of the group. Similarly, Tony Cragg, Richard Deacon and Bill Woodrow pioneered a new sculpture that was symbolic, crafted, and explored the nature of materials.

The 1990s saw a new surge in British art and these most recent movements, including the work of the so-called Young British Artists (YBAs), are well represented at Tate Britain. Damien Hirst, perhaps the most notorious of the YBAs, creates large-scale installations, but is most famous for his animals preserved in formaldehyde. Other leading figures include Tracey Emin and Sarah Lucas, who both create radically personalized work that is aesthetically confrontational, while Cornelia Parker brings a more thoughtful and poetic approach to the YBAs' characteristic use of found objects. Numerous contemporary British artists, including Tacita Dean, Sam Taylor-Wood, Douglas Gordon, Steve McQueen and the Wilson twins, use film and video as their medium – a major development of recent years and the subject of a number of special exhibitions as well as scheduled screenings at Tate Britain.

PICCADILLY AND ST JAMES'S

PICCADILLY is the main artery of the West End. Once called Portugal Street, it acquired its present name from the ruffs, or pickadills, worn by 17th-century dandies. St James's still bears traces of the 18th century, when it surrounded the royal residences, and denizens of the court and society shopped and disported

Buckingham Palace decorative lock

themselves here. Two shops in St James's Street – Lock the hatter and Berry Bros vintners – recall that era. Fortnum and Mason, on Piccadilly, has served high-quality food for nearly 300 years. Mayfair to the north is still the most fashionable address in London, while Piccadilly Circus marks the start of Soho.

SIGHTS AT A GLANCE

Historic Streets and Buildings

Piccadilly Circus ❶
Albany ❸
Burlington Arcade ❺
Ritz Hotel ❻
Spencer House ❼
St James's Palace ❽
St James's Square ❾
Royal Opera Arcade ❿
Pall Mall ⓫
The Mall ⓮
Marlborough House ⓯
Clarence House ⓱
Lancaster House ⓲
Buckingham Palace pp94–5 ⓳
Royal Mews ㉑
Wellington Arch ㉒
Shepherd Market ㉔

Museums and Galleries

Royal Academy of Arts ❹
Institute of Contemporary Arts ⓬
Queen's Gallery ⓴
Royal Mews ㉑
Apsley House ㉓
Faraday Museum ㉖

Churches

St James's Church ❷
Queen's Chapel ⓰

Parks and Gardens

St James's Park ⓭
Green Park ㉕

SEE ALSO

• *Street Finder*, maps 12, 13
• *Where to Stay* pp272–285
• *Restaurants, Pubs* pp286–311

GETTING THERE

The Piccadilly line serves Hyde Park Corner, Piccadilly Circus, and Green Park – also served by the Jubilee and Victoria lines. The Bakerloo and Northern lines serve Charing Cross. The area is served by buses 6, 9, 15, 23, 139.

| 0 metres | 500 |
| 0 yards | 500 |

KEY

	Street-by-Street map
Ⓔ	Underground station
☰	Railway station
P	Parking

Street-by-Street: Piccadilly and St James's

A S SOON AS HENRY VIII built St James's Palace in the 1530s, the area around it became the centre of fashionable London, and it has remained so ever since. The most influential people in the land strut importantly along its historic streets as they press on with the vital business of lunching in their clubs, discussing matters of pith and moment and brandishing their gold cards in the capital's most exclusive stores, or paying a visit to one of the many art galleries.

Albany
This has been one of London's smartest addresses since it opened in 1803 ❸

★Royal Academy of Arts
Sir Joshua Reynolds founded the Academy in 1768. Now it mounts large popular exhibitions ❹

★ Burlington Arcade
Uniformed beadles discourage unruly behaviour in this 19th-century mall ❺

Fortmum and Mason
was founded in 1707 by one of Queen Anne's footmen *(see p311).*

The Ritz Hotel
Named after César Ritz, and opened in 1906, it still lives up to his name ❻

Spencer House
An ancestor of Princess Diana built this house in 1766 ❼

St James's Palace
This Tudor palace is still the Court's official headquarters ❽

To the Mall

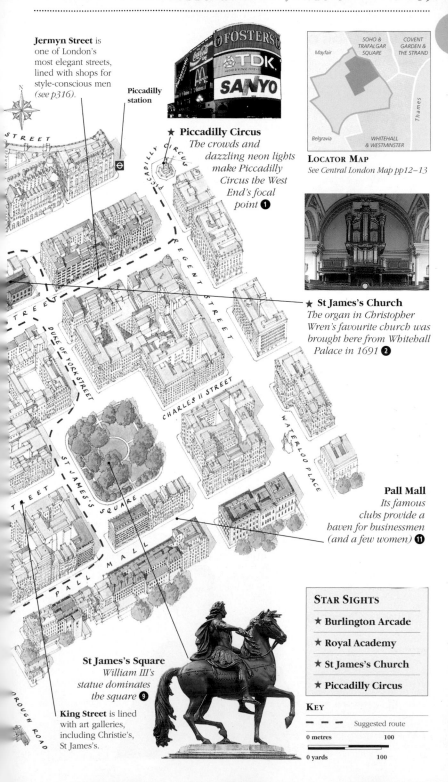

Jermyn Street is one of London's most elegant streets, lined with shops for style-conscious men *(see p316).*

Piccadilly station

LOCATOR MAP
See Central London Map pp12–13

★ **Piccadilly Circus**
The crowds and dazzling neon lights make Piccadilly Circus the West End's focal point ❶

★ **St James's Church**
The organ in Christopher Wren's favourite church was brought here from Whitehall Palace in 1691 ❷

Pall Mall
Its famous clubs provide a haven for businessmen (and a few women) ⓫

St James's Square
William III's statue dominates the square ❾

King Street is lined with art galleries, including Christie's, St James's.

STAR SIGHTS

★ Burlington Arcade

★ Royal Academy

★ St James's Church

★ Piccadilly Circus

KEY

– – –   Suggested route

| 0 metres | 100 |
| 0 yards | 100 |

Piccadilly Circus ❶

W1. **Map** 13 A3. 🚇 *Piccadilly Circus.*

Alfred Gilbert's statue of Eros

FOR YEARS PEOPLE have congregated beneath the symbolic figure of Eros, originally intended as an angel of mercy but renamed after the Greek god of love. Poised delicately with his bow, Eros has become almost a trade mark for the capital. It was erected in 1892 as a memorial to the Earl of Shaftesbury, the Victorian philanthropist. Part of Nash's master plan for Regent Street, Piccadilly Circus has been considerably altered in recent years and consists for the most part of shopping malls. One of them can be found behind the façade of the London Pavilion (1885), once a popular music hall. The circus has London's gaudiest array of neon advertising signs marking the entrance to the city's lively entertainment district with cinemas, theatres, night clubs, restaurants and pubs.

St James's Church ❷

197 Piccadilly W1. **Map** 13 A3.
📞 *020-7734 4511.* 🚇 *Piccadilly Circus, Green Park.* **Open** *8am–6.30pm daily.* **Craft market** *10am–6pm Wed–Sat,* **antiques market** *10am–6pm Tue (except Easter).* 🚫 *during services.* 🖥 *Concerts, talks, events.*

AMONG THE many churches Wren designed *(see p47),* this is said to be one of his favourites. It has been altered

over the years and was half-wrecked by a bomb in 1940, but it maintains its essential features from 1684 – the tall, arched windows, thin spire (a 1966 fibreglass replica of the original) and a light, dignified interior. The ornate screen behind the altar is one of the finest works of the 17th-century master carver Grinling Gibbons, who also made the exquisite marble font, with a scene depicting Adam and Eve standing by the Tree of Life. Artist and poet William Blake and Prime Minister Pitt the Elder were both baptized here. More of Gibbons's carvings can be seen above the grandiose organ, made for Whitehall Palace chapel but installed here in 1691. Today the church has a full calendar of events, and runs the vegetarian Wren Coffee House.

Albany ❸

Albany Court Yard, Piccadilly W1.
Map 12 F3. 🚇 *Green Park, Piccadilly Circus.* **Closed** *to the public.*

THESE DESIRABLE and discreet bachelor apartments, half hidden through an entrance off Piccadilly, were built in 1803 by Henry Holland. Notable residents have included the poet Lord Byron, novelist Graham Greene, two Prime Ministers (William Gladstone and Edward Heath) and the actor Terence Stamp. Married men were admitted in 1878 but could not bring their wives to live with them until 1919. Women are now allowed to live here in their own right.

Lord Byron lived in Albany

Royal Academy of Arts ❹

Burlington House, Piccadilly W1.
Map 12 F3. 📞 *020-7300 8000.* 🚇 *Piccadilly Circus, Green Park.* **Open** *10am–6pm Sun–Thu, 10am–10pm Fri.* **Closed** *24–25 Dec, Good Fri.* **Adm charge.** 🚫 ♿ 📷 *book in advance* 🎧 🍴 🖥 📷 **Lectures.**

Michelangelo's Madonnna and Child

THE COURTYARD in front of Burlington House, one of the West End's few surviving mansions from the early 18th century, is often crammed with people waiting to get into one of the prestigious visiting art exhibitions on show at the Royal Academy (founded 1768). The famous annual summer exhibition, which has now been held for over 200 years, comprises around 1,200 new works by both established and unknown painters, sculptors and architects. Any artist, regardless of background or talent, may submit work.

The airy Sackler Galleries (1991), designed by Norman Foster in the former diploma galleries, show visiting exhibitions. There are permanent items in the sculpture promenade outside the galleries, notably a Michelangelo relief of the Madonna and Child (1505). The exceptional permanent collection (not all on display) includes one work by each current and former Academician. There is a good shop on the first floor which sells cards and other items that are designed by Academy members for the RA.

Burlington Arcade ❺

Piccadilly W1. **Map** 12 F3. 🚇 *Green Park, Piccadilly Circus. See* **Shops and Markets** *p320.*

THIS IS ONE OF four 19th-century arcades of small shops which sell traditional British luxuries. (The Princes and Piccadilly Arcades are on the south side of Piccadilly, while the Royal Opera Arcade is off Pall Mall.) It was built for Lord Cavendish in 1819 to stop rubbish being thrown into his garden. The arcade is still patrolled by beadles who make sure an atmosphere of refinement is maintained. They have authority to eject anyone who sings, whistles, runs or opens an umbrella; those powers are infrequently invoked now, perhaps because the dictates of commerce take precedence over those of decorum.

Ritz Hotel ❻

Piccadilly W1. **Map** 12 F3. 📞 *020-7493 8181.* 🚇 *Green Park.* **Open** *to non-residents for tea or restaurant meals.* 🚹 🅿 *See* **Where to Stay** *p282 and* **Restaurants and Pubs** *p309–11.*

CESAR RITZ, the famed Swiss hotelier who inspired the adjective "ritzy", had virtually retired by the time this hotel was built and named after him in 1906. The colonnaded frontal aspect of the imposing château-style building was meant to suggest Paris, where the very grandest and most fashionable hotels were to be found around the turn of the century. It still manages to maintain its Edwardian air of *fin de siècle* opulence and is a popular stop, among those who are suitably dressed, for genteel afternoon tea. The atmosphere of chic suavity is enhanced by the tea dances and fashion parades which are held in the Palm Court.

The exquisite Palm Room of Spencer House

Spencer House ❼

27 St James's Pl SW1. **Map** 12 F4. 📞 *020-7499 8620.* 🚇 *Green Park.* **Open** *10.30am–5.30pm Sun (last adm: 4.45pm). Garden open one Sunday in June 2pm–5pm.* **Closed** *Jan & Aug.* **Adm charge. Children** *not under 10.* 🚫 🚹 📷 *compulsory.*

THIS PALLADIAN PALACE, built in 1766 for the first Earl Spencer, an ancestor of the late Princess of Wales, has been completely restored to its 18th-century splendour (thanks to an £18 million renovation project). It contains some wonderful paintings and contemporary furniture; one of the real highlights is the beautifully decorated Painted Room. The house is open to the public for guided tours, receptions and meetings.

St James's Tudor gatehouse

St James's Palace ❽

Pall Mall SW1. **Map** 12 F4. 🚇 *Green Park.* **Not open** *to the public.*

BUILT BY HENRY VIII in the late 1530s on the site of a former leper hospital, it was a primary royal residence only briefly, mainly during the reign of Elizabeth I and during the late 17th and early 18th centuries. In 1952 Queen Elizabeth II made her first speech as queen here, and foreign ambassadors are still officially accredited to the Court of St James. Its northern gatehouse, seen from St James's Street, is one of London's most evocative Tudor landmarks. Behind it the palace buildings are now occupied by privileged Crown servants.

Afternoon tea served in the opulent Palm Court of the Ritz

Royal Opera Arcade

St James's Square ⑨

SW1. **Map** 13 A3. 🚇 *Green Park, Piccadilly Circus.*

Oᴺᴇ ᴏꜰ ʟᴏɴᴅᴏɴ's earliest squares, it was laid out in the 1670s and lined by exclusive houses for those whose business made it vital for them to live near St James's Palace. Many of the buildings date from the 18th and 19th centuries and have had many illustrious residents. During World War II Generals Eisenhower and de Gaulle both had headquarters here.

Today No. 10 on the north side is Chatham House (1736), home of the Royal Institute for International Affairs and, in the northwest corner, can be found the London Library (1896), a private lending library founded in 1841 by historian Thomas Carlyle *(see p196)* and others. The lovely gardens in the middle contain an equestrian statue of William III, here since 1808.

Royal Opera Arcade ⑩

SW1. **Map** 13 A3. 🚇 *Piccadilly Circus.*

Lᴏɴᴅᴏɴ's ꜰɪʀsᴛ shopping arcade was designed by John Nash and completed in 1818, behind the Haymarket Opera House (now called Her Majesty's Theatre). It beat the Burlington Arcade *(see p91)* by a year or so. Farlows sells shooting equipment, fishing tackle and a broad range of essentials for traditional country living, including the famous Hunter's green Wellington boots, from the Pall Mall side of this arcade.

Pall Mall ⑪

SW1. **Map** 13 A4. 🚇 *Charing Cross, Green Park, Piccadilly Circus.*

The Duke of Wellington (1842): a frequent visitor to Pall Mall

Tʜɪs ᴅɪɢɴɪꜰɪᴇᴅ street is named from the game of *palle-maille*, a cross between croquet and golf, which was played here in the early 17th century. For more than 150 years Pall Mall has been at the heart of London's clubland. Here exclusive gentlemen's clubs were formed to provide members with a refuge from their womenfolk.

The clubhouses now amount to a text book of the most fashionable architects of the era. From the east end, on the left is the colonnaded entrance to No. 116, Nash's United Services Club (1827). This was the favourite club of the Duke of Wellington and now houses the Institute of Directors. Facing it, on the other side of Waterloo Place, is the Athenaeum (No. 107), designed three years later by Decimus Burton, and long the power house of the British establishment. Next door are two clubs by Sir Charles Barry, architect of the Houses of Parliament *(see pp72–3)*; the Travellers' is at No. 106 and the Reform at No. 104. The clubs' stately interiors are well preserved but only members and their guests are admitted.

Institute of Contemporary Arts ⑫

The Mall SW1. **Map** 13 B3. 📞 *020-7930 3647.* 🚇 *Charing Cross, Piccadilly Circus.* **Open** *noon–10.30pm Sun, noon–11pm Mon, noon–1am Tue–Sat.* **Closed** *24–26 Dec, 1–2 Jan, public hols.* **Adm charge.** ♿ *notify in advance.* 📷 🖳 🎭 🎞 *Concerts, theatre, dance, lectures, films, exhibitions.* See **Entertainment** *pp334–5.*

Tʜᴇ ɪɴsᴛɪᴛᴜᴛᴇ (ICA) was established in 1947 in an effort to offer British artists some of the facilities which were available to United States artists at the Museum of Modern Art in New York. Originally on Dover Street, it has been situated in John Nash's Classical Carlton House Terrace (1833) since 1968.

With its entrance on The Mall, this extensive warren contains a cinema, auditorium, bookshop, art gallery, bar and a fine restaurant. It also offers exhibitions, lectures, concerts, films and plays. Non-members have to pay a charge.

Institute of Contemporary Arts, Carlton House Terrace

St James's Park ⓭

SW1. **Map** 13 A4. 📞 020-7930 1793. 🚇 *St James's Park.* **Open** *dawn to dusk daily.* 🏛 *Open daily.* ♿ **Concerts** *twice daily on summer weekends and public hols, weather permitting.* **Bird collection.**

IN SUMMER office workers sunbathe between the dazzling flower beds of this, the capital's most ornamental park. In winter overcoated civil servants discuss affairs of state as they stroll by the lake and eye its ducks, geese and pelicans. Originally a marsh, the park was drained by Henry VIII and incorporated into his hunting grounds. Later Charles II redesigned it for pedestrian pleasures, with an aviary along its southern edge (hence Birdcage Walk, the street where the aviary was). It is still a popular place to take the air, with an appealing view of Whitehall rooftops. In the summer there are concerts on the bandstand.

The Mall ⓮

SW1. **Map** 13 A4. 🚇 *Charing Cross, Green Park, Piccadilly Circus.*

THIS BROAD triumphal approach to Buckingham Palace was created by Aston Webb when he redesigned the front of the palace and the Victoria Monument in 1911 *(see picture p96)*. It follows the course of the old path at the edge of St James's Park, laid out in the reign of Charles II when it became London's most fashionable promenade. On the flagpoles down both sides of The Mall fly national flags of foreign heads of state during official visits.

Marlborough House ⓯

Pall Mall SW1. **Map** 13 A4. 📞 020-7839 3411. 🚇 *St James's Park, Green Park.* **Open** *one Sat in Sep only (phone for details).*

MARLBOROUGH HOUSE was designed by Christopher Wren *(see p47)* for the Duchess of Marlborough, and

finished in 1711. It was substantially enlarged in the 19th century and used by members of the Royal Family. From 1863 until he became Edward VII in 1901, it was the home of the Prince and Princess of Wales and the social centre of London. An Art Nouveau memorial in the Marlborough Road wall of the house commemorates Edward's queen, Alexandra. The building now houses the Commonwealth Secretariat.

Queen's Chapel ⓰

Marlborough Rd SW1. **Map** 13 A4. 📞 020-7930 4832. 🚇 *Green Park.* **Open** *Easter day–end July: Sun only.*

THIS EXQUISITE WORK of the architect Inigo Jones was built for Charles I's French wife, Henrietta Maria, in 1627, and was the first Classical church in England. It was initially intended to be part

Queen's Chapel

of St James's Palace but is now separated from it by Marlborough Gate. George III married his queen, Charlotte of Mecklenburg-Strelitz (who was to bear him 15 children), here in 1761.

The interior of the chapel, with its wonderful Annibale Caracci altarpiece and glorious 17th-century fittings is, unfortunately, open only to regular worshippers during the spring and early summer.

Early summer in St James's Park

Buckingham Palace ⑲

BUCKINGHAM PALACE is both office and home to the British monarchy. It is also used for ceremonial state occasions such as banquets for visiting heads of state. About 300 people work at the palace, including officers of the Royal Household and domestic staff.

John Nash converted the original Buckingham House into a palace for George IV (reigned 1820–30). Both he and his brother, William IV (reigned 1830–7), died before work was completed, and Queen Victoria was the first monarch to live there. For Queen Elizabeth II, who lives there now, the year 2002 marks the golden jubilee of her accession to the throne. The present east front, facing The Mall, was added in 1913.

Music Room
State guests are presented and royal christenings take place in this room, which boasts a beautiful, original parquet floor by Nash.

The State Dining Room is where meals that are less formal than state banquets are held.

The Picture Gallery houses a selection of The Queen's priceless collection of paintings.

Kitchen and staff quarters

Blue Drawing Room
Imitation onyx columns, created by John Nash, decorate this room.

Private post office

State Ballroom
The Georgian baroque ballroom is used for state banquets and investitures.

Changing the Guard
During the summer the palace guard is changed regularly in a colourful ceremony (see pp52–5).

VISITORS' CHECKLIST

SW1. **Map** 12 F5. **☎** 020-7839
1377. **⊖** St James's Park, Victoria.
🚌 2B, 11, 16, 24, 25, 36, 38,
52, 73, 135, C1. **🚈** Victoria.
State rooms open Aug–Sep:
9.30am– 5.30pm daily (last adm:
4.30pm). **Adm charge. 🚫**
Changing the Guard: Apr–Jul:
11.30am daily; Aug–Mar: alternate
days. **☎** 0906 866 3344 (London
Tourist Board Information Line).

The garden is a haven for wildlife and is overlooked by most
of the lavishly decorated state
rooms at the back of the palace.

The White Drawing Room is
where the Royal Family assemble
before passing into the State
Dining Room or Ball Room.

The Throne Room is
illuminated by seven
magnificent chandeliers.

A swimming pool lies
in the palace grounds as
does a private cinema.

**The Green Drawing
Room** is the first of the
state rooms entered by
guests at royal functions.

**Queen's Audience
Chamber**
*This is one of The Queen's
12 private rooms on
the first floor of
the palace.*

**The Royal
Standard** flies
when The Queen
is in residence.

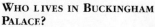

**WHO LIVES IN BUCKINGHAM
PALACE?**

The palace is the London
residence of The Queen and
her husband, the Duke of
Edinburgh. Prince Edward also
has an apartment here, as do
Princess Anne and the Duke
of York. About 50 domestic
staff have rooms in the
palace. There are more staff
homes situated in the Royal
Mews (see p96).

View over The Mall
*Traditionally, The Royal
Family waves to eager crowds
from the palace balcony.*

Clarence House ⑰

Stable Yard SW1. **Map** 12 F4.
🚇 *Green Park, St James's Park.*
Not open *to the public.*

OVERLOOKING THE MALL, it
was designed in 1827 by
John Nash for Queen Vic-
toria's predecessor, William,
Duke of Clarence, who lived
here after he became king in
1830. It is now the Queen
Mother's London home.

Lancaster House ⑱

Stable Yard SW1. **Map** 12 F4.
🚇 *Green Park, St James's Park.*
Not open *to the public.*

Lancaster House

THIS ROYAL residence was
built for the Duke of York
by Benjamin Wyatt, architect
of Apsley House, in 1825. In
1848 Chopin played here for
Queen Victoria, Prince Albert
and the Duke of Wellington.
It is now a conference centre.

Buckingham Palace ⑲

See pp94–5.

Queen's Gallery ⑳

Buckingham Palace Rd SW1.
Map 12 F5. 🕻 *020-7839 1377.*
🚇 *St James's Park, Victoria.* **Closed**
for refurbishment until early 2002.
Adm charge. 🚫

THE QUEEN POSSESSES one
of the finest and most
valuable collections of
paintings in the world, rich in
the work of such old masters

as Vermeer and Leonardo.
(For 30 years her art adviser
was Sir Anthony Blunt, until
he was finally exposed as a
Soviet spy in 1979 and then
stripped of his knighthood.)
   A selection of the works is
on display in this small
gallery (at the side of the
Palace), which was used as a
conservatory until 1962. The
building was once also used
as a chapel, and there is
still an area which is entirely
devoted to private worship
and is screened off from the
public. The exhibitions here
are based on a specific theme
and change regularly.

Royal Mews ㉑

Buckingham Palace Rd SW1.
Map 12 E5. 🕻 *020-7839 1377.*
🚇 *St James's Park, Victoria.*
Open *Aug–Sep: 10.30am–4.30pm*
Mon–Thu (last adm: 4pm). Subject to
closure at short notice (phone
first). **Adm charge.** ♿ 📷 ▯

ALTHOUGH OPEN
for only
a few hours a week, the
Mews is worth catching
for all lovers of horses
and of royal pomp. The
stables and coach
houses, designed by
Nash in 1825,
accommodate the
horses and coaches
used by the Royal
Family on state
occasions. The
star exhibit is the
gold state coach,
built for George III
in 1761, with fine
panels by Giovanni
Cipriani. Among the
other

Fabergé egg, Queen's Gallery

vehicles are the Irish state
coach, bought by Queen
Victoria for the State Opening
of Parliament; the open-
topped royal landau; and the
glass coach which was used
for royal weddings and for
transporting foreign ambassadors. The elaborate horses'
harnesses are also on display,
and so are some of the
splendid animals
that wear them.
   The Mews remains
open during the week
of the Royal Ascot race
meeting in June. For this
event, however, the Mews
vehicles go to the
Berkshire course,
where they transport
the royal party past
the grandstand before
the first race. There
is also a shop here
selling a selection
of interesting royal
merchandise and
souvenirs, open daily
from 9.30am
until 5pm.

The Victoria Monument outside Buckingham Palace

Wellington Arch ㉒

SW1. **Map** 12 D4. **〔** 020-7973 3494.
⊝ Hyde Park Corner. **Open** Apr–Sep:
10am–6pm Wed–Sun; Oct–Mar:
10am–4pm Wed–Sun. **Closed** 24–25
Dec, 1 Jan. **Adm charge**. **&**

AFTER NEARLY A century of debate about what to do with the patch of land in front of Apsley House, Wellington Arch, designed by Decimus Burton, was erected in 1828. The sculpture, by Adrian Jones, was added in 1912. Before it was installed Jones seated eight people for dinner in the body of one of the horses.

A recent conservation project restored the arch. The public now has access to the inner rooms with exhibitions on the city's statues and war memorials, and to the viewing platform under the sculpture with superb views over London.

Interior of Apsley House

Wellington Arch

Apsley House ㉓

Hyde Park Corner W1. **Map** 12 D4.
〔 020-7495 8525. **⊝** Hyde Park
Corner. **Open** 11am–5pm Tue–Sun.
Closed 24–26 Dec, 1 Jan, Good Fri,
May Day. **◎ & ⌂ ⬛** phone first.
⬛ www.apsleyhouse.org.uk

APSLEY HOUSE, on the southeast corner of Hyde Park, was completed by Robert Adam for Baron Apsley in 1778. Fifty years later it was enlarged and altered by the architects Benjamin and Philip Wyatt, to provide a suitably grand home for the Duke of Wellington, whose dual career as politician and soldier brought him victory against Napoleon at Waterloo (1815), and two terms as prime minister (1828-30, 1834). It is now a museum of Wellington memorabilia and some of his

trophies, and is dominated by Canova's startling, double life-size statue of Napoleon, who was Wellington's arch-enemy, wearing only a fig leaf. This once stood in the Louvre in Paris. Most of the paintings are of Wellington's contemporaries and victories, but there are also some old masters from his collection. The few remaining Adam interiors are worth seeing.

Shepherd Market ㉔

W1. **Map** 12 E4. **⊝** Green Park.

THIS ATTRACTIVE and bijou pedestrianized enclave of small shops, restaurants, and outdoor cafés, between Piccadilly and Curzon Street, was named after Edward Shepherd, who built it in the middle of the 18th century. During the 17th century the annual 15-day May Fair (from which the name of the area is derived) took place on this site, and today Shepherd Market is still very much the centre of Mayfair.

Green Park ㉕

SW1. **Map** 12 E4. **〔** 020-7930
1793. **⊝** Green Park, Hyde Park
Corner. **Open** 5am–midnight daily.

ONCE PART OF Henry VIII's hunting ground, it was, like St James's Park, adapted for public enjoyment by Charles II in the 1660s and is a natural, undulating landscape of grass and trees

(with a good spring show of daffodils). It was a favourite site for duels during the 18th century; in 1771 the poet Alfieri was wounded here by his mistress's husband, Viscount Ligonier, but then rushed back to the Haymarket Theatre still in time to catch the last act of a play. Today the park is popular with guests staying at the Mayfair hotels as a place to jog.

Faraday Museum ㉖

The Royal Institution, 21 Albemarle St
W1. **Map** 12 F3. **〔** 020-7409 2992.
⊝ Green Park. **Open** 10am–5.30pm
Mon–Fri. **Closed** 24 Dec–7 Jan. **Adm
charge**. **◎ ⬛** phone first. **Lectures**.

MICHAEL FARADAY was a 19th-century pioneer of the uses of electricity. His laboratory of the 1850s has been reconstructed in the basement here, and is on display together with a small museum showing some of Faraday's scientific apparatus together with personal effects.

Michael Faraday

SOHO AND TRAFALGAR SQUARE

SOHO HAS BEEN renowned for pleasures of the table, the flesh and the intellect ever since it was first developed in the late 17th century. For its first century the area was one of London's most fashionable, and Soho residents of the time have gone down in history for their extravagant parties.

During the later part of the 20th century, Soho consolidated its reputation as a centre for entertainment. With a

Clock on Liberty's department store

cosmopolitan mix of people, visitors here enjoy the many pleasant bars, restaurants and cafes – popular with everyone from tourists to locals, office workers and London's gay community.

Soho is one of London's most multi-cultural districts. The first immigrants were 18th-century Huguenots from France *(see Christ Church, Spitalfields p170)*. Soho is also famous as a Chinatown; Gerrard Street is lined with Chinese restaurants.

SIGHTS AT A GLANCE

Historic Streets and Buildings
Trafalgar Square ❶
Admiralty Arch ❷
Leicester Square ❻
Shaftesbury Avenue ❽
Chinatown ❾
Charing Cross Road ❿
Soho Square ⓬
Carnaby Street ⓮

Shops and Markets
Berwick Street Market ⓭
Liberty's ⓯

Churches
St Martin-in-the-Fields ❹

Museums and Galleries
National Gallery pp104–7 ❸
National Portrait Gallery ❺

Theatres
Palace Theatre ⓫
Theatre Royal ❼

KEY
◻ Street-by-Street map
❷ Underground station
✈ Railway station
P Parking

GETTING THERE
This area is served by the Central, Piccadilly, Bakerloo, Victoria and Northern lines. Many buses pass through Trafalgar Square and Piccadilly Circus. Rail services run from Charing Cross.

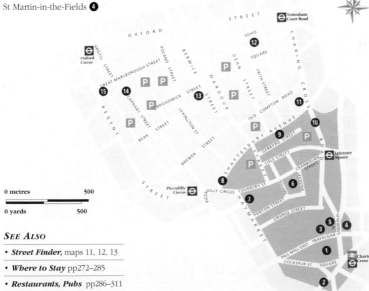

0 metres 500
0 yards 500

SEE ALSO

St Martin-in-the-Fields and Trafalgar Square

Street-by-Street: Trafalgar Square

THEATRES, cinemas, night-clubs and restaurants make this London's prime area for entertainment; there are also vast official buildings and narrow, shop-lined streets nearby.

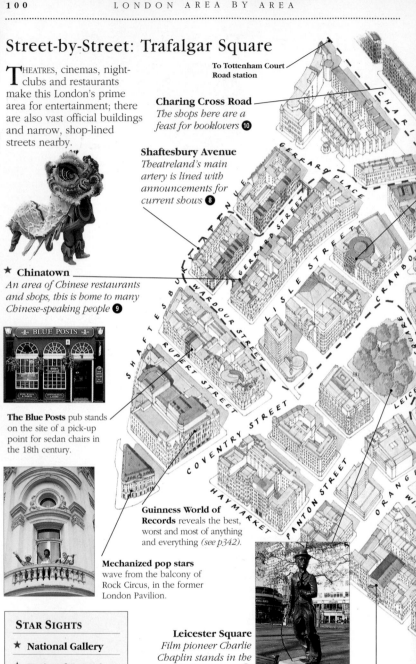

To Tottenham Court Road station

Charing Cross Road
The shops here are a feast for booklovers ❿

Shaftesbury Avenue
Theatreland's main artery is lined with announcements for current shows ❽

★ **Chinatown**
An area of Chinese restaurants and shops, this is home to many Chinese-speaking people ❾

The Blue Posts pub stands on the site of a pick-up point for sedan chairs in the 18th century.

BLUE POSTS

Guinness World of Records reveals the best, worst and most of anything and everything *(see p342).*

Mechanized pop stars wave from the balcony of Rock Circus, in the former London Pavilion.

Leicester Square
Film pioneer Charlie Chaplin stands in the traffic-free square ❻

Theatre Royal
On the site of an older theatre, it is graced by a John Nash portico ❼

STAR SIGHTS

★ **National Gallery**

★ **National Portrait Gallery**

★ **St Martin-in-the-Fields**

★ **Chinatown**

★ **Trafalgar Square**

KEY

— — — Suggested route

| 0 metres | 100 |
| 0 yards | 100 |

Notre Dame, once a theatre, was converted into a church in 1855. The Jean Cocteau murals inside date from 1960.

LOCATOR MAP
See Central London Map pp12–13

The Hippodrome, a disco and nightclub *(see pp336–7)*, was once a variety theatre.

Cecil Court is lined with shops selling old books and prints.

★ **National Gallery**
The national collection of art is housed in these buildings ③

★ **St Martin-in-the-Fields**
James Gibbs's masterpiece set the US "colonial" style ④

Leicester Square station

★ **National Portrait Gallery**
Portraits of prominent Britons from Tudor times to the present day adorn the walls here ⑤

Charing Cross station

Admiralty Arch
The Mall's regal entrance was built in 1910 ②

★ **Trafalgar Square**
Millions of tourists come here to feed the pigeons and admire the fountains ①

Nelson's Column

Trafalgar Square ❶

WC2. **Map** 13 B3. 🚇 *Charing Cross.*

Lᴏɴᴅᴏɴ's ᴍᴀɪɴ venue for rallies and outdoor public meetings was conceived by John Nash and was mostly constructed during the 1830s. The 50-m (165-ft) column commemorates Admiral Lord Nelson, Britain's most famous sea lord, who died heroically at the Battle of Trafalgar against Napoleon in 1805. It dates from 1842; 14 stone-masons held a dinner on its flat top before the statue of Nelson was finally installed. Edwin Landseer's four lions were added to guard its base 25 years later. The north side of the square is now taken up by the National Gallery and its annexe *(see pp104–7)*, with Canada House on the west side, and South Africa House on the east. The restored Grand Buildings on the south side, with their fine arcade, were built in 1880 as the Grand Hotel. It is hoped that the pedestrianization of the square is set to begin in 2002, with an enlarged central staircase descending from the National Gallery.

Nelson's statue overlooking the square

Admiralty Arch ❷

The Mall SW1. **Map** 13 B3. 🚇 *Charing Cross.*

Dᴇsɪɢɴᴇᴅ ɪɴ 1911, this triple archway was part of Aston Webb's scheme to rebuild The Mall as a grand processional route honouring Queen Victoria. The arch effectively seals the eastern end of The Mall, although traffic passes through the smaller side gates, and separates courtly London from the hurly-burly of Trafalgar Square. The central gate is opened only for royal processions, making a fine setting for the coaches and horses trotting through.

Filming *Howard's End* at Admiralty Arch

National Gallery ❸

See pp104–7.

St Martin-in-the-Fields ❹

Trafalgar Sq WC2. **Map** 13 B3. 📞 020-7766 1100. 🚇 *Charing Cross.* **Open** 8am–6.30pm daily. ♿ 11.30am Sun. 🚻 📷 🛍 *London* **Brass Rubbing Centre** 📞 020-7930 9306. **Open** 10am–6pm Mon–Sat, noon–6pm Sun. **Concerts** *see* **Entertainment** *pp332–3.*

Tʜᴇʀᴇ ʜᴀs ʙᴇᴇɴ a church on this site since the 13th century. Many famous people were buried here, including Charles II's mistress, Nell Gwynne, and the painters William Hogarth and Joshua Reynolds. The present church was designed by James Gibbs and completed in 1726. In architectural terms it was one of the most influential ever built; it was much copied in the United States where it became a model for the Colonial style of church-building. An unusual feature of St Martin's spacious interior is the royal box at gallery level on the left of the altar.

From 1914 until 1927 the crypt was opened as a shelter for homeless soldiers and down-and-outs; during World War II it was an air-raid shelter. Today it still plays a role, helping the homeless and providing a lunchtime soup kitchen for them. It also houses a café and a religious bookshop as well as the London Brass Rubbing Centre. There is a good craft market in the yard outside *(see p325)* and regular lunch-time and evening concerts are held in the church.

National Portrait Gallery ❺

2 St Martin's Place WC2. **Map** 13 B3. 📞 020-7306 0055. 🌐 www.npg.org.uk 🚇 *Leicester Sq, Charing Cross.* **Open** 10am–6pm Sat–Wed, 10am–9pm Thu–Fri. **Closed** Good Fri, May Day, 24–26 Dec, 1 Jan. ♿ Orange St entrance. 📷 *during August.* 🍴 📖 **Lectures.**

Tᴏᴏ ᴏғᴛᴇɴ ɪɢɴᴏʀᴇᴅ in favour of the National Gallery next door, this fascinating museum recounts Britain's development through portraits of its main characters, giving faces to names which are familiar from the history books. There are pictures of kings, queens, poets,

Rodrigo Moynihan's portrait of Margaret Thatcher (1984)

musicians, artists, thinkers, heroes and villains from all periods since the late 14th century. The oldest works, on the fourth floor, include a Hans Holbein cartoon of Henry VIII and paintings of several of his wives.

The National Portrait Gallery's millennium development project opened in May 2000, allowing it 50 per cent more exhibition and public space. It includes a new Tudor Gallery, displaying some of the earliest and most important paintings, including one of Shakespeare and the Ditchley portrait of Elizabeth I. A new balcony provides an extra display area for portraits from the 1960s to the 1990s.

The gallery has a new rooftop restaurant that is accessible outside normal opening hours, and the spacious lecture theatre in the basement can also be used for drama and film events.

The gallery also houses temporary exhibitions and has an excellent shop selling books on art and literature, as well as an extensive range of cards, prints and posters featuring pictures from the main collection.

Leicester Square ❻

WC2. **Map** *13 B2.* ☉ *Leicester Sq, Piccadilly Circus.*

I T IS HARD to imagine that this, the perpetually animated heart of the West End entertainment district, was once a fashionable place to live. Laid out in 1670 south of Leicester House, a long-gone royal residence, the square's early occupants included the scientist Isaac Newton and later the artists Joshua Reynolds and William Hogarth. Reynolds made his fortune painting high society in his elegant salon at No. 46. Hogarth's house, in the south-east corner, became the Hôtel de la Sablionère in 1801, probably the area's first public restaurant.

In Victorian times several of London's most popular music halls were established here, including the Empire (today

the cinema on the same site perpetuates the name) and the Alhambra, replaced in 1937 by the Art Deco Odeon. The centre of the square has been refurbished and facilities include a useful booth that sells cut-price theatre tickets *(see p328).* There is also a statue of Charlie Chaplin (by John Doubleday), which was unveiled in 1981. The Shakespeare fountain dates from an earlier renovation in 1874.

Theatre Royal ❼

Haymarket SW1. **Map** *13 A3.* 📞 *020-7930 8800.* ☉ *Piccadilly Circus.* **Open** *performances only.*

T HE FINE FRONTAGE of this theatre, with its portico of six Corinthian columns, dates from 1821, when John Nash designed it as part of his plan for a stately route from Carlton House to his new Regent's Park. The interior is equally grand.

Shaftesbury Avenue ❽

W1. **Map** *13 A2.* ☉ *Piccadilly Circus, Leicester Sq.*

T HE MAIN ARTERY of London's theatreland, Shaftesbury Avenue has six theatres and two cinemas, all on its north side. This street was cut through an area of terrible slums between 1877 and 1886 in order to improve communications across the city's busy West End; it follows the route of a much earlier highway. It is named after the Earl of Shaftesbury (1801–85), whose attempts to improve housing conditions had helped some of the local poor. (The Earl is also commemorated by the Eros statue in Piccadilly Circus – *see p90.)* The Lyric Theatre, which was designed by C J Phipps, has been open for almost the same length of time as the avenue.

London's West End: the facade of the Gielgud Theatre

National Gallery ❸

Trafalgar Square facade

THE NATIONAL GALLERY has flourished since its inception in the early 19th century. In 1824 George IV persuaded a reluctant government to buy 38 major paintings, including works by Raphael and Rembrandt, and these became the start of a national collection. The collection grew over the years as rich benefactors contributed works and money. The main gallery building was designed in Neo-Classical style by William Wilkins and built in 1834–8. To its left lies the new Sainsbury Wing, financed by the grocery family and completed in 1991. It houses some spectacular early Renaissance art.

Stairs and lift to lower galleries

Orange St entrance ♿

Stairs to lower floor

GALLERY GUIDE

Most of the collection is housed on one floor divided into four wings. The paintings hang chronologically, with the earliest works (1260–1510) in the Sainsbury Wing. The North, West and East Wings cover 1510–1600, 1600–1700 and 1700–1900. Lesser paintings of all periods are on the lower floor.

Link to main building

Stairs to lower floors

★ Leonardo Cartoon *(1510)*
The genius of Leonardo da Vinci glows through this chalk drawing of the Virgin and Child with St Anne and John the Baptist.

KEY TO FLOORPLAN

- ☐ Painting 1260–1510
- ☐ Painting 1510–1600
- ☐ Painting 1600–1700
- ☐ Painting 1700–1900
- ☐ Special exhibitions
- ☐ Non-exhibition space

Doge Leonardo Loredan *(1501)*
Giovanni Bellini portrays this Venetian head of state as a serene father figure.

Main entrance to Sainsbury Wing ♿

★ **Rokeby Venus** (1649)
*Diego Velázquez painted it
to match a lost
Venetian
nude.*

★ **The Hay Wain** (1821)
*John Constable brilliantly
caught the effect of distance
and the changing light and
shadow of a typically
English cloudy summer day
in this famous classic.*

VISITORS' CHECKLIST

Trafalgar Sq WC2. **Map** 13 B3.
[020-7747 2885. **⊖** Charing
Cross, Leicester Sq, Piccadilly
Circus. **🚌** 3, 6, 9, 11, 12, 13,
15, 23, 24, 29, 53, 77a, 88, 91,
94, 109, 139, 159, 176. **🚆**
Charing Cross. **Open** 10am–
6pm daily (9pm Wed). **Closed**
24–26 Dec, 1 Jan, Good Fri. **🅿**
♿ Sainsbury Wing entrance.
**🎫 💻 🍴 🛒 🔼 Lectures,
film presentations, videos,
exhibitions, events, gallery
guide on CD-ROM.**
W www.nationalgallery.org.uk

Stairs to
lower floor

Bathers at Asnières (1884)
*Georges Seurat experiments here
with millions of little dots of colour,
to create a Neo-Classical portrayal
of modern urban life.*

Trafalgar
Square entrance

★ **The Ambassadors**
*The strange shape in the
foreground of this Hans
Holbein portrait (1533)
is a foreshortened skull,
a symbol of mortality.*

★ **Baptism of Christ**
*Piero della Francesca
painted this tranquil
masterpiece (1450s) of
early Renaissance
perspective for a church
in his native Umbria.*

Arnolfini Marriage
*The woman in Jan van
Eyck's famous painting
(1434) is not pregnant –
her rotund shape
conforms to contemporary
ideas of female beauty.*

STAR PICTURES

★ **Baptism of Christ
by Piero della
Francesca**

★ **Cartoon by
Leonardo da Vinci**

★ **Rokeby Venus by
Diego Velázquez**

★ **The Ambassadors
by Hans Holbein**

★ **The Haywain by
John Constable**

Exploring the National Gallery

THE NATIONAL GALLERY HAS over 2,200 paintings, most kept on permanent display. The Collection ranges from early works by Giotto, in the 13th century, to 19th-century Impressionists, but its particular strengths are in Dutch, early Renaissance Italian and 17th-century Spanish painting. The bulk of the British collections are housed in Tate Britain *(see pp82–5)* while Tate Modern specializes in international modern art *(pp178–81)*.

The Adoration of The Kings (1564) by Pieter Brueghel the Elder

EARLY RENAISSANCE (1260–1510): ITALIAN AND NORTHERN PAINTING

THREE LUSTROUS PANELS from the *Maestà*, Duccio's great altarpiece in Siena cathedral, are among the earliest paintings here. Other Italian works of the period include his outstanding *Madonna*.

The fine *Wilton Diptych* portraying England's Richard II is probably by a French artist. It displays the lyrical elegance of the International Gothic style that swept Europe.

Italian masters of this style include Pisanello and Gentile da Fabriano, whose *Madonna* often hangs beside another, by Masaccio – both date from 1426. Also shown are works by Masaccio's pupil, Filippo Lippi, as well as Botticelli and Uccello. Umbrian paintings include Piero della Francesca's *Nativity* and *Baptism*, and an excellent collection of Mantegna, Bellini and other works from the Venetian and Ferrarese schools. Antonello da Messina's *St Jerome in his Study* has been mistaken for a van Eyck; it is not hard to see why, when you compare it with van Eyck's *Arnolfini Marriage*. Important

Netherlandish pictures, including some by Rogier van der Weyden and his followers, are also here, in the Sainsbury Wing.

HIGH RENAISSANCE (1510–1600): ITALIAN, NETHERLANDISH AND GERMAN PAINTING

Christ Mocked (1490–1500) by Hieronymus Bosch

SEBASTIANO DEL PIOMBO'S *The Raising of Lazarus* was painted, with Michelangelo's assistance, to rival Raphael's great *Transfiguration*, which hangs in the Vatican in Rome.

These and other well-known names of the High (or late) Renaissance are extremely well represented, often with massive works. Look out for Parmigianino's *Madonna and Child with Saints*, Leonardo da Vinci's charcoal cartoon of the *Virgin and Child* (a full-sized drawing used for copying as a painting), and his second version of the *Virgin of the Rocks*. There are also tender and amusing works by Piero di Cosimo, and several Titians, including *Bacchus and Ariadne* – which the public found too bright and garish when it was first cleaned by the gallery in the 1840s.

The Netherlandish and German collections are weaker. Even so, they include *The Ambassadors*, a fine double portrait by Holbein; and Altdorfer's superb *Christ Taking Leave of his Mother*, bought by the gallery in 1980. There is also an Hieronymus Bosch of *Christ Mocked* (sometimes known as *The Crowning with Thorns*), and an excellent Brueghel, *The Adoration of the Kings*.

The Annunciation (1448) by Filippo Lippi

THE SAINSBURY WING

Plans for this new wing, opened in 1991, provoked a storm of dissent. An incensed Prince Charles dubbed an early design "a monstrous carbuncle on the face of a much-loved friend". The final building, by Venturi, has drawn criticism from other quarters for being a derivative compromise.

This is where major changing exhibitions are held. It also houses the Micro Gallery, a computerized database of the Collection.

DUTCH, ITALIAN, FRENCH AND SPANISH PAINTING (1600–1700)

THE SUPERB DUTCH collection gives two entire rooms to Rembrandt. There are also works by Vermeer, Van Dyck (among them his equestrian portrait of King Charles I) and Rubens (including the popular *Chapeau de Paille*).

From Italy, the works of Carracci and Caravaggio are strongly represented, and Salvatore Rosa has a glowering self-portrait.

French works on show include a magnificent portrait of Cardinal Richelieu by Philippe de Champaigne. Claude's seascape, *The Embarkation of the Queen of Sheba,* hangs beside Turner's rival painting *Dido Building Carthage,* as Turner himself had instructed.

The Spanish school has works by Murillo, Velázquez, Zurbarán and others.

Young Woman Standing at a Virginal (1670) by Jan Vermeer

The Scale of Love (1715–18) by Jean Antoine Watteau

VENETIAN, FRENCH AND ENGLISH PAINTING (1700–1800)

ONE OF THE GALLERY's most famous 18th-century works is Canaletto's *The Stone-Mason's Yard.* Other Venetians here are Longhi and Tiepolo.

The French collection includes Rococo masters such as Chardin, Watteau and Boucher, as well as land-scapists and portraitists.

Gainsborough's early, gouache *Mr and Mrs Andrews* and *The Morning Walk* are favourites with visitors; his rival, Sir Joshua Reynolds, is represented by some of his most Classical work and by more informal portraits.

ENGLISH, FRENCH AND GERMAN PAINTING (1800–1900)

THE GREAT AGE OF 19th-century landscape painting is amply represented here, with fine works by Constable and Turner, including Constable's *The Hay Wain* and Turner's *The Fighting Temeraire,* as well as works by the French artists Corot and Daubigny.

Of Romantic art, there is Géricault's vivid work, *Horse Frightened by Lightning,* and several interesting paintings by Delacroix. In contrast, the society portrait of *Mme Moitessier* by Ingres, though still Romantic, is more restrained and Classical.

Impressionists and other French avant-garde artists are well represented. Among the highlights are *Waterlilies* by Monet, Auguste Renoir's *At the Theatre,* Van Gogh's *Sunflowers,* not to mention Rousseau's *Tropical Storm with Tiger.* In Seurat's *Bathers at Asnières* he did not originally use the pointillist technique he was later to invent, but subsequently reworked areas of the picture using dots of colour.

At the Theatre (1876–7) by Pierre-Auguste Renoir

Chinatown ❾

Streets around Gerrard St W1.
Map 13 A2. ⊖ *Leicester Sq,
Piccadilly Circus.*

THERE HAS BEEN a Chinese community in London since the 19th century. Originally it was concentrated around the East End docks at Limehouse, where the opium dens of Victorian melodrama were sited. As the number of immigrants increased in the 1950s, many moved into Soho where they created an ever-expanding Chinatown. It contains scores of restaurants, and mysterious aroma-filled shops selling oriental produce. Three Chinese arches straddle Gerrard Street, where a vibrant, colourful street festival, held in late January, celebrates Chinese New Year *(see p59).*

Charing Cross Road ❿

WC2. **Map** 13 B2. ⊖ *Leicester Sq.*
See **Shops and Markets** *p318–19.*

Antiquarian books from the shops on Charing Cross Road

THE ROAD is a mecca for book-lovers, with a row of second-hand bookshops south of Cambridge Circus and, north of these, a clutch of shops that, between them, should be able to supply just about any recent volume. Visit the giants: chaotic Foyle's and busy Waterstones, and the smaller, specialist shops: try Zwemmer's for art books and Silver Moon for feminism. Sadly, huge rent rises have put this unique mix under threat. At the junction with New Oxford Street rises the 1960s skyscraper, Centre-point. It lay empty for nearly ten years after it was built, its owners finding this more profitable than renting it out.

At the Palace Theatre in 1898

Palace Theatre ⓫

Shaftesbury Ave W1. **Map** 13 B2.
☎ **Box office** *020-7434 0909.*
⊖ *Leicester Sq.* **Open** *for
performances only. See*
Entertainment *pp328–9.*

MOST WEST END theatres are disappointingly unassertive. This one, which dominates the west side of Cambridge Circus, is a splendid exception, with its sparkling terracotta exterior and opulent furnishings. Completed as an opera house in 1891, it became a music hall the following year. The ballerina Anna Pavlova made her London debut here in 1910. Now the theatre, owned by Andrew Lloyd Webber whose own musicals are all over London, stages hit shows such as *Les Misérables.*

Soho Square ⓬

W1. **Map** 13 A1. ⊖ *Tottenham
Court Rd.*

SOON AFTER it was laid out in 1681 this Square enjoyed a brief reign as the most fashionable address in London. Originally it was called King Square, after Charles II whose statue was erected in the middle. The square went out of fashion by the late 18th century and is now surrounded by bland office buildings. The mock-Tudor garden shed in the centre was added much later in Victorian times.

Berwick Street Market ⓭

W1. **Map** 13 A1. ⊖ *Piccadilly
Circus.* **Open** *9am–6pm Mon–Sat.
See* **Shops and Markets** *p324.*

THERE HAS BEEN a market here since the 1840s. Berwick Street trader Jack Smith introduced grapefruit to London in 1890. Today this is the West End's best street market, at its cheeriest and most crowded during the lunch hour. The freshest and least expensive produce for miles around is to be had here. There are also some interesting shops, including Borovick's which sells extraordinary fabrics, and a growing number of cafés and restaurants. At its southern end the street narrows into an alley on which Raymond's Revue Bar (the comparatively respectable face of Soho sleaze) has presented its festival of erotica since 1958.

Some of London's cheapest produce at Berwick Street Market

Carnaby Street 14

W1. **Map** 12 F2. ⊖ *Oxford Circus.*

DURING THE 1960s this street was so much the centre of swinging London that the Oxford English Dictionary recognized the noun "Carnaby Street" as meaning "fashionable clothing for young people". Today the street is rather down-market and caters more for tourists than for the truly fashionable. England's oldest pipe maker, Inderwick's, founded in 1797, is situated at No. 45. There are some interesting young designers' shops in nearby backstreets, notably those on Newburgh Street *(see pp316–17).*

Liberty's mock-Tudor facade

Liberty's 15

Regent St W1. **Map** 12 F2. ⊖ *Oxford Circus. See* **Shops and Markets** *p313.*

ARTHUR LASENBY LIBERTY opened his first shop, selling oriental silks, on Regent Street in 1875. Among his first customers were the artists Ruskin, Rossetti and Whistler. Soon Liberty prints and designs, by artists such as William Morris, influenced the Arts and Crafts movement of the late 19th and early 20th centuries. They are still very fashionable today.

The present mock-Tudor building with its country-house feel dates from 1925, and was built specifically to house the store.

Today the shop maintains its strong links with the East. The basement Oriental Bazaar and the top floor, which is crammed with period Art Nouveau and Arts and Crafts furniture, are particularly worth visiting.

The Heart of Soho

OLD COMPTON STREET is Soho's High Street. Its shops and restaurants reflect the variety of people who have lived in the area over the centuries. These include many great artists, writers and musicians.

Bar Italia is a coffee shop situated under the room where John Logie Baird first demonstrated television in 1926. As a child, Mozart stayed next door with his family in 1764 and 1765.

Ronnie Scott's opened in 1959, and nearly all the big names of jazz have played here *(see pp335–7).*

The Coach and Horses pub has been a centre of bohemian Soho since the 1950s and is still popular.

Wheeler's opened in 1929 as part of the London-wide fish restaurant chain.

Patisserie Valerie is a Hungarian-owned café serving delicious pastries *(see pp306–8).*

St Anne's Church Tower is all that remains after a bomb destroyed the church in 1940.

The French House was frequented by Maurice Chevalier and General de Gaulle.

The Palace Theatre has hosted many successful musicals.

Covent Garden and the Strand

T HE OPEN-AIR cafés, street entertainers, stylish shops and markets
make this area a magnet for visitors. At its centre is the Piazza, which
sheltered a wholesale market until
1974. Since then, the pretty Victorian
buildings here and in the surrounding streets have been converted into
one of the city's liveliest districts. In
medieval times the area was occupied
by a convent garden which supplied
Westminster Abbey with produce. Then
in the 1630s, Inigo Jones laid out the
Piazza as
London's first
square, with
its west side
dominated by
St Paul's Church.

The Piazza was
commissioned as a
residential develop-
ment by the Earl of Bedford, owner of
one of the mansions that lined the
Strand. Before the Embankment was
built, the Strand ran along the river.

Sights at a Glance

Historic Streets and Buildings
The Piazza and
  Central Market ❶
Neal Street and
  Neal's Yard ❼
Savoy Hotel ❸
Somerset House ❶
Roman Bath ❶
Bush House ❶
Adelphi ❷
Charing Cross ❷

Museums and Galleries
London Transport
  Museum ❸
Theatre Museum ❹
Photographers' Gallery ❶

Churches
St Paul's Church ❷
Savoy Chapel ❶
St Mary-le-Strand ❶

Monuments and Statues
Seven Dials ❾
Cleopatra's Needle ❶

Famous Theatres
Theatre Royal ❺
Royal Opera House ❻
Adelphi Theatre ❶
The London Coliseum ❷

Parks and Gardens
Victoria Embankment
  Gardens ❷

Historic Pubs, Shopping Arcades
Lamb and Flag ❶
Thomas Neal's ❽

Getting There
Covent Garden, Leicester
Square and Charing Cross
Underground stations are all
nearby. There are frequent
buses: 9, 11, 15 and 30 to the
Strand or 14, 19, 22b, 24, 29,
38 and 176 to Shaftesbury
Avenue. Charing Cross rail
station is a short walk.

Key

▨	Street-by-Street map
⊖	Underground station
≷	Railway station
P	Parking

See Also
• *Street Finder*, maps 13, 14
• *Where to Stay* pp272–285
• *Restaurants, Pubs* pp286–311

0 metres   500
0 yards   500

Enzo Piazotta's statue *The Young Dancer* (1988), opposite the Royal Opera House

Street-by-Street: Covent Garden

ONCE AN AREA of decaying streets and warehouses, Covent Garden came alive only after dark when the fruit and vegetable market traders went about their business. Now it is completely revitalized. Day and night visitors, residents and street-entertainers of every vocation throng the Piazza, much as they would have done several centuries ago.

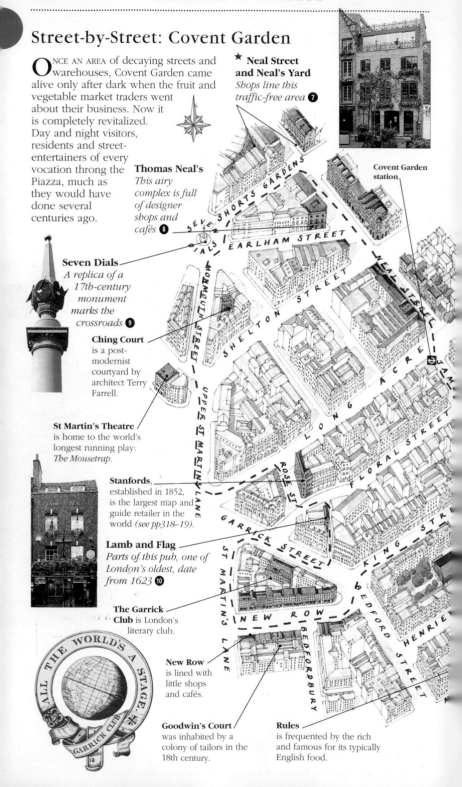

★ Neal Street and Neal's Yard
Shops line this traffic-free area ❼

Covent Garden station

Thomas Neal's
This airy complex is full of designer shops and cafés ❽

Seven Dials
A replica of a 17th-century monument marks the crossroads ❾

Ching Court
is a post-modernist courtyard by architect Terry Farrell.

St Martin's Theatre
is home to the world's longest running play: *The Mousetrap.*

Stanfords, established in 1852, is the largest map and guide retailer in the world *(see pp318–19).*

Lamb and Flag
Parts of this pub, one of London's oldest, date from 1623 ❿

The Garrick Club is London's literary club.

New Row
is lined with little shops and cafés.

Goodwin's Court
was inhabited by a colony of tailors in the 18th century.

Rules
is frequented by the rich and famous for its typically English food.

★ **The Piazza and Central Market**
Performers of all kinds – jugglers, clowns, acrobats and musicians – entertain the crowds in the square ❶

LOCATOR MAP
See Central London Map pp12–13

Royal Opera House
Most of the world's greatest singers and dancers have appeared on its stage ❻

Bow Street Police Station
housed London's first police force, the Bow Street Runners, in the 18th century. It closed in 1992.

★ **Theatre Museum**
A collection of theatrical memorabilia is housed here ❹

Theatre Royal
The old theatre now shows extravagant musicals ❺

Boswells, now a coffee house, is where Dr Johnson first met his biographer, Boswell.

Jubilee Market
sells clothes and bric-à-brac.

★ **London Transport Museum**
The history of the city's tube and buses is brought to life in this museum ❸

★ **St Paul's Church**
Despite appearances, Inigo Jones's church faces away from the Piazza – the entrance is through the churchyard ❷

STAR SIGHTS

★ **The Piazza and Central Market**

★ **St Paul's Church**

★ **London Transport Museum**

★ **Theatre Museum**

★ **Neal Street and Neal's Yard**

KEY

- - -   Suggested route

0 metres   100

0 yards   100

The Piazza and Central Market ❶

Covent Garden WC2. **Map** 13 C2.
🚇 Covent Garden. 🚶 but cobbled streets. **Street performers** 10am–dusk daily. See **Shops and Markets** p325.

THE 17TH-CENTURY architect Inigo Jones originally planned this area to be an elegant residential square, modelled on the piazza at Livorno, northern Italy. Today the buildings on and around the Piazza are almost entirely Victorian. The covered central market was designed by Charles Fowler in 1833 for fruit and vegetable whole-salers, the glass and iron roof anticipating the giant rail termini built later in the century – for instance, St Pancras (see p130) and Waterloo (see p191). It now makes a magnificent shell for an array of small shops selling designer clothes, books, arts, crafts, decorative items and antiques, all surrounded by bustling market stalls that continue south in the neighbouring Jubilee Hall, which was built in 1903.

The colonnaded Bedford Chambers, on the north side, give a hint of Inigo Jones's plan, although even they are not original: they were rebuilt and partially modified in 1879.

Street entertainment is a well-loved and now expected tradition of the area; in 1662, diarist Samuel Pepys wrote of watching a Punch and Judy show under the portico of St Paul's Church.

West entrance to St Paul's

St Paul's Church ❷

Bedford St WC2. **Map** 13 C2.
📞 020-7836 5221. 🚇 Covent Garden. **Open** 9.30am–2.30pm Mon, 9.30am–4.30pm Tue–Fri, 10am–1pm Sun. ✝ 11am Sun. 🚶

INIGO JONES built this church (completed in 1633) with the altar at the west end, so as to allow his grand portico, with its two square and two round columns, to face east into the new Piazza. Clerics objected to this unorthodox arrangement, and the altar was moved to its conventional position at the east end. Jones still went ahead with his original exterior design. Thus the church is entered from the west, and the east portico is essentially a fake door, used now as an impromptu stage for street entertainers. In 1795 the interior was destroyed by fire but was rebuilt in Jones's airy, uncomplicated style. Today the church is all that is left of Jones's original plan for the Piazza. St Paul's has long been called "the actors' church" and plaques commemorate distinguished men and women of the theatre. A 17th-century carving by Grinling Gibbons, on the west screen, is a memorial to the architect.

Punch and Judy performer

London Transport Museum ❸

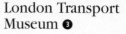

The Piazza WC2. **Map** 13 C2.
📞 020-7379 6344. 🚇 Covent Garden. **Open** 10am–6pm Sat–Thu, 11am–6pm Fri (last adm: 5.15pm). **Closed** 24–26 Dec. **Adm charge**. 📷 🚶 📹 phone in advance. 📱

London Transport Museum

YOU DO NOT have to be a train spotter or a collector of bus numbers to enjoy this exhibition. Since 1980 the intriguing collection has been housed in the picturesque Victorian Flower Market, which was built in 1872, and features past and present public transport.

The history of London's transport is in essence a social history of the capital. Bus, tram and underground route patterns first reflected the city's growth and then promoted it: the northern and western suburbs began to develop only after their tube connections were built. The museum houses a fine collection of 20th-century commercial art. London's bus and train companies have been, and still are, prolific patrons of contemporary artists, and copies of some of the finest posters on display can be bought at the well-stocked museum shop. They include the innovative Art Deco designs of E McKnight Kauffer, as well as work by renowned artists of the 1930s, such as Graham Sutherland and Paul Nash.

This museum is excellent for children. There are plenty of hands-on exhibits, and these include the opportunity for children to put themselves in the driver's seat of a London bus, or a train from the underground system.

A mid-18th-century view of the Piazza

Theatre Museum ❹

7 Russell St WC2. **Map** 13 C2.
📞 *020-7943 4700.* 🚇 *Covent
Garden.* **Open** *10am–6pm Tue–Sun.*
Closed *25–26 Dec, 1 Jan & public hols.*
Adm charge. ♿ 📷 📹 *Studio
theatre performances, events.*

A JOURNEY INTO the Theatre
Museum's subterranean
galleries with their fascinating
collection of theatrical
memorabilia is one not to be
missed. The displays include
playbills, programmes, props
and costumes from historic
productions, bits of interior
decor from theatres that have
long since vanished, as well
as paintings of actors and
scenes from plays. One
exhibit illustrates the way in
which theatre has evolved
from Shakespeare's time to
the present day and uses
models of auditoriums
through the ages. Exhibitions
are held in the Gielgud and
Irving galleries and young
theatre companies regularly
stage their own productions
in the theatre inside.

Theatre Royal ❺

Catherine St WC2. **Map** 13 C2.
📞 *020-7494 5440.* 🚇 *Covent
Garden, Holborn, Temple.* **Open**
*for performances and guided tours
(phone to check). See* **Entertainment**
pp328–9.

THE FIRST THEATRE on
this site was built in
1663 as one of only two
venues in London where
drama could legally be
staged. Nell Gwynne
acted here. Three of the
theatres built here since
then burned down,
including one designed
by Sir Christopher Wren
(see p47). The present
one, by Benjamin Wyatt,
was completed in 1812
and has one of the city's
largest auditoriums. In
the 1800s it was famous
for pantomimes – now it
stages block-buster
musicals. It is called the
Theatre Royal, Drury
Lane even though its
entrance is actually on
Catherine Street.

The glass Vilar Floral Hall, part of the recently opened Royal Opera House

Royal Opera House ❻

Covent Garden WC2. **Map** 13 C2.
📞 *020-7304 4000.* 🚇 *Covent
Garden.* **Open** *for performances and
guided tours (phone to check). See*
Entertainment *p332.*

THE FIRST THEATRE on this
site was built in 1732, and
staged plays as well as
concerts. However, like its
neighbour the Theatre Royal,
it proved prone to fire and
was destroyed in 1808 and
again in 1856. The present
opera house was designed in
1858 by E M Barry (son of the
architect of the Houses of
Parliament). John Flaxman's
portico frieze, of tragedy and
comedy, survived from the
previous building of 1809.
    The Opera House has
had both high and low
points during its history.
In 1892, the first British
performance of Wagner's
Ring was conducted
here by Gustav Mahler.
Later, during World War
I, the opera house was
used as a storehouse by
the government.
    The building is home
to the Royal Opera and
Royal Ballet Companies
– the best tickets cost
over £100 and are hard
to acquire. After two
years of extensive
renovation the building
reopened in time for the
new millennium, com-
plete with a second
auditorium and new

rehearsal rooms for its Royal
Opera and Royal Ballet companies. Backstage tours are
available, and once a month
visitors can watch the Royal
Ballet attending its daily class.

Neal Street and Neal's Yard ❼

Covent Garden WC2. **Map** 13 B1.
🚇 *Covent Garden. See* **Shops and
Markets** *pp314–15.*

A specialist shop on Neal Street

IN THIS ATTRACTIVE street,
former warehouses from
the 19th century can be
identified by the hoisting
mechanisms high on their
exterior walls. The buildings
have been converted into a
number of shops, art galleries
and restaurants. Off Neal
Street is Neal's Yard, a mock-
rustic cornucopia for lovers of
farmhouse cheeses and yogurt,
salads, wholefoods, herbs and
fresh-baked breads. Brainchild
of the late Nicholas Saunders,
it remains an oasis of alternative values amid the growing
commercialism of the area.

Café at Thomas Neal's

Thomas Neal's ❽

Earlham St WC2. **Map** 13 B2.
🚇 Covent Garden. ♿ ground floor only.

Opened in the early 1990s, this upmarket shopping complex offers an interesting range of shops, selling designer clothes and cosmetics, jewellery and accessories, antique clothing and lace. There is a coffee shop and restaurant on the lower floor. The Donmar Warehouse theatre *(see p330)* is also part of the complex, staging must-see productions such as *The Blue Room*.

Seven Dials ❾

Monmouth St WC2. **Map** 13 B2.
🚇 Covent Garden, Leicester Sq.

The pillar at this junction of seven streets incorporates six sundials (the central spike acted as a seventh). It was installed in 1989 and is a copy of a 17th-century monument. The original was removed in the 19th century because it had become a notorious meeting place for criminals.

Lamb and Flag ❿

33 Rose St WC2. **Map** 13 B2.
📞 020-7497 9504. 🚇 Covent Garden, Leicester Sq. **Open** 11am–11pm Mon–Thu, 11am–10.45pm Fri & Sat, noon–10.30pm Sun. See **Restaurants and Pubs** p311.

There has been an inn here since the 16th century. The cramped bars are still largely unmodernized. A plaque concerns satirist John Dryden, attacked in the alley outside in 1679 after lampooning the Duchess of Portsmouth (one of Charles II's mistresses).

Photographers' Gallery ⓫

5 & 8 Great Newport St WC2. **Map** 13 B2. 📞 020-7831 1772. 🚇 Leicester Sq. **Open** 11am–6pm Mon–Sat, noon–6pm Sun. 🖥 📷 ♿

This enterprising gallery is London's leading venue for photographic exhibitions, which change periodically. There are occasional lectures and theatrical events, as well as a good photographic book and print shop and a café. The plaque on the outside commemorates Sir Joshua Reynolds, the founder of the Royal Academy *(see p90)*, who lived here in the 18th century.

Adelphi Theatre ⓬

Strand WC2. **Map** 13 C3.
📞 020-7344 0055. 🚇 Charing Cross, Embankment.
Open for performances only.
See **Entertainment** pp328–9.

Built in 1806, the Adelphi was opened by John Scott, a wealthy tradesman, who was helping to launch his daughter on the stage. It was remodelled in 1930 in Art Deco style. Note the highly distinctive lettering on the frontage, and the well-kept lobby and auditorium, with their stylized motifs.

Savoy Hotel ⓭

Strand WC2. **Map** 13 C2.
📞 020-7836 4343. 🚇 Charing Cross, Embankment. See **Where to Stay** p284.

Pioneer of en-suite bathrooms and electric lighting, the grand Savoy was built in 1889 on the site of the medieval Savoy Palace. The forecourt is the only street in Britain where traffic drives on the right. Attached to the hotel are the Savoy Theatre built for D'Oyly Carte opera, Simpson's English restaurant *(see p296)*, and the Savoy Taylor's Guild with its Art Nouveau shop front. Next door is Shell Mex House which replaced the Cecil Hotel while keeping its Strand façade.

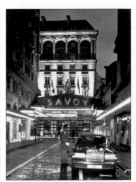

Front entrance to the Savoy Hotel

Savoy Chapel ⓮

Strand WC2. **Map** 13 C2.
📞 020-7836 7221. 🚇 Charing Cross, Embankment. **Open** 11.30am–3.30pm Tue–Fri. **Closed** Aug–Sep.
✝ 11am Sun. 🚫 📷 phone to book.

The first Savoy chapel was founded during the 16th century as the chapel for the hospital established on the site of the old Savoy Palace. Parts of the outside walls date from 1502, but most of the present building dates from the mid-19th century. In 1890 it was London's first church to be electrically lit. It became the chapel of the Royal Victorian Order in 1936, and is now a private chapel of the Queen. Nearby on Savoy Hill were the first studios of the BBC from 1922 until 1932.

Somerset House ⑮

Strand WC2. **Map** 14 D2. 📞 *020-7438 6622.* ⊖ *Temple, Embankment, Charing Cross.* **Open** *10am–6pm Mon–Sat, noon–6pm Sun.* **Closed** *24–26 Dec, 1 Jan.* **Outdoor ice rink:** *open two months in winter.* **Adm charge.** ♿ 🚻 ▢ 📷 **Courtauld Gallery.** 📞 *020-7848 2526.* **Adm charge.** 🚫 ♿ ▢ 📷 **The Gilbert Collection.** 📞 *020-7240 4080.* **Adm charge.** 🚫 🔊 ♿ ▢ 📷 ▢ 🌐 *www.somerset-house.org.uk*

THIS ELEGANT Georgian building was the creation of Sir William Chambers. It was erected in the 1770s after the first Somerset House, a Renaissance palace built for the Duke of Somerset in the mid-16th century, was pulled down following years of neglect. The replacement was the first major building to be designed for use as offices and has served to house the Navy Board (note that the classical grandeur of the Seamen's Waiting Hall and Nelson's Staircase are not to be missed), a succession of Royal Societies and, for a substantial amount of time, the Inland Revenue. Today it is home to two great collections of art – the Courtauld Gallery and the Gilbert Collection. The courtyard of Somerset House was closed to the public for nearly a century (most recently it was a dreary car park) but it has recently been cleared, as part of a £48-million restoration scheme, to make way for an attractive piazza with a 55-jet fountain, a café, the occasional classical music concert and, for a few weeks during the winter, an ice rink. From the courtyard visitors can stroll through the arches and on to a new riverside development which includes a sculpture terrace, an open-air summer café, the restored King's Barge House and pedestrian access to Waterloo Bridge and the South Bank Centre *(see pp184–91).*

Located in Somerset House, but famous in its own right, is the small but spectacular **Courtauld Gallery**. Its exquisite collection of paintings has been displayed

Partridge by Gorg Ruel (c.1600), Gilbert Collection

here since 1990 and owes its existence to the bequest of textile magnate and philanthropist Samuel Courtauld. On display are works by Botticelli, Brueghel, Bellini and Rubens (including one of his early masterpieces *The Descent from the Cross*), but it is the Courtauld's collection of Impressionist and Post-Impressionist paintings that draws the most attention. As well as works by Monet, Gauguin, Pissarro, Renoir and Modigliani, visitors can gaze captivated on Manet's *Behind the Bar at the Folies-Bergères*, Van Gogh's *Self-Portrait with Bandaged Ear*, Cezanne's *The Card Players* and some evocative studies of dancers by Degas. The Courtauld Gallery has recently been expanded to incorporate a new department devoted to digital and video art and, in addition to its permanent collection, now hosts a series of world-class temporary exhibitions which take place throughout the year.

Another treasure waiting to be discovered at Somerset House is London's recently acquired museum of decorative arts. Housed in the South Building, it is simply known as **The Gilbert Collection** and was given to the nation by the London-born property tycoon Arthur Gilbert. The bequest of this collection was the catalyst which brought about the revival of Somerset House. It is made up of 800 pieces, including an astonishing array of gold snuff boxes, Italian *pietra dura* (hard stone) mosaics, enamelled portrait miniatures and European silverware dating from the 16th to the 19th century. The informative audio guide which is included in the price of admission is an enriching accompaniment to a visit.

Van Gogh's *Self-Portrait with Bandaged Ear* (1889) at the Courtauld

St Mary-le-Strand ⑯

Strand WC2. **Map** 14 D2.
☏ *020-7836 3126.* ⊖ *Temple,
Holborn.* **Open** *11am–4pm
Mon–Fri,10am–2pm Sun.* ✝ *11am
Sun, 1.05pm Tue & Thu.* 📷 ▯

N OW BEACHED on a road
island at the east end of
the Strand, this pleasing
church was completed in
1717. It was the first public
building by James Gibbs, who
designed St-Martin-in-the-
Fields *(see p102)*. Gibbs was
influenced by Christopher
Wren, but the exuberant
external decorative detail here
was inspired by the Baroque
churches of Rome, where
Gibbs studied. Its multi-
arched tower is layered like a
wedding cake, and culminates
in a cupola and lantern. St-
Mary-le-Strand is now the
official church of the Women's
Royal Naval Service.

St-Mary-le-Strand

Roman Bath ⑰

5 Strand Lane WC2. **Map** 14 D2.
☏ *020-7641 5264.* ⊖ *Temple,
Embankment, Charing Cross.*
Open *summer: Wed; other times by
prior request.* ♿ *via Temple Pl.*

T HIS LITTLE BATH and its
surround may be seen
from a full-length window on
Surrey Street, by pressing a
light switch on the outside
wall. It is almost certainly not
Roman, for there is no other

Bush House from Kingsway

evidence of Roman habitation
in the immediate area. It is
more likely to have been part
of Arundel House, one of
several palaces which stood
on the Strand from Tudor
times until the 17th century,
when they were demolished
for new building. In the 19th
century the bath was open to
the public for cold plunges,
believed to be healthy.

Bush House ⑱

Aldwych WC2. **Map** 14 D2.
⊖ *Temple, Holborn.* **Not open** *to
the public.*

S ITUATED AT THE CENTRE of the
Aldwych crescent, this
Neo-Classical building was
first designed as manufacturers' showrooms by an
American, Irving T Bush, and
completed in 1935. It appears
especially imposing when
viewed from Kingsway, its
dramatic north entrance
graced with various statues
symbolizing Anglo-American
relations. Since 1940 it has
been used as radio studios,
and is the headquarters of the
BBC World Service, which is
due to be relocated to West
London within a few years.

Cleopatra's Needle ⑲

Embankment WC2. **Map** 13 C3.
⊖ *Embankment, Charing Cross.*

E RECTED IN HELIOPOLIS in
about 1500 BC, this
incongruous pink granite
monument is much older than
London itself. Its inscriptions

celebrate the deeds of the
pharaohs of ancient Egypt. It
was presented to Britain by
the then Viceroy of Egypt,
Mohammed Ali, in 1819 and
erected in 1878, shortly after
the Embankment was built.
It has a twin in New York's
Central Park, behind the
Metropolitan Museum of Art.
The bronze sphinxes, added
in 1882, are not Egyptian.

In its base is a Victorian
time capsule of artifacts of
the day, such as the day's
newspapers, a rail timetable
and photographs of 12
contemporary beauties.

Victoria Embankment Gardens ⑳

WC2. **Map** 13 C3. ⊖ *Embankment,
Charing Cross.* **Open** *7.30am–dusk
daily.* ♿ ▯

T HIS NARROW SLIVER of a
public park, created when
the Embankment was built,
boasts well-maintained flower
beds, a clutch of statues of
British worthies (including the
Scottish poet Robert Burns)
and, in summer, a season of
concerts. Its main historical
feature is the water gate at its
northwest corner, which was
built as a triumphal entry to
the Thames for the Duke of
Buckingham in 1626. It is a
relic of York House, which
used to stand on this site and
was the home first of the
Archbishops of York and then
of the Duke. It is still in its
original position and although
the water used to lap against
it, because of the Thames's
Embankment the gate is now
a good 100 m (330 ft) from
the river's edge.

Victoria Embankment Gardens

The new shopping and office block above Charing Cross

Adelphi ㉑

Strand WC2. **Map** 13 C3.
🚇 *Embankment, Charing Cross.*
Not open to the public.

John Adam Street, Adelphi

ADELPHI IS A PUN on *adelphoi*, the Greek word for brothers – this area was once an elegant riverside residential development designed in 1772 by brothers Robert and John Adam. The name now refers to the Art Deco office block, its entrance adorned with N A Trent's heroic reliefs of workers at toil, which in 1938 replaced the Adams' much admired Palladian-style apartment complex. That destruction is now viewed as one of the worst acts of 20th-century official vandalism. A number of the Adams' surrounding buildings fortunately survive, notably the ornate Royal Society for the Encouragement of Arts, Manufactures and Commerce just opposite. In the same exuberant idiom are Nos. 1–4 Robert Street, where Robert Adam lived for a time, and No. 7 Adam Street, decorated with honeysuckle reliefs.

Charing Cross ㉒

Strand WC2. **Map** 13 C3.
🚇 *Charing Cross, Embankment.*

THE NAME DERIVES from the last of the 12 crosses erected by Edward I to mark the funeral route in 1290 of his wife, Eleanor of Castile, from Nottinghamshire to Westminster Abbey. Today a 19th-century replica stands in the forecourt of Charing Cross station. Both the cross and the Charing Cross Hotel, built into the station frontage, were designed in 1863 by E M Barry, architect of the Royal Opera House *(see p115).*

Above the station platforms has risen an assertive shopping centre and office block, completed in 1991. Designed by Terry Farrell it resembles a giant ocean liner, with portholes looking on to Villiers Street. The new building is best seen from the river, where it dominates its neighbours. The railway arches at the rear of the station have been modernized as a suite of small shops and cafés, as well as a new venue for the Players Theatre, the last repository of Victorian music hall entertainment.

The London Coliseum ㉓

St Martin's Lane WC2. **Map** 13 B3.
📞 *020-7836 0111.* 🚇 *Leicester Sq, Charing Cross.* **Open** for performances and 🎭 (phone to arrange). 🚫 ♿ 💻 🍴 **Lectures**. See **Entertainment** pp332–3.

LONDON'S LARGEST theatre and one of its most elaborate, this flamboyant building, topped with a large globe, was designed in 1904 by Frank Matcham and was equipped with London's first revolving stage. It was also the first theatre in Europe to have lifts. A former variety house, it had a brief spell as a cinema in 1961–8. Today it is the home of the English National Opera, and well worth visiting, if only for the largely unaltered Edwardian interior with its gilded cherubs and heavy scarlet curtains.

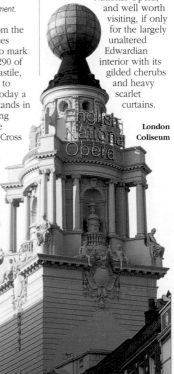

London Coliseum

BLOOMSBURY AND FITZROVIA

SINCE THE BEGINNING of the 20th century, Bloomsbury and Fitzrovia have been synonymous with literature, art and learning. The Bloomsbury Group of writers and artists were active from the early 1900s until the 1930s; the name Fitzrovia was invented by writers such as Dylan

Carving in Russell Square

Thomas who drank in the Fitzroy Tavern. Bloomsbury still boasts the University of London, the British Museum and many fine Georgian squares. But it is now also noted for its Charlotte Street restaurants and the furniture and competitively priced electrical shops lining Tottenham Court Road.

SIGHTS AT A GLANCE

**Historic Streets
and Buildings**
Bloomsbury Square **2**
Bedford Square **4**
Russell Square **5**
Queen Square **6**
British Library **8**
St Pancras Station **9**
Woburn Walk **11**
Fitzroy Square **13**
Charlotte Street **15**

Museums
British Museum pp126–9 **1**
Dickens House
  Museum **7**

Percival David Foundation of
  Chinese Art **12**
Pollock's Toy Museum **16**

Churches
St George's, Bloomsbury **3**
St Pancras Parish Church **10**

Pubs
Fitzroy Tavern **14**

SEE ALSO

• *Street Finder*, maps 4, 5, 6, 13

• *Where to Stay* pp272–285

• *Restaurants, Pubs* pp286–311

GETTING THERE
This area is served by the Circle, Northern, Piccadilly, Victoria, and Central lines. Useful buses include Nos. 8 and 98. Major railway stations are at Euston, St Pancras and King's Cross.

0 metres   500
0 yards   500

KEY

■ Street-by-Street map

⊖ Underground station

≉ Railway station

P Parking

A grand Georgian house in Bedford Square

Street-by-Street: Bloomsbury

THE BRITISH MUSEUM dominates Bloomsbury. Its earnestly intellectual atmosphere spills over into the surrounding streets, and to its north lies the main campus of London University. The area has been home to writers and artists, and is a traditional centre of the book trade. Most of the publishers have left, but there are still many book shops around.

The Senate House (1932) is the administrative headquarters of the University of London. It holds a priceless library.

Bedford Square
Uniform doorways in this square (1775) are fringed in artificial stone ❹

★ British Museum
Designed in the mid-19th century, it is extremely popular and attracts some five million visitors a year ❶

STAR SIGHTS

★ British Museum

★ Russell Square

KEY

– – – Suggested route

0 metres   100

0 yards   100

Museum Street is lined with small cafés and shops selling old books, prints and antiques.

Pizza Express occupies a charming and little-altered Victorian dairy.

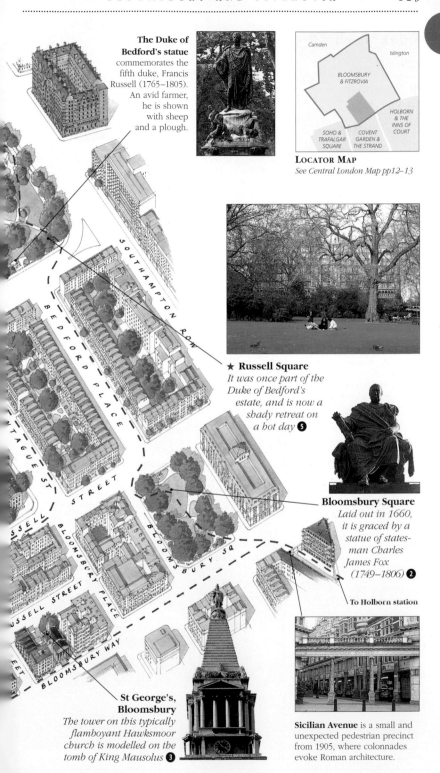

The Duke of Bedford's statue commemorates the fifth duke, Francis Russell (1765–1805). An avid farmer, he is shown with sheep and a plough.

Camden

Islington

BLOOMSBURY & FITZROVIA

HOLBORN & THE INNS OF COURT

SOHO & TRAFALGAR SQUARE

COVENT GARDEN & THE STRAND

LOCATOR MAP
See Central London Map pp12–13

SOUTHAMPTON ROW

BEDFORD PLACE

MONTAGUE ST

STREET

RUSSELL STREET

BLOOMSBURY PLACE

BLOOMSBURY SQ

BLOOMSBURY WAY

★ **Russell Square**
It was once part of the Duke of Bedford's estate, and is now a shady retreat on a hot day ❺

Bloomsbury Square
Laid out in 1660, it is graced by a statue of statesman Charles James Fox (1749–1806) ❷

To Holborn station

St George's, Bloomsbury
The tower on this typically flamboyant Hawksmoor church is modelled on the tomb of King Mausolus ❸

Sicilian Avenue is a small and unexpected pedestrian precinct from 1905, where colonnades evoke Roman architecture.

British Museum ❶

See pp126–9.

Bloomsbury Square ❷

WC1. **Map** 5 C5. 🔲 *Holborn.*

**Novelist Virginia Woolf, a
Bloomsbury resident**

THIS IS THE OLDEST of the
Bloomsbury squares. It
was laid out in 1661 by the
Earl of Southampton, who
owned the land. None of the
original buildings survives and
its shaded garden is encircled
by a busy one-way traffic
system. (Unusually for central
London, you can nearly
always find a space in the car
park under the square.)

The square has had many
famous residents; a plaque
commemorates members of
the literary and artistic
Bloomsbury Group, who
lived in the area during the
early years of the last century.
The group included novelist
Virginia Woolf, biographer
Lytton Strachey, and artists
Vanessa Bell, Duncan Grant
and Dora Carrington. Look
out for their individual
plaques throughout the area.

St George's, Bloomsbury ❸

Bloomsbury Way WC1. **Map** 13 B1.
📞 020-7405 3044.🔲 *Holborn,
Tottenham Court Rd.* **Open** 9.30am–
5.30pm Mon–Fri, for services only on
Sun. ✝ 10.30am Sun. **Recitals.**

A SLIGHTLY ECCENTRIC church,
St George's was designed
by Nicholas Hawksmoor,
Wren's pupil, and completed

in 1730. It was built as a
place of worship for the
prosperous residents of
newly-developed, fashionable
Bloomsbury. The layered
tower, modelled on the tomb
of King Mausolus (the original
mausoleum in Turkey) and
topped by a statue of George
I, was for a long time an
object of derision – the king
was thought to be presented
too heroically. There is some
good original plasterwork,
especially in the apse.

Bedford Square ❹

WC1. **Map** 5 B5. 🔲 *Tottenham
Court Rd, Goodge St.*

BUILT IN 1775, this is one of
the best-preserved of
London's 18th-century squares.
All the entrances to its brick
houses are adorned with
Coade stone, a hard-wearing
artificial stone made in

**A plaque in Bloomsbury Square
commemorating famous residents**

Lambeth (in south London) to
a formula that remained
secret for generations. The
stately houses were once
inhabited by the aristocracy.
Now all are offices, many of
them occupied until recently
by publishers most of whom
have since moved to less
expensive premises. A large
number of London's architects
have passed through the
Architectural Association at
Nos. 34–36, including
Richard Rogers who designed
the Lloyd's Building *(see p159).*

Bedford Square's lush private gardens

Russell Square ❺

WC1. **Map** 5 B5. 🚇 *Russell Sq.*
🔲 *opening hours flexible.*

ONE OF LONDON'S largest squares, the east side boasts perhaps the best of the Victorian grand hotels to survive in the capital. Charles Doll's Russell Hotel, which was opened in 1900, is a wondrous confection of red terracotta, with colonnaded balconies and prancing cherubs beneath the main columns. The exuberance is continued in the lobby, faced with marble of many colours.

The garden is open to the public. Poet T S Eliot worked at the west corner of the square, from 1925 until 1965, in what were the offices of publishers Faber and Faber.

The flamboyant Russell Hotel on Russell Square

Queen Square ❻

WC1. **Map** 5 C5. 🚇 *Russell Sq.*

IN SPITE OF being named after Queen Anne, the square contains a statue of Queen Charlotte. Her husband, George III, stayed at the house of a doctor here when he became ill with the hereditary disease that drove him mad before his death in 1820. Today the square is surrounded chiefly by hospital buildings and there are early Georgian houses on its west side.

Queen Charlotte's statue in Queen Square

Dickens House Museum ❼

48 Doughty St WC1. **Map** 6 D4.
📞 *020-7405 2127.* 🚇 *Chancery Lane, Russell Sq.* **Open** *10am–5pm Mon–Sat (last adm: 4.30pm).*
Adm charge. 🚫 📷 🔲

THE NOVELIST Charles Dickens lived in this early-19th-century terraced house for three of his most productive years (from 1837 to 1839). The popular works *Oliver Twist* and *Nicholas*

Nickleby were entirely written here, and *Pickwick Papers* was finished. Although Dickens had many London homes throughout his lifetime, this is the only one to have survived. In 1923 it was acquired by the Dickens Fellowship and it is now a well-conceived museum with some of the principal rooms laid out exactly as they were in Dickens's time. Others have been adapted to display a varied collection of articles associated with him. The exhibits include papers, portraits and pieces of furniture taken from his other homes as well as first editions of many of his best-known works. The most moving mementos are of Mary Hogarth, the author's sister-in-law, who died, aged 17, a month after the family moved here.

British Library ❽

96 Euston Rd NW1. **Map** 5 B3. 📞
020-7412 7332. 🚇 *King's Cross St Pancras.* **Open** *9.30am–6pm Mon–Fri (8pm Tue), 9.30am–5pm Sat, 11am–5pm Sun.* **Closed** *some public hols.*
🚫 📷 *phone for reservation* 🔲 📷

LONDON'S MOST important building from the late 20th century houses the national collection of books, manu-

scripts and maps, as well as the National Sound Archive. Designed in red brick by Sir Colin St John Wilson, it opened in 1998 after nearly 20 years under construction, involving controversial cost over-runs and technological problems, but is now widely admired.

A copy of nearly every printed book in the English language is held here – more than 15 million volumes in all – and can be consulted by anyone with a reader's ticket. In addition there are three exhibition galleries open to everyone. Here some of the Library's most precious items are on show, including Magna Carta, the Lindisfarne Gospels, a Gutenberg Bible and Shakespeare's First Folio. Running through six floors is a spectacular glass tower holding the 65,000 volumes of George III's library. Works of art include a statue of Sir Isaac Newton by Eduardo Paolozzi.

Page from the Lindisfarne Gospels

British Museum ❶

The innovatively designed Great Court

THE OLDEST public museum in the world, the British Museum was established in 1753 to house the collections of the physician Sir Hans Sloane (1660–1753), who also helped create the Chelsea Physic Garden *(see p197)*. Sloane's artifacts have been added to by gifts and purchases from all over the world, and the museum now contains innumerable items stretching from the present day to prehistory. Robert Smirke designed the main part of the building (1823–50), but the architectural highlight is the modern Great Court, with the world-famous Reading Room at its centre.

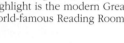

★ Egyptian Mummies

The ancient Egyptians preserved their dead in expectation of an afterlife. Animals that were believed to have sacred powers were also often mummified. This cat comes from Abydos on the Nile and dates from about 30 BC.

North entrance

Main floor

Lower floor

★ Elgin Marbles

Lord Elgin took these reliefs from the Parthenon in Athens. The British government bought them for the museum in 1816 (see p129).

Upper floor

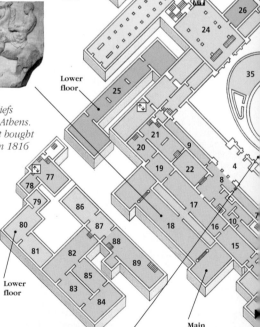

Lower floor

Main floor

Numerous large-scale sculptures are featured in the Concourse Gallery of the Great Court.

KEY TO FLOORPLAN

- ☐ Asian collection
- ☐ American Collection
- ☐ Coins, medals, prints and drawings
- ☐ Greek and Roman collection
- ☐ Egyptian collection
- ☐ Ancient Near Eastern collection
- ☐ Prehistory collection
- ☐ European collection
- ☐ African collection
- ☐ Temporary exhibitions
- ☐ Non-exhibition space

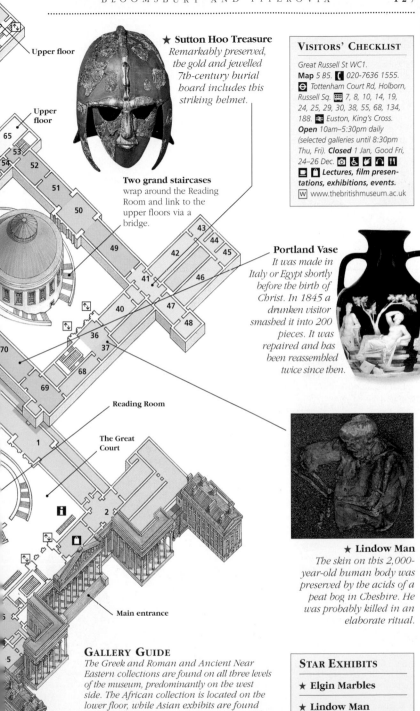

★ **Sutton Hoo Treasure**
Remarkably preserved, the gold and jewelled 7th-century burial board includes this striking helmet.

Upper floor

Upper floor

65
53
54
52
51
50
49
42
41
40
43
44
45
46
47
48
36
37
70
68
69

Two grand staircases wrap around the Reading Room and link to the upper floors via a bridge.

VISITORS' CHECKLIST

Great Russell St WC1.
Map *5 B5.* 📞 *020-7636 1555.*
🚇 *Tottenham Court Rd, Holborn, Russell Sq.* 🚌 *7, 8, 10, 14, 19, 24, 25, 29, 30, 38, 55, 68, 134, 188.* 🚃 *Euston, King's Cross.*
Open *10am–5:30pm daily (selected galleries until 8:30pm Thu, Fri).* **Closed** *1 Jan, Good Fri, 24–26 Dec.* 📷 ♿ 🎫 🛍 🍴 🎓 🎬 **Lectures, film presentations, exhibitions, events.**
🌐 *www.thebritishmuseum.ac.uk*

Portland Vase
It was made in Italy or Egypt shortly before the birth of Christ. In 1845 a drunken visitor smashed it into 200 pieces. It was repaired and has been reassembled twice since then.

Reading Room

The Great Court

1

2

Main entrance

★ **Lindow Man**
The skin on this 2,000-year-old human body was preserved by the acids of a peat bog in Cheshire. He was probably killed in an elaborate ritual.

GALLERY GUIDE
The Greek and Roman and Ancient Near Eastern collections are found on all three levels of the museum, predominantly on the west side. The African collection is located on the lower floor, while Asian exhibits are found on the main and upper floors at the rear of the Museum. The Americas collection is located in the northeast corner of the main floor. Egyptian artifacts are found west of the Great Court and on the upper floors.

STAR EXHIBITS

★ **Elgin Marbles**

★ **Lindow Man**

★ **Egyptian Mummies**

★ **Sutton Hoo Treasure**

Exploring the British Museum's Collections

THE MUSEUM'S immense hoard of treasure spans two million years of history and culture. The 94 galleries, which stretch 2.5 miles (4 km), cover civilisations from ancient Assyria to modern Japan.

Ornamental detail from a Sumerian Queen's lyre

PREHISTORIC AND ROMAN BRITAIN

1st-century BC bronze helmet dredged up from the Thames

RELICS OF PREHISTORIC Britain are on display in six separate galleries. The most impressive items include a neolithic timber trackway (or "sweet track") that once crossed the Somerset Levels; an antlered headdress worn by hunter-gatherers some 9000 years ago; and "Lindow Man", a 1st-century AD sacrificial victim who lay preserved in a bog until 1984. Some superb Celtic metalwork is also on show, alongside the silver Mildenhall Treasure and other Roman pieces. The Hinton St. Mary mosaic (4th century AD) features a roundel containing the earliest known British depiction of Christ.

EUROPE

THE SPECTACULAR Sutton Hoo ship treasure, the burial hoard of a 7th-century Anglo-Saxon life, is on display in Room 41. This superb find, made in 1939, revolutionized our understanding of Anglo-Saxon life and ritual. The artifacts include a helmet and shield, Celtic hanging bowls, the remains of a lyre, and gold and garnet jewellery.

Adjacent galleries contain a collection of clocks, watches and scientific instruments. Some exquisite timepieces are on view, including a 400-year-old clock from Prague,

designed as a model galleon; in its day it pitched, played music, and even fired a cannon. Also nearby are the famous 12th-century Lewis chessmen, and a gallery housing Baron Ferdinand Rothschild's (1839–98) remarkably varied treasures.

The museum's modern collection includes Wedgwood pottery, illustrated books, glassware, and a series of Russian revolutionary plates.

Gilded brass late-16th-century ship clock from Prague

ANCIENT NEAR EAST

THERE ARE numerous galleries devoted to the Western Asian collections, covering 7,000 years of history. The most famous items are the 7th-century BC Assyrian reliefs from King Ashurbanipal's palace at Nineveh, but of equal interest are two large human-headed bulls from 7th-century BC Khorsabad, and an inscribed Black Obelisk of Assyrian King Shalmaneser III. The upper floors contain pieces from ancient Sumeria, part of the Oxus Treasure (which lay buried for over 2,000 years), and the museum's collection of clay

cuneiform tablets. The earliest of these are inscribed with the oldest known pictographs (c.3300 BC). Also of interest is a skull discovered in Jericho in the 1950s; augmented with shells and lime plaster, the skull belonged to a hunter who lived in the area some 7,000 years ago.

EGYPT

THE MUSEUM'S Egyptian sculptures can be found in Room 4. These include a famous bronze cat with a gold nose-ring, a fine red granite head of a king, thought to be Amenophis III, and a colossal statue of king Ramses II. Also on show is the Rosetta Stone, which was used by Jean-François Champollion (1790–1832) as a primer for deciphering Egyptian hieroglyphs. An extraordinary array of mummies, jewellery and Coptic art can also be found upstairs. The various instruments used by embalmers to preserve bodies before entombment are all displayed.

Part of a colossal granite statue to Ramses II, the 13th-century BC Egyptian monarch

GREECE AND ROME

THE GREEK and Roman collections include the museum's most famous treasure, the Elgin Marbles. These 5th-century BC reliefs from the Parthenon once comprised a marble frieze which decorated Athena's temple at the Acropolis in Athens. Much of it was ruined in battle in 1687, and most of what survived was removed between 1801 and 1804 by the British diplomat Lord Elgin, and sold to the British nation. Other highlights include the Nereid Monument

Ancient Greek vase illustrating the mythical hero Hercules's fight with a bull

and sculptures and friezes from the Mausoleum at Halicarnassus. The beautiful 1st-century BC cameo-glass Portland Vase is located in the Roman Empire section.

ASIA

THE CHINESE COLLECTION is noted for its fine porcelain and ancient Shang bronzes (c.1500–1050 BC). Particularly impressive are the ceremonial ancient Chinese bronze vessels, with their enigmatic animal-head shapes. The fine Chinese ceramics range from delicate tea bowls to a model pond which is almost a thousand years old. Adjacent to these is one of the finest collections of Asian religious sculpture outside India. A major highlight is an assortment of sculpted reliefs which once covered the walls of the Buddhist temple at Amarati, and which recount stories from the life of the Buddha. A Korean section contains some gigantic works of Buddhist art.

Islamic art, including a stunning jade terrapin found in a water tank, can be found in Room 34. Rooms 92–4 house the Japanese galleries, with a

Statue of the Hindu God Shiva Nataraja, also known as the Lord of the Dance (11th century AD)

Classical teahouse in Room 92 and many delightful *netsuke* (small ivory carvings) gracing the lobby.

AFRICA

AN INTERESTING collection of African sculptures, textiles and graphic art can also be found in Room 25 in the basement. Famous bronzes from the Kingdom of Benin stand alongside modern African prints, paintings and drawings, plus an array of colourful fabrics.

THE GREAT COURT AND THE OLD READING ROOM

Surrounding the Reading Room of the former British Library, the £100-million Great Court opened to coincide with the new millennium. Designed by Sir Norman Foster, the Court is covered by a wide-span, lightweight roof, creating London's first indoor public square. The Reading Room has been restored to its original design, so visitors can sample the atmosphere which Karl Marx, Mahatma Gandhi and George Bernard Shaw found so agreeable. From the outside, however, it is scarcely recognizable; it is housed in a multi-level construction which partly supports the roof, and which also contains a Centre for Education, temporary exhibition galleries, bookshops, cafés and restaurants. Part of the Reading Room also serves as a study suite where those wishing to learn more about the Museum's collections have access to information.

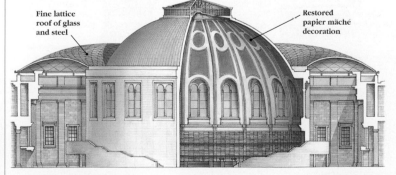

Fine lattice roof of glass and steel

Restored papier mâché decoration

The massive former Midland Grand Hotel above St Pancras Station

St Pancras Station ❾

Euston Rd NW1. **Map** 5 B2.
📞 0845 748 4950 (Rail enquiries).
🚇 King's Cross, St Pancras. **Open**
5am–11pm daily. See **Getting to London** pp360–61.

EASILY THE MOST spectacular of the three rail termini along Euston Road, its extravagant frontage, in red-brick gingerbread Gothic, is technically not part of the station. It was really Sir George Gilbert Scott's Midland Grand Hotel, opened in 1874 with 250 bedrooms as one of the most sumptuous and up-to-date hotels of its time. In 1890 London's first smoking room for women was opened here. From 1935 until the early 1980s the building was used

as offices; it is now being lavishly restored. The vast train shed behind is an out-standing example of Victorian engineering, with a roof that is 210 m (700 ft) long and 30 m (100 ft) high.

St Pancras Parish Church ❿

Euston Rd NW1. **Map** 5 B3.
📞 020-7388 1461.
🚇 Euston. **Open** 9am–2pm,
3.30–5pm Wed–Fri; 9–11am
Sat; 8am–6pm Sun. ✝ 10am
Sun 📷 ♿ **Recitals**
Mar–Sep: 1.15pm Thu.

THIS IS A STATELY Greek revival church of 1822 by William Inwood and his son Henry, both great enthusiasts for Athenian architecture. The design is based on the Erectheum on the Acropolis in Athens, and even the wooden pulpit stands on miniature Ionic columns of its own. The long, galleried interior has a dramatic severity appropriate to the church's style. The female figures on the northern outer wall were originally taller than they are now; a chunk had to be taken out of the middle of each to make them fit under the roof they were meant to be supporting.

Figures on St Pancras Church

Woburn Walk ⓫

WC1. **Map** 5 B4. 🚇 Euston,
Euston Sq.

A WELL-RESTORED street of bow-fronted shops, it was designed by Thomas Cubitt in 1822. The high pavement on the east side was to protect shop fronts from the mud thrown up by carriages. The poet W B Yeats lived at No. 5 from 1895 until 1919.

Percival David Foundation of Chinese Art ⓬

53 Gordon Sq WC1. **Map** 5 B4. 📞
020-7387 3909. 🚇 Russell Sq, Euston
Sq, Goodge St. **Open** 10.30am–5pm
Mon–Fri. **Closed** public hols. 🎫 📷

PARTICULARLY fascinating to those with a specialized interest in Chinese porcelain, but attractive also to the non-specialist, this is an important collection of exquisite wares made between the 10th and 18th centuries. Percival David presented his fine collection, much of it uniquely well preserved, to the University of London in 1950, and it is now administered by the School of Oriental and African Studies. The foundation includes a research library and, as well as the permanent collection, houses occasional special exhibitions of east Asian art.

Blue temple vase from David's collection

Fitzroy Square ⓭

W1. **Map** 4 F4. 🚇 Warren St,
Great Portland St.

DESIGNED BY Robert Adam in 1794, the square's south and east sides survive in their original form, in dignified Portland stone. Blue plaques record the homes of many artists, writers and statesmen: George Bernard Shaw and Virginia Woolf both lived at No. 29 – although not at the same time. Shaw gave money to the artist Roger Fry to establish the Omega workshop at No. 33 in 1913. Here young artists were paid a fixed wage to produce Post-Impressionist furniture, pottery, carpets and paintings for sale to the public.

No. 29 Fitzroy Square

Fitzroy Tavern ⓮

16 Charlotte St W1. **Map** 4 F5.
020-7580 3714. Goodge St.
Open 11am–11pm Mon–Sat,
noon–10.30pm Sun. See
Restaurants and Pubs pp309–11.

THIS TRADITIONAL PUB was a meeting place between World Wars I and II for a group of writers and artists who dubbed the area around Fitzroy Square and Charlotte Street "Fitzrovia". A basement "Writers and Artists Bar" contains pictures of former customers, including the writers Dylan Thomas and George Orwell, and the artist Augustus John.

Charlotte Street ⓯

W1. **Map** 5 A5. Goodge St.

AS THE UPPER classes moved west from Bloomsbury in the early 19th century, a flood of artists and European immigrants moved in, turning the area into a northern appendage to Soho (see pp98–109). The artist John Constable lived and worked for many years at No. 76. Some of the new residents established small workshops

to service the clothing shops on Oxford Street and the furniture stores on Tottenham Court Road. Others set up reasonably-priced restaurants. The street still boasts a great variety of eating places. It is overshadowed from the north by the 189-m (620-ft) Telecom Tower, built in 1964 as a vast TV, radio and telecommunications aerial (see p30).

Telecom Tower

Pollock's Toy Museum ⓰

1 Scala St W1. **Map** 5 A5.
020-7636 3452. Goodge St.
Open 10am–5pm Mon–Sat. **Closed**
public hols. **Adm charge.**

BENJAMIN POLLOCK was a renowned maker of toy theatres in the late 19th and early 20th centuries – the

novelist Robert Louis Stevenson was an enthusiastic customer. The museum opened in 1956 and the final room is devoted to stages and puppets from Pollock's theatres, together with a reconstruction of his workshop. This is a child-sized museum created in two largely unaltered 18th-century houses. The small rooms have been filled with a fascinating assortment of historic toys from all over the world There are dolls, puppets, trains, cars, construction sets, a fine rocking horse and a splendid collection of mainly Victorian doll's houses. Toy theatre performances are held here during school holidays and children can play games with boards and pieces lent free: but parents should beware – the exit leads through a very tempting toyshop.

Pearly king and queen dolls from Pollock's Toy Museum

HOLBORN AND THE INNS OF COURT

THIS AREA IS traditionally home to the legal and journalistic professions. The law is still here, in the Royal Courts of Justice and the Inns of Court, but most national newspapers left Fleet Street in the 1980s. Several buildings here predate the Great Fire of 1666 *(see pp22–3)*. These include the

Royal crest at Lincoln's Inn

superb facade of Staple Inn, Prince Henry's Room, and the interior of Middle Temple Hall. Holborn used to be one of the capital's main shopping districts. Times have changed the face of the area, but the jewellery and diamond dealers of Hatton Garden are still here, as are the London Silver Vaults.

SIGHTS AT A GLANCE

Historic Buildings, Sights and Streets
Lincoln's Inn ❷
Old Curiosity Shop ❹
Law Society ❺
Royal Courts of Justice ❼
Fleet Street ❾
Prince Henry's Room ❿
Temple ⓫
Dr Johnson's House ⓮
Holborn Viaduct ⓰
Hatton Garden ⓲
Staple Inn ⓳
Gray's Inn ㉑

Museums and Galleries
Sir John Soane's Museum ❶

Churches
St Clement Danes ❻

St Bride's ⓬
St Andrew, Holborn ⓯
St Etheldreda's Chapel ⓱

Monuments
Temple Bar Memorial ❽

Parks and Gardens
Lincoln's Inn Fields ❸

Pubs
Ye Olde Cheshire Cheese ⓭

Shops
London Silver Vaults ⓴

KEY

▢	Street-by-Street map
Ⓔ	Underground station
➤	Railway station
P	Parking

GETTING THERE

This area is served by the Circle, Central, District, Metropolitan and Piccadilly lines. Buses 17, 18, 45, 46, 171, 243 and 259 are among many in the area, and trains run from a number of mainline stations inside or close to the area.

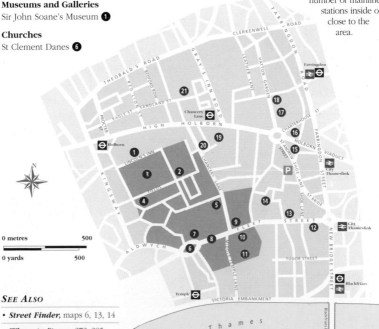

SEE ALSO

- *Street Finder,* maps 6, 13, 14
- *Where to Stay* pp272–285
- *Restaurants, Pubs* pp286–311

The Royal Courts of Justice on the Strand

Street-by-Street: Lincoln's Inn

THIS IS CALM, dignified, legal London, packed with history and interest. Lincoln's Inn, adjoining one of the city's first residential squares, has buildings dating from the late 15th century. Dark-suited lawyers carry bundles of briefs between their offices here and the Neo-Gothic Law Courts. Nearby is the Temple, another historic legal district with a famous 13th-century round church.

★ Sir John Soane's Museum
The Georgian architect made this his London home and left it, with his collection, to the nation ❶

To Kingsway

★ Lincoln's Inn Fields
The mock-Tudor archway, leading to Lincoln's Inn and built in 1845, overlooks the Fields ❸

Old Curiosity Shop
This is a rare 17th-century, pre-Great Fire building which is now a shop ❹

The Royal College of Surgeons was designed in 1836 by Sir Charles Barry. Inside there are laboratories for research and teaching as well as a museum of anatomical specimens.

LINCOLN'S INN FIELDS

LINCOLN'S INN FIELDS

PORTSMOUTH ST

PORTUGAL STREET

CAREY

SER

STAR SIGHTS

★ Sir John Soane's Museum

★ Temple

★ Lincoln's Inn Fields

★ Lincoln's Inn

KEY

– – – Suggested route

0 metres   100

0 yards   100

Twinings has been selling tea from here since 1706. The door-way dates from 1787 when the shop was called the Golden Lion.

The Gladstone Statue was erected in 1905 to commemorate William Gladstone, the Victorian statesman who was Prime Minister four times.

★ **Lincoln's Inn**
The Court of Chancery sat here, in Old Hall, from 1835 until 1858. Sir John Taylor Coleridge was a well-known judge of the time **2**

LOCATOR MAP
See Central London Map pp12–13

Royal Courts of Justice
The country's main court for civil cases and appeals was built in 1882. It is made out of 35 million bricks faced with Portland stone **7**

Law Society
Look for the gold lions on the railings of this superb building **5**

Fleet Street
For two centuries this was the centre of the national press. Today the newspaper offices are gone **9**

El Vino is a venerable wine bar, where journalists still mingle with lawyers.

Prince Henry's Room
There is an authentic 17th-century room in this former gatehouse **10**

St Clement Danes
Designed by Wren (1679), it is the Royal Air Force church **6**

Temple Bar Memorial
A griffin marks where the City of London meets Westminster **8**

★**Temple**
It was built for the Knights Templar in the 13th century, but today lawyers stroll here **11**

Wigged barristers on their way to their offices in Lincoln's Inn

Lincoln's Inn ❷

WC2. **Map** 14 D1. ☎ 020-7405 6360.
🚇 *Holborn, Chancery Lane.*
Grounds open 7am–7pm Mon–Fri.
Chapel open 12.30–2pm Mon–Fri.
Hall enquire at chapel. 🚻 grounds
only. 📷

SOME OF THE BUILDINGS in Lincoln's Inn, the best-preserved of London's Inns of Court, go back to the late 15th century. The coat of arms above the arch of the Chancery Lane gatehouse is Henry VIII's, and the heavy oak door is of the same vintage. Shakespeare's contemporary, Ben Jonson, is believed to have laid some of the bricks of Lincoln's Inn during the reign of Elizabeth I. The chapel is early-17th-century Gothic. Women were not allowed to be buried here until 1839, when the grieving Lord Brougham petitioned to have the rule changed so that his beloved daughter could be interred in the chapel, to wait for him to join her.

Lincoln's Inn has its share of famous alumni. Oliver Cromwell and John Donne,

Sir John Soane's Museum ❶

13 Lincoln's Inn Fields WC2.
Map 14 D1. ☎ 020-7405 2107.
🚇 *Holborn.* **Open** 10am–5pm
Tue–Sat, 6–9pm first Tue of month.
Closed 24–26 Dec, 1 Jan, Easter,
public hols. 🎞 Sat 2.30pm.
🚻 ground floor only.

ONE OF THE MOST surprising museums in London, this house was left to the nation by Sir John Soane in 1837, with a far-sighted stipulation that nothing at all should be changed. One of Britain's leading 19th-century architects, responsible for designing the Bank of England, Soane was the son of a bricklayer. After prudently marrying the niece of a wealthy builder, whose fortune he inherited, he bought and reconstructed No. 12 Lincoln's Inn Fields. In 1813 he and his wife moved into No. 13 and later, in 1824, he rebuilt No. 14. Today, true to Soane's wishes, the collec-

tions are much as he left them – an eclectic gathering of beautiful, peculiar and often instructional objects.

The building itself abounds with architectural surprises and illusions. In the main ground floor room, with its deep red and green colouring, cunningly placed mirrors play tricks with light and space. The upstairs picture gallery is lined with layers of folding panels to increase its capacity. The panels open out to reveal galleried extensions to the room itself. Among other works here are many of Soane's own exotic designs, including those for Pitshanger Manor *(see p258)* and the Bank of England *(see p147)*. Here also is William Hogarth's *Rake's Progress* series.

In the centre of the low-ceilinged basement an atrium stretches up to the roof. A glass dome lights galleries, on every floor, that are laden with Classical statuary.

A glass dome allows light into the basement.

A vast sarcophagus stands on the floor of the basement.

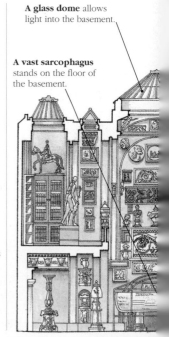

the 17th-century poet, were both students here, as was William Penn, founder of the US state of Pennsylvania.

Lincoln's Inn Fields ❸

WC2. **Map** 14 D1. 🚇 *Holborn.* **Open** *dawn–dusk daily.* **Public tennis courts** 📞 *020-7242 1626 (to book).*

THIS USED TO BE a public execution site. Under the Tudors and the Stuarts, many religious martyrs, and those suspected of treachery to the Crown, perished here.

When the developer William Newton wanted to build here in the 1640s, students at Lincoln's Inn and other residents made him undertake that the land in the centre would remain a public area for ever. Thanks to this early environmental pressure group, lawyers today play tennis here throughout the summer, or read their briefs in the fresh air. In recent years it has also become the site of a soup kitchen for some of London's homeless.

Old Curiosity Shop sign

Old Curiosity Shop ❹

13–14 Portsmouth St WC2. **Map** 14 D1. 🚇 *Holborn.*

WHETHER IT IS or is not the original for Charles Dickens's novel of the same name, this is a genuine 17th-century building and almost certainly the oldest shop in central London. With its overhanging first floor, it gives a rare impression of a London streetscape from before the Great Fire of 1666.

The Old Curiosity Shop maintains its retailing tradition, and currently operates as a shoe shop. A preservation order guarantees the long-term future of the building.

Law Society ❺

113 Chancery Lane WC2. **Map** 14 E1. 📞 *020-7242 1222.* 🚇 *Chancery Lane.* **Not open** to the public.

THE HEADQUARTERS of the solicitors' professional body is, architecturally, one of the most interesting buildings in the legal quarter. The main part, dominated by four Ionic columns, was completed in 1832. More significant is the northern extension, an early work of Charles Holden, an Arts and Crafts enthusiast who later made his name as a designer of London Underground stations. In his window arches the four seated figures depict truth, justice, liberty and mercy.

The building is on the corner of Carey Street, the site of the bankruptcy court whose name, corrupted to "Queer Street", entered the language to describe a state of destitution.

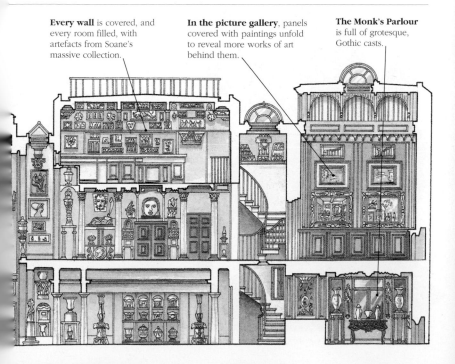

Every wall is covered, and every room filled, with artefacts from Soane's massive collection.

In the picture gallery, panels covered with paintings unfold to reveal more works of art behind them.

The Monk's Parlour is full of grotesque, Gothic casts.

St Clement Danes ❻

Strand WC2. **Map** 14 D2. ☎ *020-7242 8282.* ⊖ *Temple.* **Open** *8.30am–4pm Mon–Fri, 8.30am–3.30pm Sat, 9am–12.30pm Sun.* **Closed** *noon 25 Dec–27 Dec; public hols.* ⛪ *11am Sun. See* **Ceremonial London** *p55.*

CHRISTOPHER WREN designed this wonderful church in 1680. Its name derives from an earlier church built here by the descendants of Danish invaders whom Alfred the Great had allowed to remain in London in the 9th century. During the 17th, 18th and 19th centuries many people were buried in the crypt. The chain now hanging on the crypt wall was probably used to secure coffin lids against body snatchers who stole fresh corpses and sold them to the teaching hospitals.

St Clement Danes sits proudly isolated on a traffic island. It is now the Royal Air Force (RAF) church, and the interior decor is dominated by

Clock at the Victorian law courts

RAF symbols, memorials and monuments. Outside, to the east, is a statue (1910) of Dr Samuel Johnson *(see p140)* who, during the 18th century, often came to services here. The church's bells ring to the tune of the English nursery rhyme *Oranges and Lemons* at 9am, noon, 3pm and 6pm daily, and there is an annual oranges and lemons service.

Royal Courts of Justice (the Law Courts) ❼

Strand WC2. **Map** 14 D2. ☎ *020-7947 6000.* ⊖ *Holborn, Temple, Chancery Lane.* **Open** *9.30am–4.30pm Mon–Fri.* **Closed** *public hols.* ♿ *limited.* ☐

KNOTS OF demonstrators and television cameras can often be seen outside this sprawling and fanciful Victorian Gothic building, waiting for the result of a contentious case. These are the nation's main civil courts, dealing with such matters as divorce, libel, civil liability and appeals. Criminals are dealt with at the Old Bailey *(see p147)*, ten minutes' walk to the east. The public are admitted to all the court rooms and a list tells you which case is being heard in which court.

The massive Gothic building was completed in 1882. It is said to contain 1,000 rooms and 5.6 km (3.5 miles) of corridors.

Temple Bar Memorial ❽

Fleet St EC4. **Map** 14 D2. ⊖ *Holborn, Temple, Chancery Lane.*

THE MONUMENT in the middle of Fleet Street, outside the Law Courts, dates from 1880 and marks the entrance to the City of London. On state occasions it is a longstanding tradition for the monarch to have to pause here and ask permission of the Lord Mayor to enter. Temple Bar, a huge archway designed by Wren, used to stand here. You can see what it used to look like from one of the four reliefs that surround the base of the present monument.

Fleet Street ❾

EC4. **Map** 14 E1. ⊖ *Temple, Blackfriars, St Paul's.*

ENGLAND'S FIRST printing press was set up here in the late 15th century by William Caxton's assistant,

The griffon, symbol of the City, at the entrance to the City at Temple Bar

William Capon's engraving of Fleet Street in 1799

and Fleet Street has been a centre of London's publishing industry ever since. Playwrights Shakespeare and Ben Jonson were patrons of the old Mitre Tavern, now No. 37 Fleet Street. In 1702 the first newspaper, *The Daily Courant*, was issued from Fleet Street – conveniently placed for the City and Westminster which were the main sources of news. Later the street became synonymous with the Press.

The printing presses underneath the newspaper offices were abandoned in 1987, when new technology made it easy to produce papers away from the centre of town in areas such as Wapping and the Docklands. Today the newspapers have left their Fleet Street offices and only the agencies, Reuters and the Press Association, remain.

El Vino wine bar, at the western end opposite Fetter Lane, is a traditional haunt of journalists and lawyers.

Effigies in Temple Church

Prince Henry's Room ⓾

17 Fleet St EC4. **Map** 14 E1.
📞 020-7936 2710. 🚇 *Temple,
Chancery Lane.* **Open** *11am–2pm
Mon–Sat.* **Closed** *public hols.* 📷

B UILT IN 1610 as part of a Fleet Street tavern, this gets its name from the Prince of Wales's coat of arms and the initials PH in the centre of the ceiling. They were probably put there to mark the investiture as Prince of Wales of Henry, James I's eldest son who died before he became king.

The fine half-timbered front, alongside the gateway to Inner Temple, is original and so is some of the room's oak panelling. It contains an exhibition about the diarist Samuel Pepys.

Temple ⓫

Inner Temple, King's Bench Walk
EC4. **Map** 14 E2. 📞 *020-7797
8250.* 🚇 *Temple.* **Open** *10am–4pm
Mon–Fri (grounds only).* 📷 ♿
Middle Temple Hall, Middle Temple
Lane EC4. **Map** 14 E2. 📞 *020-7427
4800.* 🚇 *Temple.* **Open** *10am–
noon, 3–4pm Mon–Fri.* **Closed** *at
short notice for functions.* ✎ 📷

T HIS EMBRACES TWO of the four Inns of Court, the Middle Temple and the Inner Temple. (The remaining two are Lincoln's and Gray's Inns – *see p136 and p141.*)

The name derives from the Knights Templar, a chivalrous order which used to protect pilgrims to the Holy Land. The order was based here until it was suppressed by the Crown because its power was viewed as a threat. Initiations probably took place in the crypt of Temple Church and there are 13th-century effigies of Knights Templar in the nave.

Among some other ancient buildings is the wonderful Middle Temple Hall. Its fine Elizabethan interior survives – Shakespeare's *Twelfth Night* was performed here in 1601. Behind Temple, peaceful lawns stretch lazily down towards the Embankment.

St Bride's ⓬

Fleet St EC4. **Map** 14 F2. 📞 *020-
7427 0133.* 🚇 *Blackfriars, St Paul's.*
Open *8am–5pm Mon–Fri (last adm:
4.45pm), 10am–4pm Sat, 9.30am–
12.30pm, 5.30–7.30pm Sun.* **Closed**
public hols. 📷 ♿ ✝ *11am–
6.30pm Sun.* **Concerts.**

St Bride's, church of the Press

S T BRIDE'S IS ONE OF Wren's best-loved churches. Its position just off Fleet Street has made it the traditional venue for memorial services to departed journalists. Wall plaques commemorate Fleet Street journalists and printers.

The marvellous octagonal layered spire has been the model for tiered wedding cakes since shortly after it was added in 1703. Bombed in 1940, the interior was faithfully restored after World War II. The fascinating crypt contains remnants of earlier churches on the site, and a section of Roman pavement.

Ye Olde Cheshire Cheese ⑬

145 Fleet St EC4. **Map** 14 E1. 🚇
020-7353 6170. ⊖ Blackfriars. **Open**
11.30am–11pm Mon–Fri, noon–3pm,
5.30–11pm Sat, noon–3pm Sun. See
Restaurants and Pubs pp310–11.

THERE HAS BEEN an inn here
for centuries; parts of this
building date back to 1667,
when the Cheshire Cheese
was rebuilt after the Great
Fire. The diarist Samuel Pepys
often drank here in the 17th
century, but it was Dr Samuel
Johnson's association with
"the Cheese" which made it
a place of pilgrimage for 19th-
century literati. These included
novelists Mark Twain and
Charles Dickens.

This is one of the few pubs
to have kept the 18th-century
arrangement of small rooms
with fireplaces, tables and
benches, instead of knocking
them into larger bars.

Dr Johnson's House ⑭

17 Gough Sq EC4. **Map** 14 E1.
🚇 020-7353 3745. ⊖ Blackfriars,
Chancery Lane, Temple. **Open**
Apr–Sep: 11am–5.30pm Mon–Sat;
Oct–Mar: 11am–5pm Mon–Sat.
Closed 24–26 Dec, 1 Jan, Good Fri,
public hols. **Adm charge.** 📷 small
charge. 📦 📷 for groups of more
than ten (call to arrange).

DR SAMUEL JOHNSON was an
18th-century scholar
famous for the many witty
(and often contentious)

19th-century St Andrew schoolgirl

remarks that his biographer,
James Boswell, recorded and
published. Johnson lived here
from 1748 to 1759. He
compiled the first definitive
English dictionary (published
in 1755) in the attic, where
six scribes and assistants
stood all day at high desks.

The house, built before
1700, is sparsely furnished
with 18th-century pieces and
a small collection of exhibits
relating to Johnson and the
times in which he lived. These
include a tea set belonging to
his friend Mrs Thrale and
pictures of the great man
himself, his contemporaries
and their houses.

Reconstructed interior of Dr Johnson's house

St Andrew, Holborn ⑮

Holborn Circus EC4. **Map** 14 E1.
🚇 020-7583 7394. ⊖ Chancery
Lane. **Open** 9am–4.30pm Mon–Fri. 📷

THE MEDIEVAL CHURCH here
survived the Great Fire of
1666. In 1686 Christopher
Wren was, however, asked to
redesign it, and the lower part
of the tower is virtually all
that remains of the earlier
church. One of Wren's most
spacious churches, it was
gutted during World War II
but faithfully restored as the
church of the London trade
guilds. Benjamin Disraeli, the
Jewish-born Prime Minister,
was baptized here in 1817, at
the age of 12. In the 19th
century a charity school was
attached to the church.

Holborn Viaduct ⑯

EC1. **Map** 14 F1. ⊖ Farringdon, St
Paul's, Chancery Lane.

Civic symbol on Holborn Viaduct

THIS PIECE of Victorian
ironwork was erected in
the 1860s as part of a much-
needed traffic scheme. It is
best seen from Farringdon
Street which is linked to the
bridge by a staircase. Climb
up and see the status of City
heroes and bronze images of
Commerce, Agriculture,
Science and Fine Arts.

St Etheldreda's Chapel ⑰

14 Ely Place EC1. **Map** 6 E5. 🚇 020-
7405 1061. ⊖ Chancery Lane,
Farringdon. **Open** 8am–6.30pm daily.
📷 💻 11.30am–2.30pm Mon–Fri.

THIS IS A RARE 13th-century
survivor, the chapel and
crypt of Ely House, where the
Bishops of Ely lived until the

Reformation. Then it was acquired by an Elizabethan courtier, Sir Christopher Hatton, whose descendants demolished the house but kept the chapel and turned it into a Protestant church. It passed through various hands and, in 1874, reverted to the Catholic faith.

Hatton Garden ⑱

EC1. **Map** 6 E5. Ⓔ *Chancery Lane, Farringdon.*

Bᵁᴵᴸᵀ ᴼᴺ ᴸᴬᴺᴰ that used to be the garden of Hatton House, this is London's diamond and jewellery district. Gems ranging from the priceless to the mundane are traded from scores of small shops with sparkling window displays, and even from the pavements. One of the city's few remaining pawnbrokers is here – look for its traditional sign of three brass balls above the door.

Staple Inn ⑲

Holborn WC1. **Map** 14 E1.
Ⓔ *Chancery Lane.* **Courtyard open** *9am–5pm Mon–Fri.* 📷

Tᴴᴵˢ ʙᵁᴵᴸᴰᴵᴺᴳ was once the wool staple, where wool was weighed and taxed. The frontage overlooks Holborn and is the only real example of Elizabethan half-timbering left in central London. Although now much restored, it would still be recognizable by someone who had known it in 1586, when it was built. The shops at street level have the feel of the 19th century, and there are some 18th-century buildings in the courtyard.

London Silver Vaults ⑳

53–64 Chancery Lane WC2.
Map 14 D1. Ⓔ *Chancery Lane. See* **Shops and Markets** *pp324–5.*

Tᴴᴱˢᴱ ˢᴵᴸᴹᴱᴿ ᵛᴬᵁᴸᵀˢ originate from the Chancery Lane Safe Deposit Company, established in 1885. After

Staple Inn, a survivor from 1586

descending a staircase you pass through formidable steel security doors and reach a nest of underground shops sparkling with antique and modern silverware. London silver makers have been renowned for centuries, reaching their peak in the Georgian era. The best examples sell for many thousands of pounds but most shops also offer modest pieces at realistic prices.

Coffee pot (1716): Silver Vaults

Gray's Inn ㉑

Gray's Inn Rd WC1. **Map** 6 D5.
☎ *020-7458 7800.* Ⓔ *Chancery Lane, Holborn.* **Grounds open** *6am–midnight daily.* 📷 ♿

Tᴴᴵˢ ᴬᴺᶜᴵᴱᴺᵀ ᴸᴱᴳᴬᴸ centre and law school goes back to the 14th century. Like many of the buildings in this area, it was badly damaged by World War II bombs but much of it has been rebuilt. At least one of Shakespeare's plays *(A Comedy of Errors)* was first performed in Gray's Inn hall in 1594. The hall's 16th-century interior screen still survives.

More recently, the young Charles Dickens was employed as a clerk here in 1827–8. Today the garden, once a convenient site for staging duels, is open to lunchtime strollers for part of the year, and typifies the cloistered calm of the four Inns of Court. The buildings may be visited only by prior arrangement.

THE CITY

LONDON'S FINANCIAL district is built on the site of the original Roman settlement. Its full title is the City of London, but it is usually referred to as the City. Most traces of the early City were obliterated by the Great Fire of 1666 and World War II *(see pp22–3 and 31).* Today glossy modern offices stand among a plethora of banks, with marbled halls and stately pillars. It is the

Traditional bank sign on Lombard Street

contrast between dour, warren-like Victorian buildings and shiny new ones that gives the City its distinctive character. Though it hums with activity in business hours, few people have lived here since the 19th century, when it was one of London's main residential centres. Today only the churches, many of them by Christopher Wren *(see p47),* are a reminder of those past times.

SIGHTS AT A GLANCE

Historic Streets and Buildings
Mansion House **1**
Royal Exchange **3**
Old Bailey **7**
Apothecaries' Hall **8**
Fishmongers' Hall **9**
Tower of London pp154-7 **16**
Tower Bridge **17**
Stock Exchange **19**
Lloyd's of London **23**

Museums and Galleries
Bank of England Museum **4**
Guildhall Art Gallery **24**

Historic Markets
Billingsgate **12**
Leadenhall Market **22**

Monuments
Monument **11**

Churches and Cathedrals
St Stephen Walbrook **2**
St Mary-le-Bow **5**
St Paul's Cathedral pp148-51 **6**
St Magnus the Martyr **10**
St Mary-at-Hill **13**
St Margaret Pattens **14**
All Hallows by the Tower **15**
St Helen's Bishopsgate **20**
St Katharine Cree **21**

Docks
St Katharine's Dock **18**

GETTING THERE
The City is served by the DLR and the Circle, Central, District, Northern and Metropolitan lines, and bus numbers 6, 8, 9, 11, 15, 15B, 22B, 25, 133 and 501. There are many Thameslink and mainline railway stations.

KEY
▨	Street-by-Street map
⊖	Underground station
⇌	Railway station
P	Car park

SEE ALSO
- *Street Finder,* maps 14, 15, 16
- *Where to Stay* pp272–285
- *Restaurants* pp286–311

St Paul's Cathedral with the former NatWest Tower (1980) to its left

Street-by-Street: The City

THIS IS THE BUSINESS CENTRE of London, home to vast financial institutions such as the Stock Exchange and the Bank of England. But in contrast to these 19th- and 20th-century buildings are the older survivors. A walk through the City is in part a pilgrimage through the architectural visions of Christopher Wren, England's most sublime and probably most prolific architect. After the Great Fire of 1666 he supervised the rebuilding of 52 churches within the area, and enough survive to testify to his genius.

St Mary-le-Bow
Anyone born within earshot of the bells of this Wren church (the historic Bow Bells) is said to be a true Londoner or Cockney **5**

The Temple of Mithras is an important Roman relic whose foundations were revealed by a World War II bomb.

★ St Paul's
Wren's masterpiece still dominates the City skyline **6**

St Paul's station

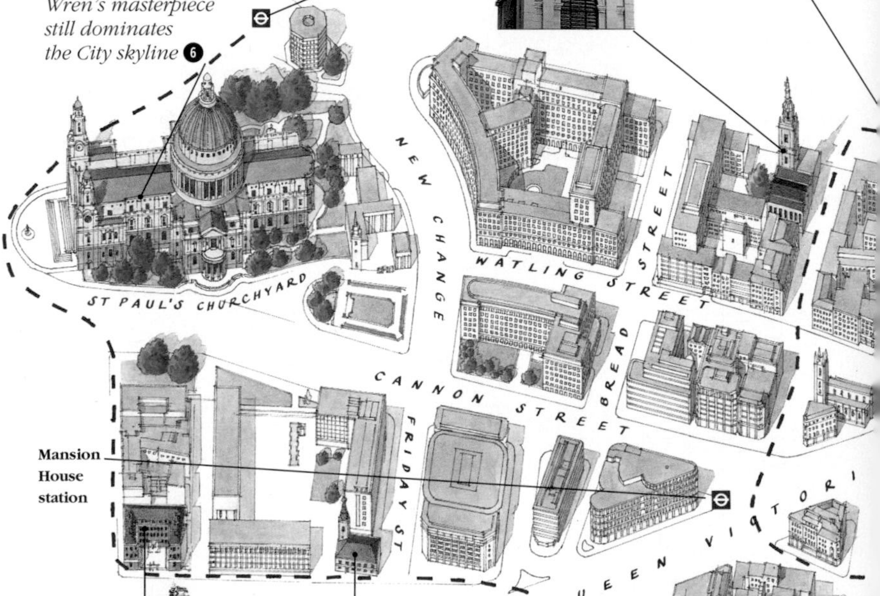

NEW CHANGE

ST PAUL'S CHURCHYARD

WATLING STREET

BREAD STREET

CANNON STREET

FRIDAY ST

Mansion House station

QUEEN VICTORI

St Nicholas Cole was the first church Wren built in the City (in 1677). Like many others, it had to be restored after World War II bomb damage.

COLLEGE · OF · ARMS

The College of Arms received its royal charter in 1484 from Richard III. Still active today, it assesses who has a legitimate claim to a British family coat of arms.

St James Garlickhythe contains unusual sword rests and hat stands, beneath Wren's elegant spire of 1717.

STAR SIGHTS

★ St Paul's

★ St Stephen Walbrook

★ Bank of England Museum

KEY

– – – Suggested route

0 metres	100
0 yards	100

Skinners' Hall is the Italianate 18th-century guild hall for the leather trade.

Mansion House
The official home of London's mayor, this building contains a small prison ❶

★ **Bank of England Museum**
The intriguing story of England's financial system is vividly displayed here ❹

LOCATOR MAP
See Central London Map pp12–13

SMITHFIELD & SPITALFIELDS

THE CITY

Thames

SOUTHWARK & BANKSIDE

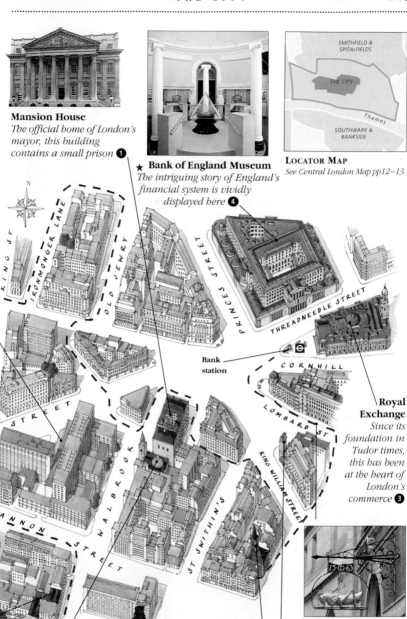

KING ST

IRONMONGER LANE

OLD JEWRY

PRINCES STREET

THREADNEEDLE STREET

EET

STREET

CORNHILL

LOMBARD ST

WALBROOK

KING WILLIAM STREET

ST SWITHIN'S

CANNON STREET

Bank station

Royal Exchange
Since its foundation in Tudor times, this has been at the heart of London's commerce ❸

Lombard Street
is named after Italian bankers who settled here from Lombardy in the 13th century. It is still a banking centre.

★ **St Stephen Walbrook**
Experimenting for St Paul's, Wren created its unique dome. The interior contains original features, such as this font ❷

St Mary Abchurch
owes its unusually spacious feel to Wren's large dome. The altar carving is by Grinling Gibbons.

St Mary Woolnoth is a characteristically powerful work by Wren's pupil, Nicholas Hawksmoor.

15·G·63

Mansion House ❶

Walbrook EC4. **Map** 15 B2.
☎ 020-7626 2500. **🚇** Bank, Mansion
House. **Open** to the public by
appointment only (call to arrange).

THE OFFICIAL RESIDENCE of the
Lord Mayor, it was
completed in 1753 to the
design of George Dance the
Elder, whose designs are now
in John Soane's Museum *(see
pp136–7)*. The Palladian front
with its six large Corinthian
columns is one of the most
familiar City landmarks. The
state rooms have a dignity
appropriate to the office of
mayor, one of the most
spectacular being the 27-m
(90-ft) Egyptian Hall.

Hidden from view are 11
holding cells (10 for men and
1, "the birdcage", for women),
a reminder of the building's
other function as a magistrate's court; the Mayor is
chief magistrate of the City
during his year of office.
Emmeline Pankhurst, who
campaigned for women's
suffrage in the early 20th
century, was once held here.

Egyptian Hall in Mansion House

St Stephen Walbrook ❷

39 Walbrook EC4. **Map** 15 B2. **☎**
020-7626 8242. **🚇** Bank, Cannon St.
Open 10am–4pm Mon–Thu, 10am–
3pm Fri. **✝** 12.45pm Thu, sung
Mass. **📷**   **Organ recitals** Fri.

THE LORD MAYOR'S parish
church was built by
Christopher Wren in 1672–9.
Architectural writers consider
it to be the finest of his City
churches *(see p47)*. The deep,
coffered dome, with its ornate
plasterwork, was a forerunner
of St Paul's. St Stephen's airy
columned interior comes as a
surprise after its plain exterior.
The font cover and pulpit
canopy are decorated with
exquisite carved figures that
contrast strongly with the
stark simplicity of Henry
Moore's massive white stone
altar (1987).

However, perhaps the most
moving monument of all is a
telephone in a glass box. This
is a tribute to Rector Chad
Varah who, in 1953, founded
the Samaritans, a voluntarily
staffed telephone help-line for
people in emotional need.

*The Martyrdom of St
Stephen,* which hangs on the
north wall, is by American
painter Benjamin West, who
became a Royal Academician
(see p90) in 1768.

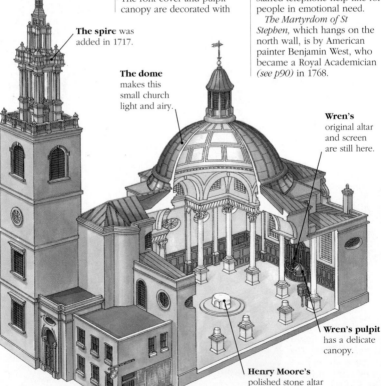

The spire was
added in 1717.

The dome
makes this
small church
light and airy.

Wren's
original altar
and screen
are still here.

Wren's pulpit
has a delicate
canopy.

Henry Moore's
polished stone altar
was added in 1987.

Royal Exchange ❸

EC3. **Map** 15 C2. **〔** 020-7623 0444.
⊖ Bank. **Not open** to the public.

Sᴵʀ ᴛʜᴏᴍᴀs ɢʀᴇsʜᴀᴍ, the Elizabethan merchant and courtier, founded the Royal Exchange in 1565 as a centre for commerce of all kinds. The original building was centred on a vast courtyard where merchants and trades-men did business. Queen Elizabeth I gave it its Royal title and it is still one of the sites from which new kings and queens are announced. Dating from 1844, this is the third splendid building on the site since Gresham's.

Britain's first public lavatories were built in the forecourt here in 1855. Exclusively for male use, they symbolized the era's unenlightened attitudes.

Bank of England Museum ❹

Bartholomew Lane EC2. **Map** 15 B1.
〔 020-7601 5545. **〔** 020-7601 5792. ⊖ Bank. **Open** 10am–5pm Mon–Fri. **Closed** public hols. ⊘ ♿ (loop system). ⬚ ⬚
Filmshows, lectures.

The facade of William Tite's Royal Exchange of 1844

The Duke of Wellington (1884) opposite the Bank of England

Tʜᴇ ʙᴀɴᴋ ᴏꜰ ᴇɴɢʟᴀɴᴅ was set up in 1694 to raise money for foreign wars. It grew to become Britain's central bank, and also issues currency notes.

Sir John Soane (see pp136–7) was the architect of the 1788 bank building on this site, but only the exterior wall of his design has survived. The rest was destroyed in the 1920s and 1930s when the Bank was enlarged. There is now a reconstruction of Soane's stock office of 1793.

Glittering gold bars, silver plated decoration and a Roman mosaic floor, discovered during the rebuilding, are among the items on display. The museum illustrates the work of the Bank and the financial system. The gift shop sells paperweights which are made out of used banknotes.

St Mary-le-Bow ❺

(Bow Church) Cheapside EC2.
Map 15 A2. **〔** 020-7248 5139.
⊖ Mansion House. **Open** 6.30am–6pm Mon–Wed, 6.30am–6.30pm Thu, 6.30am–4pm Fri. ✝ 5.45pm Thu. ⬚

Tʜᴇ ᴄʜᴜʀᴄʜ ᴛᴀᴋᴇs its name from the bow arches in the Norman crypt. When Wren rebuilt the church (in 1670–80) after the Great Fire (see pp22–3), he continued this architectural pattern through the graceful arches on the steeple. The weather-vane, dating from 1674, is an enormous dragon.

The church was bombed in 1941 leaving only the steeple and two outer walls standing. It was restored in 1956–62 when the bells were recast and rehung. Bow bells are important to Londoners: traditionally only those born within their sound can lay claim to being true Cockneys.

St Paul's ❻

See pp148–51.

Old Bailey ❼

EC4. **Map** 14 F1. **〔** 020-7248 3277.
⊖ St Paul's. **Open** 10.30am–1pm, 2–4.30pm Mon–Fri (but opening hours vary from court to court).
Closed Christmas, New Year, Easter, public hols. ⊘

Old Bailey's rooftop Justice

Tʜɪs sʜᴏʀᴛ sᴛʀᴇᴇᴛ has a long association with crime and punishment. The new Central Criminal Courts opened here in 1907 on the site of the notorious and malodorous Newgate prison (on special days in the legal calendar judges still carry small posies to court as a reminder of those times). Across the road, the Magpie and Stump served "execution breakfasts" until 1868, when mass public hangings outside the prison gates were stopped.

Today, when the courts are in session, they are open to members of the public.

St Paul's Cathedral ❻

FOLLOWING THE Great Fire of London in 1666, the medieval cathedral of St Paul's was left in ruins. The authorities turned to Christopher Wren to rebuild it, but his ideas met with considerable resistance from the conservative and tightfisted Dean and Chapter. Wren's 1672 Great Model plan was not at all popular with them, and so a watered-down plan was finally agreed in 1675. Wren's determination paid off though, as can be seen from the grandeur of the present cathedral.

Stone statuary outside the South Transept

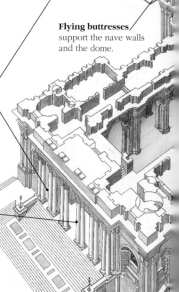

★ **The Inner and Outer Dome**
At 110 m (360 ft) high it is the second biggest dome in the world, after St Peter's in Rome, as spectacular from inside as outside.

The balustrade along the top was added in 1718 against Wren's wishes.

The pediment carvings, dating from 1706, show the Conversion of St Paul.

★ **The West Front and Towers**
The towers were not on Wren's original plan – he added them in 1707, when he was 75 years old. Both were designed to have clocks.

Flying buttresses support the nave walls and the dome.

The West Portico comprises two tiers of columns rather than the single colonnade that Wren intended.

STAR SIGHTS

★ **West Front and Towers**

★ **Inner and Outer Dome**

★ **Whispering Gallery**

The West Porch, approached from Ludgate Hill, is the main entrance to St Paul's.

Queen Anne's Statue
An 1886 copy of Francis Bird's 1712 original now stands on the forecourt.

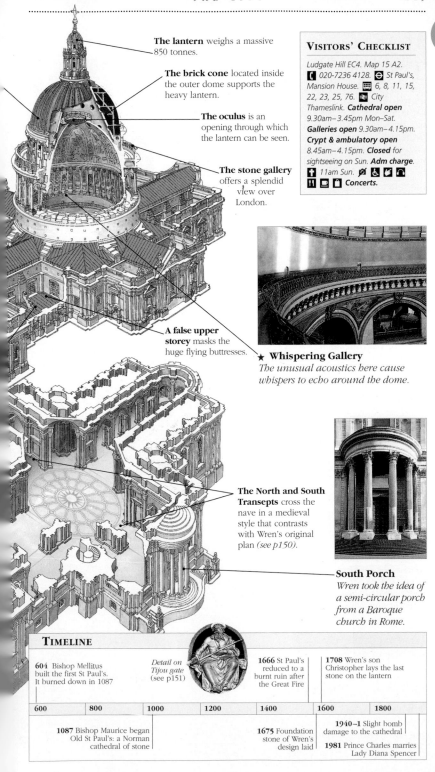

The lantern weighs a massive 850 tonnes.

The brick cone located inside the outer dome supports the heavy lantern.

The oculus is an opening through which the lantern can be seen.

The stone gallery offers a splendid view over London.

A false upper storey masks the huge flying buttresses.

The North and South Transepts cross the nave in a medieval style that contrasts with Wren's original plan (*see p150*).

(*see p150*)

VISITORS' CHECKLIST

Ludgate Hill EC4. Map 15 A2.
📞 *020-7236 4128.* 🚇 *St Paul's, Mansion House.* 🚌 *6, 8, 11, 15, 22, 23, 25, 76.* 🚆 *City Thameslink.* **Cathedral open** *9.30am–3.45pm Mon–Sat.* **Galleries open** *9.30am–4.15pm.* **Crypt & ambulatory open** *8.45am–4.15pm.* **Closed** *for sightseeing on Sun.* **Adm charge.**
⛪ *11am Sun.* ♿ ♿ 📷 🔊
🍴 🛍 🎵 *Concerts.*

★ **Whispering Gallery**
The unusual acoustics here cause whispers to echo around the dome.

South Porch
Wren took the idea of a semi-circular porch from a Baroque church in Rome.

TIMELINE

604 Bishop Mellitus built the first St Paul's. It burned down in 1087	*Detail on Tijou gate (see p151)*			**1666** St Paul's reduced to a burnt ruin after the Great Fire	**1708** Wren's son Christopher lays the last stone on the lantern	
600	800	1000	1200	1400	1600	1800
	1087 Bishop Maurice began Old St Paul's: a Norman cathedral of stone			**1675** Foundation stone of Wren's design laid	**1940–1** Slight bomb damage to the cathedral **1981** Prince Charles marries Lady Diana Spencer	

A Guided Tour of St Paul's

THE VISITOR TO ST PAUL'S will be immediately impressed by its cool, beautifully ordered and extremely spacious interior. The nave, transepts and choir are arranged in the shape of a cross, as in a medieval cathedral, but Wren's Classical vision shines through this conservative floor plan, forced on him by the cathedral authorities. Aided by some of the finest craftsmen of his day, he created an interior of grand majesty and Baroque splendour, a worthy setting for the many great ceremonial events that have taken place here. These include the funeral of Winston Churchill in 1965 and the wedding of Prince Charles and Lady Diana Spencer in 1981.

The mosaics on the choir ceiling were completed in the 1890s by William Richmond.

① The Nave
Take in the full glory of the massive arches and the succession of saucer domes that open out into a huge space below the main dome.

② The North Aisle
As you walk along the North Aisle, look above: the aisles are vaulted with small domes mimicking those of the nave ceiling.

⑨ South Aisle
From here the brave can ascend the 259 steps to the Whispering Gallery and test the acoustics.

Entrance to Whispering Gallery

⑧ Florence Nightingale's Tomb
Famous for her pioneering work in nursing standards, Florence Nightingale was the first woman to receive the Award of Merit.

Main entrances

The Geometrical Staircase is a spiral of 92 stone steps giving access to the cathedral library.

⑦ Wren's Tomb
Wren's burial place is marked by a slab. The inscription states: "Reader, if you seek his memorial look all around you."

KEY

— — — Tour route

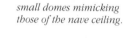

③ The Crossing
The climax of Wren's interior is this great open space. The vast dome is decorated with monochrome frescoes by Sir James Thornhill, the leading architectural painter of Wren's time.

Entrance to crypt

④ The Choir
Jean Tijou, a Huguenot refugee, created much of the cathedral's fine wrought ironwork, such as these screens in the choir aisles.

John Donne's tomb, from 1631, was the only monument to survive the Great Fire of 1666. The poet posed for it in his lifetime.

⑤ The High Altar
The canopy over the altar was replaced after World War II. It is based on Wren's original Baroque drawings.

Grinling Gibbons's work can be found on the choir stalls, with typically intricate carvings of cherubs, fruits and garlands.

TE Lawrence, or Lawrence of Arabia, the British World War I hero who earned his nickname by fighting alongside Arab tribes in their resistance to Turkish rule in 1915, is commemorated by this bust in the crypt.

⑥ The Crypt
Memorials to famous figures and popular heroes, such as Lord Nelson, can be seen in the crypt.

Apothecaries' Hall ⑧

Blackfriars Lane EC4. **Map** 14 F2.
C *020-7236 1189.* ⊖ *Blackfriars.*
Courtyard open *9am–5pm Mon–Fri.*
Closed *public hols.* **Phone Hall** *for
appt to visit (for groups only).* &

Apothecaries' Hall, rebuilt in 1670

LONDON HAS had livery
companies, or guilds, to
protect and regulate specific
trades since early medieval
times. The Apothecaries'
Society was founded in 1617
for those who prepared,
prescribed or sold drugs. It
has some surprising alumni,
including Oliver Cromwell
and the poet John Keats. Now
nearly all the members are
physicians or surgeons.

Fishmongers' Hall ⑨

London Bridge EC4. **Map** 15 B3.
C *020-7626 3531.* ⊖ *Monument.*
Not open *to the public.*

THIS IS ONE of the oldest
livery companies, estab-
lished in 1272. Lord Mayor
Walworth, a member of the
Fishmongers' Company, killed
Wat Tyler, leader and prime
motivator of the Peasants'
Revolt, in 1381 *(see p162).*
Today it still fulfils its original
role; all the fish sold in the
City must be inspected by
Company officials. The
building dates from 1834.

St Magnus the Martyr ⑩

Lower Thames St EC3. **Map** 15 C3.
C *020-7626 4481.* ⊖ *Monument.*
Open *10am–4pm Tue–Fri, 10.15am–
2pm Sun.* ♁ *11am Sun.*

THERE HAS BEEN a church
here for over 1,000 years.
Its patron saint, St Magnus,
Earl of the Orkney Islands
and a renowned Norwegian
Christian leader, was brutally
murdered in 1110.

When Christopher Wren
built this church in 1671–6, it
was at the foot of old London
Bridge, until 1738 the only
bridge across the Thames in
London. Anyone going south
from the city would have
passed under Wren's
magnificent arched porch
spanning the flagstones
leading to the old bridge.

Highlights of the church
include the carved musical
instruments that decorate the
organ case. Wren's pulpit,
with its slender supporting
stem, was restored in 1924.

Monument ⑪

Monument St EC3. **Map** 15 C2.
C *020-7626 2717.* ⊖ *Monument.*
Open *10am–5.40pm daily.*
Closed *25–26 Dec, 1 Jan.*
Adm charge. ▣

THE COLUMN, designed by
Christopher Wren to
commemorate the Great Fire
of London which devastated
the original walled city in
September 1666, is the tallest
isolated stone column in the
world. It is 62 m (205 ft) high
and is said to be 62 m west of
where the fire started in
Pudding Lane. It was sited on
the direct approach to old
London Bridge, which was a
few steps downstream from
the present one. Reliefs
around the column's base

The altar of St Magnus the Martyr

show Charles II restoring the
city. The 311 steps to the top
lead to a viewing platform.
In 1842 this was enclosed
with railings after a suicide.
The views are spectacular.

Billingsgate ⑫

Lower Thames St EC3. **Map** 15 C3.
⊖ *Monument.* **Not open** *to the
public.*

Fish weathervane at Billingsgate

LONDON'S MAIN fish market
was based here for 900
years, on one of the city's
earliest quays. During the
19th and early 20th centuries
400 tonnes of fish were sold
here every day, much of it
delivered by boat. It was
London's noisiest market,
renowned, even in
Shakespeare's day, for foul
language. In 1982 the market
moved from this building
(1877) to the Isle of Dogs.

St Mary-at-Hill ⑬

Lovat Lane EC3. **Map** 15 C2.
C *020-7626 4184.* ⊖ *Monument.*
Concerts. Open *10am–3pm Mon–Fri.*

THE INTERIOR and east end
of St Mary-at-Hill were
Wren's first church designs
(1670–6). The Greek cross
design was a prototype for
his St Paul's proposals.

Ironically, the delicate
plasterwork and rich 17th-
century fittings, which had
survived both the Victorian
mania for refurbishment and
the bombs of World War II,
were lost in a fire in 1988.

The building was then restored to its original appearance, only to be damaged again, this time by an IRA bomb in 1992.

St Margaret Pattens ⑭

Rood Lane and Eastcheap EC3. **Map** 15 C2. 020-7623 6630. Monument. **Open** 8am–4pm Mon–Fri. **Closed** Christmas week. 1.15pm Thu.

W REN'S CHURCH from 1684–7 was named after a type of overshoe made near here. Its Portland stone walls are a good contrast to the Georgian stucco shopfront in the forecourt. The simple interior retains 17th-century canopied pews and an ornate font.

All Hallows by the Tower ⑮

Byward St EC3. **Map** 16 D3. 020-7481 2928. Tower Hill. **Open** 9am–5.30pm Mon–Fri, 10am–5pm Sat–Sun. **Closed** 26 Dec–2 Jan. 11am Sun.

T HE FIRST CHURCH on this site was Saxon. The arch in the southwest corner, which contains Roman tiles, dates from that period and so do some crosses now in the crypt. There is also a well-preserved Roman pavement in the crypt, but this is irregularly open to the public. Most of the interior has been altered by restoration, but a limewood font cover, carved by Grinling Gibbons in 1682, still survives. William Penn

Roman tile from All Hallows

(founder of Pennsylvania) was baptized here in 1644 and John Quincy Adams married in 1797 before he was US president. Samuel Pepys watched the Great Fire from the church tower.

Tower of London ⑯

See pp154–7.

Tower Bridge ⑰

SE1. **Map** 16 D3. 020-7378 1928. Tower Hill. **The Tower Bridge Experience Open** Apr–Oct: 10am–6.30pm daily (last adm: 5.15pm); Nov–Mar: 9.30am–6pm daily (last adm: 4.45pm). **Closed** 24–26 Dec, 1 Jan. **Adm charge.** Video.

C OMPLETED IN 1894, this flamboyant piece of Victorian engineering quickly became a symbol of London. Its pinnacled towers and linking catwalk support the mechanism for raising the roadway when big ships have to pass through, or for special and historic occasions.

The bridge now houses The Tower Bridge Experience, with interactive displays bringing the bridge's history to life, river views from the catwalk and a close-up look at the steam engine which powered the lifting machinery until 1976, when the system was electrified.

The catwalk, which is now open to the public, affords a beautiful view along the river.

When raised, the bridge is 40 m (135 ft) high and 60 m (200 ft) wide. In its heyday it was opened five times a day.

There are nearly 300 stairs to the top of the towers.

The Victorian winding machinery was powered by steam until 1976.

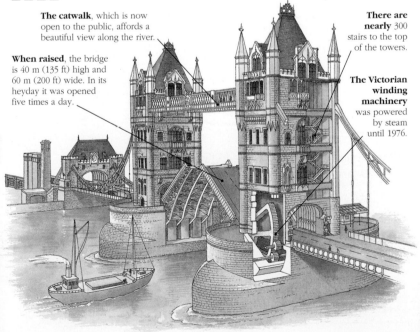

Tower of London ⓰

FOR MUCH OF ITS 900-year history the
Tower was an object of fear. Those
who had offended the monarch were
held within its dank walls. A lucky few
lived in comparative comfort,
but the majority had to put
up with appalling conditions.
Many did not get out alive,
and were tortured before
meeting cruelly violent
deaths on nearby
Tower Hill.

★ **The White Tower**
*When it was finished, c.1097,
it was the tallest building in
London – 30 m (90 ft) high.*

★ **The Jewel House** is
where the magnificent
English Crown Jewels
are housed *(see p156).*

"Beefeaters"
*Forty Yeoman
Warders guard the
Tower and live here.*

**Beauchamp
Tower**
*Many high-ranking
prisoners were held here,
often with their own
retinues of servants.*

Tower Green was where the
most favoured prisoners were
executed, away from the ghoulish
crowds on Tower Hill.
Only seven people died
here – including two of
Henry VIII's six wives –
but hundreds had to
bear more public
executions.

STAR BUILDINGS

★ **White Tower**

★ **Jewel House**

★ **Chapel of St John**

★ **Traitors' Gate**

Main entrance

THE RAVENS

The Tower's most
celebrated residents are a
colony of seven ravens. It
is not known when they
first settled here, but there
is a legend that should they
desert the Tower, the
kingdom will fall. In fact
the birds have their wings
clipped on one side,
making flight impossible.
The Ravenmaster, one of
the Yeoman Warders,
looks after the birds.

A memorial in the moat
commemorates some of the
ravens who have died at
the Tower since the 1950s.

Queen's House
*This is the official
residence of the
Tower's governor.*

★ **Chapel of St John**
Stone for this austerely beautiful Romanesque chapel was brought from France.

Wakefield Tower, part of the Medieval Palace, has been carefully refurbished to match its original appearance in the 13th century.

VISITORS' CHECKLIST

Tower Hill EC3. **Map** 16 D3.
📞 020-7709 0765. 🚇 *Tower Hill, London Bridge.* 🚌 *15, X15, 25, 42, 78, 100.* 🚉 Fenchurch Street. **Docklands Light Railway** *Tower Gateway.*
Open *Mar–Oct: 9am–6pm Tue–Sat, 10am–6pm Sun; Nov–Feb: 9am–5pm Mon–Sat, 10am–5pm Sun & Mon.*
Tower closed *24–26 Dec, 1 Jan.*
Adm charge. 🚻 🚫 *Ceremony of the Keys 9.30pm daily (tickets to be booked in advance). See pp53–5.* 🎦 📷

The Bloody Tower
is associated with the two princes who disappeared from here in 1483 (see p157).

Medieval Palace
This was created by Henry III in 1220. It was enlarged by his son, Edward I, who added Traitors' Gate.

★ **Traitors' Gate**
Prisoners, many on their way to die, entered the Tower by boat here.

TIMELINE

1078 White Tower started	**1536** Anne Boleyn executed			**1810–15** Mint moves from the Tower and arms stop being manufactured here	
	1483 Princes probably murdered in the Tower		**1553–4** Lady Jane Grey held and executed		
1050	**1250**	**1450**	**1650**	**1850**	**1950**
1066 William I erects a temporary castle			**1671** "Colonel Blood" tries to steal Crown Jewels	**1834** Menagerie moves out of Tower	
	1534–5 Thomas More imprisoned and executed		**1603–16** Walter Raleigh imprisoned in Tower	**1941** Rudolph Hess is the last prisoner held in Queen's House	

Inside the Tower

THE TOWER HAS been a tourist attraction since the reign of Charles II (1660–85), when both the Crown Jewels and the collection of armour were first shown to the public. They remain powerful reminders of royal might and wealth.

The Orb, symbolizing the power and Empire of Christ the Redeemer

THE CROWN JEWELS

THE CROWN JEWELS comprise the regalia of crowns, sceptres, orbs and swords used at coronations and other state occasions. They are impossible to price but their worth is irrelevant beside their enormous significance in the historical and religious life of the kingdom. Most of the Crown Jewels date from 1661, when a new set was made for the coronation of Charles II; Parliament had destroyed the previous crowns and sceptres after the execution of Charles I in 1649. Only a few pieces survived, hidden by the clergy of Westminster Abbey until the Restoration.

The Imperial State Crown, containing more than 2,800 diamonds, 273 pearls as well as other gems

The Coronation Ceremony
Many elements in this solemn and mystical ceremony date from the days of Edward the Confessor. The king or queen proceeds to Westminster Abbey, accompanied by parts of the regalia, including the State Sword which represents the monarch's own sword. He or she is then anointed with holy oil, to signify divine approval, and invested with ornaments and royal robes. Each of the jewels represents an aspect of the monarch's role as head of the state and church. The climax comes when St Edward's Crown is placed on the sovereign's head; there is a cry of "God Save the King" (or Queen), the trumpets sound, and guns at the Tower are fired. The last coronation was Elizabeth II's in 1953.

The crowns
There are 10 crowns on display at the Tower. Many of these have not been worn for years, but the Imperial State Crown is in frequent use. The Queen wears it at the Opening of Parliament (see p73). The crown was made in 1937 for George VI, and is similar to the one made for Queen Victoria. The sapphire set in the cross is said to have been worn in a ring by Edward the Confessor (ruled 1042 – 66).

The most recent crown is not at the Tower, however. It was made for Prince Charles's investiture as Prince of Wales at Caernavon Castle in north Wales in 1969, and is kept at the Museum of Wales in Cardiff. The Queen Mother's crown was made for the coronation of her husband, George VI, in 1937. It is the only one to be made out of platinum – all the other crowns on display at the Tower are made of gold.

Other regalia
Apart from the crowns, there are other pieces of the Crown Jewels that are essential to coronations. Among these are three Swords of Justice, symbolizing mercy, spiritual and temporal justice. The orb is a hollow gold sphere encrusted with jewels and weighing about 1.3 kg (3 lbs). The Sceptre with the Cross contains the biggest cut diamond in the world, the 530-carat First Star of Africa. The rough stone it comes from weighed 3,106 carats.

The Sovereign's Ring, sometimes referred to as "the wedding ring of England"

Plate Collection
The Jewel House also holds a collection of elaborate gold and silver plate. The Maundy Dish is still used on Maundy Thursday when the monarch distributes money to selected old people. The Exeter Salt (a very grand salt cellar from the days when salt was a valuable commodity) was given by the citizens of Exeter, in west England, to Charles II; during the 1640s' Civil War Exeter was a Royalist stronghold.

The Sceptre with the Cross (1660), rebuilt in 1910 after Edward VII was presented with the First Star of Africa diamond

The hilt and solid-gold scabbard of the Jewelled State Sword, one of the most valuable swords in the world

THE WHITE TOWER

THIS IS THE OLDEST surviving building in the Tower of London, begun by William I in 1077 and completed before 1100. For centuries it served as an armoury, and much of the national collection of arms and armour was held here. In the 1990s many exhibits moved to Leeds or Portsmouth but some of the most historic items, especially those connected with the history of the Tower, have stayed here. The extra space allows the remaining exhibits to be displayed more effectively, and also highlights architectural features of the building itself.

The Royal Castle and Armour Gallery

These two chambers on the first floor were the main ceremonial rooms of the original Norman castle. The first one, to the east, is the smaller, probably an antechamber to the banqueting Hall beyond, and contains exhibits setting out the history of the White Tower. It adjoins St John's Chapel, a rare surviving early Norman tower virtually intact, a powerfully solid interior with little ornamentation. Originally the two main rooms were twice their present height; a pitched roof was removed in 1490 to allow extra floors to be built on top. Suits of armour from Tudor and Stuart times are here, including three made for Henry VIII, one covering his horse as well. A suit made in Holland for Charles I is decorated in gold leaf.

Japanese armour presented to James I in 1613

The Ordnance Gallery

This and the temporary exhibition gallery next door were chambers created in 1490 when the roof was raised. They were used chiefly for storage and in 1603 a new floor was installed to allow gunpowder to be kept here: by 1667 some 10,000 barrels of it were stored in the Tower. Among the displays are gilt panels and ornament from the barge of the Master of the Ordnance built in 1700.

The Small Armoury and Crypt

The westerly room on the ground floor may originally have been a living area, and has traces of the oldest fireplaces known in England. Pistols, muskets, swords, pikes and bayonets are mounted on the walls and panels in elaborate symmetrical patterns based on displays in the Tower armouries in the 18th and 19th centuries. They were shown in the Grand Storehouse until it burned down in 1841. A collection of weapons taken from the men who planned to assassinate William III in 1696 is on show, and next door is a wooden block made in 1747 for the execution of Lord Lovat – the last public beheading in England. The crypt now houses a shop.

The Line of Kings

The Line of Kings, ten life-size carvings of prominent English Monarchs, wearing armour and seated on horseback, originated in Tudor times, when eight such figures adorned the royal palace at Greenwich. Two more had been added by the time they first appeared in the Tower in 1660, celebrating the Restoration of Charles II. In 1688, 17 new horses and heads were commissioned, some from the great carver Grinling Gibbons (the third from the left is reputed to be his work).

Henry VIII's armour (1540)

THE PRINCES IN THE TOWER

One of the Tower's darkest mysteries concerns two boy princes, sons and heirs of Edward IV. They were put into the Tower by their uncle, Richard of Gloucester, when their father died in 1483. Neither was seen again and Richard was crowned later that year. In 1674 the skeletons of two children were found nearby.

The yacht haven of the restored St Katharine's Dock

St Katharine's Dock ⑱

E1. **Map** 16 E3. 📞 *020-7481 8350.* 🚇 *Tower Hill.* ♿ 🍴 🛒 🏠

T HIS MOST CENTRAL of all London's docks was designed by Thomas Telford and opened in 1828 on the site of St Katharine's hospital. Commodities as diverse as tea, marble and live turtles (turtle soup was a Victorian delicacy) were unloaded here.

During the 19th and early 20th centuries the docks flourished, but by the mid-20th century cargo ships were delivering vast, bulky cargoes in massive containers. The old docks became too small and new ones had to be built downstream. St Katharine's closed in 1968 and the others followed within 15 years.

St Katharine's is now one of London's most successful developments, with its commercial, residential and entertainment facilities, including a hotel and a yacht haven. Old warehouse

buildings have shops and restaurants on their ground floors, and offices above.

On the north side of the dock is LIFFE Commodity Products, trading in commodities such as coffee, sugar and oil. There is no public gallery but, if you ask at the door, you may be able to look down from the glass-walled reception area on to the frenzied trading floors. The dock is worth wandering through after visiting the Tower or Tower Bridge *(see pp154–7 and p153).*

Stock Exchange ⑲

Old Broad St EC4. **Map** 15 B1. 🚇 *Bank.* **Not open** *to the public.*

T HE FIRST STOCK exchange was established in Threadneedle Street in 1773 by a group of stockbrokers who previously met and did business in nearby City coffee houses. By the 19th century the rules of exchange were laid down, and for a hundred years London's was the biggest stock exchange in the world. Nevertheless, the rise of the American and Japanese economies during the 20th century gradually challenged London's dominance, and today its exchange is third in size after Tokyo and New York. Unlike most exchanges, however, London's is free from government legislation.

The present building, which dates from 1969, used to house the frenzied trading floor, but in 1986 the business was computerized and the floor made redundant. The former public viewing gallery stayed open for a while, but was closed after a terrorist bomb attempt.

St Helen's Bishopsgate ⑳

Great St Helen's EC3. **Map** 15 C1. 📞 *020-7283 2231.* 🚇 *Liverpool St.* **Open** *9am–5pm Mon, Wed–Fri.* ✝ *12.35pm & 1.15pm Tue, 10.15am & 7pm Sun.* ♿

T HE CURIOUS, bisected appearance of this 13th-century church is due to its origins as two places of worship: one a parish church, the other the chapel of a long-gone nunnery next door. (The medieval nuns of St Helen's were notorious for their "secular kissing".)

Among its monuments is the tomb of Sir Thomas Gresham, who founded the Royal Exchange *(see p147).*

St Katharine Cree ㉑

86 Leadenhall St EC3. **Map** 16 D1. 📞 *020-7283 5733.* 🚇 *Aldgate, Tower Hill.* **Open** *10.30am–4.30pm Mon–Fri.* **Closed** *Christmas, Easter.* 📷 *in services.* ✝ *1.05pm Thu.*

The organ at St Katharine Cree

A RARE PRE-WREN 17th-century church with a medieval tower, this was one of only eight churches in the City to survive the fire of 1666. Some of the elaborate plasterwork on and beneath the high ceiling of the nave portrays the coats of arms of the guilds, with which the church has special links. The 17th-century organ, supported on magnificent carved wooden columns, was played by both Purcell and Handel.

St Helen's Bishopsgate

Leadenhall Market ㉒

Whittington Ave EC3. **Map** 15 C2.
🚇 Bank, Monument. **Open**
7am–4pm Mon–Fri. See **Shops and Markets** pp324–5.

THERE HAS BEEN a food market here, on the site of the Roman forum *(see pp16–17)*, since the Middle Ages. Its name is derived from a lead-roofed mansion that stood nearby in the 14th century. The ornate, Victorian covered shopping precinct of today was designed in 1881 by Sir Horace Jones, the architect of Billingsgate fish market *(see p152)*.

Essentially a food market, offering traditional game, poultry, fish, and meat, Leadenhall also has a number of independent shops, which offer all kinds of fare from chocolates to wine. The area is busiest during breakfast and lunch hours, and is best seen at Christmas when all the stores are decorated. It is particularly popular among local City workers, many of whom work in the adjacent Lloyd's of London building.

Lloyd's of London ㉓

1 Lime St EC3. **Map** 15 C2.
📞 020-7327 1000. 🚇 Bank,
Monument, Liverpool St, Aldgate.
Not open to the public.

LLOYD'S WAS FOUNDED in the late 17th century and takes its name from the coffee house where underwriters and shipowners used to meet to arrange marine insurance contracts. Lloyd's soon became the world's main insurers, issuing policies on everything from oil tankers to Betty Grable's legs.

The present building, by Richard Rogers, dates from 1986 and is one of the most interesting modern buildings in London *(see p30)*. Its exaggerated stainless steel external piping and high-tech ducts echo Rogers's forceful Pompidou Centre in Paris. Lloyd's is a far more elegant building and particularly worth seeing floodlit at night.

Leadenhall Market in 1881

Guildhall Art Gallery ㉔

Guildhall Yard EC2. **Map** 15 B1.
📞 020-7332 3700. 🚇 St Paul's.
Open 10am–5pm Mon–Sat, noon–4pm Sun (last adm 30 mins before close). **Closed** 25–26 Dec, 1 Jan. ♿
Guildhall Gresham St EC2. 📞 020-7606 3030. **Open** phone for details.

FOUNDED IN 1885 the Guildhall Art Gallery was built to house the paintings and sculptures of the Corporation of London – one of the city's oldest local governments, encompassing London's financial centre.

The paintings include the studio collection of 20th-century artist Sir Matthew Smith, portraits from the 16th century to the present day, a gallery of 18th-century works, including John Singleton Copley's *Defeat of the Floating Batteries at Gibraltar*, and numerous Victorian works. The Main Gallery is devoted to paintings of the Square Mile (London's financial heart), and include pictures of the Lord Mayor's Show and Queen Victoria's Diamond Jubilee Service of 1897.

The adjacent Guildhall itself has been the administrative centre of the City for at least 800 years. For centuries the hall was used for trials and many people were condemned to death here, including Henry Garnet, one of the Gunpowder Plot conspirators *(see p22)*. Today, a few days after the Lord Mayor's parade *(see pp54–5)*, the Prime Minister addresses a banquet here.

Richard Rogers's Lloyd's building illuminated at night

SMITHFIELD AND SPITALFIELDS

THE AREAS JUST north of the City walls have always been a refuge for those that did not want to come under its jurisdiction, or were not welcome there. These included Huguenots in the 17th century, and, in later times, other immigrants from Europe and then Bengal. They founded small industries and brought with them their restaurants and places of worship. The name Spitalfields comes

Stone dragon in Smithfield Market

from the medieval priory of St Mary Spital. Middlesex Street became known as Petticoat Lane in the 16th century, for its clothing stalls; it is still the hub of a popular Sunday morning street market that spreads as far east as Brick Lane, today lined with aromatic Bengali food shops. London's meat market is at Smithfield, and nearby is the Barbican, a 20th century residential and arts complex.

SIGHTS AT A GLANCE

Historic Streets and Buildings
Charterhouse **4**
Cloth Fair **5**
Barbican Centre **7**
Whitbread's Brewery **9**
Wesley's Chapel–Leysian Centre **11**
Broadgate Centre **12**
Petticoat Lane **13**
Fournier Street **16**
Spitalfields Centre Museum of Immigration **18**
Brick Lane **19**
Dennis Severs House **20**

Museums and Galleries
Museum of London pp166–7 **3**
Whitechapel Gallery **14**

Churches and Mosques
St Botolph, Aldersgate **2**
St Bartholomew-the-Great **6**
St Giles, Cripplegate **8**

Christ Church, Spitalfields **15**
London Jamme Masjid **17**

Cemeteries
Bunhill Fields **10**

Markets
Smithfield Market **1**
Columbia Road Market **21**

GETTING THERE
This area is served by the Northern, Hammersmith and City, Central and Circle Underground lines and by rail. The Nos. 8, 15 and many other buses run close by.

KEY
Street-by-Street map
⊖ Underground station
⇌ Railway station
P Parking

SEE ALSO
- *Street Finder*, maps 6, 7, 8, 15, 16
- *Where to Stay* pp272–85
- *Restaurants, Pubs* pp286–311

Columbia Road flower and plant market

Street-by-Street: Smithfield

THIS AREA IS AMONG the most historic in London. It contains one of the capital's oldest churches, some rare Jacobean houses, vestiges of the Roman wall (near the Museum of London) and central London's only surviving wholesale food market.

Smithfield's long history is also bloody. In 1381 the rebel peasant leader, Wat Tyler, was killed here by an ally of Richard I as he presented the king with demands for lower taxes. Later, in the reign of Mary I (1553–8), scores of Protestant religious martyrs were burned at the stake here.

**The Fat Boy:
the Great Fire
ended here**

The Fox and Anchor pub is open from 7am for hearty breakfasts, washed down with ale by the market traders of Smithfield.

CHARTERHOUSE STREET

LON

WEST SMITHFIELD

★ **Smithfield Market**
A contemporary print shows Horace Jones's stately building for the meat market when it was completed in 1867 ❶

Fat Boy

SMITHFIELD STREET

SITE OF THE
SARACEN'S HEAD
INN
DEMOLISHED
1868

COCK LANE

GILTSPUR STREET

The Saracen's Head, an historic inn, stood on this site until the 1860s when it was demolished to make way for Holborn Viaduct *(see p140)*.

SNOW HILL

St Bartholomew-the-Less has a 15th-century tower and vestry. Its links to the hospital are shown by this early-20th-century stained glass of a nurse; a gift of the Worshipful Company of Glaziers.

St Bartholomew's Hospital has stood on this site since 1123. Some of the existing buildings date from 1759.

KEY

– – – – – Suggested route

0 metres   100

0 yards   100

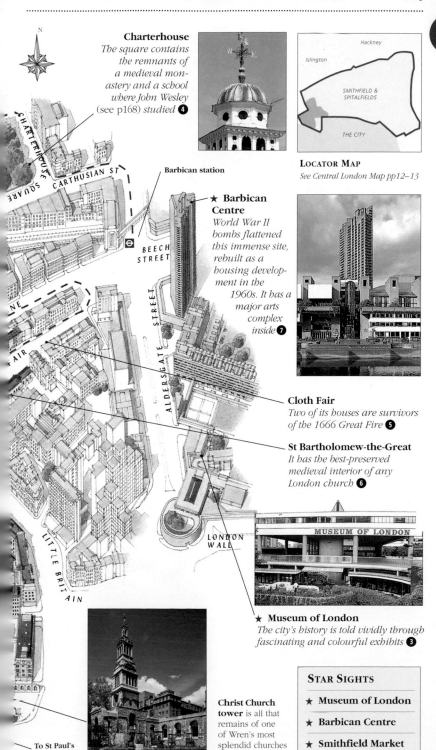

N

Charterhouse
The square contains the remnants of a medieval monastery and a school where John Wesley (see p168) studied ➍

LOCATOR MAP
See Central London Map pp12–13

Hackney

Islington

SMITHFIELD & SPITALFIELDS

THE CITY

Barbican station

★ **Barbican Centre**
World War II bombs flattened this immense site, rebuilt as a housing development in the 1960s. It has a major arts complex inside ➐

CHARTERHOUSE SQUARE

CARTHUSIAN ST

BEECH STREET

ALDERSGATE STREET

Cloth Fair
Two of its houses are survivors of the 1666 Great Fire ➎

St Bartholomew-the-Great
It has the best-preserved medieval interior of any London church ➏

LONDON WALL

MUSEUM OF LONDON

★ **Museum of London**
The city's history is told vividly through fascinating and colourful exhibits ➌

LITTLE BRITAIN

Christ Church tower is all that remains of one of Wren's most splendid churches (1704).

To St Paul's station

STAR SIGHTS

★ **Museum of London**

★ **Barbican Centre**

★ **Smithfield Market**

Smithfield Market, now officially known as London Central Markets

from the nearby Post Office headquarters. In the late 19th century, the Victorian artist G F Watts dedicated one of the walls to a quirky collection of plaques that commemorate acts of bravery and self-sacrifice by ordinary people. Some of these plaques are still here and can be viewed. In the year 1973, an impressive and powerful modern bronze minotaur, the work of sculptor Michael Ayrton, was erected.

Museum of London ❸

See pp166–7.

Charterhouse ❹

Charterhouse Sq EC1. **Map** 6 F5.
📞 *020-7253 9503.* ⊖ *Barbican.*
Open *Apr–Jul: 2.15pm Wed.* **Adm charge.** 📷 🎦

T HE 14TH-CENTURY gateway on the north side of the square leads to the site of a former Carthusian monastery which was dissolved under Henry VIII. In 1611 the buildings were converted into a hospital for poor pensioners, and a charity school – called Charterhouse – whose impressive intake of pupils included such famous names as John Wesley *(see p168)*, writer William Thackeray and Robert Baden-Powell, the founder of the Boy Scouts.

In 1872 the school, which these days is an exclusive boarding school for fee-paying boys, transferred its location to Godalming in Surrey. The original site was subsequently taken over by St Bartholomew's Hospital medical school. Some of the old buildings survived. These include the chapel and part of the cloisters.

Charterhouse: stone carving

Smithfield Market ❶

Charterhouse St EC1. **Map** 6 F5.
⊖ *Farringdon, Barbican.* **Open** *5–9am Mon–Fri.*

A NIMALS HAVE been traded here since the 12th century, but the spot was granted its first official charter in 1400. In 1648 it was officially established as a cattle market and live cattle continued to be sold here until the mid-19th century. It now confines itself to mainly wholesale trading in dead meat and poultry. It was originally sited in Smithfield outside the city walls, London's prime location for public executions. Although moved to its present location in Charterhouse Street in the 1850s and called the London Central Meat Market, the original name stuck. The old buildings are by Sir Horace Jones, the Victorian market architect, but there are 20th-century additions. Some pubs in the area keep market hours and, from dawn, serve hearty breakfasts, washed down with ale, to market traders and early-rising office workers.

St Botolph, Aldersgate ❷

Aldersgate St EC1. **Map** 15 A1.
📞 *020-7283 1670.* ⊖ *St Paul's.*
Open *10am–3pm Mon–Fri.*
🕆 *1.10pm Thu.* ♿

A MODEST LATE-Georgian exterior (completed in the late 18th century) conceals a flamboyant, well-preserved interior which has a finely-decorated plaster ceiling, a rich brown wooden organ case and galleries, as well as an oak pulpit resting on a carved palm tree. The original box pews have been kept in the galleries rather than in the body of the church. Some of the memorials come from a 14th-century church that originally existed on the site.

The former churchyard alongside was converted in 1880 into a relaxing green space known as Postman's Park, because it was used by workers

Cloth Fair ❺

EC1. **Map** 6 F5. 🚇 *Barbican.*

THIS PRETTY STREET is named after the notoriously rowdy Bartholomew Fair, which was the main cloth fair in medieval and Elizabethan England, held annually at Smithfield until 1855. Nos. 41 and 42 are fine 17th-century houses and have distinctive two-storeyed wooden bay windows, although their ground floors have since been modernized. The former poet laureate John Betjeman, who died in 1984, lived in No. 43 for most of his life. It has now been turned into a wine bar named after him.

17th-century houses: Cloth Fair

St Bartholomew-the-Great ❻

West Smithfield EC1. **Map** 6 F5. ☎ 020-7606 5171. 🚇 *Barbican.* **Open** 8.30am–5pm (4pm in winter) Mon–Fri, 10.30am–1.30pm Sat, 2–6pm Sun. 🕆 9am, 11am, 6.30pm Sun. 📷 🚻 🎫 ⛪ **Concerts.**

ONE OF LONDON'S OLDEST churches was founded in 1123 by a monk named Rahere whose tomb is inside. He had been Henry I's court jester until he had a dream in which St Bartholomew saved him from a winged monster.
The 13th-century arch used to be the door to the church until the nave of that earlier building was pulled down when Henry VIII dissolved the priory. Today the arch leads from Little Britain to the small burial ground – the gatehouse above it is from a later period. The present building retains the crossing and chancel of the original, with its round arches and other fine Norman detailing. There are also good examples of Tudor and other monuments. The painter William Hogarth *(see p259)* was baptized here in 1697.
From time to time parts of the church were used for secular purposes, including housing a blacksmith's forge and a hop store. In 1725 US statesman Benjamin Franklin worked for a printer in the Lady Chapel.

Barbican Centre ❼

Silk St EC2. **Map** 7 A5. ☎ 020-7638 8891. ☎ 020-7638 4141. 🚇 *Barbican, Moorgate.* **Open** 9am–10.30pm Mon–Sat, noon–11pm Sun, public hols. ♿ *induction loop.* 🎫 📺 🍴 📶 ⛪ **Filmshows, concerts, exhibitions.** See *Entertainment pp326–37.*

AN AMBITIOUS PIECE of 1960s city planning, this large residential, commercial and arts complex was begun in 1962 on a site devastated by World War II bombs, and not completed for nearly 20 years. Tall residential tower blocks surround an arts centre, which also includes an ornamental lake, fountains and lawns.
The old city wall turned a corner here and substantial remains are still clearly visible (particularly so from the Museum of London – *see pp166–7*). The word barbican means a defensive tower over a gate – perhaps the architects

St Bartholomew's gatehouse

were trying to live up to the name when they designed this self-sufficient community with formidable defences against the outside world. Obscure entrances and raised walkways remove pedestrians from the cramped bustle of the City, but, in spite of the signposts, and yellow lines on the pavement, the centre can be difficult to navigate.
As well as two theatres and a concert hall, the Barbican includes cinemas, one of London's largest art galleries for major touring exhibitions, a convention and exhibition hall, a library and a music school (the Guildhall School of Music). There is also a surprising conservatory above the arts centre.

The well-stocked conservatory at the Barbican Centre

Museum of London ❸

O PENED IN 1976 on the edge of the Barbican, the museum provides a lively account of London life from prehistoric times to the present day. Reconstructed interiors and street scenes are alternated with displays of original domestic artefacts and items found in the museum's archaeological digs. Look out for the working model of the Great Fire of 1666, accompanied by readings from Samuel Pepys' eyewitness account.

GALLERY GUIDE
The chronological arrangement of the galleries creates an easy route, which takes about 90 minutes to complete.

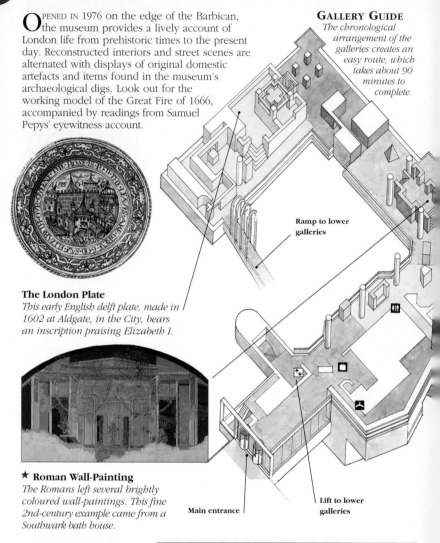

Ramp to lower galleries

The London Plate
This early English delft plate, made in 1602 at Aldgate, in the City, bears an inscription praising Elizabeth I.

★ **Roman Wall-Painting**
The Romans left several brightly coloured wall-paintings. This fine 2nd-century example came from a Southwark bath house.

Main entrance

Lift to lower galleries

Museum entrance

ALDERSGATE STREET

LONDON WALL

To St Paul's station

STAR EXHIBITS

★ **Roman Wall-Painting**

★ **Late Stuart Interior**

★ **Victorian Shop Fronts**

ORIENTATION

The museum is in a modern building above street-level where Aldersgate Street meets London Wall. Access is by signposted steps and ramps.

KEY

☐ Museum buildings

▉ Raised walkways

☐ Roads

VISITORS' CHECKLIST

London Wall EC2. **Map** 15 A1.
☎ 0120-7600 3699.
Ⓔ Barbican, St Paul's, Moorgate.
🚌 4, 6, 8, 9, 11, 15, 22, 25,
141, 279A, 501, 513, 502.
🚉 City Thameslink.
Open 10am–5.50pm Mon–Sat,
noon–5.50pm Sun. **Closed**
24–26 Dec. **Adm charge** Free
after 4.30pm. 📷 ♿ 🔊
Induction loops fitted. 🍴 🖥 🎞
Lectures, film presentations.

★ **Victorian Shop Fronts**
The atmosphere of 19th-century London is recreated by several authentic shop interiors, like this grocer's.

Twentieth-century London is illustrated by displays exploring the major historical events of this century. Votes for women, World War II, the rise of cinema and Swinging London are all here.

Garden

18th-Century Dress
Luxuriously worked Spitalfields silk was used to make this dress in 1753. It was worn over light-weight cane hoops.

Lift to upper galleries

KEY TO FLOORPLAN
- Prehistoric London
- Roman London
- Dark Age and Saxon London
- Medieval London
- Tudor and Early Stuart London
- Late Stuart London
- 18th-century London
- Victorian London and the Imperial Capital
- 20th-century London
- Lord Mayor's coach
- Temporary exhibitions
- Non-exhibition space

★ **Late Stuart Interior**
Outstanding features from several grand houses of the late 17th century were used to reconstruct this room.

St Giles, Cripplegate ❽

Fore St EC2. **Map** 7 A5. ☎ *020-7638 1997.* ⊖ *Barbican, Moorgate.* **Open** *11am–4pm Mon–Fri, 9.30am–noon Sat, 7.30am–noon Sun.* ✝ *8am, 10am Sun (family service 11.30am third Sun of each month).* ⓰ ⓰

COMPLETED IN 1550, this church managed to survive the ravages of the Great Fire in 1666, but was so badly damaged by a World War II bomb that only the tower survived. St Giles was refurbished during the 1950s to serve as the parish church of the Barbican development, and now stands awkwardly amid the uncompromising modernity of the Barbican.

Oliver Cromwell married Elizabeth Bourchier here in 1620 and the poet John Milton was buried here in 1674. Well-preserved remains of London's Roman and medieval walls can be seen to the south.

Whitbread's Brewery ❾

Chiswell St EC1. **Map** 7 B5. ⊖ *Barbican, Moorgate.* **Not open** to *the public.*

IN 1736, WHEN HE was aged just 16, Samuel Whitbread became an apprentice brewer in Bedford. By the time of his death in 1796, his Chiswell Street brewery (which he had

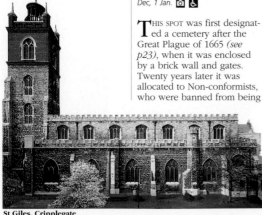
St Giles, Cripplegate

Blake's gravestone at Bunhill Fields

bought in 1750) was brewing 909,200 litres (200,000 gal) a year. The building has not been used as a brewery since 1976 when it was converted into rooms hired out for private functions – they are no longer open to the public. The Porter Tun room, which is now used as a banqueting suite, boasts the largest timber post roof in Europe, and has a huge span of 18 m (60 ft).

The street's 18th-century buildings are well-preserved examples of their period, and are worth a look from the outside. A plaque on one commemorates a visit to the brewery in 1787 by George III and Queen Charlotte.

Bunhill Fields ❿

City Rd EC1. **Map** 7 B4. ☎ *020-8472 3584.* ⊖ *Old St.* **Open** *7.30am–7pm Mon–Fri, 9.30am–4pm Sat, Sun.* **Closed** *25–26 Dec, 1 Jan.* ⓰ ⓰

THIS SPOT was first designated a cemetery after the Great Plague of 1665 (see p23), when it was enclosed by a brick wall and gates. Twenty years later it was allocated to Non-conformists, who were banned from being

buried in churchyards because of their refusal to use the Church of England prayer book. Visitors to this location, which is situated on the edge of the City, and shaded by large plane trees, can see monuments to the well-known writers Daniel Defoe, John Bunyan and William Blake, as well as to members of the Cromwell family.

John Milton wrote his famous epic poem *Paradise Lost* while he lived in Bunhill Row, located on the west side of the cemetery. It was a poem he created in the years that led up to his death in 1674.

Wesley's Chapel–Leysian Centre ⓫

49 City Rd EC1. **Map** 7 B4. ☎ *020-7253 2262.* ⊖ *Old St.* **House, chapel and museum open** *10am–4pm Mon–Sat, noon– 2pm Sun.* **Adm charge** *(except Sun).* ⓰ ✝ *9.45am, 11am Sun, 12.45pm Thu.* ⓰ ⓰ *Films, exhibitions.*

Wesley's Chapel

JOHN WESLEY, the founder of the Methodist church, laid the chapel's foundation stone in 1777. He preached here until his death in 1791, and is buried behind the chapel. Next door is the house where he lived, and today some of his furniture, books and other assorted possessions can be seen on display there.

The chapel, adorned in a spartan style, in accordance with Wesley's austere religious principles, has columns made from ships' masts. Beneath it is a small museum that explores the history of the Methodist church. Baroness Thatcher, the first British woman Prime Minister, in office from 1979 to 1990, was married in the chapel.

Broadgate Centre ⓬

Exchange Sq EC2. **Map** 7 C5.
📞 020-7505 4608. 🚇 Liverpool St.
♿ 🚻 🛒 📷

Broadgate Centre skating rink

SITUATED ABOVE and around Liverpool Street station, the terminus for trains to eastern England, this is one of the most successful recent (1985–91) shop and office developments. Each of the squares has its own distinctive character. Broadgate Arena emulates New York's Rockefeller Center, doubling as a skating rink in winter and a venue for refreshments and entertainment in summer.

Among the many sculptures dotted about the complex are George Segal's *Rush Hour Group*, and Barry Flanagan's *Leaping Hare on Crescent and Bell*. Don't miss the spectacular view of Liverpool Street station and its glass-roofed train shed, seen from Exchange Square to the north.

Petticoat Lane ⓭

Middlesex St E1. **Map** 16 D1.
🚇 Aldgate East, Aldgate, Liverpool St. **Open** 9am–2pm Sun. See **Shops and Markets** pp324–5.

IN QUEEN VICTORIA'S prudish reign the name of this street, long famous for its market, was changed to the respectable but colourless Middlesex Street. That is still its official designation, but the old name, derived from its many years as a centre of the clothing trade, has stuck, and

is now applied to the market held every Sunday morning in this and the surrounding streets. Numerous attempts have been made to stop the market, but with no success. An enormous variety of goods is sold but there is still a bias towards clothing, especially leather coats. The atmosphere is noisy and cheerful, with Cockney stall-holders making use of their wit and insolence to attract custom. There are scores of snack bars, and many of these sell traditional Jewish food such as salt beef sandwiches and bagels with smoked salmon.

Whitechapel Art Gallery ⓮

Whitechapel High St E1. **Map** 16 E1.
📞 020-7522 7878. 🚇 Aldgate East, Aldgate. **Open** 11am–5pm Tue–Sun, 11am–8pm Wed. **Closed** 25–26 Dec, 1 Jan, for exhibition installations.
Occasional adm charge. ♿ 🎦 🚻
💻 📷 **Films, lectures.**

A STRIKING ART NOUVEAU facade by C Harrison Townsend fronts this light, airy gallery founded in 1901.

Entrance to Whitechapel Gallery

Its aim is to bring art to the people of East London. Today this independent gallery enjoys an excellent international reputation for high-quality shows of major contemporary artists; these are interspersed with exhibitions reflecting the rich cultural origins of the people in the local community. In the 1950s and 1960s the likes of Jackson Pollock, Robert Rauschenberg, Anthony Caro and John Hoyland all displayed their work here. In 1970 David Hockney's first exhibition was held here.

The gallery also has a well-stocked arts bookshop, and there is a café here, serving a range of appetizing and healthy wholefoods in a relaxed atmosphere.

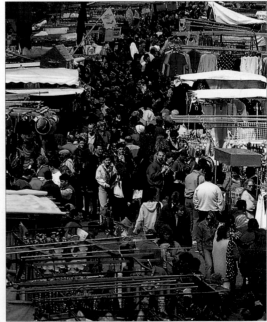

Bustling Petticoat Lane Market

18th-century Fournier Street

Christk Church, Spitalfields **⑮**

Commercial St E1. **Map** 8 E5.
📞 020-7247 7202. **⊖** Aldgate East,
Liverpool St. **Open** 1pm–3pm
Mon–Fri,. **✚** 10.30am, 7pm Sun.
♿ Concerts in June and December.

THE FINEST of Nicholas
Hawksmoor's six London
churches, started in 1714
and completed in 1729, was
mauled by Victorian alterations.
Christ Church still dominates
the surrounding streets,
however. Its portico and spire
are best seen from the western
end of Brushfield Street,
showing the four Tuscan
columns on pediments
supporting the arched roof of
the church's portico.

Christ Church was com-
missioned by parliament in
the Fifty New Churches Act of
1711. The act's purpose was
to combat the spread of Non-
conformism (to the established
Church of England) and a
church needed to make a
strong statement here, in an
area that was fast becoming a
Huguenot stronghold. The
Protestant Huguenots had fled
from religious persecution in
Catholic France and came to
Spitalfields to work in the
local silkweaving industry.

The church's impression of
size and strength is reinforced
inside by the high ceiling, the
sturdy wooden canopy over
the west door and the gallery.
In Hawksmoor's original plan
the gallery extends around the
north and south sides joining
the organ gallery at the west

end. The organ dates from
1735; the royal coat of arms,
in Coade stone, from 1822.

During the 19th century the
hand silkweaving industry
declined as machinery took
over, leaving Spitalfields too
poor to maintain a church. By
the early 20th century Christ
Church was in disrepair. In
1958 it was closed for worship
because it was dangerous.
Restoration began in 1964
and the church reopened in
1987. Since 1965 the crypt has
provided shelter to recovering
alcoholics.

Fournier Street **⑯**

E1. **Map** 8 E5. **⊖** Aldgate East,
Liverpool Street.

THE 18TH-CENTURY houses
on the north side of this
street have attics with broad
windows that were designed
to give maximum light to the
silkweaving French Huguenot
community who lived here.
Even now, the textile trade
lives on, in this and nearby
streets, still dependent on
immigrant labour. Today it is
Bengalis who toil at sewing
machines in workrooms that
are as cramped as they were
when the Huguenots used
them. Working conditions are
improving, however, and
many of the sweatshops have
been converted into show-
rooms for companies which
now have modern factories
away from the town centre.

Christ Church, Spitalfields

Bengali sweet factory: Brick Lane

London Jamme Masjid **⑰**

Brick Lane E1. **Map** 8 E5.
⊖ Liverpool St, Aldgate East.

LOCAL MUSLIMS NOW worship
here, in a building whose
life story as a religious site
reflects the fascinating history
of immigration into the area.
Built in 1743 as a Huguenot
chapel, it became a synagogue
in the 19th century, was used
as a Methodist chapel in the
early 20th century, and is
now a mosque. The sundial
above the entrance bears the
Latin inscription *Umbra
sumus* – "we are shadows".

Spitalfields Centre Museum of Immigration **⑱**

19 Princelet St E1. **Map** 8 E5.
📞 020-7247 5352. **⊖** Aldgate East,
Liverpool St. **Open** call for times.

A LITTLE VICTORIAN synagogue
hidden behind a 1719
Huguenot silk merchant's
house is the setting for exhibitions celebrating the lives of
Jewish and other peoples who
arrived as immigrants and
settled in London's East End.

Brick Lane **⑲**

E1. **Map** 8 E5. **⊖** Liverpool St,
Aldgate East, Shoreditch. **Market
open** dawn–noon Sun. See **Shops
and Markets** pp324–5.

ONCE A LANE running through
brickfields, this is now
the busy centre of London's
Bengali district. Its shops and

The grand bedroom of Dennis Severs House

houses, some dating from the 18th century, have seen waves of immigrants of many nationalities, and most now sell food, spices, silks and sarees. The first Bengalis to live here were sailors who came in the 19th century. In those days it was a predominantly Jewish quarter, and there are still a few Jewish shops left, including a popular 24-hour bagel shop at No. 159.

On Sundays a large market is held here and in the surrounding streets, complementing Petticoat Lane *(see p169)*. At the northern end of Brick Lane is the former Black Eagle Brewery, a medley of 18th- and 19th-century industrial architecture, now reflected in, and set off by, a sympathetic mirror-glassed extension.

18th-century portrait: Dennis Severs House

Dennis Severs House ⑳

18 Folgate St E1. **Map** 8 D5.
📞 020-7247 4013. 🚇 *Liverpool St.*
Open *first Sun of month 2–5pm, each Mon evening (book in advance).* **Adm charge. Evening performances.**
🌐 www.dennissevershouse.co.uk

A T NO. 18 Folgate Street, built in 1724, the late designer and performer, Dennis Severs, recreated an historical interior, that takes you an a journey from the 17th to the 19th centuries. It offers what he called "an adventure of the imagination,… a visit to a time-mode rather than… merely a look at a house". The rooms are like a series of *tableaux vivants*, as if the occupants had simply left for a moment. There is broken bread on the plates, wine in the glasses, fruit in the bowl; the candles flicker and horses' hooves clatter on the cobbles outside. This highly theatrical experience is quite removed from more usual museum recreations and is not suitable for children under 12. Praised by many, including artist David Hockney, it is truly unique. The house's motto is "you either see it or you don't".

Around the corner on Elder Street are two of London's earliest surviving terraces, also built in the 1720s, where many of the orderly Georgian red-brick houses have been carefully restored.

Columbia Road Market ㉑

Columbia Rd E2. **Map** 8 D3.
🚇 *Liverpool St, Old St, Bethnal Green.* **Open** *8.30am–1pm Sun.*
See **Shops and Markets** *pp322–3.*

A VISIT TO this flower and plant market is one of the most delightful things to do on a Sunday morning in London, whether you want to take advantage of the exotic species on offer there or not. Set in a well-preserved street of small Victorian shops, it is a lively, sweet-smelling and colourful event. Apart from the stalls, there are several shops selling, among other things, home-made bread and farmhouse cheeses, antiques and interesting objects, many of them flower-related. There is also a Spanish delicatessen and an excellent snack bar that sells bagels and welcome mugs of hot chocolate on chilly winter mornings.

Columbia Road flower market

SOUTHWARK AND BANKSIDE

SOUTHWARK ONCE offered an escape route from the City, where many forms of pleasure were banned. Borough High Street was lined with taverns: the medieval courtyards that still run off it mark where they stood. The George survives as the only galleried London inn. Prostitution thrived in houses facing the river, and theatres and bear gardens were established here in the late 16th century.

Shakespeare window at Southwark Cathedral

Shakespeare's company was based at the Globe Theatre, which has now been rebuilt close to its original site. Today the south bank of the river has undergone extensive renovation to reclaim the title of London's most historic borough. The Millennium Mile stretches from Westminster Bridge to the Design Museum. Its attractions include Southwark Cathedral and the new Tate Modern at Bankside.

SIGHTS AT A GLANCE

Historic Streets and Buildings
Hop Exchange ❷
The Old Operating Theatre ❺
Cardinal's Wharf ❼

Museums and Galleries
Clink Prison Museum ❶❷
Shakespeare's Globe ❻
Tate Modern ❾

Bankside Gallery ❽
Vinopolis ❶❶
London Dungeon ❶❹
Design Museum ❶❺

Cathedrals
Southwark Cathedral ❶

Pubs
George Inn ❹
The Anchor ❶⓪

Markets
Borough Market ❸
Bermondsey Antiques Market ❶❸

Historic Ships
HMS Belfast ❶❻

0 metres	500
0 yards	500

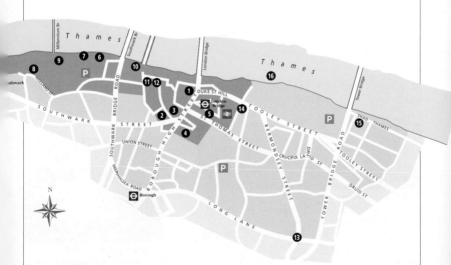

GETTING THERE
The Northern line runs a regular Underground service to this area. Nearly every train from Charing Cross or Cannon Street stops at London Bridge and the Jubilee line offers connections from east and west London.

SEE ALSO
• **Street Finder**, maps 14, 15, 16
• **Where to Stay** pp272–285
• **Restaurants, Pubs** pp286–311

KEY
Street-by-Street map
🚇 Underground station
🚉 Rail station
P Parking

The Millennium Bridge located opposite the Tate Modern

Street-by-Street: Southwark

FROM MEDIEVAL TIMES until the 18th century, Southwark was a popular venue for the pursuit of illicit pleasures. It was south of the Thames and out of the jurisdiction of the City authorities. The 18th and 19th centuries brought docks, warehouses and factories. Now Southwark is once again of London's most exciting boroughs, with the arrival of Tate Modern, a regenerated Borough Market and the stunning re-creation of Shakespeare's Globe Theatre.

Southwark Bridge
was opened in 1912
to replace a bridge
of 1819.

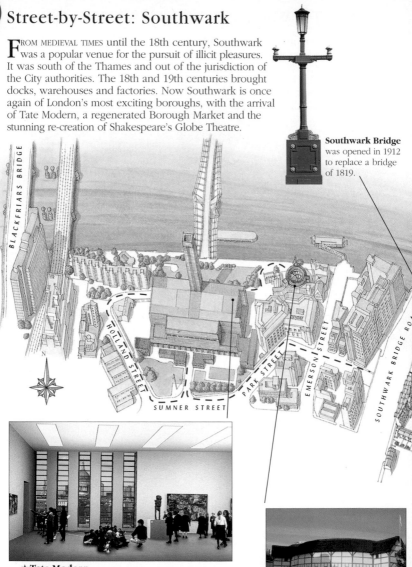

★Shakespeare's Globe
*This brilliant recreation of an
Elizabethan theatre has open-
air performances in the
summer months* ❻

★Tate Modern
*The former Bankside Power Station is now a
powerhouse of contemporary art, its spectacular
open spaces showing off exhibits to perfection* ❾

STAR SIGHTS

★**Southwark
Cathedral**

★**Tate Modern**

★**Shakespeare's
Globe**

0 metres   100

0 yards   100

KEY

– – –   Suggested route

Southwark Quayside

LOCATOR MAP
See Central London Map pp12–13

The Anchor
For centuries it has been a favourite riverside pub with fine views ⑩

Vinopolis
This new attraction is a city of wine on the banks of the river ⑪

Clink Prison Museum
This museum, on the site of the notorious old prison, looks back at Southwark's colourful past ⑫

Rose window

Replica of Sir Francis Drake's *Golden Hind*

★Southwark Cathedral
Despite major alterations, it still contains medieval elements ①

London Bridge, in its various forms, was the only river crossing in London from Roman times until 1750. The present bridge, completed in 1972, replaced the one of 1831 now in the US.

Borough Market
There has been a market on or near this site since 1276. Now it is a flourishing fine food market ③

The War Memorial, commemorating soldiers who fell in World War I, was erected in 1924 on Borough High Street where it has become a powerful landmark.

George Inn
This is London's only surviving traditional, galleried inn ④

THE GEORGE

Southwark Cathedral ❶

Montague Close SE1. **Map** 15 B3.
📞 *020-7367 6700.* 🚇 *London Bridge.* **Open** *9am–6pm daily.* 🕐 *11am Sun.* 🍴 🎵 **Concerts.**

THIS CHURCH DID not become a cathedral until 1905. However, some parts of it date back to the 12th century, when the building was attached to a priory, and many of its medieval features remain. The memorials are fascinating, including a late 13th-century wooden effigy of a knight. John Harvard, who went on to found Harvard University, was baptized here in 1607 and there is a chapel named after him.

The cathedral has recently been cleaned and restored as part of a multi-million pound restoration programme. This includes the addition of new buildings, which comprise a beautiful shop, an exciting interactive multi-media Visitor Centre and a new restaurant. The exterior has been extensively landscaped to create a herb garden and an attractive Millennium Courtyard that leads to the riverside.

Shakespeare Window in Cathedral

Hop Exchange ❷

Southwark St SE1. **Map** 15 B4. 🚇 *London Bridge.* **Not open** *to the public.*

SOUTHWARK, with its easy access to Kent where hops are grown, was a natural venue for brewing beer and trading hops. In 1866 this building was constructed as the centre of that trade. Now

The George Inn, now owned by the National Trust

offices, it retains its original pediment complete with carved scenes showing the hop harvest, and iron gates with a hop motif.

Borough Market ❸

8 Southwark St SE1. **Map** 15 B4. 🚇 *London Bridge.* **Retail market open** *Fri noon–6pm, Sat 9am–4pm.*

BOROUGH MARKET was until recently an exclusively wholesale fruit and vegetable market, which had its origins in medieval times, and moved to its current atmospheric position beneath the railway tracks in 1756. A popular fine food market has now been introduced, selling gourmet foods from Britain and Europe, as well as quality fruit and vegetables, to locals and tourists alike.

George Inn ❹

77 Borough High St SE1. **Map** 15 B4.
📞 *020-7407 2056.* 🚇 *London Bridge, Borough.* **Open** *11am–11pm Mon–Sat, noon–10.30pm Sun.* 🍴
See **Restaurants and Pubs** *pp309–11.*

DATING FROM THE 17th century, this building is the only example of a traditional galleried coaching inn left in London and is mentioned by Dickens in *Little Dorrit.* It was rebuilt after the Southwark fire of 1676 in a style that dates back to the Middle Ages.

Originally there would have been three wings around a courtyard where plays were staged in the 17th century. In 1889 the north and east wings were demolished, so there is only one wing remaining.

The inn, now owned by the National Trust, is still a restaurant. Perfect on a cold wet day, the pub has a well-worn, comfortable atmosphere. In the summer, the yard fills with picnic tables and patrons are occasionally entertained by actors and morris dancers.

The Old Operating Theatre ❺

9a St Thomas St SE1. **Map** 15 B4.
📞 *020-7955 4791.* 🚇 *London Bridge.* **Open** *10.30am–5pm daily.* **Closed** *15 Dec–5 Jan.*
Adm charge. 🚻

ST THOMAS'S HOSPITAL, one of the oldest in Britain, stood here from its foundation in the 12th century until it was moved west in 1862. At this time nearly all of its buildings were demolished in order to make way for the railway. The women's operating

19th-century surgical tools

theatre (The Old Operating Theatre Museum and Herb Garret) survived only because it was located away from the main buildings, in a garret over the hospital church (now the Chapter House of Southwark Cathedral). It lay, bricked up and forgotten, until the 1950s. It has now been fitted out just as it would have been in the early 19th century, before the discovery of either anaesthetics or antiseptics. The display shows how patients were blindfolded, gagged and bound to the wooden operating table, while a box of sawdust underneath was used to catch the blood.

Shakespeare's Henry IV (performed at the Globe Theatre around 1600)

Shakespeare's Globe **❻**

New Globe Walk SE1. **Map** 15 A3. **☎** 020-7902 1400. **☎** box office 020-7401 9919. **⊖** London Bridge, Mansion House. **Exhibition open** mid-May–Sep: 9am–12pm; Oct–mid-May: 10am–5pm daily. **Performances** mid-May–Sep. **Adm charge**. **📷** **⚲** every 30 mins. **🖥 🍴 📖**

BUILT ON THE BANKS of the Thames, Shakespeare's Globe is an impressive reconstruction of the Elizabethan theatre where many of his plays were first performed. The wooden, circular structure is open in the middle, leaving some of the audience exposed to the elements. Those holding seat tickets have a roof over their heads. The performances operate only in summer, and seeing a play here can be a lively experience,

with the "groundlings" standing in front of the stage encouraged to cheer or jeer. When there is no performance, visitors are taken on an informative tour. Beneath the theatre is Shakespeare's Globe Exhibition, where aspects of his work are brought to life with modern technology and traditional crafts.

Cardinal's Wharf **❼**

SE1. **Map** 15 A3. **⊖** London Bridge.

A SMALL GROUP OF 17th-century houses still survives here in the shadow of the new Tate Modern art gallery (see pp178–81). A plaque commemorates Christopher Wren's stay here while St Paul's Cathedral (see pp148–51) was being built. He would have had a particularly fine view of the works. It is thought that the wharf got its name from Cardinal Wolsey who was Bishop of Winchester in 1529.

Bankside Gallery **❽**

48 Hopton St SE1. **Map** 14 F3. **☎** 020-7928 7521. **⊖** Blackfriars, Southwark. **Open** 10am–8pm Tue, 10am–5pm Wed–Fri,11am–5pm Sat & Sun. **Closed** Christmas week–2 Jan. **Adm charge**. **♿ 📖** Lectures.

THIS MODERN RIVERSIDE gallery is the headquarters of two historic British societies, namely the Royal Watercolour Society and the Royal Society of Painter-

View from the Founders' Arms

Printmakers. The members of these societies are elected by their peers in a tradition that dates back almost 200 years. Their work embraces both established and experimental practices. The gallery's permanent collection is not on show here but there are constantly changing temporary displays of contemporary watercolours and original artists' prints. The exhibitions feature the work of both societies and many of the pieces on display are for sale. There is also a superb specialist art shop that sells both books and materials.

There is an unparalleled view of St Paul's Cathedral from the nearby pub, the Founders' Arms – built on the site of the foundry where the cathedral's bells were cast. South of here, on Hopton Street, is a series of almshouses dating from 1752.

Row of 17th-century houses on Cardinal's Wharf

Tate Modern ❾

L OOMING OVER THE SOUTHERN bank of the Thames, Tate
Modern occupies the converted Bankside power
station, a dynamic space for one of the world's premier
collections of 20th-century art. Up until 2000, the massive
Tate collection was drawn from by three Tate galleries:
Tate St Ives, Tate Liverpool and the Tate Gallery, now
Tate Britain *(see pp82–85)*. When Tate Modern joined this
family of galleries, space was created for an ever-expanding collection of contemporary art. The regular rotation of
pieces and the installation of numerous special exhibitions
result in compelling displays that change continuously.

★ **Composition (Man
and Woman)** *(1927)*
*Alberto Giacometti's sculp-
ture portrays the human
form trapped in urban life.*

**Do We Turn Round
Inside Houses, or Is It
Houses which Turn
Around Us?** *(1977/85)*
*Mario Merz's igloo
installations question the
relationship of humans
to the natural world.*

**Death from Death Hope Life
Fear** *(1984)*
*Gilbert and George explore the
spiritual conundrum of man.*

KEY TO FLOORPLAN

- Turbine Hall
- Still life / Object / Real Life
- Landscape / Matter / Environment
- Nude / Action / Body
- History / Memory / Society
- Temporary exhibition space
- Non-exhibition space

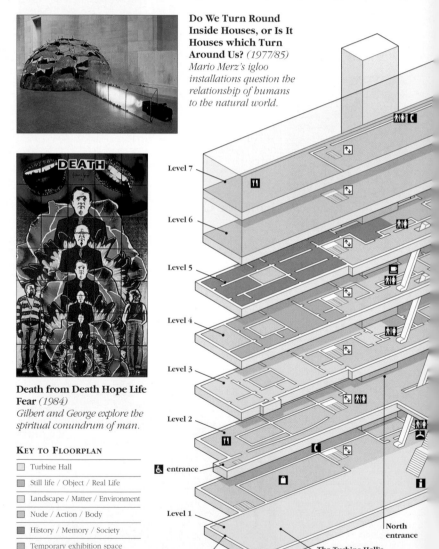

Level 7

Level 6

Level 5

Level 4

Level 3

Level 2

Level 1

& entrance

**North
entrance**

The Turbine Hall's
massive scale creates a
challenge for the artists
who install pieces here.

West entrance

Standing by the Rags
(1988–89)
Lucian Freud's honest depictions of the human form encourage viewers to re-think their own notion of the human body. Freud's nudes are considered his finest works and this is a superlative example.

The **"light beam"**, a two-storey glass box, allows light to filter into the upper galleries.

Two reading rooms offer a selection of art books and comfortable seating.

A balcony gives great views of St Paul's Cathedral *(pp148–51)* across the river.

Soft Drainpipe – Blue (Cool) Version *(1967)*
An advert for a drainpipe was the inspiration for this sculpture by Pop artist Claes Oldenburg. Like many of his pieces, Soft Drainpipe uses pliable material to represent hard surfaces, and thus renders a familiar object strange.

GALLERY GUIDE
The main west entrance opens into the expansive, sloped Turbine Hall. From here, a flight of stairs leads to the café and foyer of level 2, or an escalator whisks visitors straight up to gallery level 3. Temporary exhibitions are on level 4, while level 5 is again devoted to galleries. Level 6 is members' access only, but a superb restaurant and spectacular city views can be found on level 7.

★ **Light Red Over Black** *(1957)*
This moody painting of blurred rectangles on a vertical back drop is typical of Mark Rothko's later work.

★ **The Kiss** *(1901–4)*
Auguste Rodin's sculpture of a kissing couple pays homage to classical sculpture yet disregards petty convention by leaving part of the rough marble standing.

STAR EXHIBITS

★ **Composition by Giacometti**

★ **Light Red Over Black by Rothko**

★ **The Kiss by Rodin**

Exploring Tate Modern

IN A BREAK WITH CONVENTION, Tate Modern organizes its
pieces by theme rather than chronology or school, a
practice which cuts across movements and mixes up
media. Four topics based on traditional genres (Still
Life/Object/Real Life; Landscape/Matter/Environment;
Nude/Action/Body; History/Memory/Society) reveal how
traditions have been confronted, extended or rejected by
artists throughout the 20th and into the 21st centuries.

After Lunch (1975) by Patrick Caulfield

STILL LIFE/OBJECT/REAL LIFE

JUST AS THERE CAN be great
music without great words,
so there can be a great
painting without an important
subject. This discovery, the
thought behind the still life,
was only fully appreciated in
the 17th century when artists
began to represent the sheer
poetry of the physical world.
At the beginning of the 20th
century artists such as Paul
Cézanne, and later Pablo
Picasso and Georges Braque,
took this a stage further by
including reality
(newspaper, wallpaper,
etc.) in the work itself.
In the 1930s Surrealists
brought a touch of
humour and psycho-
sexual content to the
still life; Salvador Dali's
*Lobster Telephone (see
p41)* being a fine
example. Marcel
Duchamp radically
re-interpreted the
notion of the still life
with his series of
works that presented
everyday objects as
art (most famously a
urinal in *Fountain*).
In the latter half of the 20th
century this idea has been
explored further by artists
such as Cathy de Monchaux
and Claes Oldenburg and,
perhaps most notoriously, by
Carl Andre whose *Equivalent
VIII* looks to the uninitiated
like a pile of bricks. Patrick
Caulfield explores still life
versus real life in his
paintings by turning the
relationship of representation
and reality on its head. In
After Lunch, the idealized
landscape hanging on the
wall appears more realistic
than its graphically painted
everyday surroundings.

LANDSCAPE/MATTER/ENVIRONMENT

LANDSCAPE PAINTING became
popular in the 19th century
as industrialisation threatened
to swallow up the countryside.
In this suite of rooms, Tate
Modern looks at how 20th-
century artists have taken up
the challenge of representing
our environment, beginning
with the radical transforma-
tions of the Impressionists.
Artists such as Cézanne with
*The Grounds of the Château
Noir* and Henri Matisse in *La
Plage Rouge* tried to capture
the essence of nature by
painting what they saw rather
than what they thought they
should see. In one room,
Claude Monet's *Water Lilies*
(circa 1914) is placed alongside
Richard Long's *Red Slate Circle*
(1988) in order to draw out
both artists' sense of immer-
sion in landscape. Jackson
Pollock's exuberant abstracts
and Mark Rothko's magical
colour fields are also found in
these rooms, as are the bio-
morphic sculpture of Barbara
Hepworth and Henry Moore,
both of whom attempted to
represent nature in a three-
dimensional abstract form.

NUDE/ACTION/BODY

FROM GREEK ART onwards, the
human figure has been a
central preoccupation of
western art. Tate Modern has
assembled 20th-century artists
who have attempted to re-
shape the body. Among the
paintings and sculpture on

BANKSIDE POWER STATION

This forbidding fortress was designed in 1947 by Sir Giles
Gilbert Scott, the architect of Battersea Power Station, Waterloo
Bridge and London's famous red telephone boxes. The power
station is of a steel-framed brick skin construction, comprising
over 4.2 million bricks. The Turbine Hall was designed to
accommodate huge oil-burning generators and three vast oil
tanks are still in situ, buried under the ground just south of
the building. The tanks are to be employed in a future stage
of Tate Modern development. The power station itself was converted by Swiss architects Herzog and de Meuron who designed
the two-storey glass box, or lightbeam, which runs the length
of the building. This serves to flood the upper galleries with
light and also provides wonderful views of London.

The façade, chimney and light beam of Tate Modern

Summertime: Number 9A (1948) by Jackson Pollock

display are Francis Bacon's anguished *Three Studies for Figures at the Base of a Crucifixion* and Picasso's oddly proportioned figures in *The Three Dancers*. With his sculpture *Man Pointing*, Alberto Giacometti joins Amedeo Modigliani in re-interpreting how the human form is represented in African art.

In *The Bath*, Pierre Bonnard has created a sensual yet sad depiction of the human form by placing a softly coloured subject in a constraining geometric composition. Lucian Freud's detailed depictions of the body express a blunt honesty towards the human figure.

Beginning in the 1960s, Performance art utilized the artist's own body as the central means of expression, and often involved photography or film to document the work. Contemporary artists, such as Gilbert and George and Steve McQueen, use a combination of photographic media and shock tactics to extend the exploration of the body yet further.

HISTORY/MEMORY/SOCIETY

TAKING ITS CUE FROM a genre that covers ancient myth, literature and historical events, this suite of rooms collects together a number of 20th-century artists who engage with the moral, social or political world. Umberto Boccioni's striding figure *Unique Forms of Continuity in Space* embodies speed, strength and mechanization – virtues idealized by the Futurist movement. Picasso's *Weeping Woman* is both a personal piece and a representation of the suffering of the Spanish

Unique Forms of Continuity in Space (1913) by Umberto Boccioni

nation during the Civil War. One room is given over to the artists of De Stijl ("Style" or "The Way"), a Dutch movement which sought to create a purely abstract essential art that would be accessible to all. The best known De Stijl artist is Piet Mondrian, whose delicate abstract paintings are exhibited next to Dan Flavin's brash fluorescent tube sculptures.

As elsewhere in Tate Modern, such unexpected groupings challenge the visitor to question why certain pieces have been displayed together and to ask what they could have in common. Also on display are Modernist avant-garde artists who seek not to engage with the past or present but to erase it. Through absurd pieces such as *Fluxipingpong*, which involves a game played with impossible bats, the Fluxus collective invite visitors to see everything as art except for those works that are found in museums and galleries.

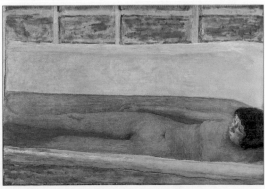

Maman (2000) by Louise Bourgeois

SPECIAL EXHIBITIONS

TO COMPLEMENT its permanent collection, Tate Modern presents a dynamic programme of temporary exhibitions including three large-scale shows a year (either retrospectives of modern masters or surveys of important movements). Smaller scale projects are dotted around, and occasionally outside, the gallery. Once a year Tate Modern challenges an artist to create a work capable of occupying the vast Turbine Hall. Louise Bourgeois was the first artist to install here. She created three giant towers with spiralling staircases and a massive 9 m-high overseeing spider.

The Bath (1925) by Pierre Bonnard

The Anchor ⑩

34 Park St SE1. **Map** 15 A3.
☎ *020-7407 1577.* 🚇 *London Bridge.* **Open** *11am–11pm Mon–Sat, noon–10.30pm Sun.* 🍽

T HIS IS ONE OF London's most famous riverside pubs. It dates from after the Southwark fire of 1676, which devastated the area *(see pp22–3)*. The present building is 18th-century, but traces of much earlier hostelries have been found beneath it. The inn was once connected with a brewery on the other side of the road that belonged to Henry Thrale, a close friend of Dr Samuel Johnson *(see p140)*. When Thrale died in 1781, Dr Johnson went to the brewery sale and encouraged the bidders with a phrase that has passed into the English language: "The potential of growing rich beyond the dreams of avarice."

Pub sign at the Anchor Inn

Vinopolis ⑪

1 Bank End SE1. **Map** 15 B3.
☎ *0870 444 4777.* 🚇 *London Bridge.* **Open** *11am-9pm (last entrance 7pm) Mon, 11am–6pm (last entrance 4pm) Tue-Fri & Sun, 11am-8pm (last entrance 6pm) Sat.*
Adm charge. 🎟 🅿 🍽 🚻 ♿

V INOPOLIS IS a unique attraction devoted to the enjoyment of wine. Its blend of interactive fun and educational exhibits has made it a popular destination for anyone who wishes to know more about making and drinking wine. Set within cavernous Victorian railway arches, Vinopolis explores the history of the grape from earliest times and illuminates the process of wine-making from planting the vines through to labelling the bottles. "Tasting stations" provide an opportunity to savour the subject matter along the way. A selection of choice vintages can be purchased from the wine warehouse after the tour, while the shop has a vast assortment of wine-related merchandise ranging from novelty corkscrews to crystal Champagne flutes.

Clink Prison Museum ⑫

1 Clink St SE1. **Map** 15 B3.
☎ *020-7378 1558.* 🚇 *London Bridge.* **Open** *Jun–Sep 10am–10pm daily; Oct–May 10am–6pm daily.* **Closed** *25 Dec.* **Adm charge.**
📷 🚻 ♿ *for groups (phone first).*

N OW A MACABRE museum, the prison that was once located here first opened in the 12th century. It was owned by successive Bishops of Winchester, who lived in the adjoining palace just east of the museum, of which all that now remains is a lovely rose window. During the 15th century, the prison became known as the "Clink", and finally closed in 1780.

The museum illustrates the history of the prison and the armoury that later occupied the premises. Tales of the inmates are told, including

Replica of Civil War trouper's helmet made in the Clink

Antiques stall at Bermondsey Market

those of numerous prostitutes, debtors and priests. Hands-on displays of torturing and restraining devices leave little to the imagination and are not for the faint-hearted.

Bermondsey Antiques Market ⑬

(New Caledonian Market) Long Lane and Bermondsey St SE1. **Map** 15 C5.
🚇 *London Bridge, Borough.* **Open** *5am–3pm Fri, starts closing midday.* See **Shops and Markets** pp324–5.

B ERMONDSEY MARKET became one of London's main antique markets during the 1960s, when the old Caledonian Market in Islington closed for redevelopment. Each Friday at dawn, seriously committed antique dealers trade their latest acquisitions at Bermondsey. There are occasional press reports about long-lost masterpieces changing hands here for a song, and early-rising optimists are welcome to try their luck and test their judgment. A trip to the market is many people's idea of a perfect day out in London. However, be warned that trading starts at the crack of dawn, and the best bargains tend to go long before most people are even awake.

Several nearby antique shops are open throughout the week. The most interesting of these are situated in a row of old warehouses on Tower Bridge Road.

London Dungeon ⑭

Tooley St SE1. **Map** 15 C3. ☎ 020-7403 7221. ⊖ London Bridge. **Open** Jul–Sep 10am–8pm daily; Oct-Jun 10am–5.30pm daily (last adm 30 mins before closing). **Closed** 25 Dec. **Adm charge**. ♿ 🖵 📷

IN EFFECT a much expanded version of the chamber of horrors at Madame Tussaud's *(see p224)*, this museum is a great hit with children. It illustrates the most blood-thirsty events in British history. It is played strictly for terror, and screams abound as Druids perform a human sacrifice at Stonehenge, Anne Boleyn is beheaded on the orders of her husband Henry VIII, and a room full of people die in agony during the Great Plague. Torture, murder and witchcraft fill the gaps between these spectacles.

Eduardo Paolozzi sculpture outside the Design Museum

Design Museum ⑮

Butlers Wharf, Shad Thames SE1. **Map** 16 E4. ☎ 020-7403 6933. ☎ 020-7940 8790. ⊖ Tower Hill, London Bridge. **Open** 11.30am–6pm Mon–Fri (last adm: 5.30pm); 10.30am–6pm Sat & Sun. **Closed** 24–26 Dec. **Adm charge** ♿ 📷 🍴 020-7378 7031 (booking advised). 🖵 📷

THIS MUSEUM was the first in the world to be devoted solely to the design of mass-produced everyday objects and to explain their function and appearance. The permanent collection offers a nostalgic look at furniture, office equipment, cars, radios and TV sets, as well as house-hold utensils from the past. Temporary exhibitions of

Spooky London Dungeon logo, an indication of the gruesome displays

international design in the Review and Collections galleries provide a taste of what is familiar to us and what may become common-place in the future. The Collections gallery is arranged thematically in a way that shows how the use, meaning, form and technology of design objects have changed through time. The collection includes pieces that date from the introduction of industrially mass-produced goods. The Review gallery, on the other hand, is devoted to the most innovative current designs, concepts and prototypes, which in their own way are shaping the future of the world we live in. Displays here include designs from the fields of engineering, tech-nology, furniture, fashion and architecture.

On the first floor is the Blueprint Café restaurant, which is a great place to get wonderful views of the Thames, especially after dark.

HMS Belfast ⑯

Morgan's Lane, Tooley St SE1. **Map** 16 D3. ☎ 020-7940 6328. ⊖ London Bridge, Tower Hill. ⛴ Tower Pier. **Open** 10am–5pm daily. **Closed** 24–26 Dec. **Adm charge**. ♿ except for café. 📷 🖵 📷

ORIGINALLY LAUNCHED in 1938 to serve in World War II, HMS Belfast was instrumental in the destruc-tion of the German battle cruiser, *Scharnhorst*, in the battle of North Cape, and also played an important role in the Normandy Landings.

After the war, the battle cruiser, designed for offensive action and for supporting amphibious operations, was sent to work for the United Nations in Korea. The ship remained in service with the British navy until 1965.

Since 1971, the cruiser has been used as a floating naval museum. Part of it has been atmospherically recreated to show what the ship was like in 1943, when it participated in sinking the German battle cruiser. Other displays portray life on board during World War II and there are also general exhibits relating to the history of the Royal Navy.

As well as being a great family day out, it is also possible for children to take part in educational activity weekends on board the ship.

The now familiar sight of the naval gunship HMS Belfast on the Thames

SOUTH BANK

FOLLOWING the Festival of Britain in 1951, the South Bank arts centre grew up around the newly erected Royal Festival Hall. The architecture has been criticized, especially the chunky concrete Hayward Gallery, but the area functions well, and is crowded with culture-seekers most evenings and afternoons. As well as theatres, concert halls and galleries, the South Bank also has the National Film Institute and London's most striking cinema, the IMAX *(see p331)*. In keeping with Festival of Britain tradition, the South Bank is a focal point for the new millennium, with the raising of the world's highest observation wheel.

Signpost at the South Bank Centre

SIGHTS AT A GLANCE

Historic Streets and Buildings
Lambeth Palace **8**
Gabriel's Wharf **11**
Waterloo Station **12**

Museums and Galleries
Hayward Gallery **2**
Florence Nightingale Museum **6**
Museum of Garden History **7**
Imperial War Museum **9**

Attractions
London Aquarium **4**
British Airways London Eye **5**

Theatres and Concert Halls
Royal National Theatre **1**
Royal Festival Hall **3**
Old Vic **10**

GETTING THERE
The Northern, Bakerloo and Jubilee lines pass through Waterloo station, which is also a major rail terminus. A few buses, such as Nos. 12, 53 and 176 run via Oxford Circus and Trafalgar Square, and stop south of the river a short walk from the South Bank Centre.

0 metres 500
0 yards 500

SEE ALSO

- **Street Finder**, maps 13, 22
- **Where to Stay** pp272–285
- **Restaurants, Pubs** pp286–311

KEY
- ▮ Street-by-Street map
- 🚇 Underground station
- 🚆 Railway station
- 🅿 Parking

Thameside promenade at the South Bank Centre

Street-by-Street: South Bank Centre

ORIGINALLY THIS WAS an area of wharves and factories which was much damaged by bombing during World War II. In 1951 it was chosen as the site of the Festival of Britain *(see p30)*, celebrating the centenary of the Great Exhibition *(see pp26–7)*. The Royal Festival Hall is the only building from 1951 to remain, but since then London's main arts centre has been created around it, including the national showplaces for theatre, music and film, and a major art gallery.

Memorial to the International Brigade of the Spanish Civil War

To the Strand

The National Film Theatre was established in 1953 to show historic films *(see pp330–31)*.

Festival Pier

The Queen Elizabeth Hall stages more intimate concerts than the Festival Hall. The adjoining Purcell Room is for chamber music *(see pp332–3)*.

★ Royal National Theatre
Its three auditoriums offer a choice of plays ranging from the classics to the sharpest modern writing **①**

Hayward Gallery
The concrete interior of this venue for important exhibitions is well suited to many modern works **②**

★ Royal Festival Hall
The London Philharmonic is one of many world-class orchestras to perform here in the focal point of the South Bank Centre **③**

Hungerford Bridge was built in 1864 to carry both trains and pedestrians to Charing Cross.

STAR SIGHTS

- ★ British Airways London Eye
- ★ Royal National Theatre
- ★ Royal Festival Hall

KEY

– – – Suggested route

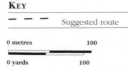

0 metres   100

0 yards   100

★British Airways London Eye
The world's largest observation wheel offers a unique view of London **⑤**

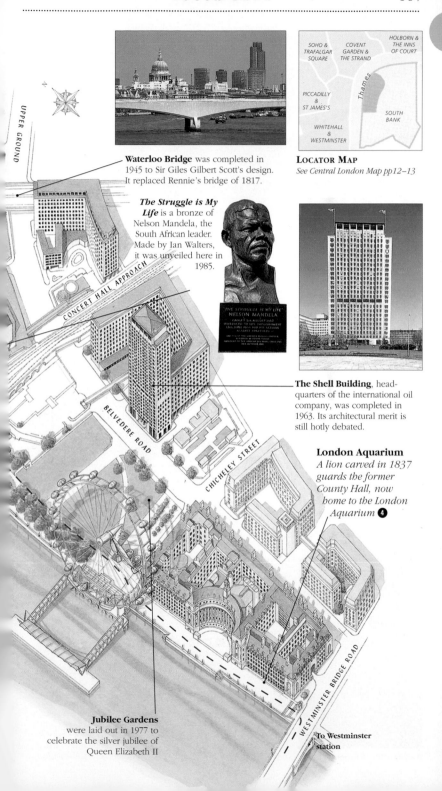

Waterloo Bridge was completed in 1945 to Sir Giles Gilbert Scott's design. It replaced Rennie's bridge of 1817.

LOCATOR MAP
See Central London Map pp12–13

The Struggle is My Life is a bronze of Nelson Mandela, the South African leader. Made by Ian Walters, it was unveiled here in 1985.

"THE STRUGGLE IS MY LIFE"
NELSON MANDELA

The Shell Building, head-quarters of the international oil company, was completed in 1963. Its architectural merit is still hotly debated.

London Aquarium
A lion carved in 1837 guards the former County Hall, now home to the London Aquarium ❹

Jubilee Gardens
were laid out in 1977 to celebrate the silver jubilee of Queen Elizabeth II

To Westminster station

The stark concrete facade of the Hayward Gallery

Royal National Theatre ❶

South Bank Centre SE1. **Map** 14 D3.
[i] 020-7452 3000. 🚇 Waterloo.
Open 10am–11pm Mon–Sat. **Closed**
24–25 Dec. 🚫 during performances.
♿ 🍴 🏪 🏛 **Concerts** at 6pm,
exhibitions. See **Entertainment**
pp326–7.

Even if you don't want to see a play, this well-appointed complex is worth a visit. Sir Denys Lasdun's building was opened in 1976 after 200 years of debate about whether there should be a national theatre and where it should be sited. The company was formed in 1963, under Laurence (later Lord) Olivier, Britain's leading 20th-century actor. The largest of the three theatres is named after him – the others, the Cottesloe and the Lyttleton, commemorate administrators.

Festival of Britain: symbol of 1951

Hayward Gallery ❷

South Bank Centre SE1. **Map** 14 D3.
[i] 020-7928 3144. 🚇 Waterloo.
Open 10am–8pm Tue–Wed, 10am–
6pm Thu–Mon. **Closed** 24–26 Dec,
1 Jan, Good Fri, May Day, between
exhibitions. **Adm charge.** 🚫 ♿ 🎧
🏪 🏛

The Hayward Gallery is one of London's main venues for large art exhibitions. Its slabby grey concrete exterior is too starkly modern for some tastes and there has been pressure for it to be pulled down or severely modified almost ever since it opened in October 1968.

Hayward exhibitions cover classical and contemporary art, but the work of British contemporary artists is particularly well represented. You may have to queue, especially at weekends.

Royal Festival Hall ❸

South Bank Centre SE1. **Map** 14 D4.
[i] 020-7960 4242. 🚇 Waterloo.
Open 10am–10pm daily.
Closed 25 Dec. 🚫 during
performances. ♿ 🍴 🏪 🏛
**Pre-concert talks, exhibitions,
free concerts.** See **Entertainment**
p330.

This was the only structure in the 1951 Festival of Britain (see p30) designed for permanence. Sir Robert Matthew and Sir Leslie Martin's concert hall was the first major public building in London following World War II. It has stood the test of time so well that many of the capital's major arts institutions have gathered round it. The hall's interior has always attracted much admiration; its sweeping staircases lead up majestically from the lobby to create a tremendous sense of occasion while also remaining highly functional. The stage has hosted renowned musicians, including the cellist Jacqueline du Pré and the conductor Georg Solti. The organ was installed in 1954. There are cafés and book stalls on the lower floors. Backstage tours are available.

London Aquarium ❹

County Hall, York Rd SE1. **Map** 13 C4.
[i] 020-7967 8000. 🚇 Waterloo,
Westminster. **Open** 10am–6pm daily.
Adm charge. ♿ 🏛

Shark in a scenic tank at the
London Aquarium

This modern aquarium, one of the largest in Europe, occupies part of the grandiose former headquarters of the Greater London Council. That London-wide authority was abolished in 1986 and the building stood empty for years. Now, fish and other aquatic creatures are shown in tanks that as far as possible simulate their native habitats, the two largest devoted to the Atlantic and Pacific Oceans. Other parts of County Hall have been converted to house two hotels, several restaurants, a multimedia games centre with a bowling alley, and a Salvador Dali exhibition.

British Airways London Eye 5

THE LONDON EYE IS A 135-m (443-ft) high observation wheel. Erected in 2000 as part of London's
millennium celebrations, it immediately became
one of the city's most recognizable landmarks,
notable not only for its size, but for its circularity
amid the block-shaped buildings flanking it. Thirty-
two capsules, each holding up to 25 people, take a
gentle 30-minute round trip. On a clear day, the
Eye affords a unique 40-km (25-mile) view which
sweeps over the capital in all directions and on to
the countryside and hills beyond.

The glass capsules
are mounted on the
outside of the rim,
allowing unobstructed
360-degree views.

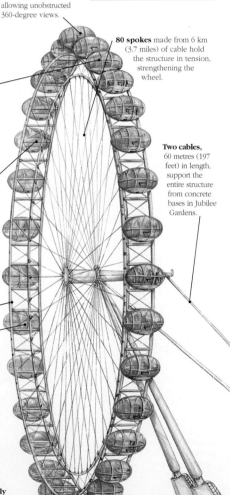

80 spokes made from 6 km
(3.7 miles) of cable hold
the structure in tension,
strengthening the
wheel.

Houses of Parliament
*Seventeen minutes into the flight,
the spectacular aerial view of
Westminster should not be missed.*

Battersea Power Station
*After 15 minutes,
the distinctive
white smokestacks
of this old power
station are visible.*

Two cables,
60 metres (197
feet) in length,
support the
entire structure
from concrete
bases in Jubilee
Gardens.

The wheel rim
was floated down
the Thames in
sections and then
assembled on site.

Buckingham Palace
*Ten minutes into the journey,
the Queen's official residence
glides into view.*

The Eye turns continuously
and moves slowly enough that the
capsules are boarded here while
moving. The wheel is halted for
those requiring assistance.

Florence Nightingale Museum ❻

2 Lambeth Palace Rd SE1. **Map** 14 D5.
📞 *020-7620 0374.* ➡ *Waterloo,
Westminster.* **Open** *10am–5pm
Mon–Fri, 11.30am–4.30pm Sat, Sun &
public hols (last adm one hour before
closing).* **Closed** *24 Dec–2 Jan, Good
Fri, Easter Sun.* **Adm charge.** 🚫 ♿
📹 *Videos, lectures.*

THIS DETERMINED woman
captured the nation's
imagination as the "Lady of
the Lamp", who nursed the
wounded soldiers of the
Crimea War (1853 – 6). She
also founded Britain's first
school of nursing at old St
Thomas's Hospital in 1860.
Obscurely sited near the
entrance to the new
St Thomas's Hospital, the
museum is worth finding. It
gives a fascinating account
of Nightingale's career
through displays of
original documents,
photographs and personal
memorabilia. They
illustrate her life and
the developments she
pioneered in health
care and sanitation, un-
til her death in 1910,
aged 90.

Florence Nightingale

Museum of Garden History ❼

Lambeth Palace Rd SE1. **Map** 21 C1.
📞 *020-7401 8865.* ➡ *Waterloo,
Vauxhall, Lambeth North,
Westminster.* **Open** *10.30am–4pm
Mon–Fri, 10.30am–5pm Sun.* **Closed**
2nd Sun Dec–1st Sun Mar. 📷 *small
charge.* ♿ 📖 📹 *Lectures,
filmshows.*

HOUSED IN AND AROUND the
14th-century tower of St
Mary's Church, this museum
opened in 1979. In the churchyard is the tomb of a father
and son both called John
Tradescant. The Tradescants
were gardeners to the 17th-
century monarchs and were
also pioneer plant hunters in
the Americas, Russia and
Europe. Their collection of
rare plant types formed the
basis of the Ashmolean
Museum, in Oxford.

The museum here consists of
a history of gardening in
Britain, illustrated by ancient
implements, plans and
documents. A knot garden
outside is devoted to plants
from the Tradescants' era.
There is a shop with a stock
of garden-related items, for
freshly-inspired gardeners.

Lambeth Palace ❽

SE1. **Map** 21 C1. ➡ *Lambeth North,
Westminster, Waterloo, Vauxhall.* **Not
open** *to the public.*

THIS HAS BEEN the London
base of the Archbishop of
Canterbury, the senior cleric
in the Church of England, for
800 years. The chapel and its
undercroft contain elements
from the 13th century, but a
large part of the rest of the
building is far more
recent. It has been
frequently restored,
most recently by
Edward Blore in 1828.
The Tudor gatehouse,
however, dates from
1485 and is one of
London's most
pleasing and
familiar riverside
landmarks.
Until the first
Westminster Bridge
was built, the
horse ferry that operated
between here and Millbank
was a principal river crossing.
The revenues from it went to
the Archbishop, who received
compensation for loss of
business when the bridge
opened in 1750.

The Tudor gatehouse

Imperial War Museum ❾

Lambeth Rd SE1. **Map** 22 E1.
📞 *020-7416 5000.* 📠 *020-7820
1683.* ➡ *Lambeth North, Elephant
& Castle.* **Open** *10am–6pm daily.*
Closed *24–26 Dec.* **Adm charge**,
*free for children and OAPs, free after
4.30pm.* 📷 ♿ 🍴
📖 📹 *Filmshows, lectures.*
🌐 *www.iwm.org.uk*

IN SPITE OF THE TWO colossal
guns that point up the
drive from the main entrance,
this is not just a display of the
engines of modern warfare.
Massive tanks, artillery, bombs
and aircraft *are* on show, yet
some of the most fascinating
exhibits in the museum relate
more to the impact on the lives
of people at home than to the
business of fighting. There are
displays about food rationing,
air raid precautions, censor-
ship and morale-boosting.
The arts are well represented,
with extracts from wartime
films, radio programmes and
literature, plus many

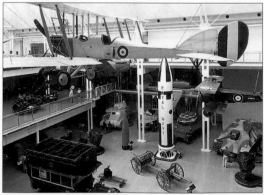

The machinery of war through the ages

hundreds of photographs, paintings by Graham Sutherland and Paul Nash, and sculpture by Jacob Epstein. Henry Moore did some evocative drawings of life during the Blitz of 1940, when many Londoners slept in underground stations in order to protect themselves from falling bombs.

The museum is kept up to date with exhibits relating to recent military engagements of British forces, including the Gulf War of 1991. It is housed in part of what used to be Bethlehem Hospital for the Insane ("Bedlam"), built in 1811. In the 19th century, visitors would come for the afternoon to enjoy the antics of the patients. The hospital moved out to new premises in Surrey in 1930, leaving this vast building empty. Its two large, flanking wings were pulled down and this central block converted into the museum which moved here from its former South Kensington site in 1936.

The memorial to the dead of World War I at Waterloo Station

The Old Vic's facade from 1816

Old Vic 🔟

Waterloo Rd SE1. **Map** 14 E5.
📞 020-7928 7616. 📠 020-7928 7618. 🚇 Waterloo. **Open** for performances only. 🎭 See **Entertainment** pp328–9.

THIS SPLENDID building dates from 1816, when it was opened as the Royal Coburg Theatre. In 1833 the name was changed to the Royal Victoria in honour of the future queen. Shortly after this the theatre became a centre for "music hall", the immensely popular Victorian entertainment in which singers, comedians and other acts were introduced by a chairman, who needed a booming voice to control unruly audiences.

In 1912 Lillian Baylis took over as manager and in 1914 introduced Shakespearean plays to the Old Vic. From 1914 to 1923 she staged all of Shakespeare's plays here. Between 1963 and 1976 it was the first home of the National Theatre *(see p184)*. In 1983 it was sold to Ed Mirvish who restored it. Since then it has operated as a conventional West End theatre.

Gabriel's Wharf 1️⃣1️⃣

56 Upper Ground SE1. **Map** 14 E3.
🚇 Waterloo. See **Shops and Markets** pp324–5.

THIS PLEASANT enclave of boutiques, craft shops and cafés was the product of a long and stormy debate over the future of what was once an industrial riverside area. Residents of Waterloo strongly opposed various schemes for office developments before a community association was able to acquire the site in 1984 and build co-operative housing around the wharf.

Adjoining the market is a small garden and a riverside walkway with marvellous views to the north of the City. The "OXO tower" to the east, built in 1928 surreptitiously to advertise a meat extract by means of its window shapes, is now the setting for a fine restaurant *(see p296)*.

Waterloo Station 1️⃣2️⃣

York Rd SE1. **Map** 14 D4.
📞 0345 484950 🚇 Waterloo. See **Getting to London** pp358–9.

THE TERMINUS FOR trains to southwest England, Waterloo station was originally built in 1848 but completely remodelled in the early 20th century, with the addition of a grand formal entrance on the northeast corner. Today the spacious concourse, lined with shops, cafés and bars, makes it one of the most practical of the London rail terminals

Towards the end of the 20th century the station was enlarged again to serve as London's first Channel Tunnel rail link to Europe. Despite the controversy surrounding the rail link when it was first built, it is now the favoured mode of travel to Europe for many people. The area around Waterloo has a great community feel and it is worth passing down Bayliss Street with its shops, eateries and street market.

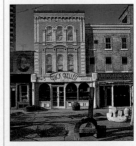

Illusionistic painting on the buildings around Gabriel's Wharf

CHELSEA

THE SHOWY young shoppers who paraded along the King's Road from the 1960s until the 1980s have more or less gone, along with Chelsea's reputation for extreme behaviour established by the bohemian

Cow's head outside the Old Dairy on Old Church Street

Chelsea Set of writers and artists in the 19th century. Formerly a riverside village, Chelsea became fashionable in Tudor times. Henry VIII liked it so much that he built a small palace (long vanished) here. Artists, including Turner, Whistler and Rossetti, were attracted by the river views from

Cheyne Walk. The historian Thomas Carlyle and the essayist Leigh Hunt arrived in the 1830s and began a literary tradition continued by writers such as the poet Swinburne. Yet Chelsea has always had a raffish element, too: in the 18th century the pleasure gardens were noted for beautiful courtesans and the Chelsea Arts Club has had riotous balls for nearly a century. Chelsea is too expensive for most artists now, but the artistic connection is maintained by many galleries and antique shops.

SIGHTS AT A GLANCE

Historic Streets and Buildings
King's Road ❶
Carlyle's House ❷
Cheyne Walk ❺
Royal Hospital ❽
Sloane Square ❾

Museums
National Army Museum ❼

Churches
Chelsea Old Church ❸

Gardens
Roper's Garden ❹
Chelsea Physic Garden ❻

GETTING THERE
The District and Circle Underground lines serve Sloane Square; the Piccadilly line passes just outside this area, through South Kensington. Buses 11, 19 and 22 all stop on the King's Road.

SEE ALSO

• *Street Finder*, maps 19, 20

• *Where to Stay* pp272–285

• *Restaurants, Pubs* pp286–311

• *Chelsea and Battersea Walk* pp266–7

No. 56 Oakley Street, where the polar explorer, R F Scott, once lived

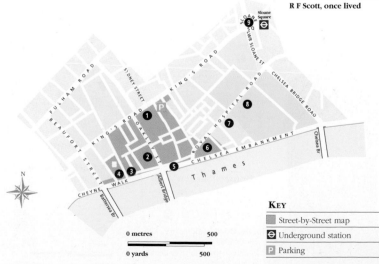

KEY

▢ Street-by-Street map

Ⓔ Underground station

Ⓟ Parking

0 metres 500

0 yards 500

Picturesque Chelsea residences in a cul-de-sac off the King's Road

Street-by-Street: Chelsea

Once a peaceful riverside village, Chelsea has been fashionable since Tudor times when Sir Thomas More, Henry VIII's Lord Chancellor, lived here. Artists, including Turner, Whistler and Rossetti, were attracted by the views from Cheyne Walk, before a busy main road disturbed its peace. Chelsea's

King's Road
In the 1960s and 1970s it was the boutique-lined centre of fashionable London and is still a main shopping street ❶

artistic connection is maintained by its galleries and antique shops, while enclaves of 18th-century houses preserve its old village atmosphere.

The Old Dairy, at 46 Old Church Street, was built in 1796, when cows still grazed in the surrounding fields. The tiling is original.

To King's Road

Carlyle's House
The historian and philosopher lived here from 1834 until his death in 1882 ❷

Chelsea Old Church
Although severely damaged during World War II, it still holds some fine Tudor monuments ❸

Roper's Garden
It includes a sculpture by Jacob Epstein who had a studio here ❹

Thomas More, sculpted in 1969 by L Cubitt Bevis, gazes calmly across the river near where he lived.

STAR SIGHT

★ **Chelsea Physic Garden**

KEY

- - - - Suggested route

0 metres   100

0 yards   100

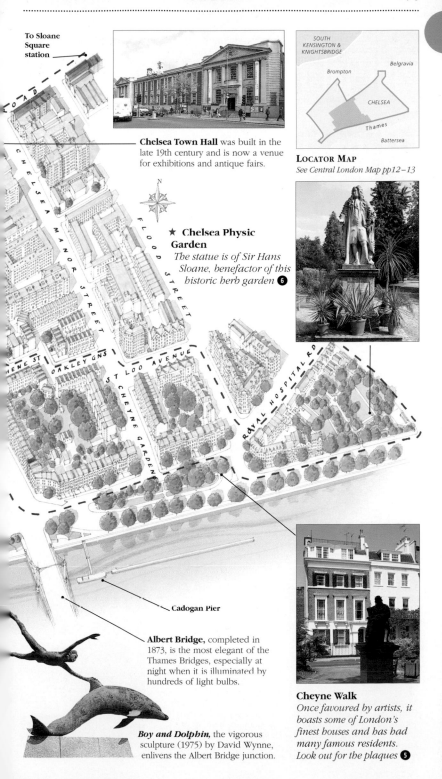

To Sloane
Square
station

Chelsea Town Hall was built in the late 19th century and is now a venue for exhibitions and antique fairs.

SOUTH
KENSINGTON &
KNIGHTSBRIDGE

Brompton

Belgravia

CHELSEA

Thames

Battersea

LOCATOR MAP
See Central London Map pp12–13

★ **Chelsea Physic Garden**
The statue is of Sir Hans Sloane, benefactor of this historic herb garden **6**

Cadogan Pier

Albert Bridge, completed in 1873, is the most elegant of the Thames Bridges, especially at night when it is illuminated by hundreds of light bulbs.

Cheyne Walk
Once favoured by artists, it boasts some of London's finest houses and has had many famous residents. Look out for the plaques **5**

Boy and Dolphin, the vigorous sculpture (1975) by David Wynne, enlivens the Albert Bridge junction.

The Pheasantry, King's Road

King's Road ❶

SW3 and SW10. **Map** 19 B3.
🚇 *Sloane Square. See* **Shops and Markets** *pp312–25.*

THIS IS CHELSEA'S central artery, with its wealth of small fashion shops packed with young people looking for avant-garde fashions. The mini-skirt revolution of the 1960s began here and so have many subsequent style trends, perhaps the most famous of them being punk.

Look out for the Pheasantry at No. 152, with its columns and statuary. It was built in 1881 as the shop-front of a furniture maker's premises but now conceals a modern restaurant. Antique-lovers will find three warrens of stalls on the south side of the King's Road: Antiquarius at No. 137, the Chenil Galleries at Nos. 181–3 and the Chelsea Antiques Market at No. 253.

Carlyle's House ❷

24 Cheyne Row SW3. **Map** 19 B4.
📞 020-7352 7087. 🚇 *Sloane Square, South Kensington.* **Open** *Apr–Nov: 11am–5pm Wed–Sun, public hols (last adm: 4.30pm).* **Closed** *Good Fri.* **Adm charge.** 🚫 📷 *by arrangement.*

THE HISTORIAN, and founder of the London Library *(see St James's Square p96)*, Thomas Carlyle moved into this modest 18th-century house in 1834, and wrote many of his best-known books here, most notably *The French Revolution*

and *Frederick the Great*. His presence made Chelsea more fashionable and the house became a mecca for some of the great literary figures of the 19th century. The novelists Charles Dickens and William Thackeray, poet Alfred Lord Tennyson, naturalist Charles Darwin and philosopher John Stuart Mill were all regular visitors here. The house has been restored so that it looks as it did during Carlyle's lifetime, and is now a museum dedicated to his life and work.

Chelsea Old Church ❸

Cheyne Walk SW3. **Map** 19 A4. 📞
020-7795 1019. 🚇 *Sloane Square, South Kensington.* **Open** *10am–1pm, 2–5pm Mon–Sat, 1.30–6pm Sun.* ♿
📷 *most days.* ✝ *10am, 11am Sun.*

Chelsea Old Church in 1860

REBUILT AFTER World War II, this square-towered building does not look old from the outside. However, early prints confirm that it is a careful replica of the medieval church that was destroyed by World War II bombs.

The glory of this church is its Tudor monuments. One to Sir Thomas More, who built a chapel here in 1528, contains an inscription he wrote (in Latin), asking to be buried next to his wife. Among other monuments is a chapel to Sir Thomas Lawrence, who was an Elizabethan merchant, and a 17th-century memorial to Lady Jane Cheyne, after whose husband Cheyne Walk was named. Outside the church is a statue in memory of Sir Thomas More, "statesman, scholar, saint", gazing piously across the river.

Roper's Garden ❹

Cheyne Walk SW3. **Map** 19 A4.
🚇 *Sloane Square, South Kensington.*

THIS IS A SMALL PARK outside Chelsea Old Church. It is named after Margaret Roper, Sir Thomas More's daughter, and her husband William, who wrote More's biography. The sculptor Sir Jacob Epstein worked at a studio on the site between 1909 and 1914, and there is a stone carving by him commemorating the fact. The park also contains a figure of a nude woman by Gilbert Carter.

Cheyne Walk ❺

SW3. **Map** 19 B4. 🚇 *Sloane Square, South Kensington.*

UNTIL CHELSEA Embankment was constructed in 1874, Cheyne Walk was a pleasant riverside promenade. Now it overlooks a busy road that has destroyed much of its charm. Many of the 18th-century houses remain, though, bristling with blue plaques celebrating some of the famous people who have lived in them. Most were writers and artists, including J M W Turner who lived incognito at No. 119, George Eliot who died at No. 4 and a clutch of writers (Henry James, T S Eliot and Ian Fleming) in Carlyle Mansions.

Thomas More on Cheyne Walk

Chelsea Physic Garden 6

Swan Walk SW3. **Map** 19 C4.
📞 020-7352 5646. 🚇 *Sloane Square.* **Open** *Apr–Oct: noon–5pm Wed, 2–6pm Sun.* **Adm charge.**
♿ 💻 *3.15–4.45pm.* 🎫 **Annual exhibition** *during Chelsea Flower Show, see p56.* **Gardening school.**

ESTABLISHED BY the Society of Apothecaries in 1673 to study plants for medicinal use, this garden has survived to the present day. It was saved from closure in 1722 by a gift from Sir Hans Sloane, whose statue adorns it. The garden has since broadened its range of plants but parts of it would be recognizable to Sir Hans today.

Many new varieties have been nurtured in its glasshouses, including cotton sent to the plantations of the southern United States. Today, visitors can see ancient trees, an historical walk and one of Britain's first rock gardens, installed in 1772.

Chelsea Physic Garden in spring

National Army Museum 7

Royal Hospital Rd SW3. **Map** 19 C4.
📞 020-7730 0717. 🚇 *Sloane Square.* **Open** *10am–5.30pm daily.* **Closed** *24–26 Dec, 1 Jan, Good Fri, May Day.* ♿ 💻 🎫

A VIVID AND LIVELY account of the history of British land forces from 1485 to the present day can be found here. Tableaux, dioramas and archive film clips illustrate major engagements and give a taste of what life behind the lines was like. There are fine paintings of battle scenes as well as portraits of soldiers. The attached museum shop offers a good range of military books and model soldiers.

Royal Hospital 8

Royal Hospital Rd SW3. **Map** 20 D3.
📞 020-7730 0161. 🚇 *Sloane Square.* **Open** *8.30am–12.30pm, 2.30–4.30pm Mon–Sat, 2–4pm Sun.* **Closed** *public hols.*

THIS GRACEFUL COMPLEX was commissioned by Charles II from Christopher Wren in 1682 as a retirement home for old or wounded soldiers, who have been known as Chelsea Pensioners ever since. The hospital opened ten years later and is still home to about 400 retired soldiers, who are instantly recognizable in their scarlet coats and tricorne hats, a distinctive uniform which dates from the 17th century.

A Chelsea Pensioner in uniform

Flanking the northern entrance are Wren's two main public rooms: the chapel, which is notable for its wonderful simplicity, and the panelled Great Hall, still used today as the dining room. A small museum explains the history of the Pensioners.

A statue of Charles II by Grinling Gibbons is to be found on the terrace outside, and there is a fine view of the remains of Battersea Power Station across the river.

Sloane Square 9

SW1. **Map** 20 D2. 🚇 *Sloane Square.*

Sloane Square fountain

THIS PLEASANT SMALL square (rectangle to be precise) has a paved centre with a flower stall and fountain depicting Venus. Laid out in the late 18th century, it was named after Sir Hans Sloane, the wealthy physician and collector who bought the manor of Chelsea in 1712. Opposite Peter Jones, the 1936 department store on the square's west side, is the Royal Court Theatre, which for over a century has fostered new drama.

SOUTH KENSINGTON AND KNIGHTSBRIDGE

BRISTLING WITH embassies and consulates, South Kensington and Knightsbridge are among London's most desirable, and expensive, areas. The proximity of Kensington Palace, a royal residence, means they have remained fairly unchanged.

The prestige shops of Knightsbridge serve their wealthy residents. With Hyde Park to the north, and museums that celebrated Victorian learning at its heart, visitors to this part of London can expect to find a unique combination of the serene and the grandiose.

SIGHTS AT A GLANCE

Historic Streets and Buildings
Royal College of Music **5**
Royal College of Art **7**
Kensington Palace **10**
Speakers' Corner **13**

Churches
Brompton Oratory **4**

Museums and Galleries
Natural History Museum pp208–9 **1**
Science Museum pp212–13 **2**
Victoria and Albert Museum pp202–5 **3**

Serpentine Gallery **9**

Parks and Gardens
Kensington Gardens **11**
Hyde Park **12**

Monuments
Albert Memorial **8**
Marble Arch **14**

Concert Halls
Royal Albert Hall **6**

Shops
Harrod's **15**

Decorative relief outside the Natural History Museum

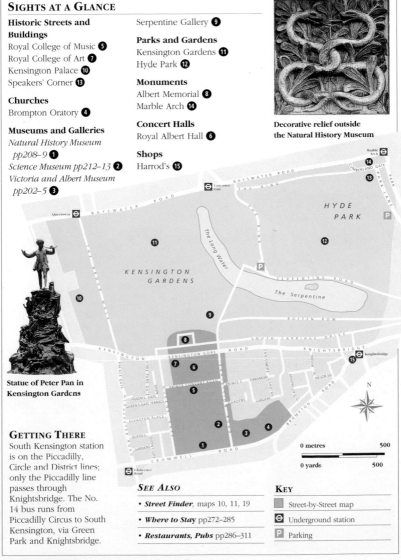

KENSINGTON GARDENS

HYDE PARK

The Long Water

The Serpentine

Statue of Peter Pan in Kensington Gardens

GETTING THERE
South Kensington station is on the Piccadilly, Circle and District lines; only the Piccadilly line passes through Knightsbridge. The No. 14 bus runs from Piccadilly Circus to South Kensington, via Green Park and Knightsbridge.

SEE ALSO

KEY
	Street-by-Street map
🚇	Underground station
🅿	Parking

0 metres 500
0 yards 500

The Albert Memorial, opposite the Royal Albert Hall

Street-by-Street: South Kensington

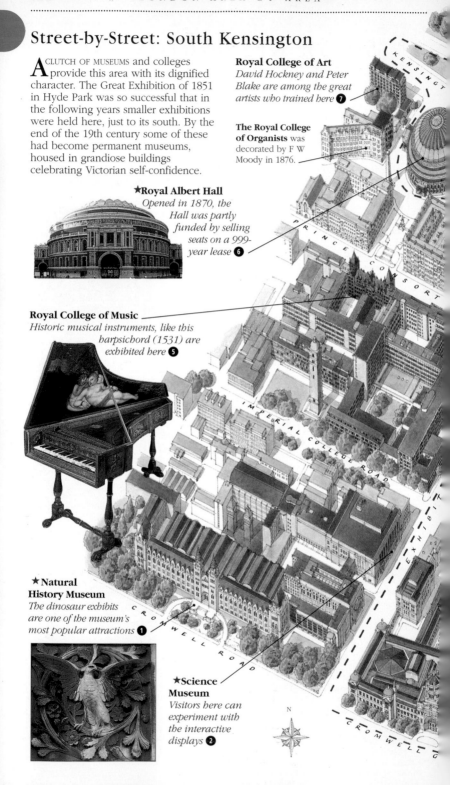

A CLUTCH OF MUSEUMS and colleges provide this area with its dignified character. The Great Exhibition of 1851 in Hyde Park was so successful that in the following years smaller exhibitions were held here, just to its south. By the end of the 19th century some of these had become permanent museums, housed in grandiose buildings celebrating Victorian self-confidence.

Royal College of Art
David Hockney and Peter Blake are among the great artists who trained here **7**

The Royal College of Organists was decorated by F W Moody in 1876.

★Royal Albert Hall
Opened in 1870, the Hall was partly funded by selling seats on a 999-year lease **6**

Royal College of Music
Historic musical instruments, like this harpsichord (1531) are exhibited here **5**

★Natural History Museum
The dinosaur exhibits are one of the museum's most popular attractions **1**

★Science Museum
Visitors here can experiment with the interactive displays **2**

N

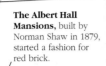

The Albert Hall Mansions, built by Norman Shaw in 1879, started a fashion for red brick.

Albert Memorial
This memorial was built to commemorate Queen Victoria's consort **8**

LOCATOR MAP
See Central London Map pp12–13

KEY

– – – Suggested route

0 metres   100

0 yards   100

The Royal Geographical Society was founded in 1830. Scottish missionary and explorer David Livingstone (1813–73) was a member.

Imperial College, part of London University, is one of the country's leading scientific institutions.

★ Victoria and Albert Museum
A range of objects and a stunning photo gallery illustrate the nation's history of design and decoration **3**

Brompton Oratory
The Oratory was built during the 19th-century Catholic revival **4**

Brompton Square, begun in 1821, established this as a fashionable residential area.

Holy Trinity church dates from the 19th-century and is located in a calm backwater among cottages.

To Knightsbridge station

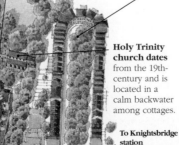

STAR SIGHTS

★ **Victoria and Albert Museum**

★ **Natural History Museum**

★ **Science Museum**

★ **Royal Albert Hall**

Victoria and Albert Museum ❸

Main entrance

THE VICTORIA AND ALBERT MUSEUM (or V&A) contains one of the world's widest collections of decorative arts. The exhibits range from early Christian devotional objects to Doc Marten boots, from the paintings of John Constable to the mystical art of southeast Asia. The V&A also houses impressive collections of sculpture, water-colours, jewellery and musical instruments. The recently opened British Galleries tell the story of Britain's culture – its design, art, society and taste – from 1500 to 1900.

Twentieth-Century Gallery
This gallery shows modern design like Daniel Weil's Radio in a Bag *(1983).*

GALLERY GUIDE
The V&A has a 7-mile (11-km) labyrinthine layout of 145 galleries occupying four main floor levels. Galleries are devoted to a particular culture or time period, for example the Italian Renaissance, or to a specific material or form of art. The ground floor contains fine collections of non-Western art representing the cultures of Japan, China, India and the Islamic world. Also on the ground floor are Medieval and Renaissance treasures, post-Classical sculpture and the Costume Court. The new British Galleries are on the first and second floors. Galleries devoted to glass, silver, cera-mics, ironwork and textiles are on the upper levels. The Henry Cole wing is situated on the northwest side of the main building and contains the Museum's collections of paintings, drawings, prints and photographs. It also houses the Frank Lloyd Wright Gallery.

★ British Galleries
In these recently opened galleries, dis-plays of evocative objects, such as King Henry VIII's writing desk, illustrate Britain's fascinating history.

Henry Cole Wing

Exhibition Road entrance

Constable Collection
Located in the Henry Cole Wing, A Windmill Among Houses by John Constable (1776–1837) vividly captures the East Anglian landscape.

KEY TO FLOORPLAN

☐	Lower ground floor
☐	Ground floor
☐	Upper ground floor
☐	First floor
☐	Upper first floor
☐	Second floor
☐	Henry Cole Wing

STAR EXHIBITS

★ **British Galleries**

★ **Dress Collection**

★ **Medieval Treasury**

★ **Morris and Gamble Rooms**

★ **Nehru Gallery of Indian Art**

★ **Morris and Gamble Rooms**
The Victorian decorations here draw on past styles and the modern materials of an industrial age.

VISITORS' CHECKLIST

Cromwell Rd SW7. **Map** 19 A1.
📞 020-7942 2000.
📠 0870 442 0808.
🚇 South Kensington. 🚌 14, 74, C1. **Open** 10am–5.45pm daily (10am–10pm Wed and last Fri of every month). **Closed** 24–26 Dec. ♿ 🎧 🚻 🍴 🛍
Lectures, presentations, concerts, exhibitions, events.
🌐 www.vam.ac.uk

T T Tsui Gallery of Chinese Art
This ancestor portrait, in watercolour on silk, is from the Qing Dynasty (1644–1912).

Pirelli Garden

★ **Medieval Treasury**
The Eltenberg Reliquary (c.1180) is one of the museum's masterpieces of medieval craftsmanship.

★ **Nehru Gallery of Indian Art**
Much of this collection dates from when Britain ruled India. The Emperor Shah Jehan's jade wine cup was made in 1657.

Main entrance

★ **Dress Collection**
Clothing here dates from 1600 to the present. This dress is from the 1880s.

Exploring the V&A's Collections

THE V&A WAS FOUNDED in 1852 as a Museum of Manufactures to inspire students of design. It was renamed by Queen Victoria, in memory of Prince Albert, in 1899. Many of the exhibits originate from parts of the British Empire, and among the wealth of artefacts is the greatest collection of Indian art outside India. The museum also houses the National Art Library, which contains works on aspects of art and design, items illustrating the art of book production since the Middle Ages, and artists' diaries and correspondence.

German Castle Cup (15th century)

BRITISH GALLERIES

A SEQUENCE OF grand rooms on the first and second floors are devoted to the British Galleries, the biggest attraction of the museum. Four hundred years of design, from 1500 to 1900, chart Britain's rise from obscurity to becoming the "workshop of the world". Four themes run through the displays, which are arranged chronologically; *Style* explores the way things looked; *Who led Taste?* identifies the periods' leading figures; *What was New?* examines the evolution of design; and *Fashionable Living* looks at changing habits and lifestyles. The Great Bed of Ware *(see box)*, James II's wedding suit, Roubiliac's statue of Handel, and numerous designs by Robert Adam, William Morris, Thomas Chippendale, and Charles Rennie Mackintosh are among the galleries' highlights. Interactive displays explain the making and workings of many interesting objects.

SCULPTURE

POST-CLASSICAL sculpture can be found across twenty six galleries, one of which features a marble relief of *The Ascension* by Donatello. Alabasters, ivories, bronzes and casts are also on view, plus various pieces from India, the Middle East and the Far East.

CERAMICS AND GLASS

EXAMPLES OF 2,000 years of pottery, porcelain and glass are exhibited across numerous galleries. These contain superb porcelain from major European china factories such as Meissen, Sèvres, Royal Copenhagen and Royal Worcester; stained glass, including some lovely medieval "Labours of the Months"; studio pottery, with rare pieces by William De Morgan, Picasso and Bernard Leach; and intricately patterned Persian and Turkish tiles.

Russian porcelain (1862)

METALWORK

INTRICATELY WROUGHT CUPS and decanters, medals, arms and armour, hunting horns, watches and clocks are among more than 35,000 objects from Europe and the Near East which are on display across 22 of the museum's galleries. Highlights include the 16th-century Burghley Nef (Room 26), a great silver salt cellar which was used to indicate the position of the host at the dinner table; and the 15th-century German Castle Cup (Room 27), a castellated, turreted copper gilt extravaganza. The new English Silver galleries also explore the history and techniques of silver making.

THE GREAT BED OF WARE

Made in about 1590 of oak with inlaid and painted decoration, the Great Bed of Ware measures some 3.6 by 3.6 m (12 by 12 ft) and is 2.6 m (8 ft 9 inches) high. It is the V&A's most celebrated piece of furniture. Elaborately carved and decorated, the bed is a superb example of the art of the English woodworker. Its name derives from the town of Ware in Hertfordshire, about a day's ride north of London, where it resided in a number of inns. The Great Bed's enormous size made it an early tourist attraction, and no doubt interest was boosted by Shakespeare's reference to it in *Twelfth Night*, which he wrote in 1601.

Recently re-decorated and re-furbished, the bed is located in the British Galleries.

Tippoo's Tiger, carved in wood for the Sultan of Mysore in about 1790, is depicted mauling a European soldier.

INDIAN ART

THE NEHRU GALLERY of Indian Art forms the centrepiece of the museum's extensive collection of Indian art from 1550 to 1900, a period that includes the opulent Mughal Empire and the India of the British Raj. Textiles, weapons, jewellery, metalwork, glass and paintings, both secular and religious, are on display. Highlights of the collection include a Mughal tent of hanging painted cotton (1640) decorated with birds, trees and a double-headed eagle (Room 41). Also look out for an 11th-century bronze depicting the Hindu deity Shiva as Lord of the Eternal Dance (Room 47B).

Indian panel of painted and dyed cotton from the 18th century

TEXTILES AND DRESS

THE WORLD-RENOWNED Dress Collection, displayed in Room 40, is devoted to fashionable clothing from about 1600 to the present day. The figures are fully dressed, complete with accessories; in addition, small cases display collections of such items as buttons, shoes, hats and parasols. The scope of the textile collection, displayed in 18 galleries, is very broad,

starting with ancient Egypt. English textiles of the last three centuries are particularly well represented.

The four great medieval tapestries in Room 94, from the collection of the Duke of Devonshire, depict fascinating scenes of courtly pastimes, while the Syon Cope, from 1300–20, is an exquisite example of *opus anglicanum*, a type of English embroidery which was popular in Europe during the Middle Ages.

FAR EASTERN ART

EIGHT GALLERIES are devoted to the arts of China, Japan, Korea and other Far Eastern countries. Under a dramatic arc of burnished steel fins representing the spine of a Chinese dragon, the T T Tsui Gallery of Chinese Art shows how the artefacts displayed would have been used in everyday life. Among the highlights of the collection are a giant Buddha's head from 700–900 AD, a huge Ming canopied bed, and rare jade and ceramics (Room 44). Japanese art is concentrated in the Toshiba Gallery, which is particularly notable for lacquer, ceramics, textiles,

Mantle for Buddhist priest from the mid-19th century

Samurai armour and woodblock prints. Especially fine exhibits include a 17th-century wooden writing table inlaid with gold and silver lacquer and the Akita Armour, dating from 1714, both in Room 38A.

PAINTINGS, PRINTS, DRAWINGS AND PHOTOGRAPHS

MOST OF THESE collections are housed in the Henry Cole Wing. Highlights include British paintings from 1700 to 1900, English portrait miniatures, European paintings from 1500 to 1900, and the largest collection of works by John Constable. The Print Room is a public study room with more than half a million watercolours, engravings, etchings and ephemera. In the main museum, the Raphael Gallery displays seven tapestry designs by the artist.

Nicholas Hilliard's *A Young Man Among Roses* (1588)

Natural History Museum ❶

See pp208–9.

Relief: Natural History Museum

Science Museum ❷

See pp212–13.

Victoria and Albert Museum ❸

See pp202–205.

Brompton Oratory ❹

Brompton Rd SW7. **Map** 19 A1.
020-7808 0900. South
Kensington. **Open** 6.30am–8pm daily.
11am Sun sung Latin Mass.

THE ITALIANATE Oratory is a rich (some think a little too rich) monument to the English Catholic revival of the late 19th century. The Oratory was established by John Henry Newman (who later became Cardinal Newman). Father Frederick William Faber (1814–63) had already founded a London community of priests at Charing Cross. The community had moved to Brompton, then an outlying London district, and this was to be its oratory. Newman and Faber (both Anglican converts to Catholicism) were following the example of St Philip Neri, who established a community of secular priests living without vows and based in large cities.

The present church was opened in 1884. Its facade and dome were added in the 1890s, and the interior has been progressively enriched ever since. Herbert Gribble, the architect, who was yet another new convert to Catholicism, was only 29 when he triumphed in the highly prestigious competition to design it. Inside, all the most eye-catching treasures predate the church – many of them were transported here from Italian churches. Giuseppe Mazzuoli carved the huge marble figures of the 12 apostles for Siena Cathedral in the late 17th century. The beautifully elaborate Lady Altar was originally created in 1693 for the Dominican church in Brescia, and the 18th-century altar in St Wilfrid's Chapel was actually imported from Rochefort in Belgium.

The Oratory has always been famous for its splendid musical tradition.

Royal College of Music ❺

Prince Consort Rd SW7. **Map** 10 F5.
020-7589 3643. High St
Kensington, Knightsbridge, South
Kensington. **Museum of Musical
Instruments open** 2–4.30pm Wed
in term time. **Adm charge.**

SIR ARTHUR BLOMFIELD designed the turretted Gothic palace, with Bavarian overtones, that has housed this distinguished institution since 1894. The college was founded in 1882 by George Grove, who also compiled the famous *Dictionary of Music*; famous pupils have included English composers Benjamin Britten and Ralph Vaughan Williams. You have to be smart to catch the Museum of Musical Instruments, which is rarely open; but, if you do manage to get in, you will see instruments from the earliest times and from many parts of the world. Some of the exhibits were played by such greats as Handel and Haydn.

17th-century viol at the Royal College of Music

The sumptuous interior of Brompton Oratory

Joseph Durham's statue of Prince Albert (1858) by the Royal Albert Hall

Royal Albert Hall ❻

Kensington Gore SW7. **Map** 10 F5.
☎ 020-7589 3203. ☻ *High St
Kensington, South Kensington
Knightsbridge.* **Open** *for
performances.* 🚫 ♿ 🅿 *See
Entertainment pp332–3.*

DESIGNED BY AN engineer,
Francis Fowke, and
completed in 1871, this huge
concert hall was modelled on
Roman amphitheatres and is
easier on the eye than most
Victorian structures. On the
red-brick exterior the only
ostentation is a pretty frieze
symbolizing the triumph of
arts and science. In plans the
building was called the Hall
of Arts and Science but
Queen Victoria changed it to
the Albert Hall, in memory of
her husband, when she laid
the foundation stone in 1868.
  The hall is often used for
Classical concerts, most
famously the "Proms", but it
also accommodates every

other kind of large gathering
such as boxing matches (first
held here in 1919), comedy
shows, rock concerts and
major business conferences.

Royal College of Art ❼

Kensington Gore SW7. **Map** 10 F5.
☎ 020-7590 4444. ☻ *High St
Kensington, South Kensington,
Knightsbridge.* **Open** *10am–6pm
Mon–Fri (phone first).* 🅿 🚻
*Lectures, events, film
presentations, exhibitions.*

SIR HUGH CASSON'S mainly
glass-fronted building
(1973) is in stark contrast to
the Victoriana around it. The
college was founded in 1837
as a school of design and
practical art for the manufac-
turing industries. It became
noted for modern art in the
1950s and 1960s when David
Hockney, Peter Blake and
Eduardo Paolozzi were there.

Albert Memorial ❽

South Carriage Drive, Kensington
Gdns SW7. **Map** 10 F5. ☻ *High St
Kensington, Knightsbridge, South
Kensington.*

THIS GRANDIOSE but dignified
memorial to Queen
Victoria's beloved consort was
completed in 1876, 15 years
after his death. Albert was a
German prince and a cousin of
Queen Victoria's. When he
died from typhoid in 1861 he
was only 41 and they had been
happily married for 21 years,
producing nine children. It is
fitting that the monument is
near the site of the 1851
Exhibition *(see pp26–7)*, for
Prince Albert was closely
identified with the Exhibition
itself and with the scientific
advances it celebrated. The
larger than life statue, by John
Foley, shows him with an exhibition catalogue on his knee.
  The desolate Queen chose
Sir George Gilbert Scott to
design the monument which
stands 55 m (175 ft) high. It is
loosely based on a medieval
market cross – although many
times more elaborate, with a
black and gilded spire, multi-
coloured marble canopy,
stones, mosaics, enamels,
wrought iron and nearly 200
sculpted figures. In October
1998 the re-gilded statue was
unveiled by Elizabeth II, it had
not been gilded since 1915
when it was painted black to
avoid attracting attention during
World War I.

Victoria and Albert at the Great
Exhibition opening (1851)

Natural History Museum ❶

Museum's main entrance

LIFE ON EARTH and the Earth itself are vividly explained at the Natural History Museum. Combining the latest interactive techniques with traditional displays, the exhibits tackle some fundamental issues, such as the delicate ecology of our planet and its gradual evolution over millions of years, the origin of species and how human beings evolved. The vast, cathedral-like museum building is a masterpiece in itself. It opened in 1881 and was designed by Alfred Waterhouse using revolutionary Victorian building techniques. It is built on an iron and steel framework concealed behind arches and columns, richly decorated with sculptures of plants and animals.

★ **Creepy Crawlies**
Eight out of ten animal species are arthropods from the world of insects and spiders, like this tarantula.

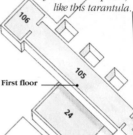

First floor

Ground floor

★ **Dinosaurs**
The killer dinosaur Deinonychus is one of the life-size robotic models in the museum.

Cromwell Road entrance – Life Galleries

Access to basement

GALLERY GUIDE
The museum is divided into two sets of galleries, the Life Galleries and the Earth Galleries. A 26-m (85-ft) skeleton of the dinosaur Diplodocus dominates the entrance hall (10) in the Life Galleries – the Dinosaur Exhibition (21), together with Human Biology (22) and Mammals (23–24), is to the left of the hall, with Creepy Crawlies (33) and Ecology (32) to the right. Reptiles and Fish (12) are behind the main hall. On the first floor are found Origin of Species (105) and Minerals and Meteorites (102–3).

The giant escalator in Visions of Earth (60) leads through a stunning globe to Earth Galleries highlights The Power Within (61) and Earth's Treasury (64).

★ **Ecology**
A small rainforest buzzing with the sounds of life begins an exploration of the complex web of the natural world and man's role in it.

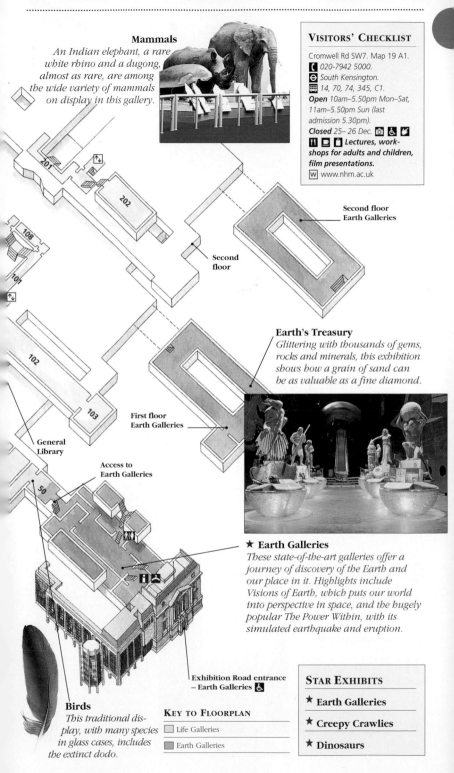

Mammals
An Indian elephant, a rare white rhino and a dugong, almost as rare, are among the wide variety of mammals on display in this gallery.

VISITORS' CHECKLIST

Cromwell Rd SW7. Map 19 A1.
📞 020-7942 5000.
⊖ South Kensington.
🚌 14, 70, 74, 345, C1.
Open 10am–5.50pm Mon–Sat, 11am–5.50pm Sun (last admission 5.30pm).
Closed 25–26 Dec. 🔲 🔲 🔲
🔲 🔲 🔲 *Lectures, work-shops for adults and children, film presentations.*
🔲 www.nhm.ac.uk

Second floor Earth Galleries

Second floor

Earth's Treasury
Glittering with thousands of gems, rocks and minerals, this exhibition shows how a grain of sand can be as valuable as a fine diamond.

First floor Earth Galleries

General Library

Access to Earth Galleries

★ Earth Galleries
These state-of-the-art galleries offer a journey of discovery of the Earth and our place in it. Highlights include Visions of Earth, which puts our world into perspective in space, and the hugely popular The Power Within, with its simulated earthquake and eruption.

Exhibition Road entrance – Earth Galleries ♿

Birds
This traditional display, with many species in glass cases, includes the extinct dodo.

KEY TO FLOORPLAN
◻ Life Galleries
◻ Earth Galleries

STAR EXHIBITS

★ **Earth Galleries**

★ **Creepy Crawlies**

★ **Dinosaurs**

Statue of young Queen Victoria by her daughter Princess Louise outside Kensington Palace

Serpentine Gallery **9**

Kensington Gdns W2. **Map** 10 F4. 020-7402 6075. ⊖ *Lancaster Gate, South Kensington.* **Open** *10am–6pm daily.* **Closed** *for exhibition installations, Christmas week.* ♿ 🛍 *major art bookshop.* **Lectures** *on current exhibition 3pm Sat.*

IN THE SOUTHEAST corner of Kensington Gardens is the Serpentine Gallery, which houses temporary exhibitions of contemporary painting and sculpture. The building is a former tea pavilion built in 1912; exhibits often spill out into the surrounding park. Its tiny bookshop has a remarkable stock of art books.

Kensington Palace **10**

Kensington Palace Gdns W8. **Map** 10 D4. 020-7937 9561. ⊖ *High St Kensington, Queensway.* **Open** *Summer: 10am–6pm daily; Winter: 10am–5pm daily (last adm: 1 hr earlier).* **Closed** *22–26 Dec, 1 Jan, Good Fri.* **Adm charge.** 🚫 ♿ *ground floor only.* 🖥 🛍 **Exhibitions, holiday activities.**

HALF OF THIS SPACIOUS palace is used as lavish royal apartments; the other half, which includes the 18th-century state rooms, is open to the public. When William III and his wife Mary came to the throne in 1689 they bought a mansion, dating from 1605, and commissioned Christopher

Wren to convert it into a royal palace. He created separate suites of rooms for the king and queen, and today visiting members of public use the queen's entrance.

Highlights include the finely decorated state rooms and, on the ground floor, an exhibition of court dress from 1760 to the present.

The palace has seen some important royal events. In 1714 Queen Anne died here from a fit of apoplexy brought on by over-eating and, on 20 June 1837, Princess Victoria of Kent was woken at 5am to be told that her uncle William IV had died and she was now queen – the start of her 64-year reign. After the death in 1997 of Diana, Princess of Wales, the gates became a focal point for mourners in their thousands, who turned the surrounding area into a field of bouquets.

Detail of the Coalbrookdale gate, Kensington Gardens

Henry Moore's *Arch* (1979), Kensington Gardens

Kensington Gardens **11**

W8. **Map** 10 E4. 020-7262 5484. ⊖ *Bayswater, High St Kensington, Queensway, Lancaster Gate.* **Open** *dawn–dusk daily.*

THE FORMER GROUNDS of Kensington Palace became a public park in 1841. A small part of it has been dedicated as a memorial garden to Diana, Princess of Wales (*see p219*). The gardens are full of charm, starting with Sir George Frampton's statue (1912) of J M Barrie's fictional Peter Pan, the boy who never grew up, playing his pipes to the bronze fairies and animals that cling to the column below. Often surrounded by parents, nannies and their charges, the statue stands near the west bank of the Serpentine, not far from where Harriet, wife of the poet Percy Bysshe Shelley drowned herself in 1816. Just north of here are the ornamental fountains and statues, including Jacob Epstein's *Rima*, at the lake's head. George Frederick Watts's statue of a muscular horse and rider, *Physical Energy*, stands to the south. Not far away are a summer house designed by William Kent in 1735, and the Serpentine Gallery.

The Round Pond, created in 1728 just east of the palace, is often packed with model boats navigated by children and older enthusiasts. In winter it is occasionally fit for skating. In the north, near Lancaster Gate, is a dogs' cemetery, started in 1880 by the Duke of Cambridge while mourning one of his pets.

Hyde Park ⓬

W2. **Map** 11 B3. 📞 020-7262 5484. ⊖ Hyde Park Corner, Knightsbridge, Lancaster Gate, Marble Arch. **Open** 5am– midnight daily. ▢ **Sporting facilities**.

Riding on Rotten Row, Hyde Park

THE ANCIENT MANOR of Hyde was part of the lands of Westminster Abbey seized by Henry VIII at the Dissolution of the Monasteries in 1536. It has remained a royal park ever since. Henry used it for hunting but James I opened it to the public in the early 17th century, and it became one of the city's most prized public spaces. The Serpentine, an artificial lake used for boating and bathing, was created when Caroline, George II's queen, dammed the flow of the Westbourne River in 1730.

In its time the park has been a venue for duelling, horse racing, highwaymen, political demonstrations, music (Mick Jagger and Luciano Pavarotti have each had a concert here) and parades. The 1851 Exhibition was held here in a vast glass palace (see pp26–7). The aristocracy drove their carriages on the outer roads.

Speakers' Corner ⓭

Hyde Park W2. **Map** 11 C2. ⊖ Marble Arch.

AN 1872 LAW made it legal to assemble an audience and address them on whatever topic you chose; since then this corner of Hyde Park has become the established venue for budding orators and a fair number of eccentrics. It is well worth spending time here on a Sunday: speakers from fringe groups and one-member political parties reveal their plans for the betterment of mankind while the assembled onlookers heckle them without mercy.

Marble Arch ⓮

Park Lane W1. **Map** 11 C2. ⊖ Marble Arch.

JOHN NASH designed the arch in 1827 as the main entrance to Buckingham Palace. It was, however, too narrow for the grandest coaches and was moved here in 1851. Now, only senior members of the Royal Family and one of the royal artillery regiments are allowed to pass under it.

The arch stands near the site of the old Tyburn gallows (marked by a plaque), where until 1783 the city's most notorious criminals were hanged in front of crowds of bloodthirsty spectators.

An orator at Speakers' Corner

Harrod's ⓯

Knightsbridge SW1. **Map** 11 C5. 📞 020-7730 1234. ⊖ Knightsbridge. **Open** 10am–7pm Mon–Sat. 🚫 ♿ 🍴 ▢ See **Shops and Markets** p313.

LONDON'S MOST famous department store had its beginnings in 1849 when Henry Charles Harrod opened a small grocery shop nearby on Brompton Road. By concentrating on good quality and impeccable service (rather than on low prices) the store was soon popular enough to expand over the surrounding area.

It used to be claimed that Harrod's could supply anything from a packet of pins to an elephant – not quite true today, but the range of stock is still phenomenal.

Harrod's at night, lit by 11,500 lights

Science Museum ❷

CENTURIES OF CONTINUING scientific and technological development lie at the heart of the Science Museum's massive collections. The hardware displayed is magnificent: from steam engines to aeroengines; spacecraft to the very first mechanical computers. Equally important is the social context of science – what discoveries and inventions mean for day-to-day life – and the process of discovery itself. The new Wellcome Wing has an IMAX 3D Cinema and many exciting interactive displays.

Science Museum facade

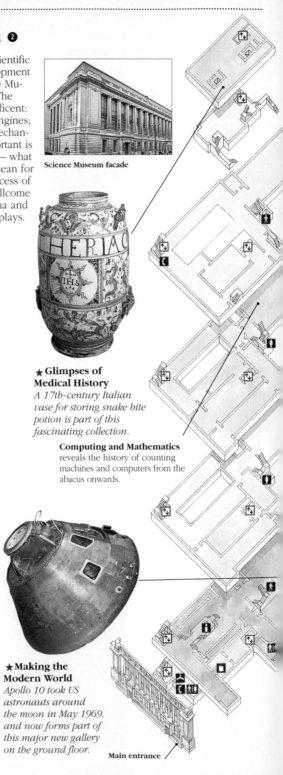

★ Launch Pad
A plasma ball is one of many hands-on exhibits for children in this basement gallery where basic scientific principles are demonstrated.

GALLERY GUIDE
There are seven floors. The Basement features The Garden *for younger children, as well as* Things, Launch Pad *and* The Secret Life of the Home *for older children. Steam power dominates the ground floor; here too are* Space *and* Making the Modern World. *The first floor has the* Challenge of Materials *gallery as well as* Food for Thought. *On the second floor is a range of such diverse galleries as nuclear power, ships, printing and computing. The third floor includes* Flight *and* Science in the 18th Century. *The fourth and fifth floors house the* Science and Art of Medicine *and* Veterinary History *galleries. The new Wellcome Wing has four floors of interactive space devoted to contemporary science and technology.*

★ Glimpses of Medical History
A 17th-century Italian vase for storing snake bite potion is part of this fascinating collection.

Computing and Mathematics reveals the history of counting machines and computers from the abacus onwards.

★ Making the Modern World
Apollo 10 took US astronauts around the moon in May 1969, and now forms part of this major new gallery on the ground floor.

Main entrance

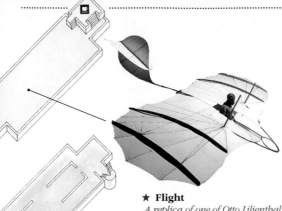

VISITORS' CHECKLIST

Exhibition Rd SW7. **Map** 19 A1.
 020-7942 4000.
 South Kensington. 9, 10,
49, 52, 74, 345, C1.
Open 10am–6pm daily.
Closed 24–26 Dec.
**Lectures, films, workshops,
demonstrations.**
 www.sciencemuseum.org.uk

★ Flight
*A replica of one of Otto Lilienthal's
gliders (1895) is one of the displays
that range from man's early
dreams of flight to today's jets.*

Marine Engineering
*The display of navigational
equipment includes this
ornately decorated circum-
ferentor (1676) by the
architect Joannes Macarius.*

Food for Thought
*The science and social history
of food is explored through
demonstrations and historic
reconstructions in this gallery.*

Picture Gallery
*The second floor has a
display of art on scientific
themes, such as this 16th-
century painting of a comet.*

KEY TO FLOORPLAN

☐	Basement
☐	Ground floor
☐	First floor
☐	Second floor
☐	Third floor
☐	Fourth floor
☐	Fifth floor

★ Challenge of Materials
*Our expectations of materials
are confounded with exhibits
like this steel wedding dress,
or a bridge made of glass.*

STAR EXHIBITS

★ **Launch Pad**

★ **Making the
Modern World**

★ **Challenge of
Materials**

★ **Flight**

★ **Glimpses of
Medical History**

KENSINGTON AND HOLLAND PARK

THE WESTERN and northern perimeters of Kensington Gardens are a rich residential area including many foreign embassies. Here, the shops on Kensington High Street are almost as smart as the ones on Knightsbridge, and Kensington Church Street is a good source of quality antiques. Around Holland Park are some magnificent late Victorian houses, two of them open to the public. But as you cross into Bayswater and Notting Hill you enter a more vibrant, cosmopolitan part of London. Its stucco terraces are lined with medium-priced hotels and a huge number of inexpensive restaurants. Westbourne Grove has become increasingly popular with

Tiled crest from Holland House

the young and trendy crowd. Whiteleys, in Queensway, is one of the many historic buidings in the area. Built in 1912 by Belcher and Joass as a fashionable department store it was converted in the 1980s into a vibrant shopping centre. Further west Portobello Road is a popular street market selling anything from food to antiques. Notting Hill is perhaps best known for its flamboyant Caribbean carnival which took to the streets of London in 1966 and has been staged every year since, during the last weekend in August *(see p57)*.

SIGHTS AT A GLANCE

Historic Streets and Buildings
Holland House **2**
Leighton House **3**
Linley Sambourne House **4**
Kensington Square **6**
Kensington Palace
 Gardens **7**
Queensway **9**

Parks and Gardens
Holland Park **1**
Kensington Roof
 Gardens **5**
The Diana, Princess
 of Wales Memorial
 Playground **8**

Markets
Portobello Road **10**

Historic Areas
Notting Hill **11**

GETTING THERE
The District, Circle and Central lines serve the area. Bus numbers 9, 10, 73, 27, 28, 49, 52, 70, C1, 31 stop on Kensington High Street; 12, 27, 28, 31, 52, 70, 94, go to Notting Hill Gate; and 70, 7, 15, 23, 27, 36, 12, 94 cross Bayswater.

| 0 metres | 500 |
| 0 yards | 500 |

SEE ALSO
- *Street Finder*, maps 9, 17
- *Where to Stay* pp272–285
- *Restaurants, Pubs* pp286–311

KEY
	Street-by-Street map
⊖	Underground station

Entrance to a house in Edwardes Square, Kensington

Street-by-Street: Kensington and Holland Park

ALTHOUGH NOW PART of central London, as recently as the 1830s this was a country village of market gardens and mansions. Outstanding among these was Holland House; part of its grounds are now Holland Park. The area grew up rapidly in the mid-19th century and most of its buildings date from then – mainly expensive apartments, mansion flats and fashionable shops.

Holland House
The rambling Jacobean mansion, started in 1605 and pictured here in 1795, was largely demolished in the 1950s ❷

★ **Holland Park**
Parts of the old formal gardens of Holland House have been retained to grace this delightful public park ❶

The Orangery, now a restaurant, has parts that date from the 1630s when it was in the grounds of Holland House.

Melbury Road is lined with large, Victorian houses. Many were built for fashionable artists of the time.

The Victorian letter box on the High Street is one of the oldest in London.

★ **Leighton House**
It is preserved as it was when the Victorian painter, Lord Leighton, lived here. He had a passion for Middle Eastern tiles ❸

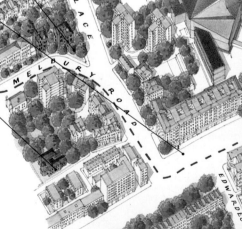

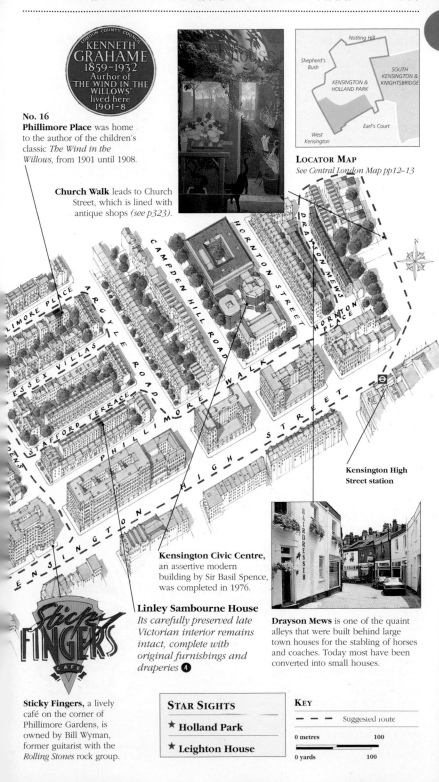

**No. 16
Phillimore Place** was home
to the author of the children's
classic *The Wind in the
Willows*, from 1901 until 1908.

Church Walk leads to Church
Street, which is lined with
antique shops *(see p323)*.

LOCATOR MAP
See Central London Map pp12–13

**Kensington High
Street station**

Kensington Civic Centre,
an assertive modern
building by Sir Basil Spence,
was completed in 1976.

Linley Sambourne House
*Its carefully preserved late
Victorian interior remains
intact, complete with
original furnishings and
draperies* **4**

Drayson Mews is one of the quaint
alleys that were built behind large
town houses for the stabling of horses
and coaches. Today most have been
converted into small houses.

Sticky Fingers, a lively
café on the corner of
Phillimore Gardens, is
owned by Bill Wyman,
former guitarist with the
Rolling Stones rock group.

STAR SIGHTS

★ **Holland Park**

★ **Leighton House**

KEY

‒ ‒ ‒   Suggested route

0 metres   100

0 yards   100

Holland Park ●

Abbotsbury Rd W14. **Map** 9 B4.
[020-7602 9487. ● Holland Park,
High St Kensington, Notting Hill Gate.
Open Apr–late Oct: 7.30am–10pm
daily (but flexible); late Oct–Mar:
7.45am–4.30pm (11pm floodlit areas).
❙❙ ▣ **Open-air opera, theatre,
dance. Art exhibitions** Apr–Oct.
See **Entertainment** pp328–9.

THIS SMALL but delightful
park, more wooded and
intimate than the large royal
parks to its east (Hyde Park
and Kensington Gardens,
see pp206–7), was opened in
1952 on what remained of the
grounds of Holland House –
the rest had been sold off in
the late 19th century for the
construction of large houses
and terraces to the north and
west. The park still contains
some of the formal gardens,
laid out in the early 19th
century for Holland House.
There is also a Japanese
garden, created for the 1991
London Festival of Japan. The
park has an abundance of
wildlife, including peacocks.

Holland House ●

Holland Park W8. **Map** 9 B5.
Youth Hostel [020-7937 0748.
● Holland Park, High Street
Kensington. ♿

Original tiling in Holland House

DURING ITS HEYDAY in the
19th century, this was a
noted centre of social and
political intrigue. Statesmen
such as Lord Palmerston
mixed here with the likes of
the poet Byron. The remains
of the house are now used
as a youth hostel.
  The outhouses are put to
various uses: exhibitions
are held in the orangery and
the ice house (a forerunner of
the fridge), and the old Garden
Ballroom is now a restaurant.

The café in Holland Park

Leighton House ●

12 Holland Park Rd W14. **Map** 17 B1.
[020-7602 3316. ● High St
Kensington. **Open** 11am–5.30pm
Mon, Wed–Sat. **Closed** public hols.
✎ noon Wed–Thu or by arrangement. ❒ **Concerts, exhibitions.**
W www.rbkc.gov.uk/
leightonhousemuseum

BUILT FOR Pre-Raphaelite
painter Lord Leighton in
1866, the house has been
preserved with its opulent
decoration as an extraordinary monument to Victorian
Aesthetics. The highlight is
the Arab hall, added in 1879
to house Leighton's collection
of Islamic tiles, some of which
are inscribed with pieces from
the Koran. The best paintings,
including some by Edward
Burne-Jones, John Millais and
Leighton, can be seen in the
downstairs reception rooms.

Linley Sambourne House ●

18 Stafford Terrace W8. **Map** 9 C5.
[020-8994 1019.
● High St Kensington.
Open Mar–Oct: 10am–4pm Wed,
2–5pm Sun. **Closed** Nov–Feb.
Adm charge. ✗ ❒

THE HOUSE, built in about
1870, has hardly changed
since Linley Sambourne
furnished it in the cluttered
Victorian manner, with china
ornaments and heavy velvet
drapes. Sambourne was a
cartoonist for the satirical
magazine *Punch* and
drawings, including some of

his own, cram the walls.
Some rooms have William
Morris wallpaper (see p249),
and even the lavatory is a
Victorian gem.

Kensington Roof Gardens ●

99 High Street W8 (entrance in Derry
Street). **Map** 10 D5. [020 7937
7994. **Open** 9am–5pm daily (but call
ahead). ▣ ❙❙

A HUNDRED FEET above the
bustle of Kensington High
Street is one of London's best
kept secrets – a 6,000 square-
metre roof garden. First planted
in the 1930s by the owners of
Derry and Toms department
store below (now a branch of
BHS stores), the themed
gardens are a lavish flight of
fancy and feature a woodland
garden (with its own stream),

**Logo for *Punch* magazine
(1841–1992)**

a Spanish garden (with palm trees, fountains and a white-walled convent) and a formal English garden (with a pond, live ducks and a pair of pink flamingos). Best of all, it's free to come up and wander round, though there is no access when the gardens have been booked for events.

Kensington Square 6

W8. **Map** 10 D5. High St Kensington.

THIS IS ONE of London's oldest squares. It was laid out in the 1680s, and a few early 18th-century houses still remain. (Nos. 11 and 12 are the oldest.) The renowned philosopher John Stuart Mill lived at No. 18, and the Pre-Raphaelite painter and illustrator Edward Burne-Jones at No.41.

JOHN STUART MILL 1806-1873 Philosopher Lived Here

Resident's plaque in Kensington Square

Kensington Palace Gardens 7

W8. **Map** 10 D3. High St Kensington, Notting Hill Gate, Queensway.

THIS PRIVATE ROAD of luxury mansions occupies the site of the former kitchen gardens of Kensington Palace (see p210). It changes its name half-way down; the southern part is known as Palace Green. It is open to pedestrians but closed to cars, unless they have specific business here. Most of the houses are occupied by embassies and their staff. At cocktail hour, you can watch black limousines with diplomatic number plates sweep beneath the raised barriers at each end of the road.

Queensway shop front

The Diana, Princess of Wales Memorial Playground 8

Kensington Gardens. **Map** 10 E3. 020 7298 2141. Bayswater, Queensway. **Open** 10am–6.45pm daily.

THE NEWEST OF Kensington Gardens' three playgrounds was opened in 2000 and is dedicated to the memory of the late Princess Diana. Located close to the park's Peter Pan statue (Peter Pan's creator, J M Barrie, funded the first playground to be built here), this innovative new adventure playground takes the boy who didn't want to grow up as its theme and is packed with novel ideas and activities including a beach cove with a 50-ft pirates' galleon, a tree house with walkways and ramps and a mermaid's fountain with a half-submerged slumbering crocodile (careful not to rouse him!). Though all children must be accompanied by an adult, experienced staff are on hand to make sure the children are safe. Many features of the playground, such as the musical garden, have been designed to be accessible to children with special needs.

Queensway 9

W2. **Map** 10 D2. Queensway, Bayswater.

ONE OF LONDON'S most cosmopolitan streets, Queensway has the heaviest concentration of eating places outside Soho. Newsagents are abundantly stocked with foreign newspapers. At the northern end is Whiteley's shopping centre. Founded by William Whiteley, who was born in Yorkshire in 1863, it was probably the world's first department store. The present building dates from 1911.

The street is named after Queen Victoria, who rode here as a princess.

Portobello Road 10

W11. **Map** 9 C3. Notting Hill Gate, Ladbroke Grove. **Antiques market open** 9.30am–4pm Fri, 8am–5pm Sat. See also **Shops and Markets** p325.

THERE HAS been a market here since 1837. These days the southern end consists almost exclusively of stalls that sell antiques, jewellery, souvenirs and many other collectables. The market is extremely popular with tourists and tends to be very crowded on summer week-ends. However, it is well worth visiting just to experience its bustling and cheerful atmosphere even if you don't intend to buy anything. If you do decide to buy, be warned – you are unlikely to get a real bargain, since the stallholders have a sound idea of the value of what they are selling.

Antique shop on Portobello Road

Notting Hill 11

W11. **Map** 9 C3. Notting Hill Gate.

NOW THE HOME of Europe's biggest street carnival, most of this area was farm-land until the 19th century.

In the 1950s and 1960s Notting Hill became a centre for the Caribbean community, many of whom lived here when they first arrived in Britain. The carnival started in 1966 and takes over the area every August over the holiday weekend (see p57) when costumed parades flood through the streets.

REGENT'S PARK AND MARYLEBONE

THE AREA south of Regent's Park, incorporating the medieval village of Marylebone, has London's highest concentration of quality Georgian housing. It was developed by Robert Harley, Earl of Oxford, as London shifted west in the 18th century. Terraces by John Nash adorn the southern edge of Regent's Park, the busiest of the royal parks, while to its northwest lies St John's Wood, a smart inner suburb.

GETTING THERE

Regent's Park and Baker Street are the nearest tube stations. Marylebone is served by tube and rail. Buses 13, 139 and 159 run from Trafalgar Square to near Baker Street, and numerous buses run along Oxford St, Baker St and Gloucester Pl.

SIGHTS AT A GLANCE

Historic Streets and Buildings

Harley Street **4**
Portland Place **5**
Broadcasting House **6**
Cumberland Terrace **15**

Museums and Galleries

Wallace Collection **10**
Sherlock Holmes Museum **11**

Churches and Mosques

St Marylebone Parish Church **3**
All Souls, Langham Place **7**
London Central Mosque **12**

Parks and Gardens

Regent's Park **2**

Entertainment

Madame Tussauds and the Planetarium **1**
Wigmore Hall **9**
London Zoo **14**

Historic Hotels

Langham Hilton Hotel **8**

Historic Waterways

Regent's Canal **13**

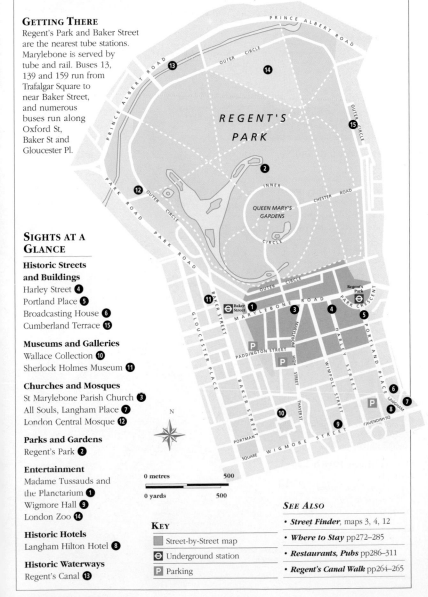

KEY

▢	Street-by-Street map
Ⓔ	Underground station
🅿	Parking

SEE ALSO

- *Street Finder*, maps 3, 4, 12
- *Where to Stay* pp272–285
- *Restaurants, Pubs* pp286–311
- *Regent's Canal Walk* pp264–265

St Andrew's Place, Regent's Park

Street-by-Street: Marylebone

S OUTH OF REGENT'S PARK, the medieval village of
Marylebone (originally Maryburne, the stream by
St Mary's church) has London's highest concentration of genteel Georgian housing. Until the 18th
century it was surrounded by fields and a pleasure
garden, but these were built over as fashionable
London drifted west. In the mid-19th century,
professional people, especially doctors,
used the spacious houses to receive
wealthy clients. The area has maintained
both its medical connection and its elegance.

Tiananmen
Square
memorial:
Portland Place

★ **Regent's Park**
*John Nash laid out the
royal park in 1812 as
a setting for Classically
designed villas and
terraces* ❷

**The Royal Academy of
Music,** England's first
music academy, was
founded in 1774. The
present brick building,
with its own concert
hall, is from 1911.

To Regent's
Park

★ **Madame Tussauds and the
Planetarium**
*The wax museum of famous people,
historical and contemporary, is one
of London's most popular attractions.
Next door, a planetarium shows
models of the sky at night* ❶

**St Marylebone Parish
Church**
*Poets Robert Browning
and Elizabeth Barrett
married in this church* ❸

KEY

– – –   Suggested route

0 metres   100
0 yards   100

**Baker Street
station**

Park Crescent's breathtaking facades by Nash have been preserved, although the interiors were rebuilt as offices in the 1960s. The crescent seals the north end of Nash's ceremonial route from St James's to Regent's Park, via Regent Street and Portland Place.

LOCATOR MAP
See Central London Map pp12–13

The London Clinic is one of the best-known private hospitals in this medical district.

Regent's Park station

Portland Place
In the centre of this broad street stands a statue of Field Marshal Sir George Stuart White, who won the Victoria Cross for gallantry in the Afghan War of 1879 **5**

The Royal Institute of British Architects is housed in a controversial Art Deco building designed by Grey Wornum in 1934.

Harley Street
Consulting rooms of eminent medical specialists have been here for more than a century **4**

STAR SIGHTS

★ **Madame Tussauds and the Planetarium**

★ **Regent's Park**

Mme Tussauds and the Planetarium ❶

Marylebone Rd NW1. **Map** 4 D5.
📞 0870-400 3000. ⊖ Baker St.
Open 10am–5.30pm daily (Planetarium), 9.30am–5.30pm (Mme Tussauds). **Closed** 25 Dec. **Adm charge.** ♿ phone first. 📷 🖥 🚻

Traditional wax-modelling at Madame Tussauds

Madame Tussaud began her wax-modelling career rather morbidly, taking death masks of many of the best-known victims of the French Revolution. In 1835 she set up an exhibition of her work in Baker Street, not far from the collection's present site.

The 1990s collection still relies upon traditional wax-modelling techniques to recreate politicians, film and television actors, rock stars and sporting heroes.

The main sections of the exhibition are the "Garden Party", where visitors mingle with extraordinarily lifelike models of celebrities; "Super Stars", devoted to the giants of the entertainment world; and the "Grand Hall", containing a collection of royalty, statesmen and world leaders, writers and artists. Where else on earth could Lenin, Martin Luther King and William Shakespeare all rub shoulders?

The Chamber of Horrors is the most renowned part of Madame Tussauds. It includes recreations of the most gruesome episodes in the grim catalogue of crime and punishment: the murderers Dr Crippen and Ethel le Neve; Gary Gilmore facing a firing squad; and the chill gloom of a Victorian street in Jack the Ripper's London.

The "Spirit of London" is the finale. Visitors travel in stylized London taxi-cabs and participate in momentous events of the city, from the Great Fire of 1666 to 1960s Swinging London.

Situated next door, and part of the same great complex, is the London Planetarium, where a spectacular star show explores and reveals some of the mysteries of the planets and the solar system. The interactive Space Trail exhibition contains many detailed models of the planets, satellites and spacecraft.

Waxwork of Elizabeth II

Tulip time at Queen Mary's Gardens in Regent's Park

Regent's Park ❷

NW1. **Map** 3 C2. 📞 020-7486 7905.
⊖ Regent's Park, Baker St, Great Portland St. **Open** 5am–dusk daily.
♿ 🖥 **Open air theatre.** See **Entertainment** pp328–9.

This area of land became enclosed as a park in 1812. John Nash designed the scheme and originally envisaged a kind of garden suburb, dotted with 56 villas in a variety of Classical styles, with a pleasure palace for the Prince Regent. At the end of the day only eight villas – but no palace – were built inside the park (three survive round the edge of the Inner Circle).

The boating lake, which has many varieties of water birds, is marvellously romantic, especially when music drifts across from the bandstand in the distance. Queen Mary's Gardens are a mass of wonderful sights and smells in summer, when visitors can enjoy Shakespeare productions at the Open Air Theatre nearby. Broad Walk provides a picturesque stroll north from Park Square.

Nash's master plan for Regent's Park continues just beyond its northeastern edge in Park Village East and West. These captivating buildings in elegant stucco were completed in 1828, some adorned with Wedgwood-style medallions.

St Marylebone Parish Church ❸

Marylebone Rd NW1. **Map** 4 D5.
📞 020-7935 7315. ⊖ Regent's Park.
Open 12.30–1.30pm Mon–Fri, Sun mornings. ♿ 📷 ✝ 11am Sun. 🖥

This is where the poets Robert Browning and Elizabeth Barrett were married in 1846 after eloping from her strict family home on nearby Wimpole Street. The large, stately church by Thomas Hardwick was consecrated in 1817 after the former church, where Lord Byron was christened in 1778, had become too small. Hardwick was determined that the same should not happen to his new church – so everything is on a grand scale.

Commemorative window in St Marylebone Parish Church

Harley Street ❹

W1. **Map** 4 E5. Ⓔ *Regent's Park, Oxford Circus, Bond St, Great Portland St.*

THE LARGE HOUSES on this late 18th-century street were popular with successful doctors and specialists in the middle of the 19th century when it was a rich residential area. The doctors' practices stayed and lend the street an air of hushed order, unusual in central London. There are very few private houses or apartments here now, but William Gladstone lived at No. 73 from 1876 to 1882.

Portland Place ❺

W1. **Map** 4 E5. Ⓔ *Regent's Park, Oxford Circus.*

THE ADAM BROTHERS, Robert and James, laid this street out in 1773. Only a few of the original houses remain, the best being 27 to 47 on the west side, south of Devonshire Street. John Nash added the street to his processional route from Carlton House to Regent's Park and sealed its northern end with Park Crescent.

The building of the Royal Institute of British Architects (1934) at No. 66 is adorned with symbolic statues and reliefs. Its bronze front doors depict London's buildings and the River Thames.

Broadcasting House ❻

Portland Place W1. **Map** 12 E1. Ⓔ *Oxford Circus.* **Not open** to the public. **BBC Backstage Tours** BBC Television Centre, Wood Lane. ☏ *0870-603 0304.* Ⓔ *White City.* **Adm charge.** ♿ ✔ *compulsory, call to book. No children under 10.*

BROADCASTING HOUSE was built in 1931 as a suitably modern Art Deco headquarters for the brand-new medium of broadcasting. Its front, curving with the street, is dominated by Eric Gill's stylized relief of Prospero and Ariel. As the invisible spirit of the air, Shakespeare's Ariel was considered an appropriate personification of broadcasting. The character appears in two other sculptures on the western frontage, and again over the eastern entrance in "Arial Piping to Children". Leslie French, who was playing Ariel in the Old Vic's presentation of *The Tempest* at the time, acted as Gill's model for the reliefs.

Broadcasting House is now occupied by management, as most BBC studios migrated to west London in the 1990s. Fascinating tours of the BBC TV Centre in White City are available. Each tour is unique, as the itinerary depends on programming and events of the day.

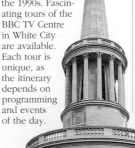

All Souls, Langham Place (1824)

Relief on the Royal Institute of British Architects on Portland Place

All Souls, Langham Place ❼

Langham Place W1. **Map** 12 F1. ☏ *020-7580 3522.* Ⓔ *Oxford Circus.* **Open** *9.30am–6pm Mon–Fri, 9am–9pm Sun.* ♿ ✝ *11.30am Sun.*

JOHN NASH designed this church in 1824. Its quirky round frontage is best seen from Regent Street. When it was first built, the spire was ridiculed as it appeared too slender and flimsy.

The only Nash church in London, it had close links with the BBC, formerly based opposite at Broadcasting House, and has often doubled as a recording studio for the daily broadcast service.

Langham Hilton Hotel ❽

1 Portland Place W1. **Map** 12 E1. ☏ *020-7636 1000.* Ⓔ *Oxford Circus. See* **Where to Stay** *p282.*

THIS WAS LONDON'S grandest hotel after it was opened in 1865. The writers Oscar Wilde and Mark Twain and composer Antonin Dvořák were among its many distinguished guests. The hotel was, for a time, used by the BBC, but since then has been restored behind its original facade. Its marble-lined entrance hall leads into the Palm Court, where there is piano music at tea-time. Colonial days are recalled in the Memories of the Empire restaurant and the Chukka bar.

Wigmore Hall [9]

36 Wigmore St W1. **Map** 12 E1.
[020-7935 2141. ⊖ Bond St,
Oxford Cir. See **Entertainment** p333.

THIS APPEALING little concert
hall for chamber music
was designed by T E Collcutt,
architect of the Savoy Hotel
(see p284), in 1900. At first it
was called Bechstein Hall
because it was attached to the
Bechstein piano showroom:
the area used to be the heart
of London's piano trade.
Opposite is the white-tiled Art
Nouveau emporium built in
1907 as Debenham and
Freebody's department store –
the forerunner of today's
Debenham's on Oxford Street.

Wallace Collection [10]

Hertford House, Manchester Square
W1. **Map** 12 D1. [020-7935
0687. ⊖ Bond St. **Open** 10am–5pm
Mon–Sat, 2–5pm Sun. **Closed** 24–26
Dec, 1 Jan, Good Fri. Ø
[&] [ ] [ ] **Lectures.**

**16th-century Italian dish from
the Wallace Collection**

THIS IS ONE OF the world's
finest private collections
of art. It has remained intact
since it was bequeathed to
the government in 1897 with
the stipulation that it should
go on permanent public
display with nothing added or
taken away. The product of
passionate collecting for four
generations of the Hertford
family, it is a must for anyone
with even a passing interest
in the progress of European
art up to the late 19th century.
Most of its highlights are in
gallery 22, which contains
some 70 master works. Frans
Hals's *The Laughing Cavalier*

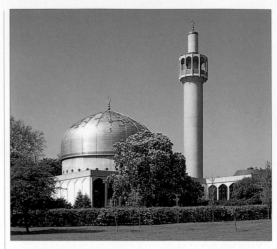

The Mosque on the edge of Regent's Park

is here, and Rembrandt's
Titus, along with Titian's
Perseus and Andromeda and
Nicolas Poussin's *A Dance to
the Music of Time*. There are
also superb English portraits
by Reynolds, Gainsborough
and Romney. The 25 galleries
contain fine Sèvres porcelain
and sculpture by Houdon,
Roubiliac and Rysbrack. There
is also an armour collection.

Sherlock Holmes Museum [11]

221b Baker St NW1. **Map** 3 C5.
[020-7935 8866. ⊖ Baker St.
Open 9.30am–6pm daily. **Closed**
25 Dec. **Adm charge**. [ ] [ ] [ ]

SIR ARTHUR CONAN DOYLE'S
fictional detective was
supposed to have lived at
221b Baker Street – this

Conan Doyle's Sherlock Holmes

museum, which boasts the
right number, actually sits
between Nos. 237 and 239.
Visitors are greeted by
Holmes's "housekeeper" and
shown to his recreated rooms
on the first floor. The fourth
floor shop sells copies of the
stories and deerstalker hats.

London Central Mosque [12]

146 Park Rd NW8. **Map** 3 B3.
[020-7724 3363. ⊖ Marylebone,
St John's Wood, Baker St. **Open**
dawn–dusk daily. [&] [ ] **Lectures.**

SURROUNDED BY TREES on the
edge of Regent's Park, this
large, golden-domed mosque
was designed by Sir Frederick
Gibberd and completed in
1978. It was built to cater for
the increasing number of
Muslim residents and visitors
in London. The mosque's
main hall of worship, which
is capable of holding 1,800
people, is a plain square
chamber with a domed roof.
It is sparsely furnished apart
from a magnificent carpet and
a colossal chandelier. The
dome is lined in a traditional
Islamic pattern of broken
shapes, predominantly blue.
Visitors must remove their
shoes before entering the
mosque, and women, for
whom there is a separate
gallery, should also remember
to cover their heads.

Regent's Canal ⓭

NW1 & NW8. **Map** 3 C1. 📞 *020-7482 2660.* ⊖ *Camden Town, St John's Wood, Warwick Ave.* **Canal towpaths open** *dawn – dusk daily.* See **Three Guided Walks** *pp264–5.*

A boat trip on Regent's Canal

JOHN NASH was extremely enthusiastic about this waterway, opened in 1820 to link the Grand Junction Canal, which ended at Little Venice in Paddington in the west, with the London docks at Limehouse in the east. He saw it as an added attraction for his new Regent's Park, and originally wanted the canal to run through the middle of that park. He was persuaded out of that by those who thought that the bargees' bad language would offend the genteel residents of the area. Perhaps this was just as well – the steam tugs that hauled the barges were dirty and sometimes dangerous.

In 1874 a barge carrying gunpowder blew up in the cutting by London Zoo, killing the crew, destroying a bridge and terrifying the populace, and the animals. After an initial period of prosperity the canal began to be hit by increasing competition from the new railways and so gradually slipped into decline.

Today it has been revived as a leisure amenity; the towpath is paved as a pleasant walkway and short boat trips are offered between Little Venice and Camden Lock, where there is a thriving crafts market. Visitors to the zoo can use the landing stage that is situated alongside it.

London Zoo ⓮

Regent's Park NW1. **Map** 4 D2. 📱 *020-7722 3333.* ⊖ *Camden Town.* **Open** *10am – 4pm daily (last adm 3pm).* **Closed** *25 Dec.* **Adm charge.** Ⓦ *www.zsl.org*

OPENED IN 1828, the zoo has been one of London's biggest tourist attractions ever since, and is also a major research and conservation centre. London Zoo has over 600 species of animal, from Sumatran tigers and black rhinos to Mexican red-kneed bird-eating spiders. One of

London Zoo's aviary designed by Lord Snowdon (1964)

the newest exhibits is the astonishing Web of Life which takes you through the vast range of life forms found in Earth's major habitats.

Cumberland Terrace ⓯

NW1. **Map** 4 E2. ⊖ *Great Portland St, Regent's Park, Camden Town.*

JAMES THOMSON is credited with the detailed design of this, the longest and most elaborate of the Nash terraces around Regent's Park. Its imposing central block of raised Ionic columns is topped with a decorated triangular pediment. Completed in 1828, it was designed to be visible from the palace Nash planned for the Prince Regent (later George IV). The palace was never built because the Prince was too busy with his plans for Buckingham Palace *(see pp94–5).*

Nash's Cumberland Terrace, dating from 1828

HAMPSTEAD

HAMPSTEAD HAS ALWAYS stayed aloof from London, looking down from its site on the high ridge north of the metropolis. Today it is essentially a Georgian village. The heath separating Hampstead from Highgate reinforces its appeal, isolating it further from the hurly-burly of the modern city. A stroll around the charming village streets, followed by a tramp across the heath, makes for one of the finest walks in London.

SIGHTS AT A GLANCE

Historic Streets and Buildings
Flask Walk and Well Walk ❶
Church Row ❺
Downshire Hill ❻
Vale of Health ⓭

Museums and Galleries
Burgh House ❷
Fenton House ❹
Keats House ❼
Kenwood House ❿

Parks and Gardens
Hampstead Heath ❽
Parliament Hill ❾
The Hill ⓬

Pubs and Restaurants
Jack Straw's Castle ❸
Spaniards Inn ⓫

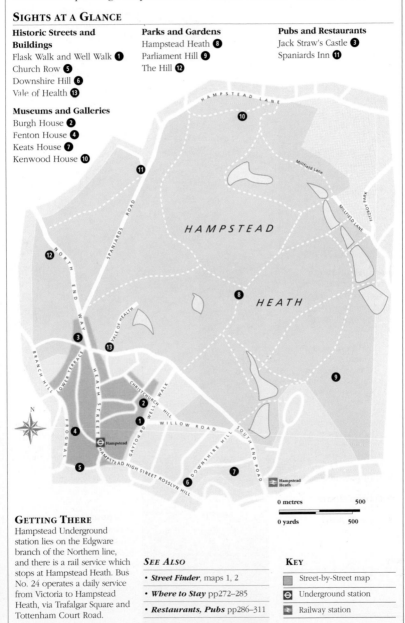

GETTING THERE
Hampstead Underground station lies on the Edgware branch of the Northern line, and there is a rail service which stops at Hampstead Heath. Bus No. 24 operates a daily service from Victoria to Hampstead Heath, via Trafalgar Square and Tottenham Court Road.

| 0 metres | 500 |
| 0 yards | 500 |

SEE ALSO
• *Street Finder*, maps 1, 2
• *Where to Stay* pp272–285
• *Restaurants, Pubs* pp286–311

KEY
▢ Street-by-Street map
⊖ Underground station
⊞ Railway station

View across Hampstead Heath from Holly Hill

Street-by-Street: Hampstead

PERCHED AWKWARDLY on a hilltop, with its broad heath to the north, Hampstead has kept its villagey atmosphere and sense of being aloof from urban pressures. This has attracted artists and writers since Georgian times and made it one of London's most desirable residential areas. Its mansions and town houses are perfectly maintained and a stroll through Hampstead's narrow streets is one of London's quieter pleasures.

Jack Straw's Castle
The pub on the edge of the Heath is named after a 14th-century rebel ❸

★ Hampstead Heath
A welcome retreat from the city, its broad open spaces include bathing ponds, meadows and lakes ❽

Whitestone Pond takes its name from the old white milestone nearby. It is 4.5 miles (7 km) from Holborn *(see pp132–41).*

Grove Lodge was home to novelist John Galsworthy (1867–1933), author of the *Forsyte Saga*, for the last 15 years of his life.

Admiral's House dates from about 1700. Built for a sea captain, its name derives from its external maritime motifs. No admiral ever actually lived in it.

STAR SIGHTS

- ★ **Burgh House**
- ★ **Hampstead Heath**
- ★ **Fenton House**
- ★ **Church Row**

★ Fenton House
Summer visitors should seek out this late 17th-century house and its exquisite walled garden, which are well hidden in the jumble of streets near the heath ❹

KEY

– – – Suggested route

0 metres 100

0 yards 100

★ **Burgh House**
Built in 1702 but much altered since, the house contains an intriguing local history museum and a café overlooking the small garden ❷

LOCATOR MAP
See Greater London Map pp10–11

The New End Theatre
produces rare but significant work. The building used to be a morgue.

No. 40 Well Walk is where artist John Constable lived while working on his many Hampstead pictures.

Flask Walk and Well Walk
An alley of charming specialist shops broadens into a residential village street ❶

Hampstead station

The Everyman Cinema
has been an art cinema since 1933.

★ **Church Row**
The tall houses are rich in original detail. Notice the superb iron-work on what is probably London's finest Georgian street ❺

Jack Straw's Castle in the 19th century

Flask Walk and Well Walk ❶

NW3. **Map** 1 B5. ⊖ *Hampstead.*

FLASK WALK IS named after the Flask pub. Here, in the 18th century, therapeutic spa water from what was then the separate village of Hampstead was put into flasks and sold to visitors or sent to London. The water, rich in iron salts, came from nearby Well Walk where a disused fountain now marks the site of the well. The Wells Tavern, almost opposite the spring, used to be a hostelry that specialized in accommodating those who engaged in the illicit liaisons for which the spa became notorious.

In later times, there have been many notable residents of Well Walk including artist John Constable (at No. 40), novelists D H Lawrence and J B Priestley and the poet John Keats, before he moved to his better-known house in what is now Keats Grove.

Site of the well on Well Walk

At the High Street end, Flask Walk is narrow and lined with old shops. Beyond the pub (note the Victorian tiled panels outside) it broadens into a row of Regency houses, one of which used to belong to the novelist Kingsley Amis.

Burgh House ❷

New End Sq NW3. **Map** 1 B4.
📞 020-7431 0144. ⊖ *Hampstead.*
Open noon–5pm Wed–Sun, 2–5pm public hols. **Closed** Christmas week.
📷 🍴 ♿ **Music recitals.**

THE LAST PRIVATE tenant of Burgh House was the son-in-law of the writer Rudyard Kipling, who visited here occasionally in the last years of his life until 1936. After a period under the ownership of Hampstead Borough Council, the house was let to the independent Burgh House Trust. Since 1979 the Trust has run it as the Hampstead Museum, which illustrates the history of the area and concentrates on some of its most celebrated residents.

One room is devoted entirely to the life of John Constable, who painted an extraordinary series of studies of clouds from Hampstead Heath. The house also has sections on Lawrence, Keats, the artist Stanley Spencer and others who lived and worked in the area. There is a display about Hampstead as a spa in the 18th and 19th centuries, which is also well worth a visit. Burgh House regularly accomodates exhibitions by contemporary local artists. The house itself was built in

1703 but is named after a 19th-century resident, the Reverend Allatson Burgh. It has been much altered inside, and today the marvellously carved staircase is a highlight of the interior. Also worth seeing is the music room which was reconstructed in 1920, but contains good 18th-century pine panelling from another house. In the 1720s Dr William Gibbons, chief physician to the then thriving Hampstead spa, lived here.

There is a moderately priced café in the basement, with a terrace that overlooks the house's pretty garden.

Burgh House staircase

Jack Straw's Castle ❸

12 North End Way NW3. **Map** 1 A3.
📞 020-7435 8885. ⊖ *Hampstead.*
Open daily 12 noon–8pm. ♿

THIS PUB IS NAMED after one of Wat Tyler's lieutenants in the Peasants' Revolt of 1381 *(see p162)*. Jack Straw is believed to have built an encampment here, from which he planned to march on London. However, before he could do that he was captured and hanged by the king's men. There has certainly been a pub here for many years – Charles Dickens was a customer – but the present building, a mock castle, dates only from 1962. It is a huge place, and there are good views across the Heath from the restaurant and Turret Bar on the second floor.

Fenton House ❹

20 Hampstead Grove NW3.
Map 1 A4. ☎ *020-7435 3471.*
🚇 *Hampstead.* **Open** *2–5pm
Wed–Fri, 11am–5pm Sat, Sun, public
hols.* **Closed** *Nov–Mar.* **Adm charge**.
🎵 **Summer concerts** *8pm Wed.*

Bᴜɪʟᴛ ɪɴ 1693, this splendid
William and Mary house
is the oldest mansion in
Hampstead. It contains two
specialized exhibitions that
are open to the public during
the summer: the Benton-
Fletcher collection of early
keyboard instruments, which
includes a harpsichord dating
from 1612, said to have been
played by Handel; and a fine
collection of porcelain. The
instruments are kept in full
working order and are
actually used for concerts
held in the house. The
porcelain collection was
largely accumulated by
Lady Binning, who, in
1952, bequeathed the
house and all of its
contents to the
National Trust.

Church Row ❺

NW3. **Map** 1 A5. 🚇 *Hampstead.*

Tʜᴇ ʀᴏᴡ ɪs ᴏɴᴇ of the most
complete Georgian streets
in London. Much of its
original detail has survived,
notably the ironwork.
    At the west end is St John's,
Hampstead's parish church,
built in 1745. The iron gates
are earlier and come from
Canons Park in Edgware.
Inside the church is a bust of
John Keats. John Constable's
grave is in the churchyard,
and many Hampstead
luminaries are buried in the
adjoining cemetery.

Downshire Hill ❻

NW3. **Map** 1 C5. 🚇 *Hampstead.*

A ʙᴇᴀᴜᴛɪꜰᴜʟ sᴛʀᴇᴇᴛ of mainly
Regency houses, it lent its
name to a group of artists,
including Stanley Spencer and
Mark Gertler, who would
gather at No. 47 between the
two World Wars. That same

house had been the meeting-
place of Pre-Raphaelite artists,
among them Dante Gabriel
Rossetti and Edward Burne-
Jones. A more recent resident,
at No. 5, was the late Jim
Henson, the creator of the television puppets, *The Muppets*.
    The church on the corner
(the second Hampstead church
to be called St John's) was
built in 1823 to serve the
Hill's residents. Inside, it still
has its original box pews.

Keats House ❼

Keats Grove NW3. **Map** 1 C5.
☎ *020-7435 2062.* 🚇 *Hampstead,
Belsize Park.* **Open** *noon–5pm
Tue–Sun (8pm Wed).* **Closed**
*periodically for renovation. Phone in
advance for further information.* 📷
Poetry readings, talks, lectures.

Lock of John Keats's hair

Oʀɪɢɪɴᴀʟʟʏ ᴛᴡᴏ semi-
detached houses built in
1816, the smaller one became
Keats's home in 1818 when
persuaded by a friend to

St John's, Downshire Hill

move in. Keats spent two
productive years here: *Ode to
a Nightingale*, perhaps his
most celebrated poem, was
written under a plum tree in
the garden. The Brawne
family moved into the larger
house a year later and Keats
became engaged to their
daughter, Fanny. However,
the marriage never took place
because Keats died of
consumption in Rome before
two years had passed. He was
only 25 years old.
    One of Keats's love letters
to Fanny, the engagement
ring he offered her, and a
lock of her hair are among
the mementos that are now
exhibited at the house – it
was first opened to the public
in 1925. Visitors are also able
to see some of Keats's original
manuscripts and books, part
of a collection that serves as
an evocative and memorable
tribute to his life and work.

Fenton House's 17th-century facade

View over London from Hampstead Heath

Hampstead Heath 8

NW3. **Map** 1 C2. 020-8348 9945.
Belsize Park, Hampstead. **Open**
24hrs daily. **Special walks** on
Sundays. **Concerts, poetry readings,
children's activities** in summer.
**Sports facilities, bathing ponds.
Sports bookings** 020-8458 4548.

THE BEST TIME to stride
across these broad 3 sq
miles (8 sq km) is Sunday
afternoon, when the local
residents walk off their roast
beef lunches, discussing the
contents of the Sunday
papers. Separating the hilltop
villages of Hampstead and

Highgate *(see p246)*, the Heath
was made from the grounds
of several, formerly separate,
properties and embraces a
variety of landscapes –
woods, meadows, hills, ponds
and lakes. It remains
uncluttered by the haphazard
buildings and statues that
embellish the central London
parks, and its open spaces
have become increasingly
precious to Londoners as
the areas around it get more
crowded. There are ponds for
bathing and fishing and, on
three holiday weekends –
Easter, late spring and late
summer – the southern part
of the Heath is taken over by
a popular funfair *(see pp56–9)*.

Parliament Hill 9

NW5. **Map** 2 E4. 020-7485 4491.
Belsize Park, Hampstead.
Concerts, children's activities in
summer. **Sporting facilities.**

AN UNLIKELY BUT romantic
explanation for the area's
name is that it is where Guy
Fawkes's fellow-plotters
gathered on 5 November 1605
in the vain hope of watching
the Houses of Parliament
blow up after they had
planted gunpowder there *(see
p22)*. More probably it was a
gun emplacement for the
Parliamentary side during the
Civil War 40 years later. The
gunners would have enjoyed

Kenwood House 10

Hampstead Lane NW3. **Map** 1 C1.
020-8348 1286. Highgate,
Archway. **Open** Apr–Sep: 10am–6pm
daily; Oct–Mar: 10am–4pm daily.
Closed 24–25 Dec.
Lakeside concerts in summer.
**Exhibitions, poetry readings,
recitals.** See **Entertainment**
pp332–3.

THIS IS A MAGNIFICENT Adam
mansion, filled with Old
Master paintings, including
works by Vermeer, Turner and
Romney (who lived in
Hampstead). It is situated in
landscaped grounds high on
the edge of Hampstead Heath.
There has been a house here
since 1616 – the present one

was remodelled by Robert
Adam in 1764 for the Earl of
Mansfield, the Lord Chancellor.
Adam refitted existing rooms
and added to the original
building. Most of his interiors
have survived, the highlight
being the library. A Rembrandt
self-portrait is the star attraction
of the collection, and there
are also works by Van Dyck,
Hals, Reynolds and others.

The orangery is
now used for
occasional concerts
and recitals.

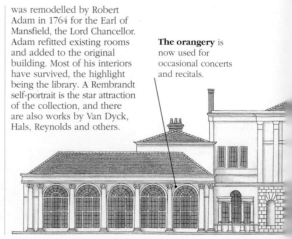

a broad view across London: even today, when many tall buildings have intervened, it provides one of the most spectacular views over the capital. From here the dome of St Paul's is prominent.

Parliament Hill is also a popular place for flying kites and sailing model boats.

Spaniards Inn ⓫

Spaniards Rd NW3. **Map** 1 B1.
📞 020-8731 6571. ⊜ *Hampstead, Golders Green.* **Open** *11am– 11pm Mon–Sat, noon–10.30pm Sun.* ♿ *See* **Restaurants and Pubs** *pp286–311.*

The historic Spaniards Inn

Dᴵᴄᴷ ᴛᴜʀᴘᴵɴ, the notorious 18th-century highwayman, is said to have frequented this pub. When he wasn't holding up stage-coaches on their way to and from London, he stabled his horse, Black Bess, at the stables nearby. The building certainly dates from Turpin's time and, although the bar downstairs has been altered frequently, the small upstairs Turpin Bar is original. A pair of guns over the bar were reputedly taken from anti-Catholic rioters, who came to Hampstead to burn the Lord Chancellor's house at Kenwood during the Gordon Riots of 1780. The landlord detained them by offering pint after pint of free beer and, when they were drunk, disarmed them.

Among the pub's noted patrons have been the poets Shelley, Keats and Byron, the actor David Garrick and the artist Sir Joshua Reynolds.

The toll house has been restored; it juts into the road so that, in the days when tolls were levied, traffic could not race past without paying.

The Hill ⓬

North End Way NW3. **Map** 1 A2.
📞 020-8455 5183. ⊜ *Hampstead, Golders Green.* **Open** *9am–one hour before dusk daily.*

Tʜᴵꜱ ᴄʜᴀʀᴍᴵɴɢ garden was created by the Edwardian soap manufacturer and patron of the arts, Lord Leverhulme. It was originally the grounds to his house, and is now part of Hampstead Heath. It boasts a pergola walkway, best seen in summer when the plants are in flower; the garden also has a beautiful formal pond.

The pergola walk at The Hill

Vale of Health ⓭

NW3. **Map** 1 B4. ⊜ *Hampstead.*

Tʜᴵꜱ ᴀʀᴇᴀ was famous as a distinctly unhealthy swamp before it was drained in 1770; until then it was known as Hatches Bottom. Its newer name may derive from people fleeing here from cholera in London at the end of the 18th century. Alternatively, the name could have been the hype of a property developer, when it was first recorded in 1801.

The poet James Henry Leigh Hunt put it on the literary map when he moved here in 1815, and played host to Coleridge, Byron Shelley and Keats.

D H Lawrence lived here briefly and Stanley Spencer painted in a room above the Vale of Health Hotel, demolished in 1964.

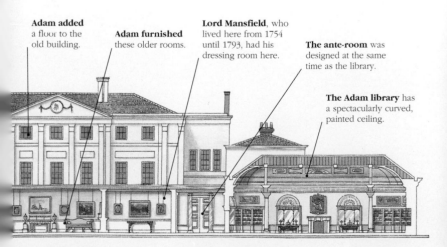

Adam added a floor to the old building.

Adam furnished these older rooms.

Lord Mansfield, who lived here from 1754 until 1793, had his dressing room here.

The ante-room was designed at the same time as the library.

The Adam library has a spectacularly curved, painted ceiling.

GREENWICH AND BLACKHEATH

BEST KNOWN AS the place from which the world's time is measured, Greenwich marks the historic eastern approach to London by land and water. Home to the National Maritime Museum and the exquisite Queen's House, Greenwich avoided the industrialization of its neighbours in the 19th century and today remains an elegant oasis of bookshops, antique shops and markets. Blackheath lies just to the south.

SIGHTS AT A GLANCE

Historic Streets and Buildings
Queen's House 2
Royal Naval College 7
Old Royal Observatory 9
Croom's Hill 12

Museums
National Maritime Museum 1
Fan Museum 13

Churches
St Alfege Church 3

Parks and Gardens
Greenwich Park 10
Blackheath 11

Walkway
Greenwich Foot Tunnel 6

Pubs and Restaurants
Trafalgar Tavern 8

Ships
Gipsy Moth IV 4
Cutty Sark 5

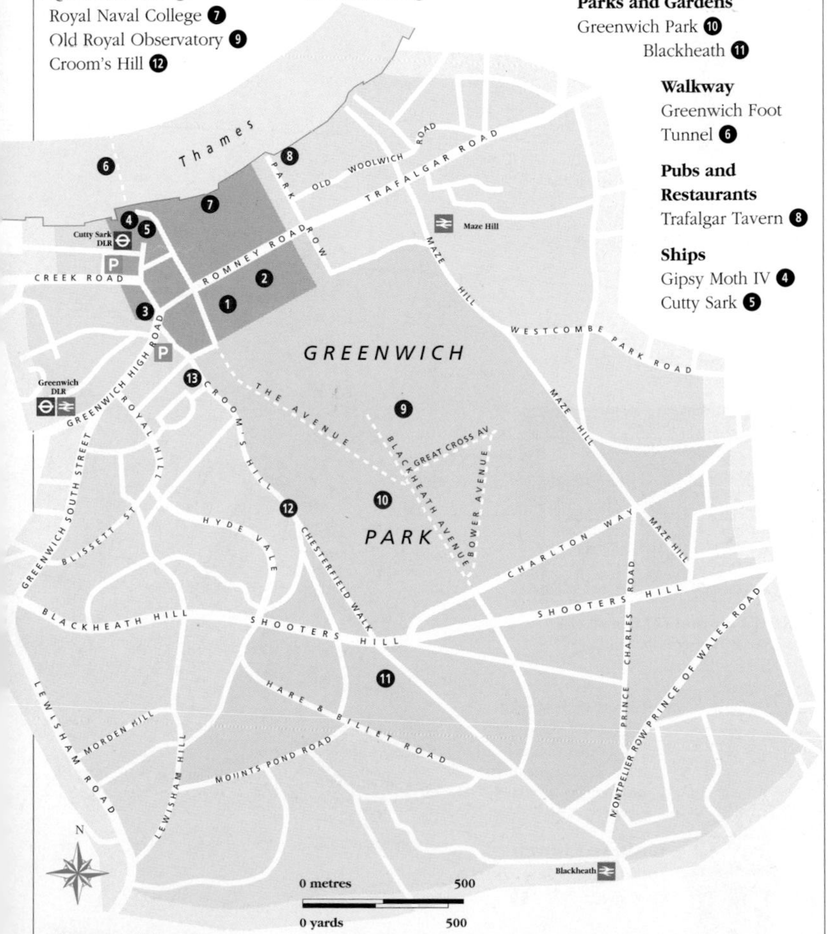

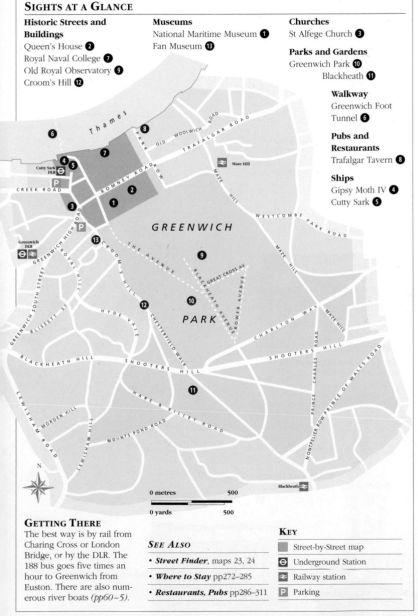

GETTING THERE

The best way is by rail from Charing Cross or London Bridge, or by the DLR. The 188 bus goes five times an hour to Greenwich from Euston. There are also numerous river boats *(pp60–5)*.

SEE ALSO

- ***Street Finder***, maps 23, 24
- ***Where to Stay*** pp272–285
- ***Restaurants, Pubs*** pp286–311

KEY

- Street-by-Street map
- Underground Station
- Railway station
- Parking

View north across the Thames from Greenwich Park, overlooking Queen's House

Street-by-Street: Greenwich

T HIS HISTORIC TOWN marks the eastern approach to London and is best visited by river *(see pp60–5)*. In Tudor times it was the site of a palace much enjoyed by Henry VIII, near a fine hunting ground and his naval base. He and his daughters Elizabeth I and Mary were born here but the old palace is gone, leaving Inigo Jones's exquisite Queen's House, built for James I's wife. Museums, book and antique shops, markets, Wren's architecture and the magnificent park make Greenwich an enjoyable day's excursion.

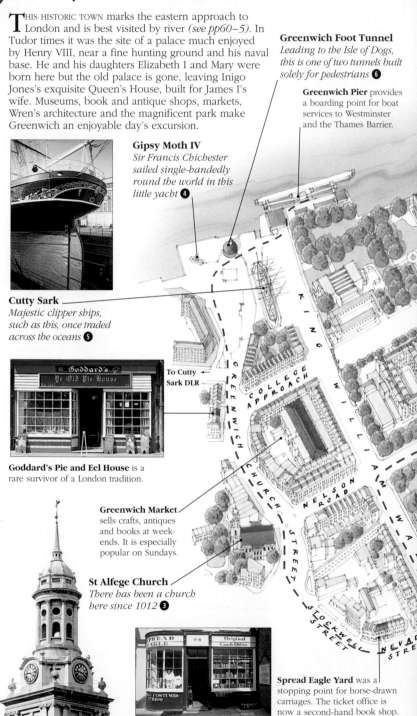

Greenwich Foot Tunnel
Leading to the Isle of Dogs, this is one of two tunnels built solely for pedestrians ❻

Greenwich Pier provides a boarding point for boat services to Westminster and the Thames Barrier.

Gipsy Moth IV
Sir Francis Chichester sailed single-handedly round the world in this little yacht ❹

Cutty Sark
Majestic clipper ships, such as this, once traded across the oceans ❺

Goddard's Pie and Eel House is a rare survivor of a London tradition.

Greenwich Market sells crafts, antiques and books at weekends. It is especially popular on Sundays.

St Alfege Church
There has been a church here since 1012 ❸

Spread Eagle Yard was a stopping point for horse-drawn carriages. The ticket office is now a second-hand book shop.

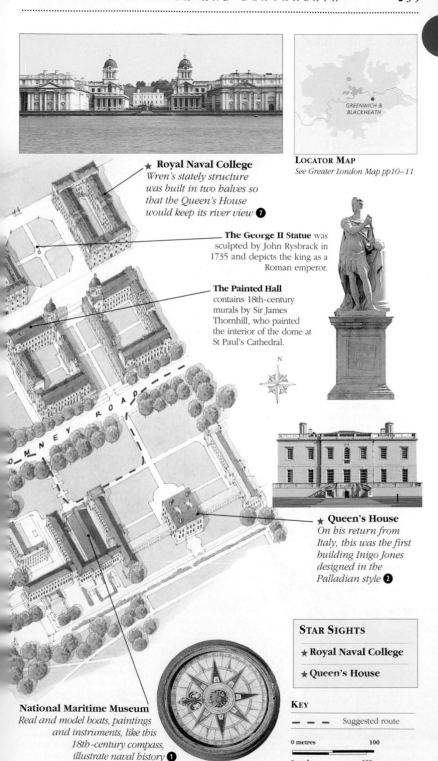

★ **Royal Naval College**
Wren's stately structure was built in two halves so that the Queen's House would keep its river view ❼

The George II Statue was sculpted by John Rysbrack in 1735 and depicts the king as a Roman emperor.

The Painted Hall contains 18th-century murals by Sir James Thornhill, who painted the interior of the dome at St Paul's Cathedral.

ROMNEY ROAD

N

★ **Queen's House**
On his return from Italy, this was the first building Inigo Jones designed in the Palladian style ❷

National Maritime Museum
Real and model boats, paintings and instruments, like this 18th-century compass, illustrate naval history ❶

STAR SIGHTS

★ **Royal Naval College**

★ **Queen's House**

KEY

– – – Suggested route

0 metres   100

0 yards   100

National Maritime Museum ❶

Romney Rd SE10. **Map** 23 C2.
📞 *020-8858 4422*. 🔵 *Cutty Sark DLR.* 🚇 *Maze Hill.* **Open** *10am–5pm daily (last adm: 30 mins before closing).* **Closed** *24–26 Dec.* **Adm charge.** 🔋 *to most of museum.* **Lectures, exhibitions.** 💻 📷

THE SEA HAS ALWAYS played an extremely important role in British history as a means of both defence and expansion, and this museum celebrates the "island nation's" seafaring heritage. Exhibits include everything from the earliest coracles (primitive hollow canoes) made from wood and leather, through early models of Elizabethan galleons to modern cargo, passenger and naval ships. There are sections devoted to trade and empire, the exploratory expeditions of Captain Cook and others, and the Napoleonic Wars.

One of the star exhibits is the uniform that Lord Horatio Nelson was wearing when he was shot at the Battle of Trafalgar in October 1805: you can easily see the bullet hole and the bloodstains.

Rather more spectacular, however, are the royal barges in the basement, most notably one that was built for Prince Frederick in 1732, elaborately decorated with gilded mermaids, shells, garlands and his Prince of Wales's feathers on the stern. Throughout the museum, which was built in the 19th century as a school for sailors' children, are scores of exquisitely crafted models of ships and historic paintings.

St Alfege's altar with rails by Jean Tijou

Prince Frederick's barge at the National Maritime Musueum

Queen's House ❷

Romney Rd SE10. **Map** 23 C2.
📞 *020-8858 4422*. 🔵 *Cutty Sark DLR.* 🚇 *Maze Hill.* **Open** *10am–5pm daily (last adm: 4.30pm).* **Adm charge.** 🚫 🍴 💻 📷 *Lectures, concerts, exhibitions.*

THE HOUSE WAS designed by Inigo Jones after his return from Italy and was completed in 1637. It was originally meant to be the home of Anne of Denmark, wife of James I, but she died while it was still being built and it was finished for Charles I's queen, Henrietta Maria. She fell in love with it and called it her house of delights. After the Civil War it was briefly occupied by Henrietta as dowager queen, but was not much used by the royal family after that.

The house is furnished as it would have been in the late 17th century, with brightly coloured wallhangings and fabrics. It was built as two halves, with one on each side of the road from Woolwich to Deptford. These two halves were linked by a bridge. Later the road was diverted; its former course is marked by cobbles in the courtyard. The main hall is a perfect cube, 12 m (40 ft) in all three dimensions. Another feature is the spiral "tulip staircase" (named after the design on its balustrades), curving sinuously upwards without a central support.

St Alfege Church ❸

Greenwich Church St SE10.
Map 23 B2. 📞 *020-8853 2703.*
🔵 *Cutty Sark DLR.* **Open** *12.30–4pm Mon, Wed & Fri, 9am–11pm Sat.* ⛪ *9.30am, 11.15am Sun.* 📷
🔋 📹 *Concerts, exhibitions.*

THIS IS ONE OF Nicholas Hawksmoor's distinctive and powerful designs, with its gigantic columns and pediments topped by urns. It was completed in 1714 on the site of an older church which marked the martyrdom of St Alfege, the then Archbishop of Canterbury, killed on this spot by Danish invaders in 1012.

Some of the carved wood inside is by Grinling Gibbons, but much of it was badly damaged by a World War II bomb and has been restored. The wrought iron of the altar and gallery rails is original, attributed to Jean Tijou. There is a reproduction of the register entry recording the baptism of Henry VIII in the former church, and a brass plate denoting the tomb of General Wolfe, who died fighting the French in Quebec in 1759. A window commemorates Thomas Tallis, the 16th-century composer and organist, who is buried here.

Gipsy Moth IV ➍

King William Walk SE10.
Map 23 B2. 020-8858 3445.
Cutty Sark DLR.
Greenwich Pier.
Not open to the public.

Gipsy Moth IV

SIR FRANCIS CHICHESTER sailed single-handed around the world in this little yacht. The journey, in 1966–7, took 226 lonely days to cover the 30,000 miles (48,000 km). He had to endure very cramped conditions on this 16-m (54-ft) vessel. The Queen knighted him on board using the sword with which Elizabeth I had knighted that earlier English seaman, Sir Francis Drake.

The domed terminal of the Greenwich Foot Tunnel

Cutty Sark ➎

King William Walk SE10. **Map** 23 B2.
020-8858 3445. 020-8853 3589. Cutty Sark DLR. Greenwich Pier. **Open** 10am–5pm daily. **Closed** 24–26 Dec. **Adm charge**. restricted. **Filmshows, videos**.

THIS MAJESTIC vessel is a survivor of the clippers that crossed the Atlantic and Pacific Oceans in the 19th century. Launched in 1869 as a tea carrier, it was something of a speed machine in its day, winning the annual clippers' race from China to London in 1871 in a time of 107 days. It made its final voyage in 1938 and was put on display here in 1957. On board you can see where the seamen slept, ate, worked and pursued their interests. Exhibits show the history of sailing and of trade in the Pacific and there is also an interesting collection of old carved ships' figureheads.

Greenwich Foot Tunnel ➏

Between Greenwich Pier SE10 and Isle of Dogs E14. **Map** 23 B1.
Island Gardens, Cutty Sark DLR.
Greenwich Pier.
Open 24hrs daily.
Lifts open 5am–9pm daily.
when lifts open.

THIS 370-M (1,200-FT) long tunnel was opened in 1902 to allow south London labourers to walk to work in Millwall Docks. Today it is worth crossing for the wonderful views – across the river, of Christopher Wren's Royal Naval College and of Inigo Jones's Queen's House.

Matching round red-brick terminals, with glass domes, mark the top of the lift shafts on either side of the river. The tunnel is about 2.5 m (9 ft) high and is lined with 200,000 tiles. Both ends of the tunnel are close to stations on the new Docklands Light Railway (DLR), with trains to Canary Wharf (see p249), Limehouse, East London, Tower Hill and Lewisham. Although there are security cameras, the tunnel can be eerie at night.

A late 19th-century figurehead in the Cutty Sark

Royal Naval College ❼

Greenwich SE10. **Map** 23 C2. [fi]
020-8269 4747. 🄴 🚄 *Greenwich,*
Maze Hill. **Open** *10am–5pm Mon–*
Sat, noon–5pm Sun (last adm:
4.45pm). **Closed** *public hols.* 🚫

THESE AMBITIOUS buildings
by Sir Christopher Wren
were built on the site of the
old 15th-century royal palace,
where Henry VIII, Mary I and
Elizabeth I lived. The chapel
and hall are the only parts of
the college that are open to
the public. The west front
was completed by Vanbrugh.

The chapel, by Wren, was
destroyed by fire in 1779.
The present Rococo interior,
designed by James Stuart, is
marvellously light and airy,
and has dainty plasterwork
decorations. The altar rail and
communion table, as well as
the candelabra, are gilded.

The Painted Hall was
opulently decorated by Sir
James Thornhill in the first
quarter of the 18th century.
The magnificent ceiling
paintings are supported by
his illusionistic pillars and
friezes. At the foot of one of
his paintings on the west
wall, the artist himself is
shown, apparently extending
his hand for more money.

Thornhill's painting of King William in the Hall of the Naval College

Trafalgar Tavern ❽

Park Row SE10. **Map** 23 C1. [C] *020-*
8858 2437. 🄴 *Greenwich. See*
Restaurants and Pubs *pp286–311.*

THIS CHARMING panelled pub
was built in 1837 and
quickly became established,
along with other waterside
inns in Greenwich, as a
venue for "whitebait dinners".
Government ministers, legal
luminaries and the like would
arrive from Westminster and
Charing Cross by water on
celebratory occasions and
feast on the tiny fish, which
could in those days be caught
locally. The last such meeting
of government ministers was
held here in 1885. Whitebait
still features, when they are
in season, on the menu at
the pub's restaurant, although
they are no longer fished
from the Thames.

This is another of Charles
Dickens's haunts. He drank
here with one of his novels'
most famous illustrators, the
engraver George Cruickshank.

In 1915 the pub became an
institution for old merchant
seamen. It was restored in 1965
after a spell of being used as
a club for working men.

Old Royal Observatory ❾

Greenwich Park SE10. **Map** 23 C3.
[C] *020-8858 4422.* 🄴 🚄 *Maze*
Hill, Greenwich. **Open** *10am–5pm*
daily (last adm: 4.30pm). **Closed** *23-*
26 Dec. **Adm charge.** 🚫 [ᐃ]

THE MERIDIAN (0° longtitude)
that divides the earth's
eastern and western hemi-
spheres passes through here,
and millions of visitors have
taken the opportunity of being
photographed standing with a
foot on either side of it. In
1884, Greenwich Mean Time
became the basis of time
measurement for most of the
world, following an important
international agreement.

The original building, still
standing, is Flamsteed House,
designed by Wren. It has a
distinctive octagonal room at
the top, hidden by square
outer walls and crowned with
two turrets. Above one of
them is a ball on a rod which
has dropped at 1pm every
day since 1833, so that sailors
on ships on the Thames, and
makers of chronometers
(navigators' clocks), could set
their clocks by it.

Flamsteed was the first
Astronomer Royal, appointed
by Charles II, and this was
the official government
observatory from 1675 until
1948, when the lights of

Trafalgar Tavern viewed from the Thames

London became too bright and the astronomers moved to darker Sussex. Today the Astronomer Royal is based in Cambridge and in the old Observatory there is housed an intriguing exhibition of astronomical instruments, chronometers and clocks.

A rare 24-hour clock at the Old Royal Observatory

Greenwich Park ⑩

SE10. **Map** 23 C3. **(** 020-8858 2608. ⊖ ⇌ *Greenwich, Blackheath, Maze Hill.* **Open** 6am–6pm daily. & **Children's shows, music, sports.** **Ranger's House,** Chesterfield Walk, Greenwich Park SE10. **Map** 23 C4. **(** 020-8853 0035. **Open** 1 Apr– 30 Sep: 10am–6pm daily; 1–21 Oct: 10am– 5pm daily; 22 Oct–31 Mar 10am–4pm Wed–Sun. **Closed** 24–25 Dec. **book in advance.**

ORIGINALLY THE GROUNDS of a royal palace and still owned by the Crown, the park was enclosed in 1433 and its brick wall built in the reign of James I. Later, in the 17th century, the French royal landscape gardener André Le Nôtre, who laid out the gardens at Versailles, was invited to design one at Greenwich. The broad avenue, rising south up the hill, was part of

his plan. There are great river views from the hilltop and on a fine day most of London can be seen. To the southeast of the park is the Ranger's House (1688), allotted in 1815 to the Park Ranger, but today housing an architectural study centre, the fine Suffolk Collection of 17th-century English portraits by Larkin, Lely and others, and a display of historic musical instruments.

Ranger's House in Greenwich Park

Blackheath ⑪

SE3. **Map** 24 D5. ⇌ *Blackheath.*

THIS OPEN HEATH used to be a rallying point for large groups entering London from the east, including Wat Tyler's band of rebels at the time of the Peasants' Revolt in 1381. It is also the place where James I introduced the game of golf, from his native Scotland, to the then largely sceptical English.

Today the heath is well worth exploring for the stately Georgian houses and terraces that surround it. In the prettily-named Tranquil Vale to the south, there are shops selling books, prints and antiques.

Croom's Hill ⑫

SE10. **Map** 23 C3. ⇌ *Greenwich.*

THIS IS ONE of the best kept 17th- to early 19th-century streets in London. The oldest buildings are at the southern end, near

Blackheath: the Manor House of 1695; near it, No. 68, from about the same date; and No. 66 the oldest of all.

Famous residents of Croom's Hill have included General James Wolfe (buried in St Alfege), and the Irish actor Daniel Day Lewis.

Fan Museum ⑬

12 Croom's Hill SE10. **Map** 23 B3. **(** 020-8858 7879. ⇌ *Greenwich.* **Open** 11am–5pm Mon–Sat, noon– 5pm Sun. **Adm charge** but reductions for pensioners and disabled. & **Lectures, fan-making work- shops first Saturday of the month.**

ONE OF LONDON'S most unlikely museums – the only one of its kind in the world – was opened here in 1989. It owes its existence and appeal to the enthusiasm of Helene Alexander, whose personal collection of 2,000 fans from the 17th century onwards has been augmented by gifts from others, including several fans that were made for the stage. The exhibitions are changed regularly in order to highlight a wide-ranging craft which embraces design, miniature painting, carving and embroidery. If there, Ms Alexander will guide you around the exhibits.

Stage fan used in a D'Oyly Carte operetta

FURTHER AFIELD

MANY OF THE GREAT houses originally built as country retreats for London's high and mighty were overrun by sprawling suburbs in the Victorian era. Fortunately several have survived as museums in these now less-rustic surroundings. Most are less than an hour's journey from central London. Richmond Park and Wimbledon Common give a taste of the country, while a trip to the Thames Barrier is an adventure.

SIGHTS AT A GLANCE

Historic Streets and Buildings
Sutton House **11**
Charlton House **19**
Eltham Palace **20**
Hampton Court pp254–5 **28**
Ham House **29**
Orleans House **30**
Marble Hill House **31**
Syon House **33**
Osterley Park House **35**
Pitshanger Manor and Gallery **36**
Strand on the Green **39**
Chiswick House **40**
Fulham Palace **42**

Churches
St Mary, Rotherhithe **13**
St Anne's, Limehouse **14**
St Mary's, Battersea **24**

Museums and Galleries
Lord's Cricket Ground **1**
Saatchi Collection **2**
Freud Museum **3**
The Jewish Museum **6**
St John's Gate **7**
Crafts Council Gallery **8**
Geffrye Museum **10**
Bethnal Green Museum of Childhood **12**
William Morris Gallery **16**
Horniman Museum **21**
Dulwich Picture Gallery **22**
Wimbledon Lawn Tennis Museum **25**
Wimbledon Windmill Museum **26**
Musical Museum **34**
Kew Bridge Steam Museum **37**
Hogarth's House **41**

Parks and Gardens
Battersea Park **23**
Richmond Park **27**
Kew Gardens pp260–61 **38**

Cemeteries
Highgate Cemetery **5**

Modern Architecture
Canary Wharf **15**
The Dome **18**
Chelsea Harbour **43**

Historic Districts
Highgate **4**
Islington **9**
Richmond **32**

Modern Technology
Thames Barrier **17**

All the sights in this section lie inside the M25 motorway *(see pp10–11).*

KEY

Main sightseeing areas

Motorway

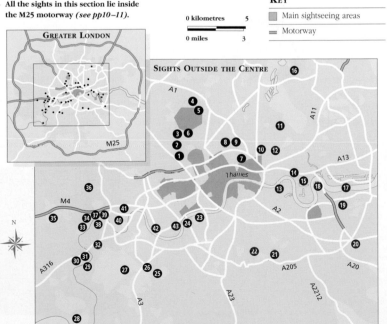

Riverside pub in Richmond

North of the Centre

Lord's Cricket Ground ❶

NW8. **Map** 3 A3. 📞 020-7289 1611. 🚇 St John's Wood. **Open** for guided tours and ticket-holders to matches only. **Closed** 25 Dec. **Adm charge.** 📷 ♿ 🎬 Mid-Sep–mid-Apr: noon, 2pm; mid-Apr–mid-Sep: 10am, noon, 2pm. 🅿 See **Entertainment** pp338–9. 🆆 www.lords.org.

T HE HEADQUARTERS of Britain's chief summer sport contains a museum, including a stuffed sparrow killed by a cricket ball as well as the Ashes (burned wood in an urn), the object of ferocious competition between the English and Australian national teams. The museum explains the history of the game, while paintings and mementos of notable cricketers make it a place of pilgrimage for devotees of the sport.

Cricket pioneer Thomas Lord moved his ground here in 1814. The Pavilion (1890), from which women were excluded until 1999, is late Victorian. There are tours of Lord's even when there is no game being played.

The Ashes at Lord's

Saatchi Collection ❷

98a Boundary Rd NW8. 📞 020-7624 8299. 🚇 St John's Wood, Swiss Cottage. **Open** noon–6pm Thu–Sun. **Adm charge**. 🎬 (phone to arrange). 🅿 **Lectures.**

C HARLES SAATCHI, who is an advertising executive, and his former wife established this gallery of contemporary art in a converted warehouse. (There is no sign outside so take care not to miss it.) He owns approximately 600 works by artists such as Andy Warhol, Carl André and Frank Stella, and selections are put on display in exhibitions that are changed every few months.

Sigmund Freud's famous couch

Freud Museum ❸

20 Maresfield Gdns NW3. 📞 020-7435 2002. 🚇 Finchley Rd. **Open** noon–5pm Wed–Sun. **Closed** 24–26 Dec. **Adm charge.** 📷 ♿ 🅿 **Videos, lectures.** 🆆 www.freud.org.uk

I N 1938 SIGMUND FREUD, the founder of psychoanalysis, fled from Nazi persecution in Vienna to this Hampstead house. Making use of the possessions he brought with him, his family recreated the atmos- phere of his Vienna consulting rooms. After Freud died in 1939 his daughter Anna (who was a pioneer of child psychoanalysis) kept the house as it was. In 1986 the house was opened to the public as a mu- seum dedicated to Freud. The most famous item is the couch on which patients lay for analysis. A compilation of 1930s home movies shows cheerful moments with his dog as well as scenes of Nazi attacks on his apartment. The museum's bookshop has a large collection of his works.

Highgate ❹

N6. 🚇 Highgate.

T HERE HAS BEEN a settlement here since at least the early Middle Ages, when an important staging post on the Great North Road from London was established here with a gate to control access. Like Hampstead across the Heath (see pp234–5), it soon became fashionable for its unpolluted air, and noblemen

built country houses here. It still has an exclusive feel, with a Georgian High Street and expensive houses. On Highgate Hill, a statue of a black cat marks the spot where a dejected Richard Whittington and his pet are said to have paused. He was about to leave London, when he heard the sound of Bow Bells telling him to turn back – to become Lord Mayor three times (see p39).

Highgate Cemetery ❺

Swain's Lane N6. 📞 020-8340 1834. 🚇 Archway. **Eastern Cemetery open** Apr–Oct: 10am–5pm Mon–Fri, 11am–5pm Sat–Sun; Nov–Mar: 10am– 4pm daily. **Western Cemetery open** 🎬 only Apr–Oct: noon, 2pm, 4pm Mon–Fri, 11am–4pm Sat, Sun; Nov– Mar: 11am–3pm Sat, Sun. **Closed** 25–26 Dec, during funerals – phone to check. **Adm charge.** ♿

T HE WESTERN part of this early Victorian gem opened in 1839. Its graves and tombs perfectly reflect high Victorian taste. For many years it lay neglected until a voluntary group, the Friends of Highgate Cemetery, stepped in to save it from further decline. They have restored the Egyptian Avenue, a street of family vaults built in a style based on ancient Egyptian tombs, and the Circle of Lebanon, more vaults in a ring, topped by a cedar tree. In the eastern section lies Karl Marx, beneath a gigantic black bust of his image. The novelist George Eliot (real name, Mary Anne Cross) is also buried here.

George Wombwell's Memorial at Highgate Cemetery

Jewish Bakers' Union banner, c.1926, Jewish Museum, Camden

The Jewish Museum ⑥

Raymond Burton House, 129–31 Albert Street, NW1. **Map** 4 C1. [020-7824 1997. ⊖ Camden Town. 80 East End Road, Finchley N3. [020-8349 1143. ⊖ Finchley Central. **Open** 10am–4pm Mon–Fri, 10am–5pm Sun. **Closed** Fri, Sat, Jewish hols. **Adm charge.** ⛔ ◻

L ONDON'S JEWISH MUSEUM was founded in 1932. Today it is spread across two sites. The Camden branch has three galleries celebrating Jewish life in this country from the Middle Ages. The museum is packed with memorabilia and inter-active displays and is seen as nationally important for its col-lections of Jewish ceremonial art, including Hanukkah lamps, a collection of Jewish marriage rings and some illuminated marriage contracts. However, the highlight of this collection is an ornate 16th-century carved and gilded walnut Venetian synagogue ark.

The Finchley site houses the museum's social history collections which feature taped and photographic archives as well as reconstructions of East End tailoring and cabinet-making workshops and a moving exhibition devoted to the Holocaust.

St John's Gate ⑦

St John's Lane EC1. **Map** 6 F4. [020-7253 6644. ⊖ Farringdon. **Museum open** 10am–5pm Mon–Fri, 10am–4pm Sat. **Closed** public hol weekends. **Adm charge.** ⛔ ◻ ◻ 11am, 2.30pm Tue, Fri, Sat. ◻

T HE TUDOR GATEHOUSE and parts of the 12th-century church are all that remain of the priory of the Knights of

St John, which flourished here for 400 years and was the precursor of the St John Ambulance. Over the years, the priory buildings have had many uses, including as offices for Elizabeth I's Master of the Revels, a pub, a coffee shop run by artist William Hogarth's father, and the offices of the *Gentlemen's Magazine* (1731–54). A museum of the order's history is open daily, but to see the rest of the building, join a guided tour.

The Crafts Council Gallery

Crafts Council Gallery ⑧

44a Pentonville Rd N1. **Map** 6 D2. [020-7278 7700. ⊖ Angel. **Open** 11am–6pm Tue–Sat, 2–6pm Sun. **Closed** 25–26 Dec, 1 Jan. ⛔ ◻ ◻ **Lectures**.

T HE COUNCIL is the national body for promoting the creation and appreciation of crafts in Britain. It has a collection of contemporary British crafts, some of which is displayed here, along with special exhibitions. There is a reference library and inform-ation service and a bookshop which also sells many good examples of modern crafts.

Islington ⑨

N1. **Map** 6 E1. ⊖ Angel, Highbury & Islington.

I SLINGTON WAS ONCE a highly fashionable spa, but the rich began to move out in the late 18th century, and the area deteriorated rapidly. During the 20th century, writers such as Evelyn Waugh, George Orwell and Joe Orton lived here. Now Islington has again returned to fashion as one of London's first areas to become "gentrified", with many young professionals buying and refurbishing old houses.

An older relic is Canonbury Tower, the remains of a medi-eval manor house converted into apartments in the 18th century. Writers such as Washington Irving and Oliver Goldsmith lived here and today it houses the Tower Theatre. On Islington Green there is a statue of Sir Hugh Myddleton, who built a canal through Islington in 1613 to bring water to London from Hertfordshire; today a pleas-ant landscaped walk along its banks runs between Essex Road and Canonbury stations. There are two markets close to the Angel station (*see p324*): Chapel Road selling fresh food and cheap clothing, and the nearby Camden Passage, selling expensive antiques.

St John's Priory: today, only the gatehouse remains intact

East of the Centre

Geffrye Museum's Victorian Room

Geffrye Museum ⑩

Kingsland Rd E2. **020-7739 9893**.
🚇 *Liverpool St, Old St.* **Open** *10am–5pm Tue–Sat, noon–5pm Sun (also noon–5pm Mon public hols).* **Closed** *24–26 Dec, 1 Jan, Good Fri.* ♿ ⑪
📷 *Exhibitions, lectures, events.*
🌐 www.geffrye-museum.org.uk

THIS DELIGHTFUL MUSEUM is housed in a set of almshouses built in 1715 on land bequeathed by Sir Robert Geffrye, a 17th-century Lord Mayor of London who made his fortune through trade, including the slave trade. The almshouses (for ironworkers and their widows) have been adapted into typical room settings of specific periods, and provide an insight into the history of family life and the evolution of interior design. The historic room settings begin with Elizabethan (which contains magnificent panelling) and run through various major styles, including Art Nouveau, while an airy, glass and red-brick extension houses more modern settings, such as an example of 1990s "loft living".

Each room contains superb examples of the furniture of the period collected from all over Britain. In the middle, the chapel has not been altered significantly from its original appearance, with box pews. There are attractive garden settings outside the museum, which include a walled herb garden.

Sutton House ⑪

2–4 Homerton High St E9.
📞 *020-8986 2264.* 🚇 *Bethnal Green then bus 253.* **Open** *Feb–Nov: 11.30am–5pm Wed, Sun.* **Closed** *Dec, Jan, Good Fri.* **Adm charge.** 🚫 ♿
📷 🖥 📷 *Concerts, lectures.*

ONE OF THE FEW London Tudor merchants' houses to survive in something like its original form, it is now being restored. Built in 1535 for Ralph Sadleir, a courtier to Henry VIII, it was owned by several wealthy families before becoming a girls' school in the 17th century. In the 18th century the front was altered, but the Tudor fabric remains surprisingly intact, with much original brickwork, large fireplaces and linenfold panelling.

Bethnal Green Museum of Childhood ⑫

Cambridge Heath Rd E2.
📞 *020-8983 5200.*
🚆 *Cambridge Heath.* 🚇 *Bethnal Green.* **Open** *10am–5.50pm Mon–Thu, Sat & Sun.* **Closed** *24–26 Dec, 1 Jan.* 📷 ♿ 📷 *Workshop, children's activities.*
🌐 www.museumofchildhood.org.uk

THIS BRANCH of the Victoria and Albert Museum *(see pp202–205)* is more usefully described as a toy museum, although there are plans to broaden its range by showing exhibits on the social history of childhood. Its array of dolls, lavish dolls' houses (some

Tate "Baby" house made in 1760

donated by royalty), games, model trains, theatres, puppets and some large play equipment are well explained and enticingly displayed.

The purpose-built museum building was erected on the V&A site. In 1872, when the V&A was extended, it was dismantled and reassembled here to bring the light of learning to the East End. The toy collection began early this century and Bethnal Green became a dedicated toy museum in 1974.

St Mary, Rotherhithe ⑬

St Marychurch St SE16.
📞 *020-7231 2465.* 🚇 *Rotherhithe.* **Open** *7.30am–6pm daily.* 🕐 *9.30am, 6pm Sun.* 🚫 ♿ *restricted.*

St Mary, Rotherhithe

THIS BRIGHT CHURCH was built in 1715 on the site of a medieval church, traces of which remain in the tower. It has nautical connotations, most notably a memorial to Christopher Jones, captain of the *Mayflower* on which the Founding Fathers sailed to North America. The barrel roof resembles an inverted hull. The communion table is made from the timbers of the *Temeraire*, a warship whose final journey to the breaker's yard at Rotherhithe was evocatively recorded in Turner's painting at the National Gallery *(see pp104–7)*.

William Morris tapestry (1885)

St Anne's, Limehouse ⓮

Commercial Rd E14.
[020-7987 1502. **Docklands Light Railway** Westferry. **Open** 2–4pm Mon–Fri, 2.30–5pm Sat, Sun (viewing by appointment only).
[10.30am, 6pm Sun. ▣ ▣
Concerts, lectures.

THIS IS ONE of the group of East End churches designed by Nicholas Hawksmoor. It was completed in 1724. Its 40-m (130-ft) tower very soon became a landmark for ships using the East End docks – St Anne's still has the highest church clock in London. The church was damaged by fire in 1850 and, while it was being restored, the architect Philip Hardwick Victorianized its interior. It was bombed in World War II and is today in need of further restoration.

Canary Wharf ⓯

E14. ⊖ **Docklands Light Railway** Canary Wharf. ♿ ▮▮ ▣ ▣
Information centre, concerts, exhibitions. See **The History of London** pp30–1.

LONDON'S MOST ambitious commercial development opened in 1991, when the first tenants moved into the

50-storey Canada Tower, designed by Argentine architect Cesar Pelli. At 250 m (800 ft) it dominates the city's eastern skyline and is the tallest office building in Europe. It stands on what was the West India Dock, closed, like all the London docks, between the 1960s and the 1980s, when trade moved to the modern container port down river at Tilbury. After almost a decade of recession-related uncertainty, Canary Wharf is growing and thriving. When completed, it will have 21 office buildings plus shops and leisure facilities.

William Morris Gallery ⓰

Lloyd Park, Forest Rd E17. **[** 020-8527 3782. ⊖ Walthamstow Central. **Open** 10am–1pm, 2–5pm Tue–Sat, 10am–1pm, 2–5pm first Sun each month. **Closed** 24–26 Dec and public hols. ♿ ▣ **Lectures.**

THE MOST influential designer of the Victorian era, born in 1834, lived in this imposing 18th-century house as a youth. It is now a beguiling and well-presented museum giving a full account of William Morris the artist, designer, writer, craftsman and pioneer socialist. It has choice examples of his work and that of various other members of the Arts and Crafts movement that he inspired – furniture by A H Mackmurdo, Kelmscott Press books, tiles by de Morgan, and paintings by members of the Pre-Raphaelite Brotherhood.

Canada Tower at Canary Wharf

Thames Barrier ⓱

Unity Way SE18. **[** 020-8854 1373. ⇌ Charlton, Silvertown. **Open** 10am–5pm Mon–Fri (Oct–Feb 10am–4pm), 10.30am–5.30pm Sat, Sun. **Closed** 25–26 Dec. **Adm charge.** ▣ ♿ ▣
[Multi-media show, exhibition.

IN 1236 THE THAMES rose so high that people rowed across Westminster Hall; London flooded again in 1663, 1928 and in 1953. Something had to be done, and in 1965 the Greater London Council invited proposals. The Thames Barrier was completed in 1984 and is 520 m (1,700 ft) across. Its 10 gates, which pivot from being flat on the river bed, swing up to 1.6 m (6 ft) above the level reached by the tide in 1953. The barrier seldom has to be raised more than twice a year and is best visited by boat.

Unique structure of the Dome

The Dome ⓲

North Greenwich SE10.
⊖ North Greenwich/The Dome (Jubilee Line). **Closed** to the public.

THE DOME was the focal point of Britain's celebration of the year 2000. Controversial from its earliest days, it is nonetheless a spectacular feat of engineering. Its base is ten times that of St Paul's Cathedral, and Nelson's Column could stand beneath its roof. Its canopy is made from 100,000 sq m (109,000 sq yards) of Teflon-coated spun glass-fibre, and is held by over 70 km (43 miles) of steel cable rigged to twelve 100-m (328-ft) masts.

The intention had been to sell the building to the most convincing bidder after the year 2000. However, while some have come close, so far there has been no confirmed buyer nor any clear idea what to do with it.

South of the Centre

A Jacobean fireplace at Charlton House

Charlton House ⑲

Charlton Rd SE7. [020-8856 3951.
≋ Charlton. **Open** 9am–10pm
Mon–Fri, 10am–5pm Sat (phone to
arrange). **Closed** public hols.
◎ by arrangement. ⊠ ⊟

THE HOUSE was completed
in 1612 for Adam Newton,
tutor to Prince Henry. It has
good river views and is the
best-preserved Jacobean mansion in the London area – well
worth the tricky journey for
enthusiasts of that period. It is
now used as a community
centre but many of the original ceilings and fireplaces
survive intact, as does the
carved main staircase, all with
an astonishing quantity of
ornament. Some parts of the
wood panelling, too, are
original, and the ceilings have
been restored using the original
moulds. In the grounds is a
summer house that, according
to tradition, was designed by
Inigo Jones, and a mulberry
tree (probably the oldest in
England) said to have been
planted by James I in 1608 as
part of his failed attempt to
start an English silk industry.

Eltham Palace ⑳

Court Yard SE9. [020-8294 2548.
≋ Eltham, then a 15-minute walk.
Open Wed–Fri, Sun. Apr–Sep: 10am–
6pm; Oct: 10am–5pm; Nov–Mar:
10am–4pm. **Adm charge.** ◎ ⅙ ⊟

THIS UNIQUE property lets
visitors relive the grand
life of two very different eras.
In the 14th century, English
kings spent Christmas in a
splendid palace here. The
Tudors used it as a base for
deer-hunting but it fell to ruin
after the Civil War (1642–8). In
1932 Stephen Courtauld, a film
director and member of the
wealthy textile family, restored
the hall which, apart from the
bridge over the moat, was the
only part of the medieval palace to survive. Next to it he
built a house described as "a
wonderful combination of
Hollywood glamour and Art
Deco design". This has now
been superbly restored and is
open in addition to the old
hall, the carp-filled moat and
the superb 1930s garden, with
its marvellous London views.

Horniman Museum ㉑

100 London Rd SE23. [020-8699
1872. ≋ Forest Hill. **Gardens open**
8am–dusk daily. **Museum open**
10.30am–5.30pm Mon–Sat, 2–5.30pm
Sun. **Closed** 24–26 Dec. ⅙ ⊟ ⊟
Concerts, lectures, events.

FREDERICK HORNIMAN, the tea
merchant, had this museum
built in 1901 to house the
curios he had collected on his
travels. It has a distinctly
Victorian feel, from the
inspirational mosaic on the
front (representing Humanity
in the House of Circumstance)
to the overstuffed walrus
inside. As you would expect,
there is also an exhibition of
tea-making paraphernalia.

Dulwich Picture Gallery ㉒

College Rd SE21. [020-8693 8000.
≋ West Dulwich, North Dulwich.
Open 10am–5pm Tue–Fri, 11am–
5pm Sat, 2–5pm Sun (last adm:
4.45pm). **Closed** all public hols except
Bank Holiday Mondays. **Adm charge.**
free Fri. ◎ ⅙ ⊠ ⊟ ⊟ **Concerts,**
events, lectures, art classes.

ENGLAND'S OLDEST public art
gallery, it was opened in
1817 and designed by Sir
John Soane (see pp136–7). Its
imaginative use of skylights

Rembrandt's *Jacob II de Gheyn* at
Dulwich Picture Gallery

made it the prototype of most art galleries built since. The gallery was commissioned to house the collection of nearby Dulwich College. (The College, by Charles Barry, was opened in 1870.).

This superb collection has works by Rembrandt (whose *Jacob II de Gheyn* has been stolen from here four times), Canaletto, Poussin, Watteau, Claude, Murillo and Raphael.

The building houses Soane's mausoleum to Desenfans and Bourgeois, original founders of the collection.

Tennis racket and net from 1888, Wimbledon Lawn Tennis Museum

Battersea Park ❷❸

Albert Bridge Rd SW11. **Map** 19 C5. ☎ *020-8871 7530.* ⊖ *Sloane Square then bus 137.* ⇌ *Battersea Park.* **Open** *dawn–dusk daily.* ⃠ ⃟ **Thrive Battersea Park Garden Project** ☎ *020-7720 2212.* ⃞ **Events.** *See* **Three Guided Walks** *pp266–7.*

Peace Pagoda, Battersea Park

THIS WAS THE second public park created to relieve the growing urban stresses on Victorian Londoners (the first was Victoria Park in the East End). It opened in 1858 on the former Battersea Fields – a swampy area notorious for every kind of vice, centred around the Old Red House, a disreputable pub.

The new park immediately became popular, especially for its man-made boating lake, with its romantic rocks, gardens and waterfalls. Later it became a great site for the new craze of cycling.

In 1985 a peace pagoda – one of more than 70 throughout the world – was opened. Buddhist nuns and monks took 11 months to build the 35-m (100-ft) high monument. There is also a small zoo.

St Mary's, Battersea ❷❹

Battersea Church Rd SW11. ☎ *020-7228 9648.* ⊖ *Sloane Square then bus 19 or 219.* **Open** *Jun–Sep: 11am–3pm Tue & Wed, or by arrangement.* ⃠ *11am, 6.30pm Sun.* ⃠ **Concerts.**

THERE HAS BEEN a church here since at least the 10th century. The present brick building dates from 1775; but the 17th-century stained glass, commemorating Tudor monarchs, comes from the former church.

In 1782 the poet and artist William Blake was married in the church to the daughter of a Battersea market gardener. Later J M W Turner was to paint some of his marvellous views of the Thames from the church tower. Nearby is Old Battersea House (1699).

Wimbledon Lawn Tennis Museum ❷❺

Church Rd SW19. ☎ *020-8946 6131.* ⊖ *Southfields.* **Open** *10.30am–5pm daily (not during Championships except to ticket holders).* **Closed** *Good Fri, 25 Dec, 1 Jan.* **Adm charge.** ⃟ ⃞ ⃟ **Exhibitions.**

EVEN THOSE with only a passing interest in the sport will find plenty to enjoy at this lively museum. It traces tennis's development from its invention in the 1860s as a diversion for country house parties, to the sport it is today. Alongside strange 19th-century equipment are film clips showing the great players of the past. More recent matches may be viewed in the video theatre.

Wimbledon Windmill Museum ❷❻

Windmill Rd SW19. ☎ *020-8947 2825.* ⊖ ⇌ *Wimbledon then 30-min walk.* **Open** *Easter–31 Oct: 2–5pm Mon–Sat, 11am–5pm Sun.* **Closed** *1 Nov–Easter (except groups, by arrangement).* **Adm charge.** ⃟ ⃟ ⃞ ⃟ *by arrangement.*

THE MILL on Wimbledon Common was built in 1817. The building at its base was turned into cottages in 1864. Boy Scout founder, Lord Baden-Powell, lived in the mill house. The site is now a museum.

St Mary's, Battersea

West of the Centre

Ham House

Richmond Park ㉗

Kingston Vale SW15. **(** 020-8948 3209. ⊖ ⇌ *Richmond then bus 65 or 71.* **Open** *Oct–Mar: 7.30am–dusk daily; Apr–Sep: 7am–dusk daily.* **Fishing, golf, riding, cycling.**

Deer in Richmond Park

CHARLES I, WHEN he was Prince of Wales in 1637, built a wall 8 miles (13 km) round to enclose the royal park as a hunting ground. Deer still graze warily among the chestnuts, birches and oaks, no longer hunted but still discreetly culled. They have learned to co-exist with the many thousands of human visitors who stroll here on fine weekends.

In late spring the highlight is the Isabella Plantation with its spectacular display of rhododendrons, while the nearby Pen Ponds are very popular with optimistic anglers. (Adam's Pond is for model boats.) The rest of the park is heath, bracken and trees. Richmond Gate, in the northwest corner, was designed by the landscape gardener Capability Brown in 1798. Nearby is Henry VIII Mound, where in 1536 the king, staying in Richmond Palace, awaited the signal that his former wife, Anne Boleyn, had been executed. The Palladian White Lodge, built for George II in 1729, is home to the Royal Ballet School.

Hampton Court ㉘

See pp254–7.

Ham House ㉙

Ham St, Richmond. **(** 020-8940 1950. ⊖ ⇌ *Richmond then bus 65 or 371.* **Open** *Apr–Oct: 1–5pm Sat–Wed.* **Closed** *Nov–Mar.* **Adm charge.** & ✔ *by prior arrangement only.* 🍴 🎁

THIS MAGNIFICENT HOUSE by the Thames was built in 1610 but had its heyday later, when it was the home of the Duke of Lauderdale, confidant to Charles II and Secretary of

Marble Hill House

State for Scotland. His wife, the Countess of Dysart, inherited the house from her father who had been Charles I's "whipping boy" – meaning that he was punished for the future king's misdemeanours. From 1672 the Duke and Countess started to modernize the house, and it was soon regarded as one of the finest in Britain. The diarist John Evelyn admired their garden, which has now been restored to its 17th-century form.

On some days in summer, a foot passenger ferry runs from here to Marble Hill House and Orleans House at Twickenham.

Orleans House ㉚

Orleans Rd, Twickenham. **(** 020-8892 0221. ⊖ ⇌ *Richmond then bus 33, 90, 290, R68 or R70.* **Open** *Apr–Sep: 1–5.30pm Tue–Sat, 2–5.30pm Sun, public hols. Oct–Mar: 1.30–4.30pm Tue–Sat, 2–4.30pm Sun, public hols.* **Closed** *24–26 Dec, Good Fri.* & *restricted.* 🎁 **Concerts, lectures.**

ONLY THE OCTAGON, designed by James Gibbs for James Johnson in 1720, remains of this early 18th-century house. It is named after Louis Philippe, the exiled Duke of Orleans, who lived here between 1800 and 1817, before becoming king of France in 1830. The lively interior plasterwork of the Octagon still remains intact. The adjacent gallery shows temporary exhibitions, and these include some local history displays of the area.

Marble Hill House ㉛

Richmond Rd, Twickenham. **(** 020-8892 5115. ⊖ ⇌ *Richmond then bus 33, 90, 290, R68 or R70.* **Open** *Apr–Sep: 10am–6pm daily; Oct–Mar: 10am–5pm Wed–Sun.* **Closed** *24–26 Dec.* 🚫 & *restricted.* 🎧 🍴 🎁 **Concerts, fireworks** *on summer weekends. See* **Entertainment** *p333.*

BUILT IN 1729 for George II's mistress, the house and its grounds have been open to the public since 1903. It has now been largely restored to its

Georgian appearance, but is not yet fully furnished. There are paintings by William Hogarth and a view of the river and house in 1762 by Richard Wilson, who is regarded as the father of English landscape painting.

Richmond ㉜

SW15. ⊖ ⇄ *Richmond.*

Richmond side street

THIS ATTRACTIVE London village took its name from the palace that Henry VII built here in 1500. Many early 18th-century houses survive near the river and off Richmond Hill, notably Maids of Honour Row, which was built in 1724. The beautiful view of the river from the top of the hill has been captured by many artists, and is largely unspoiled.

Syon House ㉝

London Rd, Brentford. **[** 020-8560 0881. ⊖ *Gunnersbury then bus 237 or 267.* **House open** *mid-Mar–Oct: 11am–5pm Wed–Thu, Sun (last adm 4.15pm).* **House closed** *Nov–mid-Mar.* **Gardens open** *10am–6pm (or dusk, whichever is earlier) daily.* **Adm charge.** ⊘ **[** *to gardens only.* **[** **[** **[** **[**

THE EARLS and Dukes of Northumberland have lived here for 400 years – it is the only large mansion in the London area still in its heredi-

tary ownership. Outbuildings house a butterfly house, an aquarium, an indoor adventure playground, an art centre, a garden centre, a National Trust souvenir and gift shop and two restaurants. The house itself will always be the star exhibit, with lavish interiors by Robert Adam. Some rooms have Spitalfields silk wall-hangings and there are many beautiful pictures. The tranquil gardens include a rosarium and an enchanting conservatory built in 1830.

Musical Museum ㉞

368 High St, Brentford. **[** 020-8560 8108. ⊖ *Gunnersbury, South Ealing then bus 65, 237 or 267.* **Open** *Apr–Jun, Sep–Oct: 2–5pm Sat, Sun; Jul & Aug: 2–4pm Wed.* **Closed** *Nov–Mar.* **Adm charge.** ▢ ⅋ ⅋ **[** **[**

THE COLLECTION comprises chiefly large instruments, including player (or auto-matic) pianos and organs, miniature and cinema pianos, and what is thought to be the only surviving self-playing Wurlitzer organ in Europe.

Drawing room: Osterley Park House

Osterley Park House ㉟

Isleworth. **[** 020-8232 5050. ⊖ *Osterley.* **Open** *1–4.30pm Wed–Sun (last adm: 4pm).* **Closed** *1 Nov –31 Mar, Good Fri.* **[** **[** **Garden open** *9am–dusk.*

OSTERLEY is ranked among Robert Adam's finest works, and its colonnaded portico and multi-coloured library ceiling are the proof. Much of the furniture was designed by Adam, and the garden and its temple are by William Chambers, architect of Somerset House *(see p117)*. The greenhouse is by Adam.

Robert Adam's red drawing room at Syon House

Hampton Court ❷⁸

CARDINAL WOLSEY, powerful Arch-bishop of York to Henry VIII, began building Hampton Court in 1514. Originally it was not a royal palace, but was

Ceiling decoration from the Queen's Drawing Room intended as Wolsey's river-side country residence.

Later, in 1528, in the hope of retaining royal favour, Wolsey offered it to the king. After the royal takeover, Hampton Court was twice rebuilt and extended, first by Henry himself and then, in the 1690s, by William and Mary, who employed Christopher Wren as architect.

There is a striking contrast between Wren's Classical royal apartments and the Tudor turrets, gables and chimneys elsewhere. The inspiration for the gardens as they are today comes largely from the time of William and Mary, for whom Wren created a vast, formal Baroque land-scape, with radiating avenues of majestic limes and many collections of exotic plants.

★ **The Maze**
Lose yourself in one of the garden's most popular features.

Royal tennis court

River boat pier

Main entrance

River Thames

Privy Garden

★ **The Great Vine**
The vine was planted in 1768, and, in the 19th century, produced up to 910 kg (2,000 lbs) of black grapes.

The Pond Garden
This sunken water garden was part of Henry VIII's elaborate designs.

★ **The Mantegna Gallery**
Andrea Mantegna's nine canvases depicting The Triumphs of Caesar *(1490s) are housed here.*

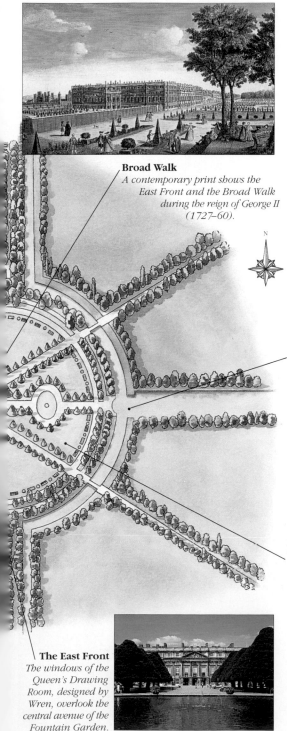

Broad Walk
A contemporary print shows the East Front and the Broad Walk during the reign of George II (1727–60).

N

Long Water
A man-made lake runs parallel to the Thames, from the Fountain Garden across the Home Park.

Fountain Garden
A few of the clipped yews here were planted in the reign of William and Mary.

The East Front
The windows of the Queen's Drawing Room, designed by Wren, overlook the central avenue of the Fountain Garden.

STAR FEATURES

★ **The Great Vine**

★ **The Mantegna Gallery**

★ **The Maze**

Exploring the Palace

AS AN HISTORIC royal palace, Hampton Court bears traces of many of the kings and queens of England from Henry VIII to the present day. The building itself

Carving on the roof of the Great Hall

is an harmonious blend of Tudor and English Baroque architecture. Inside, visitors can see the Great Hall, built by Henry VIII, as well as state apartments of the Tudor court. Many of the state apartments, including those above Fountain Court by Christopher Wren, are decorated with furniture, tapestries and old masters from the Royal Collection.

Tudor Chimneys
Ornate chimneys, some original, some careful restorations, adorn the roof of the Tudor palace.

Queen's Presence Chamber

Queen's Guard Chamber

Haunted Gallery

★ Chapel Royal
The Tudor chapel was re-fitted by Wren except for the carved and gilded vaulted ceiling.

★ Great Hall
The stained-glass window in the Tudor Great Hall shows Henry VIII flanked by the coats of arms of his six wives.

STAR FEATURES

★ **Great Hall**

★ **Fountain Court**

★ **Clock Court**

★ **Chapel Royal**

★ Clock Court
Anne Boleyn's Gateway is at the entrance to Clock Court. The Astronomical Clock, created for Henry VIII in 1540, is also located here.

King's Great Bedchamber
William III bought the crimson bed from his Lord Chamberlain.

Wren's east facade

Queen's Gallery
This marble chimneypiece by John Nost adorns the Queen's Gallery, where entertainments were often staged.

CARDINAL WOLSEY
Thomas Wolsey (c.1475–1530), simultaneously a cardinal, Archbishop of York and chancellor, was, after the king, the most powerful man in England. However, when he was unable to persuade the pope to allow Henry VIII to divorce his first wife, Catherine of Aragon, Wolsey fell from royal favour. He died while making his way to face trial for treason.

★ **Fountain Court**
The windows of state apartments are visible above the cloisters of Fountain Court.

King's Staircase
Leading to the state apartments, the King's Staircase has wall paintings by Antonio Verrio.

TIMELINE

1514 Construction of palace begins			**1734** William Kent decorates the Queen's Staircase	**1838** Public first admitted to the palace	**1986** State apartments partly damaged by fire
1532 Henry starts new hall		**1647** Charles I imprisoned by Cromwell			
1500	**1600**	**1700**	**1800**		**1900**
1528 Wolsey gives the palace to Henry VIII	**1689** William and Mary move to Hampton Court		**1770** Great Gatehouse reduced by two storeys		**1992** Damaged apartments are reopened
Henry VIII painted by Hans Holbein		**c. 1727** Queen's apartments are finally completed			

Pitshanger Manor and Gallery **36**

Mattock Lane W5. **C** *020-8567 1227.*
e *Ealing Broadway.* **Open** *10am–5pm Tue–Sat.* **Closed** *public hols.*
Exhibitions, courses, lectures.

SIR JOHN SOANE, architect of the Bank of England *(see p147)*, designed this house on the site of an earlier one. Completed in 1803 it was to become his own country residence. There are clear echoes of his elaborately constructed town house in Lincoln's Inn Fields *(see pp136–7)*, especially in the library, with its imaginative use of mirrors, in the darkly-painted breakfast room opposite and in the "monk's dining room" which is located on the basement level.

Soane retained two of the principal formal rooms: the drawing room and the dining room. These were designed in 1768 by George Dance the Younger, with whom Soane had worked before establishing his own reputation.

A sympathetic 20th-century extension has been refurbished as a gallery offering a wide range of contemporary art exhibitions and associated events.

The house also contains a large exhibition of Martinware, highly decorated glazed pottery made in nearby Southall between 1877 and

Martinware bird at Pitshanger Manor

1915 and fashionable in late Victorian times. The gardens of Pitshanger Manor are now a pleasant public park and provide a welcome contrast to the bustle of nearby Ealing.

Kew Bridge Steam Museum **37**

Green Dragon Lane, Brentford.
C *020-8568 4757.* **e** *Kew Bridge, Gunnersbury then bus 237 or 267.*
Open *11am–5pm daily.* **Closed** *week to Christmas, Good Fri.* **Adm charge.**
book in advance.
W *www.kbsm. org*

THE 19TH-CENTURY water pumping station, near the north end of Kew Bridge, is now a museum of steam power. Its main exhibits are five giant Cornish beam engines which used to pump the water here from the river, to be distributed in London. The earliest engines, which date from 1820, were designed to pump water out of the Cornish tin and copper mines. See them in operation at weekends and on public holidays.

Kew Gardens **38**

See pp260–61.

City Barge: Strand on the Green

Strand on the Green **39**

W4. **e** *Gunnersbury then bus 237 or 267.* **≷** *Kew Bridge.*

THIS CHARMING Thames-side walk passes some fine 18th-century houses as well as rows of more modest cottages once inhabited by fishermen. The oldest of its three pubs is the City Barge *(see pp309–11)*, parts of which date from the 15th century: the name is older and derives from the time when the Lord Mayor's barge was moored on the Thames outside.

Chiswick House **40**

Burlington Lane W4. **C** *020-8995 0508.* **e** *Chiswick.* **Open** *Easter–Oct: 10am–6pm daily; Nov–Good Friday: 10am–4pm Wed–Sun.* **Adm charge.**

COMPLETED IN 1729 to the design of the third Earl of Burlington, this is a textbook example of a Palladian villa. Burlington revered both Palladio and his disciple Inigo

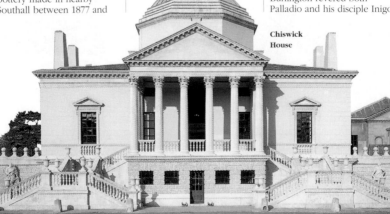

Chiswick House

Jones, and their statues stand outside. Built round a central octagonal room, the house is packed with references to ancient Rome and Palladian devices, such as rooms whose dimensions form perfect cubes.

Chiswick was Burlington's country residence and this house was built as an annexe to a larger, older house, which was later demolished. It was designed for recreation and entertaining – Lord Hervey, Burlington's enemy, dismissed it as "too little to live in and too big to hang on a watch chain". Some of the ceiling paintings are by William Kent, who also laid out the gardens.

The house was a private mental home from 1892 until 1928 when a long process of restoration began. The restorers are still searching for pieces of its original furniture, but the layout of the garden, now a public park, is much as Kent designed it.

Attractive residential and leisure development in Chelsea Harbour

Plaque on Hogarth's House

Hogarth's House ④

Hogarth Lane, W4. 📞 020-8994 6757.
🚇 Turnham Green. **Open** Apr–Oct:
1–5pm Tue–Fri, 1–6pm Sat, Sun;
Nov–Dec & Feb–Mar: 1–4pm Tue–Fri,
1–5pm Sat, Sun. **Closed** Jan. 📷 🚫
🦽 ground floor only. 🚻

WHEN THE PAINTER William Hogarth lived here from 1749 until his death in 1764, he called it "a little country box by the Thames" and painted bucolic views from its windows – he had moved from Leicester Square (see p103). Today heavy traffic roars by along the Great West Road, on its way to and from Heathrow Airport – rush hour traffic is also notoriously bad here. In an environment as

hostile as this, and following years of neglect and then bombing during World War II, the house has done well to survive. It has now been turned into a small museum and gallery, which is filled mostly with a collection of engraved copies of the moralistic cartoon-style pictures with which Hogarth made his name. Salutary tales, such as *The Rake's Progress* (in Sir John Soane's Museum – see pp136–7), *Marriage à la Mode, An Election Entertainment* and many others, can all be seen here.

Fulham Palace ④

Bishops Ave SW6. 📞 020-7736 3233.
🚇 Putney Bridge. **Open** Wed–Sun,
public hol Mon, Mar–Oct: 2–5pm;
Nov–Mar: 1–4pm Thu–Sun. **Closed**
Good Fri, 25–26 Dec. **Park open**
daylight hrs. **Adm charge** for
museum. 🦽 🚫 🚻 **Events,**
concerts, lectures.

THE HOME of the Bishops of London from the 8th century until 1973, the oldest parts of Fulham Palace to survive date from the 15th century. The palace stands in its own landscaped gardens northwest of Putney Bridge. It is here that the annual Oxford versus Cambridge Boat Race begins (see p56).

Chelsea Harbour ④

SW10. 🚇 Fulham Broadway. 🦽
Exhibitions. 📺 🚻

THIS IS AN impressive development of modern apartments, shops, offices, restaurants, a hotel and a marina. It is near the site of Cremorne Pleasure Gardens, which closed in 1877 after more than 40 years as a venue for dances and circuses. The centrepiece is the Belvedere, a 20-storey apartment tower with an external glass lift and pyramid roof, topped with a golden ball on a rod that rises and falls with the tide.

Eye-catching entrance to Fulham Palace dating from Tudor times

Kew Gardens 🔟

THE ROYAL BOTANIC GARDENS at Kew are the most complete public gardens in the world. Their reputation was first established by Sir Joseph Banks, the British naturalist and plant hunter, who worked here in the late 18th century. In 1841 the former royal gardens were given to the nation and now display about 40,000 different kinds of plant. Kew is also a centre for scholarly research into horticulture and botany and garden enthusiasts will want a full day for their visit.

Princess Augusta
King George III's mother established the first garden on a nine-acre (3.6 ha) site here in 1759.

Queen Charlotte's Cottage

★ **Temperate House**
The building dates from 1899. Delicate woody plants are arranged here according to their geographical origins.

★ **Pagoda**
Britain's fascination with the Orient influenced William Chambers's pagoda, built in 1762.

Evolution House
gives a detailed history of plant life on Earth.

Lion Gate entrance

Flagpole

Marianne North Gallery
The Victorian flower painter, Marianne North, gave her works to Kew and paid for this gallery of 1882.

HIGHLIGHTS

Spring
Flowering cherries ①
Crocus "carpet" ②

Summer
Rock Garden ③
Rose Garden ④

Autumn
Autumn foliage ⑤

Winter
Alpine House ⑥
Witch Hazels ⑦

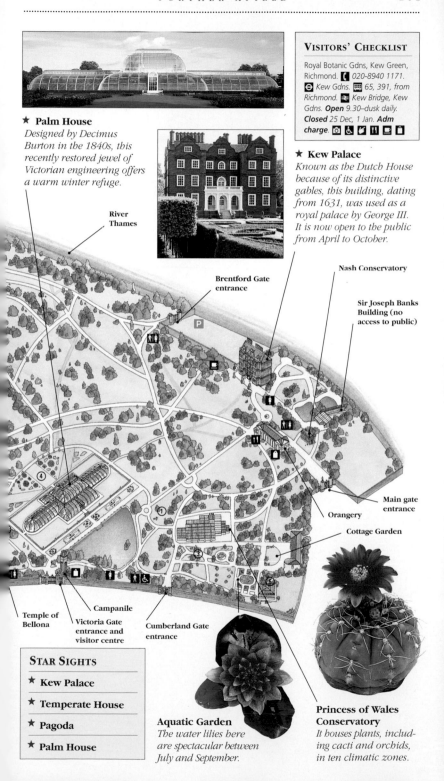

★ **Palm House**
Designed by Decimus Burton in the 1840s, this recently restored jewel of Victorian engineering offers a warm winter refuge.

River Thames

★ **Kew Palace**
Known as the Dutch House because of its distinctive gables, this building, dating from 1631, was used as a royal palace by George III. It is now open to the public from April to October.

Brentford Gate entrance

Nash Conservatory

Sir Joseph Banks Building (no access to public)

Main gate entrance

Orangery

Cottage Garden

Temple of Bellona

Campanile

Victoria Gate entrance and visitor centre

Cumberland Gate entrance

STAR SIGHTS

★ **Kew Palace**

★ **Temperate House**

★ **Pagoda**

★ **Palm House**

Aquatic Garden
The water lilies here are spectacular between July and September.

Princess of Wales Conservatory
It houses plants, including cacti and orchids, in ten climatic zones.

THREE GUIDED WALKS

LONDON IS AN EXCELLENT city for walkers. Although it is much more spread out than most European capitals, many of the main tourist attractions are fairly close to each other *(see pp12–13)*. Central London is full of parks and gardens *(see pp48–51)*, and there are also several walk routes planned by the tourist board and local history societies. These include footpaths along canals and the Thames, and the Silver Jubilee Walk. Planned in 1977 to commemorate the Queen's Silver Jubilee, the walk runs for 12 miles (19 km) between Lambeth Bridge in the west and Tower Bridge in the east; the London Tourist Board *(see p347)* has maps of the route, which is marked by silver-coloured plaques placed at intervals on the pavement.

Statue of boy and dolphin in Regent's Park

Each of the 16 areas described in the *Area-by-Area* section of this book has a short walk marked on its *Street-by-Street* map. These walks will take you past many of the most interesting sights in that area. On the following eight pages are routes for four walks that take you through areas of London not covered in detail elsewhere. These range from the bustling, fashionable King's Road *(see pp266–7)* to the wide open spaces of riverside Richmond and Kew *(see pp268–9)*.

Several companies offer guided walks *(see below)*. Most of these have themes, such as ghosts or Shakespeare's London. Look in listings magazines *(see p326)* for details.

Useful numbers The Original London Walks ☎ 020-7624 3978. W www.walks.com

CHOOSING A WALK

The Three Walks
This map shows the location of the four guided walks in relation to the main sightseeing areas of London.

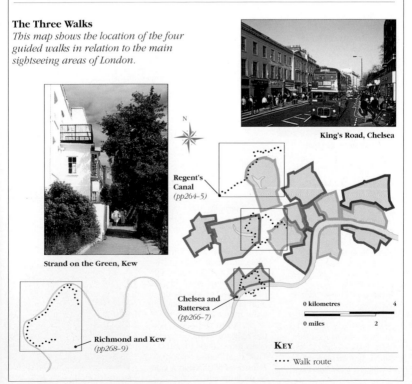

King's Road, Chelsea

Strand on the Green, Kew

N

Regent's Canal *(pp264–5)*

Chelsea and Battersea *(pp266–7)*

Richmond and Kew *(pp268–9)*

0 kilometres   4

0 miles   2

KEY

•••• Walk route

Houseboats on Regent's Canal, Little Venice

A Two-Hour Walk along the Regent's Canal

MASTER BUILDER John Nash wanted the Regent's Canal to pass through Regent's Park, but instead it circles north of the park. Opened in 1820, it is long defunct as a commercial waterway but is today a valuable leisure amenity. This walk starts at Little Venice and ends at Camden Lock market, diverting briefly to take in the view from Primrose Hill. For more details on the sights near the Regent's Canal, see pages 220–27.

Houseboat on the canal ③

From Little Venice to Lisson Grove

At Warwick Avenue station ① take the left-hand exit and walk straight to the traffic lights by the canal bridge at Blomfield Road. Turn right and descend to the canal through an iron gate ② opposite No. 42, marked "Lady Rose of Regent". The pretty basin with moored narrow boats is Little Venice ③. At the foot of the steps turn left to walk back beneath the blue iron bridge ④. You soon have to climb up to street level again because this stretch of the towpath is reserved for access to the

The Warwick Castle, near Warwick Avenue

barges. Cross Edgware Road and walk down Aberdeen Place. When the road turns to the left by a pub, Crockers ⑤, follow the signposted Canal Way down to the right of some modern flats. Continue your route along the canal towpath, crossing Park Road at street level. The scenery along this stretch is unremarkable, but it is not long before a splash of green to your right announces that you are now walking alongside Regent's Park ⑥.

Houseboats moored at Little Venice ③

KEY

— Walk route
☆ Good viewing point
🚇 Underground station
🚉 Railway station

Regent's Park

Soon you see four mansions ⑦. A bridge on huge pillars marked "Coalbrookdale" ⑧ carries Avenue Road into the park. Cross the next bridge, with London Zoo ⑨ on your right, then turn left up a slope. A few steps later, take the right fork, and turn left to cross Prince Albert Road. Turn right before entering Primrose Hill through a gate ⑩ on your left.

Mansion with riverside gardens ⑦

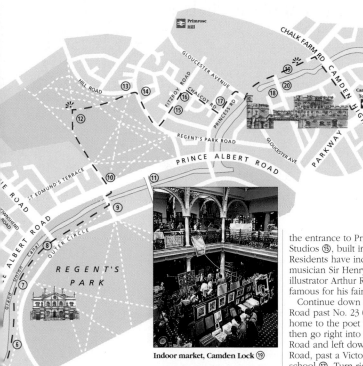

Primrose Lodge, Primrose Hill ⑩

Primrose Hill

From here there is a view of
the zoo aviary ⑪, designed
by Lord Snowdon and
opened in 1965. Inside the
park, keep to the left-hand
path that climbs to the top of
the hill. Soon you fork right
to the summit, which offers a
fine view of the city skyline.
A viewing panel ⑫ helps
identify the landmarks but it
does not include the 1990
skyscraper at Canary Wharf,
with its pyramid crown, on
the left. Descend on the left,
making for the park gate at
the junction of Regent's Park
Road and Primrose Hill Road.

Indoor market, Camden Lock ⑲

Towards Camden

Almost opposite the gate is
the Queens ⑬, a Victorian
pub and, just to the left, is No.
122 Regent's Park Road ⑭.
This was for 24 years the
home of the communist philosopher Friedrich Engels; he
was often visited there by his
friend Karl Marx.

Turn right and walk down
Regent's Park Road for 135 m
(150 yd) then turn left up
Fitzroy Road. On the right,
between Nos. 41 and 39, is

the entrance to Primrose Hill
Studios ⑮, built in 1882.
Residents have included the
musician Sir Henry Wood and
illustrator Arthur Rackham,
famous for his fairy pictures.

Continue down Fitzroy
Road past No. 23 ⑯, once
home to the poet W B Yeats,
then go right into Chalcot
Road and left down Princess
Road, past a Victorian board
school ⑰. Turn right and
rejoin the canal down steps
across Gloucester Avenue.
Turn left under the railway
bridge and past the Pirate
Castle ⑱, a water sports
centre. Cross a hump bridge
and enter Camden Lock
Market ⑲ *(see p324)* through
an arch on your left. After
browsing there you can take
the water bus ⑳ back to Little
Venice or turn right into
Chalk Farm Road and walk
up to Camden Town Under-
ground station.

Pedestrian bridge over the canal at Camden Lock ⑲

A Three-Hour Walk in Chelsea and Battersea

Royal Hospital ③

THIS DELIGHTFUL CIRCULAR WALK ambles through the grounds of the Royal Hospital and across the river to Battersea Park, with its romantic Victorian landscaping. It then returns to the narrow village streets of Chelsea and the stylish shops on the King's Road. For more details on the sights in Chelsea see pages 192–7.

Sloane Square to Battersea Park

From the station ①, turn left and walk down Holbein Place. The Renaissance painter's connection with Chelsea stems from his friendship with Sir Thomas More who lived nearby. Pass the cluster of good antique shops ② as you turn on to Royal Hospital Road. Enter the grounds of the Royal Hospital ③, designed by Christopher Wren, and turn left into the informal Ranelagh Gardens ④. The small pavilion by John Soane ⑤ displays a history of the gardens as a Georgian pleasure resort – it was the most fashionable meeting place for London society.

Galleon on
Chelsea Bridge

Charles II statue in
Royal Hospital ⑥

Leave the gardens for fine views of the hospital and Grinling Gibbons's bronze of Charles II ⑥. The granite obelisk ⑦ commemorates the 1849 battle at Chilianwalla, in what is now Pakistan, and forms the centrepiece of the main marquee at the Chelsea Flower Show (see p56).

Battersea Park

When crossing the Chelsea Bridge ⑧ (1937), look up at the four gilded galleons on top of the pillars at each end. Turn into Battersea Park ⑨ (see p251), one of London's liveliest, and follow the main path along the river to enjoy the excellent views of Chelsea. Turn left at the exotic Buddhist Peace Pagoda ⑩ to the main part of the park.

Past the bowling greens lies Henry Moore's carving of *Three Standing Figures* ⑪ (1948) and the lake, a favoured spot for wildfowl. (There are boats for hire.) Just beyond the sculpture head northwest and, after crossing the central avenue, fork right and make for the wooden gate into the rustic Old English Garden ⑫. Leave the garden by the metal gate and return to Chelsea via the Victorian Albert Bridge ⑬.

Three Standing Figures by
Henry Moore ⑪

KEY

— Walk route

☀ Good viewing point

🚇 Underground station

TIPS FOR WALKERS

Starting point: Sloane Square.
Length: 4 miles (6.5 km).
Getting there: Sloane Square is the nearest tube. There are frequent buses 11, 19, 22 and 349 to Sloane Square and along the King's Road.
Royal Hospital Grounds are open only 10am–6pm Mon–Sat, 2–6pm Sun.
Stopping-off points: There is a café in Battersea Park, by the lake. The King's Head and Eight Bells, on Cheyne Walk, is a well known local pub. There are several other pubs, restaurants and sandwich shops to be found along the King's Road. The Chelsea Farmers' Market on Sydney Street has several cafés.

Old English Garden in Battersea Park ⑫

Albert Bridge ⑬

much of its original character. Where Glebe Place meets the King's Road are three pretty, early 18th-century houses ㉓. Cross Dovehouse Green opposite (it used to be a burial ground), to Chelsea Farmers' Market ㉔, an enclave of cafés and craft shops.

The King's Road

Leave the market on Sydney Street and cross into the garden of St Luke's Church ㉕, where the writer Charles Dickens was married. The walk then winds through pretty back streets until it rejoins the King's Road ㉖ (see p196), which was very fashionable in the 1960s. On the left is The Pheasantry ㉗. Look down the side streets on both left and right to see the squares and terraces: Wellington Square ㉘, then Royal Avenue ㉙, intended as a triumphal way to the Royal Hospital, and Blacklands Terrace ㉚, where book-lovers will want to visit John Sandoe's shop. The Duke of York's Territorial Headquarters ㉛ (1803) on the right marks the approach to Sloane Square ㉜ and the Royal Court Theatre (see Sloane Square p197).

Thomas Carlyle statue ⑮

The Back Streets of Chelsea

Over the bridge is David Wynne's sculpture of a boy and dolphin ⑭ (1975). Pass the sought-after residences on Cheyne Walk and the statues of historian Thomas Carlyle ⑮, and Sir Thomas More ⑯. The area was renowned for gatherings of intellectuals. Past Chelsea Old Church ⑰ is Roper's Gardens ⑱ with

its carving by Jacob Epstein. Just beyond these is the old, medieval Crosby Hall ⑲. Justice Walk ⑳ has a nice view of two early Georgian houses – Duke's House and Monmouth House. Turn left to pass the site of the Chelsea porcelain factory ㉑, which used to make highly fashionable (and today very highly collectable) wares in the late 18th century. Glebe Place ㉒ has retained

Royal Court Theatre ㉜

A 90-Minute Walk around Richmond and Kew

THIS DELIGHTFUL RIVERSIDE walk begins in historic Richmond by the remains of Henry VII's once-splendid palace and ends at Kew, Britain's premier botanic garden. For more details on the sights in Richmond and Kew, turn to pages 252–8.

The river at low tide

Richmond Green

From Richmond station ①, proceed to Oriel House ②, which is practically opposite. Take the alleyway beneath it, and turn left towards the red-brick and terracotta Richmond Theatre ③, built in 1899. The remarkable Edmund Kean, whose brief, meteoric career in the early 19th century had a lasting impact on English acting, was closely associated with the previous theatre on the site. Opposite is Richmond Green ④. Cross it diagonally and go through the entrance arch ⑤ of the old Tudor palace, which is adorned with the arms of Henry VII.

Old Palace: carving over entrance ⑤

remnants, much modified, of the 16th-century buildings.

Leave Old Palace Yard at the right-hand corner ⑥, following a sign "To the River", and turn left to pass the White Swan pub ⑦. At the river, go right along the towpath under the iron railway bridge and then the concrete Twickenham Bridge ⑧, completed in 1933, to reach Richmond Lock ⑨, with its cast-iron footbridge built in 1894. The Thames is tidal as far as Teddington, some 3 miles (5 km) upstream, and the lock is used to make the river continuously navigable.

Richmond Theatre ③

Richmond

Richmond owes much of its importance – as well as its name – to Henry, victor of the Wars of the Roses and the first Tudor monarch. On becoming king in 1485 he spent a lot of time at an earlier residence on this site, Sheen Palace, dating from the 12th century. The palace burned down in 1499 and Henry had it rebuilt, naming it Richmond after the town in Yorkshire where he held an earldom. In 1603 Henry's daughter, Elizabeth I, died here. The houses inside the archway on the left contain

The Riverside

Do not cross the bridge but continue along the wooded path by the river to Isleworth Ait ⑩, a large island where herons may be standing warily on the river bank. Just beyond it, on the far shore, is All Saints' Church ⑪, where the 15th-century tower has survived several rebuildings, most recently in the 1960s. Further round the inlet, Isleworth ⑫, once a small riverside village with a busy harbour, is now a dormitory for central London. Here there will be river traffic to watch: barges, yachts and, in summer, the passenger boats that ply up-river to Hampton Court (see pp254–7). Rowers are out at most times of year, training for races and regattas. The most prestigious occasions are the Henley Regatta in July and the Oxford v Cambridge boat race, every spring from Putney to

Herons fish the river

KEY

— Walk route

꙳ Good viewing point

⊖ Underground station

⊞ Railway station

Mortlake *(see p56)*.

Kew

After a while the appearance of iron railings on your right marks where Old Deer Park ⑬ turns into Kew Gardens ⑭ (correctly the Royal Botanic Gardens – *see pp260–61*). There used to be a riverside entrance for visitors arriving on foot or by water, but the

Kew Palace in Kew Gardens ⑲

laid out in the 18th century. Just beyond are modern waterside apartments at Brentford ⑰. This was originally an industrial suburb, sited where the Grand Union Canal runs into the Thames, and its residential potential has only recently been exploited. You can pick out the tall chimney of the waterworks ⑱, now a museum dedicated to steam power. On the right, behind the Kew Gardens car park, there is soon a view of Kew Palace ⑲, a gloomy edifice in red brick built in 1631.

Beyond the car park, leave the river by Ferry Lane on to Kew Green ⑳. Now you could spend the rest of the day in Kew Gardens or cross Kew Bridge and turn right on to Strand on the Green ㉑, a fine riverside walkway with atmospheric pubs, the oldest of them the City Barge ㉒. Head south down Kew Road if you need to get back, then turn left at Kew Gardens Road to depart from Kew Gardens Underground station

Steam Museum ⑱

TIPS FOR WALKERS

Starting point: Richmond station, District Line.
Length: 3 miles (5 km).
Getting there: Richmond Underground or railway station. Bus 415 comes from Victoria; 391 and R68 from Kew.
Stopping-off points: There are many cafés, pubs and tearooms in Richmond. The famous Maids of Honour tearoom is at Kew, as is Jasper's Bun in the Oven, a good restaurant.

0 metres   500
0 yards   500

gate ⑮ is now closed and the nearest entrance is to the north, near the car park.

Across the river, there are magnificent views of Syon House ⑯, seat of the Dukes of Northumberland since 1594. Part of the present house dates from the 16th century but it was largely redesigned by Robert Adam in the 1760s. You are looking at it across the garden Capability Brown

The river bank between Richmond and Kew

TRAVELLERS' NEEDS

WHERE TO STAY

THE HIGH COST of accommodation in London is one of the biggest drawbacks for visitors. At the top end of the market, there is no shortage of expensive pedigree hotels, such as the Savoy and the Ritz. Mid-range hotels, while there are many, tend to be slightly further out of the centre of town. Sadly, most of the budget hotels are seedy and unappealing, a problem exacerbated by rising land and property prices. However, there are ways to stay in the capital without breaking the bank. Low-cost hotel chains such as Travel Inn, Express by Holiday Inn and Ibis have been established in many convenient locations throughout the city, offering good-quality if standardized accommodation at affordable prices. We have inspected more than 250 hotels and apartment complexes across a range of price brackets and localities and have more than 120 of the best of their kind. For further details on these, turn to the listings on pages 276–285. Self-catering apartments and private homes *(see pp274–5)* are available at a wide range of prices. Student halls and hostels, even a few camping sites on London's outskirts, are additional possibilities for budget travellers *(see p275).*

Hilton doorman

WHERE TO LOOK

THE MOST expensive hotels tend to be in smart West End areas such as Mayfair and Belgravia. Often large and opulent, with uniformed staff, they are not always the most relaxing places to stay. For smaller, more personal, but still luxurious hotels, try South Kensington or Holland Park.

The streets off Earl's Court Road are full of hotels at the lower end of the price range. Several of the big railway stations are well served with budget hotels too. Try Ebury Street near Victoria, or Sussex Gardens near Paddington. Close to Euston or Waterloo and in the City and Docklands, well-known chain hotels cater for travellers at a range of prices. The area immediately north of King's Cross is best avoided at night.

There are also inexpensive hotels in the suburbs, such as Ealing, Hendon, Wembley, Bromley or Harrow. From here you can get into town on public transport. Take care not to miss the last train back.

If you get stranded at an airport or have to catch a very early morning flight, consult the list on page 361.

For further information, advice and reservation services, contact the **London Tourist Board** which publishes several annually updated booklets on accommodation in Greater London.

DISCOUNT RATES

PRICES IN the capital tend to stay high all year round, but there are bargains. Many hotels, especially the groups, offer reduced rates for weekends and special breaks *(see p274).* Others work on a more ad hoc basis, depending on how busy they are. If a hotel isn't full, it is always worth trying to negotiate a discount (see Booking On-line below). Older budget hotels may have rooms without showers or private bathrooms. These usually cost less than those with private facilities.

HIDDEN EXTRAS

READ THE SMALL print carefully. Most hotels quote room rates rather than rates per person, but not all. Service charges are usually included in the quoted price but in some cases they are added on later. Beware of high mark-ups on telephone calls. A hotel with a high room tariff may be even more expensive than at first appears, which means that the the final bill can come as a shock to many visitors.

The Tearoom at Le Meridien Waldorf *(see p284)*

The Raddisson Edwardian Hampshire hotel *(see p282)*

Breakfast may not be included in room rates, though it generally is in cheaper hotels. The definition of breakfast ranges from 'full English' (a hearty, traditional fry-up which will see you through the most hectic sightseeing programme), to a 'Continental' cup of coffee and a roll or croissant. Buffet breakfasts with lavish spreads of fruit, muesli and yoghurt are increasingly popular with health-conscious visitors.

Tipping is expected in the more expensive hotels, but there is no need to tip staff other than porters, except perhaps a helpful concierge for arranging theatre tickets or phoning for taxis.

Single travellers are usually charged a "supplement" and end up paying about 80 per cent of the double room rate, even if they are occupying a "single" room – so don't accept anything substandard.

The elegant hallway of The Gore hotel in Kensington *(see p276)*

FACILITIES

ROOM SIZES in London hotels at all price ranges tend to be on the small side, but the majority of hotels now provide telephones, televisions and private baths or showers in all their rooms. At the top end of the scale, hotels compete to provide the very latest sound-and-video systems, computer equipment and high-tech gadgetry. A recent luxury craze is mini-television screens in the bathroom. Whatever the hotel, you will be expected to vacate your room by noon on the day you leave, sometimes earlier.

HOW TO BOOK

IT IS ALWAYS advisable to book well in advance, as room availability fluctuates and better quality hotels are in constant demand. Direct bookings can be made by letter, phone, fax, or increasingly, via the internet. This generally entails giving some kind of guarantee: either a credit card number from which a cancellation fee can be deducted, or remitting a one-night deposit (some hotels will expect more for longer stays). Don't forget that if you subsequently cancel for any reason, part or all of the room price may be charged unless the hotel can relet the accommodation. Insurance cover is advised.

The London Tourist Board (LTB) provides a free booking service. To take advantage of this, write, at least six weeks in advance, to the Accommodation Service's Advance Booking Office stating how much you want to spend. Remember to confirm any bookings they make for you. If you give less than six weeks notice, a small booking fee is charged, plus a deposit for your stay which is deducted from the final bill. You can book by credit card over the phone, or turn up at an LTB Tourist Information Centre at Victoria or Liverpool Street stations or at Heathrow (on the underground station concourse for terminals 1, 2 and 3). The LTB also has branches at Harrods,

One of the stylish bathrooms at the Portobello hotel *(see p277)*

Selfridges and the Tower of London. It publishes a couple of accommodation booklets providing information on where to stay in London.

Accommodation booking services are also available at the British Travel Centre on Regent Street. A number of non-LTB booking agencies operate from booths in the major railway stations, charging a small fee to personal callers. Unidentified touts, who hang around at railway and coach stations offering cheap accommodation to tourists, should be avoided.

BOOKING ON-LINE

MANY HOTELS have their own websites and the information available on these is often more regularly updated than the hotel brochure. If you are familiar with the technology, internet bookings can be quick and efficient. There are also some good deals available by booking on-line, especially at larger hotels. Accommodation agencies and travel websites also use the internet as a cost-effective way of doing business and, in most cases, at least some of the savings are passed on to customers. Increasingly, the internet demonstrates the fluidity of many hotel "rack rates" (i.e. the prices printed on the tariff sheet), which, far from being fixed in stone, fluctuate widely according to the laws of supply and demand.

SPECIAL BREAKS

MANY TRAVEL agencies carry brochures from the major hotel chains listing special offers, which are usually costed on a minimum two-night stay. Some are extraordinarily good value compared to the usual tariff. For most leisure travellers or families with children, this is the best way to get value for money out of London hotels so that you can spend time in the city without breaking the bank.

City-break packages are organised by specialist operators, ferry companies and airlines, and some privately owned hotels too. Sometimes the same hotel may be featured in several brochures at widely differing prices and with different perks. It's worth asking the hotel directly what special rates they offer, and checking their websites too.

DISABLED TRAVELLERS

INFORMATION ABOUT wheelchair access is based largely on hotels' own assessments, but travellers with special needs should always confirm when booking whether an establishment is suitable. If forewarned, many hotels will go out of their way to help disabled visitors. The nationwide *Tourism for All*

1920s Savoy poster

scheme provides details on accommodation standards and facilities for visitors with mobility problems. For more information on hotels that meet the three-tier 'National Accessible Standard', contact the **LTB** or the **Holiday Care Service**. A booklet, *Access in London*, can be obtained from **RADAR**.

TRAVELLING WITH CHILDREN

LONDON HOTELS are no longer the notorious child-free zones they used to be. A large number now make a concerted effort to cater for the needs of people travelling with children, providing cots, high-chairs, baby-sitting services and special meal arrangements. Always ask whether the hotel offers special deals for children – some have special rates, or allow children to stay free of charge if they sleep in their parents' room. The hotel recommendations in our listing *(see pp272–285)* point out whether particular hotels offer child facilities, or whether on the other hand they have age restrictions.

SELF-CATERING FLATS

MANY AGENCIES offer self-catering accommodation in flats, usually for stays of a week or more. Prices,

depending on size and location, start at about £300 per week. Some luxury complexes are fully serviced, so you don't need to cook, shop or clean. **Bridge Street Accommodations** has over 550 London apartments in smart locations. It caters mainly for corporate and professional travellers, but its properties can be rented for short-term lets whenever they are available.

The **Landmark Trust** rents apartments in historic or unusual buildings. These include rooms in Hampton Court *(see pp250–3)* and flats in a pretty 18th-century terrace in the City: one of them was the home of the late poet laureate, Sir John Betjeman. A handbook of Landmark Trust properties is available for a small charge.

STAYING IN PRIVATE HOMES

A NUMBER OF agencies organize stays in private homes; several are registered with the LTB. Credit card reservations can be made through LTB's telephone booking service *(see box)*. Several agencies have minimum stays of anything up to a week. Prices depend on location, starting at around £20 per person per night. Sometimes you will enjoy family hospitality, but this isn't guaranteed, so enquire when you book. Deposits may be requested and cancellation fees imposed. The **Bed & Breakfast and Homestay Association (BBHA)** is an umbrella organisation for several reputable agencies whose properties are inspected regularly. Several BBHA members are listed in the Directory *(see box)*.

Uptown Reservations arranges upmarket B&B in interesting, well-located London homes which have been inspected for their welcome, security and comfort. Prices start at £85 per night for a double room. It works in tandem with **Wolsey Lodges**, a nationwide consortium of distinctive private

Classical opulence at Claridge's Hotel *(see p281)*

homes, often of historic or architectural interest, offering individual hospitality and a good dinner. Wolsey Lodges lists a couple of charming London properties.

BUDGET ACCOMMODATION

DESPITE THE HIGH cost of many London hotels, budget accommodation does exist, and not only for young travellers.

Dormitory accommodation and youth hostels
These can be booked through the LTB's information centre at Victoria Station for a small fee plus a refundable deposit. Some private hostels near Earl's Court charge little more than £10 a night for a dormitory bed with breakfast. The **London Hostel Association** has a selection of very reasonably priced accommodation throughout central London.

City of London Youth Hostel

The **Youth Hostels Association (YHA)** runs seven hostels in London. There is no age limit, though non-members pay a small joining fee. One of the most interesting and popular is Holland House, a Jacobean mansion in Holland Park.

Halls of residence
Many student rooms are available at Easter and from July to September at very reasonable prices. Some of these are in central locations such as South Kensington. Advance booking is recommended, but places are sometimes available at short notice. Try **City University**, or, if you need accommodation in a hurry, **King's College** or **Imperial College** may be able to find you something.

CAMPING SITES

IN HACKNEY, east of the city centre, there is a place called **Tent City** (open June-Aug). This is a canal-side tented hostel and campsite with basic facilities. There are also sites in Edmonton, Leyton, Chingford and Crystal Palace which have rather more elaborate facilities and also have caravan spaces. The LTB publishes a leaflet detailing the locations and facilities of camping sites in London.

DIRECTORY

RESERVATIONS AND INFORMATION

London Tourist Board (LTB)
Glen House, Stag Place, SW1E 5LT.
📞 020-7932 2020
(advance credit card booking for accommodation).
🖥 www.londontown.com

British Hotel Reservation Centre
13 Grosvenor Gardens SW1W 0BD.
📞 0800 282888.
🖥 www.bhrconline.com

DISABLED TRAVELLERS

Holiday Care Service
2nd Floor, Imperial Buildings, Victoria Road, Horley, Surrey RH6 7BZ.
📞 01293 771500.

RADAR
250 City Road EC1V 8AF.
📞 020-7250 3222.

SELF-CATERING AGENCIES

Bridge Street Accommodations
42 Lower Sloane St SW1W 8BP.
📞 020-7792 2222.
🖥 www.bridgestreet.com

Landmark Trust
Shottesbrooke, Maiden-head, Berks SL6 3SW.
📞 01628 825925.
🖥 www.landmarktrust.co.uk

AGENCIES FOR STAYS IN PRIVATE HOMES

Bed & Breakfast and Homestay Association
🖥 www.bbha.org.uk

Host and Guest Services
103 Dawes Road SW6 7DU
📞 020-7385 9922.
🖥 www.host-guest.co.uk

London Bed and Breakfast Agency
71 Fellows Road NW3 3JY
📞 020-7586 2768.
🖥 www.londonbb.com

Uptown Reservations
41 Paradise Walk SW3 4JL.
📞 020-7351 3445.
🖥 www.uptownres.co.uk

Wolsey Lodges
9 Market Place, Hadleigh, Ipswich, Suffolk, IP7 5DL.
📞 01473 822058.
🖥 www.wolsey-lodges.co.uk

HOSTEL ADDRESSES

London Hostel Association
54 Eccleston Sq SW1V 1PG.
📞 020-7834 1545.
🖥 www.london-hostels.co.uk

Youth Hostels Association
Trevelyan House, 8 St Stephen's Hill, St Albans, Herts AL1 2DY.
📞 01727 855215.

CAMPING SITES

Tent City
Millfields Road, Hackney E5 0AR.
📞 020-8985 7656.
🖥 www.tentcity.co.uk

BOOKING ADDRESSES FOR RESIDENCE HALLS

City University Accommodation and Conference Service
Northampton Sq EC1V 0HB.
📞 020-7477 8037.

Imperial College Summer Accommodation Centre
Watts Way Princes Gdns SW7 1LU.
📞 020-7594 9507.

King's Campus Vacation Bureau
127 Stamford St, SE1 9NQ.
📞 020-7928 3777.

Choosing a Hotel

THESE HOTELS have been selected across a wide price range for their good value, facilities and location; they are listed by area. Starting with west and southwestern districts of London, the guide moves through central parts of the city and on to eastern districts, eventually looking at hotels further outside the city. For map references, see pages 370–407.

BAYSWATER, PADDINGTON

Hotel	Credit Cards	Number of Rooms	Restaurant	Children's Facilities	Quiet Location
DELMERE 130 Sussex Gardens, W2. Map 11 A2. ££ — 020 7706 3344. FAX 020 7262 1863. W www.delmerehotels.com — A well-managed, welcoming hotel that stands out in a street packed with budget accommodation. Bedrooms are small but tidy.	AE DC JCB MC V	38	■		
PAVILION 34–36 Sussex Gardens, W2. Map 11 A1. ££ — 020 7262 0905. FAX 020 7262 1324. W www.msi.com.mt/pavilion — A funky but inexpensive place, where bedrooms are outrageously themed. There's a party in the Silver Salon most nights.	AE DC JCB MC V	27			
MORNINGTON 12 Lancaster Gate, W2. Map 10 F2. £££ — 020 7262 7361. FAX 020 7706 1028. W www.mornington.se — Cool bedrooms contrast with the masculine clubbiness of the bar at this Swedish hotel which offers *Smorgasbord* buffet breakfasts.	AE DC JCB MC V	66		●	■
QUALITY 8–14 Talbot Square, W2. Map 11 A2. £££ — 020 7262 6699. FAX 020 7229 3333. W www.choicehotelslondon.com — Friendly service and smart contemporary decor grace this handsome townhouse chain hotel on a quiet, tree-lined square.	AE DC JCB MC V	75		●	■
HEMPEL 31 Craven Hill Gardens, W2. £££ — 020 7298 9000. FAX 020 7402 4666. W www.the-hempel.co.uk — Anouska Hempel's ultra-chic design statement combines innovative decor, superb service and state-of-the-art technology.	AE DC JCB MC V	47	■	●	■

NORTH KENSINGTON, EARL'S COURT

Hotel	Credit Cards	Number of Rooms	Restaurant	Children's Facilities	Quiet Location
ABBEY HOUSE 11 Vicarage Gate, W8. Map 10 D4. £ — 020 7727 2594. W www.abbeyhousekensington.com — A realistic assessment of budget travellers' needs keeps tariffs down in this popular townhouse B&B. The location is smart; rooms simple and clean.	AE DC JCB MC V	16		●	■
47 WARWICK GARDENS 47 Warwick Gardens, W14. Map 17 C2. ££ — 020 7603 7614. FAX 020 7602 5473. @ nanette@stylianou.fsnet.co.uk — A beautifully kept home-from-home with good transport links nearby and a pretty rear garden for drinks outside, and an excellent breakfast.	MC V	3			
RUSHMORE 11 Trebovir Road, SW5. Map 17 C2. ££ — 020 7370 3839. FAX 020 7370 0274. — Conveniently close to Earl's Court Tube, this well-kept Victorian townhouse offers interestingly decorated rooms.	AE DC JCB MC V	22		●	■
KENSINGTON HOUSE 15–16 Prince of Wales Terrace, W8. Map 10 E5. £££ — 020 7937 2345. FAX 020 7368 6700. W www.kenhouse.com — This smart, newly opened townhouse hotel combines period interest with understated contemporary style.	AE DC JCB MC V	41	■	●	■
ROYAL GARDEN 2–24 Kensington High St, W8. Map 10 5E. £££ — 020 7937 8000. FAX 020 7361 1991. W www.royalgardenhotel.co.uk — Views over Kensington Gardens add to the pleasure of staying in this smart business hotel. It has polished service and a car park.	AE DC JCB MC V	396	■	●	■
TWENTY NEVERN SQUARE 20 Nevern Square, SW5. Map 17 C2. £££ — 020 7565 9555. FAX 020 7565 9444. @ hotel@twentynevernsquare.co.uk — A sumptuously furnished townhouse making imaginative use of natural fabrics and oriental artifacts.	AE DC JCB MC V	20	■		■
THE GORE 189 Queen's Gate, SW7. Map 10 F5. ££££ — 020 7584 6601. FAX 020 7589 8127. W www.gorehotel.com — A quirky Victorian hotel with blizzards of pictures, curios and period features. Two excellent restaurants. Closed Christmas.	AE DC JCB MC V	53	■	●	■

Price categories for a standard double room per night, inclusive of breakfast, service charges and any additional taxes such as VAT:

£ under £80
££ £80–£120
£££ £120–£180
££££ £180–£220
£££££ £220 plus.

CREDIT CARDS
Indicates which credit cards are accepted: *AE* American Express; *DC* Diners Club; *JCB* Japan Credit Bureau; *MC* MasterCard/Access; *V* Visa.

RESTAURANT
Hotel restaurant or dining room serving more than just breakfast – may or may not be open to non-residents.

CHILDREN'S FACILITIES
Any or all of the following: cots, highchairs, babysitting or baby listening, child meal portions, toys, family rooms.

QUIET LOCATION
Not too much passing traffic at night.

	CREDIT CARDS	NUMBER OF ROOMS	RESTAURANT	CHILDREN'S FACILITIES	QUIET LOCATION
THE MILESTONE 1 Kensington Court, W8. **Map** 10 E5. ☎ 020 7917 1000. FAX 020 7917 1010. W www.redcarnationhotels.com Lavish conversion of two townhouses opposite Kensington Gardens. Excellent facilities. Suites and apartments offered. £££££	AE DC JCB MC V	57	■	●	

NOTTING HILL, HOLLAND PARK

	CREDIT CARDS	NUMBER OF ROOMS	RESTAURANT	CHILDREN'S FACILITIES	QUIET LOCATION
ABBEY COURT 20 Pembridge Gardens, W2. **Map** 9 C3. ☎ 020 7221 7518. FAX 020 7792 0858. W www.abbeycourthotel.co.uk Quiet rooms furnished with books and personal touches mark this Victorian townhouse near Notting Hill Gate. £££	AE DC JCB MC V	22		●	■
PEMBRIDGE COURT 34 Pembridge Gardens, W2. **Map** 9 C3. ☎ 020 7229 9977. FAX 020 7727 4982. W www.pemct.co.uk A family-friendly hotel full of Victorian curios. A cheerful cellar bar offers light fare. £££	AE DC MC V	20		●	■
PORTOBELLO 21 Stanley Gardens, W11. **Map** 9 B2. ☎ 020 7727 2777. FAX 020 7792 9641. W www.portobello-hotel.co.uk Delightfully eccentric hotel full of entertaining antiques. Bedrooms bristle with exoticism. Closed Christmas and New Year. ££££	AE MC V	24	■		
MILLERS 111a Westbourne Grove, W2. **Map** 10 D2. ☎ 020 7243 1024. FAX 020 7243 1064. W www.millersuk.com This hotel is an *Aladdin's Cave* of fascinating *objets d'art* collected by antiques guru Martin Miller. ££££	AE MC V	7			
WESTBOURNE 165 Westbourne Grove, W11. **Map** 9 B2. ☎ 020 7243 6008. FAX 020 7229 7201. W www.zoohotels.com The mood of this streamlined hangout in the heart of Notting Hill is chic and contemporary. Many original works of art. ££££	AE DC JCB MC V	20			
HALCYON 81 Holland Park, W11. **Map** 9 A4. ☎ 020 727 7288. FAX 020 7229 8516. W www.thehalcyon.com This romantic hideaway in elegant Holland Park is the last word in luxury exuding classic charm at every turn. £££££	AE DC JCB MC V	42	■	●	■

KNIGHTSBRIDGE, BROMPTON, BELGRAVIA

	CREDIT CARDS	NUMBER OF ROOMS	RESTAURANT	CHILDREN'S FACILITIES	QUIET LOCATION
WILLETT 32 Sloane Gardens, SW1. **Map** 20 D2. ☎ 020 7824 8415. FAX 020 7730 4830. W www.eeh.co.uk This elegant B&B is discreetly tucked away just off Sloane Square. Its rates are modest for this smart location. ££	AE DC JCB MC V	19		●	■
CLAVERLEY 13–14 Beaufort Gardens, SW3. **Map** 19 B1. ☎ 020 7589 8541. FAX 020 7584 3410. @ reservations@claverleyhotel.co.uk A good-value B&B in a peaceful, tree-lined cul-de-sac. Bedrooms are handsome (best have the tall windows on the first floor). £££	AE DC JCB MC V	33		●	■
KNIGHTSBRIDGE GREEN 159 Knightsbridge, SW1. **Map** 11 C5. ☎ 020 7584 6274. FAX 020 7225 1635. W www.thekghotel.co.uk An immaculate hotel, ideally placed for Knightsbridge shopping and serving three-tier breakfasts in spacious bedrooms. £££	AE DC MC V	28		●	■
SEARCY'S ROOF GARDEN 30 Pavilion Road, SW1. **Map** 11 C5. ☎ 020 7584 4921. FAX 020 7823 8694. W www.searcys.co.uk These elegant mews apartments are a real find. Access is via an ancient and eccentric goods lift. £££	AE MC V	11			■
57 POND ST 57 Pond St, SW1. **Map** 19 C1. ☎ 020 7590 1090. FAX 020 7590 1099. W www.no57.com Glamorous hotel with state-of-the-art design features, cool, uncluttered decor and an intimate basement bar-lounge. ££££	AE DC JCB MC V	22	■	●	

For key to symbols see back flap

Price categories for a standard double room per night, inclusive of breakfast, service charges and any additional taxes such as VAT:

£ under £80
££ £80–£120
£££ £120–£180
££££ £180–£220
£££££ £220 plus.

CREDIT CARDS
Indicates which credit cards are accepted: AE American Express; DC Diners Club; JCB Japan Credit Bureau; MC MasterCard/Access; V Visa.

RESTAURANT
Hotel restaurant or dining room serving more than just breakfast – may or may not be open to non-residents.

CHILDREN'S FACILITIES
Any or all of the following: cots, highchairs, babysitting or baby listening, child meal portions, toys, family rooms.

QUIET LOCATION
Not too much passing traffic at night.

	Credit Cards	Number of Rooms	Restaurant	Children's Facilities	Quiet Location
BEAUFORT 33 Beaufort Gardens, SW3. Map 19 B1. ££££ — 020 7584 5252. FAX 020 7589 2834. W www.thebeaufort.co.uk — An aristocratic hideaway in a quiet square with beautifully decorated rooms. Room service and free health club membership.	AE DC JCB MC V	28		●	■
L'HOTEL 28 Basil St, SW3. Map 11 C5. ££££ — 020 7589 6286. FAX 020 7823 7826. W www.lhotel.co.uk — Modestly described as a B&B, this hotel has refined bedrooms and an urbane basement wine bar (Le Metro) serving imaginative dishes.	AE DC JCB MC V	12	■		■
BEAUFORT HOUSE 45 Beaufort Gardens, SW3. Map 19 B1. £££££ — 020 7584 2600. FAX 020 7584 6532. W www.beauforthouse.co.uk — Beautifully furnished apartments in a quiet cul-de-sac. Rates include daily maid service and membership of Champneys health club.	AE DC MC V			●	■
BASIL STREET 23 Basil St, SW3. Map 11 C5. £££££ — 020 7581 3311. FAX 020 7581 3693. W www.thebasil.com — An enduringly popular hotel just off Sloane Street. It has a long history and lots of personality.	AE DC JCB MC V	80	■	●	■
BERKELEY Wilton Place, SW1. Map 12 D5. £££££ — 020 7235 6000. FAX 020 7235 4330. W www.savoy-group.co.uk — This elegant hotel has two top restaurants (Vong and Tante Claire), as well as a Christian Dior health club.	AE DC JCB MC V	168	■	●	
CAPITAL 22–24 Basil St, SW3. Map 11 C5. £££££ — 020 7589 5171. FAX 020 7225 0011. W www.capitalhotel.co.uk — A celebrated restaurant is a main attraction at this small hotel, but the accommodation is managed with similar panache.	AE DC JCB MC V	48	■	●	
EGERTON HOUSE Egerton Terrace, SW3. Map 19 B1. £££££ — 020 7589 2412. FAX 020 7584 6540. W www.egertonhousehotel.co.uk — An intimate townhouse setting overlooking two quiet tree-lined squares, this hotel offers classic furnishings and high standards.	AE DC MC V	29		●	■
HALKIN 5 Halkin St, SW1. Map 12 D5. £££££ — 020 7333 1000. FAX 020 7333 1100. W www.halkin.co.uk — Sophisticated Italian design with oriental touches combined with Stephano Cavallini's understated restaurant overlooking a courtyard garden makes this hotel a startling experience.	AE DC JCB MC V	41	■	●	■
MANDARIN ORIENTAL 66 Knightsbridge, SW1. Map 11 C5. £££££ — 020 7235 2000. FAX 020 7235 4552. W www.mandarinoriental.com — This landmark hotel overlooking Hyde Park offers superb rooms and facilities and an oriental health spa.	AE DC MC V	200	■	●	

SOUTH KENSINGTON, CHELSEA

	Credit Cards	Number of Rooms	Restaurant	Children's Facilities	Quiet Location
HOTEL 167 167 Old Brompton Road, SW5. Map 18 E3. ££ — 020 7373 0672. FAX 020 7373 3360. W www.hotel167.com — An affordable B&B in an elegant part of South Kensington. Bedrooms are unexpectedly stylish.	AE DC JCB MC V	19			
SWISS HOUSE 171 Old Brompton Road, SW5. Map 18 E3. ££ — 020 7373 2769. FAX 020 7373 4983. W www.swiss-hh.demon.co.uk — Friendly, well-kept guesthouse with many thoughtful touches. Bedrooms are charming in warm, fresh schemes with good bathrooms.	AE DC MC V	16		●	
ASTONS APARTMENTS 31 Rosary Gardens, SW7. Map 18 E3. ££ — 020 7590 6000. FAX 020 7590 6060. W www.astons-apartments.com — These self-contained studio apartments vary in size and facilities and offer more freedom and lower costs than staying in a hotel.	AE DC JCB MC V	54		●	■

ASTER HOUSE 3 Sumner Place, SW7. **Map** 19 A2.   £££
📞 020 7581 5888. **FAX** 020 7584 4925. [W] asterhouse.com
A welcoming B&B in an elegant, tranquil street. Practical, tidy bedrooms
and a charming rear garden. Strictly non-smoking. 🚗 ⤢
Cards: JCB, MC, V — Rooms: 14

FIVE SUMNER PLACE 5 Sumner Place, SW7. **Map** 19 A2.   £££
📞 020 7584 7586. **FAX** 020 7823 9962. [W] www.sumnerplace.com
A small hotel with a quiet, courteous welcome and good facilities.
Breakfast is served with complimentary newspapers. 🚗 📺 ⤢
Cards: AE, JCB, MC, V — Rooms: 15

GAINSBOROUGH 7–11 Queensberry Place, SW7. **Map** 18 F2.   £££
📞 020 7957 0000. **FAX** 020 7957 0001. [W] www.eeh.co.uk
Located near South Kensington's museums, this hotel has handsomely
ornate, comfortable bedrooms with a 24-hour butler service. 🚗 📺 🛏 ☰
Cards: AE, DC, JCB, MC, V — Rooms: 49

GALLERY 8–10 Queensbury Place, SW7. **Map** 18 F2.   £££
📞 020 7915 0000. **FAX** 020 7915 4400. [W] www.eeh.co.uk
Under the same management as the Gainsborough (above), this hotel has
elegant bedrooms and many original paintings. 🚗 📺 🛏 ☰
Cards: AE, DC, JCB, MC, V — Rooms: 36

CRANLEY 10–12 Bina Gardens, SW5. **Map** 18 E2.   ££££
📞 020 7373 0123. **FAX** 020 7373 9497. [W] www.thecranley.com
A townhouse graced with antiques and attractive interior design.
Complimentary aperitifs and afternoon teas. 🚗 📺 ⤢ 🛏 ☰
Cards: AE, DC, JCB, MC, V — Rooms: 38

LONDON OUTPOST 69 Cadogan Gardens, SW3. **Map** 19 C2.   ££££
📞 020 7589 7333. **FAX** 020 7531 4958. [W] www.carnegie.club.co.uk
In dignified Edwardian premises off Sloane Street, this hotel comes with
billiard room, newspapers and button-back armchairs. 🚗 📺 ⤢ 🛏 ☰
Cards: AE, DC, JCB, MC, V — Rooms: 11

NUMBER SIXTEEN 16 Sumner Place, SW7. **Map** 19 A2.   ££££
📞 020 7589 5232. **FAX** 020 7584 8615. [W] www.numbersixteenhotel.co.uk
Antiques, flowers and beautiful fabrics give this townhouse hotel the
glossy magazine touch. It also has a charming garden. 🚗 📺
Cards: AE, MC, V — Rooms: 37

PELHAM 15 Cromwell Place, SW7. **Map** 19 A2.   ££££
📞 020 7589 8288. **FAX** 020 7584 8444. [W] www.firmdale.com
Every square inch of the interior of this hotel is a designer's dream, with
odd touches of eccentricity. 🚗 📺 🛏 ☰
Cards: AE, MC, V — Rooms: 51

BLAKES 33 Roland Gardens, SW7. **Map** 18 F3.   £££££
📞 020 7370 6701. **FAX** 020 7373 0442.
An opulent hotel, with each room a fantasy of natural materials and
fascinating antiques. It also has secluded gardens and an oriental-style
restaurant. 🚗 📺 🛏 ☰
Cards: AE, DC, JCB, MC, V — Rooms: 50

CADOGAN 75 Sloane St, SW1. **Map** 19 C1.   £££££
📞 020 7235 7141. **FAX** 020 7245 0994. [W] www.cadogan.com
These premises evoke the grandeur and formality of yesteryear. Now solidly
respectable, mobiles and laptops are banned in public areas. 🚗 📺 ♿ ⤢ 🛏 ☰
Cards: AE, MC, V — Rooms: 65

CLIVEDEN TOWN HOUSE 26 Cadogan Gardens, SW3. **Map** 19 C1.   £££££
📞 020 7730 6466. **FAX** 020 7730 0236. [W] www.clivedentownhouse.co.uk
Standards are very high in this grand hotel with its luxurious Edwardian-
style rooms and suites and secluded gardens. 🚗 📺 🛏 ☰
Cards: AE, DC, JCB, MC, V — Rooms: 35

DRAYCOTT HOUSE APARTMENTS 10 Draycott Av, SW3. **Map** 19 C2.   £££££
📞 020 7584 4659. **FAX** 020 7225 3694. [W] www.draycotthouse.co.uk
These luxurious serviced apartments in an elegant Chelsea mansion block are
equipped with every imaginable appliance; some even have private balconies.
🚗 📺 🛏 ☰
Cards: AE, DC, JCB, MC, V — Rooms: 13

VICTORIA, WESTMINSTER, PIMLICO

MORGAN HOUSE 120 Ebury St, SW1. **Map** 20 E2.   £
📞 020 7730 2384. **FAX** 020 7730 8442. [W] www.morganhouse.co.uk
This stylish budget B&B in a Georgian terrace has light, modern decor;
just three rooms have private bathrooms. ⤢
Cards: MC, V — Rooms: 11

LIME TREE 135–137 Ebury St, SW1. **Map** 20 E2.   ££
📞 020 7730 8191. **FAX** 020 7730 7865. [W] www.limetreehotel.co.uk
Attractive B&B with breakfast served in a cheerful room overlooking rose
gardens. No children under five. 🚗 ⤢
Cards: AE, DC, JCB, MC, V — Rooms: 26

Price categories for a standard double room per night, inclusive of breakfast, service charges and any additional taxes such as VAT:

£ under £80
££ £80–£120
£££ £120–£180
££££ £180–£220
£££££ £220 plus.

CREDIT CARDS
Indicates which credit cards are accepted: *AE* American Express; *DC* Diners Club; *JCB* Japan Credit Bureau; *MC* MasterCard/Access; *V* Visa.

RESTAURANT
Hotel restaurant or dining room serving more than just breakfast – may or may not be open to non-residents.

CHILDREN'S FACILITIES
Any or all of the following: cots, highchairs, babysitting or baby listening, child meal portions, toys, family rooms.

QUIET LOCATION
Not too much passing traffic at night.

	CREDIT CARDS	NUMBER OF ROOMS	RESTAURANT	CHILDREN'S FACILITIES	QUIET LOCATION
WINDERMERE 142–144 Warwick St, SW1. **Map** 20 E2. **££** 020 7834 5163. FAX 020 7630 8831. W www.tophams.co.uk Friendly hotel with varied, carefully maintained bedrooms; the attractive basement restaurant serves a good range of tasty menus.	AE JCB MC V	22	■	●	
DOLPHIN SQUARE Chichester St, SW1. **Map** 21 A3. **£££** 020 7834 3800. FAX 020 7798 8735. W www.dolphinsquarehotel.co.uk A smart complex of fresh suites and studios near Tate Britain. Facilities include gardens, sports courts, a pool, a shopping mall, a Gary Rhodes restaurant and a brasserie.	AE DC MC V	148	■	●	
TOPHAMS BELGRAVIA 28 Ebury St, SW1. **Map** 20 E1. **£££** 020 7730 8147. FAX 020 7823 5966. W www.tophams.co.uk A long-established, family-run hotel close to Victoria station, occupying several adjacent townhouses. The tariff is good value.	AE DC JCB MC V	39	■		
41 41 Buckingham Palace Road, SW1. **Map** 12 F5. **£££££** 020 7300 0041. FAX 020 7300 0141. W www.redcarnationhotels.com A stunning boutique hotel opposite Buckingham Palace. Rates include lots of extras. Dashing black-and-white decor.	AE DC JCB MC V	20		●	
CROWNE PLAZA Buckingham Gate, SW1. **Map** 12 F5. **£££££** 020 7834 6655. FAX 020 7630 7587. W www.london.crowneplaza.com Facilities at these Edwardian premises near St James's Park include a fully equipped gym and three acclaimed restaurants.	AE DC JCB MC V	458	■		
GORING Beeston Place, SW1. **£££££** 020 7396 9000. FAX 020 7834 4393. W www.goringhotel.co.uk Fine Belgravia hotel with elegant furnishings and a warm welcome. Immaculate gardens make a pleasant backdrop.	AE DC MC V	75	■	●	■
JOLLY ST ERMIN'S 2 Caxton St, SW1. **Map** 13 A5. **£££££** 020 7222 7888. FAX 020 7222 6814. W www.jollyhotels.it/eng/ Late-Victorian hotel with eye-catching plasterwork conveniently close to Westminster and much favoured by politicians.	AE DC JCB MC V	290	■	●	
ROYAL HORSEGUARDS Whitehall Court, SW1. **Map** 13 C4. **£££££** 020 7839 3400. FAX 020 7925 2263. W www.thistlehotels.com A grand building between Whitehall and the Thames. Some rooms enjoy river views. The interior is smartly traditional.	AE DC JCB MC V	280	■		

MAYFAIR, ST JAMES'S

	CREDIT CARDS	NUMBER OF ROOMS	RESTAURANT	CHILDREN'S FACILITIES	QUIET LOCATION
CHESTERFIELD 35 Charles St, W1. **Map** 12 E3. **££££** 020 7491 2622. FAX 020 7491 4793. W www.redcarnationhotels.com This quiet well-kept place near Berkeley Square is decked with fruit and flowers, bedrooms are deluxe, staff welcoming.	AE DC MC V	110	■		■
22 JERMYN STREET 22 Jermyn St, SW1. **Map** 13 A3. **£££££** 020 7734 2353. FAX 020 7734 9750. W www.22jermyn.com A luxurious complex of suites and studios with round-the-clock service, a video library and use of the nearby health club.	AE DC JCB MC V	18		●	■
ASCOTT 49 Hill St, W1. **Map** 12 E3. **£££££** 020 7499 6868. FAX 020 7499 0705. W www.the-ascott.com Apartments with every facility for business, home entertainment or private dining.	AE DC JCB MC V	56		●	■
ATHENAEUM 116 Piccadilly, W1. **Map** 12 E4. **£££££** 020 7499 3464. FAX 020 7493 1860. W www.athenaeumhotel.com Despite a smart location and plush facilities, this hotel feels cosy and intimate, unlike some grand Mayfair establishments. Beautifully fitted apartments as well as conventional bedrooms.	AE DC JCB MC V	157	■	●	

BROWN'S Albemarle St, W1. **Map** 12 F3.   £££££
020 7493 6020. FAX 020 7493 9381. W www.brownshotel.com
A long-established and highly traditional hotel which rambles through 11
townhouses and offers classic bedrooms.

| AE DC JCB MC V | 118 |

CLARIDGE'S Brook St, W1. **Map** 12 E2.   £££££
020 7235 6000. FAX 020 7235 4330. W www.savoy-group.co.uk
A recent facelift has rejuvenated this grand old dame, but time-honoured
virtues of personal service and period charm linger on amid in-room
entertainment systems and fitness facilities.

| AE DC JCB MC V | 197 |

CONNAUGHT Carlos Place, W1. **Map** 12 E3.   £££££
020 7499 7070. FAX 020 7495 3262. W www.savoy-group.co.uk
The Connaught's century-old laurels remain undimmed. Staff are
surprisingly unstuffy, and bedrooms contain plenty of discreetly
concealed modern gadgetry.

| AE DC JCB MC V | 90 |

DORCHESTER Park Lane, W1. **Map** 12 D3.   £££££
020 7629 8888. FAX 020 7409 0114. W www.dorchesterhotel.com
The Dorchester is a fantasy world of gilding, mirror glass and statuary
with sumptuous bedrooms. Tea in the Promenade is a treat; so too is the
Art Deco spa and either of its famed restaurants.

| AE DC JCB MC V | 250 |

DUKES St James's Place, SW1. **Map** 12 F4.   £££££
020 7491 4840. FAX 020 7493 1264. W www.dukeshotel.co.uk
In its tiny courtyard enclave, Dukes feels completely secluded. Classic
country-house furnishings deck its elegant interior. The cosy bar serves
legendary martinis and vintage cognacs.

| AE DC JCB MC V | 89 |

LE MERIDIEN PICCADILLY 21 Piccadilly, W1. **Map** 12 F3.   £££££
0870 400 8400. FAX 020 7437 3574. W www.lemeridien-piccadilly.com
This plush business hotel scores highly for its rightly acclaimed Oak
Room restaurant. An additional bonus is that Champney's health club
is here too.

| AE DC JCB MC V | 266 |

METROPOLITAN Old Park Lane, W1. **Map** 12 E1.   £££££
020 7447 1000. FAX 020 7447 1100. W www.metropolitan.co.uk
This trendy hotel offers Japanese cuisine, cardiovascular gym equipment,
the Met Bar and views over Hyde Park.

| AE DC JCB MC V | 155 |

NO.5 MADDOX STREET 5 Maddox St, W1. **Map** 12 F2.   £££££
020 7647 0200. FAX 020 7647 0300. W www.living-rooms.co.uk
Minimalist urban cocoons are offered here with chocolate and ivory
suites and kitchens stocked with Ben and Jerry's ice cream.

| AE DC JCB MC V | 12 |

RITZ 150 Piccadilly, W1. **Map** 12 F3.   £££££
020 7493 8181. FAX 020 7493 2687. W www.theritzlondon.com
Dripping with Louis XVI furnishings and big flowers, the Ritz's public
areas make a natural stage for famous faces and the most exclusive
afternoon teas. Views over Green Park.

| AE DC JCB MC V | 133 |

STAFFORD 16–18 St James's Place, SW1. **Map** 12 F4.   £££££
020 7493 0111. FAX 020 7493 7121. W www.thestaffordhotel.co.uk
This long-established hotel is liked for its dedicated staff and excellent facilities.
The American Bar is famous for its decor and its dry martinis.

| AE DC JCB MC V | 81 |

OXFORD STREET, SOHO

EDWARD LEAR 30 Seymour St, W1. **Map** 11 C2.   ££
020 7402 5401. FAX 020 7706 3766. W www.edlear.com
This former home of the famous Victorian limerick writer, Edward Lear,
makes an inexpensive base. It also offers free internet access from a
small guest lounge.

| MC V | 31 |

PARKWOOD 4 Stanhope Place, W2. **Map** 11 B2.   ££
020 7402 2241. FAX 020 7402 1574. W www.parkwoodhotel.com
A family-run B&B in a well-kept townhouse conveniently close to Marble
Arch and Hyde Park. A refurbishment progamme is gradually upgrading
all the bedrooms.

| MC V | 14 |

10 MANCHESTER STREET 10 Manchester St, W1. **Map** 12 D1.   £££
020 7486 6669. FAX 020 7224 0348. W www.10manchesterstreet.com
This attractive "boutique" hotel in a secluded townhouse has well-
equipped bedrooms with tastefully muted decor.

| AE MC V | 46 |

For key to symbols see back flap

		CREDIT CARDS	NUMBER OF ROOMS	RESTAURANT	CHILDREN'S FACILITIES	QUIET LOCATION

Price categories for a standard double room per night, inclusive of breakfast, service charges and any additional taxes such as VAT:

£ under £80
££ £80–£120
£££ £120–£180
££££ £180–£220
£££££ £220 plus.

CREDIT CARDS
Indicates which credit cards are accepted: *AE* American Express; *DC* Diners Club; *JCB* Japan Credit Bureau; *MC* MasterCard/Access; *V* Visa.
RESTAURANT
Hotel restaurant or dining room serving more than just breakfast – may or may not be open to non-residents.
CHILDREN'S FACILITIES
Any or all of the following: cots, highchairs, babysitting or baby listening, child meal portions, toys, family rooms.
QUIET LOCATION
Not too much passing traffic at night.

DURRANTS George St, W1. **Map** 12 D1.   £££
020 7935 8131. FAX 020 7487 3510. W www.durrantshotel.co.uk
This well-loved hotel with its courteous staff retains the air of an old-fashioned coaching inn. Bedrooms are traditional.

| | AE MC V | 92 | ■ | ● | |

HAZLITT'S 6 Frith St, W1. **Map** 13 A2.   ££££
020 7434 1771. FAX 020 7439 1524. W www.hazlittshotel.com
Three 18th-century houses in the heart of Soho make a peaceful bolthole for artistic temperaments of many kinds. The interior is furnished with Victorian antiques with mod cons unobtrusively incorporated.

| | AE DC JCB MC V | 23 | | | |

THE LEONARD 15 Seymour St, W1. **Map** 11 C2.   ££££
020 7925 2010. FAX 020 7935 6700. W www.theleonard.com
This smartly furnished hotel offers thoroughly modern standards of gadgetry and interior design. Some suites have kitchens.

| | AE DC JCB MC V | 29 | ■ | ● | |

RADISSON EDWARDIAN HAMPSHIRE 31–36 Leicester Sq WC2.   £££££
Map 11 C2. 020 7839 9399. FAX 020 7930 8122. W www.radissonedwardian.com
The central location, handsome architecture and exemplary facilities of this hotel go some way towards justifying the high tariff.

| | AE DC JCB MC V | 124 | | | |

SANDERSON 50 Berners St, W1. **Map** 12 F1.   £££££
020 7300 1400. FAX 020 7300 1401. @ reservation@sanderson.schragerhotels.com
One of London's sleekest hotels. Decor is truly eyecatching with courtyard fountains and voguish bedrooms.

| | AE DC JCB MC V | 150 | ■ | ● | ■ |

REGENT'S PARK, MARYLEBONE

22 **Map** 3 C5.   ££
020 7224 2990. FAX 020 7224 1990. W www.myrtle-cottage.co.uk
Charming townhouse B&B in a family home full of period features. All guest bedrooms are elegantly furnished. Book well in advance.

| | AE DC MC V | 10 | | | ■ |

BICKENHALL 119 Gloucester Place, W1. **Map** 3 C5.   ££
020 7935 2418. FAX 020 7935 4547. W www.bickenhallhotel.co.uk
Modest but civilized townhouse B&B with period Georgian features not far from Marylebone Road. Bedrooms are pleasantly furnished and airy.

| | AE MC V | 20 | | ● | |

FOUR SEASONS 173–183 Gloucester Place, NW1. **Map** 3 C4.   ££
020 7724 3461. FAX 020 7402 5594. W www.4seasonshotel.co.uk
More modestly priced than its plush namesakes elsewhere in town, this townhouse just south of Regent's Park has smart bedrooms.

| | AE DC JCB MC V | 28 | | | |

LA PLACE 17 Nottingham Place, W1. **Map** 4 D5.   £££
020 7486 2323. FAX 020 7486 4335. W www.hotellaplace
Small hotel near Baker Street. Rooms and suites provide good facilities for business visitors and women travelling alone.

| | AE DC JCB MC V | 20 | ■ | ● | ■ |

DORSET SQUARE 39 Dorset Square, NW1. **Map** 3 C5.   ££££
020 7723 7874. FAX 020 7724 3328. W www.firmdale.com
Exquisitely furnished townhouse on a tree-lined garden square. Bedrooms are individually designed for comfort and luxury.

| | AE MC V | 38 | ■ | ● | ■ |

THE LANDMARK 222 Marylebone Road, NW1. **Map** 3 B5.   £££££
020 7631 8000. FAX 020 7631 8092. W www.landmarklondon.co.uk
Palatially restored, Marylebone's railway hotel now boasts an eye-popping atrium of soaring palm trees.

| | AE DC MC V | 299 | ■ | ● | |

LANGHAM HILTON 1c Portland Place, W1. **Map** 12 E1.   £££££
020 7636 1000. FAX 020 7323 2340.
Decked in quasi-Victorian splendour, this grand old stalwart presents a mix of colonial public rooms and suavely equipped bedrooms. A lavish health spa adds to its attractions.

| | AE DC JCB MC V | 379 | ■ | ● | |

BLOOMSBURY, FITZROVIA

GENERATOR Compton Place, 37 Tavistock Place, WC1. **Map** 5 B4. £
020 7388 7666. **FAX** 020 7388 7644. **W** www.the-generator.co.uk
Somewhere between sci-fi and industrial chic, this youth-orientated
hostel provides budget solutions for impecunious travellers.
| MC V | 200 |

MABLEDON COURT 10–11 Mabledon Place, WC1. **Map** 5 B3. £
020 7388 3866. **FAX** 020 7387 5686. **@** book@mabledoncourt.com
No-frills B&B, handy for London's northerly mainline rail stations. Rooms
are neat and practical with useful mod cons.
| AE DC JCB MC V | 43 |

THANET 8 Bedford Place, WC1. **Map** 5 C5. ££
020 7636 2869. **FAX** 020 7323 6676. **W** www.freepages.co.uk/thanet_hotel/
Modest but friendly B&B in a townhouse near the British Museum. The plain
but serviceable rooms are steadily being upgraded.
| AE MC V | 17 |

ACADEMY 21 Gower St, WC1. **Map** 5 A5. £££
020 7631 4115. **FAX** 020 7636 3442. **W** www.etontownhouse.com
Five Georgian townhouses in the university quarter make up this
beautifully furnished hotel with courtyard gardens.
| AE DC JCB MC V | 49 |

BONNINGTON IN BLOOMSBURY 92 Southampton Row, WC1. **Map** 5 C5. £££
020 7242 2828. **FAX** 020 7831 9170. **@** sales@bonnington.com
This hotel with its friendly hospitality boasts bright, contemporary
furnishings and sparkling bathrooms.
| AE DC MC V | 215 |

BLOOMS 7 Montague St, WC1. **Map** 5 B5. ££££
020 7323 1717. **FAX** 020 7636 6498. **W** www.bloomshotel.com
This elegant townhouse has a basement bar offering a range of malts and
wines and light meals. Picturesque courtyard garden.
| AE DC JCB MC V | 27 |

MONTAGUE ON THE GARDENS 15 Montague St, WC1. **Map** 5 B5. ££££
020 7637 1001. **FAX** 020 7637 2516. **W** www.redcarnationhotels.com
Well-furnished public rooms ramble to a plant-filled conservatory and
terrace bar overlooking a charming rear garden. Bedrooms are equally
handsome in ornate individual schemes.
| AE DC JCB MC V | 104 |

CHARLOTTE STREET 15 Charlotte St, W1. **Map** 13 A1. £££££
020 7806 2000. **FAX** 020 7806 2002. **W** www.charlottestreethotel.com
The "Bloomsbury" theme incorporates original period art in the spacious
public areas, while bedrooms run to mini-TV screens in the granite
bathrooms and exemplary high-tech facilities.
| AE DC JCB MC V | 52 |

GRANGE HOLBORN 50–60 Southampton Row, WC1. **Map** 5 C5. £££££
020 7611 5800. **FAX** 020 7242 0057. **W** www.grangehotels.co.uk
An efficient and comfortable business hotel with marquetry-effect
rosewood furnishings and offering luxuries like a sushi restaurant,
a pool and fitness centre.
| AE DC JCB MC V | 160 |

MYHOTEL BLOOMSBURY 11–13 Bayley St, WC1. **Map** 5 A5. £££££
020 7667 6000. **FAX** 020 7667 6001. **W** www.myhotels.co.uk
Chic hotel just off Tottenham Court Road. Inside, all is Oriental calm,
from the sushi bar to the holistic centre. Bedrooms are immaculate with
crisp bedlinen and big cushions.
| AE DC MC V | 76 |

COVENT GARDEN, STRAND, HOLBORN

FIELDING 4 Broad Court, Bow St, WC2. **Map** 12 C2. ££
020 7836 8305. **FAX** 020 7497 0064. **W** www.the-fielding-hotel.co.uk
A good-value hotel near the Royal Opera House with limited but clean
facilities. No meals are served. No children under 12.
| AE DC JCB MC V | 24 |

COVENT GARDEN 10 Monmouth St, WC2. **Map** 13 B2. £££££
020 7806 1000. **FAX** 020 7806 1100. **W** www.firmdale.com
Situated on one of Covent Garden's most interesting streets, this discreet five-star
is at the same time a fascinatingly theatrical place to stay and is a tour-de-force of
dramatic interior design.
| AE MC V | 58 |

KINGSWAY HALL Great Queen St, WC2. **Map** 13 C1. £££££
020 7309 0909. **FAX** 020 7309 9696. **W** www.kingswayhall.co.uk
This contemporary new business venture is extremely handy for
London's theatres and its sophisticated restaurant offers pre-theatre
dinners.
| AE DC JCB MC V | 170 |

For key to symbols see back flap

Price categories for a standard double room per night, inclusive of breakfast, service charges and any additional taxes such as VAT:

£ under £80
££ £80–£120
£££ £120–£180
££££ £180–£220
£££££ £220 plus.

CREDIT CARDS
Indicates which credit cards are accepted: *AE* American Express; *DC* Diners Club; *JCB* Japan Credit Bureau; *MC* MasterCard/Access; *V* Visa.
RESTAURANT
Hotel restaurant or dining room serving more than just breakfast – may or may not be open to non-residents.
CHILDREN'S FACILITIES
Any or all of the following: cots, highchairs, babysitting or baby listening, child meal portions, toys, family rooms.
QUIET LOCATION
Not too much passing traffic at night.

	CREDIT CARDS	NUMBER OF ROOMS	RESTAURANT	CHILDREN'S FACILITIES	QUIET LOCATION
LE MERIDIEN WALDORF Aldwych, WC2. **Map** 14 D2. £££££ 0870 400 8484. FAX 020 7836 7244. A handsome Edwardian hotel, well placed for Covent Garden and the City and serving pre-theatre dinners.	AE DC JCB MC V	292	■	●	
ONE ALDWYCH Aldwych, WC2. **Map** 13 C2. £££££ 020 7300 1000. FAX 020 7300 1001. W www.onealdwych.co.uk Filled with contemporary works of art, every inch of this hotel is imaginative with well-thought-out rooms. Underwater classical music plays in the swimming pool.	AE DC JCB MC V	105	■	●	
RENAISSANCE LONDON CHANCERY COURT £££££ 252 High Holborn, WC1. **Map** 13 C1. 020 7829 9888. FAX 020 7829 9889. W www.renaissancehotels.com/loncc Sumptuous transformation of the stately former Pearl Assurance headquarters – location set of several films and television dramas.	AE DC JCB MC V	357	■	●	
SAVOY Strand, WC2. **Map** 13 C2. £££££ 020 7836 4343. FAX 020 7872 8901. W www.savoy-group.co.uk Flamboyant Art Deco hotel with glorious waterfront views, combining period character with modern comforts.	AE DC JCB MC V	207	■	●	■

SOUTHWARK, LAMBETH

	CREDIT CARDS	NUMBER OF ROOMS	RESTAURANT	CHILDREN'S FACILITIES	QUIET LOCATION
COUNTY HALL TRAVEL INN CAPITAL Belvedere Road, SE1. **Map** 14 D4. £ 020 7902 1600. FAX 020 7902 1619. W www.travelinn.co.uk Excellent value in the old GLC building near the London Eye. This chain hotel provides practical and surprisingly spacious rooms. The low tariff and central location make it extremely popular. Book well in advance.	AE DC MC V	313	■	●	
MAD HATTER 3–7 Stamford St, SE1. **Map** 14 E3. ££ 020 7401 9222. FAX 020 7401 7111. @ madhatter@fullers.demon.co.uk This Victorian-style Fullers pub-hotel offers good-quality, well-equipped bedrooms and a lively bar-restaurant.	AE DC MC V	30	■	●	
NOVOTEL WATERLOO 113 Lambeth Road, SE1. **Map** 22 D1. £££ 020 7793 1010. FAX 020 7793 0202. W www.novotel.com A bland but convenient chain hotel with spacious rooms ideal for business visitors and families. On-site parking.	AE DC JCB MC V	187	■	●	
LONDON BRIDGE 8–18 London Bridge St, SE1. **Map** 15 B4. ££££ 020 7855 2200. FAX 020 7855 2233. W www.london-bridge-hotel.co.uk A smart new South Bank or City base with state-of-the art business and fitness facilities and a Simply Nico restaurant.	AE DC JCB MC V	138	■	●	
LONDON MARRIOTT COUNTY HALL County Hall, SE1. **Map** 13 C5. £££££ 020 7982 5200. FAX 020 7928 5300. W www.marriott.com/marriott/lonch A business hotel in monumental surroundings. Magnificent river and Westminster views from some rooms. On-site healthclub and pool.	AE DC JCB MC V	200	■	●	

CITY, CLERKENWELL

	CREDIT CARDS	NUMBER OF ROOMS	RESTAURANT	CHILDREN'S FACILITIES	QUIET LOCATION
NOVOTEL TOWER BRIDGE 10 Pepys St, EC3. **Map** 16 D2. £££ 020 7265 6000. FAX 020 7265 6060. W www.novotel.com This newly opened chain hotel in a fascinating part of London has well-equipped, pleasing bedrooms. Good value for families.	AE DC JCB MC V	203	■	●	■
THE KING'S WARDROBE 6 Wardrobe Place, EC4. **Map** 14 F2. ££££ 020 7248 0222. FAX 020 7248 0011. W www.bridgestreet.com Luxury serviced apartments in a quiet, leafy courtyard a stone's throw from St Paul's Cathedral. Designed to sophisticated specifications, this stylish complex has architectural distinction and a fascinating history.	AE DC JCB MC V	63	■	●	

GREAT EASTERN Liverpool St, EC2. **Map** 15 C1. £££££
020 7618 5010. FAX 020 7618 5011. W www.great-eastern-hotel.co.uk
A superb restoration of Liverpool Street's grand railway hotel which
offers smart restaurants and elegant bedrooms. 🛏 ⬆ & ⚡ 📺 🔒 ≣
AE DC MC V — 267

ROOKERY Peter's Lane, Cowcross St, EC1. **Map** 6 F5. £££££
020 7336 0931. FAX 020 7336 0932. W www.hampsteadguesthouse.com
Lovingly restored B&B in several 18th-century cottages near Smithfield
market. The Rook's Nest with its lantern gallery is the *pièce de résistance*,
but all rooms have handsome period furnishings. 🛏 ⚡ 🔒
AE DC JCB MC V — 33

THISTLE TOWER St Katharine's Way, E1. **Map** 16 E3. ££££
020 7841 2575. FAX 020 7488 4106. W www.thistlehotels.com
This huge concrete edifice is no beauty, but the waterfront location is
spectacular and the interior comfortable. 🛏 ⬆ & ⚡ 📺 🔒 ≣
AE DC JCB MC V — 801

CANARY WHARF, GREENWICH

IBIS GREENWICH 30 Stockwell St, Greenwich SE10. **Map** 23 B2. £
020 8305 1177. FAX 020 ... W www.ibishotel.com
This no-frills budget chain hotel is remarkable value. Rooms are clean
and neat. The hotel is close to transport links and also offers free car
parking space. 🛏 ⬆ & ⚡
AE DC MC V — 82

MITRE 291 Greenwich High Road, SE10. **Map** 23 B2. £
020 8355 6760. FAX 020 293 0037.
Bustling pub-with-rooms close to sights and transport links. Originally an
18th-century coffee shop, this old inn has been part of the Greenwich
townscape since the 1700s. Parking available. 🛏 ⬆ & ⚡ 🔒
DC MC V — 16

FOUR SEASONS CANARY WHARF 46 Westferry Circus, E14. £££££
020 7510 1999. FAX 020 7510 1998. W www.fourseasons.com
A stunning complex with superb waterfront views and facilities, and the
Holmes Place leisure centre just next door. 🛏 ⬆ & ⚡ 📺 ≋ 🔒 ≣
AE DC JCB MC V — 139

HAMPSTEAD

HAMPSTEAD VILLAGE GUESTHOUSE 2 Kemplay Road, NW3. **Map** 1 B5. ££
020 7435 8679. FAX 020 7794 0254. W www.hampsteadguesthouse.com
This Victorian family home has bedrooms crammed with books and
fascinating bygones, as well as practicalities. 🛏 ⚡ 🔒
AE DC MC V — 9

LA GAFFE 107–111 Heath St, NW3. **Map** 1 A4. ££
020 7435 8965. FAX 020 7794 7592. W www.lagaffe.co.uk
A cheerful, family-run Italian restaurant-with-rooms in the heart of
Hampstead village. Bedrooms are simple, but pretty. 🛏 ⚡ 🔒
AE MC V — 18

LANGORF 20 Frognal, NW3. **Map** 1 A5. ££
020 7794 4483. FAX 020 7435 9055. W www.langorfhotel.com
Three townhouses comprise this hotel. Light room-service meals are
offered and there are five self-catering apartments. 🛏 ⬆ 🔒 ≣
AE DC JCB MC V — 36

FURTHER AFIELD

PETERSHAM Nightingale Lane, Richmond, Surrey, TW10. ££
020 8940 7471. FAX 020 8939 1098. W www.petershamhotel.co.uk
A striking building with a spectacular view of the Thames. The romantic
setting, along with excellent food, makes this a popular venue. 🛏 ⬆ 🔒
AE DC MC V — 60

COLONNADE 2 Warrington Crescent, W9. £££
020 7286 1052. FAX 020 7286 1057. W www.etontownhouse.com
A charming base in Little Venice. This elegant Victorian townhouse boasts
dashing rooms and comfortable public areas. 🛏 ⬆ ⚡ 🔒 ≣
AE DC MC V — 43

HOLIDAY INN NELSON DOCK 265 Rotherhithe St, SE16. ££££
020 7231 1001. FAX 020 7231 0599. W www.holiday-inn.com/lon-nelsondock
This family-friendly riverside hotel has good facilities; elegant bedrooms;
courtesy shuttle to Canada Water and parking. 🛏 ⬆ & ⚡ 📺 ≋ 🔒 ≣
AE DC JCB MC V — 386

CANNIZARO HOUSE West Side, Wimbledon Common, SW19. £££££
020 8879 1464. FAX 020 8944 6515. W www.thistlehotels.com
This Georgian mansion near Wimbledon Common is elegant and formal;
the surrounding grounds large and tranquil. Parking. 🛏 ⬆ & ⚡ 🔒 ≣
AE DC JCB MC V — 45

For key to symbols see back flap

RESTAURANTS AND PUBS

HAILED AS THE world's dining capital, London thrives on an extraordinary culinary diversity. From a traditional forte of Indian, Chinese, French and Italian restaurants, eating out in London now enables your palate to take a gastronomic journey around the world, from America to Africa, taking in a pan-European tour, as well as the Middle East, Asia, and the Pacific Rim.

A pre-theatre menu board

included. *Choosing a Restaurant* on pages 290–93 summarizes key features of the restaurants, listed according to their geographical area. More details are in the listings on pages 294–305, where restaurants are grouped according to cuisine.

London's café scene has become much more dynamic over the past few years, with good coffee and snacks readily available throughout the day. Pubs have also evolved, with many modernizing their decor and placing far more emphasis on serving good food, ranging from classic British snacks to ethnic dishes. For a selection of mainly informal places to eat and drink, including pubs, see pages 306–11.

CHOOSING YOUR TABLE

The restaurants listed in this guide represent a comprehensive range of styles and prices. They are spread across the main tourist areas, although some that merit a special trip further afield are also

LONDON RESTAURANTS

THE BROADEST choice of restaurants can be found in Covent Garden, Piccadilly, Mayfair, Soho and Leicester Square. Knightsbridge, Kensington and Chelsea also offer a good range of restaurants. Central London has very few riverside restaurants, but there is a cluster along Chelsea Harbour, in Chelsea, and Butler's Wharf on the south bank of the Thames. While traditional British food can be enjoyed, the style is not so readily available. Some chefs such as Gary Rhodes

Commissionaire at the Hard Rock Café *(see p294)*

are revitalizing British dishes, but the emphasis is on Modern British cooking which combines a variety of culinary influences and techniques from around the world. Home-grown chefs such as Sally Clarke, Alastair Little and Marco Pierre White have been instrumental in helping to elevate restaurant dining over the past two decades. Alongside great improvements in cuisine, the standard of service has risen, and there has never been so much focus on interior design. This has also added to the "diversity" of London's restaurants, which offer anything from classically ornate and romantic decor, to modern and post-modern minimalism. London has long been a paradise for Indian, Chinese, French and Italian food, with more restaurants specializing in regional cuisine. Asian food is increasingly popular, particularly Thai and Japanese, with Soho offering plenty of choice. Most restaurants provide at least one vegetarian option, and some have a separate vegetarian menu, while a growing number of specialist vegetarian restaurants offer more adventurous dishes. Fish and seafood is another speciality, with both traditional and modern-style restaurants.

Coast *(see p303)*

OTHER PLACES TO EAT

MANY HOTELS have excellent restaurants open to non-residents, which in some cases includes a menu composed by, or even the actual dishes prepared by, a star chef. These restaurants range from the very formal to the fun and flamboyant, and prices tend to be at the top end of the scale. There are also increasing numbers of pizza, pasta and brasserie chains serving reliable, good-value food across the city. Among these dramatic improvements are also "gastro-pubs" and wine bars that serve anything from standard staples to Thai curries, accompanied by global wine lists. Otherwise, you can grab a quick, cheap snack from any number of sandwich bars or cafés.

Bibendum *(see p298)*

TIPS ON EATING OUT

MOST LONDON restaurants serve lunch between 12.30pm and 2.30pm, with dinner from 7pm until 11pm, which usually means that last orders are taken at 11pm. Ethnic restaurants may stay open slightly longer, until midnight or even later. Some restaurants may close for either lunch or dinner during the weekend, and it is always best to check opening times first. All-day cafés and brasseries may now serve alcohol without restriction during licensing hours (11am–11pm). The traditional British Sunday lunch *(see p289)* appears in many pubs and restaurants, although more informal brunches are increasingly popular. It is worth checking beforehand, however, unless traditional Sunday lunch is what you particularly want, as even high-class restaurants may now suspend their normal menu on Sundays.

Some of the most formal restaurants insist on a jacket and tie, or a jacket. Booking is advisable, especially at recently opened or celebrity-chef-run restaurants.

PRICE AND SERVICE

AS LONDON IS ONE of the world's most expensive cities, restaurant prices can often seem exorbitant to visitors, with an average three-course meal and a few glasses of house wine, at a medium-priced central London restaurant costing around £25–35 per person. Many restaurants have set-price menus which are generally significantly less expensive than ordering à la carte and, in some instances, the price includes coffee and service. Similarly, various West End restaurants serve pre-theatre set menus (typically from around 5.30–6pm). Although geared towards a quick turn-around, this provides an opportunity to eat at quality restaurants at a competitive price. Lower prices (around £10–15 a head) apply at smaller, more modest ethnic and vegetarian restaurants, wine bars and pubs, where the food can nevertheless be well prepared and offer good value. However, some of these establishments will only accept cash or cheques, not credit cards.

Before ordering, check the small print at the bottom of the menu. Prices will include Value Added Tax (VAT) and may add an optional service charge (between 10 and 15 per cent). Some restaurants may also impose a cover charge (£1–2 a head), or a minimum charge during the busiest periods, while some do not accept certain credit cards. Beware of the old trick where service is included in the bill but staff leave the "total" box on your credit slip blank, hoping you will add another 10 per cent. Expect different types of service in different types of restaurant. This can range from cheerful and breezy in fast-food joints to discreet yet attentive in more expensive venues. At peak dining times you will usually have to wait longer to be served.

EATING WITH CHILDREN

EXCEPT IN Italian restaurants, fast-food establishments and a few other venues such as The Rainforest Café on Shaftesbury Avenue (a tropical haven geared towards young diners), children tend to be simply tolerated in London restaurants as a rule rather than warmly welcomed.

However, with the growing trend for a more informal style of dining, more and more restaurants are learning to become child-friendly, offering a special children's menu or smaller portions and high chairs *(see pp290–93)*, while some provide colouring books and even put on live entertainment to keep the little diners happy. See page 341 for suggested places that cater for children of a wide range of ages.

Clarke's Restaurant *(see p303)*

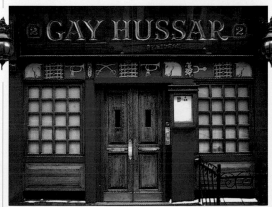

London's top Hungarian restaurant *(see p304)*

What to Eat in London

THE TRADITIONAL SUNDAY lunch displays what is best about British food – good ingredients prepared simply but well. A joint of roast meat (usually lamb or beef) served with appropriate accompaniments (mint sauce or redcurrant jelly for lamb, mustard or horseradish sauce for beef) is the centrepiece of the meal;

Fish and Chips
The battered fish (usually haddock or cod) and chips are deep fried.

wonderful homely puddings and fine British cheeses served with cheese biscuits are obligatory "afters". Sunday lunch is still an institution for Londoners and you will find versions of it in many restaurants and cafés as well as in hotels and pubs all over the capital. The legendary English breakfast may be less ambitious than the five-course feast enjoyed by the Victorians, but it is still a hearty meal and the perfect start to a hard day's sightseeing. Afternoon tea (which is usually taken at around 4pm) is another treat, when the British genius for cakes and their fondness for tea-drinking come together. The smell of fish and chips will often greet you as you wander around the city, and this classic British meal is best eaten in the open air, direct from its paper wrapping.

Full English Breakfast
This favourite meal consists of bacon, egg, tomato, fried bread and a variety of sausages.

Toast and Marmalade
Breakfast is usually finished off with slices of toast spread with orange marmalade.

Cheeses
British cheeses are mostly hard or semi-hard, such as Cheshire, Leicester and the most famous of all, Cheddar. Stilton is blue-veined.

Cheddar

Sage Derby

Ploughman's Lunch
Crusty bread, cheese and sweet pickle are at the heart of this simple pub lunch.

Cheshire

Stilton

Red Leicester

Bread and Butter Pudding
Served hot, the layers of bread and dried fruit are baked in a creamy custard.

Strawberries and Cream
Strawberries served with sugar and cream are a favourite summer dessert.

Summer Pudding
The outer bread lining is soaked in the juice of the many soft fruits inside.

Cucumber Sandwiches
Wafer-thin cucumber sandwiches are a traditional part of an English tea.

Jam and Cream Scones
Halfway between a cake and a bun, scones are served with cream and jam.

Tea
A cup of tea, served with milk or lemon, is still the British national drink.

Meat dishes are usually served with at least one green vegetable.

Horseradish sauce

Yorkshire pudding

Roast beef

Steak and Kidney Pie
Chunks of beef and pigs' kidneys are braised in a thick gravy and topped off with a browned pastry crust.

Roast potatoes

Roast Beef and Yorkshire Pudding
Yorkshire pudding, a savoury batter baked in the oven, is the traditional accompaniment to roast beef along with horseradish sauce, roast potatoes and a meat gravy.

Shepherd's Pie
This is made with stewed minced lamb, vegetables and a mashed potato topping.

What to Drink
Beer is the British drink. The many different kinds (see p309) range from light lager to stout and bitter. Dry gin originally came from London. Pimms, usually mixed with lemonade, fruit and mint, is a cooling drink on those hot summer days.

Stout (Guinness)   Bitter   Lager

Pimms   Gin and tonic

Choosing a Restaurant

THE RESTAURANTS IN this section have been selected for their good value or exceptional food. This chart highlights some of the main factors which may influence your choice. For more details about the restaurants see pages 294–305; light meals and snack places are on pages 306–8; and pubs on pages 309–11.

Restaurant	Price	Page Number	Set-Price Menu	Late Opening	Child Friendly	Live Music	Tables Outside	Non-Smoking Areas	Air Conditioning
BAYSWATER, PADDINGTON									
40 Degrees At Veronica's (British)	££	295	●		●	■	●		
KENSINGTON, HOLLAND PARK, NOTTING HILL									
L'Anis (French)	££	297	●		●				●
Kensington Place (Modern International)	££	303	●		●				●
Mandola (African)	££	294			●				
Sticky Fingers (Modern International)	££	303			●				
Wódka (Other European)	££	304	●						●
Bali Sugar (Modern International)	£££	302					●	■	
Dakota (The Americas)	£££	294	●				●	■	●
Clarke's (Modern International)	££££	303	●		●		●	■	●
SOUTH KENSINGTON, GLOUCESTER ROAD									
Bibendum (French)	£££	298	●					■	●
Bombay Brasserie (Indian)	£££	300			●			■	●
KNIGHTSBRIDGE, BROMPTON, BELGRAVIA, PIMLICO, VICTORIA									
Emporio Armani Café (Italian)	££	301			●		■		
Osteria d'Isola (Italian)	££	301	●		●			■	●
Boisdale (British)	£££	296	●					■	●
Drones (Modern International)	£££	303	●		●				●
The Fifth Floor (British)	£££	296	●					■	●
L'Incontro (Italian)	£££	301	●					■	
Isola (Italian)	£££	301			●				●
Restaurant One-O-One (Fish and Seafood)	£££	297	●		●	■			
Rhodes in the Square (British)	£££	296	●					■	●
Salloos (Indian)	£££	300	●						
Zafferano (Italian)	£££	302	●		●				●
Roussillon (French)	££££	299	●		●			■	●
La Tante Claire (French)	£££££	299	●		●				●
CHELSEA, FULHAM									
The New Culture Revolution (Chinese)	£	296						■	●
Bluebird (Modern International)	££	303	●					■	●
Nikita's (Other European)	££	304	●						
Soviet Canteen (Other European)	££	304	●					■	●
Cactus Blue (The Americas)	£££	294					■		●
Vama (Indian)	£££	300	●		●		●		
Zaika (Indian)	£££	300	●						●
PICCADILLY, MAYFAIR, BAKER STREET									
Sofra (Greek and Middle Eastern)	£	299	●	■	●		●	■	●
L'Artiste Musclé (French)	££	297				■	●		
Carluccio's (Italian)	££	301			●	■	●		●
Getti (Italian)	££	301			●			■	●
Giraffe (Modern International)	££	303	●		●			■	●
Spighetta (Italian)	££	301	●					■	
Hard Rock Café (The Americas)	££	294			●		●	■	

Price categories are for a three-course meal per person including tax, service and half a bottle of house wine (unless required to supply your own):
£ under £15
££ £15–£35
£££ £35–£55
££££ £55–£75
£££££ £75 plus.

PAGE NUMBER – of restaurant review.
SET-PRICE MENU – at lunch or dinner.
LATE OPENING Last orders taken at or after 11.30pm.
CHILD FRIENDLY Children's portions and/or high chairs.
LIVE MUSIC Live musicians feature at the restaurant.
TABLES OUTSIDE Al fresco dining weather permitting.
NON-SMOKING AREAS No smoking permitted in designated areas.
AIR CONDITIONING Restaurant is fully air-conditioned.

Restaurant	Price	Page Number	Set-Price Menu	Late Opening	Child Friendly	Live Music	Tables Outside	Non-Smoking Areas	Air Conditioning
Al Duca (Italian)	££	300	●		●				●
L'Oranger (French)	££	298	●				●	■	●
Mash Mayfair (British)	££	295	●		●		●		●
Mulligan's of Mayfair (Other European)	££	304							
Al Hamra (Greek and Middle Eastern)	££	299	●				●	■	
Teca (Italian)	££	301	●		●			■	
Alloro (Italian)	££	301	●		●			■	
Veeraswamy (Indian)	£££	300	●			■		■	
Just Oriental (Southeast Asian)	£££	305	●						
Chor Bizarre (Indian)	£££	300	●		●				
The Avenue (British)	£££	295	●	■	●	■		■	
Che (Modern International)	£££	303	●					■	
Criterion Brasserie (French)	£££	298	●						●
F. Miyama (Japanese)	£££	302	●		●				
Green's Restaurant & Oyster Bar (Fish & Seafood)	£££	297	●		●				●
Just St James (British)	£££	296	●		●				
Momo (Greek and Middle Eastern)	£££	299	●				●		
L'Odéon (Modern European)	£££	303	●		●				
Quaglino's (British)	£££	296	●	■					
Royal China (Chinese)	£££	297	●						
Tamarind (Indian)	£££	300	●						●
Coast (Modern International)	££££	303	●	■	●			■	
Mirabelle (French)	££££	298	●				●		
Chez Nico (French)	£££££	299	●		●				●
Le Gavroche (French)	£££££	299	●						●
Nobu (Japanese)	£££££	302	●		●	■		■	●

SOHO

Restaurant	Price	Page Number	Set-Price Menu	Late Opening	Child Friendly	Live Music	Tables Outside	Non-Smoking Areas	Air Conditioning
New World (Chinese)	£	297	●		●			■	
Yo! Sushi (Japanese)	£	302	●		●			■	
Blue's Bistro and Bar (The Americas)	££	294	●		●			■	
Fung Shing (Chinese)	££	297	●						
The Gay Hussar (Other European)	££	304	●		●				●
Harbour City (Chinese)	££	297	●						
Mela (Indian)	££	300	●		●			■	
Melati (Southeast Asian)	££	305	●		●				
Mezzonine (Southeast Asian)	££	305	●	■					
Mildred's (Vegetarian)	££	305			●		●		
Spiga Soho (Italian)	££	301	●		●	■			
Sri Siam (Southeast Asian)	££	305	●		●				●
Tokyo Diner (Japanese)	££	302						■	
Alastair Little (Modern International)	£££	302	●		●				
Circus (Modern European)	£££	303	●		●				●
Mezzo (Modern European)	£££	304	●	■					
Richard Corrigan (Other European)	£££	305	●		●				●
Nobu (Japanese)	£££££	302	●	■		■		■	●
The Sugar Club (Modern International)	£££££	303	●		●	■			●

Price categories are for a three-course meal per person including tax, service and half a bottle of house wine (unless required to supply your own):
£ under £15
££ £15–£35
£££ £35–£55
££££ £55–£75
£££££ £75 plus.

PAGE NUMBER – of restaurant review.
SET PRICE MENU – at lunch or dinner.
LATE OPENING
Last orders taken at or after 11.30pm.
CHILD FRIENDLY
Children's portions and/or high chairs.
LIVE MUSIC
Live musicians feature at the restaurant.
TABLES OUTSIDE
Al fresco dining weather permitting.
NON-SMOKING AREAS
No smoking permitted in designated areas.
AIR CONDITIONING
Restaurant is fully air-conditioned.

Restaurant	Price	Page Number	Set-Price Menu	Late Opening	Child Friendly	Live Music	Tables Outside	Non-Smoking Areas	Air Conditioning
COVENT GARDEN, STRAND									
Calabash *(African)*	£	294			●	●			●
Food for Thought *(Vegetarian)*	£	305					●	●	●
World Food Café *(Vegetarian)*	£	305				●		●	●
Alfred *(British)*	££	295	●	●	●	●			●
Belgo Centraal *(Other European)*	££	304	●		●				
Café Pacífico *(The Americas)*	££	294							
Navajo Joe *(The Americas)*	££	294			●				●
Palms *(Other European)*	££	304							
La Perla *(The Americas)*	££	294			●				
Bank Aldwych *(Modern International)*	£££	302	●		●				
Chez Gerard *(French)*	£££	298	●			●	●	●	●
Christopher's *(The Americas)*	£££	294			●				●
The Ivy *(Modern European)*	£££	303	●	●	●				
Mon Plaisir *(French)*	£££	298	●					●	
Orso *(Italian)*	£££	301	●					●	
Le Palais du Jardin *(French)*	£££	298	●		●		●		
River Restaurant *(Modern European)*	£££	304	●		●				
Rules *(British)*	£££	296			●	●		●	●
Simpson's-in-the-Strand *(British)*	£££	296	●	●					
Tuscan Steak *(Italian)*	£££	301			●		●		●
BLOOMSBURY, FITZROVIA									
Wagamama *(Japanese)*	£	302			●			●	
Bertorelli's *(Italian)*	££	301	●		●	●		●	●
Table Café *(Italian)*	££	301	●		●			●	
Hakkasan *(Chinese)*	£££	297							
Pied à Terre *(French)*	£££	298	●						●
Spoon + *(French)*	£££	298			●	●	●		●
CAMDEN TOWN, HAMPSTEAD									
Daphne *(Greek and Middle Eastern)*	££	299	●		●		●		
Lemonia *(Greek and Middle Eastern)*	££	299	●		●		●		
Sauce Bar Organic Diner *(British)*	££	295	●		●				●
SPITALFIELDS, CLERKENWELL									
Nazrul *(Indian)*	£	300	●		●				●
Cicada *(Southeast Asian)*	££	305	●		●		●	●	
Moro *(Modern International)*	££	303	●		●		●		
Quality Chop House *(British)*	££	295	●		●			●	
Maison Novelli *(French)*	££££	298			●		●	●	
THE CITY, SOUTH BANK									
The Place Below *(Vegetarian)*	£	305	●			●	●	●	
Wine Wharf at Vinopolis *(Modern European)*	£	303							●
Baltic *(Other European)*	££	304	●		●			●	●
Café Seven *(British)*	££	295	●		●		●	●	
Club Gascon *(French)*	££	298							●
Livebait *(Fish and Seafood)*	££	297						●	●

Restaurant	Price	Page
The People's Palace (*Modern European*)	££	303
Searcy's Restaurant (*British*)	££	295
Café Spice Namaste (*Indian*)	£££	300
City Rhodes (*British*)	£££	296
The Oxo Tower (*British*)	£££	296
Le Pont de la Tour (*French*)	£££	298
Prism (*British*)	£££	296
Sweetings (*Fish and Seafood*)	£££	297
FURTHER AFIELD		
Madhu's Brilliant (*Indian*)	£	299
Chez Bruce (*British*)	££	295
Istanbul Iskembecisi (*Greek and Middle Eastern*)	££	299
Manna (*Vegetarian*)	££	305
Sonny's (*British*)	££	295
River Café (*Italian*)	££££	302

Choosing a Cuisine

THE RESTAURANTS IN THIS GUIDE have been selected across a wide range of price categories for their value, good food and atmosphere; they are listed by type of cuisine, starting with African and American and within each food category they are listed in order of the average price you might expect to pay. For map references, see the Street Finder, pages 384–407.

	CREDIT CARDS	VEGETARIAN SPECIALITIES	HIGHLY RECOMMENDED	EXCELLENT WINE LIST

AFRICAN

Given London's multi-ethnic population, there are fewer African restaurants than you might expect. Common dishes are fried plantain (a type of banana) with a hot sauce, spicy stews and soups.

CALABASH £
Africa Centre, 38 King St, WC2. **Map** 13 C2. 📞 *020 7836 1976.* **FAX** *020 7836 7736.*
Friendly African restaurant serving the likes of Nigerian *egusi* (meat soup cooked with palm oil and melon seeds). ● *Christmas and public hols.* 🍸
— MC V — ● — —

MANDOLA ££
139–143 Westbourne Grove, W11. **Map** 9 C2. 📞 *020 7229 4734.*
Sudanese cuisine served in a "traditional Khartoum" setting. Bring your own wine. Minimal corkage charge. ● *Christmas, New Year.*
— MC V — ● — —

THE AMERICAS

Apart from the ubiquitous burger bars (see pp306–7), authentic and creative food from the Americas is a comparatively recent addition to London's repertoire. Beyond Mexican and Tex-Mex, a growing number offer East-Coast as well as South-West American specialities.

BLUE'S BISTRO AND BAR Ⓦ www.bluebistro.com ££
42–43 Dean St, W1. **Map** 13 A2. 📞 *020 7494 1966.* **FAX** *020 7494 0717.*
North American-based cuisine with classics like Maryland chicken with corn fritters. Modern setting with interesting art. ● *public hols.* 🍸 ▤
— MC V — ● — ●

CAFE PACIFICO ££
5 Langley St, WC2. **Map** 13 B2. 📞 *020 7379 7728.* **FAX** *020 7836 5088.*
Traditional and modern Mexican dishes served cantina-style in a converted banana warehouse. Great range of tequilas. 🍸
— AE MC V — ● — —

HARD ROCK CAFE ££
1 Old Park Lane, W1. **Map** 12 E4. 📞 *020 7629 0382.*
No reservations means queues, but the reward is classic North American fare with rock music videos and endless memorabilia – Jimi Hendrix's guitar, Ringo's drumstick and so on. ● *25 Dec.* 🍸
— AE DC MC V — — — ●

LA PERLA ££
28 Maiden Lane, WC2. **Map** 13 C2. 📞 *020 7240 7400.* **FAX** *020 7836 5088.*
A bar with plenty of tequilas and cocktails serving modern, traditional and tapas-style Mexican cuisine from an open-plan grill. 🍸 ♿
— AE MC V — ● — —

NAVAJO JOE ££
34 King St, WC2. **Map** 13 C2. 📞 *020 7240 4008.* **FAX** *020 7240 4009.*
Southwest American cuisine served in a chic setting amid contemporary American Indian art. Good for tequila and mezcal. 🍸
— AE MC V — ● ■ ●

CACTUS BLUE £££
86 Fulham Rd, SW3. **Map** 19 A3. 📞 *020 7823 7858.* **FAX** *020 7823 8577.*
An innovative Southwest American menu that thrives on its melting pot of different influences. Its retro-modern look includes Native American Indian art. Plenty of tequilas to sip and savour. 🍸 ♿
— AE DC JCB MC V — ● — —

CHRISTOPHER'S Ⓦ www.christophersgrill.com £££
18 Wellington St, WC2. **Map** 13 C2. 📞 *020 7240 4222.* **FAX** *020 7836 3506.*
Traditional East-Coast Americana with a grand theatricality in the decor (frescoes, sweeping staircase). ● *public hols.* 🍸
— AE DC JCB MC — — ■ ●

DAKOTA £££
127 Ledbury Rd, W11. **Map** 9 C2. 📞 *020 7792 9191.* **FAX** *020 7792 9090.*
Southwestern American cuisine includes Iowa rib-eye steak and tequila-cured salmon with a corn blini. The modern streamlined look features continual art exhibitions. ● *25–26 Dec.* 🍸
— AE MC V — ● — ●

Price categories are for a three-course meal per person including tax, service and half a bottle of house wine (unless required to supply your own):
£ under £15
££ £15–£35
£££ £35–£55
££££ £55–£75
£££££ £75 plus.

CREDIT CARDS
Indicates which credit cards are accepted: *AE* American Express; *DC* Diners Club; *JCB* Japan Credit Bureau; *MC* MasterCard/Access; *V* Visa.
VEGETARIAN SPECIALITIES
Imaginative vegetarian options offered.
HIGHLY RECOMMENDED
A restaurant of particularly good value – great food and quality service.
EXCELLENT WINE LIST
An outstanding selection of wine offered.

		Credit Cards	Vegetarian Specialities	Highly Recommended	Excellent Wine List
THE GAUCHO GRILL	£££	AE DC MC V	●		●

89 Sloane Avenue, SW3. **Map** 19 B2. 020 7584 9901.
Argentine beef cooked over charcoal on an *asado*, as used by *gauchos* (Argentinian cowboys), is a speciality.

BRITISH/MODERN BRITISH

Restaurants serving traditional or updated British classics have a very loyal following. Modern British, meanwhile, is a hybrid of international influences and ingredients.

		Credit Cards	Vegetarian Specialities	Highly Recommended	Excellent Wine List
ALFRED	££	AE DC JCB MC V	●	■	

245 Shaftesbury Avenue, WC2. **Map** 13 B1. 020 7240 2566.
Minimal retro decor, reminiscent of a post-war café, in which updated English and Modern British food is served. Dishes include crispy belly of pork and sticky toffee pudding. 24 Dec–2 Jan, public hols.

		Credit Cards	Vegetarian Specialities	Highly Recommended	Excellent Wine List
CAFE SEVEN	££	AE DC MC V	●		●

7th Floor, Tate Modern, Bankside, SE1. **Map** 15 A3. 020 7401 5020.
Modern British ranging from fish and chips to Chinese duck salad in a modern, minimalist setting with an annually changing mural by a recognised artist. Views of St Paul's. 25–26 Dec.

		Credit Cards	Vegetarian Specialities	Highly Recommended	Excellent Wine List
CHEZ BRUCE	££	AE DC MC V		■	●

2 Bellevue Rd, SW17. 020 8767 6648.
Overlooking Wandsworth Common, this "local" offers Modern British masterpieces such as roast rump of veal with Provençal tart and *sauce bourride*. Good French wines or you can bring your own bottle.

		Credit Cards	Vegetarian Specialities	Highly Recommended	Excellent Wine List
40 DEGREES AT VERONICA'S	££	AE DC MC V			●

3 Hereford Rd, W2. **Map** 10 D2. & FAX 020 7229 5079.
Veronica's offers regional, historical and Modern British cooking and a choice of differently themed dining areas. 25 Dec–7 Jan.

		Credit Cards	Vegetarian Specialities	Highly Recommended	Excellent Wine List
MASH MAYFAIR	££	AE DC MC V	●	■	

26b Albemarle St, W1. **Map** 12 F3. 020 7495 5999. FAX 020 7495 2999.
Modern British with Mediterranean influences (wood-fired stove yielding duck and plum sauce pizza). public hols.

		Credit Cards	Vegetarian Specialities	Highly Recommended	Excellent Wine List
QUALITY CHOP HOUSE	££	MC V	●		

94 Farringdon Rd, EC1. **Map** 6 E4. 020 7837 5093. FAX 020 7833 8748.
"Progressive working-class caterer" is etched on the glass window of this Victorian diner. Now it serves City workers. 23 Dec–2 Jan.

		Credit Cards	Vegetarian Specialities	Highly Recommended	Excellent Wine List
SAUCE BAR ORGANIC DINER	££	AE DC MC V	●	■	

214 Camden High St, NW1. **Map** 4 F1. 020 7482 0777.
Modern British, diner-style cuisine using organic ingredients and served in an airy basement with modern, bright decor.

		Credit Cards	Vegetarian Specialities	Highly Recommended	Excellent Wine List
SEARCY'S RESTAURANT	££	AE DC MC V	●	■	●

Level 2, The Barbican, Silk St, EC2. **Map** 7 B5. 020 7588 3008.
Views of the Barbican's central courtyard and fountain enhance dishes such as roast scallops with crispy pork and carrots.

		Credit Cards	Vegetarian Specialities	Highly Recommended	Excellent Wine List
SONNY'S	££	AE DC MC V	●	■	

94 Church Rd, Barnes SW13. 020 8748 0393. FAX 020 8748 2698.
This superior local restaurant serves Modern British dishes including roasted monkfish, crispy bacon and braised red cabbage.

		Credit Cards	Vegetarian Specialities	Highly Recommended	Excellent Wine List
THE AVENUE	£££	AE DC MC V	●	■	●

7–9 St James's St, SW1. **Map** 12 F4. 020 7321 2111. FAX 020 7321 2500.
Minimalist interiors provide a streamlined atmosphere for Modern British cuisine, including Avenue fish fingers and sticky toffee pudding with cream. Pianist Mon–Sat. 25 Dec.

Price categories are for a three-course meal per person including tax, service and half a bottle of house wine (unless required to supply your own):

£ under £15
££ £15–£35
£££ £35–£55
££££ £55–£75
£££££ £75 plus.

CREDIT CARDS
Indicates which credit cards are accepted: *AE* American Express; *DC* Diners Club; *JCB* Japan Credit Bureau; *MC* MasterCard/Access; *V* Visa.

VEGETARIAN SPECIALITIES
Imaginative vegetarian options offered.

HIGHLY RECOMMENDED
A restaurant of particularly good value – great food and quality service.

EXCELLENT WINE LIST
An outstanding selection of wine offered.

	Price	Credit Cards	Vegetarian Specialities	Highly Recommended	Excellent Wine List
BOISDALE W www.boisdale.uk.com 15 Eccleston St, SW1. **Map** 20 E1. 020 7730 6922. FAX 020 7730 0548. Traditional and Modern British with Scottish specialities such as haggis, plus over 200 wines and a great range of malt whiskies. Live jazz Mon–Sat.	£££	AE DC MC V	●		●
CITY RHODES 1 New St, EC4. **Map** 14 E1. 020 7583 1313. FAX 020 7553 1662. This was superchef Gary Rhodes' first restaurant. Dishes include pan-fried sea bream with fresh herb and oyster tartare. Over 100 wines.	£££	AE DC MC V	●	■	●
THE FIFTH FLOOR 5th Floor, Harvey Nichols, 109–125 Knightsbridge, SW1. **Map** 11 C5. 020 7235 5250. FAX 020 7823 2207. Imaginative Modern British served in an elegant setting at the top of one of London's most fashionable stores. ● 25–26 Dec.	£££	AE MC V	●	■	●
JUST ST JAMES 16 St James's St, SW1. **Map** 12 F4. 020 7976 2222. FAX 020 7976 2020. Modern British with classic European influences served in an Edwardian Baroque interior with paintings and sculpture. ● 25 Dec.	£££	AE MC V	●		
THE OXO TOWER Oxo Tower Wharf, Barge House St, SE1. **Map** 14 E3. 020 7803 3888. FAX 020 7803 3838. On the 8th floor of a landmark 1930s building, this restaurant serves exemplary Modern British accompanied by an extensive wine list.	£££	AE MC V	●	■	●
PRISM 147 Leadenhall St, EC3. **Map** 15 C2. 020 7256 3888. FAX 020 7256 3883. Housed in the former Bank of New York, the restaurant offers an impressive line-up of Modern British dishes and a good wine list.	£££	AE DC MC	●	■	●
QUAGLINO'S W www.conran.com 16 Bury St, SW1. **Map** 12 F3. 020 7930 6767. FAX 020 7839 2866. Modern British brasserie reflecting its 1930s origins and thriving on Conran design, serving classic dishes such as calves liver and bacon.	£££	AE DC MC	●		●
RHODES IN THE SQUARE Dolphin Square, Chichester St, SW1. **Map** 21 A3. 020 7798 6767. FAX 020 7798 5685. Inspired Modern British dishes, such as red wine beef lasagna with a chestnut mushroom cream sauce, served in a superior Art Deco setting.	£££	AE DC MC V	●	■	●
RULES 35 Maiden Lane, WC2. **Map** 13 C2. 020 7836 5314. FAX 020 7497 1081. London's oldest surviving restaurant serving traditional British fare since 1798 amid Edwardian decor. For a high corkage fee you can bring your own wine. ● 23–26 Dec.	£££	AE MC V	●	■	●
SIMPSON'S-IN-THE-STRAND 100 Strand, WC2. **Map** 13 C2. 020 7836 9112. FAX 020 7836 1381. A truly traditional English experience, with grand Victorian interiors reminiscent of a traditional but welcoming club. ● 25–26 Dec.	£££	AE DC MC V	●		

CHINESE

Cantonese is the archetypal style served in Chinese restaurants, which is rice-based, although the chilli-flavoured dishes of Szechuan and Hunan are increasingly popular here. At lunchtime many Cantonese restaurants serve delicious hors d'oeuvres called dim sum.

	Price	Credit Cards	Vegetarian Specialities	Highly Recommended	Excellent Wine List
THE NEW CULTURE REVOLUTION 305 Kings Rd, SW3. **Map** 19 A4. 020 7352 9281. A traditional Cantonese repertoire: soups, various noodles, dumplings, all served in a bright, modern setting. Friendly service. ● 25–26 Dec.	£	MC V	●	■	

NEW WORLD £
1 Gerrard Place, W1. **Map** 13 B2. 020 7734 0396. FAX 020 7287 3994.
Helpful staff serve a range of Cantonese, Szechuan and seafood dishes, not to
mention an exemplary dim sum selection. 25 Dec.
AE JCB MC V

FUNG SHING ££
15 Lisle St, WC2. **Map** 13 A2. 020 7437 1539. FAX 020 7734 0284.
One of the best restaurants in Chinatown, serving Chinese fare in a European
atmosphere. You can bring your own bottle. 24–26 Dec.
AE DC MC V

HARBOUR CITY ££
46 Gerrard St, W1. **Map** 13 B2. 020 7439 7120. FAX 020 7734 7745.
Cantonese and Pekinese cuisine, with speciality hot pot. European, Australian
and Chinese wines. Or you can bring a bottle. 25 Dec.
AE DC MC V

HAKKASAN £££
8 Hanway Place, W1. **Map** 13 A1. 020 7927 7000. FAX 020 7907 1889.
Dim sum is served all day, changing to à la carte for dinner, with the lounge
bar also serving dim sum during the day.
AE DC MC V

ROYAL CHINA £££
40 Baker St, W1. **Map** 3 C5. 020 7487 4688.
A restaurant specializing in Peking and Cantonese dishes, while also
renowned for lobster noodles and dim sum. 25–27 Dec.
AE JCB V

FISH AND SEAFOOD

*London boasts a thriving collection of fish restaurants, spanning the range from informal modern
to formal traditional, receiving fresh produce every morning from local markets.*

LIVEBAIT ££
43 The Cut, SE1. **Map** 14 E4. 020 7928 7211. FAX 020 7928 2299.
Retaining the original Victorian style, the fish and shellfish repertoire includes
traditional British platters as well as international dishes.
MC JCB V

GREEN'S RESTAURANT AND OYSTER BAR £££
36 Duke St, St James's, SW1. **Map** 12 F3. 020 7930 4366.
Amid classic "gentleman's club" decor, with banquettes and booths, fish and
oysters from County Cork are a particular feature. Sundays 1 May–31 Aug.
AE DC JCB MC

RESTAURANT ONE-O-ONE £££
William St, SW1. **Map** 11 C5. 020 7290 7101. FAX 020 7235 6196.
Fish and seafood prepared French style, including sea bass in rock salt,
accompanied by a choice of 100 wines.
AE DC MC V

LE SUQUET £££
104 Draycott Avenue, SW3. **Map** 19 B2. 020 7581 1785. .
Serving fish and seafood amid the maritime ambience and watercolours of
Cannes. Separate oyster bar and patio. One week at Christmas.
AE DC MC V

SWEETINGS £££
30 Queen Victoria St, EC4. **Map** 15 B2. 020 7248 3062.
This City gent's institution is renowned for oysters and classic British dishes
like grilled Dover sole. No reservations. 24 Dec–2 Jan.

CAFE FISH ££££
36–40 Rupert St, SW1. **Map** 13 A2. 020 7287 8989. FAX 020 7287 8400.
A classic French approach is applied to the fish and seafood, with favourites
including fish and chips and seafood platter.
AE DC JCB MC

FRENCH

*French food is readily available throughout the capital, ranging from regional cuisine in bistro
settings to classic favourites in brasseries and haute cuisine in deluxe settings.*

L'ANIS ££
1 Kensington High St, W8. **Map** 10 E5. 020 7795 6533. FAX 020 7937 8854.
The menu here is a French-Mediterranean rendezvous that yields rewarding
results, housed in a contemporized former banking hall.
AE MC V

L'ARTISTE MUSCLÉ ££
1 Shepherd Mkt, W1. **Map** 12 E4. 020 7493 6150. FAX 020 7495 5747.
French bistro serving boeuf Bourguignon in a classic setting with pavement
tables overlooking Shepherd Market. 25 Dec, Easter Sunday.
AE DC MC V

Price categories are for a three-course meal per person including tax, service and half a bottle of house wine (unless required to supply your own):
£ under £15
££ £15–£35
£££ £35–£55
££££ £55–£75
£££££ £75 plus.

CREDIT CARDS
Indicates which credit cards are accepted: *AE* American Express; *DC* Diners Club; *JCB* Japan Credit Bureau; *MC* MasterCard/Access; *V* Visa.

VEGETARIAN SPECIALITIES
Imaginative vegetarian options offered.

HIGHLY RECOMMENDED
A restaurant of particularly good value – great food and quality service.

EXCELLENT WINE LIST
An outstanding selection of wine offered.

	CREDIT CARDS	VEGETARIAN SPECIALITIES	HIGHLY RECOMMENDED	EXCELLENT WINE LIST
CLUB GASCON (££) 57 West Smithfield, EC1. **Map** 14 F1. 020 7796 0600. FAX 020 7960 0601. Cuisine from southwestern France, with foie gras, truffle and seafood dishes a speciality. Food also served tapas-style in the bar.	AE MC V	●	■	●
L'ORANGER (££) 5 St James's St, SW1. **Map** 12 F4. 020 7839 3774. FAX 020 7839 4330. Fine dining in elegant French style. Specialities include steamed salmon *boudin* stuffed with scallop mousse.	AE DC MC V	●	■	●
BIBENDUM (£££) 1st Floor, Michelin House, 81 Fulham Rd, SW3. **Map** 19 B2. 020 7581 5187. A retro-chic showcase for Modern French cuisine. The ground floor of the building features an oyster bar and café.	AE MC V	●		●
CHEZ GERARD (£££) Opera Terrace, The Market, Covent Garden Piazza, WC2. **Map** 13 C2. 020 7379 0666. FAX 020 7497 9060. Renowned for its classic Parisian *steak frites*, this stylish French establishment has a terrace overlooking Covent Garden Piazza.	AE JCB MC V	●	■	●
CRITERION BRASSERIE (£££) Piccadilly Circus, W1. **Map** 13 A3. 020 7930 0488. Stunning, historic interiors culminate in a glittering Neo-Byzantine mosaic ceiling. French dishes with Mediterranean influences.	AE DC MC V	●		●
MON PLAISIR (£££) 21 Monmouth St, WC2. **Map** 13 B1. 020 7836 7243. FAX 020 7240 4774. A staple of Covent Garden's theatreland, known for unpretentious French provincial dishes (coq au vin, tarte tatin). ● *public hols.*	AE DC JCB MC V	●		●
LE PALAIS DU JARDIN (£££) 136 Long Acre, WC2. **Map** 13 B2. 020 7379 5353. FAX 020 7379 1846. Vintage brasserie with a separate seafood section serving creative, reliable French dishes with an extensive international wine list.	AE MC V	●		●
PIED À TERRE W www.pied.a.terre.co.uk (£££) 34 Charlotte St, W1. **Map** 5 A5. 020 7636 1178. Modern French cuisine, along the lines of lime marinated scallop *ceviche* with scallop tartare, served in an intimate setting. Outstanding wine list.	AE MC V	●	■	●
LE PONT DE LA TOUR W www.conran.com (£££) Butlers Wharf, SE1. **Map** 16 E4. 020 7403 8403. Riverside marvel with a separate crustacea bar, nightly pianist and over 900 wines to accompany Euro-Med French cuisine. ● *public hols.*	AE DC JCB MC V	●	■	●
SPOON + (£££) Sanderson Hotel, 50 Berners St, W1. **Map** 12 F1. 020 7300 1444. A perfect combination of style and culinary content with tables on a delightfully retro-chic heated patio.	AE DC JCB MC V	●	■	●
MAISON NOVELLI (££££) 29 Clerkenwell Green, EC1. **Map** 6 E4. 020 7251 6606. FAX 020 7490 1083. Jean-Christophe Novelli's background in haute cuisine shows here where flavour is at the forefront of his modern rustic French cuisine. The chocolate plate dessert is legendary.	AE DC MC V	●		
MIRABELLE (££££) 56 Curzon St, W1. **Map** 12 E3. 020 7499 4636. FAX 020 7499 5449. A superlative restaurant offering Art Deco elegance, a delightful patio for fresco dining, superb service and creative French cuisine, beautifully presented and perfectly cooked.	AE MC V			●

ROUSSILLON £££
16 St Barnabas St, SW1. **Map** 20 D3. 020 7730 5550. FAX 020 7824 8617.
Elegant Provençal decor with neutral tones, providing a showcase for superb modern French cuisine using organic ingredients.

AE MC V

THE SQUARE ££££
6–10 Bruton St, W1. **Map** 12 E3. 020 7495 7100. FAX 020 7495 7150.
Lasagne of crab with a mousseline of scallops and basil is typical of the distinguished Modern French cuisine on offer here.

AE MC V

CHEZ NICO £££££
90 Park Lane, W1. **Map** 12 D3. 020 7409 1290.
An elegant setting for superstar chef, Nico Ladenis, to exercise his classical French gastronomic artistry. Great wine list. ● *public hols.*

AE DC MC V

LE GAVROCHE £££££
43 Upper Brook St, W1. **Map** 12 D2. 020 7408 0881. FAX 020 7491 4387.
Superlative modern and classical French cuisine in a sophisticated setting where French chic meets English club. ● *23 Dec–3 Jan.*

AE DC JCB MC V

LA TANTE CLAIRE £££££
The Berkeley Hotel, Wilton Place, SW1. **Map** 12 D5.
020 7823 2003. FAX 020 7235 6330.
A medley of lilac and mauve sets the tone in this elegant restaurant run by masterchef Pierre Koffman. ● *public hols.*

AE DC JCB MC

GREEK, TURKISH AND NORTH AFRICAN

Classic characteristics which tie these cuisines together are that they tend to be lightly seasoned yet full-flavoured – barbecued meats, salads and "dips" such as taramasalata (cod's roe) and houmous (chick pea paste) are prominent staples.

SOFRA £
18 Shepherd St, W1. **Map** 12 E4. 020 7493 3320. FAX 020 7499 8282.
One of London's best-known, best-value chains of Turkish restaurants. A main attraction is the inexpensive selection of set menus.

AE DCJ CB MC V

AL HAMRA ££
31–35 Shepherd Market, W1. **Map** 12 E4. 020 7493 1954.
Authentic Lebanese cuisine (traditional and modern) in a restaurant famed for *meze* that includes a choice of more than 60 dishes. ● *public hols.*

AE DC MC V

DAPHNE ££
83 Bayham St, NW1. **Map** 4 F1. 020 7267 7322. FAX 020 7482 3964.
Offering the best in classic and modern dishes – king prawns with aubergine and feta in filo, deep-fried. ● *25–26 Dec, 1 Jan.*

MC V

ISTANBUL ISKEMBECISI ££
9 Stoke Newington Rd, N16. 020 7254 7291.
Classic Turkish cuisine available virtually round the clock in a lively, authentic setting with great staff.

LEMONIA ££
89 Regent's Park Rd, NW1. **Map** 3 C1. 020 7586 7454.
Traditional and modern Greek dishes served within a brasserie-style setting with a lot of plants and a conservatory. ● *25–26 Dec.*

MC V

MOMO £££
25 Heddon St, W1. **Map** 12 F2. 020 7434 4040.
Housed in a wonderful "antique Moroccan palace" the restaurant combines Moroccan, Tunisian and Algerian cuisine, balancing tradition with a more modern approach. The bar is an ideal "Casablanca" rendezvous.

AE JCB MC V

INDIAN

The range and quality of Indian restaurants in London is a delight, with growing numbers specializing in specific styles of food, such as "balti", fast-cooked dishes served in a small wok. Dishes are mildly spicy (korma), medium (bhuna, dansak, dopiaza) or very hot (madras, vindaloo).

MADHU'S BRILLIANT £
39 South Rd, Southall, Middlesex UB1. 020 8574 1897.
Authentic Punjabi and East African cuisine offering great value for money making the detour to Southall well worth it. ● *Tue.*

AE DC MC V

Price categories are for a three-course meal per person including tax, service and half a bottle of house wine (unless required to supply your own):
£ under £15
££ £15–£35
£££ £35–£55
££££ £55–£75
£££££ £75 plus.

CREDIT CARDS
Indicates which credit cards are accepted: *AE* American Express; *DC* Diners Club; *JCB* Japan Credit Bureau; *MC* MasterCard/Access; *V* Visa.

VEGETARIAN SPECIALITIES
Imaginative vegetarian options offered.

HIGHLY RECOMMENDED
A restaurant of particularly good value – great food and quality service.

EXCELLENT WINE LIST
An outstanding selection of wine offered.

	Credit Cards	Vegetarian Specialities	Highly Recommended	Excellent Wine List
NAZRUL £ 130 Brick Lane, E1. **Map** 8 E4. 020 7247 2505. Classic Indian, regional and balti dishes served amid decor that includes Indian antiques. Bring your own wine. No corkage charge. 25 Dec.		●	■	
MELA ££ 152–156 Shaftesbury Avenue, WC2. **Map** 13 B2. 020 7379 0527. Country-style Indian cuisine, with a similarly themed decor, with wooden floors and furniture creating a warm and relaxing ambiance.	AE DC MC V	●		
BOMBAY BRASSERIE £££ Courtfield Close, Courtfield Rd, SW7. **Map** 18 E2. 020 7370 4040. FAX 020 7835 1669. Impressive colonial, Raj atmosphere and resident pianist. Bombay and regional cuisine includes Goan chicken with coconut and spices. 25–26 Dec.	AE DC MC V	●	■	●
CAFE SPICE NAMASTE £££ 16 Prescot St, E1. **Map** 16 E2. 020 7488 9242. FAX 020 7481 0508. A fantastic menu specializes in Parsee and Goan (Dansak, lamb with lentils) dishes with wines to match. public hols.	AE DC MC	●		●
CHOR BIZARRE £££ 16 Albemarle St, W1. **Map** 12 F3. 020 7629 9802. FAX 020 7493 7756. Amidst numerous Indian antiques (all for sale), the menu has a Kashmiri focus (*gostaba* – minced lamb with cardamom and yoghurt). 25–26 Dec.	AE MC V	●		
SALLOOS £££ 62–64 Kinnerton St, SW1. **Map** 11 C5. 020 7235 4444. FAX 020 7259 5703. North Indian and Pakistani menu specializing in chicken and lamb. Upmarket decor. You can bring your own wine. public hols.	AE DC MC V			
TAMARIND £££ 20 Queen St, W1. **Map** 12 E3. 020 7629 3561. FAX 020 7499 5034. Gilded basement with sumptuous decor. North Indian cuisine is fastidiously prepared by top chefs from the region.	AE DCJ CB MC V			
VAMA £££ 438 King's Rd, SW10. **Map** 18 F4. 020 7351 4118. FAX 020 7565 8501. A feast of northwest Indian regional cuisine, as well as Pakistani, Afghan and Iranian specialities. Live jazz on Sunday lunchtimes. 25 Dec.	AE DC MC V			
VEERASWAMY £££ Mezzanine Floor, Victory House, 99 Regent St, W1. **Map** 12 F1. 020 7734 1401. FAX 020 7439 8434. London's oldest Indian restaurant (est. 1927), it is also one of the most modern, with chic decor and inspiring Indian dishes.	AE DC JCB MC	●	■	
ZAIKA £££ 257–259 Fulham Rd, SW3. **Map** 19 A3. 020 7351 7823. FAX 020 7376 4971. Supreme modern Indian food served amid elegant, ethnic decor. Terrific degustation menu and attentive service.	AE MC V	●	■	●

ITALIAN

Going beyond staples such as pizza and pasta, menus now encompass far more comprehensive and regional Italian cuisine, which has captivated the capital's restaurant-goers.

	Credit Cards	Vegetarian Specialities	Highly Recommended	Excellent Wine List
AL DUCA ££ 4–5 Duke of York St, SW1. **Map** 13 A3. 020 7839 3090. FAX 020 7839 4050. Excellent Italian dishes, classics and regional specialities, with great-value set menus, served in a modern, colourful, yet intimate Italianate setting. Good wines and service.	AE MC V		■	●

ALLORO   ££
19–20 Dover St, W1. **Map** 12 F3. 📞 *020 7495 4768.* **FAX** *020 7629 5348.*
Traditional, imaginative Italian cuisine – black tagliolini with crab sauce –
served in an elegant setting. 🍽 ♿

BERTORELLI'S   ££
44a Floral St, WC2. **Map** 13 C2. 📞 *020 7836 3969.* **FAX** *020 7836 1868.*
Modern Italian cuisine with numerous traditional favourites served
amid warm and inviting decor. Ideal location for Covent Garden's Opera
House and theatres. 🍽

CARLUCCIO'S   ££
3–5 Barrett St, St Christopher's Place, W1. **Map** 12 D1.
📞 *020 7935 5927.* **FAX** *020 7487 5436.*
Authentic Italian dishes including soups and pastas, with the bright, warm
interior also housing a shop with Carluccio's range of Italian foods. 🍽 ♿

EMPORIO ARMANI CAFE   ££
191 Brompton Rd, SW3. **Map** 19 B1. 📞 *020 7823 8818.* **FAX** *020 7823 8854.*
Reminiscent of a chic Italian railway dining car, this in-store designer café
serves classics such as prawn and lemon risotto. ● *25–26 Dec.* 🍽 ♿

GETTI   ££
16–17 Jermyn St, SW1. **Map** 13 A3. 📞 *020 7734 7334.*
Regional Italian cuisine innovatively presented, with risotto a speciality,
accompanied by a great line-up of Italian drinks. 🍽 ♿

OSTERIA D'ISOLA   ££
145 Knightsbridge, SW1. **Map** 11 C5. 📞 *020 7838 1055.* **FAX** *020 7838 1099.*
Traditional rustic Italian cuisine (beetroot ravioli) served in a modern spacious
basement with a view into the open-plan kitchen. ● *25 Dec, 1 Jan.* 🍽

SPIGA SOHO   ££
84 Wardour St, W1. **Map** 13 A2. 📞 *020 7734 3444.* **FAX** *020 7734 3332.*
Fashionable and fun, with banquette seating and a wood-burning stove.
Classic Italian repertoire includes pizzas and pastas. 🍽 ♿

SPIGHETTA   ££
43 Blandford St, W1. **Map** 12 D1. 📞 *020 7486 7340.*
Modern Italian cuisine – pizza with fresh buffalo mozzarella, cherry tomatoes
and basil dressing – served in a relaxed family atmosphere. 🍽 ♿

TABLE CAFE   ££
Habitat, 196 Tottenham Court Rd, W1. **Map** 5 A5. 📞 *020 7636 8330.*
Modern basement cafe in a home interiors store, with traditional, regional
dishes. Around 70 per cent of the menu is vegetarian. ● *25–26 Dec.* ♿

TECA   ££
54 Brook Mews, W1. **Map** 12 E2. 📞 *020 7495 4774.* **FAX** *020 7491 3545.*
Accomplished Modern Italian cuisine making full use of seasonal ingredients.
Quietly tucked away with an elegant, stylish look. 🍽 ♿

L'INCONTRO   £££
87 Pimlico Rd, SW1. **Map** 20 D3. 📞 *020 7730 6327.* **FAX** *020 7730 5062.*
Wonderful Italian dishes leaning towards Valentian cuisine – seabass with
balsamic vinegar and olive oil – served in an elegantly contemporary,
Italianate setting. ● *24–26 Dec, Easter Sunday and lunch on public hols.*

ISOLA   £££
145 Knightsbridge, SW1. **Map** 11 C5. 📞 *020 7838 1044.* **FAX** *020 7838 1099.*
Gourmet, Italian cuisine, accompanied by over 400 wines, served amid
an impressive red and white colour scheme. ● *25 Dec, 1 Jan.* ♿

ORSO   £££
27 Wellington St, WC2. **Map** 13 C2. 📞 *020 7240 5269.* **FAX** *020 7497 2148.*
A media, theatre-goers rendezvous serving north Italian regional cuisine –
rocket salad with Parma ham and parmesan, accompanied by an all-Italian
wine list. ● *25 Dec.* 🍽

TUSCAN STEAK   £££
St Martin's Lane Hotel, St Martin's Lane, WC2. **Map** 13 B2.
📞 *020 7300 5544.* **FAX** *020 7300 5501.*
An Italian menu includes steak Italian style, and plenty of Italian drinks at the
bar. Whimsical Tuscan ambience. 🍽

Credit card columns (AE/DC/JCB/MC/V):

Restaurant	Cards				
ALLORO	AE DC MC V	●			●
BERTORELLI'S	AE DC JCB MC V	●	■		
CARLUCCIO'S	AE MC V	●	■		
EMPORIO ARMANI CAFE	AE DC MC V	●			
GETTI	AE MC V	●	■		
OSTERIA D'ISOLA	AE DC MC V	●	■		●
SPIGA SOHO	AE DC MC V	●	■		
SPIGHETTA	AE DC MC V	●			●
TABLE CAFE	MC V	●			
TECA	AE DC MC V	●	■		●
L'INCONTRO	AE DC MC V				
ISOLA	AE DC MC V		■		●
ORSO	AE MC V	●			●
TUSCAN STEAK	AE DC MC V	●	■		●

Price categories are for a three-course meal per person including tax, service and half a bottle of house wine (unless required to supply your own):
ⓔ under £15
ⓔⓔ £15–£35
ⓔⓔⓔ £35–£55
ⓔⓔⓔⓔ £55–£75
ⓔⓔⓔⓔⓔ £75 plus.

CREDIT CARDS
Indicates which credit cards are accepted: *AE* American Express; *DC* Diners Club; *JCB* Japan Credit Bureau; *MC* MasterCard/Access; *V* Visa.
VEGETARIAN SPECIALITIES
Imaginative vegetarian options offered.
HIGHLY RECOMMENDED
A restaurant of particularly good value – great food and quality service.
EXCELLENT WINE LIST
An outstanding selection of wine offered.

	Credit Cards	Vegetarian Specialities	Highly Recommended	Excellent Wine List
ZAFFERANO ⓔⓔⓔ 15 Lowndes St, SW1. **Map** 20 D1. ☎ 020 7235 5800. One of London's finest Modern Italian restaurants, with white truffle dishes among the specialities. 🕒 *Christmas week, public hols.* ♿	MC V	●	■	●
RIVER CAFE ⓔⓔⓔⓔ Thames Wharf Studios, Rainville Rd, W6. ☎ 020 7381 8824. A modern-style interior that also provides river views, serving highly praised modern interpretations of traditional Italian cuisine. 🕒 *public hols.* 🍸	AE DC MC V			●

JAPANESE

Expect the unexpected – teppan-yaki tables (sitting around a chef cooking on a hotplate), sushi passing by on a conveyor belt, or tatami rooms, where diners sit on straw mats.

	Credit Cards	Vegetarian Specialities	Highly Recommended	Excellent Wine List
TOKYO DINER ⓔⓔ 2 Newport Place, WC1. **Map** 13 B2. ☎ 020 7287 8777. ℻ 020 7434 1415. Good value in an authentic Japanese "canteen" atmosphere. The menu includes sushi, sashimi and Japanese curry. ♿	DC MC V	●		
WAGAMAMA ⓔ 4 Streatham St, WC1. **Map** 13 B1. ☎ 020 7323 9223. ℻ 020 7323 9224. Modern refectory-style in a spacious, bustling basement, serving various types of noodles in numerous rewarding formats. 🕒 *25 Dec.*	AE DC MC V	●		
YO! SUSHI ⓔ 52–53 Poland St, W1. **Map** 13 A2. ☎ 020 7287 0443. Sushi, sashimi, salads, soups and noodles pass by on a conveyor belt, in this modern, minimalist setting. 🕒 *25 Dec.* 🍸	AE DC JCB MC V	●		
F. MIYAMA ⓔⓔⓔ 38 Clarges St, W1. **Map** 12 E3. ☎ 020 7499 2443. ℻ 020 7493 1573. Elegant, European-style decor houses a teppan-yaki counter for meat and seafood, with meticulously prepared dishes. 🕒 *25 Dec. 1 Jan.* 🍸	AE DC MC V	●		
NOBU ⓔⓔⓔⓔⓔ 19 Old Park Lane, W1. **Map** 12 E4. ☎ 020 7447 4747. Stylish first-floor restaurant serving sensational Japanese-South American fusion cuisine. Extensive wine and sake list. 🕒 *public hols.* 🍸 ♿	AE DC MC V	●	■	●

MODERN INTERNATIONAL

This eclectic genre emerged in the 1990s and continues to evolve as its popularity grows. It uses ingredients and techniques from various of the world's cuisines to create an exciting "fusion" style.

	Credit Cards	Vegetarian Specialities	Highly Recommended	Excellent Wine List
ALASTAIR LITTLE ⓔⓔⓔ 49 Frith St, W1. **Map** 13 A2. ☎ 020 7734 5183. ℻ 020 7734 5206. Modern International cooking with an Italian accent. 🕒 *public hols.*	AE JCB MC V	●		
BALI SUGAR ⓔⓔⓔ 33a All Saints Rd, W11. **Map** 9 B1. ☎ 020 7221 4477. ℻ 020 7221 9955. A split-level, cleverly converted terraced house. Sashimi of seabream is a taste of what to expect. 🕒 *23–27 Dec, Easter.* ♿	AE DC MC V	●		●
BANK ALDWYCH ⓔⓔ 1 Kingsway, Aldwych, WC2. **Map** 14 D2. ☎ 020 7379 9797. Former bank that now offers classic dishes with a twist. 🍸 ♿	AE DC MC V	●		
BLUEBIRD Ⓦ www.conran.com ⓔⓔ 350 King's Rd, SW3. **Map** 19 A4. ☎ 020 7559 1000. ℻ 020 7559 1111. Inspired conversion with Classical, Neo-Georgian and Art Deco elements. Flavourful dishes with game and crustacea a speciality. 🍸 ♿	AE DC JCB MC V	●		

GIRAFFE ££ AE MC V
6–8 Blandford St, W1. **Map** 12 D1. (020 7935 2333.
Global cuisine (wok-fried noodles, Louisiana fishcakes), served amid friendly,
colourful, global decor with world music. ● 25–26 Dec.

KENSINGTON PLACE ££ AE DC MC V
205 Kensington Church St, W8. **Map** 9 C3. (020 7727 3184. FAX 020 7229 2025.
Minimalist venue attracting a dedicated crowd and serving Modern
International cuisine with exciting reinterpretations. ● Christmas. ▮ ⟐

MORO ££ AE DC MC V
34–36 Exmouth Market, EC1. **Map** 6 E4. (020 7833 8336.
A menu that changes fortnightly delivers interesting Spanish and North African
dishes, such as charcoal-grilled quail with pomegranate molasses, with
Spanish and Italian wines a feature. ● public hols. ▮ ⟐

STICKY FINGERS ££ AE MC V
1a Phillimore Gardens, W8. **Map** 9 C5. (020 7938 5338. FAX 020 7938 5337.
Rolling Stones memorabilia are the background for a menu ranging from
North American burgers to bang bang chicken. ▮ ⟐

CHE £££ AE DC MC V
23 St James's St, SW1. **Map** 12 F3. (020 7747 9380. FAX 020 7747 9382.
A range of international favourites, from Caesar salad to lobster thermidor,
served in the landmark 1964 Smithson building with the original escalators.
Renowned for its cocktail bar and cigar lounge on the ground floor. ▮

DRONES £££ AE DC MC V
1 Pont St, SW1. **Map** 20 D1. (020 7235 9555. FAX 020 7235 9566.
Classic French cuisine with Mediterranean influences, beautifully prepared
and presented amid sophisticated modern decor. ▮

THE SUGAR CLUB £££ AE DC MC V
21 Warwick St, W1. **Map** 12 F2. (020 7437 7776. FAX 020 7437 7773.
Fusion cuisine in a modern, streamlined setting – spicy kangaroo salad with
mint, peanuts and lime chilli dressing,and plenty of new world wines,
particularly from Australia and New Zealand. ▮

CLARKE'S ££££ AE MC V
124 Kensington Church St, W8. **Map** 10 D4. (020 7221 9225.
British, Californian and Italian cuisine meet in this restaurant's inspired
menus. Food is light but always tasty. ▮ ⟐

COAST ££££ AE JCB MC V
26B Albemarle St, W1. **Map** 12 F3. (020 7495 5999.
Possibly London's most extraordinary restaurant, not only because of the
goldfish bowl interior, but also for the exquisite cuisine. ▮

MODERN EUROPEAN

*Just as Modern British and Modern International cuisine celebrate a fusion of ingredients and
techniques, so Modern European thrives on innovative interpretations of classic European dishes.*

WINE WHARF AT VINOPOLIS £ AE MC V
Storey St, Borough Market, SE1. **Map** 15 B3. (020 7940 8335. FAX 020 7940 8336.
Graze on tapas-type dishes or tackle the fuller menu in this modernized
Victorian workhouse. ● 25 Dec. 1 Jan. ▮

THE PEOPLE'S PALACE ££ AE DC MC V
Level 3, Royal Festival Hall, South Bank Centre, SE1. **Map** 14 D4.
(020 7928 9999. FAX 020 7928 2355.
Set in 1950s retro, dishes include roast leg of rabbit, leek farçi, prosciutto and
mustard cream. Ideal for pre- or post-performance. ▮ ⟐

CIRCUS £££ AE DC MC V
1 Upper James St, W1. **Map** 12 F2. (020 7534 4000. FAX 020 7534 4010.
A sleek modern bar for aperitifs sets the mood for the minimalist setting
delivering maximum flavours in a Modern European repertoire. ▮ ⟐

THE IVY £££ AE DC JCB MC V
1 West St, WC2. **Map** 13 B2. (020 7836 4751. FAX 020 7240 9333.
An institution of the theatre district, this celebrity haven features 19th–20th
century artworks and sculpture, stained-glass windows and green leather
banquettes. Plenty of French and New World wines. ▮ ⟐

Price categories are for a three-course meal per person including tax, service and half a bottle of house wine (unless required to supply your own):
£ under £15
££ £15–£35
£££ £35–£55
££££ £55–£75
£££££ £75 plus.

CREDIT CARDS
Indicates which credit cards are accepted: *AE* American Express; *DC* Diners Club; *JCB* Japan Credit Bureau; *MC* MasterCard/Access; *V* Visa.

VEGETARIAN SPECIALITIES
Imaginative vegetarian options offered.

HIGHLY RECOMMENDED
A restaurant of particularly good value – great food and quality service.

EXCELLENT WINE LIST
An outstanding selection of wine offered.

Restaurant	Price	Credit Cards	Vegetarian Specialities	Highly Recommended	Excellent Wine List
L'ODEON — 65 Regent St, W1. Map 12 F3. 020 7287 1400. FAX 020 7287 1300. A Modern European menu includes French dishes, such as baked scallops, spinach with truffle en croûte. 25 Dec–1 Jan.	£££	AE DC MC V	●	■	●
MEZZO — 100 Wardour St, W1. Map 13 A2. 020 7314 4000. In a Soho landmark, Modern European dishes – bruschetta of goat's cheese, fig and San Daniela ham – are served to live music nightly.	£££	AE DC JCB MC V	●		●
RIVER RESTAURANT — The Savoy Hotel, Strand, WC2. Map 13 C2. 020 7420 2698. FAX 020 7240 6040. Wonderful views of the Thames and live music all week, with a dinner dance Friday and Saturday. Stylish 1930s decor.	£££	AE DC MC V			

OTHER EUROPEAN

The British generally favour food from climates more exotic than their own, but there is a growing number of northern and eastern European restaurants well worth seeking out.

Restaurant	Price	Credit Cards	Vegetarian Specialities	Highly Recommended	Excellent Wine List
BALTIC — 74 Blackfriars Rd, SE1. Map 14 F4. 020 7928 1111. FAX 020 7401 6917. Pan East-European dishes with some Scandinavian influences, spanning seafood, classic Georgian, Polish, Russian and Hungarian.	££	AE DC MC V	●	■	
BELGO CENTRAAL — 50 Earlham St, WC2. Map 13 B2. 020 7813 2233. FAX 020 7681 0811. An industrial lift takes you down to this monastic basement where staff in monk's habits dispense Modern Belgian dishes, with beer, mussel pots and platters a speciality. 25 Dec.	££	AE DC MC V	●		
THE GAY HUSSAR — 2 Greek St, W1. Map 13 B2. 020 7437 0973. FAX 020 7437 4631. Clubby library setting serving politicians, media and literary types chilled wild cherry soup and Transylvanian stuffed cabbage. Set lunch menus offer good value. public hols.	££	AE DC JCB MC V	●	■	
MULLIGAN'S OF MAYFAIR — 13–14 Cork St, W1. Map 12 F3. 020 7409 1370. Basement restaurant offering traditional and modern Irish dishes – Irish stew with red cabbage, with oysters a speciality. There is also a separate oyster bar. public hols.	££	AE DC JCB MC V			●
NIKITA'S — www.nikitasrestaurant.co.uk — 65 Ifield Rd, SW10. Map 18 E4. 020 7352 6326. Small, but perfectly stocked bar (for vodka), with a fantastically decorated basement restaurant serving classic Russian dishes.	££	AE DC MC V	●		●
PALMS — 39 King St, WC2. Map 13 C2. 020 7240 2939. FAX 020 7378 5035. Mediterranean cuisine, including Italian, French and Greek influences (tarragon chicken, lamb kofta) served in a relaxed setting.	££	AE MC V	●		
SOVIET CANTEEN — 430 King's Rd, SW10. Map 18 F4. 020 7795 1556. FAX 020 7795 1562. Cosy whitewashed basement hung with Soviet art, where classical Russian dishes are given a Modern British twist. Great service and extensive wine list. 24 Dec–2 Jan.	££	AE DC MC V	●	■	
WÓDKA — 12 St Alban's Grove, W8. Map 10 E5. 020 7937 6513. A mixture of classic and modern Polish food (blini with smoked salmon, roast duck) served in a modern, but warm and friendly setting.	££	AE DC MC V	●	■	●

RICHARD CORRIGAN AT LINDSAY HOUSE £££
21 Romilly St, W1. **Map** 13 A2. 020 7439 0450. FAX 020 7437 7349.
An elegant Georgian townhouse is an atmospheric setting for Modern Irish
dishes – boudin of lamb, pearl barley and rosemary.

AE
DC
JCB
MC
V

SOUTHEAST ASIAN

*Thai food has pioneered the growing popularity of Southeast Asian food, with various restaurants
offering a menu that includes Thai, Singaporean, Malaysian and Indonesian cuisine.*

CICADA ££
132–136 St John St, EC1. **Map** 6 F4. 020 7608 1550.
Renowned southeast Asian cuisine is served here using traditional recipes and
ingredients. The menu is divided into small and large dishes and includes
creations like chilli salt squid. ● *public hols.* ▮

AE
DC
MC
V

MELATI ££
21 Gt Windmill St, W1. **Map** 13 A2. 020 7437 2745. FAX 020 7734 6964.
Bustling restaurant with polite staff serving authentic Indonesian, Malaysian
and southeast Asian specialities including beef rendang (spicy beef in thick
coconut sauce). ● *Christmas.*

AE
MC
V

MEZZONINE ££
100 Wardour St, W1. **Map** 13 A2. 020 7314 4000.
Contemporary Thai specialities such as Thai beef salad, green papaya and prik
naam plaa, deep fried whole bass, chilli jam dressing, are served to the beat
provided by DJs six nights a week. ▮ ♿

AE
DC
JCB
MC
V

SRI SIAM ££
16 Old Compton St, W1. **Map** 13 A2. 020 7434 3544.
This is a perfect place for your first taste of Thai food – the heat is toned
down, but the flavours are still strong. There is an extensive vegetarian menu.
● *24–26 Dec, 1 Jan.* ▮

AE
DC
MC
V

JUST ORIENTAL £££
19 King St, SW1. **Map** 12 F4. 020 7930 9292.
Fresh, pan-Asian fast food specializing in noodles, dim sum and steamed fish,
served in an intimate setting with a feature aquarium and booth seating. ▮ ♿

AE
MC
V

VEGETARIAN

*Vegetarian cuisine has crossed over from being a substitute to being a fully fledged independent
culinary genre, often with vegetarian wines and organic drinks on offer.*

FOOD FOR THOUGHT £
31 Neal St, WC2. **Map** 13 B2. 020 7836 0239.
Daily changing menu features various quiches and stir-fried vegetables, and
includes vegan options. First floor tables overlook Covent Garden. Bring your
own wine. No corkage charge.

THE PLACE BELOW £
St Mary-le-Bow Church, Cheapside, EC2. **Map** 15 A2.
020 7329 0789. FAX 020 7248 2626.
An 11th-century church crypt is the setting for dishes such as spinach and
potato curry with dhal, while the courtyard sees tables with parasols in
summer. Bring your own wine. No reservations. ● *public hols.*

JCB
MC
V

MANNA ££
4 Erskine Rd, Primrose Hill, NW3. 020 7722 8028.
Global gourmet organic vegetarian cuisine (organic roast shallot and leek tarte
tatin with wild garlic risotto). Modern, minimalist setting yet with warm
honey-coloured walls. ● *25 Dec–1 Jan.*

MC
V

MILDRED'S ££
58 Greek St, W1. **Map** 13 A1. 020 7494 1634.
Global vegetarian cuisine, including the likes of white bean falafel with chilli
sauce and tahina wrapped in a flour tortilla, accompanied by an all-organic
wine list. No reservations. Cash or cheque only.

WORLD FOOD CAFE £
14 Neal's Yard, WC2. **Map** 13 B1. 020 7379 0298.
A great global vegetarian restaurant with specialities including West African
and Indian dishes – vegetable masala, tortillas. Airy, mellow atmosphere with
open-plan kitchen. Bring your own wine. Corkage charged.

MC
V

Light Meals and Snacks

WHEN YOU DO not have the time, the money or the appetite to sit down for a full meal, London has a range of venues serving quick, simple fare which can often be inexpensive. Many of the venues listed here are ideal for visitors snacking on a tight schedule and tight budget in need of a comfortable break.

BREAKFAST

A GOOD BREAKFAST is a key preparation for a solid day's sightseeing, with the traditional British breakfast including staples such as bacon and eggs, smoked salmon and grilled kippers. Many hotels (see pp276–85) serve traditional British breakfasts to non-residents, with restaurants such as **Simpson's-in-the-Strand** serving traditional cooked breakfasts (see pp286–7) in an historic setting. The menu includes numerous favourites like porridge, lamb's kidneys, Cumberland sausage and black pudding as part of the "10 deadly sins" set breakfast. Several pubs around Smithfield market serve the all-night meat market workers. The most famous of these is the **Cock Tavern**, dishing up good-value fare from 5.30am.

For continental breakfasts such as pastries and a cappuccino, there are many cafés to choose from. One of the most relaxed venues is **Villandry**. The modern, bright restaurant has established a reputation for a good breakfast with a contemporary touch. It is served from 8am to 10.30am every day except Sunday, and brunch will take you to 3pm. A growing number of restaurants also serve brunch at the weekend.

COFFEE AND TEA

IF YOU'RE OUT shopping, many of London's department stores have their own cafés, the most stylish of all being the new-wave Italian **Emporio Armani Express**. Both the Nicole Farhi and DKNY stores (see p317) on Bond Street have trendy bars where you can get a bite to eat and a drink and watch the models as they shop. Patisseries such as **Patisserie Valerie** and **Maison Bertaux** are a delight, with mouth-watering window displays of French pastries. For an English feed you can't beat afternoon tea. Top hotels like the Ritz and Brown's (see p281) offer pots of tea, scones with jam and cream, delicious, thin cucumber sandwiches and cakes galore. For a relaxed place in the beautiful setting of Kensington Gardens, **The Orangery** can't be beaten. Its selection of English teas and cakes tastes even better in the elegant surroundings of Sir John Vanbrugh's 18th-century building. Superb cakes (and coffee) can also be found at the **Coffee Gallery**, near the British Museum. Fortnum & Mason (see p313) serves both afternoon and high teas. In Kew, the **Maids of Honour** tea room offers pastries, reputedly enjoyed by King Henry VIII.

MUSEUM AND THEATRE CAFÉS

MOST MUSEUMS and galleries have cafés, including the Royal Academy, the Tate Modern (with wonderful views over the Thames), the National Portrait Gallery and the British Museum where many vegetarian dishes are offered. If visiting the Young Vic Theatre, **Konditor & Cook** serves delicious cakes, while there are various dining options at the Royal Opera House in Covent Garden.

SANDWICH BARS

A LEADING SANDWICH chain in London is **Prêt à Manger**, with branches throughout the centre decked out with metal-work features and serving a range of delicious pre-packed sandwiches, salads, cakes and soft drinks. Another popular sandwich chain is **Eat** which offers a daily changing menu of innovative soups and salads using seasonal ingredients as well as sandwiches made with homemade breads and tortilla wraps. For quality Italian sandwich fillings in focaccia and ciabatta breads, try Soho's **Carlton Coffee House**.

DINERS

L ONDON IS FULL of American-style fast-food joints, serving burgers, fries, fried chicken, apple pie, milk shakes and cola, particularly around Soho, Leicester Square, Shaftesbury Avenue and Covent Garden. Meanwhile, restaurant options include **Maxwell's**, a Covent Garden institution, serving great burgers and cocktails, while the **Hard Rock Café** is a firm favourite with families.

PIZZA AND PASTA

I TALIAN FOOD has never been so popular in London, with pasta and pizza now adopted as a staple dish by Londoners. Street-side booths offer variable quality, while there are well-established chains with branches throughout the centre, including **Ask**. **Pizza Express** is another popular choice, offering individually tailored outlets that serve thin-crust pizzas with a range of toppings that are a step up from the norm. Try the elegant Georgian townhouse outlet which provides an atmospheric venue on Chelsea's King's Road, or the branch in a converted dairy in Soho where there's also live jazz. **Condotti** in Mayfair and **Kettner's** in Soho are also long-standing favourites, with Kettner's serving up interesting food in historic interiors. Jazz concerts and cabaret are regularly staged at **Pizza on the Park** at Hyde Park Corner. Reliable pasta chains include **Spaghetti House** and **Café Pasta**, with inexpensive pasta served at bustling trattorias such as **Pollo** in Soho.

FOOD IN PUBS

IN LINE with London's culinary revival, pub food has also undergone a complete evolution in the last few years. While many pubs still serve traditional meals, such as ploughman's lunch (cheese, salad, pickles and bread), shepherd's pie or roast beef on Sundays, they increasingly serve more adventurous evening meals. **The Chapel**, **The Cow**, **The Eagle**, **The Engineer**, **The Crown and Goose**, **The Fire Station**, **The Lansdowne** and **The Prince Bonaparte** are among the best of the so-called gastro-pubs *(see p311)*, offering interesting food at reasonable prices. It is usually essential to book in advance.

FISH AND CHIPS

FISH AND CHIPS is typically considered the British national dish, with a "chippy" serving a choice of fish (typically cod or plaice) deep-fried in batter, accompanied by chips (thicker cut than French fries). A range of accompaniments includes bread baps for a "chip buttie" (a chip sandwich), mushy peas, pickled eggs or onions. Three of the best are the **Seashell**, **Rock & Sole Plaice**, and **Faulkner's**. Fish and chips is now being "gentrified" and increasingly available on the menu in various smart restaurants and chains such as **Fish**.

SOUP BARS

WITH LONDONERS ever more receptive to new food trends, one of the latest is soup. Branches of the aptly named **Soup Opera** and **Soup Works** can be found around the centre of London. Try all manner of tempting combinations from Stilton with spinach to chilli and chicken.

BARS

THE RANGE AND quality of London's bars has grown incredibly over the past five years. There are numerous wine bars in the centre, such as **Café des Amis du Vin** in Covent Garden, and the legendary **El Vino** in Fleet Street, as well as chains such as **Corney & Barrow** and **Balls Bros**, which also have a good reputation for food. Good-value food is also part of the success of chain bars such as **All Bar One**, with micro-breweries offering a full view of the equipment used to brew beer on the premises, as well as well-priced menus. Try one of the **Freedom Brewing Company**'s two outlets (Wardour Street and Covent Garden). A growing number of "style bars" which, as the name suggests, offer cutting-edge design for style-conscious drinkers, serve interesting bar food and cock-tails. Around Piccadilly, top style bars include **Che** and **The Met Bar**, with Soho's **Alphabet** and **Lab Bar** also serving good food. Beyond the centre, areas of east London, such as Clerkenwell, Shoreditch and Hoxton, have become very fashionable, with **The Shoreditch Electricity Showrooms**, for instance, having a good bar menu and separate restaurant.

BRASSERIES

CAPITALIZING ON the growing market for good-value, informal dining with longer opening hours, brasseries have become an integral part of the London scene. These are based on the classic French blueprint, with its Parisian ambiance and decor, serving favourites such as *steak frites* and seafood platters. Brasseries such as **Palais du Jardin** in Covent Garden also have a separate crustacea bar. Among the pick of the chains are the chandelier embellished **Dôme**, **Café Rouge** and **Café Flo**, which each have a particular take on the genre. **Randall & Aubin** is a buzzy oyster and lobster (plus champagne) bar in a former delicatessen that has retained its period charm and overlooks Soho's lively Brewer Street, while **La Brasserie** in South Kensington is another classic example of Parisian style.

JUICE BARS

AS HEALTHY eating and drinking is now considered highly fashionable, juice bars are finding they have a captive audience. Many outlets have sprung up serving a delicious and refreshing range of organic juices including favourites such as wheatgrass juice. **Planet Organic** has two branches, as do **Crussh**, and **Fluid Juice Bar**. **Ranoush Juice** is a long-standing Lebanese favourite on Edgware Road, while **Zeta** (in the Park Lane Hilton) is a popular cocktail bar which also has an interesting range of healthy drinks.

STREET FOOD

DURING THE summer, many parks have ice cream vans parked by the entrances, with **Marine Ices** serving some of the best ice cream in town. Hot roasted chestnuts, made on mini-barbecue units, are a winter delight readily found along Oxford Street. Shellfish stalls, selling ready-to-eat potted shrimps, crab, whelks and jellied eels are a feature of many street markets. At Camden Lock and Spitalfields you can wander from stall to stall choosing from falafel, satay chicken, vegeburgers, Chinese noodles and honey balls. In the East End, Jewish bakeries such as **Brick Lane Beigel Bake** are open 24 hours a day. As well as freshly baked bagels which are delicious plain, they can also be bought with a wide range of fillings, such as the classic smoked salmon and cream cheese, or salt beef.

The East End also has the largest number of pie and mash shops. These shops provide an inexpensive and satisfying "nosh-up" of jellied eels and potatoes, or meat pie with mash and liquor (green parsley sauce). Two classic venues, both on Bethnal Green Road, are **G Kelly** and **S&R Kelly**. For the real East End experience, you should drench your food in vinegar and wash it all down with a couple of mugs of strong, hot tea.

DIRECTORY

BREAKFAST

Cock Tavern
East Poultry Avenue,
Smithfield Market EC1.
Map 6 F5.

Simpson's-on-the-Strand
100 Strand WC2.
Map 13 C2.

Villandry
170 Great Portland
Street W1. **Map** 4 F5.

COFFEE AND TEA

Coffee Gallery
23 Museum St WC1.
Map 13 B1.

Emporio Armani Express
191 Brompton Rd SW3.
Map 19 B1.

Maids of Honour
288 Kew Rd
Richmond
Surrey.

Maison Bertaux
28 Greek St W1.
Map 13 A1.

The Orangery
Kensington Palace,
Kensington
Gardens W8.
Map 10 D3.

Patisserie Valerie
215 Brompton Rd SW3.
Map 19 B1.
One of several branches.

MUSEUM AND THEATRE CAFÉS

Konditor & Cook
Young Vic Theatre,
66 The Cut SE1.
Map 14 E4.

SANDWICH BARS

Carlton Coffee House
41 Broadwick St W1.
Map 13 A2.

Eat
12 Oxo Tower Wharf,
Barge House St SE1 .
Map 14 E3.

Prêt à Manger
421 Strand WC2.
Map 13 C3.

DINERS

Hard Rock Café
150 Old Park Lane W1.
Map 12 E4.

Maxwell's
89 James St WC2.
Map 13 C2.

PIZZA AND PASTA

Ask
103 St John St EC1.
Map 16 E2.

Café Pasta
15 Greek Street W1.
Map 13 2B.

Condotti
4 Mill Street W1.
Map 12 F2.

Kettner's
29 Romilly St W1.
Map 13 A2.

Pizza Express
30 Coptic St WC1.
Map 13 B1.
One of several branches.

Pizza on the Park
11 Knightsbridge SW1.
Map 12 D5.

Pollo
20 Old Compton St W1.
Map 13 A2.

Spaghetti House
15 Goodge Street W1.
Map 5 A5.

FISH AND CHIPS

Faulkner's
424–426 Kingsland Rd E8.

Fish
3B Belvedere Road SE1.
Map 14 D4.

Rock & Sole Plaice
49 Great Windmill St W1.
Map 13 A2.

Seashell
324 Upper St N1.
Map 6 F1.

SOUP BARS

Soup Opera
17 Kingsway WC2.
Map 13 C1.

Soup Works
9 D'Arblay St W1.
Map 13 A2.

BARS

All Bar One
103 Cannon St EC4.
Map 15 A2.

Alphabet Bar
61 Beak Street W1.
Map 12 F2.

Balls Bros
Hays Galleria
Tooley Street SE1.
Map 15 B3.

Café des Amis du Vin
11–14 Hanover Place WC2
Map 13 C2.

Che
23 St James's St WC1.
Map 12 F3.

Corney & Barrow
19 Broadgate Circle EC2.
Map 7 C5.

El Vino
47 Fleet Street EC4.
Map 14 E1.

Freedom Brewing Company
60-66 Wardour St W1.
Map 13 A2.
One of two branches.

Lab Bar
20 Old Compton St W1.
Map 13 A2.

The Met Bar
19 Old Park Lane W1.
Map 12 E4.

The Shoreditch Electricity Showrooms
39a Hoxton Sq N1.
Map 7 C3.

BRASSERIES

La Brasserie
272 Brompton Rd SW3.
Map 19 B2.

Dôme
32–33 Long Acre WC2.
Map 13 B2.
One of several branches.

Café Flo
51 St Martin's Lane WC2.
Map 13 B2.

Café Rouge
27 Basil St SW3.
Map 11 C5.

Palais du Jardin
136 Long Acre WC2.
Map 13 B2.

Randall & Aubin
16 Brewer St W1
Map 13 A2.

JUICE BARS

Crussh
Unit 1
1 Curzon Street W1.
Map 12 E3.

Fluid Juice Bar
Fulham Rd SW3.
Map 19 A2.

Planet Organic
22 Torrington Place WC1.
Map 5 A5.

Ranoush Juice
43 Edgware Rd W2.
Map 11 C2.

Zeta
Park Lane Hilton W1.
Map 12 E4.

STREET FOOD

Brick Lane Beigel Bake
159 Brick La E1.
Map 8 E5.

Marine Ices
8 Haverstock Hill NW3.

G Kelly S&R Kelly
Bethnal Green Road E1
Map 8 D4.

London Pubs

A FFECTIONATELY KNOWN as a "pub" as well as "boozer" and "the local", a public house was originally just that – a house in which the public could eat, drink, and even stay the night. Large inns with courtyards, such as The George Inn, were originally stopping points for horse-drawn coach services. Some pubs stand on historic public house sites, for instance the Ship, the Lamb and Flag and the City Barge. However, many of the finest pubs date from the emergence of "gin palaces" in the late 1800s, where Londoners took refuge from the misery of their poverty amid lavish interiors, often with stunning mirrors (The Salisbury) and elaborate decorations. In Maida Vale you will find Crockers Folly, probably London's finest surviving gin palace.

RULES AND CONVENTIONS

I N THEORY, pubs can now open from 11am–11pm on Monday to Saturday and noon–10.30pm on Sunday, but some may close in the afternoon or early evening and also at weekends. You must be at least 18 to buy or drink alcohol, and at least 14 to enter a pub without an adult. Children can be taken into pubs that serve food, or can use outside areas. Order at the bar, and pay when you are served; tips are not usual unless you are served food and drink at a table. "Last orders" are usually called 10 minutes before closing, then "time" is called, and a further 20 minutes is then allowed for finishing up drinks.

BRITISH BEER

T HE MOST traditional British beers are available in various different strengths and styles, and are flat (not fizzy), and served only lightly cooled. The spectrum of bottled beers goes from "light" ale, through "pale", "brown", "bitter" and the strong "old". A sweeter, lower alcohol alternative is shandy, a classic mixture of draught beer or lager and lemonade. Many traditional methods of brewing and serving beer have been preserved over the years, and there is a great variety of "real ale" in London pubs. Serious beer drinkers should look for "Free Houses", pubs that are not tied to any particular brewery. The main London brewers are Young's (try their strong "Winter Warmer" beer) and Fuller's. The **Orange Brewery** serves a good pint and excellent food, and offers tours of the brewery.

OTHER PUB DRINKS

A NOTHER TRADITIONAL English drink found in every pub is cider. Made from apples, it comes in a range of strengths and degrees of dryness. Blended Scotch whisky and malt whiskies are also staples, together with gin which is usually drunk with tonic water. During the winter, mulled wine (warm and spicy) or hot toddies (brandy or whisky with hot water and sugar) may be served. A range of non-alcoholic drinks such as mineral water and fruit juices is also always available.

HISTORIC PUBS

M ANY LONDON pubs have a fascinating history and decor, whether it is a beamed medieval snug, Victorian fantasy, or an extraordinary Arts-and-Crafts interior, as at the **Black Friar**. At the **Bunch of Grapes** the bar is divided by "snobscreens", a feature once found in many pubs to enable the upper set to enjoy a drink without mixing with their servants. The 16th-century **King's Head and Eight Bells** has a display of antiques. Many pubs have strong literary associations, such as the **Fitzroy Tavern**, a meeting place for writers and artists, **Ye Olde Cheshire Cheese** is associated with Dr Johnson, Charles Dickens frequented the **Trafalgar Tavern**, while Oscar Wilde often went to the **Salisbury**. On a less literary note, the **Bull and Bush** in north London was the subject of a well known old music-hall song. Other pubs have sinister associations, for example, some of Jack the Ripper's victims were found near the **Ten Bells**. The 18th-century highwayman Dick Turpin took refreshment at the **Spaniards Inn** in north London, and the **French House** in Soho was a meeting point for the French Resistance during the Second World War.

PUB NAMES

S IGNS HAVE hung outside public houses since 1393, when King Richard II decreed they should replace the usual bush outside the door. As most people were illiterate, names that could easily be illustrated were chosen, such as the Rose & Crown, coats of arms (Freemasons' Arms), historical figures (Princess Louise) or heraldic animals (White Lion).

PUB ENTERTAINMENT

M ANY LONDON pubs also offer live entertainment. Fringe theatre productions (see p330) are staged at the **King's Head**, the **Latchmere**, and the **Prince Albert**. Some pubs have live music: there is excellent modern jazz at the **Bull's Head** and a wide variety of music styles at the popular Mean Fiddler (see pp335–7).

OUTDOOR DRINKING

T HE LARGEST number of pubs with outdoor seating tend to be located slightly outside the centre of the city. The **Freemason's Arms** for example, near Hampstead Heath, has a very pleasant garden. Some pubs enjoy riverside locations with fine views, from the **Grapes** in Limehouse to the **White Cross** in Richmond.

MICROBREWERIES

DELICIOUS BEER is brewed on the premises at microbreweries such as **Mash** where a space-age interior makes you forget that real ale tends to be the domain of older drinkers. This bar is frequented by a young and trendy crowd. Huge orange vats indicate where the actual brewing takes place. **The Freedom Brewing Company** makes more German-style, homemade brews amidst attractive, light interiors. For the best homemade beer of all, **O'Hanlon's** in Clerkenwell looks like a normal pub, but has abnormally good ales.

THEMED PUBS AND BARS

THEME PUBS are a recent phenomenon, with Irish pubs such as **Filthy McNasty's** and the cavernous **Waxy O'Connor's** attracting a regular crowd, as do Australian bars such as **Sheila's**. Sports bars are another popular sector, with outlets such as **Shoeless Joe's** and the extensive **Sports Café**, near Piccadilly, which has three bars, a dance floor — and 120 television sets showing the sporting action from around the world on satellite TV.

BARS

LONDON'S BAR scene has been evolving rapidly since the mid-1990s, when the choice was essentially limited to either hotel bars, wine bars or pubs. Propelled by a cocktail revival, as well as the fact that eating and drinking out is now an established "lifestyle" issue for Londoners, new bars are opening all the time. Eagerly sought out by style-conscious connoisseurs, new bars are now as much a talking point as new restaurants. As a result, bars have become the latest arena for London's beautiful people, while the finest bartenders (now known as "mixologists") are also becoming media stars. **Che** is renowned for a superb selection of the finest spirits

from around the world, as well as making them into great cocktails. Bars with particular specialities include the Mexican bar/restaurant **La Perla** in Covent Garden with an extensive range of tequilas, while vodka is the draw at the **Babushka** chain. The **10 Room**, **10 Tokyo Joe** and **Lab Bar** (*see p308*) also serve excellent cocktails in designer surroundings, pounding lime, ice and spirits together to make south Central American drinks such as Caprinhas and Mojitos. The **Fridge Bar** in Brixton has DJs playing decent hip hop and deep house with lots of dancing and drinking. Other fashionable venues include the **Match** chain with branches in Oxford Circus and Clerkenwell. Try their cognac-based cocktails.

CHAIN BARS

THEY MAY NOT be the most exciting places to drink, but at least London's chain bars are a reliable option. Typically halfway between a bar and a pub, with large windows and white walls, they are also far more female-friendly than dark, smokey pubs. **All Bar One** is very popular, with chunky wood furniture. **Pitcher & Piano** has sofas and blonde wood surrounds, while **The Slug & Lettuce** chain features paintings on the walls and quiet rooms for talking.

HOTEL BARS

LONDON'S HOTEL bars continue to offer an elegant setting for classic and innovative cocktails, with **The Blue Bar** at the Berkeley Hotel and the **Long Bar** at the Sanderson Hotel prime examples. The **American Bar** at The Savoy is decorated in an Art Deco style, has a pianist, a terrific atmosphere and a great range of malt whiskies, while **Claridge's Bar** (Claridge's hotel) also offers a distinctive and sophisticated ambiance as well as excellent champagne cocktails. **Tsar's Bar** at the Langham Hilton stocks an impressive range of vod as, while **Trader Vic's** in the Park

Lane Hilton offers an exotically tropical setting in which to enjoy an amazing range of rum cocktails. At **Zeta**, also in the Park Lane Hilton, the emphasis is on healthy drinking and organic fruit juice-based drinks, while special fruit flavoured martinis are a forte of **The Met Bar** (open until 6pm to non-members), at the Metropolitan Hotel.

GAY BARS

OLD COMPTON STREET in Soho has a burgeoning gay scene. Tables spill out on to the pavements and there is a lively atmosphere tolerant of all sexual preferences. **Manto** is a well-known bar in Manchester's gay scene, and it has recently opened very successfully in London. It is situated next to the gay bar and eatery **Balans** and close to the well-known gay pub, **The Admiral Duncan**. **The Edge** is a sprawling bar and club spread over four floors on the corner of Soho Square. For a lesbian crowd, try the nearby Soho **Candy Bar** and for both straight and gay drinkers try **Freedom** on Wardour Street.

CIGAR BARS

A RECENT FASHION for cigars, particularly accompanied by the finest malt whiskies, cognacs and rums, has seen a number of venues being opened dedicated to this activity. **Che** has a cigar lounge adjoining the bar and restaurant. The bar manager will guide you through a superb selection of Cuban cigars, not to mention a specialist range of digestifs. Meanwhile at **Boisdale** and **The Churchill Bar & Cigar Divan** (Churchill Inter-continental hotel), you can choose from a superlative range of malt whiskies to sip with a cigar. The **Havana** bar on Leicester Square may not seem like a place for a good smoke. It's loud and tacky but the Cuban cigars go well with the enticing selection of tasty rum cocktails on offer.

DIRECTORY

SOHO, PICCADILLY

10 Room
10 Air St W1.
Map 13 A2.

10 Tokyo Joe
85 Piccadilly W1.
Map 12 F3.

Admiral Duncan
Old Compton St W1.
Map 13 A2.

Balans
60 Old Compton St W1.
Map 13 A2.

Candy Bar
4 Carlisle St W1.
Map 13 A2.

Che
23 St James's St WC1.
Map 12 F3.

Churchill Bar & Cigar Divan
30 Portman Sq W1.
Map 12 D1.

Claridge's
Brook St W1. Map 12 E2.

Coach and Horses
29 Greek St WC2.
Map 14 F2.

Edge
11 Soho Sq W1.
Map 13 A1.

Freedom Brewing Company
60–66 Wardour St W1.
Map 13 A2.

French House
49 Dean St W1.
Map 13 A2.

Long Bar
50 Berners Street.
Map 12 F1.

Manto
Old Compton St W1.
Map 13 A2.

Mash
19–21 Great Portland St
W1. Map 12 F1.

Met Bar
19 Old Park Lane W1.
Map 12 E4.

Pitcher & Piano
70 Dean St W1.
Map 13 A1.

Sports Café
80 Haymarket SW1.
Map 13 A3.

Trader Vic's
22 Park Lane. Map 12 D3.

Tsar's Bar
1 Portland Pl W1. Map 4 E5.

Waxy O'Connor's
14-16 Rupert St W1.
Map 13 A2.

Zeta
Park Lane Hilton W1.
Map 12 E4..

COVENT GARDEN, STRAND

American Bar
The Savoy, Strand WC2.
Map 13 C2.

Havana
Leicester Pl WC2.
Map 13 B2.

Lamb and Flag
33 Rose St WC2.
Map 13 B2.

La Perla
28 Maiden Lane WC2.
Map 13 C2.

The Salisbury
90 St Martin's Lane WC2.
Map 13 B2.

Sheila's
14 King St WC2.
Map 13 B2.

Slug and Lettuce
14 Upper St Martin's
Lane WC2. Map 14 F2.

BLOOMSBURY, FITZROVIA

Fitzroy Tavern
16 Charlotte St W1.
Map 13 A1.

HOLBORN

Ye Olde Cheshire Cheese
145 Fleet St EC4.
Map 14 E1.

THE CITY, CLERKENWELL

All Bar One
103 Cannon St EC4.
Map 15 A2.

Babushka
The City Yacht, Addle St
EC2. Map 15 A1.

Balls Brothers
11 Blomfield St EC2.
Map 15 C1.

Black Friar
174 Queen Victoria St EC4.
Map 14 F2.

Corney & Barrow
19 Broadgate Circle EC2.
Map 7 C5.

Eagle
159 Farringdon Rd EC1.
Map 6 E4.

Filthy McNasty's
68 Amwell St EC1.
Map 6 E3.

Match
45–47 Clerkenwell Rd EC1.
Map 6 E5.

O'Hanlon's
8 Tysoe St EC1.
Map 6 E3.

Ship
23 Lime St EC3.
Map 15 C2.

Ten Bells
84 Commercial St E1.
Map 16 E1.

SOUTHWARK AND SOUTH BANK

Bunch of Grapes
St Thomas St SE1.
Map 15 C4.

Fire Station
150 Waterloo Rd SE1.
Map 14 E4.

George Inn
77 Borough High St SE1.
Map 15 B4.

CHELSEA, SOUTH KENSINGTON

Blue Bar
Wilton Pl SW1.
Map 12 D5.

Boisdale
15 Eccleston St SW1.
Map 20 E1.

King's Head and Eight Bells
50 Cheyne Walk SW3.
Map 19 A5.

Orange Brewery
37 Pimlico Rd SW1.
Map 20 D2.

Shoeless Joe's
1 Abbey Orchard St SW1.
Map 13 B5.

CAMDEN TOWN, HAMPSTEAD

Bull and Bush
North End Way NW3.
Map 1 A3.

Chapel
48 Chapel St NW1.
Map 3 B5.

Crown and Goose
100 Arlington Rd NW1.
Map 4 F1.

The Engineer
65 Gloucester Ave NW1.
Map 4 D1.

Freemasons Arms
32 Downshire Hill NW3.
Map 1 C5.

The Lansdowne
90 Gloucester Ave NW1.
Map 4 D1.

Spaniards Inn
Spaniards Way NW3.
Map 1 A3.

NOTTING HILL, MAIDA VALE

The Cow
89 Westbourne Park Rd
W11. Map 23 C1.

Crockers Folly
24 Aberdeen Pl NW8.

Prince Albert
11 Pembridge Rd W11.
Map 9 C3.

Prince Bonaparte
80 Chepstow Rd W2.
Map 9 C1.

FURTHER AFIELD

Bull's Head
373 Lonsdale Rd SW13.

City Barge
27 Strand o t Green W4.

Fridge Bar
1 Town Hall Parade SW2.

Grapes
76 Narrow St E14.

King's Head
115 Upper St N1.
Map 6 F1.

Latchmere
503 Battersea Pk Rd SW11.

Trafalgar Tavern
Park Row SE10.

White Cross
Cholmondeley Walk
Richmond, Surrey.

SHOPS AND MARKETS

LONDON IS STILL one of the most lively shopping cities in the world. Within just a few minutes' walk you can find both vast department stores, with glittering window displays, and tiny, cluttered rooms where one customer almost fills the entire shop. Many of the most famous London shops are in Knightsbridge or Regent Street, where prices can be steep, but Oxford Street, which is packed with a huge number of shops offering quality

Bags from two of the most famous West End shops

goods at a range of prices, is also worth a visit. All over London, there are plenty of places tucked away down side-streets – and don't forget to try the markets for antiques, crafts, household goods, food and clothing. You can buy virtually anything in London; specialities include clothes (from Burberry raincoats and traditional tweeds to "street fashion"); floral scents and soaps; art and antiques; and craft goods such as jewellery, ceramics and leather.

WHEN TO SHOP

IN CENTRAL LONDON, most shops open around 10am and close between 5.30pm and 6pm on weekdays; some close earlier on Saturdays. The "late night" shopping (until 7pm or 8pm) is on Thursdays in Oxford Street and the rest of the West End, and on Wednesdays in Knightsbridge and Chelsea; some shops in tourist areas, such as Covent Garden (see pp110–19) and the Trocadero, are open until 7pm or later every day, including Sundays. A few street markets (see pp324–5) and a growing number of other shops are also open on Sundays.

HOW TO PAY

MOST SHOPS WILL accept the following major credit cards: Access (Mastercard), American Express, Diners Club, Japanese Credit Bureau and Visa. Some, however, do not, notably the John Lewis and Peter Jones stores, as well as street markets and smaller shops. Some of the stores do accept traveller's cheques, especially if they're in sterling; for other currencies the rate of exchange is less favourable than in a bank. You need your passport with you. Most shops will accept a personal cheque, but only if drawn on a UK account and accompanied by a cheque guarantee card.

RIGHTS AND SERVICES

IF YOUR PURCHASE is defective you are usually entitled to a refund if you have proof of purchase and return the goods. This isn't always the case with sales goods, so inspect them carefully before you buy.

Most large stores, and some small ones, will pack goods up for you and also send them anywhere in the world.

VAT EXEMPTION

VAT (VALUE ADDED tax) is a sales tax of 17.5% which is charged on virtually all goods sold in Britain (the notable exceptions are books, food and all children's clothes). VAT is nearly always included in the advertised or marked price, although often business suppliers, including some stationers and electrical goods shops, charge it separately.

Non-European Union visitors to Britain who stay no longer than three months may claim back VAT. If you plan to do this, make sure you take along your passport when shopping. You must complete a form in the store when you buy the goods and then give a copy to Customs when you leave the country. (You may have to show your purchases to Customs, so do pack them somewhere accessible.) The tax refund may be returned to you by cheque or attributed to your credit card, but then a service charge will usually be

Harrod's elaborate Edwardian tiled food halls

deducted and most stores have a minimum purchase threshold (often £50 or £75). If you arrange to have your goods shipped directly home from the store, VAT should be deducted before you pay.

TWICE-YEARLY SALES

THE TRADITIONAL sale season is from January to February and June to July, when virtually every shop cuts its prices and sells off imperfect or unwanted stock. The department stores have some of the best reductions; one of the most famous sales is at **Harrod's** (see p211) where queues start to form outside long before opening.

BEST OF THE DEPARTMENT STORES

THE KING OF London's department stores, by tradition, is **Harrod's**, with its 300 departments and staff of 4,000. Prices are not always as high as you may well expect. The spectacular food hall, decorated with Edwardian tiles, has splendid displays of fish, cheese, fruit and vegetables; other specialities include fashions for all ages, china and glass, electronics and kitchenware. Though Harrod's is still just as popular, especially with well-heeled visitors, Londoners often head instead for nearby **Harvey Nichols**, which aims to stock the best of everything with the price tags to match. Clothes are particularly strong, with the emphasis firmly on very high fashion, with many talented British, European and American names represented. There is also an impressive menswear section. The food hall, opened in 1992, is one of the most stylish in London.

Selfridge's vast building on Oxford Street houses everything from Gucci bags and Hermès scarves to household gadgets and bed-linen. **Miss Selfridge**, the popular high street fashion chain, also has a branch in the store.

The original **John Lewis** was a draper and his shop still has a gorgeous selection of fabrics and haberdashery. Its china, glass and household items make John Lewis, and its well-known Sloane Square partner, Peter Jones, equally popular with Londoners.

Liberty (see p109) near Carnaby Street still sells the beautiful hand-blocked silks and other oriental goods it was famed for when it opened in 1875. Look out for the famous scarf department.

Fortnum and Mason's ground floor provisions department is so engrossing that often the upper floors of classic fashion remain peaceful. The food section stocks everything from tins of baked beans to beautifully prepared hampers.

Some of the best-known names in British clothes design today

DEPARTMENT STORES

Fortnum and Mason
181 Piccadilly W1. **Map** 12 F3.
020-7734 8040.

Harrod's
87–135 Brompton Rd SW1.
Map 11 C5.
020-7730 1234.

Harvey Nichols
109–125 Knightsbridge SW1.
Map 11 C5.
020-7235 5000.

John Lewis
278–306 Oxford St W1. **Map** 12 E1.
020-7629 7711.

Liberty
210–220 Regent St W1. **Map** 12 F2.
020-7734 1234.

Selfridge's
400 Oxford St W1. **Map** 12 D2.
020-7629 1234.

Doorman at Fortnum and Mason

MARKS AND SPENCER

MARKS AND SPENCER has come a long way since 1882 when Russian emigré Michael Marks had a stall in Leeds' Kirkgate market under the sign, "Don't ask the price – it's a penny!" It now has over 680 stores worldwide and everything in them is "own label". It stocks reliable versions of more expensive clothes – Marks and Spencer's underwear in particular is a staple of the British wardrobe. The food department concentrates mainly on upmarket convenience foods. The main Oxford Street branches at the Pantheon (near Oxford Circus) and Marble Arch are the most interesting and well stocked.

Penhaligon's for scents (see p320)

London's Best: Shopping Streets and Markets

LONDON'S BEST shopping areas range from the elegance of Knightsbridge, where porcelain, jewellery and *couture* clothes come at the highest prices, to colourful markets such as Brick Lane and Portobello Road. Meccas for those who enjoy searching for a bargain, London's markets also reflect the vibrant street life engendered by its enterprising multi-racial community. The city is fertile ground for specialist shoppers: there are streets crammed with antique shops, antiquarian booksellers and art galleries. Turn to pages 316–25 for more details of shops, grouped according to category.

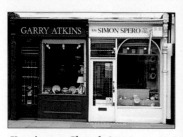

Kensington Church Street
The small book and furniture shops on this winding street still provide old-fashioned service. (See p323.)

Portobello Road Market
Over 200 stalls sell objets d'art, *jewellery, medals, paintings and silverware – plus fresh fruit and vegetables.* (See p325.)

See inset map

Regent's Park and Marylebone

Kensington and Holland Park

South Kensington and Knightsbridge

*Piccad...
and
Jame...*

Knightsbridge
Exclusive designer-wear is on sale here, at Harrod's as well as smaller stores. (See p211.)

Chelsea

King's Road
Once a centre for avant-garde fashion in the 1960s and 1970s, the street is now home to chain-stores and designer shops. There is also a good antiques market. (See p196.)

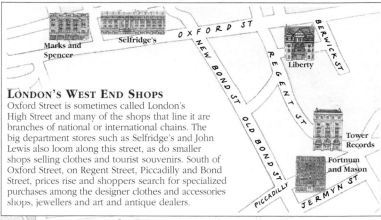

LONDON'S WEST END SHOPS

Oxford Street is sometimes called London's High Street and many of the shops that line it are branches of national or international chains. The big department stores such as Selfridge's and John Lewis also loom along this street, as do smaller shops selling clothes and tourist souvenirs. South of Oxford Street, on Regent Street, Piccadilly and Bond Street, prices rise and shoppers search for specialized purchases among the designer clothes and accessories shops, jewellers and art and antique dealers.

Brick Lane Market
In this East End street, everything from old books to new trainers is on sale. (See p324.)

Gabriel's Wharf
The wharf has been converted into small shops selling art, jewellery and crafts. (See p191.)

Petticoat Lane
London's most famous market has leather, clothes, watches, jewellery and toys (See p325.)

Charing Cross Road
Crammed shops selling old and new books line this long street. (See p318.)

Covent Garden and Neal Street
Street entertainers perform in this lively and historic market. The specialist shops of Neal Street are nearby. (See p115.)

Clothes

LONDON OFFERS the clothes-shopper a seemingly inexhaustible range of styles, price levels, quality and areas to shop in. The world's top designers are here, clustered around Knightsbridge, Bond Street and Chelsea, as are familiar chains such as Benetton and The Gap. But it is the wealth of home-based style that makes London such an exciting place to buy clothes. British designers excel in the opposite extremes of the market – traditional tailoring and street fashions.

TRADITIONAL CLOTHING

THE RUGGED country look is best found in the Regent Street/Piccadilly area. Waxed Barbour jackets are available from Farlow's *(see Royal Opera Arcade p92)* of Pall Mall and riding accessories from **Swaine Adeney**. **Kent and Curwen** is the place for cricket jumpers and **Captain Watts**, guernsey sweaters and oilskins. Try the Knightsbridge branch of **The Scotch House** for traditional tartan clothing, cashmere, Aran jerseys and Shetland shawls.

Classic town and business wear is another speciality of this area. **Burberry** sells the famous trenchcoats as well as checked clothing and some distinctive luggage from their shop on Haymarket. **Hackett** stocks traditionally tailored men's clothing. For shirts visit Jermyn Street, where you can order them made-to-measure or choose the more reasonably priced off-the-shelf ones. Many manufacturers now also sell classic women's blouses.

Liberty *(see p109)* use their famous patterned prints to make scarves, ties, blouses, pretty English rose dresses and some unusual trimmed denim jackets. **Laura Ashley** is also well renowned for its floral print dresses and frilly blouses.

For the ultimate in luxury, visit Savile Row, home of the top few tailors, including the famous **Gieves and Hawkes**.

MODERN BRITISH DESIGN AND STREET FASHION

LONDON IS one of the world's capitals for street fashion – designer **Jean-Paul Gaultier** prefers it to Paris because, he says, the street fashion is "free from the constraints of good taste". In Britain, quirky **Vivienne Westwood** won the Fashion Designer of the Year Award (1991). Other over-the-top British designers can be found in **Browns**. For more wearable styles, try the shops around Newburgh Street, West Soho. Most are predominantly for women, but **The Duffer of St George** is among the trailblazers for men. New designers very often start out with a small stall on Portobello Road – an extremely good source of more unusual clothing.

Nowadays Oxford Street shops such as **Top Shop** and **Mash** excel at copying street fashions at very low prices.

Paul Smith is one of the best-liked outlets for British high fashion. For women only, try **Browns, Whistles, Jasper Conran, Katherine Hamnett** or **Caroline Charles**.

KNITWEAR

FROM Fair Isle jumpers to Aran knits, the traditional British knitwear is famous. The best places for these are in Piccadilly – where you will find **N Peal** – and in Regent Street and Knightsbridge. Top designers such as **Patricia Roberts** and **Joseph**, and small shops such as **Jane and Dada**, stock a range of quite unusual and innovative machine- and hand-knits.

CHILDREN'S CLOTHES

You can get traditional hand-smocked dresses and romper suits from Liberty, **Young England** and **Anthea Moore Ede**, which stock

SIZE CHART

For Australian sizes follow British and American convention

Children's clothing

British	2–3	4–5	6–7	8–9	10–11	12	14	14+ (years)
American	2–3	4–5	6–6X	7–8	10	12	14	16 (size)
Continental	2–3	4–5	6–7	8–9	10–11	12	14	14+ (years)

Children's shoes

British	7^1	8	9	10	11	12	13	1	2
American	$7\frac{1}{2}$	$8\frac{1}{2}$	$9\frac{1}{2}$	$10\frac{1}{2}$	$11\frac{1}{2}$	$12\frac{1}{2}$	$13\frac{1}{2}$	$1\frac{1}{2}$	$2\frac{1}{2}$
Continental	24	$25\frac{1}{2}$	27	28	29	30	32	33	34

Women's dresses, coats and skirts

British	6	8	10	12	14	16	18	20
American	4	6	8	10	12	14	16	18
Continental	38	40	42	44	46	48	50	52

Women's blouses and sweaters

British	30	32	34	36	38	40	42
American	6	8	10	12	14	16	18
Continental	40	42	44	46	48	50	52

Women's shoes

British	3	4	5	6	7	8
American	5	6	7	8	9	10
Continental	36	37	38	39	40	41

Men's suits

British	34	36	38	40	42	44	46	48
American	34	36	38	40	42	44	46	48
Continental	44	46	48	50	52	54	56	58

Men's shirts

British	14	15	$15\frac{1}{2}$	16	$16\frac{1}{2}$	17	$17\frac{1}{2}$	18
American	14	15	$15\frac{1}{2}$	16	$16\frac{1}{2}$	17	$17\frac{1}{2}$	18
Continental	36	38	39	41	42	43	44	45

Men's shoes

British	7	$7\frac{1}{2}$	8	9	10	11	12
American	$7\frac{1}{2}$	8	$8\frac{1}{2}$	$9\frac{1}{2}$	$10\frac{1}{2}$	11	$11\frac{1}{2}$
Continental	40	41	42	43	44	45	46

smocks, gowns and tweed coats. **Trotters** offers everything from shoes to haircuts, while **Daisy and Tom** is a large children's store selling toys and clothing.

SHOES

WITH SHOES, again it is the very traditional or the very trendy British designers and manufacturers who excel.

Their ready-made traditional brogues and Oxfords are the mainstay of **Church's Shoes**. For hand-made, classic footwear, try the Royal Family's shoe-maker **John Lobb**. At the other end of the scale, **Shelly's** sells the utilitarian, trendy Dr Martens, originally designed as hard-wearing work boots. **Jimmy Choo Shoes** is an English shoe company selling much

sought-after designs that are sold worldwide. **Johnny Moke** of the King's Road or **Emma Hope** in Sloane Square both stock shoes for people looking for elegant styles. If you are on the look-out for more exquisite women's shoes visit **Manolo Blahnik**. Cheaper and less exclusive, but often equally original, designs can be found either in **Hobbs** or **Pied à Terre.**

DIRECTORY

TRADITIONAL

Burberry
18–22 Haymarket SW1.
Map 13 A3.
(020-7930 3343.

Captain Watts
7 Dover St W1.
Map 12 E3.
(020-7493 4633.

Gieves & Hawkes
1 Savile Row W1.
Map 12 E3.
(020-7434 2001.

Hackett
87 Jermyn St SW1.
Map 13 A3.
(020-7930 1300.

Kent and Curwen
39 St James's St SW1.
Map 12 F3.
(020-7409 1955.

Laura Ashley
256–258 Regent St W1.
Map 12 F1.
(020-7437 9760.

The Scotch House
2 Brompton Rd SW1.
Map 11 C5.
(020-7581 2151.

Swaine Adeney
54 St James's St SW1.
Map 12 F3.
(020-7409 7277.

MODERN/STREET FASHION

Browns
23–27 South Molton St
W1. **Map** 12 E2.
(020-7514 0000.

Caroline Charles
56–57 Beauchamp Pl SW3.
Map 19 B1.
(020-7589 5850.

The Duffer of St George
29 Shorts Gardens W2.
Map 13 B2.
(020-7379 4660.

Jaspar Conran
6 Burnsall St SW3.
Map 19 B3.
(020-7352 3572.

Jean-Paul Gaultier
171–5 Draycott Ave SW3.
Map 19 B2.
(020-7584 4648.

Katharine Hamnett at Harvey Nichols
109–125 Knightsbridge
SW1.
Map 11 C5.
(020-7235 5000.

Koh Samui
50 Monmouth St WC2.
Map 13 B2.
(020-7240 4280.

Mash
73 Oxford St W1.
Map 13 A1.
(020-7434 9609.

Nicole Farhi
158 New Bond St W1.
Map 12 E2.
(020-7499 8368.

Paul Smith
40–44 Floral St WC2.
Map 13 B2.
(020-7379 7133.

Top Shop
Oxford Circus W1.
Map 12 F1.
(020-7636 7700.

Urban Outfitters
36-38 Kensington High St
W8. **Map** 10 D5.
(020-7761 1001.

Vivienne Westwood
6 Davies St W1. **Map** 12 E2.
(020-7629 3757.

Whistles
12–14 St Christopher's Pl
W1. **Map** 12 D1.
(020-7487 4484.

KNITWEAR

Jane and Dada
20–21 St Christopher's Pl
W1. **Map** 12 D1.
(020-7486 0977.

Joseph
28 Brook St W1.
Map 12 E2.
(020-7629 6077.

N Peal
Burlington Arcade,
Piccadilly, W1. **Map** 12 F3.
(020-7493 9220.

Patricia Roberts
60 Kinnerton St SW1.
Map 11 C5.
(020-7235 4742.

CHILDREN'S

Anthea Moore Ede
16 Victoria Grove W8.
Map 18 E1.
(020-7584 8826.

Daisy and Tom
181–3 King's Road SW3.
Map 19 A4.
(020-7352 5000.

Trotters
34 King's Rd SW3.
Map 19 C2.
(020-7259 9620.

Young England
47 Elizabeth St SW1.
Map 20 E2.
(020-7259 9003.

SHOES

Church's Shoes
163 New Bond St W1.
Map 12 E2.
(020-7499 9449.

Emma Hope
53 Sloane Sq SW1.
Map 19 C2.
(020-7259 9566.

Hobbs
47 South Molton St W1.
Map 12 E2.
(020-7629 0750.

Jimmy Choo Shoes
20 Motcomb St SW1.
Map 12 D5.
(020-7235 0242.

John Lobb
9 St James's St SW1.
Map 12 F4.
(020-7930 3664.

Johnny Moke
396 King's Rd SW10.
Map 18 F4.
(020-7351 2232.

Manolo Blahnik
49–51 Old Church St,
Kings Road SW3.
Map 19 A4.
(020-7352 3863.

Pied à Terre
19 South Molton St W1.
Map 12 E2.
(020-7629 1362.

Shelly's
19–21 Foubert's Pl,
Carnaby Street, W1.
Map 12 F2.
(020-7287 0593.

Specialist Shops

L ONDON MAY BE famed for the grand department stores
such as Harrod's, but there are many specialist
shops which should also figure on the visitor's itinerary.
Some have expertise built up over a century or more,
while others cater for the new and fashionable.

FOOD

B RITISH FOOD may be much
maligned but there are
many specialities that are well
worth sampling, such as teas,
cheeses, chocolates, biscuits
and preserves (see pp286– 7).
The food halls of Fortnum
and Mason, Harrod's and
Selfridge's are good for all of
these. Otherwise, head for
Paxton and Whitfield, a
delightful shop dating from
1830 and stocking over 300
cheeses, including baby
Stiltons and Cheshire truckles,
along with pork pies, elegant
biscuits, oils and preserves.

For chocolates, the ultimate
extravagance is **Charbonnel
et Walker** on Bond Street.
Despite the name it is an
English manufacturer, and the
chocolates are all handmade.
The gift boxes are particularly
beautiful and they also do
mail order. **Maxwells** on the
Aldwych also sells pretty hand-
dipped chocolates, which are
made in Tunbridge Wells.

DRINKS

T EA, THAT MOST famous of
British drinks, comes in
all kinds of flavours. A huge
selection is available at the
Tea House in Covent Garden.
Jolly tea pots are also sold.
Strangely, the **Algerian
Coffee Stores** sells more tea
than coffee, but the selection
of coffees is excellent.

Vinopolis (see p182),
Bankside's "wine city", which
charges admission, has a vast
range of wines from which to
choose once you been on
their interactive world wine
tour and enjoyed five tastings.
You can continue to imbibe
in the restaurant or wine bar.

ONE-OFFS

T HERE ARE hundreds of odd
shops in London that
specialize in just one sort of

thing. **The Covent Garden
Candle Company** supplies
candles of every imaginable
shape and size, along with
candle holders and candle-
making equipment. Demon-
strations of the art take place
outside. **Halcyon Days**
specializes in little enamelled
copper boxes, the delightful
products of a revived English
18th-century craft.

Astleys sells pipes but not
tobacco; the range is quite
bewildering, from simple
handturned straightgrains to
weird-looking slope-domed
calabashes and Sherlock
Holmesian meerschaums. For
serious collectors of antique
scientific instruments, **Arthur
Middleton** has a fascinatingly
cluttered shop full of ancient
globes and early microscopes.
Casual browsers are not
encouraged. For equally
serious collectors of doll's
houses, the **Singing Tree** has
the ultimate in English doll's
houses, and many beautifully
crafted tiny things to put
inside them, all replicated to
precise scale in accurate
period style.

Finally, at **Anything Left-
Handed** in Soho, everything
is designed to make life easier
for the left-hander. Scissors,
corkscrews, cutlery, pens and
kitchen and garden tools are
the main sellers.

BOOKS AND MAGAZINES

B OOKSHOPS ARE high among
London's specialities.
Charing Cross Road (see p108)
is the focal point for those
searching for new, antiquarian
and second-hand volumes,
and is the home of **Foyle's**,
with its massive but notoriously
badly organized stock. Large
branches of chains such as
Borders and **Waterstone's**
are also here; so are many
specialist bookshops such as
Murder One for crime
books, **Silver Moon** for

women's and feminist writing,
and **Zwemmer** for art books.

Stanford's (see p112), with
maps and guides to cover the
globe, is in Long Acre; more
travel books can be found at
the **Travel Bookshop**. Nearby
is **Books for Cooks**, complete
with café and demonstration
kitchen. Adult comics are the
speciality at **Comic Showcase**
in Neal Street, while fantasy,
science fiction and graphic
novels abound at **Forbidden
Planet**. For gay writing, visit
the pioneering **Gay's The
Word**, near Russell Square.
The best selection of books
on movies is found at the
Cinema Bookshop.

The **PC Bookshop** sells a
huge range of books on all
aspects of computers, while
its sister shop nearby stocks
multimedia packages.

Two of the best general
bookshops are **Hatchard's** in
Piccadilly and the flagship
Dillons store in Gower
Street, both of which offer a
well-organized and extensive
choice. **Grant and Cutler** is
London's best-loved source of
foreign books and videos,
while **The Banana
Bookshop** in Covent Garden
must be the world's most
endearing remainder shop,
decorated with jungle murals
and a waterfall running
beside the stairs.

The Charing Cross Road
area is the best hunting
ground for antiquarian books.
Many shops offer a book-
finding service if the title you
want is no longer in print.

If you're looking for newspapers and magazines from
abroad, the basement of
Tower Records has the best
selection of US newspapers,
while **Capital Newsagents**
stocks (among others) Italian,
French, Spanish and Middle
Eastern publications. **Gray's
Inn News** is also worth a
visit for publications from
overseas (see pp318–9).

RECORDS AND MUSIC

A S ONE OF the world's
greatest centres of
recorded music, London has a
huge and excellent selection

of record shops catering to all manner of musical styles. The megastores such as **HMV**, **Virgin** and **Tower Records** have a very comprehensive range of classical music and are the best source of mainstream platters from pop to punk to peaceful easy listening. The small specialist shops tend to cater to the more esoteric tastes. For jazz take a trip to **Ray's Jazz** and **Honest Jon's**, while reggae fans should head down to **Daddy Kool**. **HMV** has a good selection of world music, and **Stern's** is without equal when it comes to African music. For 12-inch singles, the medium of club and dance music, **Trax** and **Black Market** are two of the most central places to look.

DIRECTORY

FOODS

Charbonnel et Walker
1 Royal Arcade, 28 Old Bond St W1. **Map** 12 F3.
📞 020-7491 0939.

Maxwells
7 Aldwych WC2.
Map 13 C2.
📞 020-7836 1846.

Paxton and Whitfield
93 Jermyn St SW1.
Map 12 F3.
📞 020-7930 0259.

DRINKS

Algerian Coffee Stores
52 Old Compton St W1.
Map 13 A2.
📞 020-7437 2480.

The Tea House
15 Neal St WC2.
Map 13 B2.
📞 020-7240 7539.

Vinopolis
1 Bank End SE1.
Map 15 B3.
📞 020-7940 8300.

ONE-OFFS

Anything Left-Handed
57 Brewer St W1.
Map 13 A2.
📞 020-7437 3910.

Arthur Middleton
12 New Row, Covent Garden WC2.
Map 13 B2.
📞 020-7836 7042.

Astleys
16 Piccadilly Arcade SW1.
Map 13 A3.
📞 020-7937 0317.

The Covent Garden Candle Company
30 The Market, Covent Garden Piazza WC2.
Map 13 C2.
📞 020-7836 9815.

Halcyon Days
14 Brook St W1.
Map 12 E2.
📞 020-7629 8811.

The Singing Tree
69 New King's Rd SW6.
📞 020-7736 4527.

BOOKS AND MAGAZINES

The Banana Bookshop
10 The Market, Covent Garden Piazza WC2.
Map 13 C2.
📞 020-7379 7475.

Books for Cooks
4 Blenheim Crescent W11.
Map 9 B2.
📞 020-7221 1992.

Borders
120 Charing Cross Rd WC2.
Map 13 B1.
📞 020-7379 6838.

Capital Newsagents
48 Old Compton St W1.
Map 13 A2.
📞 020-7437 2479.

Cinema Store
Unit 4B, Upper St Martin's Lane WC1.
Map 13 B2.
📞 020-7379 7838.

Comic Showcase
63 Charing Cross Rd WC1.
Map 13 B1.
📞 020-7434 4349.

Forbidden Planet
71 New Oxford St WC1.
Map 13 B1.
📞 020-7836 4179.

Foyle's
113–119 Charing Cross Rd WC2. **Map** 13 B1.
📞 020-7437 5660.

Gay's The Word
66 Marchmont St WC1.
Map 5 B4.
📞 020-7278 7654.

Gray's Inn News
50 Theobalds Rd WC1.
Map 6 D5.
📞 020-7405 5241.

Hatchard's
187 Piccadilly W1.
Map 12 F3.
📞 020-7439 9921.

Murder One
71–73 Charing Cross Rd WC2. **Map** 13 B2.
📞 020-7734 3485.

PC Bookshop
21 Sicilian Ave WC1.
Map 13 1C.
📞 020-7831 0022.

Silver Moon
64–68 Charing Cross Rd WC2. **Map** 13 B2.
📞 020-7836 7906.

Stanford's
12–14 Long Acre WC2.
Map 13 B2.
📞 020-7836 1321.

Travel Bookshop
13 Blenheim Crescent W11 **Map** 9 B2.
📞 020-7229 5260.

Waterstone's
121–125 Charing Cross Rd WC2. **Map** 13 B1.
📞 020-7434 4291.
also at: 82 Gower St WC1.
Map 5 A5.
📞 020-7636 1577.

The Women's Book Club
34 Great Sutton St EC1.
Map 6 F4.
📞 020-7251 3007.

Zwemmer
24 Litchfield St WC2.
Map 13 B2.
📞 020-7379 7886.

RECORDS AND MUSIC

Black Market
25 D'Arblay St W1.
Map 13 A2.
📞 020-7437 0478.

Daddy Kool Music
12 Berwick St W1.
Map 13 A2.
📞 020-7437 3535.

HMV
150 Oxford St W1.
Map 13 A1.
📞 020-7631 3423.

Honest Jon's Records
278 Portobello Rd W10.
Map 9 A1.
📞 020-7969 9822.

Ray's Jazz
180 Shaftesbury Ave WC2. **Map** 13 B1.
📞 020-7240 3969.

Rough Trade
130 Talbot Rd W11.
Map 9 C1.
📞 020-7229 8541.

Stern's
293 Euston Rd NW1.
Map 5 A4.
📞 020-7387 5550.

Tower Records
1 Piccadilly Circus W1.
Map 13 A3.
📞 020-7439 2500.

Trax
55 Greek St W1.
Map 13 A2.
📞 020-7734 0795.

Virgin Megastore
14–30 Oxford St W1.
Map 13 A1.
📞 020-7631 1234.

Gifts and Souvenirs

L ONDON IS A WONDERFUL PLACE to shop for presents. As well as an impressive array of original ceramics, jewellery, perfume and glassware, there is exotic merchandise from around the world, including jewellery from India and Africa, stationery from Europe and kitchenware from France and Italy. The elegant, Regency-period Burlington Arcade (see p91) is a popular shopping destination selling high-quality gifts, clothes, art and crafts, many of which are made in the UK.

The shops at big museums, such as the Victoria and Albert (see pp202–5), the Natural History (see pp208–9) and the Science Museum (see pp212–13) often have unusual and original items to take home as mementos of your visit, while **Contemporary Applied Arts** and the market in Covent Garden Piazza (see p114) sell a good range of British pottery, jewellery, knitwear, pictures, clothing and other crafts. If you want to buy all your gifts under one roof, go to Liberty (see p313), where beautiful stock from all over the globe fills every department and the haberdashery is one of the best in the world.

JEWELLERY

J EWELLERY SHOPS in London range from the extremely traditional to the tiny shops and stalls that huddle in areas like Covent Garden (see pp110–19), Gabriel's Wharf (see p191), and Camden Lock (see p324), which specialize in unusual pieces. **Butler and Wilson** has some of the most eye-catching costume jewellery in town, while next door **Electrum** keeps less bold but equally innovative pieces.

Past Times sells modern reproductions of ancient British designs, as do the shops at the British Museum (see pp126–9) and the V&A. The **Lesley Craze Gallery** sells new designs, while **Contemporary Applied Arts** has stylish craft jewellery. **Janet Fitch** sells fashionable silver jewellery and the best place for Gothic jewellery is **The Great Frog** on Carnaby Street. **Liberty** stocks spectacular ethnic, costume and fashion jewellery. **Manquette** is also worth visiting, for its elegant, one-off pieces in lapis lazuli, amber, coral, gold and silver.

HATS AND ACCESSORIES

T RADITIONAL MEN'S hats, from flat caps to trilbies and pith helmets, can be found at **Edward Bates** and **Herbert Johnson**. For women, truly distinctive creations come from **Herald and Heart Hatters**, while **Stephen Jones** has a wide range of designs from the everyday to the extravagant and will make hats to match any outfit if you supply your own fabric.

For a selection of the best in British accessories, try the shops on Jermyn Street or in the arcades off Piccadilly. Elsewhere, **James Smith & Sons** produces wonderful umbrellas, ideal for wet London weather. For walking sticks, canes and riding crops, pay a visit to Swaine Adeney (see p317). **Mulberry Company** stocks classically English luggage, as well as accessories such as belts, purses and wallets, and **Philip Treacey** sells some of the most breathtaking hat creations available.

At the cheaper end of the market, the **Accessorize** chain sells all manner of beads and baubles, grouped by colour to help co-ordinate your outfit.

PERFUMES AND TOILETRIES

M ANY BRITISH perfumeries use recipes that are hundreds of years old. **Floris** and **Penhaligon's**, for example, still manufacture the same flower-based scents and toiletries for men and women that they sold in the 19th century. The same goes for **Czech and Speake**, and for men's specialists **Truefitt and Hill** and **George F Trumper**, where you can buy some wonderful reproductions of antique shaving equipment as well. Both **Culpeper** and **Neal's Yard Remedies** employ traditional herbal and floral remedies as bases for their natural, therapeutic toiletries.

Other manufacturers have a more contemporary approach to their wares; **The Body Shop**, for example, uses recyclable plastic packaging for its natural cosmetics and toiletries and encourages staff and customers alike to take an interest in environmental issues. **Molton Brown** sells a range of natural cosmetics, body and haircare products, from both its own shops in South Molton Street and Hampstead and from other outlets.

STATIONERY

S OME OF THE most interesting wrapping paper on sale in London is designed by **Tessa Fantoni**, whose paper-covered boxes, photo frames and albums are sold in several specialist stationery and gift shops, as well as the Conran Shop and her own shop in Clapham.

Falkiner Fine Papers stocks a range of handmade and decorative papers. Their marbled paper makes glorious giftwrapping for a very special gift. To find luxurious writing paper, pens, pencils and desk accessories, try the Queen's stationer, **Smythson of Bond Street**. Fortnum and Mason (see p313) does handsome leather-bound diaries, blotters and pencil holders, while Liberty embellishes desk accessories with its famous Art Deco prints. For personal organizers covered in anything from vinyl to iguana skin try **The Filofax Centre**. The minuscule shop **Pencraft** is the place for classic pens by Mont Blanc, Watermans, Parker, or Sheaffer. Finally, for greetings cards, pens, gift wrapping paper and general stationery, pop into one of the branches of **Paperchase**.

INTERIORS

WEDGWOOD STILL makes the famous pale blue Jasper china that Josiah Wedgwood designed in the 18th century.

You can buy it, as well as Irish Waterford crystal at **Waterford Wedgwood** on Piccadilly. For a fine selection of original pottery, visit the **Craftsmen Potters Association of Great Britain** and **Contemporary Applied Arts**. Everything sold by **The Holding Company** holds something, and does so in a funkier fashion than

ordinary crates and boxes. Personalized gifts are also available. **Heal's**, the **Conran Shop** and **Freud's** all offer a great selection of stylish, well-designed accessories for the home. For a wealth of good-quality kitchen and various household items, **Divertimenti** and **David Mellor** are the places to go.

DIRECTORY

JEWELLERY

Butler & Wilson
20 South Molton St W1.
Map 12 E2.
020-7409 2955.

Contemporary Applied Arts
2 Percy St WC1.
Map 13 A1.
020-7436 2344.

Electrum Gallery
21 South Molton St W1.
Map 12 E2.
020-7629 6325.

The Great Frog
10 Ganton St W1.
Map 12 F2.
020-7439 9357.

Janet Fitch
188a King's Rd SW3.
Map 19 B.
020-7352 4401.
One of several branches.

Lesley Craze Gallery
34 Clerkenwell Green EC1. Map 6 E4.
020-7608 0393.

Manquette
40 Gordon Place,
Holland St W8. Map 10 D5.
020-7937 2897.

Past Times
146 Brompton Rd SW3.
Map 11 C5.
020-7581 7616.
One of several branches.

HATS AND ACCESSORIES

Accessorize
22 The Market,
Covent Garden WC2.
Map 13 C2.
020-7240 2107.
One of several branches.

Edward Bates
21a Jermyn St SW1.
Map 13 A3.
020-7734 2722.

Herald & Heart Hatters
131 St Philip's St SW8.
020-7627 2414.

Herbert Johnson
10 Old Bond St W1.
Map 12 F3.
020-7408 1174.

James Smith & Sons
53 New Oxford St WC1.
Map 13 C1.
020-7836 4731.

Mulberry Company
11–12 Gees Court, St
Christopher's Pl W1.
Map 12 D1.
020-7493 2546.

Philip Treacey
69 Elizabeth Street SW1.
Map 20 E2.
020-7259 9605.

Stephen Jones
36 Great Queen St WC2.
Map 13 C1.
020-7242 0770.

PERFUMES AND TOILETRIES

The Body Shop
32–34 Great Marlborough
St W1. Map 12 F2.
020-7437 5137.
One of several branches.

Culpeper Ltd
21 Bruton St W1. Map
12 E3. 020-7629 4559.

Czech & Speake
39c Jermyn St SW1.
Map 13 A3.
020-7439 0216.

Floris
89 Jermyn St SW1.
Map 13 A3.
020-7930 2885.

George F Trumper
9 Curzon St W1.
Map 12 E3.
020-7499 1850.

Molton Brown
54 Rosslyn Hill NW3.
Map 12 E2.
020-7794 2022.

Neal's Yard Remedies
15 Neal's Yard WC2.
Map 13 B1.
020-7379 7222.

Penhaligon's
41 Wellington St WC2.
Map 13 C2.
020-7836 2150.

Truefitt & Hill
71 St James's St SW1.
Map 12 F3.
020-7493 2961.

STATIONERY

Falkiner Fine Papers
76 Southampton Row WC1.
Map 5 C5.
020-7831 1151.

The Filofax Centre
21 Conduit St W1.
Map 12 F2.
020-7499 0457.

Paperchase
213 Tottenham Court Rd
W1. Map 5 A5.
020-7467 6200.
One of several branches.

Pencraft
119 Regent St W1.
Map 12 F1.
020-7734 4928.

Smythson of Bond Street
40 New Bond St W1.
Map 12 E2.
020-7629 8558.

Tessa Fantoni
77 Abbeville Rd SW4.
020-8673 1253.

INTERIORS

Conran Shop
Michelin House,
81 Fulham Rd SW3.
Map 19 A2.
020-7589 7401.

Craftsmen Potters Association of Great Britain
7 Marshall St W1.
Map 12 F2.
020-7437 7605.

David Mellor
4 Sloane Sq SW1.
Map 20 D2.
020-7730 4259.

Divertimenti
45 – 47 Wigmore St W1.
Map 12 E1.
020-7935 0689.

Freud's
198 Shaftesbury Ave
WC2.
Map 13 B1.
020-7831 1071.

Heal's
196 Tottenham
Court Rd W1.
Map 5 A5.
020-7636 1666.

The Holding Company
241–5 King's Rd SW3.
Map 19 A4.
020-7352 1600.

Waterford Wedgwood
173–174 Piccadilly W1.
Map 12 F3.
020-7629 2614.

Art and Antiques

LONDON'S ART AND antique shops are spread across the capital. While the more fashionable (and more expensive) dealers are concentrated in a relatively small area bounded by Mayfair and St James's, other shops and galleries catering to a more modest budget are scattered over the rest of the city. Whether your taste is for Old Masters or young modern artists, Boule or Bauhaus, you are bound to find something of beauty in London that is within your financial means.

MAYFAIR

CORK STREET is the centre of the British contemporary art world. Walk up from Piccadilly and pass, on your left, the **Piccadilly Gallery**, which sells modern British pictures. Next come several galleries, including **Boukamel Contemporary Art**, offering work in varying degrees of the avant-garde. The biggest name to look out for is **Waddington**, and if you want to discover the flavour of the month a stop here is a must. However, purchasing is only for the serious (and rich) collector. **Chat Noir** in nearby Albemarle Street is committed to selling contemporary work at a more affordable price.

Before retracing your steps down Cork Street, look into Clifford Street, where **Maas Gallery** excels in Victorian masters. Make your way back via a wide variety of artistic styles, from traditional British sporting pictures and sculpture at **Tryon and Swann** to **Mayor's** Surrealism and mainstream art at **Redfern**.

Nearby, Old Bond Street is the centre of the fine antiques trade in London. If it's Turner watercolours or Louis XV furniture you're after, this is the place. A walk up from Piccadilly takes you past the lush portals of **Richard Green** and the **Fine Art Society**, among other extremely smart galleries. For furniture and decorative arts visit **Bond Street Antiques Centre** and **Asprey**; for silver go to **S J Phillips**; and for Victorian art try **Christopher Wood's** gallery. Even if you are not a buyer these galleries are fascinating places to visit, so don't be afraid to walk in – you can learn more from an hour spent here than you can from weeks of studying text books. Also on Old Bond Street are two of the big four London auction houses, **Phillips** and **Sotheby's**. In Bury Street the well-heeled can visit the **Malcolm Innes** gallery, where there are sporting watercolours on show.

ST JAMES'S

SOUTH OF Piccadilly lies a maze of 18th-century streets. This is gentlemen's club country (see Pall Mall p92) and the galleries mostly reflect the traditional nature of the area. The centre is Duke Street, home of Old Master dealers **Johnny van Haeften** and **Harari and Johns**. At the bottom is King Street, with that leviathan of antiques dealers, **Spink**. A few doors down you will find the main salerooms of **Christie's**, the well-known auction house where Van Goghs and Picassos change hands for millions.

Walk back up Bury Street past several interesting galleries and duck into Ryder Street to take in **Chris Beetle's** gallery of works by illustrators and caricaturists.

WALTON STREET

CLOSE TO fashionable and expensive Knightsbridge, the art galleries and antique shops along this elegant little street have prices to match. A short walk away in nearby Montpelier Street is **Bonham's** the auctioneers, fourth in line of the big four and recently redecorated in chic style. Of course, fourth in line does not necessarily mean fourth in quality, and you may be lucky enough to find a bargain here.

PIMLICO ROAD

THE ANTIQUE shops that line this road tend to cater predominantly for the pricey requirements of the interior decorator – this is where to come if you are searching for an Italian leather screen or a silver-encrusted ram's skull. Of particular fascination is **Westenholz**. Nearby, **Henry Sotheran** offers fine prints.

BELGRAVIA

THIS AREA HAS a reputation for good British pictures. The real hub of art activity is Motcomb Street, which caters for most tastes. Those seeking fine but well-priced British pictures should head towards **Michael Parkin's** gallery, while Oriental-art enthusiasts will luxuriate in the **Mathaf Gallery**, with its 19th-century British and European paintings of the Arab world.

AFFORDABLE ART

THE HUGELY popular Contemporary Art Society's market takes place every autumn at the **Royal Festival Hall**, with work on sale from £100. London's East End, a growth area for contemporary art, has a cluster of small galleries as well as the magnificent **Flowers East**, which is strong on work by young artists. For sometimes brilliant shows of contemporary art, step along to Portobello and the **East-West Gallery**. A lot of the work on offer here is reasonably-priced, too. **Purdey Hicks** is a great place to go for affordable contemporary British painting.

PHOTOGRAPHY

THE LARGEST collection of original photographs for sale in the country is at the **Photographers' Gallery**. The **Special Photographers' Company** is well known for selling top-quality work – by unknown artists as well as famous photographic names. **Hamilton's** is worth visiting during its major exhibitions.

BRIC-À-BRAC AND COLLECTABLES

For smaller, more affordable pieces, it's worth going to one of the markets, such as Camden Lock (see p324), Camden Passage (p324) or Bermondsey (p324), which is the main antiques market, catering to the trade. Many high streets out of the centre of town have covered markets of specialist stalls. Finally, a browse along Kensington Church Street in west London will reveal everything from Arts and Crafts furniture to Staffordshire dogs in a concentration of small emporia.

AUCTIONS

If you are confident enough, auctions are a cheaper way to buy art or antiques but be sure to read the small print in the catalogue (which usually costs around £15). Bidding is simple – you simply register, take a number, then raise your hand when the lot you want comes up. The auctioneer will see your bid. It's as easy as that, and can be great fun. The main auction houses are Christie's, Sotheby's, Phillips and Bonham's. Don't forget Christie's saleroom in South Kensington, which offers art and antiques for the more modest budget.

DIRECTORY

MAYFAIR

Asprey
165–169 New Bond St W1. **Map** 12 E2.
☏ 020-7493 6767.

Bond Street Antiques Centre
124 New Bond St W1.
Map 12 F3.
☏ 020-7351 5353.

Boukamel Contemporary Art
9 Cork St W1. **Map** 12 F3.
☏ 020-7734 6444.

Chat Noir
35 Albemarle St W1.
Map 12 F3.
☏ 020-7495 6710.

Christopher Wood Gallery
20 Georgian House,
10 Bury St W1.
Map 12 F3.
☏ 020-7499 7411.

Fine Art Society
148 New Bond St W1.
Map 12 E2.
☏ 020-7629 5116.

Maas Gallery
15a Clifford St W1.
Map 12 F3.
☏ 020-7734 2302.

Malcolm Innes
7 Bury St W1.
Map 12 F3.
☏ 020-7839 8083.

Mayor Gallery
22a Cork St W1.
Map 12 F3.
☏ 020-7734 3558.

Piccadilly Gallery
16 Cork Street W1.
Map 12 F3.
☏ 020-7629 2875.

Redfern Art Gallery
20 Cork St W1.
Map 12 F3.
☏ 020-7734 1732.

Richard Green
4 New Bond St W1.
Map 12 E2.
☏ 020-7491 3277.

S J Phillips
139 New Bond St W1.
Map 12 E2.
☏ 020-7629 6261.

Tryon and Swann
23-24 Cork St W1.
Map 12 F3.
☏ 020-7734 6961.

Waddington Galleries
11, 12, 34 Cork St W1.
Map 12 F3.
☏ 020-7437 8611.

ST JAMES'S

Chris Beetle
8 & 10 Ryder St SW1.
Map 12 F3.
☏ 020-7839 7429.

Harari and Johns
12 Duke St SW1.
Map 12 F3.
☏ 020-7839 7671.

Johnny van Haeften
13 Duke St SW1.
Map 12 F3.
☏ 020-7930 3062.

Spink & Son
5 King St SW1. **Map** 12 F4.
☏ 020-7930 7888.

PIMLICO ROAD

Henry Sotheran Ltd
80 Pimlico Rd SW1.
Map 20 D3.
☏ 020-7730 8756.

Westenholz
76 Pimlico Rd SW1.
Map 20 D2.
☏ 020-7824 8090.

BELGRAVIA

Mathaf Gallery
24 Motcomb St SW1.
Map 12 D5.
☏ 020-7235 0010.

Michael Parkin Gallery
11 Motcomb St SW1.
Map 12 D5.
☏ 020-7235 8144.

AFFORDABLE ART

East-West Gallery
8 Blenheim Cres W11.
Map 9 A2.
☏ 020-7229 7981.

Flowers East
199–205 Richmond Rd E8.
☏ 020-8985 3333.

Purdey Hicks
65 Hopton St SE1.
Map 14 F3.
☏ 020-7401 9229.

Royal Festival Hall
South Bank Centre SE1.
Map 14 D4.
☏ 020-7928 3191.

PHOTOGRAPHY

Hamiltons Gallery
13 Carlos Place
London W1.
Map 12 E3.
☏ 020-7499 9493.

Photographers' Gallery
5 & 8 Great Newport St
WC2.
Map 13 B2.
☏ 020-7831 1772.

Special Photographers Company
21 Kensington Park Rd
W11.
Map 9 B2.
☏ 020-7221 3489.

AUCTIONS

Bonhams, W & F C, Auctioneers
Montpelier St SW7.
Map 11 B5.
☏ 020-7584 9161

Also: Chelsea Galleries,
65–69 Lots Road SW10.
Map 18 F5.
☏ 020-7351 7111.

Christie's Fine Art Auctioneers
8 King St SW1.
Map 12 F4.
☏ 020-7839 9060.

Also: 85 Old Brompton
Road SW7.
Map 18 F2.
☏ 020-7581 7611.

Phillips Auctioneers & Valuers
101 New Bond St W1.
Map 12 E2.
☏ 020-7629 6602.

Sotheby's Auctioneers
34–35 New Bond St W1.
Map 12 E2.
☏ 020-7293 5000.

Markets

L ONDON STREET MARKETS have an air of exuberant irreverence which in itself provides sufficient reason to pay them a visit. At many you will also find some of the keenest prices in the capital. Keep your wits about you and your hand on your purse and join in the fun.

Bermondsey Market (New Caledonian Market)

Long Lane and Bermondsey St SE1. **Map** 15 C5. ⊖ *London Bridge, Borough.* **Open** *5am–2pm Fri.* **Starts closing** *midday. See p183.*

Bermondsey is the gathering point for London's antique traders every Friday. Serious collectors start early and scrutinize the paintings, the silver and the vast array of old jewellery. Browsers might uncover some interesting curiosities but most bargains go before 9am.

Berwick Street Market

Berwick St W1. **Map** 13 A1. ⊖ *Piccadilly Circus, Leicester Sq.* **Open** *9am–6pm Mon–Sat. See p108.*

The spirited costermongers of Soho's Berwick Street sell the cheapest and most attractive fruit and vegetables in the West End. Spanish black radish, star fruit and Italian plum tomatoes are among the produce you might find here; Dennis's vegetable stall sells a massive range of interesting edible fungi, all immaculately presented. The market is good for fabrics and cheap household goods too, as well as for leather handbags and delicatessen. Separated from Berwick Street by a seedy passage-way is Rupert Street market, where prices tend to be higher and the traders quieter.

Brick Lane Market

Brick Lane E1. **Map** 8 E5. ⊖ *Shoreditch, Liverpool St, Aldgate East.* **Open** *daybreak to 1pm Sun. See pp170–1.*

This massively popular East End jamboree is at its best around its gloriously frayed edges. Explore the Cheshire Street lock-ups, packed with tatty furniture and old books, or the mish-mash of junk sold on Bethnal Green Road. East End spivs huddle together on Bacon Street proffering gold rings and watches, while much of Sclater Street is given over to pet foods and provisions. On the wasteland off Cygnet Street, new bicycles, fresh meat and frozen food are among the myriad of goods up for grabs. Brick Lane itself is rather more prosaic, with new goods such as handbags,

sports shoes and jeans on sale, but look out too for the wonderful range of spice shops and curry restaurants in this centre for London's Bangladeshi community.

Brixton Market

Electric Ave SW9. ⊖ *Brixton.* **Open** *8.30am–5.30pm Mon, Tue, Thu–Sat; 8.30am–1pm Wed.*

This market offers a wonderful assortment of Afro-Caribbean food, from goats' meat, pigs' tails and salt fish to plantain, yams and breadfruit. The best food is to be found in the old Granville and Market Row arcades, where exotic fish are a highlight. Afro-style wigs, strange herbs and potions, religious tracts sold by Rastafarian priests and, on Brixton Station Road, cheap second-hand clothes are also to be had. From record stalls, the bass of raw reggae pounds through this cosmopolitan market like a heartbeat.

Camden Lock Market

Chalk Farm Road NW1. ⊖ *Camden Town.* **Open** *9.30am–5.30pm Mon–Fri, 10am–6pm Sat and Sun.*

Camden Lock Market has grown swiftly since its opening in 1974. Handmade crafts, new and second-hand street fashions, wholefoods, books, records and antiques form the bulk of the goods that are on sale, although thousands of young people come here simply for the atmosphere, especially at weekends. This is enhanced by the buskers and street performers who draw the crowds to the attractive cobbled area around the canal.

Camden Passage Market

Camden Passage N1. **Map** 6 F1. ⊖ *Angel.* **Open** *10am–2pm Wed, 10am–5pm Sat.*

Camden Passage is a quiet walk-way where bookshops and restaurants nestle among bijou antique shops. Prints, silverware, 19th-century magazines, jewellery and toys are among the many collectables that are on show. There aren't very many bargains to be picked up here, as most of the traders tend to be specialists. However, it is an ideal market for those who want to indulge in some genteel browsing.

Chapel Market

Chapel Market N1. **Map** 6 E2. ⊖ *Angel.* **Open** *9am–3.30pm Tue, Wed, Fri, Sat; 9am–1pm Thu, Sun.*

This is one of London's most traditional and exuberant street markets. Weekends are best; the fruit and vegetables are varied and cheap, the fish stalls are the finest in the area, and there's a wealth of bargain household goods and clothing to be had.

Church Street and Bell Street Markets

Church St NW8 and Bell St NW1. **Map** 3 A5. ⊖ *Edgware Rd.* **Open** *8.30am–5pm Mon–Thu, 8.30am–5pm Fri, Sat.*

Like many of London's markets, Church Street reaches a crescendo at the weekend. On Friday, stalls selling electrical goods, cheap clothes, household goods, fish, cheese and antiques join the everyday fruit and vegetable stalls. Alfie's Antique Market at Nos. 13–25 houses over 300 small stalls selling anything from jewellery to old radios and gramophones. Bell Street, running parallel, has its own market where second-hand clothes, records and antiquated electrical goods are sold for a song on Saturdays.

Columbia Road Market

Columbia Rd E2. **Map** 8 D3. ⊖ *Shoreditch, Old St.* **Open** *8am–12.30pm Sun. See p171.*

This is the place to come to buy greenery and blossoms or just to enjoy the fragrances and colours. Cut flowers, plants, shrubs, seedlings and pots are all sold at about half normal prices in this charming Victorian street on a Sunday morning.

East Street Market

East St SE17. ⊖ *Elephant and Castle.* **Open** *8am–5pm Tue, Wed, Fri, Sat; 8am–2pm Thu, Sun.*

East Street Market's high spot is Sunday, when over 250 stalls fill the narrow street and a small plant and flower market is set up on Blackwood Street. Fruit and vegetable stalls are in a minority as traders of clothes (mainly new), electrical and household goods swing into action, while furtive street-hawkers proffer shoelaces and razor blades from old suitcases. Many locals come here more for the entertainment than to buy, as did the young Charlie Chaplin *(see p37)* at the beginning of the 20th century.

Gabriel's Wharf and Riverside Walk Markets

56 Upper Ground and Riverside Walk
SE1. **Map** 14 E3. ⊖ *Waterloo.*
Gabriel's Wharf open 9.30am–6pm
Fri–Sun; Riverside Walk open
10am–5pm Sat, Sun and irregular
weekdays. See p193.

Little shops filled with ceramics, paintings and jewellery surround a bandstand in Gabriel's Wharf where jazz groups sometimes play in the summer. A few stalls are set up around the courtyard, selling ethnic clothing and handmade jewellery and pottery. The nearby book market, to be found under Waterloo Bridge, includes a good selection of new and old Penguin paperbacks, as well as new and second-hand hardbacks.

Greenwich Market

College Approach SE10. **Map** 23 B2.
⊛ *Greenwich.* ⊖ *Cutty Sark DLR.*
Open *9am–5pm Sat, Sun.*

At weekends, the area west of the Hotel Ibis accommodates dozens of trestle tables piled with coins, medals and banknotes, second-hand books, Art Deco furniture, and assorted bric-à-brac. The covered crafts market specializes in wooden toys, clothes made by young designers, handmade jewellery and accessories.

Jubilee and Apple Markets

Covent Gdn Piazza WC2. **Map** 13 C2.
⊖ *Covent Gdn.* **Open** *9am–5pm*
daily.

Covent Garden has become the centre of London street-life, with some of the capital's best busking. Both these markets sell lots of interesting crafts and designs. The Apple Market, inside the Piazza where the famous fruit and vegetable market was housed *(see p114)* has chunky knitwear, leather jewellery and novelty goods; a nearby open-air section has cheap army-surplus clothes, old prints and more jewellery. Jubilee Hall sells antiques on Monday, crafts at the weekend, and a large selection of clothes, handbags, cosmetics and tacky mementoes in between.

Leadenhall Market

Whittington Ave EC3. **Map** 15 C2.
⊖ *Bank, Monument.* **Open**
7am–4pm Mon–Fri. See p159.

Leadenhall Market is a welcome culinary oasis in the City and houses some of the best food shops in the capital. The market's traditional strengths of poultry and game have been well maintained: mallard, teal, partridge and woodcock are all available when in season. There is also a fabulous display of sea food, including excellent oysters, at Ashdown. Other stores stock high-class delicatessen, cheeses and chocolate – an expensive but mouth-watering display of goods that is hard to beat.

Leather Lane Market

Leather Lane EC1. **Map** 6 E5.
⊖ *Farringdon, Chancery Lane.*
Open *10.30am–2pm Mon–Fri.*

This ancient street has played host to a market for over 300 years. The history of the Lane has nothing to do with leather (it was originally called Le Vrune Lane), but it is in this commodity that some of the best buys are to be had in modern times. The stalls selling electrical goods, cheap tapes and CDs, clothes and toiletries are also worth having a browse through.

Petticoat Lane Market

Middlesex St E1. **Map** 16 D1.
⊖ *Liverpool St, Aldgate, Aldgate*
East. **Open** *9am–2pm Sun*
(Wentworth St 10am–2.30pm
Mon–Fri). See p169.

Probably the most famous of all London's street markets, Petticoat Lane continues to attract many thousands of visitors and locals every Sunday. The prices may not be as cheap as some of those to be found elsewhere, but the sheer volume of leather goods, clothes (the Lane's traditional strong point), watches, cheap jewellery and toys more than makes up for that. A variety of fast-food sellers do a brisk trade catering for the bustling crowds.

Piccadilly Crafts Market

St James's Church, Piccadilly W1.
Map 13 A3. ⊖ *Piccadilly Circus,*
Green Park. **Open** *10am–5pm*
Wed–Sat.

Many of the markets in the Middle Ages were held in churchyards and Piccadilly Crafts Market is rekindling that ancient tradition. It is aimed mostly at visitors to London rather than locals, and the merchandise on display ranges from tacky T-shirts to genuine 19th-century prints. Warm Aran woollens, handmade greetings cards and, on a few of the stalls, antiques also compete for custom and attention. All are spread out in the shadow of Wren's beautiful church *(see p90)*.

Portobello Road Market

Portobello Rd W10. **Map** 9 C3.
⊖ *Notting Hill Gate, Ladbroke*
Grove. **Open** *antiques and junk:*
7am–5.30pm Sat. General market:
9am–5pm Mon–Wed, Fri, Sat;
9am–1pm Thu. See p219.

Portobello Road is really three or four markets rolled into one. The Notting Hill end has over 2000 stalls displaying a compendium of objets d'art, jewellery, old medals, paintings and silverware. Most stalls are managed by experts, so bargains are rare. Further down the gentle hill, antiques give way to fruit and vegetables. The next transformation comes under the Westway flyover, where cheap clothes, bric-à-brac and tacky jewellery take over. From this point on the market becomes increasingly shabby.

Ridley Road Market

Ridley Rd E8. ⊛ *Dalston.* **Open**
9am–3pm Mon–Wed. 9am–noon
Thu. 9am–5pm Fri, Sat.

Early this century Ridley Road was a centre of the Jewish community. Since then, Asians, Greeks, Turks and West Indians have also settled in the area and the market is a lively celebration of this cultural mix. Highlights include the 24-hour bagel bakery, the shanty-town shacks selling green bananas and reggae records, the colourful drapery stalls and the very cheap fruit and vegetables.

St Martin-in-the-Fields Market

St Martin-in-the-Fields Churchyard
WC2. **Map** 13 B3. ⊖ *Charing Cross.*
Open *11am–5pm Mon–Sat; noon–*
5pm Sun. See p102.

This crafts market was started in the late 1980s. T-shirts and football scarves are among the unremarkable selection of London mementoes; more interesting are the Russian dolls, the South American handicrafts and the assorted knitwear.

Shepherd's Bush Market

Goldhawk Rd W12. ⊖ *Goldhawk*
Road, Shepherd's Bush. **Open**
9.30am–5pm Mon–Wed, Fri, Sat.
9.30am–2.30pm Thu.

Like Ridley Road and Brixton, Shepherd's Bush Market is a focal point for many of the local ethnic communities. West Indian food, Afro wigs, Asian spices and cheap household and electrical goods are just some of the attractions.

ENTERTAINMENT IN LONDON

LONDON HAS THE ENORMOUS, multi-layered variety of entertainment that only the great cities of the world can provide, and, as always, the city's historical backdrop adds depth to the experience. While few things could be more contemporary than dancing the night away in style at a famed disco such as Stringfellows or Heaven, you could also choose to spend the evening picturing the ghosts of long-dead Hamlets pacing ancient boards in the shadow of one of the living legends that grace the West End theatres today. There's a healthy, innovative fringe theatre scene too, plus world-class ballet and opera in fabled venues such as Sadler's Wells, the Royal Opera House and the Coliseum. In London you'll be able to hear the

Café sign advertising free live music

best music, ranging from classical, jazz and rock to rhythm and blues, while dedicated movie buffs can choose from hundreds of different films each night, both in large, multi-screen complexes and excellent small independent cinemas. Sports fans can watch a game of cricket at Lords, cheer on oarsmen on the Thames or eat strawberries and cream at Wimbledon. Should you be feeling adventurous and sporty yourself, you could try going for a horse ride along Rotten Row in Hyde Park. There are festivals, celebrations and sports to attend, and there's plenty for children to do, too – in fact, there's plenty for everyone to do. Whatever you want, you'll be sure to find it on offer in London; it's just a question of knowing where to look.

Cultural classics: a concert at Kenwood House *(top)*; **open-air theatre at Regent's Park** *(above left)*; ***The Mikado* at the Coliseum** *(above right)*

INFORMATION SOURCES

FOR DETAILS OF events in London, check the comprehensive weekly listings and review magazine *Time Out* (published every Wednesday), sold at most newsagents and many bookshops. The weekly *What's On and Where*

to Go In London (Wednesdays) is also useful, and London's evening newspaper, the *Evening Standard*, gives brief daily listings with a detailed supplement, "Hot Tickets", every Thursday. The *Independent* has daily listings and also reviews a different arts sector every day, plus a

weekly round-up section, "The Information"; the *Guardian* has arts reviews in its G2 section every day and weekly listings on Saturday. The *Independent*, *Guardian* and *The Times* all have lists of ticket availability.

Specialized news sheets, brochures and advance listings are distributed free in the foyers of theatres, concert halls, cinemas and arts complexes such as the South Bank and Barbican. Tourist information offices and hotel foyers often have the same publications. Fly posters advertise forthcoming events on billboards everywhere.

The Society of London Theatre (SOLT) publishes an informative free broadsheet every fortnight, available in many theatre foyers. It tends to concentrate on mainstream theatres, but does provide invaluable information about what's on. The National Theatre and the Royal Shakespeare Company also publish free broadsheets detailing future performances, distributed at the theatres.

SOLT's website (www. officiallondontheatre.co.uk) provides full details of current productions. It also has news and updates, but not seat availability. For this, there is a faxback service (09069-111 311). Many theatres also operate a faxback service which enables you to see a seating plan showing the unsold seats for any performance.

Line-up from the Royal Ballet, on stage at Covent Garden

BOOKING TICKETS

SOME OF THE more popular shows and plays in London's West End – the latest Lloyd Webber musical for instance – can be totally booked out for weeks and even months ahead and you will find it impossible to purchase any tickets. This is not the norm, though, and most tickets will be available on the night, especially if you would be prepared to queue in front of the theatre for returns. However, for a stress-free holiday it helps to book tickets in advance; this will ensure that you get the day, time and seats that you want. You can book tickets from the box office in person, by telephone or by post. Quite a few hotels have concierges or porters who will give advice on where to go and arrange tickets for you.

Box offices are usually open from about 10am–8pm, and accept payment by cash, credit card, traveller's cheque or else a personal UK cheque

when supported by a cheque guarantee card. Many venues will now sell unclaimed or returned tickets just before the performance; ask at the box office for the queuing times. To reserve seats by telephone, call the box office and either pay on arrival or send payment – seats are usually held for three days. Some venues now have separate phone numbers for your credit card bookings – check before you call. Reserve your seat, and always take your credit card with you when you collect your ticket. Some smaller venues do not accept credit cards.

Palace Theatre plaque

DISABLED VISITORS

MANY LONDON venues are old buildings and were not originally designed with disabled visitors in mind, but

recently many facilities have been updated, particularly to give access to those using wheelchairs, or for those with hearing difficulties.

Telephone the box office prior to your visit to reserve the special seating places or equipment, which are often limited. Special discounts may be available: for details and information on facilities call Artsline (020-7388 2227).

TRANSPORT

NIGHT BUSES (see p367) are now the preferred late-night mode of transport, or phone for a cab from the venue. If you find yourself outside the city centre late at night, do not rely on being able to hail a taxi quickly in the street. The Underground usually runs until just after midnight but the times of last trains vary according to the lines. Check the timetables displayed in the stations (see pp364–5).

BOOKING AGENCIES

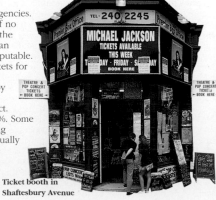

Tickets are also available from agencies. Try the theatre box office first; if no seats are available there, find out the standard prices before going to an agency. Most, but not all, are reputable. Agencies advertising top show tickets for "tonight" may really have them, and they may be a fair price. If you order by phone, tickets will be posted to you or sent to the theatre for you to collect. Commission should be a standard 22%. Some shows waive the agency fee by paying the commission themselves; this is usually advertised, and agencies should then charge standard box office prices. Always compare prices, try to avoid agencies in bureaux de change, and buy from ticket touts in the street only in desperation.

The major listings magazines

Ticket booth in Shaftesbury Avenue

London's Theatres

LONDON OFFERS AN extraordinary range of theatrical entertainment – this is one of the world's great stages, and, at its best, standards of quality are extremely high. Despite their legendary reputation for reserve, the British are passionate about theatre and London's theatres reflect every nuance of this passion. You can stroll along a street of West End theatres and find a sombre Samuel Beckett, Brecht or Chekhov play showing next door to some absurdly frothy farce like *No Sex Please, We're British!* Amid such diversity there is always something to appeal to everyone.

WEST END THEATRE

THERE IS A distinct glamour to the West End theatres. Perhaps it is the glittering lights of the foyer and the impressively ornate interiors, or maybe it is their hallowed reputations – but whatever it is, the old theatres retain a magic all of their own.

The West End billboards always feature a generous sprinkling of world-famous performers such as Judi Dench, Vanessa Redgrave, John Malkovich, Kevin Spacey and Peter O'Toole.

The major commercial theatres cluster along Shaftesbury Avenue and the Haymarket and around Covent Garden and Charing Cross Road. Unlike the national theatres, most West End theatres survive only on profits; they do not receive any state subsidy. They rely on an army of ever-hopeful "angels" (financial backers) and producers to keep the old traditions alive.

Many theatres are historical landmarks, such as the classic **Theatre Royal Drury Lane**, established in 1663 *(see p115)*, and the elegant **Theatre Royal Haymarket** – both superb examples of early 19th-century buildings. Another to note is the **Palace** *(see p108)*, with its terracotta exterior and imposing position right on Cambridge Circus.

NATIONAL THEATRE

THE **Royal National Theatre** is based in the South Bank Centre *(see p332)*. Here, the large, open-staged Olivier, the proscenium-staged Lyttelton and the small, flexible Cottesloe offer a range of size and style, making it possible to produce every kind of theatre from large, extravagant works to miniature masterpieces. The complex is also a lively social centre. Enjoy a drink with your friends before your play begins; watch the crowds and the river drift by; wander around the many free art exhibitions; relax during the free early evening concerts in the foyer or browse through the theatre bookshop.

The **Royal Shakespeare Company**, Britain's national theatre company, has its London home at the Barbican Centre. While this unique company centres its work mainly on Shakespeare's many plays, its repertoire also includes some classic Greek tragedies, gems of the Restoration theatre and a multitude of modern works. Vast productions of superb quality are staged in the magnificent Barbican Theatre, and smaller performances can be seen on the more intimate stage of The Pit, which is contained in the same complex. The centre's layout is known to be somewhat confusing so go a little early to ensure you arrive before the performance. Use any spare time to enjoy the free art and craft exhibitions in the foyer, often complementary to the plays being staged at the time, and the free musical entertainments which range from classical opera to chamber music, samba to the sound of the big brass band.

The Barbican can also supply information about RSC productions at their theatres in Stratford-upon-Avon.

NATIONAL THEATRE BOOKING ADDRESSES

Royal National Theatre
(Lyttelton, Cottesloe, Olivier)
South Bank SE1. **Map** 14 D3.
C 020-7452 3000.

Royal Shakespeare Company
Barbican Centre, Silk St EC2.
Map 7 A5.
C 020-7638 8891.

PANTOMIME

SHOULD YOU HAPPEN to be visiting London between December and February, one unmissable experience for the whole family is pantomime. Part of nearly every British child's upbringing, "panto" is an absurd tradition in which major female characters are played by men and principal male roles are played by women and the audience has to participate, shouting encouragement and stage directions to a set formula. Adults may find the whole experience rather strange, but most children love the experience.

OPEN-AIR THEATRE

A PERFORMANCE OF one of Shakespeare's airier creations, such as *Comedy of Errors, As You Like It* or *A Midsummer Night's Dream*, takes on an atmosphere of pure enchantment and magic among the green vistas of Regent's Park *(see p224)* or Holland Park *(see p218)*. Be sure to take a blanket and, to be safe, an umbrella.

Refreshments are available, or you can take a picnic.

OPEN-AIR THEATRE BOOKING ADDRESSES

Holland Park Theatre
Holland Park. **Map** 9 B4.
C 020-7602 7856.
Open Jun–Aug.

Open-Air Theatre
Inner Circle, Regent's Park NW1.
Map 4 D3.
C 020-7935 5756.
✉ 020-7486 1933.
Open May–Sep.

WEST END THEATRES

Adelphi ⓭
Strand WC2.
📞 020-7344 0055.

Albery ❶
St Martin's Lane WC2.
📞 020-7369 1730.

Aldwych ⓱
Aldwych WC2.
📞 020-7379 3367.

Apollo ⓴
Shaftesbury Ave W1.
📞 020-7494 5070.

Cambridge ㉒
Earlham St WC2.
📞 020-7494 5080.

Comedy ❽
Panton St SW1.
📞 020-7369 1731.

Criterion ❼
Piccadilly Circus W1.
📞 020-7413 1437.

Duchess ⓯
Catherine St WC2.
📞 020-7494 5075.

Duke of York's ❹
St Martin's Lane WC2.
📞 020-7836 5122.

Fortune ⓳
Russell St WC2.
📞 020-7836 2238.

Garrick ❺
Charing Cross Rd WC2.
📞 020-7494 5085.

Gielgud ㉙
Shaftesbury Ave W1.
📞 020-7494 5065.

Her Majesty's ❿
Haymarket SW1.
📞 020-7494 5400.

Lyric ㉛
Shaftesbury Ave W1.
📞 020-7494 5045.

New Ambassadors ㉔
West St WC2.
📞 020-7369 1761.

New London ⓴
Drury Lane WC2.
📞 020-7405 0072.

Palace ㉖
Shaftesbury Ave W1.
📞 020-7434 0909.

Phoenix ㉕
Charing Cross Rd WC2.
📞 020-7369 1733.

Piccadilly ㉜
Denman St W1.
📞 020-7369 1734.

Playhouse ⓬
Northumberland Ave WC2.
📞 020-7839 4401.

Prince Edward ㉗
Old Compton St W1.
📞 020-7447 5400.

Prince of Wales ❻
Coventry St W1.
📞 020-7839 5987.

Queen's ㉘
Shaftesbury Ave W1.
📞 020-7494 5040.

Shaftesbury ㉑
Shaftesbury Ave WC2.
📞 020-7379 5399.

Strand ⓰
Aldwych WC2.
📞 020-7930 8800.

St Martin's ㉓
West St WC2.
📞 020-7836 1443.

Theatre Royal:
–Drury Lane ⓲
Catherine St WC2.
📞 020-7494 5062.
–Haymarket ❾
Haymarket SW1.
📞 020-7930 8800.

Vaudeville ⓮
Strand WC2.
📞 020-7836 9987.

Whitehall ⓫
Whitehall SW1.
📞 020-7369 1735.

Wyndham's ❸
Charing Cross Rd WC2.
📞 020-7369 1736.

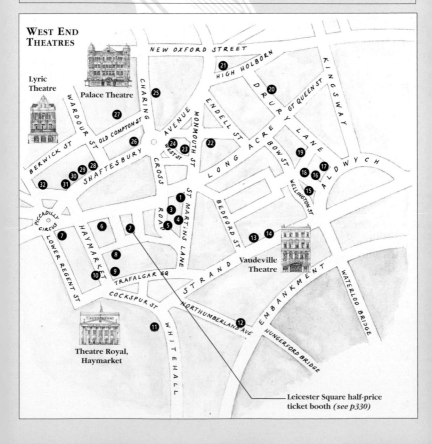

WEST END THEATRES

Leicester Square half-price ticket booth (see p330)

FRINGE THEATRE

LONDON'S FRINGE theatre acts as an outlet for new, adventurous writing and for writers from other cultures and lifestyles – works by Irish writers appear regularly, as do plays by Caribbean and Latin American authors and feminist and gay writers.

The plays are usually staged in tiny theatres based in pubs, such as the **Gate Theatre** above the Prince Albert pub in Notting Hill, the **King's Head** in Islington and the **Grace** in the Latchmere pub in Battersea, or in warehouses and spare space in larger theatres, such as the **Donmar Warehouse** and the **Studio** in the Lyric.

Venues like the **Bush**, the **Almeida** and the **Theatre Upstairs** at the Royal Court have earned their reputations for discovering outstanding new works, some of which have subsequently transferred successfully to the West End.

Foreign-language plays are sometimes performed at national cultural institutes; for example you might be able to catch Molière at the **Institut Français** or Brecht at the **Goethe Institute**; check the listings magazines.

For alternative stand-up comedy and cabaret, where you can encounter the sharp edge of satire with its brash, newsy style, try the **Comedy Store**, the birthplace of so-called "alternative" comedy, or the **Hackney Empire**, a former Victorian music hall with a once magnificent but now faded grand interior, that hosts different types of show.

BUDGET TICKETS

THERE IS A wide range of prices for seats in London theatres. The cheaper West End tickets, for example, can cost under £10, whereas the best seats for musicals hover around the £30 mark. However, it is usually quite possible to obtain cheaper tickets.

The Leicester Square Half Price Ticket Booth (see p329) sells tickets on the day of the performance for a wide range of mainstream shows. Situated in Leicester Square, the booth is open Monday to Saturday, (10am–7pm) and Sunday (noon–3:30pm) for matinees only. Payment is by cash and there is a strict limit of only four tickets for each purchaser. There is also a small service charge to pay.

You can sometimes get reduced price seats for matinee performances, press and preview nights – it is always worth checking with the box office to see what they currently have on offer.

CHOOSING SEATS

IF YOU GO TO the theatre in person, you will be able to see its seating plan and note where you can get a good view at an affordable price. If you book by telephone, you should note the following: stalls are in front of the stage and expensive. The back stalls are slightly cheaper; dress, grand or royal circles are above the stalls and cheaper again; the upper circle or balcony are the cheapest seats but you will have to climb several flights of stairs; the slips are seats that run along the very edges of the theatre; boxes are the most expensive option.

It is also as well to bear in mind that some of the cheapest seats may have a restricted view of the stage.

THEATRE-RELATED ACTIVITIES

IF YOU ARE curious about how the mechanics of the theatre work, you would probably enjoy a back-stage tour. The National Theatre and the RSC both organize these tours (contact the box office – see p326 – for details). If you enjoy a good walk, London Theatre Walks (020-7839 7438) may interest you. The Theatre Museum (see p115) is well worth a visit.

IRATE GHOSTS

Many London theatres are reputed to have ghosts; however, the two most famous spectres haunt the environs of the Garrick and the Duke of York's (see p329). The Garrick is heavily atmospheric and the ghost of Arthur Bourchier, a manager at the turn of the century, is reputed to make fairly regular appearances. He hated critics and many believe he is still trying to frighten them away. The ghost occupying the Duke of York's theatre was Violet Melnotte, an actress manager during the 1890s, who was famed for her extremely fiery temper.

FRINGE THEATRE

Almeida
Almeida St N1.
📞 020-7359 4404.

Bush
Shepherds Bush Green W12.
📞 020-7602 3703.

Comedy Store
28a Leicester Sq WC2.
Map 13 B3.
📞 020-7344 0234.

Donmar Warehouse
41 Earlham St WC2.
Map 13 B2.
📞 020-7369 1732.

Institut Français
17 Queensberry Pl SW7.
Map 18 F2.
📞 020-7589 6211.

Gate Theatre
The Prince Albert,
11 Pembridge Rd W11.
Map 9 C3.
📞 020-7229 0706.

Goethe Institute
50 Prince's Gate,
Exhibition Rd SW7.
Map 11 A5.
📞 020-7596 4000.

Grace
503 Battersea Park Rd SW11.
📞 020-7223 3549.

Hackney Empire
291 Mare St E8.
📞 020-8985 2424.

King's Head
115 Upper St N1.
Map 6 F1.
📞 020-7226 1916.

Studio
Lyric, Hammersmith,
King St W6.
📞 020-8741 2311.

Theatre Upstairs
Royal Court,
Sloane Sq SW1.
Map 19 C2.
📞 020-7565 5000.

Cinemas

IF YOU CAN'T FIND a movie you like in London, then you don't like movies. The huge choice of British, American, foreign-language, new, classic, popular and special-interest films makes London a major international film centre, with about 250 different films showing at any one time. There are about 50 cinemas in the central district of London alone, many of them ultra-modern multi-screened complexes. The big commercial chains show current smash-hits and a healthy number of independent cinemas offer some inventive programmes drawing on the whole history of film. London's listings magazines carry full details of what's on where.

WEST END CINEMAS

WEST END is a loose term for the main cinemas in the West End of London which show new releases, such as the **Odeon Leicester Square** and the **ABC** Shaftesbury Avenue, but it also includes the cinemas found in Chelsea, Fulham and Notting Hill. Programmes normally begin around midday and are then repeated every two or three hours, with the last show around 8.30pm; there are often late-night screenings on Fridays and Saturdays.

West End cinemas are very expensive, but admission is often cheaper for afternoon performances or on Mondays. Reserve your seats well in advance for screenings of the more popular films on Friday and Saturday evenings and Sunday afternoon.

BFI LONDON IMAX

THE LARGEST IMAX screen in Britain shows specially created movies accompanied by surround sound. Subjects like spaceflight or the undersea world suit this breathtaking format well, as do animations.

REPERTORY CINEMAS

THESE CINEMAS OFTEN show foreign-language and slightly more "off-beat" art films and sometimes change programmes daily or even several times each day. Some cinemas show two or three films, often on the same theme, for one entrance charge.

These include the **Prince Charles**, which is situated centrally, close to Leicester Square, the **Everyman** in north London, the ICA in the Mall, the newly refurbished **Ritzy** in South London and the National Film Theatre.

NATIONAL FILM THEATRE

THE NATIONAL FILM Theatre (NFT) is located in the South Bank Arts Complex, near Waterloo Station. The NFT has two cinemas of its own, both of which offer a huge and diverse selection of films, both British and international. The NFT also holds regular screenings of rare and restored films and television programmes taken from the National Film Archive. It is absolutely essential for movie buffs to pay a visit.

FOREIGN-LANGUAGE FILMS

THESE ARE screened at a number of repertory and independent cinemas, including the **Renoir**, the **Prince Charles**, the Curzon in Shaftesbury Avenue, the **Minema** and the **Screen** cinemas chain. Films are shown in the original language, with English subtitles.

FILM CERTIFICATES

CHILDREN ARE ALLOWED to go to a cinema unaccompanied by an adult to films which have been awarded either a U (universal) or a PG (parental guidance advised) certificate for viewing.

With other films, the numbers 12, 15 or 18 quite simply denote the minimum ages allowed for admission to the cinema. These classifications are always clearly advertised in the publicity for the film.

LONDON FILM FESTIVAL

THE MOST important cinema event in Britain is held every November, when over 100 films – some of which will have already won awards abroad – from a number of countries are screened. The NFT, several of the repertory cinemas and some of the big West End cinemas will have special showings of these films. Details are published in the listings magazines. Tickets are quite hard to come by but some "standby" tickets will generally be available to the public 30 minutes before the start of a performance.

CINEMA ADDRESSES

ABC
135 Shaftesbury Ave WC2.
Map 13 B2.
020-7836 8606.

BFI London IMAX
Waterloo Rd SE1.
Map 14 D4.
020-7902 1234.

Everyman
Hollybush Vale NW3.
Map 1 A5.
020-7431 1777.

Minema
45 Knightsbridge SW1.
Map 12 D5.
020-7369 1723.

National Film Theatre
South Bank Centre, SE1.

Map 14 D3.
020-7928 3232.

Odeon Leicester Sq
Leicester Sq, WC2.
Map 13 B2.
020-8315 4215.

Prince Charles
Leicester Pl, WC2.
Map 13 B2
020-7437 8181.

Renoir
Brunswick Sq WC1.
Map 5 C4.
020-7837 8402.

Ritzy
Brixton Rd SW2.
Map 5
020-7733 2229.

Screen Cinemas
96 Baker St NW1
Map 3 C5.
020-7935 2772.

Opera, Classical and Contemporary Music

UNTIL RECENTLY, OPERA enjoyed a somewhat elitist reputation. However, televised concerts and free outdoor concerts in Hyde Park and the Piazza, Covent Garden, have greatly increased its popularity. London is home to five world-class orchestras and a veritable host of smaller music companies and contemporary music ensembles; it also houses three permanent opera companies and numerous smaller opera groups and leads the world with its period orchestras. It is a major centre for the classical recording industry, which helps to support a large community of musicians and singers. Mainstream, obscure, traditional and innovative music are all to be found in profusion. *Time Out* magazine *(see p326)* has the most comprehensive listings of the classical music on offer around the capital.

Royal Opera House

Floral Street WC2. **Map** 13 C2.
C 020-7304 4000. See p115.

The building, with its opulent, elaborate red, white and gold interior, is very glamorous; it looks, and is, expensive. It is the home of the Royal Opera, but very often visiting opera and ballet companies also perform here. Many productions are shared with foreign opera houses, so if you are a visitor to England check that you haven't already seen the same production at home. Works are always performed in the original language, but English translations are flashed up above the stage.

Seats are usually booked well in advance, particularly if major stars such as Placido Domingo, Luciano Pavarotti or Kiri Te Kanawa are performing. The sound is best in the seats centre of stage, right in the front. Tickets range from about £5 to £200 or more for a world-class star. The cheapest seats tend to be bought first, although a number of these tickets are reserved for sale on the day. (Remember some of the cheaper seats in the Royal Opera House have extremely restricted views of the stage.) Standing passes can often be obtained right up to the time of a performance. Standby information is available on the day of the performance on 020-7836 6903 and there are often concessions on tickets. It is also worthwhile queuing for last-minute returns.

London Coliseum

St Martin's Lane WC2. **Map** 13 B3.
C 020-7836 0111.
📠 020-7632 8300. See p119.

The Coliseum, home of the English National Opera (ENO), has rather faded decor but the musical standards are extremely high. The company trains its own singers for its productions and they rehearse in the setting in which they will perform. ENO productions of the classics are nearly all sung in English. The productions are often adventurous and critics have been known to complain that the clarity of the storyline is impaired. The audiences tend to be younger than at the Royal Opera House, the seats are much cheaper and there is less corporate entertaining. The cheapest seats are infamous for being real backbreakers.

Sadler's Wells

Rosebery Ave EC1. **Map** 6 E3.
C 020-7314 8800.

Less glamorous, expensive and central than the other opera houses, Sadler's Wells does not have its own company but it provides a useful venue for many visiting companies. Among these, three have a regular season here, each presenting two works: the D'Oyly Carte company, formed in 1875 specifically to perform works by Gilbert and Sullivan, has its season in April and May; Opera 80, with a cast of 22 singers and an orchestra of 27, offers opera in English at a reasonable price in the last two weeks of May; and the British Youth Opera performs here each year in early September.

South Bank Centre

South Bank Centre SE1. **Map** 14 D4.
C 020-7921 0600. See pp186–7.

The South Bank Centre houses the Royal Festival Hall (RFH), the Queen Elizabeth Hall and the Purcell Room. There are nightly performances, mostly of classical music, interspersed with opera, ballet and modern dance seasons, jazz, festivals of contemporary and ethnic music and other one-off events running throughout the year. The largest concert hall on the South Bank is the RFH, which is ideal for the major national and international orchestras and large-scale choral works. The Purcell Room is comparatively small and tends to host string quartets and contemporary music in addition to many debut recitals of young artists. The Queen Elizabeth Hall lies somewhere in between. It stages medium-sized ensembles whose audiences, while too large for the Purcell Room, would not fill the Festival Hall. Jazz and ethnic music are performed here and the very innovative and often controversial Opera Factory makes several appearances throughout the year. It performs a range of modern interpretations of the classics, and often also com-missions and performs new works. The acoustics are very good throughout the complex.

The London Philharmonic Orchestra is resident at the South Bank. The Royal Philharmonic, the Philharmonia and the BBC Symphony Orchestra are frequent visitors, along with leading ensem-bles and soloists such as Shura Cherkassky, Stephen Kovacevich and Anne-Sofie von Otter.

The Academy of St Martin-in-the-Fields, the London Festival Orchestra, Opera Factory, the London Classical Players and the

London Mozart Players all have regular seasons. There are also frequent free foyer concerts, and throughout the summer the centre is well worth visiting as musical events take place on the terraces when the weather permits.

Barbican Concert Hall

Silk Street EC2. **Map** 7 A5.
☎ 020-7638 8891. See p165.

This stark concrete building is the permanent home of the London Symphony Orchestra (LSO), which concentrates on the work of one composer each season. The LSO Summer Pops features an impressive line-up of stars from stage, television, film and the recording world, which in the past has included famous artists such as Victor Borge and the jazz singer Barbara Cook.

The English National Opera makes regular appearances, and the Royal Philharmonic Orchestra has a spring season.

The Barbican is also renowned for its concerts of contemporary music: the BBC Symphony Orchestra holds an annual festival of 20th-century composers here and the London Sinfonietta, which specializes in 20th-century music, performs most of its London concerts at the same venue. There are free foyer concerts too.

Royal Albert Hall

Kensington Gore SW7. **Map** 10 F5.
☎ 020-7589 3203. See p207.

The beautiful Royal Albert Hall is the venue for a wide variety of events from fashion and pop shows to wrestling. However, from mid-July to mid-September it is devoted solely to the Henry Wood Promenade Concerts, the "Proms". Organized by the BBC, the season features the BBC Philharmonic Orchestra, which performs some modern symphonic music as well as classics. Visiting orchestras from around the United Kingdom and worldwide, such as the City of Birmingham Orchestra, the Chicago Symphony Orchestra and the Boston Symphony Orchestra, make up a very varied programme. Tickets for the Proms can be bought on the day of performance but long queues build up early in the day so experienced Promenaders take cushions to sit on. Tickets sell out weeks ahead for the "Last Night of the Proms", which has become a national institution. The audience wave flags and sing. Some people may consider it an evening of nationalistic fervour, although the majority just like singing the traditional *Land of Hope and Glory* without giving much thought to its possibly jingoistic words.

OUTDOOR MUSIC

London has many outdoor musical events in summer. At Kenwood House on Hampstead Heath (*see p234*), a grassy hill leads down to a lake, beyond which is the concert platform. Arrive early as the concerts are popular, particularly if fireworks are to accompany the music. Deck-chairs tend to be booked up early, so most people sit on the grass. Take a sweater and a picnic. Purists beware – people walk around, eat and talk throughout and the music is amplified so it can be a little distorted. You don't get your money back if it rains, as they have never abandoned a performance yet.

Other venues include Marble Hill House in Twickenham (*see p252*), with practices similar to Kenwood, Crystal Palace Park and Holland Park.

Wigmore Hall

36 Wigmore St W1. **Map** 12 E1.
☎ 020-7935 2141. See p226.

Because of its excellent acoustics the Wigmore Hall is a favourite with visiting artists, and attracts international names such as Jessye Norman and Julian Bream for a very wide-ranging programme of events. It presents seven evening concerts a week, and a Sunday morning concert from September through to July.

St Martin-in-the-Fields

Trafalgar Sq WC2. **Map** 13 B3.
☎ 020-7930 1862. See p102.

This elegant Gibbs church is home to the Academy of St Martin-in-the-Fields and the famous choir of the same name. These and orchestras as disparate as the Henry Wood Chamber Orchestra, the Penguin Café Orchestra and the St Martin-in-the-Fields Sinfonia provide evening concerts. The choice of each programme is, to a degree, dictated by the religious year; for example, Bach's *St John Passion* is played at Ascensiontide and Handel's *Messiah* at Christmas.

Free lunchtime concerts are given on Mondays, Tuesdays and Fridays by young artists.

St John's, Smith Square

Smith Sq SW1. **Map** 21 B1.
☎ 020-7222 1061. See p81.

This converted Baroque church has good acoustics and provides comfortable seating, making it a marvellous setting. It hosts varied concerts and recitals by groups such as the Wren Orchestra, the Vanbrugh String Quartet and the London Sonata Group. A daily series of BBC Radio lunchtime concerts covers the music and song recitals.

Broadgate Arena

3 Broadgate EC2. **Map** 7 C5.
☎ 020-7505 4068. See p169.

This is the new City-based venue for a summer season of lunchtime concerts offering varied programmes, often from up-and-coming musicians.

MUSIC VENUES

Orchestral

Barbican Concert Hall
Broadgate Arena
Queen Elizabeth Hall
Royal Albert Hall
Royal Festival Hall
St Martin-in-the-Fields
St John's, Smith Square

Chamber and Ensemble

Barbican Concert Hall
Broadgate Arena
Purcell Room
Royal Festival Hall foyer
St Martin-in-the-Fields
St John's, Smith Square
Wigmore Hall

Soloists and Recitals

Barbican Concert Hall
Purcell Room
Royal Albert Hall
St Martin-in-the-Fields
St John's, Smith Square
Wigmore Hall

Children's

Barbican Concert Hall
Royal Festival Hall

Free

Barbican Concert Hall
National Theatre foyer (see p328)
Royal Festival Hall foyer
St Martin-in-the-Fields (lunchtime)

Early Music

Purcell Room
Wigmore Hall

Contemporary Music

Barbican Concert Hall
South Bank Complex

Dance

LONDON-BASED DANCE companies present a range of styles from classical ballet to mime, jazz, experimental and ethnic dance. London is also host to visiting companies as diverse as the classic Bolshoi Ballet and the innovative Jaleo Flamenco. Most dance companies (with the exception of the resident ballets) have short seasons that seldom last longer than a fortnight and often less than a week – check the listings magazines for details *(see p326)*. Theatres that regularly feature dance are the **Royal Opera House**, the **London Coliseum**, **Sadler's Wells** and **The Place Theatre**. There are also performances at the **South Bank Centre** and other arts centres throughout the city.

dance company has a short season and runs a week of choreographic workshops in April at the **Riverside Studios**. Other venues used include the **Institute of Contemporary Arts** (ICA) *(see p92)*, the **Shaw Theatre** and the **Chisenhale Dance Space**, a centre for small and independent companies currently regarded as on the experimental fringe of contemporary dance.

BALLET

THE **Royal Opera House** *(see p115)* and the **London Coliseum** in St Martin's Lane are by far the best venues for classical ballet, providing the stage for foreign companies when they visit London. The Opera House is home to the Royal Ballet, which usually invites major international guest artists to take up residence. Book well in advance for classics such as *Swan Lake* and *Giselle*. The company also has an unusual repertoire of modern ballet; triple bills provide a mixture of new and old and seats are normally quite readily available.

The English National Ballet holds its summer season at the **London Coliseum**. It has a similar repertoire to the Royal Ballet and stages some very popular productions.

Visiting companies also perform at **Sadler's Wells** *(see p332)*, where the London City Ballet has its annual season during December and January. This company has a mainly classical repertoire.

CONTEMPORARY

A PLETHORA OF new and young companies is flourishing in London, each with its own distinctive style. **Sadler's Wells** is one of the main venues, with short seasons featuring visiting and local companies. Attached to Sadler's Wells is the Lilian Baylis Studio, a venue for smaller and often more experimental productions.

The Place is the home of contemporary and ethnic dance companies and has a year-round programme of performances from these and visiting dancers. The London Contemporary Dance Theatre, the largest of Britain's contemporary dance companies, is based here.

Jacksons Lane was opened 25 years ago as an arts and community centre and has become an acclaimed venue for innovative contemporary dance often from international dance groups, including Asian, African, Greek, Middle Eastern and Spanish. The world-renowned Rambert

ETHNIC

THERE IS A constant stream of visiting groups coming to perform traditional dance from all over the world. Both **Sadler's Wells** and the **Riverside Studios** are major venues, while classical ethnic dance companies, including Indian and Far Eastern, have seasons at the South Bank Centre, often in the **Queen Elizabeth Hall**. Check the listings magazines for details.

DANCE FESTIVALS

THERE ARE TWO major contemporary dance festivals each year in London, featuring many different companies. Spring Loaded runs from February to April, while Dance Umbrella runs from early October to early November. The listings magazines carry all details.

Other smaller festivals include Almeida Dance, from the end of April to the first week of May at the **Almeida Theatre**, and The Turning World, a festival running in April and May offering dance from all over the world.

DANCE VENUES

Almeida Theatre
Almeida St N1.
📞 020-7226 7432.

Chisenhale Dance Space
64 Chisenhale Rd E3.
📞 020-8981 6617.

ICA
Nash House,
Carlton House Terrace,

The Mall SW1.
Map 13 A4.
📞 020-7930 0493.

Jacksons Lane
269a Archway Rd N6.
📞 020-8340 5226.

London Coliseum
St Martin's Lane WC2.
Map 13 B3.
📞 020-7836 0111.
📠 020-7632 8300.

The Place
17 Duke's Rd WC1.
Map 5 B3.
📞 020-7380 1268.

Queen Elizabeth Hall
South Bank Centre SE1.
Map 14 D4.
📞 020-7960 4242.

Riverside Studios
Crisp Rd W6.
📞 020-8237 1111.

Royal Opera House
Floral St WC2.
Map 13 C2.
📞 020-7304 4000.

Sadler's Wells
Rosebery Ave EC1.
Map 6 E3.
📞 020-7863 8000.

Shaw Theatre
100 Euston Rd NW1.
Map 5 B3.
📞 020-7388 1394.

Rock, Pop, Jazz, Reggae and World Music

YOU WILL FIND THE WHOLE range of popular music being strummed and hummed, howled, growled or synthesized in London. There may be as many as 80 listed concerts on an ordinary weeknight, featuring rock, reggae, soul, folk, country, jazz, Latin and world music. In addition to the gigs, there are music festivals in the summer at parks, pubs, halls and stadiums throughout the capital *(see p337)*. Check the listings magazines and keep your eyes open for publicity posters *(see p326)*.

MAJOR VENUES

THE LARGEST venues in London are host to an extraordinary variety of music. The **London Arena** on the Isle of Dogs is one of the largest, with room for 12,500. Other places where pop idols hope to draw enormous crowds of adoring fans include the cavernous indoor **Wembley Arena**, the **Hammersmith Apollo**, or, if they take themselves rather seriously, the grand **Royal Albert Hall**.

The **Brixton Academy** and the **Town and Country Club** are next in prominence and size. Each can take well over 1,000 people, and for many Londoners these former cinemas are the capital's best venues, with seating upstairs, large dance-floors downstairs and accessible bars.

ROCK AND POP

INDIE MUSIC is one of the mainstays of London's live music output. Following the leads of Manchester and Bristol, the capital has a healthy, cross-fertilized rock scene: venues all over town offer Britpop, bratpop, hip-hop, trip-hop and the many other variations on pop which have yet to be labelled for the mass market. Kentish Town's **Bull and Gate** and the **Powerhaus** in Islington are good for goth, while rock is the order of the day at venues such as the **Astoria** in the West End and **The Shepherd's Bush Empire** among others.

The **Mean Fiddler** in Charing Cross Road is one of the best of the mid-sized venues and is famous for being the place that bands play twice – once on the way up, and again on the way down. London is the home of pub-rock, which is a vibrant blend of rhythm and blues, rock and punk that has been evolving since the 1960s as a genre in which bands frequently develop before finding their real musical identity. Such diverse bands as the Clash, Dr Feelgood and Dire Straits all started as pub rockers. While there's usually no entrance fee to pub gigs, drinks tend to be surcharged.

New bands have a popular showcase at the **Rock Garden** in Covent Garden most week nights, while **Borderline**, near to Leicester Square, is frequented by record company talent scouts. **Subterania** in Ladbroke Grove holds interesting new songwriter nights. The **Camden Palace** is very good value for money, especially on Tuesdays, when you can listen to the finest established indie pop both before and after live performances from up-and-coming indie bands. Another good venue for stimulating rock bands in North London is **The Garage** at Highbury Corner.

JAZZ

THE NUMBER of jazz venues in London has grown in the last few years – both the music and the lifestyle which is romantically imagined to go with it are officially hip once again. **Ronnie Scott's** in the West End is still the pick of the vintage crop, and since the 1950s many of the finest performers in the world have come to play here. The **100 Club** in Oxford Street is another very popular venue for confirmed jazzniks.

Jazz and food have formed a partnership at venues such as the **Palookaville** in Covent Garden, the **Dover Street Wine Bar** and the largely vegetarian **Jazz Café**. Others include the **Pizza Express** on Dean Street and the **Pizza on the Park**, by Hyde Park Corner.

The **South Bank Centre** *(see pp186–7)* and also the **Barbican** *(see p165)* feature formal jazz concerts and free jazz in the foyers.

REGGAE

LONDON'S LARGE West Indian community has made the city the European reggae capital. At the **Notting Hill Carnival** *(see p57)*, late in August, many top bands perform free.

Reggae has now become integrated with the mainstream rock music scene, and bands appear at most of London's rock venues.

WORLD MUSIC

MUSICIANS FROM every corner of the globe live in London. "World music" includes African, Latin, South American, anything exotic, and its popularity has sparked a revitalization of British and Irish folk music. **Cecil Sharp House** has regular shows for folk purists, while the **ICA** *(see p92)* hosts innovative acts. **The Weavers Arms,** near Newington Green, has a reputation for Cajun, African and Latin American music. Hot Latin nights can be found at **Down Mexico Way** near Piccadilly and at **Cuba Libre** in Islington. For all French Caribbean and African sounds you could check **Le Café de Piaf** inside Waterloo Station; and for the widest selection of African sounds and food in town, try visiting the **Africa Centre** in Covent Garden. The **Barbican Centre**, the **Royal Festival Hall** and the **Queen Elizabeth Hall** at the South Bank Centre all offer plenty of world music.

Clubs

THE OLD CLICHÉ that London dies when the pubs shut no longer holds true. Europe has long scoffed at Londoners going to bed at 11pm when the night is only just beginning in Paris, Madrid and Rome, but London has caught on at last and you can revel all night if you want to. The best clubs are not all confined to the city's centre – initial disappointment that your hotel is a half-hour tube-ride from Leicester Square can be offset by the discovery of a trendy club right on your doorstep.

ETIQUETTE

FASHIONS and club nights change very rapidly and nightspots open and close down all the time. Some of the best club nights are one-nighters – check the listings magazines (see p326). Style magazines like The Face can help you avoid humiliating comments from bouncers who don't like your appearance. Some clubs change the dress policy with each evening, so it is best to check in advance.

A few clubs require that you arrange membership 48 hours in advance, and you may also find that you have to be introduced by a member. Again, check these details in the listings magazines. Groups of men may not be welcome, so split up and find a woman to go in with; expect to queue to get in. Entrance fees may seem reasonable, but drinks tend to be over-priced.

Opening times are usually 10pm–3am Monday to Saturday, although many clubs stay open until 6am at the weekend and some open on Sunday from about 8pm to midnight.

MAINSTREAM

LONDON IS HOME to one of the best-known discos in the world: **Stringfellows** is as much a part of the tourist circuit as Madame Tussaud's. It's glitzy and expensive so jeans are out of the question. The nearby **Hippodrome** is similar. One of the world's largest discos, it has stunning lighting, several bars and also serves food.

Most of the more upmarket nightclubs in London, for example **Annabel's**, have a strict members-only policy; they require nominations by current members and have long waiting lists, so unless you mix in privileged circles you are unlikely to get in.

Traditional West End disco-type clubs which are easier to enter include **Limelight**, the sleek club **Legends** and **Café de Paris**, where you can dine and boogie the night away.

Further north, the **Forum** hosts popular club nights, which feature classic soul, funk and rhythm and blues. Similar clubs are **Equinox** in Leicester Square and the **Tattershall Castle**, a disco boat moored on the Thames.

FASHIONABLE VENUES AND CLUB NIGHTS

OVER THE LAST few years London has become one of the most innovative and sought-after club capitals in the world. It is now a major stage where trends are set. **Heaven** hosts England's premier "house" night. With its huge dance floor, excellent lasers, sound systems and lightshows it's very popular, so start queuing early. The **Ministry of Sound** is a New York-style club that set the pattern for others to follow. However, it has no alcohol licence and is also notoriously difficult to get into. If you are feeling energetic, house nights are also run at the **Gardening Club** and **Woody's**, which is home to garage as well as hardcore house, and there's always the young and trendy **Wag Club**.

As with many clubs, **Bar Rhumba** has different themes on different evenings, but if you like your dancing with a dash of spice and a lot of sauce, sashay along to its salsa night. "Talkin' Loud" club night at the **Fridge** in Brixton offers some of the funkiest jazz-based sounds.

Turnmills is London's first 24-hour club; it's cheap, plays funky jazz and also boasts a decent restaurant. For 1970s nostalgists, **Le Scandale** hosts "Carwash" – disco was never such fun. There is also cheap admission for those brave enough to dress in seventies style so what you lose in fashion points, you can re-coup for your bar budget.

Disappointingly, there are surprisingly few regular reggae nights. **Gossips** has the best dance reggae on Saturday nights and a tremendous toe-tapping tripartite rhythm riot of ska, classic soul and R 'n' B on Thursdays.

GAY

LONDON HAS a number of gay nightclubs. The best-known and most popular is **Heaven**, with its huge dance floor and bar and video lounge. The **Fridge** and the **Gardening Club** host mixed gay nights, and the Fridge holds women-only nights.

TRANSVESTITE

WATCH for the occasional "Kinky Gerlinky" night in the listings magazines, an outrageously kitsch collection of drag queens and assorted exotica. In Soho, **Madame Jojo's** revue is a fabulous whirl of glittering colour and extreme high camp.

CASINOS

TO GAMBLE in London you must be a member, or at least the guest of a member, of a licensed gaming club. Most clubs are happy to let you join but membership must be arranged 48 hours in advance. Many will let you in to use facilities other than the gambling tables until about 4am, when most close. Try the excellent restaurants and bars, which are often subject to the usual licensing laws (see p310). Many clubs also have "hostesses" – beware the cost of their company.

DIRECTORY

MAJOR MUSIC VENUES

Brixton Academy
211 Stockwell Rd SW9.
020-7924 9999.

Forum
9–17 Highgate Rd NW5.
020-7284 1001.
020-7284 2200.

Hammersmith Apollo
Queen Caroline St W6.
0870-505 0007.

London Arena
Limeharbour, Isle of
Dogs, E14.
020-7538 1212.

Royal Albert Hall
See p203.

Wembley Arena
Empire Way, Wembley,
Middlesex HA9.
0870-840 1111.

ROCK AND POP VENUES

Astoria
157 Charing Cross Rd
WC2. **Map** 13 B1.
020-7434 9592.

Borderline
Orange Yard,
Manette St WC2.
Map 13 B1.
020-7734 2095.

Bull and Gate
389 Kentish Town Rd
NW5.
020-7485 5358.

Camden Palace
1a Camden High St
NW1. **Map** 4 F2.
020-7387 0428.

The Garage
20–22 Highbury Corner,
N5.
020-7607 1818.

Limelight
136 Shaftesbury Ave
WC2. **Map** 13 B2.
020-7434 0572.

Mean Fiddler
157 Charing Cross Rd
WC2. **Map** 13 B2.
020-7434 9592.

Powerhaus
270 Seven Sisters Rd N4.
020-7836 4052.

Rock Garden
6–7 The Piazza, Covent
Garden WC2.
Map 13 C2.
020-7836 4052.
www.rockgarden.uk

Shepherd's Bush Empire
Shepherd's Bush Green W12.
020-8740 7474.

Subterania
12 Acklam Rd W10.
020-8960 4590.
020-8284 2200.

Woody's
41–43 Woodfield Rd W9.
020-7266 3030.

JAZZ VENUES

100 Club
100 Oxford St W1.
Map 13 A1.
020-7636 0933.

Barbican Hall
See p165.

Dover Street Wine Bar
8–10 Dover St W1.
Map 12 F3.
020-7629 9813.

Jazz Café
5 Parkway NW1.
Map 4 E1.
020-7916 6060.

Pizza Express
10 Dean St W1.
Map 13 A1.
020-7437 9595.

Pizza on the Park
11 Knightsbridge SW1.
Map 12 D5.
020-7235 5550.

Ronnie Scott's
47 Frith St W1.
Map 13 A2.
020-7439 0747.
www.ronniescotts.uk

Royal Festival Hall
See p184.

Vortex Jazz Bar
Stoke Newington Church St
N16.
020-7254 6516.

WORLD MUSIC

Africa Centre
38 King St WC2.
Map 13 C2.
020-7836 1973.

Barbican Centre
See p165.

Cecil Sharp House
2 Regent's Park Rd NW1.
Map 4 D1.
020-7485 2206.

Cuba Libre
72 Upper St N1. **Map** 6 F1.
020-7354 9998.

Down Mexico Way
25 Swallow St W1.
Map 12 F3.
020-7437 9895.

ICA
See p92.

Mean Fiddler
22-28A High St NW10.
020-8961 5490.

Queen Elizabeth Hall
South Bank Centre SE1.
Map 14 D4.
020-7960 4242.

Royal Festival Hall
See pp184–5.

CLUBS

Annabel's
44 Berkeley Sq W1.
Map 12 E3.
020-7629 1096.

Bar Rhumba
36 Shaftesbury Ave WC2.
Map 6 E2.
020-7287 2715.

Café de Paris
3 Coventry St W1.
Map 13 A3.
020-7734 7700.

Equinox
Leicester Sq WC2.
Map 13 B2.
020-7437 1446.

Fridge
Town Hall Parade,
Brixton Hill SW2.
020-7326 5100.

Gardening Club
6 The Market,
Covent Garden WC2.
Map 13 C2.
020-7497 3154.

Gossips
69 Dean St W1.
Map 13 A2.
020-7434 4480.

Heaven
Under the Arches,
Villiers St WC2.
Map 13 C3.
020-7930 2020.

Hippodrome
Cranbourn St WC2.
Map 13 B2.
020-7437 4311.

Legends
29 Old Burlington St
W1.
Map 12 F3.
020-7437 9933.

Madame Jojo
8–10 Brewer St W1.
Map 13 A2.
020-7734 2473.

Ministry of Sound
103 Gaunt St SE1.
020-7378 6528.

Le Scandale
53–54 Berwick St W1.
Map 13 A1.
020-7437 6830.

Stringfellows
16 Upper St Martin's
Lane WC2.
Map 13 B2.
020-7240 5534.
www.stringfellows.uk

Tattershall Castle
Victoria Embankment,
SW1. **Map** 13 C3.
020-7839 6548.

Turnmills
63 Clerkenwell Road
EC1. **Map** 6 E5.
020-7250 3409.

Wag Club
35 Wardour St W1.
Map 13 A2.
020-7437 5534.

Sport

THE RANGE OF SPORTS on offer in London is quite phenomenal. Should you feel the urge to watch a game of medieval tennis or go scuba-diving in the city centre, you've come to the right place. More likely, you'll just want to watch a football or rugby match, or play a set of tennis in a park. With far more public facilities than most European capitals, London is the place to enjoy cheap, accessible sport. What the city lacks, however, is a national stadium. The old Wembley Stadium is being demolished, to be replaced by a new one – possibly by 2004 – but the project has run into considerable political and economic difficulties.

ATHLETICS

ATHLETES WILL find a good choice of running tracks, often with free admission. **West London Stadium** has good facilities; **Regent's Park** is free; try also **Parliament Hill Fields**. For a sociable jog, meet the Bow Street Runners at **Jubilee Hall** on Tuesdays at 6pm.

CRICKET

FIVE-DAY TEST MATCHES and one-day internationals are played in summer at Lord's (*see p244*) and the Oval, near Vauxhall. Tickets for the first four days of tests and for one-day games are hard to get, but you may get in on the last day and see a thrilling finish. When Middlesex and Surrey play county games at these grounds there are always seats.

FOOTBALL (SOCCER)

THIS IS THE MOST popular spectator sport in Britain, its season running from August to May, with matches on weekends and weekday evenings. It is the most common topic of conversation in pubs, where games are often shown live on TV. Premier League and FA Cup games are frequently sold out in advance. London's top clubs include **Arsenal**, **Chelsea**, **West Ham** and **Tottenham Hotspur**.

GOLF

THERE ARE NO golf courses in central London, but a few are scattered around the outskirts. The most accessible public courses are **Hounslow Heath**, **Chessington** (nine holes, train from Waterloo) and **Richmond Park** (two courses, computerized indoor teaching room). If you didn't pack your clubs, sets can be hired at a reasonable price.

GREYHOUND RACING

AT A NIGHT "down the dogs" you can follow the races on a screen in the bar, stand by the track or watch from the restaurant (book in advance) at **Walthamstow Stadium**, **The Embassy London Stadium** or **Wimbledon Stadium**.

HORSE RACING

HIGH CLASS FLAT RACING in summer and steeple-chasing in winter can be seen at **Ascot**, **Kempton Park** and **Sandown Park**, which are all less than an hour from central London by train. Britain's most famous flat race, the Derby, is run at **Epsom** in June.

HORSE-RIDING

FOR CENTURIES, fashionable riders have exercised their steeds in Hyde Park; **Ross Nye** will provide you with a horse so that you can follow a long tradition.

ICE-SKATING

ICE-SKATERS SHOULD head for London's best-known rink, **Queens**, where you can hire skates. The most attractive ice rink, open only in winter, is in the **Broadgate** complex in the heart of the City.

RUGBY FOOTBALL

RUGBY UNION, or rugger, is a 15-a-side game, once played only by amateurs, but is now a professional sport. International matches are played at **Twickenham Rugby Football Ground**. The season runs from September to April and you can watch "friendly" weekend games at local grounds. Top London teams **Saracens** and **Rosslyn Park** can be seen at their own grounds outside the centre of town.

SQUASH

SQUASH COURTS tend to be busy, so try to book at least two days ahead. Many sports centres have squash facilities and will hire out equipment, including **Swiss Cottage Sports Centre** and **Saddlers Sports Centre**.

SWIMMING

BEST INDOOR pools include **Chelsea Sports Centre**, the **Oasis** and **Porchester Baths**; for outdoor, try **Highgate** (men), **Kenwood** (women) and **Hampstead** (mixed bathing).

TENNIS

THERE ARE hundreds of tennis courts in London's public parks, most of them cheap and easily reserved. It can be busy in the summer, so book your court two or three days ahead. You must supply your own racquet and balls. Good public tennis courts include the following: **Holland Park**, **Parliament Hill** and **Swiss Cottage**.

Tickets for the Centre Court of the **All England Lawn Tennis Club** at Wimbledon are hard to obtain – it is possibly easier to enter the tournament as a player than to obtain tickets for Centre Court; try queueing overnight, or queue for return tickets after lunch on the day – for a bargain price, you can still enjoy a good four hours of tennis. (*See p249.*)

TRADITIONAL SPORTS

AN OLD LONDON tradition is the University Boat Race, held in March or April, when teams from Oxford and Cambridge row from Putney to Mortlake *(see p56)*; a newer tradition is the London Marathon, which is run from Greenwich to The Mall at Westminster *(see p56)* on an April Sunday. You can watch croquet at the **Hurlingham Club** and medieval (real) tennis at **Queen's Club**.

WATER SPORTS

THERE ARE FACILITIES for a wide variety of water sports at the **Docklands Sailing and Water Sports Centre**. You can choose from sports such as windsurfing, dinghy sailing, powerboating, waterskiing and canoeing. Rowing boats are also available for hire by the hour on the calmer, central London waters of the **Serpentine** in Hyde Park and **Regent's Park Lake**.

WORKING OUT

MOST SPORTS centres have gymnasiums, work-out studios and health clubs. If you are a member of the YMCA, you'll be able to use the excellent facilities at the **Central YMCA**. **Jubilee Hall** and **Swiss Cottage Sports Centre** both offer a variety of aerobic classes, keep-fit and weight training. For those who have overdone it, the **Chelsea Sports Centre** has a sports injury clinic.

DIRECTORY

General Sports Information Line
☎ 020 7222 8000.

Greater London Sports Council
☎ 020-7273 1500.

All England Lawn Tennis and Croquet Club
Church Rd, Wimbledon SW19. ☎ 020-8946 2244.

Arsenal Stadium
Avenell Rd, Highbury N5.
☎ 020-7704 4000.

Ascot Racecourse
Ascot, Berkshire.
☎ 01344 622211.

Broadgate Ice Rink
Broadgate Circle EC2.
Map 7 C5.
☎ 020-7505 4068.

Central YMCA
112 Great Russell St WC1. Map 13 B1.
☎ 020-7637 8131.

Chelsea Football Club
Stamford Bridge SW6.
☎ 020-7385 5545.

Chelsea Sports Centre
Chelsea Manor St SW3.
Map 19 B3.
☎ 020-7352 6985.

Chessington Golf Course
Garrison Lane, Surrey.
☎ 020-8391 0948.

Docklands Sailing and Watersports Centre
235a Westferry Rd, E14.
☎ 020-7537 2626.

The Embassy London Stadium
Waterden Rd, E15.
☎ 020-8986 3511.

Epsom Racecourse
Epsom Downs, Surrey.
☎ 01372 726311.

Hampstead Ponds
off East Heath Rd NW3.
Map 1 C4.
☎ 020-7435 3873.

Holland Park Lawn Tennis Courts
Kensington High St W8.
Map 9 B5.
☎ 020-7602 2226.

Hounslow Heath Golf Course
Staines Rd, Hounslow, Middlesex.
☎ 020-8570 5271.

Hurlingham Club
Ranelagh Gdns SW6.
☎ 020-7736 8411.

Jubilee Hall Sports Centre
30 The Piazza, Covent Garden WC2. Map 13 C2.
☎ 020-7836 4007.

Kempton Park Racecourse
Sunbury on Thames, Middx.
☎ 01932 782292.

Kenwood and Highgate Ponds
Millfield Lane N6. Map 2 E3.
☎ 020-7485 3873.

Linford Christie Stadium
Du Cane Rd W12.
☎ 020-8743 3401.

Lord's Cricket Ground
St John's Wood NW8.

Map 3 A3.
☎ 020-7289 1611.

Oasis Swimming Pool & Sports Centre
32 Endell St WC2.
Map 13 B1.
☎ 020-7831 1804.

Oval Cricket Ground
Kennington Oval SE11.
Map 22 D4.
☎ 020-7582 6660.

Parliament Hill
Highgate Rd NW5.
Map 2 E5.
☎ 020-7435 8998 *(athletics)*.
☎ 020-7284 3779 *(tennis)*.

Porchester Centre
Queensway W2.
Map 10 D1.
☎ 020-7792 2919.

Queen's Club (Real Tennis)
Palliser Rd W14.
Map 17 A3.
☎ 020-7385 3421.

Queens Ice Skating Club
17 Queensway W2.
Map 10 E2.
☎ 020-7229 0172.

Regent's Park Lake
Regent's Park NW1.
Map 3 C3.
☎ 020-7486 7905.

Richmond Park Golf
Roehampton Gate, Priory Lane SW15.
☎ 020-8876 3205.

Rosslyn Park Rugby
Priory Lane, Upper Richmond Rd SW15.
☎ 020-8876 1879.

Ross Nye Stables
8 Bathurst Mews W2.
Map 11 A2.
☎ 020-7262 3791.

Saddlers Sports Centre
Goswell Rd EC1.
Map 6 F3.
☎ 020-7253 9285.

Sandown Park Racecourse
Esher, Surrey.
☎ 01372 463072.

Saracens Rugby Football Club
5 Vicarage Rd, Watford, Hertfordshire, WD1.
☎ 01923 496 200.

Serpentine
Hyde Park W2.
Map 11 B4.
☎ 020-7706 3422.

Swiss Cottage Sports Centre
Winchester Rd NW3.
☎ 020-7413 6490.

Tottenham Hotspur FC
White Hart Lane, 748 High Rd N17.
☎ 020-8365 5050.

Twickenham Rugby Ground
Whitton Rd, Twickenham, Middlesex.
☎ 020-8892 2000.

Walthamstow Stadium
Chingford Rd E4.
☎ 020-8498 3300.

West Ham United
Boleyn Ground, Green St, Upton Park E13.
☎ 020-8548 2700.

CHILDREN'S LONDON

LONDON OFFERS children a potential goldmine of fun, excitement and adventure. Each year finds new attractions and sights opening up and older ones being updated.

First-time visitors may want to watch traditional ceremonies *(see pp52–5)* or visit famous buildings *(see p35)*, but these are merely the tip of the iceberg. While London's parks, zoos and

Humpty Dumpty doll

adventure playgrounds provide outdoor activities there are also loads of workshops, activity centres and museums providing quizzes, hands-on experiments and interactive displays. A day out needn't be costly: children are entitled to reduced fares on London Transport and lower admission prices at museums. Some of London's star attractions, for instance all the ceremonies, are free.

PRACTICAL ADVICE

A LITTLE PLANNING is the key to a successful outing. You may want to check the opening hours of the places you plan to visit in advance, by telephone. Work out your journey thoroughly using the tube map at the end of this book. If you are travelling with very young children remember that there will be queues at the Underground stations or bus stops near popular sights. These will be long during peak hours, so buy your tickets or a Travelcard in advance *(see p362).*

Children under 5 can travel free on buses and tubes and child fares operate for all children between the ages of 5 and 15. (Children of 14 and 15, and those who look older than they are, need to have a Photocard.) Children very often enjoy using public transport, especially when it's

Punch and Judy show in the Piazza, Covent Garden

a novelty, so plan your outing carefully using one form of transport for the outward journey and another for the journey home. You can get around London easily by bus, Underground, taxi, train and riverboat *(see pp362–9).* Visiting all the exhibitions and museums as a family doesn't have to be

Covent Garden clowns

as expensive as it sounds. An annual family season ticket, usually for two adults and up to four children, is available at many of the museums and often costs only marginally more than the initial visit. In some cases you can buy a family ticket that covers a group of museums; for instance the Science, Natural History and Victoria and Albert Museums in South Kensington *(see pp198–213).* Being able to visit a sight more than once means that you won't exhaust your children and put them off museums for life by trying to see absolutely everything over one long, tiring day.

If your children want a break from sightseeing, most borough councils provide information on activities for children such as playgroups, theatres, fun-fairs and activity centres in their area. Leaflets are usually available from libraries and leisure centres, as well as local town halls. During the long summer school holidays (July to the beginning of September) there are organized activity programmes all over London.

CHILDREN AND THE LAW

C HILDREN UNDER 14 are not allowed into British pubs and wine bars (unless there is a special family room or garden) and only people over 18 can drink or buy any alcohol. In restaurants, the law is a little more relaxed. Those over 16 can drink wine or beer with their

EATING OUT WITH CHILDREN

The choosing chart (see pp290–93) in the front of the restaurants section of this book shows establishments that welcome children. But as long as your offspring are reasonably well-behaved, most of London's more informal and ethnic restaurants will be happy to serve a family. Some can also provide highchairs and booster cushions, as well as colouring mats to keep children quiet while waiting for their food to arrive. Many will also offer special children's menus with small helpings which, although fairly unadventurous, will cut the cost of your meal.

Over the weekend some restaurants (such as **Smollensky's On The Strand** and **Sticky Fingers**) provide live entertainment for children in the form of clowns, face painters and magicians. A number accept bookings for children's parties. It is always worth trying to book in advance (especially for Sunday lunch), so that you don't have to hang around waiting with tired and hungry children.

Coming up for air at Smollensky's On The Strand

London has a number of restaurants ideal for older children. Among these are the **Rainforest Cafe** and the **Hard Rock Café** on Old Park Lane.

For budget eating, try the Café in the Crypt, St Martin-in-the-Fields (see p102).

Dine with the elephants at the Rainforest Cafe

USEFUL ADDRESSES

Hard Rock Cafe
150 Old Park Lane W1. **Map** 12 E4.
020-7629 0382.

Rainforest Cafe
20 Shaftesbury Ave W1. **Map** 13 A2.
020-7434 3111.

Smollensky's On The Strand 105 Strand WC2.
Map 14 D2. 020-7497 2101.

Sticky Fingers
1a Phillimore Gdns, W8. **Map** 9 C5.
020-7938 5338.

---

meal, but you still have to be over 18 to be served spirits. In general, young children are rarely welcome anywhere they might create a nuisance. Some films are classed as unsuitable for children (see p331).

If you want to take your children by car, you must use seat belts wherever they are provided. Babies will need a special child seat. If you are in doubt, ask at any police station.

GETTING THEM OFF YOUR HANDS

MANY OF London's great museums (see pp40–43) and theatres (see pp328–30) provide weekend and holiday activities and workshops where you can leave children over a certain age for a few hours or even for a whole day, and the children's theatres are a great way to spend a rainy afternoon. A day at the fair is always a success – try Hampstead fair on summer bank holidays.

London has a great many sports centres (see pp338–9), which usually open daily and often have special clubs and activities to occupy children of every age.

If you want a total break, contact **Childminders**, **Annies Nannies, Kensington Nannies**, or **Pippa Pop-Ins**, London's hotel for children between 2 and 12.

CHILDMINDING

Annies Nannies
1 Hughes Mews, 143 Chatham Rd,
SW11. 020-7924 6464.

Childminders
9 Nottingham Street W1. **Map** 4 D5.
020-7487 5040.

Kensington Nannies
82 Kensington High St, W8.
Map 10 D5. 020-7937 2333.

Pippa Pop-Ins
430 Fulham Road SW6.
Map 18 D5.
020-7385 2458.

Airborne at the Hampstead fair

Bathtime fun at Pippa Pop-Ins

SHOPPING

All children love a visit to **Hamleys** toy shop or Harrod's toy department *(see p313)*. **Davenport's Magic Shop** and **The Doll's House** are smaller and more specialized.

Both the **Early Learning Centre** (many branches) and the **Children's Book Centre** have good selections of books. Some shops organize readings and signings by children's authors, especially during Children's Book Week, held in October.

Useful numbers Children's Book Centre [C] *020-7937 7497;* Davenport's Magic Shop [C] *020-7836 0408;* The Doll's House [C] *020-7736 4527;* Early Learning Centre [C] *020-7581 5764;* Hamleys [C] *020-7494 2000.*

Bears at Hamleys toy shop

MUSEUMS AND GALLERIES

LONDON HAS a wealth of museums, exhibitions and galleries; more information on those listed here is to be found on pages 40–43. Most have been updated over the last few years to incorporate some exciting modern display techniques. It's unlikely that you'll have to drag reluctant children around an assortment of lifeless and stuffy exhibits.

The Bethnal Green Museum of Childhood (the children's branch of the Victoria and Albert Museum) and Pollock's Toy Museum are especially good for young children.

For older children try one of London's Brass Rubbing Centres: the great Brass Rubbing Centre in the Crypt of St Martin-in-the-Fields *(p102)*, Westminster Abbey *(pp76–9)* or at St James's Church on Piccadilly *(p90)*. The Guinness World of Records Exhibitions *(p100)* at the Trocadero (close to Leicester Square), Madame Tussauds *(p224)* and Tower Bridge *(p153)* are all firm favourites with children.

The British Museum has fabulous treasures from all over the world, and the Commonwealth Experience and the Horniman Museum have colourful displays from many different cultures. The Science Museum, with over 600 working exhibits, is one of London's best attractions for children – its Launch Pad gallery will help keep them amused for hours. If you have the stamina, the Natural History Museum next door contains hundreds of amazing objects and animals from the world of nature. Included is a Dinosaur Exhibition incorporating a fabulous new model of a Tyrannosaurus Rex with movement and sound

Shirley Temple doll at Bethnal Green Museum

effects. Suits of armour built for knights and monarchs can be seen at the Tower of London. More up-to-date armoury and weapons, including aircraft and the tools of modern warfare, can be seen at the National Army Museum, and the Imperial War Museum. Also worth a visit is the Guards' Museum located on Birdcage Walk. London's colourful past is brought alive at the Museum of London.

The superb **London Aquarium** *(p189)*, on the bank of the Thames, offers close-up encounters with sea life from starfish to sharks.

THE GREAT OUTDOORS

LONDON IS FORTUNATE in having many parks and open spaces *(see pp48–51)*. Most local parks contain conventional playgrounds for children, many with modern, safe equipment. Some parks also have One O'Clock Clubs (specially enclosed areas for children under 5 with activities supervised by play-workers) as well as adventure

Puppets at the Little Angel Marionette Theatre, Highbury

Playground at Gunnersbury Park

playgrounds, nature trails, boating ponds and athletic tracks for older children and energetic adults.

Kite-flying on Blackheath (p243), Hampstead Heath or Parliament Hill can be great fun, as can boating in Regent's Park. A trip to Primrose Hill (pp266–7) can be combined with a visit to London Zoo and Regent's Canal (p227).

The large parks are one of London's greatest assets for parents who have energetic children. For a good walk or cycle ride, there is quite an abundance of parks all over London. For instance, there's Hyde Park in the city centre; Hampstead Heath up in the north; Wimbledon Common in southwest London; and Gunnersbury Park in west London. Cyclists should be sure to watch out for pedestrians and remember that some paths may be out of bounds.

Battersea Park has a children's zoo and Crystal Palace Park (Penge SE20) has a children's farm and a dinosaur park. Greenwich and Richmond Parks have herds of deer. For a relaxing trip, go and feed the ducks in St James's Park.

Tuojiangasaurus skeleton at the Natural History Museum

CHILDREN'S THEATRE

INTRODUCING CHILDREN to the theatre can be great fun for adults too. Get involved with the froth and mania at the **Little Angel Theatre,** or the floating fantasy of the **Puppet Theatre Barge** in Little Venice. **The Unicorn Theatre** offers the best range of children's theatre and the **Polka Children's Theatre** has some good shows.
Useful numbers Little Angel Theatre [C] 020-7359 8581. Polka Children's Theatre [C] 020-8543 3741. Puppet Theatre Barge Marionette Performers [C] 020-7249 6876. The Unicorn Theatre [C] 020-7700 0702.

Deer in Richmond Park

SIGHTSEEING

FOR SEEING the sights of London you can't beat the top of a double-decker bus (see pp366–7). It's a cheap and easy way of entertaining children, and if they get restless you can always jump off the bus at the next stop. London's colourful ceremonies are detailed on pages 52–5.

Children will also enjoy such spectacles as the summer fun-fairs in London's parks, the firework displays throughout London on

Boating lake near Winfield House in Regent's Park

Guy Fawkes Night (every 5 November) and the Christmas decorations in Oxford Street and Regent Street and Trafalgar Square's Christmas tree.

BEHIND THE SCENES

OLDER CHILDREN in particular will love the opportunity to look "behind the scenes" and see how famous events or institutions are run.

If you have a brood of sports enthusiasts, you should visit Twickenham Rugby Football Ground (see p339), Lord's Cricket Ground (p246), or the Wimbledon Lawn Tennis Museum (p251).

For budding theatre buffs, the Royal National Theatre (p188), the Royal Opera House (p115), and Sadler's Wells (p332) all offer tours.

Other good buildings for children to visit include the Tower of London (pp154–7), the Old Bailey law courts (p147) and the Houses of Parliament (pp72–3).

If none of the above satisfies the children, the London Fire Brigade (020-7587 4063) and the London Diamond Centre (020-7629 5511) offer more unusual guided tours.

SURVIVAL GUIDE

PRACTICAL INFORMATION

London has responded well to the demands of tourism. The range of facilities on offer to travellers, from cashpoint machines and bureaux de change to medical care and late-night transport, has expanded very quickly over the last few years. Whether or not you find London an expensive city will depend on the prevailing exchange rate between the pound and your own currency. It is known for its high hotel prices but even here there are budget options *(see pp272–5)*. Nor need you spend a lot on food if you choose carefully: for the price of a single meal at some Mayfair restaurants you could feed yourself, albeit modestly, for several days *(see pp306–8)*. The following tips will help you to make the most of your visit.

A walking tour of the City

AVOIDING THE CROWDS

Museums and galleries can be crowded with school parties, particularly at the end of terms, so it might be best to plan your visit to start after 2.30pm during term-time. At other times of the year, visit early in the day and try and avoid weekends if you can.

Coach parties are another source of congestion. They do, however, tend to follow a predictable path. To miss them, it is wise to steer well clear of Westminster Abbey in the morning, and St Paul's around the afternoon. The Tower of London is usually busy all day.

A lot of London can be seen on foot. Brown signs indicate sights and facilities of interest to tourists. Look out, too, for the blue plaques attached to many buildings *(see p39)* showing where famous citizens have lived in the past.

GUIDED TOURS

A good way to enjoy London, weather permitting, is from the top of a traditional open-topped double-decker bus. The **London Transport Sightseeing Tour** lasts around 90 minutes, and leaves every half-hour or so (10am–6pm) from various central locations. Commercial rivals, including **Back Roads Touring** and **Harrod's**, offer tours lasting anything from an hour to a full day. You can buy your tickets just before boarding, or in advance (sometimes more cheaply) at Tourist Information Centres. Private tours can also be arranged with many companies, for instance **Tour Guides Ltd** or **British Tours**. The best tour guides receive a Blue Badge qualification from the London Tourist Board.

You can also explore London by joining a walking tour *(see p263)*. Themed tours range from pub crawls to a jaunt in the steps of Charles Dickens. Check for details of the walks at tourist offices, or in listings magazines *(see p326)*.

Cruise boats operate on the River Thames – an excellent way of travelling the breadth of London *(see pp60–65)*.

Useful numbers British Tours [020-7734 8734; Back Roads Touring [020-8566 5312; Harrod's [020-7581 3603; London Transport Sightseeing Tour [020-7828 7395; Tour Guides Ltd [020-7495 5504; information for the disabled: [020-7495 5504.

OPENING HOURS

Opening times for sights have been listed in the *Area by Area* section of this book. Core visiting times in London are 10am–5pm daily, though many places stay open longer, especially in summer. Some major sights, like the British Museum, also stay open late on certain evenings. There are variations at weekends and public holidays. Opening times on Sundays are often restricted and a few museums close on Mondays.

Double-decker sightseeing bus with an open top

Queueing for a bus

ADMISSION CHARGES

MANY MAJOR sights, including London's cathedrals and some churches, either charge for admission or ask for a voluntary contribution upon entry. Charges vary greatly. The *Area by Area* listings tell you which museums charge for admission. Some sights have reduced-price visiting times and offer concessions. Telephone if you think you might be eligible.

The GoSee Card is a saver pass to 17 of London's major museums and galleries. Valid for either three or seven days, it is available from a wide range of tourist and travel centres.

Signposted information

ETIQUETTE

SMOKING IS NOW forbidden in many of London's public places. These include the bus and Underground transport systems, taxis, some railway stations, all theatres and most cinemas. Many London restaurants now have no-smoking sections. The great exception to the anti-smoking trend is pubs. ASH (Action on Smoking and Health) can give advice on smoke-free venues (020-7935 3519). Consult the Hotels and Restaurants listings (*pp278–85* and *pp295–305*) for details of places that cater for non-smokers.

Londoners queue for anything from shops, buses and post offices to theatre tickets,

takeaway food and taxis. Anyone barging in will encounter frosty glares and acid comments. The exceptions are commuter rail and rush-hour tube services, when the laws of the jungle prevail.

The words "please", "thank you" and "sorry" are used regularly in London; people sometimes apologize if you step on their feet. It may seem unnecessary to thank a barman for simply doing his job, but it should improve your chances of decent service.

Like any big city, London can seem alienating to newcomers, but Londoners are usually helpful, and most will respond generously to your request for directions. The stalwart British bobby (police constable on the beat) is also always patiently ready to help stranded tourists *(see p348).*

DISABLED VISITORS

MANY SIGHTS HAVE access for wheelchairs. Again, this information is listed in the *Area by Area* section of this book, but phone first to check that your special needs are catered for. Useful guides to buy include *Access in London*, published by Nicholson, *London for All*, published by the London Tourist Board, and a booklet from London Transport called *Access to the Underground*, available at main tube stations. **Artsline** gives free information on facilities for disabled people at cultural events and venues. **Holiday Care Service** offers many facts on hotel facilities for the disabled. **Tripscope** provides free information on transport for the elderly and the disabled.
Useful numbers Artsline [020-7388 2227; Holiday Care Service [01293 771500; Tripscope [020-8580 7021.

Box for voluntary contributions in lieu of admission charges

TOURIST INFORMATION CENTRES

THESE OFFER ADVICE on anything from day trips and guided tours to accommodation.

Tourist information symbol

If you need tourist information, including free leaflets on current events, look for the large blue symbol at the following locations:

Heathrow Airport
Location The Underground station. ⊖ *Heathrow, 1, 2, 3.* **Open** *8am–6pm daily.*

Liverpool Street Station
EC2. **Map** 7 C5.
Location The Underground station. ⊖ *Liverpool Street.* **Open** *8.15am–7pm Mon, 8.15am–6pm Tue–Sat, 8.15am–4.45pm Sun.*

Selfridge's
400 Oxford St W1. **Map** 12 D2.
Location The basement.
⊖ *Bond Street.* **Open** *9.30am–7pm Fri–Wed, 9.30–8pm Thu.*

Victoria Station
SW1. **Map** 20 F1.
Location The railway station forecourt. ⊖ *Victoria.*
Open *8am–7pm daily.*

You can also contact the London Tourist Board:
[*020-7932 2000.*
W *www.londontown.com*

Another service exists for information about the City of London area only (see pp143–59):

City of London Information Centre
St Paul's Churchyard EC4.
Map 15 A1. [*020-7332 1456.*
⊖ *St Paul's.* **Open** *Apr–Oct: 9.30am–5pm daily; Nov–Mar: 9.30am–12.30pm Sat only.*

Personal Security and Health

L ONDON IS A LARGE city which, like any other, has had its recent share of urban problems. It has also often been a terrorist target, and London life is sometimes disrupted by security alerts. Nearly all of these turn out to be false alarms, but they should always still be taken seriously. Never hesitate to approach one of London's many police constables for assistance – they are trained to help the public with any of their problems.

SUITABLE PRECAUTIONS

T HERE IS LITTLE likelihood that your stay in London will be blighted at all by the spectre of violent crime. Even in the run-down and rougher parts of the town, the risk of having your pocket picked, or your bag stolen, is not very great. It is far more likely to happen right in the middle of heaving shopping crowds in areas like Oxford Street or Camden Lock, or perhaps on a very busy tube platform.

Mounted police

Muggers and rapists prefer poorly lit or isolated places like back-streets, parks and unmanned railway stations. If you avoid these, especially at night, or travel round in a group, you should manage to stay out of danger.

Pickpockets and thieves pose a much more immediate problem. Keep your valuables securely concealed. If you carry a handbag or a case, never let it out of your sight – particularly in restaurants, theatres and cinemas, where it is not unknown for bags to vanish from between the feet of their owners.

Although London has a small population of homeless people, they do not present a threat. The very worst they are likely to trouble you with is a request for spare change.

WOMEN TRAVELLING ALONE

U NLIKE SOME European cities, it is considered quite normal in London for women to eat out on their own or go out in a group, perhaps to a pub or a bar. However, risks do exist, and caution is essential. Stick to well-lit streets with plenty of traffic. Many women avoid travelling on the tube late at night, and it is best not to travel alone on trains. If you have no companions, try to find an occupied carriage – preferably with more than one group of people. Best of all, take a taxi *(see p369)*.

Many forms of self-defence are restricted in the UK, and it is illegal for anyone to carry various offensive weapons in public places. These include knives, coshes, guns and tear-gas canisters, all of which are strictly prohibited. Personal alarm systems are permitted.

PERSONAL PROPERTY

T AKE SENSIBLE precautions with personal property at all times. Make sure that your possessions are adequately insured before you arrive, since it is difficult for visitors to arrange once in the UK.

Do not carry your valuables around with you; take just as much cash as you need, and leave the rest in a hotel safe or lock it up in your suitcase. Traveller's cheques are the safest method of carrying large amounts of money *(see p351)*. Never leave bags or briefcases unattended in tube or train stations – they will either be stolen or suspected of being bombs and therefore cause a security alert.

Report all lost items to the nearest police station (get the necessary paperwork if you plan an insurance claim). Each of the main rail stations has a lost property office on the premises. If you do leave something on a bus or tube, it may be better to call in at the address given below rather than to telephone.

Lost Property

Lost Property Offices
London Transport Lost Property Office, 200 Baker Street NW1. *Open weekdays 9am–2pm.* 020-7486 2496, *enquiries should be made in person;* Black Cab Lost Property Office. 020-7833 0996.

Woman Police Constable   **Traffic Police Officer**   **Police Constable**

Typical London police car

London ambulance

London fire engine

EMERGENCIES

LONDON'S EMERGENCY police, ambulance and fire services are on call 24 hours a day. These, like the London hospital casualty services, are strictly for emergencies only.

Services are also available to offer help in emergencies, for instance in case of rape. If there is no appropriate number in the Crisis Information box (see right) you may be able to obtain one from the directory enquiries service (dial 142 or 192). Police stations and also hospitals with casualty wards are shown on the Street Finder maps (see pp370–1).

MEDICAL TREATMENT

VISITORS TO LONDON from all countries outside the European Union (EU) are strongly advised to take out medical insurance. Any good insurance policy should cover against the cost of any emergency hospital care, specialists' fees and repatriation to your home country. Emergency treatment in a British casualty ward in a public hospital is free, but any additional medical care may be costly.

Residents of the EU and nationals of other European and Commonwealth countries are entitled to receive free medical treatment under the National Health Service (NHS). Before travelling, you should obtain a form confirming that your country of origin has adequate reciprocal health arrangements with Britain. However, even without this form, free medical treatment can still be obtained if you offer proof of your nationality, but there are exceptions for certain kinds of treatment which is why taking out medical insurance is always advisable.

If you need to see a dentist while staying in London, you will have to pay at least a small amount as dentist care is not normally free. This will vary, depending on your entitlement to NHS treatment, and whether you can find an NHS dentist. Various institutions offer emergecy dental treatment (see addresses right), but if you wish to visit a private dental surgeon, you should try looking in the Yellow Pages (see p352) or seek advice from your hotel.

MEDICINES

YOU CAN BUY most medical supplies from chemists and supermarkets throughout London. However, many medicines are available only with a doctor's prescription. If you are likely to require drugs, you should either bring your own supplies or get your doctor to write out the generic name of the drug, as opposed to the brand name. If you are not eligible to receive NHS treatment, you will be charged at the medicine's cost price; remember to get a receipt to support any medical insurance claim you may wish to make after your trip.

Boots, a chain of chemists' shops

CRISIS INFORMATION

Police, fire and ambulance services
[Dial 999 or 112. Calls are free.

Emergency Dental Care
[020-7837 3646

London Rape Crisis Centre
[020-7837 1600 (24-hour phoneline).

Samaritans
[08457-909090 (24-hour helpline). For all emotional problems.

Chelsea and Westminster Hospital
369 Fulham Rd SW10. **Map** 18 F4.
[020-8746 8999.

St Thomas's Hospital
Lambeth Palace Rd SE1.
Map 13 C5. [020-7928 9292.

University College Hospital
Gower St WC1. **Map** 5 A4.
[020-7387 9300.

Medical Express (Private Casualty Clinic)
117A Harley St W1.
Map 4 E5. [020-7486 0516.
Treatment guaranteed within 30 minutes, but a fee is charged for consultations and tests.

Eastman Dental School
256 Gray's Inn Rd WC1.
Map 6 D4. [020-7915 1000.
Private and NHS dental care.

Guy's Hospital Dental School
St Thomas's St SE1. **Map** 15 B4.
[020-7955 4317.

Late-opening chemists
Contact your local London police station for a comprehensive list.

Bliss Chemist
5–6 Marble Arch W1. **Map** 11 C2.
[020-7723 6116.
Open until midnight daily.

Boots the Chemist
Piccadilly Circus W1. **Map** 13 A3.
[020-7734 6126. **Open**
8.30am–8pm Mon–Fri, 9am–8pm Sat, noon–6pm Sun.

Banking and Local Currency

V ISITORS TO LONDON will find that banks usually offer them the best rates of exchange. Privately owned bureaux de change have variable exchange rates, and care should be taken to check the small print details relating to commission and minimum charges before completing any transaction. Bureaux de change do, however, have the advantage of staying open long after the banks have closed.

Cashpoint machine

BANKING

B ANKING HOURS vary in London. The minimum opening hours are, without exception, 9.30am–3.30pm Mon–Fri, but many stay open longer than this, especially those in the centre of London. Saturday morning opening is also more common now. All banks are closed on public holidays (known as bank holidays in the UK, *see p59*), and some may close early on the day before a holiday.

Many major banks in London have cashpoint machines that will allow you to obtain money by using your credit card and a PIN (personal identification number); some machines have clear computerized instructions in several languages. American Express cards may be used in 24-hour Lloyds Bank and Royal Bank of Scotland cash machines in London, but you must arrange to have your PIN linked by code to your personal account before you leave home. There is a 2% charge for each transaction.

Besides the main clearing banks, good places to change your traveller's cheques are **Thomas Cook** and **American Express** offices, or the bank-operated bureaux de change, which can usually be found at airports and major railway stations. Don't forget to bring along a passport if you want to change cheques.

BUREAUX DE CHANGE

American Express
30 Haymarket SW1. **Map** 13 A3.
📞 020-7484 9600.

Chequepoint
548 Oxford St W1.
Map 13 A1. 📞 020-7723 1005.

Exchange International
Victoria Station SW1.
Map 20 E1. 📞 020-7630 1107.

Thomas Cook
30 St James St
SW1. **Map** 12 F3.
📞 020-7853
6440.

Ways of paying accepted at bureaux de change

You can find facilities for changing money all over the city centre, at main stations and tourist information offices, and in most large stores. **Chequepoint** is one of the largest bureaux de change in Britain; **Exchange International** has a number of useful late-opening branches. Since, in London, there is no consumer organization to regulate the activities of the privately run bureaux de change, their prices need to be examined carefully.

CREDIT CARDS

I T IS WORTH bringing a credit card with you, particularly for hotel and restaurant bills, shopping, car hire and book-ing tickets by telephone. Visa is the most widely accepted card in London, followed by Mastercard (its local name is Access), American Express, Diners Club and JCB.

It is possible to obtain cash advances (up to your credit limit) with an internationally recognized credit card at any London bank displaying the appropriate card sign. You will be charged the credit card company's interest rate, which appears on your statement with the amount advanced.

MAIN BANKS IN LONDON

England's main clearing banks (those whose dealings are processed through a single clearing house) are Barclays, Lloyds, HSBC (formerly the Midland Bank) and National Westminster (NatWest). The Royal Bank of Scotland also has a number of branches in London with exchange facilities. The commission charged by each bank for changing money can vary, so check before going ahead with your transaction.

 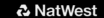

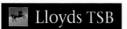 

The conspicuous logos of the main banks can be seen on most of London's principal shopping streets.

BARCLAYS

CASH AND TRAVELLER'S CHEQUES

BRITAIN'S CURRENCY is the pound sterling (£), which is divided into 100 pence (p). Since there are no exchange controls in Britain, there is no limit to how much cash you may import or export.

Traveller's cheques are the safest alternative to carrying large amounts of cash. Keep receipts from your traveller's cheques separately, and also make a note of offices where you will be able to obtain a refund if the cheques are lost or stolen. Some banks issue traveller's cheques free of commission to established customers, but the normal rate is about 1%. It is sensible to change some money into sterling before arriving in Britain, as queues at airport exchange offices can be very long. Do obtain some smaller denominations: shopkeepers may refuse to accept larger notes for small purchases.

English bank notes of all denominations always feature the Queen's head on one side

Bank Notes

English notes used in the UK are £5, £10, £20 and £50. Scotland has its own notes which, despite being legal tender throughout the UK, are not always accepted.

£20 note

£50 note

£10 note

£5 note

Coins of the Realm

Coins in circulation are £2, £1, 50p, 20p, 10p, 5p, 2p and 1p (shown here slightly smaller than actual size). They all have the Queen's head on one side.

2 pounds (£2)

1 pound (£1)

50 pence (50p)

20 pence (20p)

10 pence (10p)

5 pence (5p)

2 pence (2p)

1 penny (1p)

Using London's Phones

YOU WILL FIND A PHONEBOX on many street corners in central London and in main bus stations and every railway station. Inland calls are most expensive from 9am to 1pm on weekdays. Cheap rate applies before 8am or after 6pm on weekdays, and all day at weekends. Cheap times for overseas calls vary from country to country, but tend to be at weekends and in the evening. You can use coins, buy prepaid phonecards or use your credit card. British Telecom phonecards come in £2, £4 and £10 denominations and can be bought at some newsagents as well as post offices.

PHONEBOXES

THERE ARE two different types of BT phoneboxes found in London: old-style red phoneboxes and a new, modern style. The payphones are equipped to take either coins or cards. Other payphone companies' phoneboxes are becoming more common on London streets. Some of these accept coins only.

In those BT phones that accept cards, you can use BT phonecards, BT charge cards and most credit cards. The

Old BT phonebox   **New BT phonebox**

newer-style phoneboxes display whether cards, coins, or both, are accepted.

USING A CARD PHONE

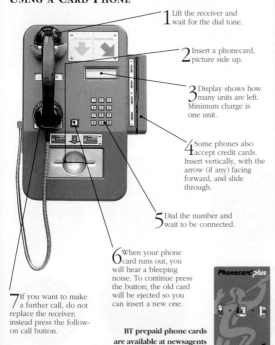

1 Lift the receiver and wait for the dial tone.

2 Insert a phonecard, picture side up.

3 Display shows how many units are left. Minimum charge is one unit.

4 Some phones also accept credit cards. Insert vertically, with the arrow (if any) facing forward, and slide through.

5 Dial the number and wait to be connected.

6 When your phone card runs out, you will hear a bleeping noise. To continue press the button; the old card will be ejected so you can insert a new one.

7 If you want to make a further call, do not replace the receiver; instead press the follow-on call button.

BT prepaid phone cards are available at newsagents and Post Offices

TELEPHONE DIRECTORIES

SHOULD YOU require any services that are not listed in this guide, try consulting one of London's telephone directories. The *Yellow Pages* comprehensively lists services throughout London, while *The Thomson Local* is area-specific. Both of these can be found at Post Offices, libraries, and often at your hotel. *Talking Pages* (0800-600 900) is a telephone service which is operated by British Telecom. It gives you the telephone number of anyone who offers the service you require in any part of London or the UK.

Directory enquiries (dial 192) can be dialled free of charge from public payphones and will give you any telephone number in the directory. You need to know the name and address of the person or business you wish to contact.

The *Yellow Pages* logo

REACHING THE RIGHT NUMBER

• All London codes were changed in April 2000.
• The area code for London is 020.
• Phone numbers in central London start with 7 and in outer areas with 8. The 020 prefix must be used if dialling between these two areas.
• Directory inquiries is 192.
• If you have any problems contacting a number, call the operator on 100.
• To make an international call, dial 00 followed by the country code (USA and Canada: 1; Australia: 61; New Zealand: 64), the area code and the number.
• The international operator is on 155.
• International directory inquiries is 153. You need a phonecard with at least £2 credit for an international call.
• **In an emergency, dial 999 or 112.**

Postal and Internet Services

Red and gold Post Office logo

BESIDES MAIN POST OFFICE branches that offer all the postal services available, London has many Post Office outlets which double as newsagents. Branches are usually open from 9am to 5.30pm Monday to Friday, and until 12.30pm on Saturday. First- and second-class stamps are available either individually or in books of six or twelve. First-class stamps can be used for letters and cards to the European Union. Post boxes – in all shapes and sizes but always red – are found throughout the city.

Old-style pillar box

POSTAL SERVICES

STAMPS CAN be bought at any outlet which displays the sign "Stamps sold here". Hotels often have post boxes in their reception areas. When writing to a UK address always make sure to include the postcode, which can be obtained from either the **Royal Mail** enquiry line or website. Letters posted within the UK can be sent first or second class. The first-class service is quicker, but more expensive, with letters usually

Air letters are all 1st class

2nd-class stamp   **1st-class stamp**

Books of twelve 1st- and 2nd-class stamps

reaching their destination the following day (except on Sunday); second-class mail takes a day or two longer.

Royal Mail
C 0845 7740740.
W www.royalmail.com

POSTE RESTANTE

IT IS POSSIBLE to receive mail in London by *poste restante*. This is a service where letters can be sent for collection. To use the service be sure to print the surname clearly so it will be filed away correctly. Send it to *Poste Restante* followed by the address of the post office. To collect your post you will have to show your existing passport or another form of identification. Post will be kept for one month. London's main post office branch is in William IV Street, WC2. Also, the American Express office at 30 Haymarket, London SW1 provides a *poste restante* service for its customers.

POST BOXES

THESE MAY BE either free-standing "pillar boxes" or wall safes, both painted bright red. Some pillar boxes have separate slots, which are clearly labelled, one slot for overseas and first-class mail, another for second-class mail. Initials found on the outside of the older style post boxes indicate the monarch at the time it was erected. Collections are usually made several times a day during weekdays (less often on Saturdays and Sundays); times are marked on the box.

ACCESSING THE INTERNET

LONDON HAS plenty of public access to computers and the Internet. Free Internet access is often available at public libraries, but you may have to book in advance. Internet cafés usually charge by the minute for computer use, and charges build up quickly, especially when including the cost of printed pages. EasyEverything, a chain of massive Internet cafés, has four main branches in central London: 9–16 Tottenham Court Road, 358 Oxford Street, 7 Strand (Trafalgar Square), and 9–13 Wilton Road (Victoria). Internet access is cheapest during off-peak times.

24-hour Internet access at the Europe-wide chain EasyEverything

POSTING ABROAD

AIR LETTERS go by Royal Mail's fast airmail service anywhere in the world and cost the same regardless of their destination. On average, it usually takes 3 days for them to reach cities in Europe, and 4–6 days for destinations elsewhere. Sending post by surface mail is more economical, but it can take up to 8 weeks to reach its destination. For express deliveries use the Royal Mail's **Swiftair** service. **Parcelforce Worldwide**, the national courier service, is comparable in price to **DHL**, **Crossflight** or **Expressair**.

Crossflight
C 01753 776000.

DHL
C 0845 710 0300.

Expressair
C 020-8897 6568.

Parcelforce Worldwide
C 0800 224466.

Swiftair
C 0845 774 0740.

INSURANCE

IT IS SENSIBLE to take out travel insurance to cover cancellation or curtailment of your trip, theft or loss of money and possessions and the cost of any medical treatment (see p349). If your country has a reciprocal medical arrangement with Britain (for example, Australia, New Zealand, and the EU), you can obtain free treatment under the National Health Service, but there are a number of forms to fill out. North American and Canadian health plans or student identity cards may give you some protection against costs, but check the small print.

If you want to drive a car in London it is advisable to take out fully comprehensive insurance, and you must always carry a valid driver's licence.

CUSTOMS AND IMMIGRATION

A VALID PASSPORT is needed to enter the UK. Visitors from the EU, the US, Canada, Australia and New Zealand do not require a visa to enter, nor are any inoculations or vaccinations necessary.

When you arrive at one of Britain's ports you will find separate queues at immigration control – one for EU nationals, others for everyone else.

European union has led to changes in UK customs and immigration policy. Travellers entering the UK from outside the EU still have to pass through customs channels: red exit routes for people carrying goods on which duty has to be paid; green routes for those with no payment to make (nothing to "declare"). If, however, you are travelling from within the EU you will find that these have been replaced by a blue channel – EU residents no longer have to "declare" goods. Random checks are made to guard against drugs traffickers.

EU residents are no longer entitled to a Value Added Tax refund on goods bought in the UK. Travellers from outside the EU can obtain one if they leave the UK within three months of the purchase.

International Student Identity Card

STUDENT TRAVELLERS

AN ISIC CARD (International Student Identity Card) entitles full-time students to discounts on things from travel to sports events. For students from the US, the ISIC also includes some medical cover, though this may not be sufficient on its own. If you don't have an ISIC, it can be obtained (with proof of student status) from the **University of London Students' Union** (ULSU) or branches of **STA Travel**. ULSU offers many social and sports facilities to valid union card holders and reciprocating educational establishments. **International Youth Hostel Federation** membership is also worth having for cheap accommodation in London.

EU nationals do not require a permit to work in the UK. Commonwealth citizens under the age of 27 are allowed to work in the UK for up to two years. Visiting students from the US can get a blue card which enables them to work for up to six months (you must get this before you arrive). **BUNAC** is a student club organizing work exchange schemes for students from Australia, the United States, Canada and Jamaica.

USEFUL ADDRESSES AND TELEPHONE NUMBERS

BUNAC
16 Bowling Green Lane EC1.
Map 6 E4. [020-7251 3472.

International Youth Hostel Federation
[01707-324170.

STA Travel
86 Old Brompton Rd SW7.
Map 18 F2. [020-7581 1022.

University of London Students' Union
Malet St WC1. **Map** 5 A5.
[020-7664 2000.

NEWSPAPERS, TELEVISION AND RADIO

LONDON'S PRINCIPAL newspaper is the *Evening Standard*, available from about midday, Monday to Friday. The Friday edition is worth getting for its listings section and reviews. International

---

PUBLIC TOILETS

Although many older-style, supervised public conveniences still exist, these have largely been replaced by coin-operated "Superloos". Young children should never use these devices on their own – they will find it almost impossible to operate the inner door handle.

1 If the green "vacant" light is shown, insert the required fee. The door located on your left will slide open.

"Vacant" light   Coin slot

2 Once inside, the door slides closed and locks.

3 To exit, pull down the inner door handle.

London newspaper stand

newspapers are sold in many newsagents. The *International Herald Tribune* is available on the day of issue; others may appear a day or more later. Five television channels can be seen with conventional receiving equipment: two run by the BBC (BBC1 and BBC2), and three independent (ITV and Channels 4 and 5). Satellite and cable networks are both available in the UK, and many hotels have these facilities for their guests.

The BBC's local and national radio stations are supplemented by many independent local companies, like London's Capital Radio (95.8 FM), a pop music station, and easy-listening Classic FM (101.9 FM).

EMBASSIES AND CONSULATES

Australian High Commission
Australia House, Strand WC2.
Map 13 C2.
[020-7379 4334.

Canadian High Commission
Haut Commissariat du Canada,
Macdonald House, 1 Grosvenor Square W1. **Map** 12 D2.
[020-7258 6600.

New Zealand High Commission
New Zealand House,
80 Haymarket SW1. **Map** 13 A3.
[020-7930 8422.

United States Embassy
24 Grosvenor Square W1.
Map 12 D2. [020-7499 9000.

INTERNATIONAL NEWSAGENTS

Gray's Inn News
50 Theobalds Rd WC1. **Map** 5 C5.
[020-7405 5241.

A Moroni and Son
68 Old Compton Street W1.
Map 13 A2. [020-7437 2847.

D S Radford
61 Fleet St EC4. **Map** 14 E1.
[020-7583 7166.

LONDON TIME

L ONDON IS ON Greenwich Mean Time (GMT) during the winter months, five hours ahead of Eastern Standard Time and ten hours behind Sydney. From late March to late October, clocks are set forward one hour to British Summer Time (equivalent to Central European Time). At any time of year you can check the correct time by dialling 123 to contact the 24-hour **Speaking Clock** service.

Standard British plug

ELECTRICAL ADAPTORS

T HE VOLTAGE in London is 240V AC. Plugs have three square pins and take fuses of 3, 5 and 13 amps. Visitors will need an adaptor for appliances.

CONVERSION CHART

O FFICIALLY THE metric system is used, but imperial measures are still common.

Imperial to metric
1 inch = 2.5 centimetres
1 foot = 30 centimetres
1 mile = 1.6 kilometres
1 ounce = 28 grams
1 pound = 454 grams
1 pint = 0.6 litre
1 gallon = 4.6 litres

Metric to imperial
1 millimetre = 0.04 inch
1 centimetre = 0.4 inch
1 metre = 3 feet 3 inches
1 kilometre = 0.6 mile
1 gram = 0.04 ounce
1 kilogram = 2.2 pounds

RELIGIOUS SERVICES

T HE FOLLOWING organizations can help you find a place to worship.

Church of England
St Paul's Cathedral EC4.
Map 15 A2. [020-7236 4128.

Roman Catholic
Westminster Cathedral,
Victoria St SW1. **Map** 20 F1.
[020-7798 9055.

Jewish
Liberal Jewish Synagogue,
28 St John's Wood Rd NW8.
Map 3 A3. [020-7286 5181.
United Synagogue (Orthodox)
735 High Rd N12.
[020-8343 8989.

Moslem
Islamic Cultural Centre,
146 Park Rd NW8. **Map** 3 B3.
[020-7724 3363.

Baptist
London Baptist Association,
235 Shaftesbury Ave WC2.
Map 13 B1. [020-7692 5592.

Quakers
Religious Society of Quakers,
173–7 Euston Rd NW1.
Map 5 A4. [020-7663 1000.

Evangelical
Whitefield House, 186
Kennington Park Rd SE11.
Map 22 E4.
[020-7582 0228.

Buddhist
The Buddhist Society,
58 Eccleston Sq SW1.
Map 20 F2. [020-7834 5858.

St Martin-in-the-Fields,
Trafalgar Square *(see p102)*

GETTING TO LONDON

L ONDON IS ONE of Europe's central routing points for international air and sea travel. By air, travellers face a bewildering choice of carriers serving Europe, North America, Australasia and the Far East. Stiff competition on some routes means that low fares are occasionally introduced to attract new passengers, but after a while fares always seem to level out again. Long-distance sea travel is a different proposition as few transatlantic liners operate these days. Cunard offers the only regular services on the *Queen*

British Airways 737

Elizabeth 2. There are efficient and regular ferry services from Europe. About 20 passenger and car ferry routes, served by large ferries, jetfoils and catamarans, cross the North Sea and the English Channel to Britain. Since 1995 the Channel Tunnel has provided a new, efficient high-speed train link – Eurostar – running between Europe and the UK, although work on the new rail line on the English side of the Channel will not be complete for some years. The tunnel also enables drivers to cross the Channel in a little over half an hour.

AIR TRAVEL

T HE MAIN United States airlines offering scheduled flights to London include Delta, **United**, **American Airlines** and USAir. Two major British operators are **British Airways** and **Virgin Atlantic**. From Canada, the main carriers are British Airways and **Air Canada**. The flight time from New York is about six and a half hours, and from Los Angeles about 10 hours.

There are regular scheduled flights to London from all the major European cities, as well as from numerous other parts of the UK itself, including northern England, Scotland and Northern Ireland.

The choice of carriers from Australasia is enormous. Well over 20 airlines share around two dozen different routes. The more indirect your route, the cheaper the fare; but remember that lengthy jet travel is bound to be stressful. **Qantas**, **Air New Zealand** and British Airways may be

Passenger jet landing at Luton

your first thoughts for comfort and speed, but all the Far Eastern operators and several European airlines offer interesting alternatives.

Getting a good deal
Cheap deals are available from good travel agents and package operators, and are advertised in newspapers and travel magazines. Students, senior citizens and regular or business travellers may well be able to obtain a discount. Children under two (who do not occupy a separate seat) pay 10% of the adult fare; older children up to 12 also travel at lower fares.

Ticket types
Excursion tickets can be good buys, but they need to be booked up to a month in advance. They are subject to restrictions and cannot be changed without penalty. There are usually minimum (and maximum) length of stay requirements. Fares on scheduled flights are available through specialist agents at much lower rates. Charter flights offer even cheaper seats, but have less flexible departure times and can be less punctual.

If you book a cheap deal with a discount agent, check whether you will get a refund if the agent or operator ceases trading, and do not part with

the full fare until you see the ticket; you will have to pay a deposit to hold it. Do not forget to check with the relevant airline to ensure that your seat has been confirmed.

AIRLINE INFORMATION

Major Carriers
Air Canada
W www.aircanada.ca

Air New Zealand
W www.airnz.com

American Airlines
W www.aa.com

British Airways
W www.britishairways.com

Qantas
W www.qantas.com.aus

Singapore Airlines
W www.singaporeair.com

United Airlines
W www.united.com

Virgin Atlantic
W www.virgin-atlantic.com

Discount ticket agents
ATAB (Air Travel Advisory Bureau)
This regulatory organization will recommend a discount agency.
C 020-7636 5000.
W www.atab.co.uk

Trailfinders *(European and worldwide travel)* C 020-7937 5400.
W www.trailfinders.com

Flight Centre *(worldwide travel)*
C 0807-566 6677.
W www.flightcentre.com

TRAVELLING BY RAIL

LONDON HAS EIGHT main rail stations at which InterCity express trains terminate. These are scattered in a ring around the city centre. Paddington in west London serves the West Country, Wales and the South Midlands; Liverpool Street in the City covers East Anglia and Essex. In north London, Euston, St Pancras and King's Cross serve northern and central Britain. In the south, Charing Cross, Victoria and Waterloo serve the whole of southern England and are also the termini for travel by ferry and train from Europe. Since 1995, **Eurostar** has operated the Channel Tunnel rail service, with trains running from Waterloo International to Paris and Brussels.

All of London's stations have had recent facelifts and are now smart and modern

Station concourse at Liverpool Street

Rail information point *(see p347)*

with many facilities for the traveller, such as bureaux de change and shops selling food, books and confectionery.

Information about rail services is quite easy to find; most rail stations have an information point detailing times, prices and destinations. In addition, constantly updated details of services are screened on monitors dotted around the stations. Railway staff are usually helpful and courteous.

If your ferry ticket does not include the price of rail travel to the centre of London, tickets can be bought at the clearly signed ticket offices or automatic machines *(see p368)*. You may decide to buy a Travelcard from the first day you are in London *(see p362)*.

Eurostar London Waterloo International
☎ 0870 600 0792.
W www.eurostar.com
National Rail Enquiries
☎ 0845 748 4950.

COACH SERVICES

THE MAIN COACH station in London is on Buckingham Palace Road (about 10 minutes' walk from Victoria railway station). You can travel to London by coach from many European cities, but the majority of services travelling through London are from within the UK. National Express runs to about 1,000 British destinations, but other companies depart from this station, too. Coach travel is cheaper than the railway, but journeys are longer and arrival times can be unpredictable. **National Express** coaches can be very comfortable and normally have sophisticated facilities. **London Country** buses operate within 40 miles (64 km) of London.

Coach companies London Country Bus ☎ 01737-240501; National Express ☎ 0870-580 8080.

CROSSING THE CHANNEL

Britain's sea links with Europe were finally joined by a landlink in 1995, when the Channel Tunnel opened. **Eurotunnel** operates a drive-on-drive-off train service for cars between Folkestone and Calais which runs about three times an hour with a journey time of 35 minutes.

A network of ferry services also operates between British and Continental ports. Ferry crossings to and from the Continent are operated by **P&O Stena Line, P&O Portsmouth, SeaFrance** and **Brittany Ferries**. Fast catamaran Seacat services between Dover and Calais and Dover and Ostend are run by **Hoverspeed**, which also operates between Newhaven and Dieppe. The shortest crossings are not necessarily the cheapest; you pay both for the speed of your journey and the convenience.

Cross-channel ferry

Contact Brittany Ferries W www.brittany-ferries.com ☎ 0870 536 0360; Eurotunnel W www.eurotunnel. co.uk ☎ 0870 535 3535; Hoverspeed W www.hoverspeed.com ☎ 0870 524 0241; P&O Portsmouth W www.poportsmouth.com ☎ 0870 242 4999; P&O Stena Line W www.posl. com ☎ 0870 600 0600; SeaFrance W www. seafrance.com ☎ 0870 571 1711.

London's Airports

LONDON'S TWO MAIN airports, Heathrow and Gatwick, are supported by Luton, Stansted and London City airports *(see p361)*. Heathrow is well connected to the city centre by tube, while the rest of the airports have convenient train or coach links. Each airport has facilities from banks and bureaux de change to shops, restaurants and nearby hotels. Check which airport you are landing at so you can plan the last stages of your journey.

Access to the Underground in the arrival terminal at Heathrow

British Airways passenger jet at Heathrow airport

HEATHROW (LHR)

HEATHROW IN WEST London (airport information 0870-0000123) is the world's busiest international airport. Mainly scheduled long-haul aircraft land here, and a fifth terminal is being planned to cope with the rising levels of air traffic to the UK. Money exchange and left luggage facilities, chemists, baby care rooms, shops and restaurants are found in all terminals.

All of the four terminals are linked to the Underground system by a variety of moving walkways, passageways and lifts. Just follow the clearly marked directions posted throughout the terminals and you can't go wrong. London Underground runs a regular service on the Piccadilly line. The tube journey into central London normally takes about 40 minutes (add 10 minutes more from terminal 4).

Road links for Heathrow can be very congested, and are not recommended if your schedule is tight.

The best way to travel into London from Heathrow is the Heathrow Express to Paddington. Trains run every 15 minutes between 5am and 11.30pm. The journey takes a

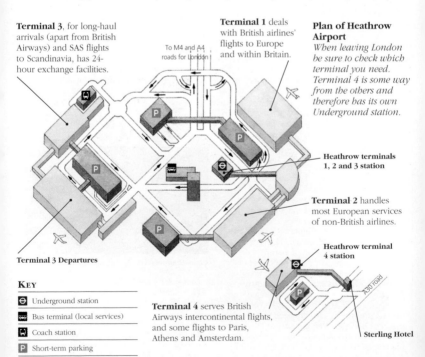

Terminal 3, for long-haul arrivals (apart from British Airways) and SAS flights to Scandinavia, has 24-hour exchange facilities.

Terminal 1 deals with British airlines' flights to Europe and within Britain.

To M4 and A4 roads for London

Plan of Heathrow Airport
When leaving London be sure to check which terminal you need. Terminal 4 is some way from the others and therefore has its own Underground station.

Heathrow terminals 1, 2 and 3 station

Terminal 2 handles most European services of non-British airlines.

Terminal 3 Departures

Heathrow terminal 4 station

Terminal 4 serves British Airways intercontinental flights, and some flights to Paris, Athens and Amsterdam.

Sterling Hotel

KEY

⊖	Underground station
🚌	Bus terminal (local services)
🚍	Coach station
P	Short-term parking
⇶	Direction of traffic flow

mere 15 minutes (allow 8 extra minutes for terminal 4). Paddington operates a check-in service for your return flight, serving most major airlines, accepting hold baggage and issuing boarding cards and seat numbers. Check-in is a minimum of 2 hours prior to your departure (1 hour if you have hand luggage only). Most participating airlines' check-in desks are open from 5am–9pm daily.

GATWICK (LGW)

GATWICK AIRPORT (airport information: 01293-535 353) is south of London, on the Surrey–Sussex border.

Distinctive logo of the Gatwick Express service

Unlike Heathrow, it handles scheduled and charter flights.

A large volume of package holiday traffic passes through Gatwick. This can cause long queues at immigration desks and security checks, so make sure to leave plenty of time in which to check in on your return journey if you want to avoid being rushed. Make certain, too, that you know from which terminal your flight home leaves.

Gatwick has fewer business facilities than Heathrow, but has a number of 24-hour restaurants, banks, exchange facilities and duty-free shops in each terminal.

Gatwick has convenient rail links with the capital, including Thameslink. The Gatwick Express train provides a fast, regular service into Victoria station. Journey time is 30 minutes; departures are every 15 minutes from 6.05am to 12.50am and hourly through the night.

Driving from Gatwick to central London can take a couple of hours. A taxi will cost from £50 to £60.

Gatwick's free monorail service linking the two terminals

KEY

⊉	Railway station
⊟	Coach station
P	Short-term parking
⊟	Police station
⊒	Direction of traffic flow

Plan of Gatwick Airport
There are two terminals at Gatwick: north and south. They are linked by a free monorail service, and the journey between them takes only a couple of minutes. Near the railway station entrance (which, if you are not arriving by rail, is clearly marked) you will find boards that state which terminal serves your carrier.

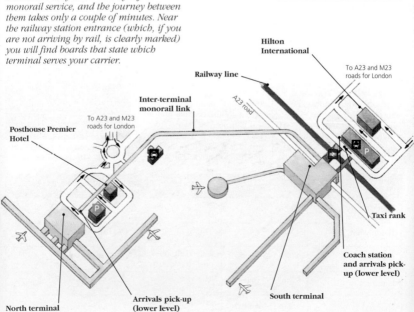

Hilton International

To A23 and M23 roads for London

Railway line

A23 road

Inter-terminal monorail link

Posthouse Premier Hotel

To A23 and M23 roads for London

Taxi rank

Coach station and arrivals pick-up (lower level)

North terminal

Arrivals pick-up (lower level)

South terminal

Entrance to Stansted's spacious modern passenger terminal

STANSTED (STN)

STANSTED IS IN ESSEX (airport information 0870-0000 303), to the northeast of London. It is the UK's fourth largest airport, and London's fastest growing, with a £500 million investment to bring its capacity up to 15 million passengers per year. It has been particularly successful as a base for the growing number of low-cost airlines. Its passenger terminal was designed by Sir Norman Foster, and was opened in 1991. All standard facilities are present including restaurants, bureaux de change and car rental desks. Two satellite buildings help to serve the growing number of passengers, making Stansted still a pleasant airport to use. Rapid-transit driverless trains shuttle between the three locations.

A rail link with London's Liverpool Street station, the Stansted Skytrain, runs every 30 minutes (journey time is 41 minutes). It stops at Tottenham Hale for direct access to the Victoria Line under-ground. A coach station is adjacent to the terminal. The M11 motorway links Stansted to central London by road.

LUTON (LTN)

LUTON AIRPORT (airport information 01582-405 100) is to the north of London, close to junction 10 of the M1 motorway, the UK's main arterial road. Its new passenger terminal opened in November 1999, along with a dedicated train station, Luton Parkway, with frequent trains to King's Cross station (journey time less than 40 minutes). A free shuttle bus links the airport with the station. A range of coach services also links it to London, with pick-up and set-down points directly outside the terminal. Following a £5 million refurbishment of the original terminal in summer 2000 as a departures/arrivals area, it should be fully able to deal with its 5 million passengers each year. Luton Airport is the base for the no-frills budget airline easyJet.

LONDON CITY AIRPORT (LCY)

LONDON CITY (airport information 020-7646 0088) is the capital's newest airport, having opened in 1987. It now serves over 1 million passengers each year. Not surprisingly, given its location just 10 km (6 miles) from the city, it is very popular with business travellers, a fact reflected in the standard of dedicated facilities (including meeting rooms, secretarial services and private dining rooms) in addition to the more usual airport essentials. An additional incentive is the check-in time: 10 minutes. While an estimated 70 per cent of passengers reach City Airport by private car or taxi (parking is adjacent to the terminal), public transport is also on hand. Shuttle buses link City Airport to the Jubilee line (30 minutes to the West End) and the Docklands Light Railway system.

London City airport, within sight of the city's Docklands area

AIRPORT	FROM CITY CENTRE	AVERAGE JOURNEY TIME	AVERAGE TAXI FARE
London City	10 km (6 miles)	Tube: 20 minutes DLR: 20 minutes	£8–12
Heathrow	23km (14 miles)	Rail: 15 minutes Tube: 45 minutes	£25–30
Gatwick	45km (28 miles)	Rail: 30 minutes Bus: 70 minutes	£40–50
Luton	51km (32 miles)	Rail: 35 minutes Bus: 70 minutes	£45–55
Stansted	55km (34 miles)	Rail: 41 minutes Bus: 75 minutes	£45–55

AIRPORT HOTELS

HEATHROW

Hilton London Heathrow
☎ 020-8759 7755.

Posthouse Premier
☎ 0870-400 8595.

Crowne Plaza
☎ 01895-445555.

Posthouse Heathrow
☎ 020-8759 2535.

GATWICK

Thistle Gatwick
☎ 01293-786992.

Hilton International
☎ 01293-518080.

Le Meridien Gatwick Airport
☎ 0870-400 8494.

Posthouse Gatwick
☎ 0870-400 9030.

STANSTED

Hilton London Stansted
☎ 01279-680800.

Harlow Stansted Moat House
☎ 01279-829988.

Swallow Churchgate
☎ 01279-420246.

LUTON

Ibis Luton Airport
☎ 01582-424488.

Luton Travelodge
☎ 01582-575955.

Hertfordshire Moat House
☎ 01582-449988.

LONDON CITY

Four Seasons Canary Wharf
☎ 020-7510 1999.

Ibis Greenwich
☎ 020-8305 1177.

Relaxing bar of the popular
Posthouse Heathrow hotel

KEY

🚉	Railway stations
Ⓔ	Tube stations
✈	Airport
▬	Motorway
▬	'A' road

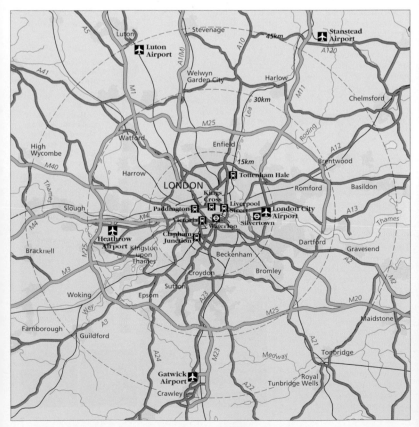

GETTING AROUND LONDON

LONDON'S PUBLIC TRANSPORT system is one of the busiest and largest in Europe, and has all the over-crowding problems to match. The worst and busiest times to travel are in the two rush hours, between 8am and 9.30am or later, from 4.30pm to 6.30pm. Within London and its suburbs, most of the public transport is organized by London Regional Transport (LRT). This consists of various types of bus, the Underground system, and Connex South Central (a privately operated overground train system). For any information you require about fares, routes and timings of the various transport services, ring 020-7222 1234 *(see p347)*, or visit one of the LRT Travel Information Centres which are to be found at Euston, King's Cross and Victoria mainline stations, as well as at Oxford Circus and Piccadilly Circus underground stations and Heathrow Airport.

Routemaster bus

THE TRANSPORT SYSTEM

THE UNDERGROUND (the "tube") is usually by far the quickest way of travelling around London. Services are, however, prone to delays and the trains are often crowded. Changing lines may involve a longish walk at some stations.

London is so large that some sights are a long way, even a bus journey, from any Underground station. There are also areas, often in the south, with no Underground service. Bus travel can be slow, and walking may be quicker.

Photocard and Weekly Travelcard

TRAVEL ZONES AND TRAVELCARDS

PUBLIC TRANSPORT in London is expensive compared with many cities in Europe. Short trips are relatively more expensive than the longer journeys; it is rarely worth-while getting on a tube to travel just one stop.

By far the most economical tickets are Travelcards – daily, weekly or monthly passes that allow unlimited travel on all forms of transport in the zones you require. (Six bands, called travel zones, extend from the city centre into the outer suburbs; most of London's main sights are located in Zone One.)

Travelcards are bought in train or Underground stations *(see p364)* and at newsagents displaying a red "pass agent" sign. For weekly and monthly tickets you need a passport-sized photo for a Photocard. One-day Travelcards (no photo needed) cannot be used before 9.30am from Monday to Friday. There are no restrictions on weekend, weekly or monthly Travelcards. If you are in London for four days or more, a one- or two-zone weekly Travelcard is probably the best pass to buy.

You can also buy a "carnet" of ten single-zone tickets for roughly 25% off full price.

LONDON ON FOOT

Once you get used to traffic driving on the left, London can be safely explored on foot but take care when crossing the road. There are two types of pedestrian crossing in London: striped zebra crossings marked by beacons, and push-button crossings at traffic lights. Traffic should stop for you if you are waiting at a zebra crossing, but at push-button crossings cars will not stop until the green man lights up. Look out for instructions written on the road; these tell you from which direction you can expect the traffic to come.

Beacons mark London's older-style zebra crossings

Pushing the button makes the red man, located on a pillar across the road, turn into a green man

Zebra crossing

Push-button control

Do not cross   Cross the road

Driving a Car in London

Sign for a car park

MOST VISITORS ARE BETTER off not driving in central London. Traffic moves at an average speed of about 11 mph (18 km/h) during the rush hour, and parking is hard to find. Many Londoners only take their car out at weekends and after 6.30pm on weekdays, when you are allowed to park on some single yellow lines and at parking meters free of charge. Remember that you must drive on the left.

Double yellow lines on road, meaning no parking at any time

PARKING REGULATIONS

PARKING IN London is scarce, and you should look closely at any restrictions (usually attached to lampposts). Meters close to the centre are expensive during working hours (usually 8.00am–6.30pm Mon–Sat). You will also need plenty of coins *(see p351)* to feed them. Two hours is usually the maximum time you can stay at any meter. National Car Parks (marked with the logo NCP) are available in central areas and are easy to find. NCP produces a free London Parking Guide showing its parks; write to 21 Bryanston Street, W1A 4NH or call 020-7499 7050.

Parking meter

You are not allowed to park along red routes or on double yellow lines at any time. Parking on single yellow lines is prohibited during working hours but you can park on them during the evenings or on Sundays provided you are not causing an obstruction. Resident permit zones are unenforceable outside posted hours, but remove your car before 8am. Steer clear of any parking areas marked "cardholders only". Parking near pedestrian crossings is always forbidden. In Pay-and-Display areas, you should buy a ticket for the appropriate time span to display on your windscreen.

CLAMPING AND TOWING

IF YOU PARK illegally or allow a meter to run out, you may well find your car has been clamped. A large notice slapped across your windscreen will inform you which Payment Centre you need to visit to get your car released (after paying a hefty fine). If you cannot find your car at all, it is quite likely to have been removed by a team of London's feared and hated car impounders. Their speed and efficiency are remarkable, the cost and inconvenience to drivers enormous: it is rarely worth taking the risk. The main car pounds are at Hyde Park, Kensington and Camden Town. Ring 020-7747 7474 and you will be told if they do have your car and whereabouts it is being held.

Traffic Signs
Every driver should read the UK Highway Code *manual (available from bookshops) and familiarize themselves with London's traffic signs.*

Illegally parked car immobilized by wheel clamp

CAR HIRE AGENCIES

Avis Rent a Car
📞 0870 606 0100. 🌐 www.avis.com

Europcar
📞 0870 607 5005.
🌐 www.europcar.co.uk

Hertz Rent a Car
📞 0870 840 0084. 🌐 www.hertz.com

Thrifty Car Rental
📞 01494 751600.
🌐 www.thrifty.co.uk

No stopping   **30 mph (48 km/h) speed limit**

No entry   **Give way to all vehicles**   **One-way traffic**   **No right turn allowed**

CYCLING AROUND LONDON

London's busy roads can be quite hazardous for cyclists, but the parks and quieter districts make excellent cycling routes. Use a solid lock to deter thieves, and wear weatherproof reflective clothing. Cycle helmets are not compulsory but are strongly recommended. You might also wear a protective mask to counteract traffic pollution. Bikes can be hired from **On Your Bike**.

Hire shop numbers and addresses On Your Bike, 52–54 Tooley St SE1. 📞 020-7378 6669.

Travelling by Underground

BAKER STREET

Underground sign outside a station

THE UNDERGROUND system, known as the "tube" to Londoners, has 273 stations, each clearly marked with the Underground logo. Trains run every day, except Christmas Day, from about 5.30am until just after midnight, but a few lines or sections of lines have an irregular service. Check when the last train leaves if you are relying on it after 11.30pm, and remember that fewer trains run on Sundays. The Docklands Light Railway links key tube stations to much of southeast London.

London Underground train

Reading the Underground Map

The 11 Underground lines are colour-coded and maps (see inside cover) called Journey Planners are posted at every station. Maps of the central section are displayed in the trains. The map shows how to change lines to travel from where you are to any station on the Underground system. Some lines, such as the Victoria and Jubilee, are simple single-branch routes; others, such as the Northern line, have more than one branch. The Circle line is a continuous loop around central London. Distances shown on the map are not to scale and the routes that lines are seen to take should not be relied upon for directions.

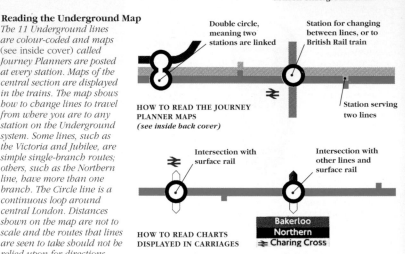

Double circle, meaning two stations are linked

Station for changing between lines, or to British Rail train

HOW TO READ THE JOURNEY PLANNER MAPS *(see inside back cover)*

Station serving two lines

Intersection with surface rail

Intersection with other lines and surface rail

HOW TO READ CHARTS DISPLAYED IN CARRIAGES

Bakerloo
Northern
≷ Charing Cross

BUYING A TICKET

If you are likely to be making more than two trips a day on London's Underground, the best ticket to buy is a Travelcard *(see p362)*. You can also buy single tickets or return tickets which are available from ticket offices and either of two types of automatic machine. The large machines *(see below)* take coins and £5 or £10 notes, and normally give change. You select the ticket type you need, then the station you

are travelling to, and the cost of the fare is automatically displayed. The smaller machines only show a choice of fare prices from which you select the correct one for your journey. They do not take notes, seldom give change, and are geared towards regular Underground travellers, who know the cost of their journey. All destinations fall within six specified London transport zones *(see p362)*.

1 Select the type of ticket you need from those shown: adult or child, single, return, or one-day Travelcard.

2 Press the button for the station you want to travel to.

3 The fare is shown here. Also indicated is whether you need to give exact money or if change can be given.

4 Insert either coins or a bank note. The machine will give you change if it has enough coins.

5 Collect your tickets and any change.

Tickets
Keep your ticket – you will need it at the end of your journey.

MAKING A JOURNEY BY UNDERGROUND

1 When you first enter the station, check which line, or lines, you will need to take. If you have any difficulty planning your route, ask the clerk at the ticket office for help.

Journey planner

Feed your ticket or Travelcard into the slot found at the front of the machine.

2 Buy your ticket or Travelcard from one of the automatic machines (see facing page) or the ticket office located in each station. If you wish to make a return journey by Underground, you will normally be given one ticket which you must keep until you have completed both journeys.

As soon as your ticket emerges, withdraw it and the gate will open.

The ticket office is near the ticket barriers in most stations.

3 The platforms are on the other side of the ticket barriers. These are easy to use if you follow the correct procedure.

Central line →

4 Follow the directions to the line on which you need to travel. In some cases this can be a complicated route, so keep your eyes open.

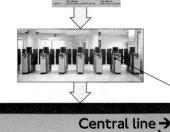

Central line Westbound platform 5 →

5 You will eventually find yourself with a choice of platforms for the line you want. Look at the list of stations if you are not sure which direction to take.

6 Most platforms now have electronic indicators displaying the destination of the next two or three trains and the length of time that you will have to wait before they arrive.

1 HAINAULT via Newbury Park
2 EPPING   5 mins

7 Once you have boarded the train and begun your journey, you can check on your progress using the line chart displayed in every carriage. As you pull into each station, you will see its name posted along the length of the walls.

On some trains, you must push a button to open the carriage doors.

Way out →

⇌ British Rail

Hammersmith & City →
Metropolitan and Circle lines

8 After leaving the train, look for signs giving directions to exits or to platforms for any connecting lines.

London's Buses

Distinctive logo used on London bus stops

Oᴺᴇ ᴏꜰ ʟᴏɴᴅᴏɴ'ꜱ most recognizable symbols is the old-fashioned, red double-decker Routemaster bus, but it is a less common sight now than it once was. Today, the need to modernize the buses has resulted in the production of many new vehicles which offer wheelchair access and more comfortable seating, but not all of which are of the traditional red colour. If you are able to get a seat, a bus journey is an undemanding and enjoyable way to see London. If you are in a hurry, however, it can be an extremely frustrating experience. London's traffic is notoriously congested and bus journeys can take a long time, especially during the morning and evening rush hours (8–10am and 4–7pm).

Bus Stops
Buses always pause at stops marked with the London Buses symbol (far left). At request stops (below), hail the driver by raising your arm. In practice it pays to do this at any stop.

Tickets on Routemasters
The conductor will issue you with the right ticket for your journey. Try not to pay with a large note.

Fɪɴᴅɪɴɢ ᴛʜᴇ Rɪɢʜᴛ Bᴜꜱ

Eᴀᴄʜ ʙᴜꜱ ꜱᴛᴏᴘ in central London has a list of main destinations showing which bus routes you need. There may also be a local street plan with each nearby bus stop letter-coded. Make sure you catch a bus going in the right direction; if in doubt, check with the driver. For details, contact **London Travel Information**.

London Travel Information
020-7222 1234.
www.transportforlondon.com

Usɪɴɢ Lᴏɴᴅᴏɴ'ꜱ Bᴜꜱᴇꜱ

Bᴜꜱᴇꜱ ᴀʟᴡᴀʏꜱ ʜᴀʟᴛ at bus stops marked with the London Buses symbol (see above), unless they are labelled "request" stops. Route numbers and destinations are displayed clearly on the front and rear of the bus. The newer buses have only a driver, who takes fares as passengers board. Routemaster services have both a driver and a conductor who collects fares during the journey. The driver or conductor will tell you the fare for your destination and give change (but not for

large notes). There are only two fares for buses in the capital. In central London, or Zone 1 (see p362), all journeys cost £1, while trips in outer zones (Zones 2–6) are 70p. Travel from any outer zone into Central London costs £1. Buying a Travelcard (see p362) is more economical, especially if you are making several journeys a day.

When you want to get off the bus, ring the bell as the bus approaches your stop.

Bus Conductor
Conductors sell tickets on London's Routemaster buses.

Usᴇꜰᴜʟ Bᴜꜱ Rᴏᴜᴛᴇꜱ

Several of London's bus routes are convenient for many of the capital's main sights and shops. If you arm yourself with a Travelcard and are in no particular hurry, sightseeing or shopping by bus can be great fun. The cost of a journey by public transport is far less than any of the charges levied by tour operators, but you won't have the commentary that tour companies give you as you pass sights (see p346).

There are also some sights or areas in London that are inaccessible by Underground. Buses run regularly from the city centre to, for instance, the Albert Hall (see p201), Chelsea (see pp192–97), and Clerkenwell (see p247).

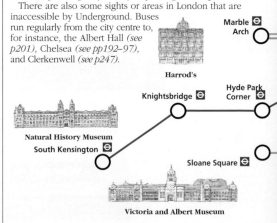

Harrod's

Natural History Museum
South Kensington 🚇

Knightsbridge 🚇

Marble Arch 🚇

Hyde Park Corner 🚇

Sloane Square 🚇

Victoria and Albert Museum

To stop the bus, press the bell located by the doors or near the stairs, just once.

Destinations are shown on the front and rear of buses.

To buy a ticket, have your money ready before you board.

Routemaster Bus
Board these buses at the rear. The conductor asks for your fare after you have boarded and found a seat.

Night Buses
These services run through the night from stops with this logo. One-day Travelcards are valid on them until 4:30am.

New-Style Bus
These buses are controlled by the driver and do not have a conductor. The driver collects fares as passengers board.

NIGHT BUSES

L ONDON'S NIGHT-TIME services run on several popular routes from 11pm until 6am. The routes are prefixed with the letter "N" before blue or yellow numbers. All these services pass through Trafalgar Square, so if you are out late, head there to get a ride at least part of the way. Be sure to plan your journey carefully; London is so big that even if you board a bus going in the right direction you could end up completely lost, or a long walk from your accommodation. As always, make sure that you employ a little common sense when travelling on a night bus. Sitting all alone on the top deck is not a good idea; night buses never have a conductor. Travel information centres can supply you with details of routes and time-tables for night buses, which are also posted at bus stops.

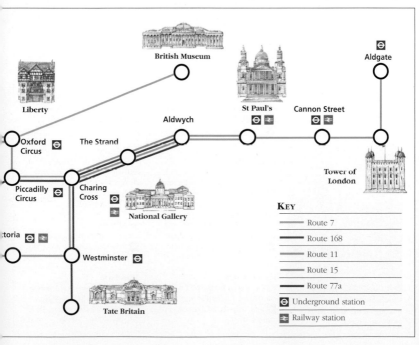

KEY

- Route 7
- Route 168
- Route 11
- Route 15
- Route 77a
- Underground station
- Railway station

Seeing London by Rail

Paddington

Railway station sign

Londons's train service is used by many hundreds of thousands of commuters daily. As far as tourists are concerned, rail services are useful for trips to the outskirts of the capital, especially south of the river where the Underground hardly extends. Trains are also ideal for day trips and longer excursions around Britain.

USEFUL ROUTES

Perhaps the most useful rail line for visitors to London is the one that starts off from Charing Cross or Cannon Street stations (services from here only run on weekdays) and goes via London Bridge to Greenwich *(see pp236–43).*

The Thameslink service also connects Luton Airport with south London, Gatwick Airport and Brighton via West Hampstead and Blackfriars.

USING THE TRAINS

London has eight main railway stations serving the whole of the southeast of England and beyond. Rail services travel overground and vary between slow stopping trains, express services to major towns and Intercity trains which travel throughout the UK. Make sure that you study the platform indicators carefully so that you get on the most direct train to the correct destination.

Some train doors will open automatically, others at the touch of a button or else by means of a handle. To open the older-style manual doors from inside, you need to pull down the window and reach outside. Keep well away from the doors while the train is travelling, and if you have to stand, make sure you hold on firmly to a strap or hand-rail.

RAIL TICKETS

All tickets must be bought in person, either from a travel agent or from a railway station. Most credit cards are accepted. Queues for ticket offices can often be long, so use the automatic machines similar to those on the Underground *(see p364).*

A bewildering range of train tickets exists, but two main options stand out: for travel within Greater London, Travel-cards *(see p362)* offer the most flexibility, while for longer journeys, Cheap Day Return tickets offer excellent value compared to the standard return fares. However, these are both only obtainable and usable after 9.30am.

Cheap Day Return tickets

DAY TRIPS

Southeast England has a lot more besides the capital to offer visitors. Getting out of London is fast and very easy by rail. For details of sights ring the English Tourist Board (020-8846 9000). Passenger Enquiries (0845 748 4950) will give you details of all rail services.

Boating on the River Thames at Windsor Castle

Audley End
Village with a stunning Jacobean mansion nearby.
≥ *from Liverpool Street. 40 miles (64 km); 1 hr.*

Bath
Beautiful Georgian city which has escaped redevelopment. It also has Roman remains.
≥ *from Paddington. 107 miles (172 km); 1 hr 25 mins.*

Brighton
Lively and attractive seaside resort. See the Royal Pavilion.
≥ *from Victoria. 53 miles (85 km); 1 hr.*

Cambridge
University city with fine art gallery and ancient colleges.
≥ *from Liverpool Street or King's Cross. 54 miles (86 km); 1 hr.*

Canterbury
Its cathedral is one of England's oldest and greatest sights.
≥ *from Victoria. 84 miles (98 km); 1 hr 25 mins.*

Hatfield House
Elizabethan palace with remarkable contents.
≥ *from King's Cross or Moorgate. 21 miles (33 km); 20 mins.*

Oxford
Like Cambridge, famous for its ancient university.
≥ *from Paddington. 56 miles (86 km); 1 hr.*

Salisbury
Famous for its cathedral, Salisbury is within driving distance of Stonehenge.
≥ *from Waterloo. 84 miles (135 km); 1 hr 40 mins.*

St Albans
Once a great Roman city.
≥ *from King's Cross or Moorgate. 25 miles (40km); 30 mins.*

Windsor
Riverside town; royal castle damaged by fire in 1992.
≥ *from Paddington, change Slough. 20 miles (32 km); approx. 30 mins.*

Getting a Taxi

The modern colours of
traditional London cabs

LONDON'S WELL-KNOWN black cabs are almost as much of an institution as its red buses. But they, too, are being modernized, and you may well see blue, green, red or even white cabs, with some carrying advertising. Black-cab drivers have to take a stringent test on their knowledge of London's streets and its quickest traffic routes before they are awarded a licence. Contrary to popular opinion, they are also among London's safest drivers, if only because they are forbidden to drive a cab with damaged bodywork.

London taxi rank

FINDING A CAB

LICENSED CABS MUST carry a "For Hire" sign, which is lit up whenever they are free. You can ring for them, hail them on the streets or find them at ranks, especially near large stations and some major hotels. Raise your arm and wave purposefully. The cab will stop and you simply tell the driver your destination. If a cab stops, it must take you anywhere within a radius of 6 miles (9.6 km) as long as it is in the Metropolitan Police district, which includes most of the Greater London area and Heathrow Airport.

An alternative to black cabs are mini-cabs, saloon cars summoned by ringing a firm or going into one of their offices, which are usually open 24 hours a day. Do not take a mini-cab in the street as they often operate illegally, without proper insurance, and can be dangerous. Negotiate your fare before setting off. Mini-cab firms are listed in the Yellow Pages (see p352).

TAXI FARES

ALL LICENSED CABS have meters which will start ticking at around £1.40 as soon as the taxidriver accepts your custom. The fare increases by minute or for each 311 m (340 yds) travelled. Surcharges are then added for every piece of luggage, each extra passenger and unsocial hours such as late at night. Fares should be displayed in the vehicle.

USEFUL NUMBERS

Computer Cabs (licensed)
020-7286 0286.

Radio Taxis (licensed)
020-7272 0272.

Ladycabs (women-only drivers) 020-7254 3501.

Lost property
020-7833 0996.
Open 9am–4pm Mon–Fri.

Complaints
020-7230 1631.
You will need to know the cab's serial number.

The light, when lit, shows the cab is available and whether there is wheelchair access.

The meter displays your fare as it increases, and surcharges for extra passengers, luggage or unsocial hours. Fares are the same in all licensed cabs.

Fare   Surcharges

Licensed Cabs
London's cabs are a safe way of travelling around the capital. They have two fold-down seats, can carry a maximum of five passengers and have ample luggage space.

H301 XYW

STREET FINDER

THE MAP REFERENCES given with all sights, hotels, restaurants, shops and entertainment venues described in this book refer to the maps in this section *(see* How Map References Work *opposite)*. A complete index of street names and all the places of interest marked on the maps can be found on the following pages.

The key map shows the area of London covered by the *Street Finder*, with the postal codes of all the various districts. The maps include the sightseeing areas (which are colour-coded), as well as the whole of central London with all the districts important for hotels, restaurants, pubs and entertainment venues.

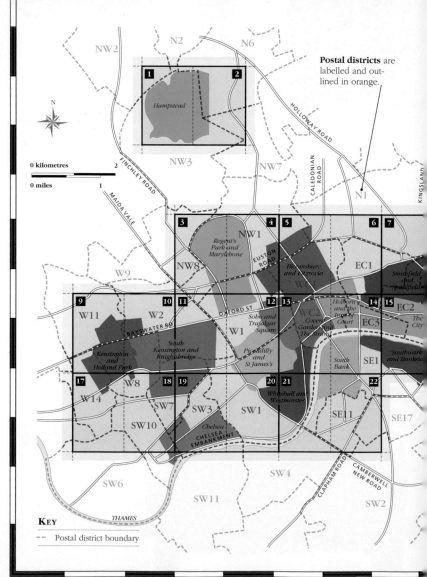

Postal districts are labelled and outlined in orange.

0 kilometres 2

0 miles 1

KEY

- - - Postal district boundary

HOW THE MAP REFERENCES WORK

The first figure tells you which Street Finder map to turn to.

Wesley's House and Chapel ⑫

49 City Rd EC1. **Map 7** **B4**.
☎ 020-7253 2262. ⊖ Old St.
House open 10am–4pm Mon–Sat.
Adm charge. ⬜ ♿ ✝ 11 am Sun.
🎞 📷 Films, exhibitions.

A letter and number give the grid reference. Letters go across the map's top and bottom; figures on its sides.

The map continues on map 15 of the Street Finder.

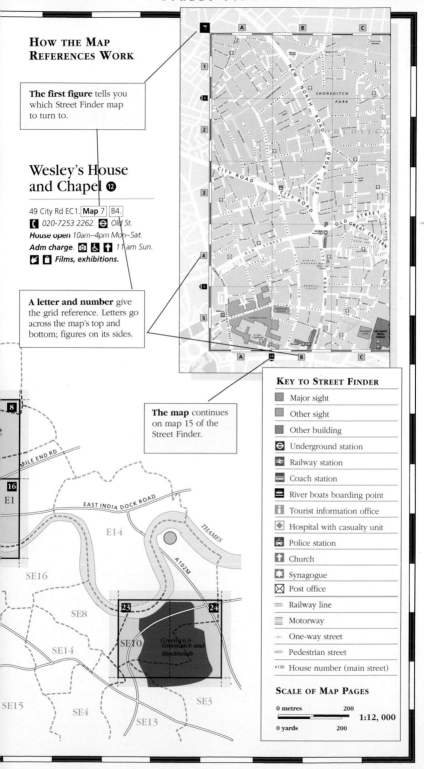

KEY TO STREET FINDER

🟥	Major sight
🟪	Other sight
⬜	Other building
⊖	Underground station
🚉	Railway station
🚍	Coach station
🚢	River boats boarding point
ℹ	Tourist information office
✚	Hospital with casualty unit
🚔	Police station
✝	Church
✡	Synagogue
⊠	Post office
═	Railway line
▬	Motorway
→	One-way street
▬	Pedestrian street
◄¹³⁰	House number (main street)

SCALE OF MAP PAGES

0 metres   200
0 yards   200

1:12,000

Street Finder Index

Each place name is followed by its postal district, and then by its Street Finder reference

Each place name is followed by its postal district, and then by its Street Finder reference

Each place name is followed by its postal district, and then by its Street Finder reference

Each place name is followed by its postal district, and then by its Street Finder reference

Each place name is followed by its postal district, and then by its Street Finder reference

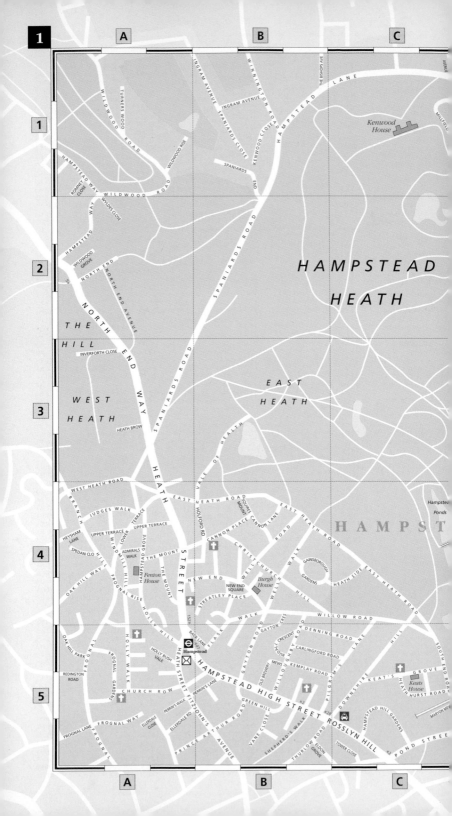

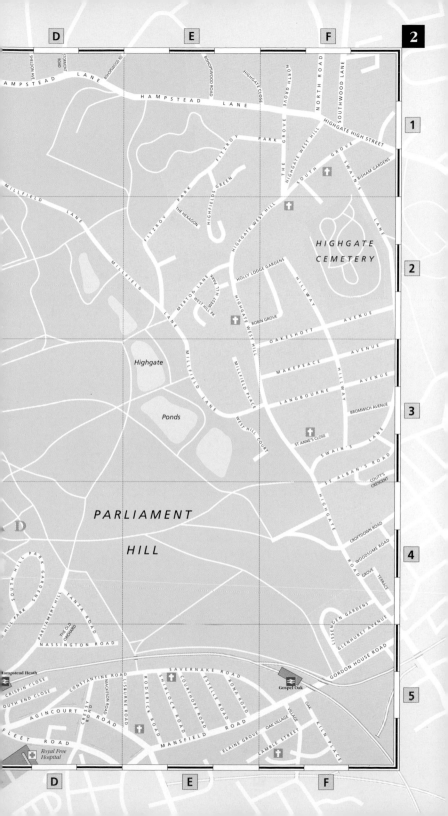

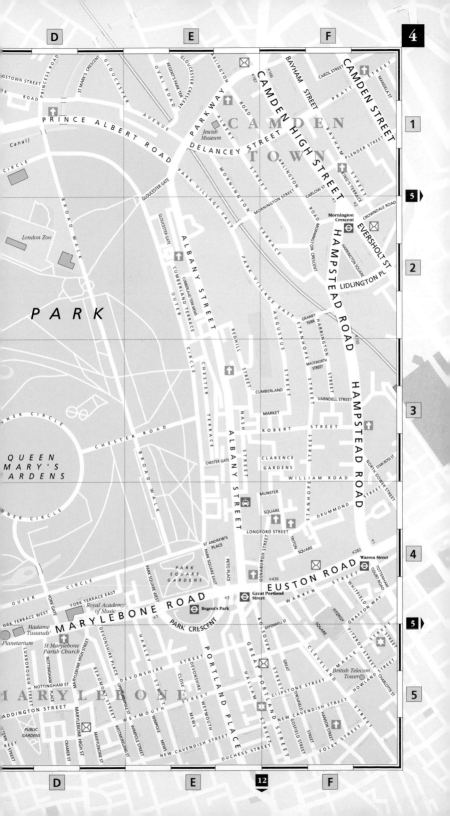

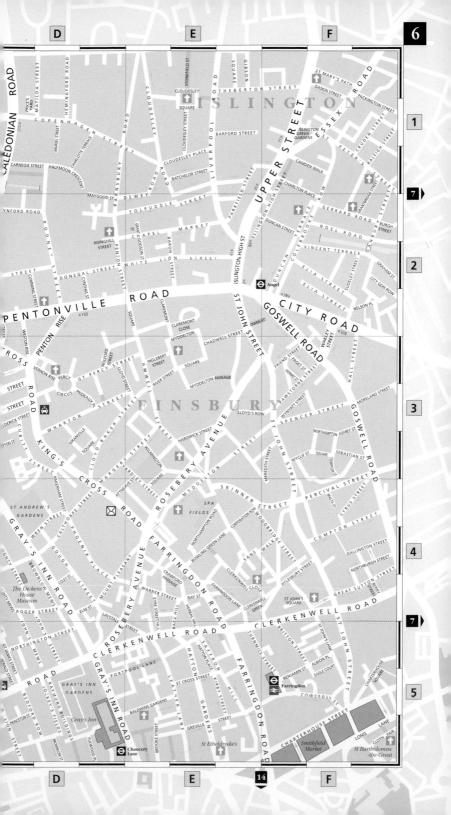

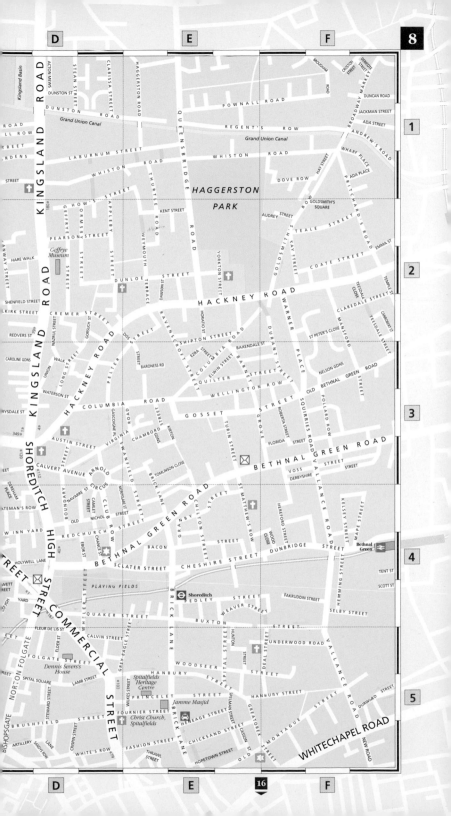

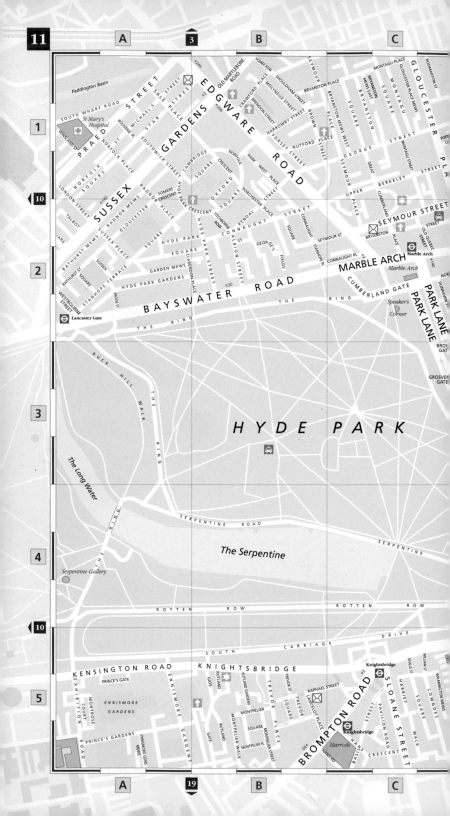

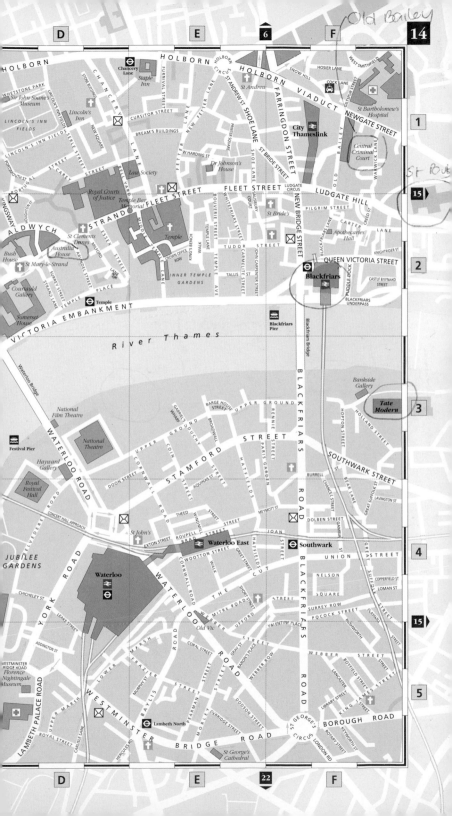

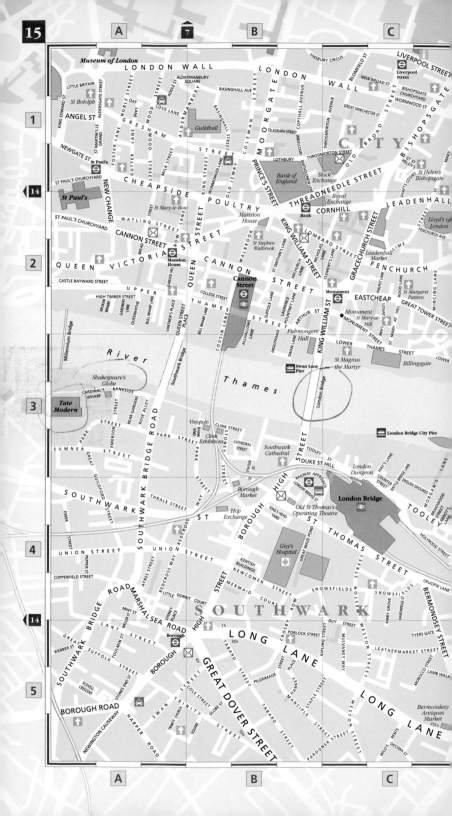

A   **7**   **B**   **C**

Museum of London

LONDON WALL

Little Britain
St Botolph
KING EDWARD ST
ALDERSGATE STREET
ALDERMANBURY SQUARE
LONDON
BASINGHALL AVE
LONDON WALL
FINSBURY CIRCUS
LIVERPOOL STREET
NEW BROAD ST
Liverpool Street
BISHOPSGATE CHURCHYARD
WORMWOOD ST

1
ANGEL ST
ST MARTIN'S LE GRAND
NEWGATE ST
St Paul's
NOBLE STREET
OAT LANE
LOVE LANE
WOOD STREET
ADDLE ST
ALDERMANBURY
Guildhall
GRESHAM STREET
BASINGHALL STREET
COLEMAN STREET
MOORGATE
THROGMORTON AVENUE
TELEGRAPH STREET
LOTHBURY
THROGMORTON STREET
GREAT WINCHESTER ST
OLD BROAD STREET
BISHOPSGATE
CITY
GT ST
ST HELEN'S
St Helen's Bishopsgate

14
ST PAUL'S CHURCHYARD
NEW CHANGE
St Paul's
ST PAUL'S CHURCHYARD
FOSTER LANE
GUTTER LANE
WOOD STREET
MILK STREET
KING STREET
IRONMONGER LANE
OLD JEWRY
PRINCE'S STREET
Bank of England
Stock Exchange
THREADNEEDLE STREET
Royal Exchange
Bank
CORNHILL
LEADENHALL
Lloyd's of London
FENCHURCH AVE

CHEAPSIDE
St Mary-le-Bow
POULTRY
Mansion House
LOMBARD STREET
GRACECHURCH STREET
FENCHURCH
Leadenhall Market

2
QUEEN VICTORIA STREET
WATLING STREET
Mansion House
CANNON STREET
QUEEN STREET
BOW LANE
GARLICK HILL
CANNON
St Stephen Walbrook
WALBROOK
KING WILLIAM STREET
ST SWITHIN'S LANE
CLEMENT'S LANE
NICHOLAS LANE
ABCHURCH LANE
GRACECHURCH STREET
FENCHURCH
St Margaret Pattens
ROOD LANE
MINCING LANE

CASTLE BAYWARD STREET
UPPER
HIGH TIMBER STREET
BRICKER WHARF
GARDNER'S LANE
QUEENHITHE
BULL WHARF LANE
VINTNER'S PLACE
QUEEN STREET PLACE
COLLEGE STREET
SUFFOLK LANE
LAURENCE POUNTNEY LANE
ARTHUR STREET
EASTCHEAP
Monument
Monument
St Mary-at-Hill
MONUMENT STREET
MARY AT HILL
GREAT TOWER STREET

Millennium Bridge
River
Thames
Shakespeare's Globe
CARDINAL'S WHARF
BANKSIDE
Tate Modern
Southwark Bridge
CANNON STREET
Cannon Street
THAMES
BELL WHARF LANE
COUSIN LANE
ALLHALLOWS LANE
ANGELPASSAGE
SWAN LANE
Fishmongers' Hall
KING WILLIAM ST
Swan Lane Pier
London Bridge
LOWER THAMES STREET
St Magnus the Martyr
Billingsgate
LOWER

3
Tate Modern
PARK STREET
EMERSON STREET
BEAR GARDENS
ROSE ALLEY
SOUTHWARK BRIDGE ROAD
PARK STREET
PARK
Vinopolis
BANK END
CLINK STREET
Clink Exhibitions
STONEY STREET
CATHEDRAL STREET
Southwark Cathedral
TOOLEY ST
London Bridge City Pier
London Dungeon
HAY'S LANE
BATTLE BRIDGE LANE
ENGLISH GROUNDS
MORGAN'S LANE
SHAD THAMES

SUMNER STREET
GREAT GUILDFORD STREET
THRALE STREET
BOROUGH MARKET
Borough Market
BEDALE ST
DUKE ST HILL
TOOLEY STREET
COUNTER STREET
BERMONDSEY STREET

4
SOUTHWARK
Hop Exchange
KING'S HEAD YARD
Old St Thomas's Operating Theatre
RAILWAY APPROACH
London Bridge
London Bridge
ST THOMAS STREET
HOLYROOD STREET
CRUCIFIX LANE

EWER STREET
UNION STREET
SOUTHWARK BRIDGE ROAD
UNION STREET
REDCROSS WAY
BOROUGH HIGH STREET
Guy's Hospital
KENTISH BUILDINGS
NEWCOMEN STREET
SNOWSFIELDS
SNOWSFIELDS
KIRBY GROVE
HARDWIDGE ST
TYERS GATE
LEATHERMARKET STREET

COPPERFIELD STREET
PEPPER ST
AYRES STREET
LITTLE DORRIT COURT
DISNEY PLACE
MERMAID COURT
CROSBY ROW
GUY STREET
WESTON STREET
MORROCCO STREET
LAMB WALK

14
SOUTHWARK BRIDGE ROAD
MARSHALSEA ROAD
LANT STREET
MINT ST
BOROUGH HIGH STREET
Borough
LONG LANE
PORLOCK STREET
KIPLING STREET
MULVANEY WAY
LEATHERMARKET STREET

5
SOUTHWARK BRIDGE ROAD
SUFFOLK STREET
TOULMIN STREET
STONES END ST
WEBBER STREET
SCOVELL CRESCENT
BOROUGH ROAD
NEWINGTON CAUSEWAY
GREAT DOVER STREET
SWAN STREET
NICOLE STREET
TRINITY SQUARE
TRINITY CHURCH SQUARE
GLOBE ST
PILGRIMAGE STREET
TABARD STREET
HANKEY PLACE
MANCIPLE STREET
STAPLE STREET
PARDONER STREET
WILD'S RENTS
DECIMA ST
LONG LANE
Bermondsey Antiques Market
HARPER ROAD

A   **B**   **C**

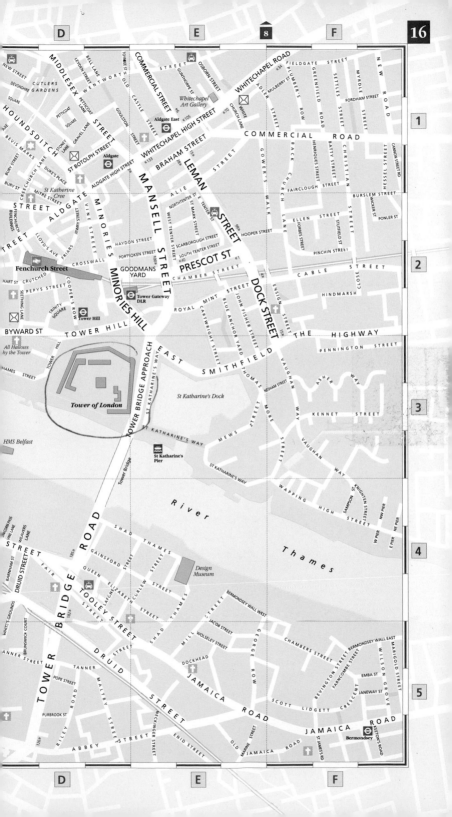

NEW STREET
DEVONSHIRE SQUARE
CUTLERS GARDENS
MIDDLESEX STREET
BELL LANE
LEYDEN STREET
WENTWORTH
TOWER STREET
OLD CASTLE STREET
COMMERCIAL STREET
GUNTHORPE STREET
OSBORN STREET
WHITECHAPEL ROAD
ADLER STREET
FIELDGATE STREET
MULBERRY STREET
PLUMBER'S ROW
GREENFIELD ROAD
SETTLES STREET
MYRDLE STREET
FORDHAM STREET
NEW ROAD

HOUNDSDITCH
AVE
BEVIS MARKS
BURY STREET
CREECHURCH LANE
DUKE'S PLACE
MITRE STREET
PETTICOAT SQUARE
GOULSTON STREET
CASTLE STREET
WHITECHAPEL HIGH STREET
Whitechapel Art Gallery
Aldgate East
BRAHAM STREET
COMMERCIAL ROAD
GOWER'S WALK
BACK CHURCH LANE
HENRIQUES STREET
BATTY STREET
CHRISTIAN STREET
FAIRCLOUGH STREET
ELLEN STREET
FORBES STREET
STUTFIELD STREET
BURSLEM STREET
WICKER ST
HESSEL STREET
CANNON STREET RD
PONLER ST

1

St Botolph Street
Aldgate
ST KATHERINE CREE
VINE STREET
MINORIES
GRAVEL LANE
STONEY LANE
JEWRY STREET
ALDGATE HIGH STREET
ALIE STREET
NORTHUMBERLAND ST
ST MARK STREET
WEST TENTER STREET
EAST TENTER ST
LEMAN STREET
HOOPER STREET
PINCHIN STREET

STREET
ALDGATE
FENCHURCH BUILDINGS
LLOYD'S AVE
FRIARS
CROSSWALL
MANSELL STREET
HAYDON STREET
PORTSOKEN STREET
SCARBOROUGH STREET
SOUTH TENTER STREET
CHAMBER STREET
CABLE STREET
HINDMARSH

Fenchurch Street
HART ST
CRUTCHED FRIARS
PEPYS STREET
SEETHING LANE
COOPER'S ROW
GOODMANS YARD
PRESCOT ST
ROYAL MINT STREET
JOHN FISHER STREET
BLUE ANCHOR YARD
ENSIGN STREET

2

TRINITY SQUARE
COOPER'S ROW
Tower Gateway DLR
MINORIES HILL
CARTWRIGHT STREET
DOCK STREET
VAUGHAN WAY

BYWARD ST
Tower Hill
TOWER HILL
EAST SMITHFIELD
THOMAS MORE STREET
NEDHAM STREET
THE HIGHWAY
PENNINGTON STREET

All Hallows by the Tower
TOWER HILL
St Katharine's Dock
ST KATHARINE'S WAY
ASHER WAY
KENNET STREET

3

THAMES STREET
Tower of London
St Katharine's Way
VAUGHAN WAY

HMS Belfast
St Katharine's Pier
Tower Bridge
ST KATHARINE'S WAY
MEWS STREET
MORE STREET
WAPPING HIGH STREET
SIMPSONS
KNIGHTEN STREET
W PIER
WW PIER
E PIER
NE PIER

River
Thames

4

UNICORN PAS
VINE LANE
WEAVERS LANE
BARNHAM ST
TOWER BRIDGE ROAD
SHAD THAMES
GAINSFORD STREET
QUEEN ELIZABETH STREET
CURLEW STREET
Design Museum
BERMONDSEY WALL WEST

ANNER STREET
WHITE'S GROUNDS
BRUNSWICK COURT
DRUID STREET
TOOLEY STREET
SHAD THAMES
MILL STREET
WOLSELEY STREET
DOCKHEAD
JACOB STREET
GEORGE ROW
CHAMBERS STREET
BEVINGTON STREET
BERMONDSEY WALL EAST
FARNCOMBE STREET
WILSON GROVE
MARIGOLD STREET

TANNER STREET
POPE STREET
DRUID STREET
JAMAICA ROAD
SCOTT
LIDGETT CRESCENT
EMBA ST
JANEWAY STREET
KEETON'S ROAD

5

PURBROOK ST
RILEY STREET
MALTBY STREET
ABBEY STREET
NECKINGER STREET
ENID STREET
OLD JAMAICA
MARINE STREET
JAMAICA ROAD
ST JAMES'S RD
Bermondsey

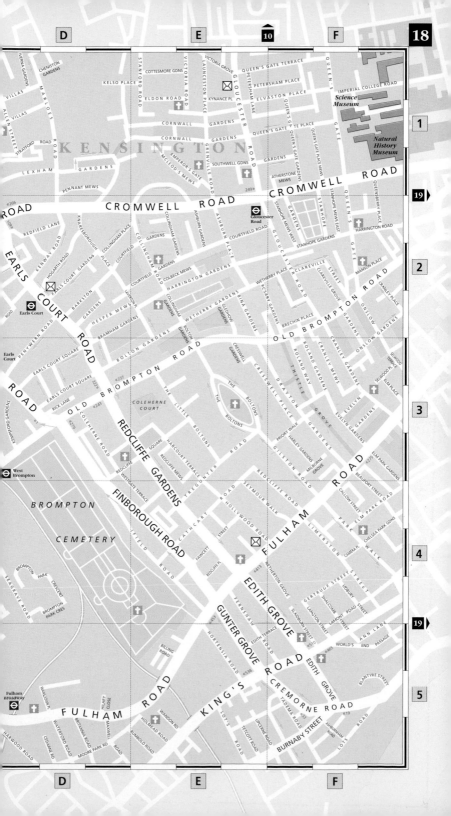

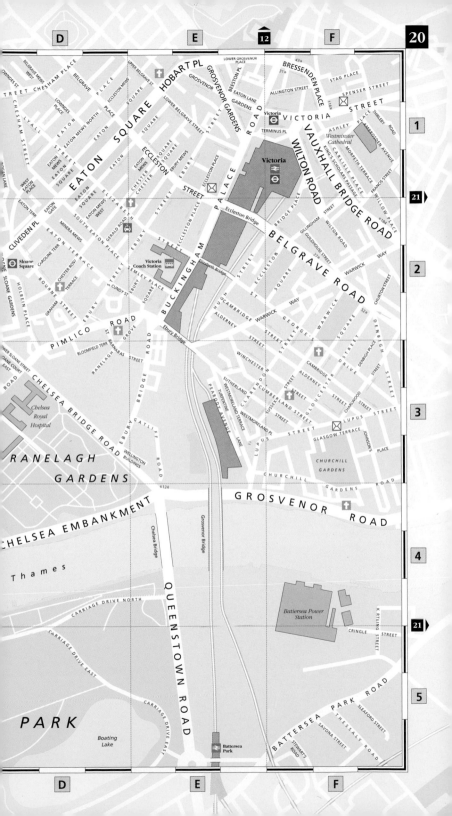

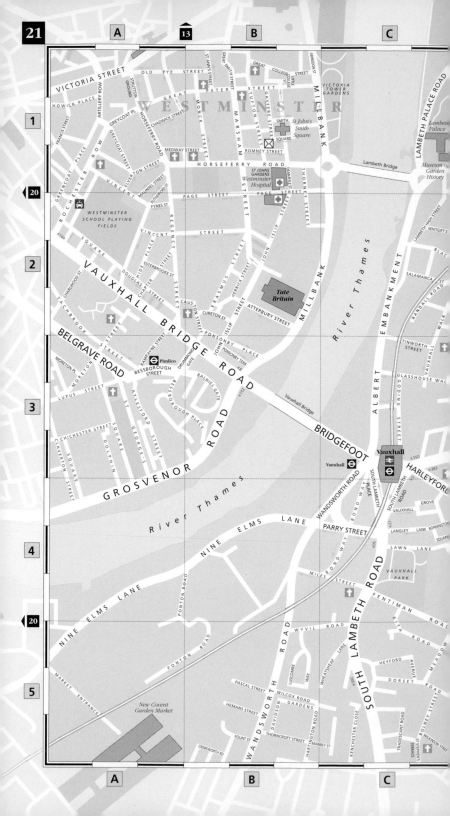

ARCHBISHOP'S PARK

CARLISLE LANE

HERCULES ROAD

COSSER STREET

KENNINGTON ROAD

KING EDWARD WALK

LAMBETH ROAD

ST GEORGE'S ROAD

GARDEN ROW

LONDON ROAD

ONTARIO STREET

GLADSTONE STREET

COLNBROOK ST

GERALDINE ST

Elephant & Castle

GERALDINE MARY HARMSWORTH PARK

Imperial War Museum

SAIL WALK

LAMBETH ROAD

BROOK DRIVE

WEST SQUARE

AUSTRAL STREET

HAYLES STREET

ELLIOTT'S ROW

BROOK DRIVE

GOSWIN STREET

PRATT WALK

SALL WALK

LAMBETH WALK

WALNUT TREE WALK

FITZALAN STREET

WALCOT SQUARE

ST MARY'S WALK

WALCOT SQUARE

LAMLASH ST

BROOK

LONGVILLE ROAD

HOLYOAK ROAD

DANTE ROAD

PLAYING FIELDS

NEWPORT STREET

SAVANT ROAD

GIBSON ROAD

LOLLARD STREET

OAKDEN STREET

WINCOTT STREET

GILBERT ROAD

MONKTON STREET

KEMPSFORD ROAD

RENFREW ROAD

WINCHESTER CLOSE

LAMBETH

L A M B E T H

PRINCE ROAD

BEAUFOY WALK

MARYLEE WAY

BLACK PRINCE ROAD

KENNINGTON ROAD

REEDWORTH STREET

CHESTER WAY

DENNY STREET

KENNINGTON LANE

NEWINGTON BUTTS

OVAL STREET

COTTINGTON CLOSE

COTTINGTON CF

CANTERBURY PLACE

PENTON PLACE

JONATHAN STREET

WICKHAM STREET

VAUXHALL STREET

ORSETT STREET

SANCROFT STREET

BLACK PRINCE ROAD

NEWBURN STREET

COURTENAY STREET

CARDIGAN STREET

STREET

KENNINGTON PARK ROAD

CLEAVER STREET

CLEAVER SQUARE

KENNINGTON

Kennington

BRAGANZA STREET

ALBERTA STREET

AMELIA STREET

DELVERTON ROAD

MANOR PLACE

CHAPTER RD

TYERS TERRACE

LOUGHBOROUGH STREET

AVELINE STREET

MONTFORD PLACE

METHLEY STREET

MILVERTON STREET

RAVENSDON STREET

LAUD STREET

DE HARMSWORTH

GAZA STREET

FAUNCE STREET

DODDINGTON GROVE

WESTCOTT ROAD

LORRIMORE SQ

KENNINGTON LANE

VAUXHALL STREET

GASHOLDER PLACE

STANNARY STREET

KENNINGTON PARK PLACE

ROYAL ROAD

DODDINGTON PLACE

COOK'S ROAD

FLEMING ROAD

FORSYTH GARDENS

LORRIMORE ROAD

DONALD'S PLACE

KENNINGTON GROVE

OVAL WAY

FARNHAM ROYAL

CLAYTON STREET

BOWLING GREEN STREET

KENNINGTON PARK ROAD

The Oval

KENNINGTON OVAL

DURHAM ST ROAD

KENNINGTON OVAL

KENNINGTON PARK

ST AGNES PLACE

KENNINGTON PARK GARDENS

HILLINGDON STREET

RUSKIN

BETHWIN RD

Oval

PRIMA ROAD

CLAYLANDS ROAD

PALFREY PLACE

CLAPHAM ROAD

BRIXTON ROAD

OFFLEY ROAD

CAMBERWELL NEW ROAD

JOHN RUSKIN STREET

WARHAM STREET

FARMER'S ROAD

FENTIMAN ROAD

RICHBORNE TERRACE

HANFORTH ROAD

CRANMER ROAD

FOXLEY ROAD

KENDAL CLOSE

WYNDHAM ROAD

OVAL PLACE

PALFREY PLACE

CREWDSON ROAD

CHRYSSELL ROAD

HOLLAND GROVE

LANGTON RD

DORSET ROAD

RALEIGH PLACE

SOUTH ISLAND PLACE

MOWLL ST

MANDELA STREET

VASSALL ROAD

HACKFORD RD

A **B** **C**

WYNAN ROAD
PONTERS CLOSE
WEST FERRY ROAD MANCHESTER ROAD Island Gardens
EAST FERRY ROAD
FERRY STREET
SAUNDERS NESS ROAD
ISLAND GARDENS
FERRY STREET
MIDLAND PLACE

1

River *Thames*
Greenwich Foot Tunnel
BALLA LASSE
HOSKINS STREET
CRANE STREET HIGH BRIDGE
EASTNEY STREET
OLD WOOLWICH RO
Greenwich Pier
Royal Naval College
PARK ROW
FEATHERS PLACE
PARK R
Gipsy Moth IV
Cutty Sark
ROMNEY ROAD
Queen's House

2

STOWAGE
THAMES STREET
NORWAY ST
HORSEFERRY PLACE
WILLIAM STREET
Cutty Sark DLR 39
CREEK ROAD
COPPERAS STREET
BARDSLEY LANE
ROAD
THORNHAM STREET
HADDO STREET
GREENWICH CHURCH STREET
St Alfege
NELSON ROAD
KING WILLIAM WALK
National Maritime Museum
GRE
Queen's House
CLAREMONT STREET
RANDALL PLACE
ROAN STREET
STRAIGHTSMOUTH STREET
STOCKWELL ST
NEVADA ST

3

NORMAN ROAD
TARVES WAY
HIGH
Fan Museum
CROOM'S HILL GROVE
Old Royal Observatory
GREENWICH DLR
GREENWICH ROAD
ROYAL
BURNEY STREET
GLOUCESTER CIRCUS
CROOM'S
THE AVENUE
LANGDALE ROAD
CIRCUS STREET
PRIOR STREET
GEORGETTE PLACE
HILL
GREENWICH SOUTH STREET
ASHBURNHAM PLACE
BRAND STREET
HILL
GEORGE
LUTON PL

4

DEVONSHIRE DRIVE
CATHERINE GROVE
ASHBURNHAM GROVE
ROYAL HILL
KING GEORGE
HYDE
Ranger's House
EGERTON DRIVE
GUILDFORD GROVE
DRIVE
BLISSET STREET
WINFORTON STREET
DIAMOND TERRACE
WESTGROVE
VALE
CHESTERFIELD ROAD
GENERAL WOLFE ROAD
BLACKHEATH RD
DABIN CRESCENT
MAIDENSTONE HILL
POINT HILL
WEST GROVE
LANE
CASCADE
WALK
DITCH ALLEY
BLACKHEATH HILL SHOOTERS HILL ROAD
HOLLYMOUNT CLOSE
DARTMOUTH HILL
HARE AND BILLET ROAD
WHITFIELD ROAD

5

JOHN PENN STREET
SPARTA STREET
LEWISHAM
DARTMOUTH ROW
DARTMOUTH GROVE
BECK CLOSE
MORDEN STREET
LETHBRIDGE CLOSE
COLDBATH STREET
BENNETT GROVE
ORCHARD HILL
NECTARINE WAY
ROAD
MORDEN HILL
ST AUSTELL ROAD
OAKCROFT ROAD
WHITFIELD ROAD
BLISS CRESCENT
RAVENSBOURNE PLACE
RUSSETT WAY
ROSEWOOD GARDENS
CONINGTON RD
MORDEN CLOSE
BLACKHEATH RISE
PRINCE'S RISE
LEWISHAM HILL
ELIOT HILL ROAD
POND ROAD
GRANVILLE PARK
ABERDEEN TERRACE
THE ORCHARD
ELIOT VAL
BROOKMILL ROAD
ELVERSON ROAD
LEATHWELL ROAD
ROCONINGTON ROAD
159A
ST TYLER
MOUNTS PASCOE
PAGODA GARDENS

A **B** **C**

D   **E**   **F**

1

2

3

4

5

EMKERBY STREET
SPELTON
GIBANNING STREET
HADRIAN STREET
CARADOC STREET
WOOLWICH ROAD
GIBSON STREET
ORLOP STREET
STREET

BELLOT ST
CHRISTCHURCH WAY
WHITWORTH ST
CANNERELL ST
CONLEY STREET
CAMBERSL ST
BLACKWALL LANE
ROOMARE STREET
COLOMB STREET
ROAD
213²
39
VANBRUGH HILL
ARMITAGE RD
GLENISTER RD

WOOLWICH ROAD

FINGAL STREET
CHILVER ST
DENHAM ST
COMBEDALE ROAD
KEMSING ROAD
HALSTOW ROAD
A102 (M)
1129¹

TRAFALGAR ROAD
TOATYLER ROAD
EARLSWOOD STREET
WALNUT TREE ROAD
WOODLAND GROVE
CALVERT ROAD
ANNANDALE ROAD
CHEVENING ROAD
WESTCOMBE HILL
WESTERDALE ROAD

Greenwich District Hospital

ROYAL HOSPITAL CEMETERY

ORMISTON ROAD
Westcombe Park

TUSKAR STREET
WOODLANDS
PARK ROAD
ANNANDALE ROAD
HUMBER
RUTHIN ROAD

Maze Hill
TOM SMITH CLOSE
RESTELL CLOSE
DINSDALE ROAD
HUMBER ROAD
PEACHUM ROAD
COLERAINE ROAD
BEACONSFIELD ROAD
MYCENAE ROAD

VISTA
MAZE HILL

NWICH

PARK

WESTCOMBE
VANBRUGH HILL
ULUNDI ROAD
FOYLE ROAD
WEBB ROAD
COLERAINE ROAD
BELFAST GARDENS
HARDY ROAD
INGLESIDE GROVE
BEACONSFIELD ROAD
BEACONSFIELD CLOSE
BEACONSFIELD

HIGHMORE ROAD
LYNDALE CLOSE
VANBRUGH FIELDS
WESTCOMBE PARK ROAD

MAZE HILL
VANBRUGH PARK
WYCHERLEY CLOSE
VANBRUGH PARK ROAD
COMBE AVENUE
VANBRUGH PARK ROAD WEST
COMBE MEWS
OAKBRIDGE CLOSE

VANBRUGH
PARK

CHARLTON WAY
BLACKHEATH AVENUE
BOWER AVENUE
MAZE HILL ROAD
MANDEVILLE CLOSE
VANBRUGH ST
JOHN'S PARK
HEATH WAY
WAY

SHOOTERS HILL ROAD
CHARLES ROAD
MAZE HILL ROAD
VANBRUGH TERRACE
ANGERSTEIN LANE
LANGTON ROAD
STRATHEDEN ROAD
ST GERMAN'S PLACE
37⁵

BLACKHEATH
LONG POND ROAD
HUMPHREY
PRINCE OF WALES ROAD
ROW
THE PARAGON
MORDEN ROAD
KIDBROOKE GARDENS
REGENTS PLACE

GOFFERS
MOUNTS POND ROAD
TALBOT PLACE
BLACKHEATH VALE
ALL SAINTS DRIVE
ROYAL PARADE
MONTPELIER ROW
PRINCE OF WALES ROAD
SOUTH PARAGON PLACE
RYCULF SQUARE
POND ROAD
FULTHOR
MERRYFIELD
MORDEN ROAD MEWS

HARE AND BILLET ROAD
ORCHARD
ELIOT PLACE
GROTE'S PLACE
TRANQUIL VALE
FALCONWOOD COURT
MERRYFIELD
THE KEEP

General Index

Acknowledgments

DORLING KINDERSLEY would like to thank the following people whose help and assistance contributed to the preparation of this book.

MAIN CONTRIBUTOR

Michael Leapman was born in London in 1938 and has been a journalist since he was 20. He has worked for most British national newspapers and writes about travel and other subjects for several publications, among them *The Independent, Independent on Sunday, The Economist* and *Country Life*. He has written ten books, including *London's River* (1991) and the award-winning *Companion Guide to New York* (1983, revised 1991). In 1989 he edited the acclaimed *Book of London*.

CONTRIBUTORS

James Aufenast, Yvonne Deutch, Guy Dimond, George Foster, Iain Gale, Fiona Holman, Phil Harriss, Lindsay Hunt, Christopher Middleton, Steven Parissien, Christopher Pick, Bazyli Solowij, Matthew Tanner, Mark Wareham, Jude Welton, Ian Wisniewski.

DORLING KINDERSLEY wishes to thank the following editors and researchers at Webster's International Publishers: Sandy Carr, Matthew Barrell, Siobhan Bremner, Serena Cross, Annie Galpin, Miriam Lloyd, Ava-Lee Tanner.

ADDITIONAL PHOTOGRAPHY

Max Alexander, Peter Anderson, June Buck, Peter Chadwick, Michael Dent, Philip Dowell, Mike Dunning, Philip Enticknap, Andreas Einsiedel, Steve Gorton, Christi Graham, Alison Harris, Peter Hayman, Stephen Hayward, Roger Hilton, Ed Ironside, Colin Keates, Dave King, Neil Mersh, Nick Nichols, Robert O'Dea, Vincent Oliver, John Parker, Tim Ridley, Kim Sayer, Chris Stevens, James Stevenson, James Strachan, Doug Traverso, David Ward, Mathew Ward, Steven Wooster and Nick Wright.

ADDITIONAL ILLUSTRATIONS

Ann Child, Gary Cross, Tim Hayward, Fiona M Macpherson, Janos Marffy, David More, Chris D Orr, Richard Phipps, Michelle Ross and John Woodcock.

CARTOGRAPHY

Andrew Heritage, James Mills-Hicks, Chez Picthall, John Plumer (DK Cartography). Advanced Illustration (Cheshire), Contour Publishing (Derby), Euromap Ltd (Berkshire). Street Finder maps: ERA Maptec Ltd (Dublin) adapted with permission from original survey and mapping from Shobunsha (Japan).

CARTOGRAPHIC RESEARCH

James Anderson, Roger Bullen, Tony Chambers, Ruth Duxbury, Jason Gough, Ailsa Heritage, Jayne Parsons, Donna Rispoli, Jill Tinsley, Andrew Thompson, Iorwerth Watkins.

DESIGN AND EDITORIAL

MANAGING EDITOR Douglas Amrine
MANAGING ART EDITOR Geoff Manders
SENIOR EDITOR Georgina Matthews
EDITORIAL DIRECTOR David Lamb
ART DIRECTOR Anne-Marie Bulat
PRODUCTION CONTROLLER Hilary Stephens
PICTURE RESEARCH Ellen Root
DTP EDITOR Siri Lowe
REVISIONS EDITOR Kathryn Lane

Keith Addison, Elizabeth Atherton, Sam Atkinson, Oliver Bennett, Michelle Clark, Carey Combe, Vanessa Courtier, Lorna Damms, Jessica Doyle, Jane Ewart, Simon Farbrother, Gadi Farfour, Fay Franklin, Simon Hall, Marcus Hardy, Sasha Heseltine, Paul Hines, Stephanie Jackson, Gail Jones, Nancy Jones, Stephen Knowlden, Esther Labi, Chris Lascelles, Jeanette Leung, Ferdie McDonald, Jane Middleton, Rebecca Milner, Fiona Morgan, Louise Parsons, Andrea Powell, Leigh Priest, Liz Rowe, Simon Ryder, Susannah Steel, Kathryn Steve, Anna Streiffert, Andrew Szudek, Hugh Thompson, Diana Vowles, Andy Wilkinson.

SPECIAL ASSISTANCE

Christine Brandt at Kew Gardens, Sheila Brown at The Bank of England, John Cattermole at London Buses Northern, the DK picture department, especially Jenny Rayner, Pippa Grimes at the V & A, Emma Healy at Bethnal Green Museum of Childhood, Alan Hills at the British Museum, Emma Hutton and Cooling Brown Partnership, Gavin Morgan at the Musuem of London, Clare Murphy at Historic Royal Palaces, Ali Naqei at the Science Museum, Patrizio Semproni, Caroline Shaw at the Natural History Museum, Gary Smith at British Rail, Monica Thurnauer at The Tate, Simon Wilson at the Tate, and Alistair Wardle.

PHOTOGRAPHIC REFERENCE

The London Aerial Photo Library, and P and P F James.

PHOTOGRAPHY PERMISSIONS

DORLING KINDERSLEY would like to thank all the museums, galleries, churches and other sights that allowed us to photograph at their establishments.

PICTURE CREDITS

t = top; tl = top left; tc = top centre; tr = top right; cla = centre left above; ca = centre above; cra = centre right above; cl = centre left; c = centre; cr = centre right; clb = centre left below; cb = centre below; crb = centre right below; bl = bottom left; b = bottom; bc = bottom centre; br = bottom right.

Works of art have been reproduced with the permission of the following copyright holders:

The Bath, 1925, Pierre Bonnard © ADAGP, Paris and DACS, London 2001 181b; *After Lunch*, 1975 © Patrick Caulfield. All rights Reserved, DACS 2001 180t; *Lobster Telephone*, 1936 © Salvador Dali, Gala-Salvador Dali Foundation/DACS 2001 41cr; *Standing by the Rags*, 1988 © Lucian Freud 179tl; *Composition: Man and Woman*, 1927, Alberto Giacometti © ADAGP, Paris and DACS, London 2001 178tr; *Death* from *Death Hope Life Fear* (d) 1984 © Gilbert and George 178lb; *Mr. and Mrs. Clark and Percy* (1970–71) © David Hockney 85t; Bust of *Lawrence of Arabia* © The Family of Eric H. Kennington, RA 151bl; *Do We Turn Round Inside Houses, Or is It Houses*, 1977–85 © Mario Merz 178la; *Cold Dark Matter: An Exploded View*, 1991 © Cornelia Parker 85b; The works by Henry Moore illustrated on the following pages have been reproduced by kind permission of the Henry Moore Foundation: 45c, 85c, 206b, 266cb. *Soft Drainpipe – Blue (Cool) version*, 1967 © Claes Oldenburg 179c; *Maman*, 2000 © Louise Bourgeois/VAGA, New York/DACS, London 2001 181cr; *Summertime: Number 9A*, 1948, Jackson Pollock © ARS, New York and DACS, London 2001 181t; *Light Red Over Black*, 1957 © 1998 Kate Rothko Prizel and Christopher Rothko/DACS 179cr.

The Publishers are grateful to the following individuals, companies and picture libraries for permission to reproduce their photographs: Printed by kind permission of THE ALBERMARLE CONNECTION: 91T; ARCAID: Richard Bryant, Architect Foster and Partners 126t; Richard Bryant 249cr; ARCBLUE: Peter Durant 189cl; THE ART ARCHIVE: 19bl, 26c, 26bc, 27bl, 28br, 29cra, 29clb, 33tc, 33cr, 36bl, 188b, 188bl; British Library, London 18cr; Imperial War Museum, London 30bc; Museum of London 15b, 27br, 28bl; Science Museum, London 27cla; Stoke Museum Staffordshire Polytechnic 23bl, 25cl, 33bc; Victoria and Albert Museum, London 20c, 21bc, 25tr; AXIOM: James Morris 164tl.

GOVERNOR AND COMPANY OF THE BANK OF ENGLAND: 145tr; BRIDGEMAN ART LIBRARY, London: 21t, 28t; British Library, London 14, 19tr, (detail) 21br, 24cb, (detail) 32tl, 32bl; Courtesy of the Institute of Directors, London 29cla; Guildhall Art Gallery, Corporation of London (detail) 26t; Guildhall Library, Corporation of London 24br, 76c; ML Holmes Jamestown – Yorktown Educational Trust, VA (detail) 17bc; Master and Fellows, Magdalene College, Cambridge (detail) 23clb; Marylebone Cricket Club, London 246c; William Morris Gallery, Walthamstow 19tl, 249tl; Museum of London 22–3; O'Shea Gallery, London (detail) 22cl; Royal Holloway & Bedford New

College 157bl; Russell Cotes Art Gallery and Museum, Bournemouth 38tr; Thyssen-Bornemisza Collection, Lugano Casta 257b; Westminster Abbey, London (detail) 32bc; White House, Bond Street, London 28cb. BRITISH AIRWAYS: Adrian Meredith Photography: 356t, 358tl; reproduced with permission of the BRITISH LIBRARY BOARD: 125b; © THE BRITISH MUSEUM: 16t, 16ca, 17tl, 40t, 91c, 126–7 all pics except 126t, 128–9 all pics.

CAMERA PRESS, London: P. Abbey - LNS 73cb; Cecil Beaton 79tl; HRH Prince Andrew 95bl; Allan Warren 31cb; COLLECTIONS: John Miller 163bl; COLORIFIC!: Steve Benbow 55t; David Levenson 66–7; CONRAN RESTAURANTS 291cb, 314bc; CORBIS: 259t; Angelo Hornak 183b; London Aerial Photo Library 189bl, 189t; Courtesy of the CORPORATION OF LONDON: 55c, 146t; COURTAULD INSTITUTE GALLERIES, London: 41c, 117b.

PERCIVAL DAVID FOUNDATION OF CHINESE ART: 130c; Copyright: Dean & Chapter of Westminster 78bl, 79tr; DEPARTMENT OF TRANSPORT (Crown Copyright): 363b; Courtesy of the GOVERNORS AND THE DIRECTORS DULWICH PICTURE GALLERY: 43bl, 250bl.

EASYJET: 356b; EASY EVERYTHING: James Hamilton 353cr; ENGLISH HERITAGE: 252b, 258b; ENGLISH LIFE PUBLICATIONS LTD: 252b; PHILIP ENTICKNAP: 255tr; MARY EVANS PICTURE LIBRARY: 16bl, 16br, 17bl, 17br, 20bl, 22bl, 24t, 25bc, 25br, 27t, 27cb, 27bc, 30bl, 32br, 33tl, 33cl, 33bl, 33br, 36t, 36c, 38tl, 39bl, 72cb, 72b, 90b, 112b, 114b, 135t, 139t, 155bl, 159t, 162ca, 174ca, 177l, 207b, 216t, 226b.

Courtesy of the FAN MUSEUM (The Helene Alexander Collection) 243b; FREUD MUSEUM, London: 246t.

GATWICK EXPRESS: 359t; THE GORE HOTEL, London: 273b; GILBERT COLLECTION: 117t.

ROBERT HARDING PICTURE LIBRARY: 31ca, 42c, 52ca, 169tl, 327t, 349cb, 368b; Philip Craven 210t; Brian Hawkes 21clb; Michael Jenner 21cra, 242t; 58t; 227t; Mark Mawson 113tl; Nick Wood 63bl; HARROD'S (printed by kind permission of Mohamed al Fayed): 310b; HAYES-DAVIDSON (computer generated images: 174bl; Reproduced with permission of HER MAJESTY'S STATIONERY OFFICE (Crown Copyright): 156 all pics; JOHN HESELTINE: 12tr, 13tl, 13tr, 13cb, 13br, 51tr, 63br, 98, 124b, 132, 142, 172, 220; FRIENDS OF HIGHGATE CEMETERY: 37tr, 244, 246b; HISTORIC ROYAL PALACES (Crown Copyright): 5t, 35tc, 254–255 all except 254br, 256–7 all except 257b; THE HORNIMAN MUSEUM, London: 256br; HOVERSPEED LTD: 361b; HULTON GETTY: 24bl, 124tl, 135cr, 232t.

THE IMAGE BANK, London: Gio Barto 55b; Derek Berwin 31t, 272t; Romilly Lockyer 72t, 94br; Leo Mason 56t; Terry Williams 139b; Courtesy of ISIC, UK: 354t.

PETER JACKSON COLLECTION: 24–5; JEWISH MUSEUM, London: 247tl.

LEIGHTON HOUSE: 216b; LITTLE ANGEL MARIONETTE THEATRE: 343tl; LONDON AMBULANCE SERVICE: 349ca; LONDON AQUARIUM 188c, 188r; LONDON CITY AIRPORT: 360b; LONDON DUNGEON: 183t; LONDON PALLADIUM: 103; LONDON REGIONAL TRANSPORT: 364t; LONDON TRANSPORT MUSEUM: 28ca, 364–5 all maps and tickets.

MADAME TUSSAUDS: 222c, 224t; MANSELL COLLECTION: 19br, 20t, 20br, 21bl, 22t, 22cl, 23br, 27ca, 32tr; METROPOLITAN POLICE SERVICE: 348t, 349t; ROB MOORE: 115t; MUSEUM OF LONDON: 16cb, 17tr, 17cb, 18t, 21crb, 41tc, 166–7 all pics.

NATIONAL EXPRESS LTD: 360; Reproduced by courtesy of the TRUSTEES, THE NATIONAL GALLERY, London: (detail) 35c, 104–5 all except 104t, 106–7 all except 107t; NATIONAL PORTRAIT GALLERY, London: 4t, 41tl, 101cb, (detail) 102b; NATIONAL POSTAL MUSEUM, London: 26bl; By permission of the KEEPER OF THE NATIONAL RAILWAY MUSEUM, York: 28–9; NATIONAL TRUST PHOTOGRAPHIC LIBRARY: Wendy Aldiss 23ca; John Bethell 252t, 253t; Michael Boys 38b; NATURAL HISTORY MUSEUM, LONDON: 209t, 209cr; Derek Adams 208b; John Downs 208c; NEW SHAKESPEARE THEATRE CO: 326bl.

P&O STENA LINE LTD: 337b; PA PHOTOS LTD: 31cr; PALACE THEATRE ARCHIVE: 108t; PICTOR INTERNATIONAL, London: 61t, 174br; PICTURES COLOUR LIBRARY: 54br; PIPPA POP-INS CHILDREN'S HOTEL, London: 341b; PITSHANGER MANOR MUSEUM: 258c; POPPERFOTO: 29tl, 29crb, 30tl, 30tr, 30c, 33tr, 39br; THE PORTOBELLO HOTEL: 273tr; POST HOUSE HEATHROW: Tim Young 361t; PRESS ASSOCIATION LTD: 29bl, 29br; PUBLIC RECORD OFFICE (Crown Copyright): 18b.

BILL RAFFERTY: 326br; RAINFOREST CAFE: 341cl; REX FEATURES LTD: 53tl; Peter Brooker 53tr; Andrew Laenen 54c; THE RITZ, London: 91b;

ROCK CIRCUS: 100cb; ROYAL ACADEMY OF ARTS, London: 90tr; THE BOARD OF TRUSTEES OF THE ROYAL ARMOURIES: 41tr, 155tl, 157t, 157br; ROYAL BOTANIC GARDENS, KEW: Andrew McRob 48cl, 56b, 260–61 all pics except 260t & 260br; ROYAL COLLECTION, ST JAMES'S PALACE © HM THE QUEEN: 8–9, 53b, 88t, 93t, 94–5 all pics except 94br & 95bl, 96t, 254br; ROYAL COLLEGE OF MUSIC, London: 200c, 206c.

THE SAVOY GROUP: 116cr, 274t, 274b; SCIENCE MUSEUM, London: 212cr, 212b, 213cl, 213 cra, 213bl, 213br; SCIENCE PHOTO LIBRARY: Maptec International Ltd 10b; SPENCER HOUSE LTD: 88b; SOUTHBANK PRESS OFFICE: 186bl; SYNDICATION INTERNATIONAL: 31bl, 35tr, 52cb, 53c, 58bl, 59t, 136; Library of Congress 25bl.

TATE LONDON 2001: 41cr, 43br, 82–3 all pics, 84–5 all pics, 178–9 all pics, 180–81 all pics.

Courtesy of the BOARD OF TRUSTEES OF THE VICTORIA AND ALBERT MUSEUM: 35br, 40b, 201cl; 202–3 all pics, 204–5 all pics, 254b, 342t.

THE WALDORF, London: 272b; THE WALLACE COLLECTION, London: 40ca, 226c; PHILIP WAY PHOTOGRAPHY: 64lb, 150clb, 177b; Courtesy of the TRUSTEES OF THE WEDGWOOD MUSEUM, Barlaston, Stoke-on-Trent, Staffs, England: 26br; VIVIENNE WESTWOOD: Patrick Fetherstonhaugh 31br; THE WIMBLEDON LAWN TENNIS MUSEUM: Micky White 251t; Photo © WOODMANSTERNE: Jeremy Marks 35tl, 149t; GREGORY WRONA 267r.

YOUTH HOSTEL ASSOCIATION: 277; ZEFA: 10t, 52b, 326c; Bob Croxford 57t; Clive Sawyer 57b.

Front Endpaper: all special or additional photography except THE IMAGE BANK, London: Romilly Lockyer bl, crb; MUSEUM OF LONDON: bcr; NATURAL HISTORY MUSEUM: John Downs cl; TATE GALLERY: bcl; BOARD OF TRUSTEES OF THE VICTORIA AND ALBERT MUSEUM: cla.
Cover: All special photography by Max Alexander, Philip Enticknap, John Heseltine, Stephen Oliver, Mathew Ward, Steven Wooster, except: LONDON TRANSPORT MUSEUM: front cover cla; PICTOR INTERNATIONAL: back cover bl.

EYEWITNESS *TRAVEL GUIDES*

COUNTRY GUIDES

AUSTRALIA • CANADA • CRUISE GUIDE TO EUROPE AND THE
MEDITERRANEAN • CUBA • EGYPT • FRANCE • GERMANY
GREAT BRITAIN • GREECE: ATHENS & THE MAINLAND
THE GREEK ISLANDS • IRELAND • ITALY • JAPAN
MEXICO • POLAND • PORTUGAL • SCOTLAND
SINGAPORE • SOUTH AFRICA • SPAIN
THAILAND • GREAT PLACES TO STAY
IN EUROPE • A TASTE OF SCOTLAND

REGIONAL GUIDES

BALI & LOMBOK • BARCELONA & CATALONIA • CALIFORNIA
EUROPE • FLORENCE & TUSCANY • FLORIDA • HAWAII
JERUSALEM & THE HOLY LAND • LOIRE VALLEY
MILAN & THE LAKES • MUNICH & THE BAVARIAN ALPS • NAPLES WITH
POMPEII & THE AMALFI COAST • NEW ENGLAND • NEW ZEALAND
PROVENCE & THE COTE D'AZUR • SARDINIA
SEVILLE & ANDALUSIA • SICILY • SOUTHWEST USA & LAS VEGAS
A TASTE OF TUSCANY • VENICE & THE VENETO

CITY GUIDES

AMSTERDAM • BERLIN • BOSTON • BRUSSELS • BUDAPEST
CHICAGO • CRACOW • DELHI, AGRA & JAIPUR • DUBLIN
ISTANBUL • LISBON • LONDON • MADRID
MOSCOW • NEW YORK • PARIS • PRAGUE • ROME
SAN FRANCISCO • STOCKHOLM • ST PETERSBURG
SYDNEY • VIENNA • WARSAW • WASHINGTON, DC

NEW FOR AUTUMN 2002

INDIA • MOROCCO • NEW ORLEANS • TURKEY

FOR INFORMATION ON OUR NEW <u>EYEWITNESS TOP TEN</u> POCKET SERIES
AND ON
<u>DK TRAVEL MAPS</u> & <u>PHRASEBOOKS</u>

VISIT US AT
www.dk.com

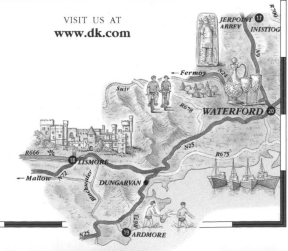

The London Underground

UNDERGROUND

London Travel Information
020 7222 1234
24 hours

Textphone
020 7918 3015

© Transport for London